## ALSO BY BARRY DAY

*This Wooden "O": Shakespeare's Globe Reborn*

*My Life with Noël Coward* (with Graham Payn)

*Noël Coward: The Complete Lyrics*

*Noël Coward: In His Own Words*

*Noël Coward: Complete Sketches and Parodies*

*Theatrical Companion to Coward* (with Sheridan Morley)

*The Unknown Noël: New Writing from the Coward Archives*

*Coward on Film: The Cinema of Noël Coward*

*Oscar Wilde: A Life in Quotes*

*P. G. Wodehouse: In His Own Words*

*P. G. Wodehouse: The Complete Lyrics*

*Dorothy Parker: In Her Own Words*

*Sherlock Holmes: In His Own Words and the Words of Those Who Knew Him*

*Sherlock Holmes and the Shakespeare Globe Murders*

*Sherlock Holmes and the Alice in Wonderland Murders*

*Sherlock Holmes and the Copycat Murders*

*Sherlock Holmes and the Apocalypse Murders*

*Sherlock Holmes and the Seven Deadly Sins Murders*

*Murder, My Dear Watson* (contributor)

# THE LETTERS OF NOËL COWARD

# THE LETTERS OF

# NOËL COWARD

EDITED AND WITH COMMENTARY BY

## BARRY DAY

ALFRED A. KNOPF ✦ NEW YORK 2007

*Grateful acknowledgment is made to Methuen Drama for permission to reprint excerpts*
*from the following Noël Coward songs: "Faraway Land," "I Travel Alone,"*
*"Mad About the Boy," "Poor Little Rich Girl," "Sail Away," "Twentieth Century Blues,"*
*"Where Are the Songs We Sung," "Why Must the Show Go On?," and "World Weary."*
*Reprinted by permission of Methuen Drama, an imprint of A&C Black Publishers Ltd.,*
*a division of Bloomsbury Publishing Plc., London.*

*Library of Congress Cataloging-in-Publication Data*
*Coward, Noël, 1899–1973.*
*{Correspondence. Selections}*
*The letters of Noël Coward / edited and with an introduction by Barry Day. — 1st ed.*
*p.    cm.*
*ISBN 978-0-375-42303-1*
1. *Coward, Noël, 1899–1973—Correspondence.    2. Dramatists, English—20th*
*century—Correspondence.    3. Actors—Great Britain—Correspondence.    4. Coward,*
*Noël, 1899–1973—Friends and associates.    5. Coward, Noël, 1899–1973—Family.*
*I. Day, Barry.    II. Title.*
*PR6005.O85Z48 2007*
*822'.912—dc22*
*{B}      2007012316*

FOR LYNNE

PRIMA INTER PARES

# CONTENTS

# ILLUSTRATIONS

# THE LETTERS OF NOËL COWARD

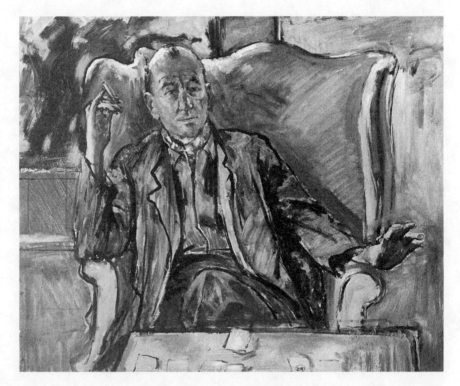

Noël—by Derek Hill.
Noël warned Hill at the outset: "Derek, dear, remember I have painted my own face
in the theatre over the last fifty years, so I know it much better than you ever will."
Even though he felt "my eyes are too close together," it remained his favorite portrait.

# INTRODUCTION

A T A PARTY in London's Savoy Hotel to celebrate Noël's seventieth birthday his longtime friend Lord Louis Mountbatten said of him:

> There are probably greater painters than Noël, greater novelists than Noël, greater librettists, greater composers of music, greater singers, greater dancers, greater comedians, greater tragedians, greater stage producers, greater film directors, greater cabaret artists, greater TV stars. If there are, they are twelve different people. Only one man combined all twelve labels—The Master.

He might easily have gone on to enumerate Noël's several other roles in social and political life on both sides of the Atlantic and well beyond, for over and above his many artistic talents he was for most of his seventy-three years what John Osborne was to call "his own invention"—and a contribution to his century. Noël Coward, an early role model for that twentieth-century phenomenon the "celebrity," someone "well known for being famous and famous for being well known."

During his life Noël collected people and was just as avidly collected by them. And since this was an age in which people still wrote letters, they wrote to him and he wrote back. (One wonders what history will make of the present illiterate e-mail era.) He conducted a dialogue with others in the arts like the Lunts, Marlene Dietrich, John Gielgud, Edna Ferber, Alexander Woollcott, Vivien Leigh, Diana Cooper, Alec Guinness, Virginia Woolf, Edith Sitwell . . . he debated current events with politicians . . . he gossiped with friends and the "family" he created as a personal cocoon. By his own admission he was a dyed-in-the-wool "Royal snob," and many—like the Queen Mother—became personal friends. And running like a thread through it all, until the day she died in 1954, was his correspondence with his mother, Violet Coward, the woman whose ambition sparked him and whose golden opinions drove him on. To her he would confide not merely the happenings but the feelings they engendered.

And that, essentially, is the dimension *The Letters* provides. Anyone interested in Coward is familiar with at least an outline of the events of his life. That is not the purpose of this book, although the letters are set in a chronological context to "fix" them. Having said that, the published accounts—Noël's own and his biographers'—do differ in a number of slight but significant ways. Cole Lesley, Noël's right-hand man, found a number of such differences when he came to write his life of The Master and compared the material Noël had left behind—in terms of diaries and notebooks—with Noël's own published autobiography.

This should not be too surprising.

Many people in the public eye smooth off personal rough edges, sometimes without being aware of what they're doing. Many more reshape an anecdote so that it makes a better story. And whatever disclaimers they may make, everyone who keeps a detailed journal has at the back of his or her mind the thought—perhaps the hope—that one day it will be read and admired by others. (Even Noël mentions "the benefit of future historians who might avidly read this journal.") Diarists write their story as they'd like it to be remembered. As the script for John Ford's *The Man Who Shot Liberty Valance* has it, "When you have the facts and the legend, print the legend."

Two unrehearsed moments in an ordered life.
In the rocking chair, Noël considers what went wrong with *Point Valaine* (1935).

Coward-san. Drawing by Makoto Wada.

Noël's *Diaries,* to my mind, fall into that category. What may have started out as a series of notes for the still-to-be-written autobiography of his later years becomes more and more a piece of literature with an eye on posterity.

But letters are different. Two letters with virtually identical content to two different people will vary in their tonality and say just as much about the individual relationships as they do about the matters being discussed. Which is why in this collection I have chosen to break the convention of Collected Letters by using letters to as well as from Noël. Alexander Pope called letters "the very *déshabillé* of understanding"—and one can see what he meant.

The letters that do remain—at least the ones I have been able to unearth—tell the story of a life. Not a complete story, to be sure, but aspects of one, and certainly Noël's abiding preoccupations with his work, family, and friends clearly emerge as the years go by and we can share what he felt at the time: the high youthful hopes, the disappointments, the exhilaration of success, the numbness of being banished to the wings, the immense relief of "Dad's Renaissance." This is what it was like for him in real time, not as recollections in relative tranquillity. The letters complete the portrait of what it was like to be Noël Coward.

They also reveal the repeating pattern in his life—the need to compete and succeed, at one and the same time, in all the creative areas his multiple talents opened up to him; the winding up of his personal mainspring until mind and body force him to stop and draw reluctant breath . . . and then the game is afoot once more. So much to do, so little time. If anyone was ever driven, Noël was driven by the need to succeed and please those few whose approval he sought.

He was always a man in a hurry—a hurry to get on to the next thing and the next place. Which is why he was particularly fond of the telegram as a means of communication. Not only was it necessarily brief and to the point but it lent itself to the kind of verbal jokes that he dearly loved. Western Union should have given him shares.

There is the famous (and probably apocryphal) story of the occasion when Noël tried to send a telegram by phone when he was in New York. Being fond of signing both his letters and cables with fanciful names, he dictated as his signature "Fiorello La Guardia."

There was a moment of outraged silence on the line. Then . . .

"Are you *really* Mayor La Guardia?"

"No."

"Then you can't *sign* it 'Fiorello La Guardia.' What is your *real* name?"

"Noël Coward."

"Are you *really* Noël Coward?"

"Yes."

"Then you may sign it 'Fiorello La Guardia.' "

•

I HAVE TRIED as far as possible to avoid endless footnotes. The linking narrative covers most of the necessary context, and I have inserted key information, such as a surname or the title of a play, in the letter itself.

I have also, in the main, adhered to the misspellings in the original letters—Noël's and his correspondents'. Occasionally I have indicated the correct spelling, so as not to drive the proofreader mad, but it seemed to me that you are probably as sick of *sic* as I am. So what you see is what Noël got—and gave.

When he was asked in a final TV interview to sum up his life in a single word, Noël thought for a long moment before saying, "Love . . . To know that you are among people you love and who love you. That has made all the successes wonderful—much more wonderful than they'd have been anyway. And that's it, really."

Apart from time's wingèd chariot, the thread that goes through this life in letters is, indeed, love. Not the homosexual definition of love that can now not only speak but positively shout its name. That was not the Coward style. As his friend Rebecca West always maintained, "He was a very dignified man . . . There was an impeccable dignity in his sexual life,

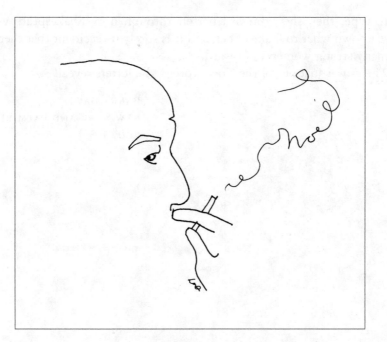

Drawing by Lynne Carey.

which was reticent but untainted by pretence." He would not have been well pleased to become a gay icon at the expense of his work or to observe, for instance, a generation of young gay directors giving us Coward plays, "as darling Noël *would* have produced them," had he been able to in the prehistory of sexual liberation.

No, the love expressed in the letters is an almost childlike affection for family and friends, with Noël anxious to see the qualities he wanted to see in them, even in those cases—such as Jack Wilson—when the signs increasingly indicated otherwise. Noël continued to travel hopefully and to see what he *wanted* to see for as long as he could.

And of all of his correspondents, the most important for those first fifty-four years of his life was his mother, Violet Coward. He wrote to her once a week, regular as clockwork, whenever he was away from her, telling her what he was doing, how he was feeling, seeking her approval. In them and in her replies one can see the balance of the relationship shift as fame and a degree of fortune take over the son and turn the nurturing mother into the dependant, now demanding the love she feels is hers by right.

No sweet little old lady contentedly crocheting in a rose-bowered cottage, she emerges as a strong-minded, not to say imperious, woman, determined to see her son succeed and making her love conditional on his efforts to do so. If contemporary society insisted on trapping her in a social stereotype, then she expressed herself through him. Shakespeare would have known what to make of her, and it is surely no accident that there are so many strong women in Coward.

Theirs was just one of the "love stories" the letters reveal.

BARRY DAY
NEW YORK AND PALM BEACH
2007

# PREFACE

Hail, starry dawn and dark December morn,
Clash on the cymbals, blow the hunting horn,
Let joy be unconfined and flags unfurled
To honour Noël's advent in the world.
Not long since that auspicious winter day
When he, an innocent pink cherub, lay
In swaddling clothes, and sucked and coo-ed and cried
While his Mamma beamed down on him with pride.
Yet even she could not foretell his fame,
Nor did she spot the Muses when they came
By Comet from Parnassus (V.I.P.
Nine spritely sisters, and their baggage, free.)
To place their gifts upon the bassinette,
And make this sleeping babe their special pet.
Melpomene, Terpsichore (Terps to you)
Polymnia, Clio and Euterpe too,
With harpsichord and palette, brush and pen,
To bless this babe, most fortunate of men.
Came their Papa, in his triumphal car,
(The spirit of Winston, minus his cigar)
Quoth he, "That high-brow stuff may go down well
On Mount Olympus, but down here, it's hell.
Wit is the saving grace of this world, and hereafter,
So I endow your prodigy with laughter."
The Norns (or Maughams? I always get them mixed)
Wove pretty woofs with N.C. on them fixed,
While Pan (not Peter, but his adult prototype)
Composed a new allegro for the pipe,
And danced to it in moonlit woods, for joy,
(Which shows this was no ordinary boy)
Sweet and beguiling ladies, merry gents,
Pray charge your goblets while you still make sense,
And to the ancient air you know so well,
Sing with the Waits outside
No–ël, No–ël!

**KATE MARY BRUCE**
*(Somerset Maugham's favorite niece)*

# PART ONE

# "BEGINNERS, PLEASE!"

# CHAPTER 1

# THE BOY ACTOR

## (1899–1919)

*I never cared who scored the goal*
*Or which side won the silver cup,*
*I never learned to bat or bowl*
*But I heard the curtain going up.*

UNTIL THE DAY she died, Violet Agnes Veitch Coward made sure she was the single most important person in her son Noël's life. In a very real sense her own determination shaped what he became.

She suffered—like a lot of late-Victorian, lower-middle-class women—from having a native intelligence that was largely uneducated and from having to settle, through lack of alternatives, for the boring domestic round. Married to the ineffectual Arthur Coward, she found herself in the poverty trap, forced to take in lodgers to make ends meet. The role of cook, bottle washer, and all-round skivvy was not one she relished or thought she deserved. Some generations back, she would remind people, her own family had had "connections." Noël wrote that his mother came from a "good family . . . brought up in the tradition of being a gentlewoman." Living in suburban Teddington, Middlesex, with her sometime piano salesman husband, that must have seemed a world away.

In 1928—with Noël at the height of his fame—Violet decided to put her version of the family history on the record:

Mr. Noël Coward, author of *This Year of Grace,* is the descendant of a very old Scotch family on his mother's side, Veitch of Dawick in Peebleshire. The beautiful and finely wooded estate of Dawick which extended for 4 miles along the banks of the river Tweed was held by the Veitches from the 13th to the close of the 17th century, when an heiress inherited and married James MacSuelt, 2nd baronet, known as the "Deil o'Dawick." The ruins of the old house are still in exis-

Noël's mother, Violet Agnes Coward (1863–1954).

tence but nearby has been built a beautiful castellated mansion. There is a celebrated avenue of silver firs.

Mrs. Coward's great grandfather, Mr. Henry Veitch was Her Majesty's agent and Consul General of her Island of Madeira for 30 years. His great uncle was Sir George Harrison, assistant secretary to the treasury who lived at Spring Gardens and wrote several learned books which with his portrait are preserved in the British Museum. His grandfather entered the British Navy and became Captain but retired at an early age on account of his health and went to Madeira with his wife and family, where they lived for some years. On his death his widow returned to England and settled in what was in those days the pretty riverside village of Teddington on Thames. There his youngest daughter met Mr. Coward, who was a member of a large and very medical family who did much to help with their talents in the work of the Parish and services in the beautiful church of St. Alban. The vicar, Francis Boy of Toronto, Canada, was a great friend of the family and was afterwards Vicar of St. Paul's, Knightsbridge.

Noël Coward's grandfather on his father's side was organist of the Crystal Palace when it was at the height of its popularity and was one of the most celebrated glee writers of his day.

The Veitch coat of arms is three bulls' heads and the motto—"We

Noël's maternal grandmother,
Mary Kathleen Synch (1837–1908).

extend our fame by our deeds", which seems singularly appropriate to their present descendant.

Violet Coward
December 9th 1928

Being a woman of spirit, though, she was always looking for a way out of the sexual and social prison society had imposed on her and women like her and she knew she would have to find that way out for herself.

To add to her burdens, her beloved first son, Russell, died at the age of six of spinal meningitis. He was "so lovely and so clever, too clever," she would recall.

And then, on December 16, her second son, Noël Peirce, was born—the "Noël" the Cowards considered appropriate because Christmas was just around the corner and this was the best Christmas present Violet could imagine.

"I was looking forward with joy and longing to my little newcomer," Violet wrote in the notes she left behind, "little knowing the great happiness and pride I was to have in him, and how he was to alter all our lives. It seems almost incredible to think that I should have been destined to be the mother of a genius."

It was a present she would cherish for the next half century. In fact, she came to live her life through it.

Aunt Vidal Sarah ("Vida")
Veitch (1854–1946).

When she died, "Mum's Suitcase" came to light and it became obvious that she had kept every last relic of her remarkable second son. There was the little blue book marked "Baby's Record" that came to new mothers with the compliments of Mellin's Food for Babies ("Used by the Royal Mother of the Future King of England"). With her sharp sense of humor, Violet must have positively enjoyed writing in the column marked "Baby Food" the names of Mellin's two major competitors!

She also noted: "Baby's eyes—blue, hair 'Golden Brown,' weight: 7½ lbs." She documented his first outing: "January 10th, 1900: Baby went out for the first time in the garden. Wore hat and cloak and went for walk." And other trivia: "Bought baby's first pair of shoes and he walked out the nursery in them holding on to a chair."

Writing finis in August 1901, she concluded with the observation that he had "cut his last tooth, thank goodness!"

•

ALTHOUGH THE FAMILY had no real theatrical background, there was always music in the air. Several members of the family on both sides sang in church choirs, and like so many Victorian—or by this time, Edwardian—families, the informal sing-song round the family piano was a primary source of family entertainment in those pre–radio and TV days.

As a result, the young Noël was brought up to the sound of music and

Brother Russell Arthur Coward (1891–1898).

could remember and sing those songs and hymns word for word perfectly to the end of his life. The urge to entertain seems to have been in his genes. At two he had to be removed from church for dancing in the aisle to accompany the hymn being played, and even in old age he would still recall his disappointment that his passionate rendering of the treble solo in the church choir did not receive a round of applause but instead the shuffling of an audience kneeling to pray.

Another disappointment he suffered was the fact that he applied for but was rejected by the Chapel Royal choir. No reason was given, but it remained a contentious topic for Noël and as late as 1949 he is correcting journalist Beverley Baxter, who was preparing a profile for *The Times* and had sent Noël the draft to vet. Noël replied:

> The article is very loving and very kind and pleases me very much. Of course, you have been basely inaccurate on one point, which is that I NEVER told you that my boy's voice was awful. On the contrary, it was quite, quite beautiful and on one occasion moved the late ex–Queen of Portugal to tears. The reason that the Chapel Royal refused me was because my performance was too dramatic.

·

THE SAME URGE to entertain was evidenced in his first extant letter to Violet in that same seventh year. It became a habit to send Noël in the

summer to stay with his aunt Laura (Violet's sister) and uncle Harry Bulteel in Charlestown, near St. Austell, Cornwall. The house and grounds
were spectacular and there was a large lake with an island and a dilapi-
dated punt to get to it.

Darling Mother
I hope you are well. Girlie {his cousin Violet] has taught me to row
with two oars and I row her along. I had some little boys over yesterday afternoon to tea and I dressed up in a short dress and danced to
them and sung to them and we all went round the lake and on it.
XXXXXOOOOXO I am writing this in the kitchen with love from
Noël Coward give this to Maggie and Winnie.

Maggie and Winnie were the maids in the Coward household at that
time. No matter how straitened a family's circumstances, it was unthinkable to manage without domestic servants.
Another endless summer (1912) and another unpunctuated letter:

Dear Darling old Mother,
Thank you very much for your letter. I could not send a card and
this was scarcely odd because there were no cards to send. I am
enjoying myself very much indeed Yesterday Girlie took me round
the lake and gave me a nice swing, and in the evening she and I
went out in a boat fishing we were out nearly 3 hours and never
caught a single one. I have been out in the yaught this afternoon it
was very rough and I was fearfly sea sick and Uncle Harry took me
ashore and I was going to wait on the beach for 2 hours but a very
nice lady asked me to go to tea with her I went and had a huge tea
this is the menu 3 seed buns 2 peacies of cake 2 peacies of Bread and
jam 3 Biscuits 2 cups of tea when I thanked her she began to Preach
and said we were all put into the world to do kind things (amen) I
am afraid she did not impress me much but I wished her somewhere
I shant go in that yaught again for months and months and months.
Auntie Laura sent my washing to the village I hope you are not miserable it makes me miserable to think you are I have got to go to
bed now so goodbye from your ever loving sun Noël. Squillions of
kisses to all love to Eric the name of the lady that gave me tea is
Mrs. Penrose Walter. The dogs are so nice down here Nan and Marcus, Marcus sits on a chair and smokes a pipe he looks so funny and
if you drop anything anywhere Nan goes and fetches it. I had 3 little boys to tea yesterday each about the size of a flea. I had to amuse
them and didn't enjoy it much Elephant [Aunt Laura] sends her
love.

His brother Eric (later Erik) had entered the scene in 1905. Noël always professed to be indifferent to both his father and Erik, and certainly there is little evidence of marked affection on either side, but they rubbed along and corresponded occasionally once Noël took to the road as a touring actor.

There was room for only one emotional relationship in the Coward family and that was the rather Oedipal one between Noël and Violet. Unbeknownst to him she wrote a memoir of him that was found in Mum's Suitcase: "There is so much I could tell of his dear ways and loving affection when he was a boy, no mother ever had such a son and I always feel that I am really and truly more proud of his love for me than of his great success." But she was not complaining of that success when it came.

·

MEANWHILE, THERE WAS a small matter of Noël's education. Dancing and singing lessons were all very well, but the three *R*s were in grave need of attention by this time (1909). Matters were not helped by the fact that the Coward family were somewhat footloose and kept moving the family home. At the end of that year his parents made (for them) a difficult decision. After Christmas, Noël was sent to stay with Aunty Amy and Uncle Ran in St. George's Square, where he was tutored by Mr. Selfe, who seems to have been a minor Dickensian pedagogue. Taken away from home, the ten-year-old Noël was badly homesick, a condition that was to apply for many years to come when he was separated from his mother.

> Dear darling old Mother,
> I am still very unhappy and I shant get over it till I see you again. I would rather see you than Alladin but I suppose I cant. I saw the Portsmouth train going off the other day and I longed to get on it. I wish you would let me come back to you please do, for I do want to so I could never be happy without you. I cry every night and day and are so miserable do let me come back. I am quite alright now but I wish you were here. The dinners are alright, at school there are six new boys. I have to get up very early in the morning. Aunty Amy and Uncle Ran send there love to you . . . oh mother do send me some money to come down to you please do I am not very happy here without you . . .

A week later the Cowards returned to London from Southsea, and mother and son were reunited.

·

THE SUCCESS BEGAN in September 1910, when Violet saw an advertisement by a Miss Lila Field, who was anxious to set up a London theater for children. That particular dream eventually proved to be too grandiose, but while she was pursuing it, Miss Field decided to put on a fantasy play called *The Goldfish*. Violet wasted no time in writing to Miss Field, and soon received a reply:

> September 11th 1910
>
> Many thanks for your letter, I shall be pleased to see your little son on Tuesday next at 10:45 at my studio, 24 King Street, Baker Street, W.
>
> Yrs. v. truly, Lila Field.

*The Goldfish,* "a Fairy Play in three Acts with a Star Cast of Wonder Children," was put on at the Little Theatre on January 27, 1911, and the reviewer for the *Mirror* noted that "Great success is scored by Master Noël Coward as Prince Mussel."

Lila Field also kept in touch with her "discovery" over the years and nearly half a century later wrote to him that for her he would always be "the Goldfish to me," clearly choosing to forget that his Prince Mussel had been a strictly supporting role.

•

THAT SAME AUTUMN he was hired by Sir Charles Hawtrey (1886–1923), the well-known actor/manager, for the part of a pageboy in *The Great Name*. From Hawtrey, he would always claim, Noël learned all the basics of light comedy acting by simply watching how the actor achieved his apparently casual effects. Hawtrey taught him how to laugh onstage—an art infinitely more difficult than it appears—and how to use his hands. Both of these techniques figured largely in the mature Coward repertoire.

By the time *The Great Name* turned out to be not so great, Noël was cast as the Pageboy in Hawtrey's production of *Where the Rainbow Ends,* a Christmas show that for many years rivaled the classic *Peter Pan.*

Most of the children for the production were provided by the legendary Miss Italia Conti (1874–1946), who, with her equally formidable sister, Mrs. Murray, "a dragon in Astrakhan," ran a school that provided children for most West End productions. In this first season Noël's part was confined to the play's first act so Miss Conti shortly suggested that he might double as a hyena in act 2—a suggestion that did not find favor with either Noël or Violet. What was the point of leaping around in a hot fur suit when nobody knew or could see who was doing the leaping?

Noël retained a vivid recollection of Miss Conti's habit of dosing him regularly with Epsom salts (a well-known laxative), doubtless in the belief that the secret of all evil lay in the bowels. This merely succeeded in making rehearsals extremely convulsive for him.

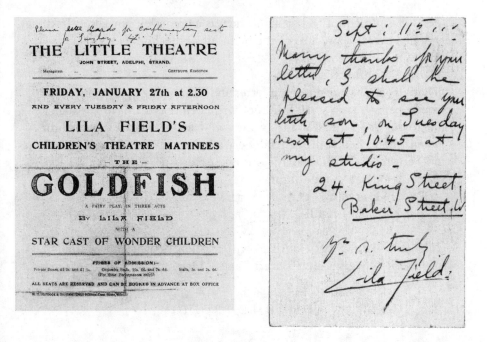

Noël's memories of the lady died hard, and even ten years later he was enclosing to his mother a verse he had written about the experience:

### ODE TO ITALIA CONTI

*Oh, Italia, with thy face so pale*
*Why must you float about the Stalls*
*Where Mr. Hawtrey sits?*
*Dost think that passing thus thou wilt prevail*
*Upon him to cut out the finest bits*
*Which we poor principals in our parts must speak?*
*We often hear the hapless ballet tremble*
*When they're corrected by your raucous squeak.*

*To principals you like not you will serve*
*Out contracts in which cheek and guile are blended*
*And then you have the most appalling nerve*
*To say they must be yours till world is ended.*
*In vain you've tried to lure us to your classes—*
*We are not such unmitigated asses.*

Noël was not simply a boy actor; he was a homesick boy actor. In these early years this was a recurrent theme in his letters home to Violet:

Darling Mummy,
Thank you for your nice long letter and Chums [a popular children's comic paper]. I am sorry I did not write before but I have got such a lot to do. You know I always want you just a very little bit at night when I go to bed and I generally cry a bit but it is nothing to speak of! You are *SUCH* a *DARLING*. Please excuse me, won't you, duckie, as it is a quarter to ten (night).
Love to everyone from your ever loving son
NOËL

In 1917, looking back on his own experiences as a child actor, Noël wrote a series of verses on "Concert Types." One of them was:

## THE CHILD PRODIGY

*An infant prodigy of nine*
*Is shoved upon the stage in white.*
*She starts off in a dismal whine*
*About a Dark and Stormy night,*
*A burglar whose heart is true,*
*Despite his wicked looking face!*
*And what a little child can do*
*To save her Mama's jewel case!*
*This may bring tears to every eye.*
*It does not set my heart on fire*
*I'd like to stand serenely by*
*And watch that Horrid child expire!*

In March 1913 Noël went away for the first time without Violet. For three weeks he was in Liverpool and Manchester to appear in Basil Dean's production of Hauptmann's *Hannele*.

In that production he met someone who was to be the second most influential woman in his life—Gertrude Dagmar Clausen Lawrence (aka Gertie Lawrence)—an overly mature fifteen-year-old. From the outset they found they shared the same irreverent sense of humor. Both were cast as angels, and on one auspicious occasion the curtain rose on this highly dramatic piece to find two angelic members of the cast, gorged on peppermints, being spectacularly sick over the scenery.

The twenty-five-year-old director, Basil Dean, was even then a martinetin-the-making. In the 1920s he was to direct five of Noël's plays, but the balance of their relationship was established right here, in 1913. Displeased by something Dean had said, the thirteen-year-old Coward warned him, "Mr. Dean, if you ever speak to me like that again, I shall go straight home to my mother."

That summer Noël spent with his aunt Vida, his mother's sister, at Lee-on-Solent and his letters were in playful mood. On the page he drew four long lines, then wrote:

Dear and most august Parent,
This is a letter, although you may not think so. These lines are to show how much I adore you. I am still as beautiful as rotten Mangold-Wurzel. I met the Douglas woman today and told her what fun I had when I was at my Zenith! (I hope that isent a rude word!!!) Farewell Beloved.
                    Your Sweet Son Noël.

In the autumn he must have felt that he was, indeed, at his "zenith." He auditioned at the Duke of York's Theatre for the annual production of *Peter Pan* and a few days later received a letter with the heading "CHARLES FROHMAN, LONDON AND NEW YORK":

Dear Master Coward,
On behalf of Mr. Frohman, I engage you to play the part of 'Slightly' in *Peter Pan* on or about December 23rd, at a salary of £4 a week. Kindly write and confirm this and oblige.
                    Yours truly,
                    W. Lestocq
                    General Manager

It was the farewell season of the legendary Peter—Pauline Chase—who had played the part for eight successive years. Naturally, most of the audience acclaim was for her, but Noël received good reviews himself and was thrilled when, on the last night, he left the theater to cries from the crowds waiting for Miss Chase of "good old Slightly!" As critic Kenneth Tynan was to comment years later, "Forty years ago he was Slightly in *Peter Pan,* and you might say that he has been wholly in *Peter Pan* ever since."

The following year there was rather less to be cheerful about. Once the *Peter Pan* tour ended, Noël was diagnosed as having a tubercular gland in his chest and packed off to Dr. Etlinger's sanatorium at Wokingham, from which he wrote to his mother with a cheerfulness that may have been a little forced. Young actors, after all, cannot turn themselves into stars without a stage.

Noël—Boy Actor as Boy Artist.

Cranham, nr. Stroud, Gloucester

Darling Mummy,
It is simply perfect down here it's a dear little cottage on the side of a
very steep hill, woods at the back and woods at the side and a lovely
valley in front with a lake, a cow, a horse, two puppies and a good
many snakes! Today I have seen an Adder, a Grass Snake, and a blind-
worm they abound, Mrs. E is so nice so is the Doctor. There is a
lovely pony I ride I am going shopping on him this afternoon. There
is a forest opposite us. Out of my bedroom window I can see and hear
a Waterfall, The Regent's Canal begins in this garden I had a grass
Snake round my neck today!!! (me don't think!). Do send my bathing
dress. I dident feel a bit homesick last night. Love to everything,
everybody, anyhow, anywhere.

Your ever loving son Noël
P.S. I was up to my calfs in mud at 7 oc this morning

·

SOON AFTER HIS return from the sanatorium, Noël met Philip
Streatfeild, an aspiring artist. One can only speculate on the relationship
between a thirty-year-old man and a fourteen-year-old precocious boy, but
clearly Violet did not disapprove. When Philip and his friend Sidney
Lomer took a motor tour that summer, she allowed Noël to go with them.

Brother Eric Vidal Coward
(1905–1933) with Noël.

Cornwall sur le Corn

Dear Darling old Mummy-snooks,

I *am* enjoying myself so much it really is perfectly Heavenly here. Donald Bain [another London friend of Philip's] has got the most ripping pair of field-glasses that ever happened in this wide universe and the next! If you see a little smoke on the Horizon and you look at it through the glasses it immediately turns into a huge liner! We are right opposite the "Eddistone Lighthouse" and it looks so tall and white standing straight up in the sun. We haven't had such very lovely weather its generally been a leetle beet to cold a wind to be really nice but we bathe from a sandy cove about a mile along the cliffs and then lie in the sun and dry. I am now the coulour of a boiled lobster with which these shores abound (not to say sharks! O-o-er-r Auntie!) This house is so perfectly ripping so beautifully furnished and its about 300 feet above the sea and I climb right down every morning to catch fish for my aquarium which is a clear pool in the rocks. Philip has bought me a net with which to catch le denizens de la deep (Bow-wow!) We have a boat in which we have been as far as the mouth (or gaping jaws) of the Harbour and then we came back because Philip said it was too rough. Philip and I are going to send you a tin of Cornish cream once a week. I received le sweater et le lettre all right and it fits me, Tres chic!!! (More Bow-wows!) I haven't been very homesick but I have been a little (bless you). I shall have to

"Little Flapper" comes of age. Noël at the theatrical garden party.
(At extreme right is Nigel Bruce.)

stoppp now as I am going to wallow in Bacon and eggs so goodbye
and love to Daddy and Eric and Florrie and Tinker and any old thing
you like to munch!

Hope you are quite well as leaves me at pres.

Your everevereverever loving

NOËL

P.S. I will write every Saturday.

And write every week he did—not just on this holiday but for the rest
of her life when he was away from her, with abject apologies when he
missed a date. In this letter, for the first time, the tone is jocular, the hand-
writing bolder; there is the playful use of French (however inaccurate!) and
already one sees the consistent use of the diaeresis in "Noël." A young man
beginning to feel self-confident in an adult world.

The mention of Eric is a rare one. The brothers were never close and the
only letter of the period is a rather stilted one from Eric.

Dear Noël.

Tink swallowed a bone today and she was sick three times and
brought it up the first time. She was a good dog yesterday she went
to her box three times running. Did you like the Forth Bridge? Good
bye for now.

From Eric.

At the end of the jaunt Philip dropped Noël off at his aunt Laura's house in Charlestown. There was the familiar lake and the garden. There were his cousins Walter and Connie Bulteel, always ready to create a little harmless chaos.

On this occasion the devilry they devised was for Noël to dress up as a girl for one dinner party to see how long he could carry off the deception. It was almost too successful, for one young man—perhaps overstimulated by fruit cup—fell madly under the spell of this bewitching young woman and declared his passion in the garden. Noël briskly steered him indoors to the safety of the crowd but managed to keep up the act until the party was over.

Next morning the young man returned to press his suit, only to be told by the Bulteels that the charming young lady had already left. However, should he care to leave a note for her . . . He did care.

> White Hart Hotel, St. Austell
> May 13th 1914

My Dear Little Flapper,
You can imagine my feelings when I arrived at the Bulteels this morning, to find you had flown. I was fearfully sick and wished your friends a long way off, as I was looking forward to spending an exceedingly pleasant morning with you on the lake and was beastly disappointed. I do call it real hard lines and I am still feeling beastly depressed. I meant to have traveled up with you as far as Plymouth and now all my nice little plans have been upset. I have got a little remembrance of you which I am loath to part with—your cigarette holder. Am I to send it to you? If so, let me know and I will grudgingly do so. When are you coming down to Cornwall again? Can't you get your Aunt to ask you to Charlestown again before August or must I wait till then before I see you again? I hope to get to town sometime in July and if so, I shall come and call on you and I shall be very bucked if I can manage that.

Now, be a dear and write and tell me how you are getting on; will you let me write to you occasionally and, if so, will you promise to answer my letters? Should I be presuming too much if I asked for your photo? I hope that I shall hear from you soon and that you are not going to ignore and forget me altogether.

Wishing you the best of luck and with best love
     Yours ever

But, strangely, "Dear Little Flapper" was never seen or heard from again. She might as well have drifted off into the mist of morning, like a character in a J. M. Barrie fantasy.

•

THE FRIENDSHIP WITH Philip Streatfeild continued, but the golden days of summer were now clouded with the prospect of war. On August 4 it was declared.

Philip enlisted as a second lieutenant in the Sherwood Foresters on November 10. Just before Noël rejoined the *Peter Pan* company for the 1914/15 season, he wrote to Violet from Philip's London address.

> 53 Glebe Place, Chelsea
> Friday
>
> Ducky old Diddleums,
> Philip is now a soldier! (cheers) and I am going to stay tonight with him as I shant see much of him when he is drilling all day. I took him to *The Little Minister* last night [a revival of J. M. Barrie's play that was at the Duke of York's Theatre in the evenings, while *Peter Pan* occupied it for matinées] and Mr. Matthews promised to let me have two more seats when I wanted them. I couldn't say anything about *Peter Pan* because he was surrounded by people but I will when I go with you. *Peter Pan* is still up in the box office so I expect it is going to be produced.
> The play is ripping the most beautiful scenery you ever saw and Marie Lohr is sweet but its all in very broad Scotch so unless we get stalls you won't hear a word. I am going to see Captain Charlton this morning and Captain Somers is going to take Philip and Captain C and yours truly to a box at a Music Hall tonight. No evening dress required. Good bye for now.
> > Ever your own
> > Dinkybobs

By June 1915 Philip was training and Noël visited him:

> The Moorings, Harpenden, Herts.
> Just a line to tell you I shall be back in time for Friday afternoon. I am having the time of my life here. I have just come back from a long day with Somer's division and I've marched 10 miles! And I'm so tired all the officers are so nice to me and all wanted to share their lunch with me. You've got a fascinating youth for your son, my dear. George is teaching me to drive the car so good bye now, darling.
> > Ever so much love,
> > Dinky

•

ALTHOUGH THE EXCITEMENT of his older male friends preparing to go to war was more immediate, there was another friend who was exercising a more important and lasting influence on Noël's life.

In that first 1911 production of *Where the Rainbow Ends* with Sir Charles Hawtrey, the leading lady was "a podgy, brown-haired little girl with a bleating voice." Her name was Esmé Wynne.

They met in January and Noël records her attending his twelfth birthday party the following December. By that time they were "best friends" and practically inseparable, according to Violet Coward.

They gave each other affectionate, if not very flattering, nicknames. She was "Stoj" and Noël was "Poj." They would spend hours discussing the key issues of the universe—sex, religion, life and death—though what conclusions they reached, if any, are not recorded. Esmé's religious convictions, though passionately held, were somewhat volatile in nature, and her anxiety to bring Noël to the latest Truth was the one source of friction between them—and one that grew as later years went by.

To mitigate the arguments, they would eventually draw up a semiformal document they called "Rules of Palship":

## RULES OF PALSHIP BETWEEN
## ESMÉ WYNNE AND NOËL COWARD

1. We must not tease one another and if we begin we must stop directly we are asked.
2. We must take it in turns to go and see one another and if one goes twice running to the other's house, the other must do the same afterwards.
3. We must *never* split on one another even if the PALSHIP is dissolved and we must hold all confidences sacred.
4. We must share all profits in any transaction made together, however slight the help of the other may be. Profits are excluded from any expenses incurred during the said transaction.
5. In case of serious quarrel a week or a fortnight may be taken to think things over before abolishing the PALSHIP.
6. If one hits the other either in anger or fun, he must allow the other to hit back. Any other offence must be paid for.
7. We must stick up for each other against anyone or anything, and stand by each other in all danger.
8. We must tell each other all secrets concerned with ourselves, other confidences may be held sacred even from one another.
9. We must not talk RELIGION unless it is inevitable.

10. When writing to mutual friends we must tell each other, we must also tell each other what we have said in the letter.
11. We must swear by "<u>HONOUR AS A PAL</u>" and hold it <u>THE</u> most sacred of bonds in the world.
12. We must tell each other what we think about the other's appearance or behaviour.
13. We must go straight to one another in case of mischief being made and believe NOTHING unless it comes from the other's own lips.
14. NO ONE, not even our Parents, may keep us from one another.
15. If any other rules are formed or thought of, they must be added (with the consent of both) at the end of this document.
16. <u>NO OTHER PERSON</u> may be admitted into our PALSHIP or SECRETS.

SIGNATURE OF BOTH

Dated August the 11th 1915

Esmé Wynne          Noël Coward

"Rules of Palship" between Noël and Esmé Wynne.

In 1932, when Noël was first contemplating his autobiography, Esmé wrote, "I found our rules of palship in an old desk the other day. Would you like a copy? It's terribly funny and shows what complete children we were in some ways, even at fifteen. I'm afraid, however, the 'religion' clause has been violated. So, where do we stand legally?"

·

ESMÉ ASPIRED to be a writer and turned out vast quantities of romantic verse ("alive with elves, mermaids, leafy glades and Pan—a good deal of Pan"). Not to be outdone by a mere girl, Noël found that his competitive spirit urged him to do the same. Frequently they would collaborate, although his efforts tended to turn to the humorous. Both became decidedly prolific. Pen skated across paper, fingers across the keys of the typewriter donated by Uncle Walter Bulteel, and neither stopped writing for the rest of their lives.

In a 1958 letter to a friend, Esmé felt she could pin down the precise moment when Noël's ambition to be a writer was fixed:

It was during the *Rainbow* at the Savoy (where we first met). Charles Hawtrey got me as "leading lady" to write a three-act fairy play [*The Prince's Bride*] for production at a special matinée [February 2, 1912].
It got a great deal of extra publicity because the censor banned it, on account of its length, so at Hawtrey's invitation, the audience had

1912. In Noël's frequent letters to his young actress friend Esmé Wynne ("Stoj" to his "Poj"), the juvenile wit was not confined to the words.

to go out of the theatre and return to witness a "dress rehearsal" of it! All this excitement and publicity, so dear, even then, to the heart of the youthful Noël determined him to write himself, and he suggested that we collaborate, as we did in excruciatingly bad sketches, stories and songs during the next few years.

When they were parted by circumstance—such as when Esmé went off to a Belgian convent school—Noël would write her whimsical letters. In the early summer of 1914 (in a letter of which the first page is missing) he writes:

Who is this Miriam of whom you speak? Give her my love and tell her that I hope she'll do some good with it because I can't. Ah! Me I am wandering again. At the beginning of August I am going to Lee [-on-Solent] avec my parents and they are going to stay about six weeks, and I don't know what I am going to do without my Stodge because there won't be any room at Lee when we are all down there.

Can't we arrange so that we can be together lots? Please go on with all your wicked ways at the Convent and get expelled and come home! DO!!!!! I am longing for you. I've got to sing at three concerts and "At Homes" (mixed) this month . . .

(Now his rendition of what happens at the "Agonising Theatre" when he does so. Outside a long line of matchstick people queue to get in. Inside onstage, Noël is singing, "My heart still clings to you." Below, the same people pour out of the emergency exit "After the 1st line.")

I am going away on the 1st July avec Philip. It will be ripping will not it?

(Another drawing captioned "I Dream of You By Night and Day." A Noël with outstretched elongated arms lies in bed and cries, "Help! Mother." Another figure [Esmé?] sits on top of a London omnibus carrying advertising slogans for "Pears Soap" and "Wait and See Liver Pills." Just to make sure there is no mistake, the figure also bears the caption "This is a Buss.")

Isn't Motor Cycling Glorious I did it a lot on my cousin's cycle down in Cornwall it certainly beats Motoring for thrills.

(Drawing of a boy and girl on a motorcycle. Her hat has been blown off.)

Goodbye now darling old Stodgekins from your ever loving Pal to all Eternity.

> Podge

N.B. You got some Romantic in your last letter.

•

NINETEEN FIFTEEN . . . and war is suddenly no longer a vaguely romantic adventure. Every family is losing a father, a brother, a husband. Philip Streatfeild, who, like so many others, enlisted so bravely in November 1914, is invalided out in the spring and dies on June 3 of tuberculosis of the lung, the same condition Noël had suffered from a year before. In *Present Indicative,* Noël would write: "Philip died . . . without ever realizing to the full the kindness he had done me."

At Christmas Noël was reengaged for the annual production of *Rainbow,* playing the part of The Slacker, half man, half dragon, and all ham— at least the way Noël played him. Again in the cast was Esmé, and as soon as the run finished, they were engaged to tour in *Charley's Aunt.* Noël was to play the title part, Charles Wyckham, and Esmé was Amy Spettigue, the ward.

The tour crisscrossed the country, which, in those days, boasted a theater of sorts—and sometimes more than one—in anything that even *called* itself a town: Hastings, Nottingham, Chester, Blackpool, Rugby, Birmingham, Manchester, Hanley, Torquay, Bristol, Wolverhampton. Sometimes the venues were geographically adjacent; more often the company went wherever a one-week slot was open, regardless of the travel involved. It was a world of boarding houses that would take "theatricals"—some of them a home-away-from-home, others rather more questionable—of packing up the show after the Saturday evening performance, and of waiting around in draughty railway

1916. *Charley's Aunt* was the homesick young Noël's first extended tour—and it showed him more of his native land than he reasonably wanted to see.

stations early every Sunday morning for a train that would arrive late and take forever to get where it was going.

It was a way of life that taught an actor his or her trade—and made them determined to get out of the provinces and into the West End as soon as possible. If they ever returned, it would be to "ride in triumph through Persepolis" (or at least Hull). In later years Noël would recall "those wonderful touring days" in song:

> *Touring days, touring days,*
> *What ages it seems to be*
> *Since the landlady at Norwich*
> *Served a mouse up in the porridge*
> *And a beetle in the morning tea.*

Every week, wherever they were playing, Noël would write home to Violet. A collage of extracts from those letters gives some idea of what his life then was like.

To begin with, Noël was not particularly happy to be cast as Charley, a character he felt was there only for the others to score off. He felt that the part of Jack Chesney offered more opportunity, and he was delighted to be able to stand in as Jack at Nottingham.

I was a great success . . . I looked so funny, like a fair edition of Vesta Tilley [the famous male impersonator in the music halls of the period]. I forgot most of his lines and had to gag a lot. I played it again on Monday and my love scene with Kitty was the funniest thing you ever knew. I said—"My hopes will be nil and my fears tremendous", instead of the other way around and, of course, Kitty collapsed like a pricked balloon. I am playing Charley again now but I quite enjoyed playing Jack for a change.

There were frequent bouts of homesickness, which Esmé shared, and one suspects that each indulged the other.
Birmingham again:

Bless your dear heart, how homesick I am sometimes. Esmé and I both wept on the stage in unison the other day.

Hanley:

My own old mother, how I am longing and longing for you. So is Esmé for her Mummy. We have both been crying hard for the last hour. Never again do I go on tour. This feeling of being so far away is too dreadful for words, but I must try not to be melancholy and cheer up but, all the same, Hanley is the most horribly depressing place I have ever been to . . .

Not surprisingly, some of their colleagues were less than sympathetic to the two tear-stained young thespians:

Ela [Norah Howard] got in an awful rage with us yesterday for crying and was very rude indeed, since then she has sulked and not spoken a word! She is very nice in some ways but Stodge and I can never stand anyone who sulks, so next week Esmé is having a bedroom and sitting room in one and I am having a room out and we are having all our meals together. I think it will be nicer, anyway it's no business of Ela's if we like to cry for our mothers and I'm sure it did us good.

Being on the road so long, of course, created certain domestic problems:

Are there two vests of mine at home? It seems to me that I have been wearing the two I have on now since the tour started. I think they are getting somewhat congealed!!! Please send me the other two.

Whenever they came to a new location and had any free time, Noël and Esmé would explore the neighborhood.

When the New Forest was nearby (Esmé recalled) "we went into the forest and heard the stillness of it all and rubbed our faces in the cool moss and I picked ferns and red and green ivy and baby leaves. The smell was earthy and good." While in Torquay they found a suitably quiet beach where they "sat on a rock and let the water run over us, then we raced about the rocks and danced on the cliffs in the nude—it was so lovely and our figures looked so pretty against the green and blue."

Not that every outing was so idyllic. At Peterborough:

Yesterday I went for a country walk with Stoj . . . and after we had walked across a rather boggy meadow I discovered I had lost one of my goloshes! I hunted for it but it was no good, so in a fit of Pique (good word that!) I threw my other one up in a tree and it stuck! So I threw Sidney (the stick) up to knock Gerald (the golosh!) down and HE stuck. I tried for three quarters of an hour to get him down but he was firmly wedged, so now I am stickless!

And at Hastings:

Stodge and Ayshie have been very bad with sunburn . . . I haven't been particularly sore but I am nearly black and peeling gracefully at all extremities. Such fun!

We had an air raid [zeppelin] the other night a few miles away, also a thunderstorm. Such excitement!

Ayshie tobogganed down a rather steep cliff on her bummy yesterday and bruised same! Little Rogue!

Torquay:

We have all been having great fun taking silly photos with Kitty's camera. [Kitty Verdun was the name of the character played by Enid Groom]. Kindly imagine me your pretty little son lying at full length on the Promenade with Ela sitting on my stomach and with an upraised penknife in her hand and Kathy Barber in the background with her hair over her face crying—"Stop—in Heaven's name—Stop!!!" We took lots more of the same style!

Tomorrow we are going out with a cigar box on a tripod and pretend to take cinema pictures. We have already shocked half of Torquay. We shall finish it off tomorrow.

Hastings:

On Sunday Ayshie and I went on the pier to listen to the band and like fools, we took the dog with us. He barked without ceasing all through *Pagliacci* and we had heated altercations with practically the entire population of Hastings. As we rose with great dignity to go, some feeble-minded rogue at the back started clapping and everyone took it up! So without any fuss and to their extreme consternation we sat down again! Stalky then resumed his barking and kept it up all afternoon.

Wolverhampton and the tour are almost over but not before they encounter another problem:

My dear, I get so fed up with relations . . . On Friday morning we were all in our sitting room, Kitty with her hair down, having just washed it, Esmé putting lace on a pair of knickers and myself painfully working through a new song at the piano, when in walked dear Dolly. She asked us all to tea that afternoon. She said it was a two penny bus fare. We all at once went into peals of hysterical laughter because, being Friday, we had exactly 1½d. between us . . . Well, Dolly thought we were laughing at her and looked rather offended, so we had to explain.

She was very scandalized at us not having any money and said how pathetic it was. We said we thought it peculiarly amusing. Anyhow, she lent us 2/6d. In the afternoon we all trooped up there. She has a lovely house and we entertained her very nicely, all singing and dancing our very Bests. Esmé and I sang "We've been married just one year," and she was most shocked. I've never met anyone so painfully provincial in all my life.

Well, on Saturday I was asked to lunch alone. I had to go to give her the 2/6d. back, and all through lunch she and her stout and corseted sister enlarged upon the dreadful Pitfalls and Perils that await a young girl on the Stage. She said if *she* had any children, *she'd never* let them go on the Stage! And how she pitied poor Esmé and Enid being on the Stage! And anyone more revolting than her husband I've never seen. He drank ale and made a noise like water running out of the bath and crammed his fork with food and shoved it into his great gullet. Altogether he made me quite sick. All through lunch he read me extracts from Lloyd George's speeches and long letters that he (Mr. Robertson) had written to the *Daily Mail* . . . I did try to drown the noise he was making with his mouth by bubbling into my lemonade, but I failed miserably.

Dear, dear, etc. It was the limit. She said she didn't want to come to *Charley's Aunt,* as she'd heard . . . that I had got such a rotten part! I said she had better not go, then and at once began to point out and paint in lurid colours the awful Trials and Temptations that await the common or garden (generally the former) typist and that having a typewriter myself, I could well believe it. I said that the Stage was *the* one moral and proper place nowadays and that thousands of respectable and be-principled Clergyman's Sons and Daughters had left comfortable and upholstered in red plush Vicarages for the staid lives of Actors and Actresses. This seemed to impress them and I left the house inwardly fuming but outwardly smiling and with a *Play Pictorial* I have been wanting for years under my coat.

Luckily, there was light at the end of the railway tunnel:

On Sunday my train arrives at Euston at 1:45 and leaves here at 11:00. We shall have to take a taxi as I shall have Bertha the Basket as well as my two bags, Hilda and Eileen, to say nothing of Joyce the Typewriter and Maurice and Oswald, the Mackintosh and Overcoat respectively but I think I shall be able to pack them as they are only boys!

•

SOMEHOW OR OTHER Noël and Esmé found the time to write together, and in 1917 two short plays by Esnomel (their clumsy joint sobriquet) were put on as curtain raisers in professional theaters: *Ida Collaborates (The Last Chapter),* played at the Theatre Royal, Aldershot, in August, and *Woman and Whisky,* in November at Wimbledon. After which their lives sharply diverged and put an end to their working together.

The old intimacy was over, though the friendship continued after Esmé's marriage, which broke up in 1929.

In later years, when Noël was making his name, Esmé would send him her work for his professional critique. His notes to her offer some interesting sidelights on his own emerging theories of drama. In many ways they comprised a first draft for the book on the theater he intended to write one day and never did.

You're at your old game—you *point* things too much. (Let the fact of there being a scarcity of men be apparent in their *attitude,* but don't mention it, because it's blatant!)

Your dinner scene is ridiculously short. You must give at least two pages to every course, if not more.

You must not abbreviate words and use suburban slang such as "vamping", "coddling", etc., unless it's essential psychologically. (It's quite appalling and the obvious result of the people you're mixing with—you never used to do it.)

You have a serene and maddening disregard for superficial details which destroys atmosphere in exactly the places where you wish to use them to create it. (One bright moment that shattered my sensibilities is the thought that Peter's room in 1915–16 being filled with lusty photographs of Marie Tempest—then about 59—and Mrs. Patrick Campbell—then about 48).

You've devoted your entire energy to the writing and haven't given a thought to *construction* or sense of the Theatre or Drama or climax—all of which are necessary in a good play.

You have a Prose mind not a dialogue mind. Novelists can't write plays and playwrights can't write novels—at least very *seldom*—Clemence Dane and Galsworthy.

·

NINETEEN THIRTY-SIX NOW, and Noël is touring with *Tonight at 8:30,* but even so, he's not too busy to spare time to write to Esmé about her latest offering:

Kings Theatre, Edinburgh

Darling Stoj

As I have been living in the country in almost complete seclusion since June working on three plays and have only spent nine nights in the gay metrollops in four months, I am *actually* more busy socially now than I was then, but even so I have found, nay *made* opportunity during these hectic crowded hours to read *Prelude to Peace* from what is known as cover to cover. I did *not* find the actual reading dull, owing to a strange new simplicity of style that you have evolved. I think the bulk of it is extraordinarily well done and, apart from just a few sentimental digressions, rigidly to the point. No intelligent reader could fail to appreciate your utter sincerity and the sound sense of your educational theories but unfortunately, as you are an idealist, *soi disant,* and I am a realist, ever so *soi disant,* I fear we shall never see human life eye to eye and tooth to tooth and cheek to cheek and bottom to bottom. At the risk of bitter postal accusations of reactionalism, I will boldly announce that it is my considered opinion that the human race (*soi disant*) is cruel, idiotic, sentimental, predatory, ungrateful, ugly, conceited and egocentric to the last ditch and that the occasional discovery of an isolated exception is as deliciously surprising as finding a sudden brazil nut in what you *know* to be five pounds of vanilla creams. These glorious moments, although not making life actually worth living, perhaps, at least make it pleasanter.

You may well imagine that with such a jaundiced view I am a very unhappy creature but this is not so—I have a very nice time all told and enjoy life keenly—I can't explain this—perhaps there will be a reckoning—perhaps I only *think* I'm happy—perhaps I shall suddenly find Jesus but I still have the grace to hope, both for his sake and for mine, that I don't!

At all events, my darling old cow, I salute your ideals with (for me) considerable reverence and I'm sending the ten pounds from the heart because, as you know, I'm just *au fond* an old beauty lover and dreamer (*soi disant*).

All love<br>POJ

All French interpolations in this letter by courtesy of the Linguaphone!

In 1934 Noël is still pondering the autobiography—and Esmé, who knows her subject better than anyone, is continuing to ponder him:

You know, it's practically impossible to talk really seriously face to face with you. I believe it's a sort of psychological armour. And it certainly has its points—and disadvantages, the chief of them being that you always see other people with a layer of artificiality over them. You prefer them like that, depth being uncomfortable.

She was one of the few people at this stage to see the phenomenon called "Noël Coward" in perspective.

I wonder if you realise how you, personally, are getting to dwarf your achievements . . . it gets more noticeable every time I see you . . . nothing to do with your writing at all—though, of course, it will affect that.

Three years later she—and everyone else—could read the result in *Present Indicative.* It contained an affectionate account of the early years of Poj and Stoj, but Esmé took strong exception to it:

Flat 3
19 Chesham Place
Brighton
8.6.37

Darling,

—even in the sense it's rather like squashing soap bubbles with a hatchet to apply the touchstone of truth to your bright and gay babblings about our early life together, but I think a little honest psychoanalysis on the subject mightn't come amiss. I can't believe you're as inaccurate when dealing with other aspects of your life as you are on the points which concern us.

I can understand you exaggerating, as you do in places, to make a good story—that's the showmanship coming out—but to invent and to twist facts until they become the reverse of facts isn't worthy of a Cynic or "a seeker after *relative* truth". I enclose a copy of corrections for you to ponder . . . I can't think why you've got this so wrong. It's as though you invent an aspect to a case which you want to believe, and then insist on believing it.

I found that part of your life when we were not together most interesting and it explained so much I'd not realized. I never understood before what you must have gone through in that epileptic ward, for instance, or during that first visit to America . . . I think the book is clever, too, in the way the writing matures with the life. The frivolous beginning and that really impressive piece of writing about the production of *Cavalcade,* which is, of course, your *chef d'oeuvre* up to date. But I wonder if you realize that to the discerning eye what you have *not* told reveals even more than what you have told, which may or may not be a good thing. On the whole, I do feel a little what you felt so strongly when Ethel Mannin wrote *her* autobiography—that it's not good policy. Meanwhile, of course, while it is earning so much money and publicity, it must be hard for you to judge.

The chief interest to me in the book is that throughout you are asking "Why?"—still seeking for truth. But there's a stumbling block that will always prevent you finding it—until you deal firmly with the stumbling block. You will accept any relative truth (the symptoms of T.B., for instance) and your one desire is not to be fooled, by any uncomfortable, fundamental Truth, which is going to interfere with your way of living, or alter your attitude towards life, you will, so far, resist to the last ditch.

Of course, this is only the fringe of a very large subject which I don't feel you want to discuss yet—anyhow with me. I used to think your habit of evading a logical issue to an argument through abuse or humour was weakness. I'm now convinced it's a protective armour— and that's another big subject.

So I will what is known as "close", writing pads being finite and time being so frightfully on the wing . . .

Fondest love—*malgré tout*—and that's charitable anyhow— though when I think of the things you *could* have said, it's a puzzle to me why you didn't keep to facts!

But there, you always were a "puckish sprite".

Eternally—
Titania.


Twelve years later the "large subject" looms even larger and Esmé has even written a book on it (*The Unity of Being*). As far as she was concerned, Noël was "dead from the neck up" when it came to religion, and it was her mission to resurrect him.

17 Gerald Road
London S.W.1.
19th October, 1949

Darling Stoj,

It was lovely to hear from you and to know you are still bright as a button and not lost and gone before.

I am writing this before reading your book, because I am at the moment in the throes of doing a new musical [*Ace of Clubs*] which is very cheerful and robust and neither Victorian nor nostalgic, and am also casting my new comedy [*Island Fling*] and putting finishing touches to the film I have just done [*The Astonished Heart*]; and as your book does not seem the sort of little book-stall number that would make an unnecessary journey go in a flash, I shall wait for two or three weeks and read it carefully. In the meantime, do you ever come up to London or are we never to meet again until I am on my deathbed and you appear with, I hope, not *extreme* unction?

You ask me how I am thinking these days; do you know, the awful thing is I don't believe I am thinking very differently from the way I always have thought. My philosophy is as simple as ever. I love smoking, drinking, moderate sexual intercourse on a diminishing scale, reading and writing (not arithmetic). I have a selfless absorption in the well-being and achievements of Noël Coward. I do not care for any Church (even the dear old Mother Church) and I don't believe there is a Universal Truth and if you have found it you are better men than I am, Gunga Din.

In spite of my unregenerate spiritual attitude, I am jolly kind to everybody and still attentive and devoted to my dear old Mother who is hale and hearty, sharp as a needle and occasionally very cross indeed.

I have built myself a little house in Jamaica on the edge of the sea where I eat bread-fruit, coconuts, yams, bananas and rather curious fish and where also I lie in the sun and relax and paint a series of pictures in oils, all of which I consider to be of great beauty but which, in reality, are amateur, inept and great fun to do.

I have not yet found Jesus but I am pegging on with my nose to the grindstone and my shoulder to the wheel and also with a great deal of love for my childhood playmate whom I should like to see again if some old Universal Truth would lead her (in an off moment) to 17 Gerald Road, S.W.1.

Love and kisses

PS Lorn sends you her best love
PPS I also drink rum in Jamaica
PPPS I am looking very pretty in a chocolate-boxy sort of way.

God bothered Noël. And Esmé was perceptive when she observed that when something became too difficult or serious for Noël to handle, he seemed to feel the need to distance himself from it—usually with a joke. Some things were too serious to be taken seriously.

In his own way he would return to the subject of God frequently for the rest of his life.

When, in 1917, John Ekins, a mutual friend of his and Esmé's, suddenly died of spinal meningitis while serving in the Royal Flying Corps, Noël expressed the depth of his feelings in verse.

### LINES TO GOD

*If I should ultimately meet my God,*
*He will not be the God of love or Battles,*
*He'll be some under God whose job it is*
*To organize sharp sounds and things that rattle.*
*He'll be the one who, all my life on earth*
*Can, most sadistically, my spirit shatter*
*With little hammerings and sudden shouts*
*And hollow ricochets of empty mirth.*

John Ekins's death—like Philip Streatfeild's—would certainly qualify as one more "hollow ricochet."

John Ekins, a mutual friend
(who died in 1917), Esmé,
and Noël (1916).

21.10.49

My darling Poj,

As to churches, I couldn't agree with you more—including "Mother"—probably principally "Mother"—as you will gather from the careful perusal of *The Unity of Being* which you've promised. But, my pet, you don't know *what* you've promised. Experienced metaphysicians blench, or blanch at the task. But there, I'm a great believer in common sense; and you always have had that. At any rate, I hope you will read it attentively enough to see that I am so far from being Church-bound that the entire book is a plea for "living the life" without benefit of the clergy. I loathe hypocrisy. And the habit of all the churches, except the Quakers, is to teach its tots the ten commandments and the sermon on the mount Sunday after Sunday and then when war comes, incite the little thugs to kill as many of their fellow men who don't happen to agree with them, as they can. And then these dolts of ministers and priests ask why the Church has lost its authority.

You say you don't believe you're thinking very differently from the way you've always thought. Might that not indicate a slight lack of progress? But in fact, your memory appears to fail you. You say "I love smoking, drinking . . ." But in the most clear-sighted period of our close companionship, you did neither, thinking it was more original and sensible not to. On the other hand, I like your Jamaican diet, except for the fish. Why take it out on the fish?

I *am* glad to hear you've still got your precious Mum in a visible state; but then you always were firm about anything you really wanted. Is she parked in England or Jamaica?

Darling, I've only been to London for three separate days in the last ten years, twice to see [her son] Jon's flat in Hampstead and once to divorce Lynden. And if that poor lad has ever regretted anything more than the fact that I married him it is the fact that I divorced him. He lost a front tooth three weeks after marriage owing to a wild Australian wife's unerring aim. (That'll teach him to break with a pacifist) and has spent the intervening months trying to get protection from her by law. See references to Karmic wheel!

Heaps of love, my pretty lamb, and big hugs.

Yours,
STOJ

In the years that followed the relationship drifted still further, but the memories of events they had shared and that had shaped the people they had become were never far from the surface. "Remember what our eight years' companionship was all about," Esmé wrote in March 1953. "If we aimed too high, at least we didn't commit the common mistake of remaining aimless."

In a letter dated February 24, 1960, she asks him:

I wonder if you remember us standing in a field during that awful *Charley's Aunt* tour, realizing (as I see it was now) *power?* We admitted to each other that we felt within us the power to achieve *anything,* and your integrated wish was to have the world at your feet, theatrically speaking. How surely that wish came true! Yet how far from it you seemed at the time. Mine—just as integrated—was to "know the Truth". It has taken much longer but it's happened.

LES AVANTS
Sur MONTREUX
March 9th 1960

My Darling Stoj,

I was so very very pleased to get your sweet letter. And what with telepathy and one thing and another it arrived just as I was thinking of you. I happened to be having my annual re-read of the E. Nesbits, which I still prefer to any other literature, and there on the fly leaf of *The Magic City* was the evocative name Charles Steuart! And I remembered without remorse how we had broken in and stolen it! Out of evil cometh good is what *I* always say and I don't believe a *word* of it. The phlebitis was a grave bore and my monotonously beautiful right leg swelled up like a pink sausage and I had to be carried about like a parcel. Fortunately I have an Italian house boy who is quite square like a biscuit box and *likes* carrying wardrobes up and down stairs, so he placed me on the loo every morning and then placed me back in bed again and the stupid old clot disappeared and the Good Mind sodden with universal truth suddenly decided that this was all too easy and so, in order to teach me a further sharp lesson, gave me congestion of the left lung which was not serious but jolly painful for three days, because of my stubborn devotion to the frivolous pleasures of life such as breathing! However that has now disappeared too and I am now scampering up and down stairs like a 60 year old and waiting eagerly for the first joyous signs of syphilis.

I was very distressed about Edwina's [Mountbatten] death but, as you say, what an enviable way to go. The sadness, as always, is reserved for those who are left. In any case so many of my friends have upped and died during the last few years that I'm becoming sort of

"Stoj" at seventy.

hardened to it. I start practically every letter now quite automatically with "Words are useless but please accept my deepest etc.,"

All I ask of my friends who are left is that they should live through dinner.

[It was a line good enough to use again and again, sometimes substituting "lunch" for "dinner."]

I remember, I remember so very, very well that long ago day in that far away field. I think we both decided then and there (if not before) that we were going to get what we wanted and, both being determined characters, to say the least of it, we succeeded. I only know that if I should happen to "pop" tomorrow that I have no complaints—I have had a very happy and full life with enough sadness here and there to highlight the happiness. I have had, to quote that classic, *Bittersweet* [*sic*], "A talent to amuse" and, with it, have been able to make many millions of my fellow creatures laugh, which, when all is said and done, is not a bad accolade to retire to the grave with! You have found peace and content in research and solitude. A rare treasure. Whether or not the truths you have discovered are transferable is not the point. The point is that *you* have discovered them. Or It. But *don't* dear perennial* reformer waste *too* much mental energy trying to impart it because that, my darling, leads to disillusion, irritation, discouragement, a thorough upset of your spiritual acids and frequently spots on the back. Just be grateful that you are *convinced* and healthy and still have a twinkle in your eye . . .

I am really in love with this house. When I first saw it it was hideous beyond belief but now, after spending forty million pounds eighteen and fourpence on it, it is lovely. The views are fabulous, lake and mountains and, at the moment, snow. In the Spring it still looks like snow because of the wild narcissi.

Kindly write again and oblige
Your ever loving
POJ

*I know this word is wrongly spelt but I have an Italian typewriter.

To which she replied:

9 Park Lane, Selsey, Sussex
14.3.60

Poj darling,
Until I found Science, I was certainly not ethical, but I WAS cautious (thank heaven or goodness knows what I'd have been landed with!) . . .

But darling, aren't you a bit unrealistic in your advice to me not to impart what I know? It is just as though I said: "Yes, Poj darling, you have indeed a talent to amuse, but don't use it to make other people laugh. Just sit in the bath and have a thoroughly good time with your own jokes." People don't search for a lifetime to find something for the good of mankind and then sit in a corner of a very stoney beach mumbling to themselves about it . . . Darling, it really isn't just a cosy "piece of mind" I've found. It is the answer to what I believe are fundamental questions, which no one ever would or could answer in my youth. Nor would I lay claim to having achieved the abounding physical fitness you credit me with. I 'ave me problems . . .

I LOVE the way you throw off here a ballet, there a light novel. But do leave yourself something to do in your early hundreds. If the first twenty years are too dull people have a tendency, at 120, to commit suicide by going to New York. Whereas the famous Irish countess still enjoyed climbing apple trees at 145. Look after your infant self, still much loved by his
STOJ
P.S. Fondest love, darling. Bits of us remain just the same as they were fifty years ago, and we're probably right to keep to them, instead of meeting and disagreeing on many issues. I really do think your letter of the 9th is the funniest I have ever had from you in my life, which is saying something when I think how letters from you preserved me from near-suicide at that dreadful convent, in 1914 . . .

Which brings me to your extremely fictional account of how we procured the [E] Nesbits. You must know perfectly well that we never "broke in and stole". We went to Steu's flat, armed with a letter from him saying that I could have anything or everything that was in the flat (which he was going to give up). I had to show the distinctly hostile landlady—a friend of his—the letter before she would admit us. And, looking back on my financial situation at the time, it is a wonder to me that I was so moderate, only taking a pink rug, a waste paper basket and a few books . . .

Noël's 1964 Christmas card seems to show him taking a more relaxed view of Esmé's religious preoccupation.

Darling Stoj,

I loved your loving my joke. I read your piece and really you do know a lot! Much more I am sure than Mary Baker Eddy. You are also very lucid. Oh dear, I do wish we saw each other more often. Let's have a try when spring breaks through again! Isn't it peculiar about me being a promising young classic and the Pride of the National Theatre? Dame Edie [Edith Evans, also a Christian Scientist] is a hundred years too old for the part [of Judith in *Hay Fever*] but certainly doesn't look it. I suspect our old friend Mary B E is at it again! Love, love, Poj (Don't be put off by this elegance. It's all a hideous mockery. I *still* pick my nose!)

There is only one more (recorded) example of their correspondence. When Noël received his long-overdue knighthood in the 1970 New Year's Honours List, Esmé sent her congratulations, and Noël promptly replied:

LES AVANTS
January 19th 1970

My Darling Stoj,

I have now had two sweet letters from you so here's one sweet letter from me. I am of course delighted to have the knighthood but what moved me most was the manner in which the Queen offered it to me. It was in the middle of a birthday lunch given for me by the beloved Queen Mother. (You know dear old democratic me—lunch with the Queen one day and Norah Howard the next). She gave me the impression (the Queen, not Norah Howard), that it was *I* who was conferring the honour on *her* instead of the other way around—how's that for Royal Grace! So from now on I shall expect a great deal more deference from you than I have received in the past. You must never sit in my presence—unless I happen to have thrown you onto the sofa and you must always address me as *Sir* Poj. I hope all this is clear in your dizzy mind.

All loving love, my darling old pal
Your devoted old Sir Poj

Norah Howard was the child actress who had appeared with them both in *Charley's Aunt.*

And that effectively was that. Esmé died in 1972.

By the time of this last letter, they had not met for several decades, and they were now two quite different people. Nonetheless, it is hard to escape the conclusion that if Poj and Stoj had never met and shared their personal lives for a while, there might never have been a *Private Lives.*

·

THAT SUMMER, Noël made his first appearance in a film—D. W. Griffith's antiwar film, *Hearts of the World,* starring Lillian and Dorothy Gish. It was a small part, consisting entirely in pushing a wheelbarrow along a "French village" street. Originally Griffith had Noël walking away from the camera, but Noël's stage experience told him that characters with their backs to the audience might as well not be on the stage. Would it not be more effective, he asked the director, if he were to push the barrow toward the camera? Not caring either way, Griffith agreed, and gave us our first view of Noël Coward on camera.

There was something about the young boy that appealed to the Gish sisters, who proceeded to take him under their wing for the duration of the shoot, and remained friends with him for the rest of their lives. As late as 1964, Lillian is writing to Noël and recollecting the experience.

There am I, waving, as you chart your course on the small river in 1917 to float down to the great seas of the world, while I remain moored to the little raft !!!

Bless that day that took us to Broadway in England to meet our dearest genius.

·

IN AUGUST Noël found himself in the company of *Wild Heather* for a three-week booking in Manchester. The booking did not start auspiciously. The country was still at war, and Noël, having witnessed several zeppelin raids, was concerned for Violet back in London. He wrote a rather dejected letter to her from the Midland Hotel:

Wednesday

Darling,

The play is going very well, I come back to Town on Sunday week. I have been very ill the last few days, it started off with a sore throat and me losing my voice . . . Manchester always affects me like this, it is a beastly hole. Most of the company are in the same boat . . . Aren't the air raids awful, please wire me if they go anywhere near our delec-

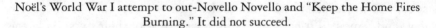

Noël's World War I attempt to out-Novello Novello and "Keep the Home Fires Burning." It did not succeed.

table residence, because I shall probably hear that Clapham has been raised to the ground.

> Farewell now, my lamb
> Ever your ownest
> Snag

Once again we see Noël's predilection for pet names. "Poj" and "Stoj," christening his personal possessions like galoshes, stick, and typewriter, and now—in his correspondence with Violet the two of them became "Snig" and "Snag" (later "Snoop"). Promising material for a psychological dissertation?

It was in Manchester that Noël first met one of his idols, Ivor Novello. Six years older than Noël, Novello was already successful as playwright, composer, actor, and profile, and in the first three respects, at least, Noël was anxious to emulate him.

The meeting was momentous—the two of them were to work together more than once in the following decade—but it was overshadowed for Noël in that particular week by two other events:

Gaiety Theatre
Manchester
Thursday

My Darling,

at the moment I am nearly mad with excitement, it is awful not having you here to tell about it all! My Dear, I am collaborating with Max Darewski in a new song, I wrote the lyric yesterday after breakfast, I hummed it to him in the Midland lounge at 12oc, we at once rushed up to his private room and he put harmonies to it, there were some other people there, when they had sung it over once or twice, Max leapt off the piano stool and danced for joy and said it was going to take London by storm! We are putting the verse to music this morning it is to be published next week and probably sung by Lee White or Phyllis Dare! I am arranging the business part of it today. I shall probably make a lot of money out of it. It is called "When You Come Home On Leave", written and composed by Noël Coward and Max Darewski. He also says he may be able to place "Bertha from Balham" [another Coward song] with Margaret Cooper. You see he is one of the most influential men in town. He owns three theatres. At last I am beginning to make my way, really Manchester has been astonishingly lucky for me. Goodbye now, my Snig. I am too mad to write about anything else. Your Baby, Snag (Dramatist and Composer)

And as if that were not enough excitement . . .

Gaiety Theatre

Darling,

I felt I must write and tell you my news, I was sent for to see Gilbert Miller at the Midland. My Dear, he had come down *specially* to see me in *Wild Heather* and he said I was *really splendid* and that I hadn't half enough to do! Also that it would be all right about the extra week now that he had seen me play, he felt absolutely certain that I should make my name in *The Saving Grace*. He says it is a terrific part and I have to play with Marie Lohr! Isn't it gorgeous. He is going back to Hawtrey today to say that he had perfect confidence in me and that I am thoroughly natural and unaffected etc.. Oh, I am a star!

Your ownest, Noël.

Gilbert Miller, a successful American impresario, was co-producing *The Saving Grace* with Charles Hawtrey later that year. In years to come he would be a key influence on Noël as a playwright, warning him that he must concentrate on plot construction—see Noël's advice to Esmé—before he indulged himself in the process of writing. The point went home, and Noël became duly conscious of "my dangerous facility for dialogue, which I must beware of. Gilbert Miller warned me about it years ago."

Darewski gave him a three-year contract to write lyrics, but few were published and none of them became a hit. Noël took the money until the three years were up and then moved on. Darewski also moved on—into bankruptcy, a situation Noël always claimed he foresaw.

*The Saving Grace* was a different matter altogether. Hawtrey and the press alike recognized Noël for the first time as an actor of stature. Violet went so far as to record that Hawtrey was

> always so very much interested in Noël, and appreciated his charms and humour, and often repeated his remarks . . . Noël was now a tall, well set up young man, very, very popular. He was always witty and amusing and made wonderful friends, who always wanted him to be with them . . . He was wrapped up in the theatre, and everything connected with it, and when people used to be so shocked to think he had had no real education, I always said and felt that he was having his education from his career.

•

AT THE BEGINNING of 1918, Violet had finally had enough of living in the cramped Clapham flat. She took over the lease of a boardinghouse at 111 Ebury Street, and the whole family, including Aunt Vida, moved into the narrow Georgian town house, with Noël ensconced in a tiny room just under the eaves.

No sooner had they settled in than he was summoned to an army medical exam. An earlier one had rejected him pro tem on account of his tubercular history; this one decided that he could serve some useful purpose, and he was immediately inducted into Company C of the Artists' Rifles. The name did nothing to placate him. What was he doing in uniform when a new fifteen-pound-a-week part awaited this rising star?

He was the first to admit in later years that his part in World War I was, to say the least, inglorious. Even Violet had to admit that "I'm afraid he was more trouble than he was worth in the Army and did not help the War along very much." He was a soldier in name only for a mere eight months, and his service involved a psychosomatic breakdown and an accident that confined him to hospital for much of the time. His official record paints a pathetic picture: "Cannot stand any noise and complains of constant headaches. Tremors of both hands plus superficial reflexes. Emotional and unstable. Family history bad."

In August he was invalided out. This anticlimactic ending to his military "career" pleased and relieved him at the time but it also haunted him, making him determined—when it became clear that "the war to end wars" had been nothing but a prelude to a yet bigger conflict—that the next time his contribution would be a significant one.

·

BY THE TIME of Peace Day, in the spring of 1919, London was alive again, full of bright lights and even brighter young things, for whom the old social taboos were a thing of the past.

Noël was a guest of actress Fay Compton at the Victory Ball in her box at the Albert Hall. The rest of the party consisted of Beatrice Lillie, who was to become a major character in Noël's life, and Billie Carleton, a perky young actress whose looks outshone her acting ability. That evening all over the country joy was considerably unconfined, and the following morning Lillie decided to check up on her young friend Billie. On arrival at the girl's hotel, the Savoy, she was told that Miss Carleton had been found dead of a cocaine overdose.

Although he did not know her well, the young woman's pointless death haunted Noël for years to come, and he spoke about it frequently. At the time it must have seemed like a portent of what the following decade might hold. War was not the only way people could destroy themselves.

"Dance, dance, dance, little lady," he would write in a song lyric, "leave tomorrow behind." The way Billie Carleton had left her own tomorrow behind would continue to bother him until it found expression in *The Vortex*.

# CHAPTER 2

# "I LIKE AMERICA"

(1919–1921)

*I like America*
*Its Society*
*Offers infinite variety . . .*

"I LIKE AMERICA," FROM *ACE OF CLUBS*

Oh, my America!
My new found land.

JOHN DONNE

ON MAY 14, 1921, Noël sailed on the SS *Aquitania* on his first visit to New York. His traveling companion was Jeffrey Holmesdale (later Lord Amherst), a young officer in the Coldstream Guards he had met a couple of months earlier and the man who would accompany him to various far-flung parts of the world for the next decade or so and remain his friend for life.

A lot had happened in the last two years, and several of the people he had met would also become lifelong friends. In 1919, at the home of an acting colleague, Betty Chester, he met Lorn MacNaughtan. She seemed "unremarkable in manner and personality, but there was authority in her quietness." As the widowed Lorn Loraine, "Lornie" became the secretary and confidante who would anchor his existence and the Coward "family" until her death in 1967.

It was time to develop social skills that were not naturally inbred in those brought up in Teddington, Clapham, or even Ebury Street. For example, there were gaucheries to be ruthlessly removed, such as those displayed when, invited to a country weekend party at the Dawson-Scotts, he announced his imminent arrival with the cable:

"I Like America," Noël said, and he was to like it even
more as the years went by. Drawing by William
Auerbach-Levy. (Reproduced by permission
of The Players Club, New York.)

ARRIVING PADSTOW 5.30 STOP TALL AND DIVINELY HANDSOME
IN GREY.

The Dawson-Scotts were not amused, and kept a close eye on their
fourteen-year-old-son, Toby.

Fortunately, Mrs. Astley Cooper, an old friend of Philip Streatfeild's,
took Noël under her wing, realizing that here was a young man who did
not need to be taught but simply had to be given the opportunity to learn.

In January of 1920, Noël made his first trip abroad—a one-week visit
to Paris that triggered his love of the city that was to play such a large part
in his later life. He even managed one night at the Ritz, and that hotel and
the social values it represented would also stay with him and crop up time
and again in his work. ("I have a Ritz mind and always have had"—

*Diaries,* April 22, 1960.) A month later he is in Alassio, as the guest of Mrs. Astley Cooper.

In May he had his first play produced. It was called *I'll Leave It to You* and it was—as Noël would say in another context—"jagged with sophistication." After an encouraging opening in Manchester, it moved to London's New Theatre, where audiences took the advice of the play's title and decided to leave it alone after a five-week run. Nonetheless, it was a start, and his name was becoming known.

While waiting for a new acting engagement to start, he took himself back to Italy and finished up again in Alassio, where Mrs. Astley Cooper was once more in residence at the Grand Hotel. This time she had another friend along, who was also to become a founding member of the Coward "family."

Asked to perform at a concert at the English Club, Noël found himself distracted by "a smartly dressed young woman in the front row, who appeared to be fighting an attack of convulsive giggles with singular lack of success." Her name was Gladys Calthrop and, as a designer as well as a friend, she was to become "intimately concerned with all my best work, and so intrinsically part of my failures and successes."

Back in London Noël appeared in a run-of-the-mill imported American farce, *Polly with a Past,* but his interest lay elsewhere. He felt himself to be a creative cornucopia, with songs, sketches, and plays waiting to pour out. It was exciting but dangerously facile.

One of the plays waiting in the wings was *The Young Idea,* based all too closely—as Noël was the first to admit—on Shaw's *You Never Can Tell,* which had been revived in 1919. The script was sent to Shaw, who took the trouble to read it carefully and return it with detailed comments such as "No you don't, young author!"

June 27th 1921

Dear Mr. Coward,

I gather from Mr. Vedrenne that he turned the play down because he had some misgivings about trying to repeat the old success of the twins in *You Never Can Tell,* and was not quite sure that you had pulled off the final scene which I suggested. But when once a manager has entertained a play at all, his reasons for discarding it are pretty sure to be business and circumstantial ones. When you put impudent people on the stage they are very amusing when the actor or actress has sufficient charm to make the audience forgive the impudence: in my youth Charles Mathews lived on impudent parts; and every comedy had a stage cynic in it. Hawtrey has kept up the tradition to some extent; but impudence has been long out of fashion; your twins will take some casting to make them pardonable. I daresay Vedrenne did not know where to lay his hands on the right pair. I have no doubt that you will succeed if you persevere, and take care never to fall into a breach of essential good manners and above all, never to see or read my plays. Unless you can get clean away from me you will begin as a back number, and be hopelessly out of it when you are forty.

> Faithfully,
> G. BERNARD SHAW

Interestingly, from the outset, established writers were prepared to take Noël almost as seriously as he took himself. Novelist Hugh Walpole (1884–1941)—to whom Philip Streatfeild had introduced him during the war—read several of Noël's early efforts and responded to one of them: "You're quite right, your punctuation is vastly better! Also the adjectives, though some of your verbs are still too complicated." As praise went it may not have been exactly effusive, but at least it was attention!

·

SHAW'S LETTER was certainly instrumental in focusing Noël's future, but rather more immediate was the news he had received in August 1919. Gilbert Miller had finally delivered on the commitment he made at the time of *Wild Heather,* up in Manchester. Noël was able to cable Violet on August 29:

> PLAY [*THE LAST TRICK*] ACCEPTED FOR AMERICA ADVANCE OF
> FIVE HUNDRED DOLLARS PASSING PEACEFULLY AWAY LOVE
> NOËL.

America . . . that was where the future lay. All it needed was—Noël Coward.

·

HE HAD A one-way ticket, a case full of manuscripts, and precisely seventeen pounds between him and starvation in a country about which he knew absolutely nothing. Had he done his homework, he might have realized that New York in June during a heat wave can be an uncomfortable place to be, which meant that many of the people he hoped to meet had left the city for the duration.

He spent the first night at the Algonquin, where the witty élite of the Round Table liked to meet and greet. Dorothy Parker, Robert Benchley, Edna Ferber, Alexander Woollcott—many of them would become close friends over the years, but for now they were just names Noël wanted to be able to add to his list of acquaintances.

"New York seemed, in spite of its hardness and irritating, noisy efficiency,
a great and exciting place."

The hotel might well have been redolent with literary history and the
ghosts of *bons mots,* but it was unfortunately lacking in adequate air-
conditioning. The next day Noël moved to the cooler (and cheaper)
Brevoort Hotel.

Since his stay was theoretically open-ended, he was concerned to set to
rest Violet's worries about his well-being. The weekly letters continued,
and in an attempt to distract her, he devised a tongue-in-cheek "Diary,"
which commingled a smattering of fact with a good deal of fantasy. He
explained:

> My publisher has informed me that it is the note of careless intimacy
> in published diaries which attracts the public. According to him, peo-
> ple love to know a bit about names and personalities that they have
> never met. For instance, if I wrote—"Tuesday—met Mrs. Fiske—how
> like she is to Auntie Clara, only without her nose"—everyone would
> be immensely thrilled. Tho' until that moment they had never heard
> of Auntie Clara, they would experience a pleasant glow of satisfaction
> in the thought of how like she was to Mrs. Fiske. An atmosphere of
> charming cameraderie would be established. Mrs. Fiske would in all
> probability receive heaps of letters likening her to their Auntie Jessie's
> and their Auntie Amy's and everyone would be pleased.

I was awfully thrilled when he suggested a diary of my American
visit. Here is the opportunity I have been waiting for, I told myself. I

The Algonquin Round Table, the self-appointed arbiters of New York literary taste in the 1920s. This mural from the Algonquin Hotel's dining room is *A Vicious Circle,* by Natalie Ascencios. (Reproduced by permission of the Algonquin Hotel.)

shall be able to be frightfully witty and everybody will talk a lot about my caustic pen, etc. I shall tell the true story of Mrs. Vernon Ball and the Parrot . . . and I shan't scruple to publish the facts of the Southampton weekend party when Mrs. Frazzle and Marie Prune did that most peculiar nautch dance in their bathing dresses.

NEW YORK DIARY

SATURDAY

I felt that some sort of scene was necessary to celebrate my first entrance into America, so I said—"Little lamb, who made thee?" to a Customs official. A fracas far exceeding my wildest dreams ensued, during which he delved down with malice aforethought to the bottom of my trunk and discovered the oddest things in my sponge bag. I think I am going to like America. I have very good letters to frightfully influential people—Daniel Blood, Dolores Harper, Senator Pinchbeck, Violet Curyon Meyer and Julia Pescod—so I ought to get along all right socially at any rate.

WEDNESDAY

For a really jolly evening I recommend the Times Square subway station. You get into any train with that delicious sensation of breathless uncertainty as to where you are going. To ask an official is sheer folly, as any tentative question is calculated to work them up to a frenzy of rage and violence. To ask your fellow passengers is equally useless, as they are generally as dazed as you are. The great thing is to keep calm and at all costs to avoid Expresses. As another means of locomotion the Elevated Railway possesses a rugged charm. The serene pleasure of gazing into frowsy bedroom windows at elderly coloured ladies in bust bodices and flannel petticoats is only equalled by the sudden thrill you experience when the two front carriages hurtle down to the street in flames.

This morning I took two of my plays to Fred Latham at the Globe Theatre. He didn't accept them for immediate production but told me of two delightful bus rides—one going up Riverside Drive and the other coming down Riverside Drive. I was very grateful, as the buses this slow moving are more or less tranquil and filled with the wittiest advertisements, which make everyone rock with laughter.

THURSDAY

Spent all last night at Coney Island. I've never known such an atmosphere of genuine carnival. We went on The Whip, the sudden convulsions of which drove the clasp of my braces sharply into my back, scarring me, I think, for life. Now I know why Americans always wear belts.

Then we went into a Haunted House, where a board gave way beneath my foot and nicked my ankle. The Giant Dipper was comfortingly tame, as I only bruised my side and cut my cheek—after which we had "Hot Dog and Stout", which the others seemed to enjoy immensely. Then—laughing gaily—we all ran through a revolving wooden wheel. At least, the others did. I inadvertently caught my foot and fell, which caused a lot of amusement. I shall not go out again with a sharp cigarette case in my pocket.

MONDAY, 23RD.

Met AW [Alexander Woollcott] at a first night. We were roguish together for hours and I liked him enormously. What a pity he's so devoted to Marie Prune—not that I actually dislike her but, really, a woman of her age ought never to behave in such an abandoned manner. Also that dreadful blouse she wore made me feel quite ill and she squinted vilely.

I went on afterwards to "Montmartre". Ina Claire was there looking lovely as usual—anyhow she's one of the cleverest artists in the world. I noticed poor Vera Frazzle at the next table. She was rather

ABOVE LEFT: Laurette Taylor (1884–1946). The inspiration for
Judith Bliss in *Hay Fever*. After she saw the play, Taylor didn't
speak to Noël for several years (hence "Silently Yours").
ABOVE RIGHT: "Do you remember Lynn Fontanne?" Noël wrote
to his mother from New York in 1921. "She played some small parts
in London, was 'adopted' by Laurette Taylor . . . and came to New York."

drunk and obviously upset about her sister running away with a Chi-
naman. After all, who wouldn't be?

SATURDAY 4TH
Met the Theatre Guild and played Hide and Seek with them in the
park. Helen Westley fell into the pond—how we laughed. Lunched
at the Algonquin with the *crème de la crème* of the artistic world. Francis Carson, George Kaufman and notably, Cynthia Burdleheim, who
ate her food quite disgustingly and was wearing imitation pearls the
size of hen's eggs. Later on we went and had tea at Mesa Malmean's
Studio, which was most attractive. She is a perfect hostess and there
was an air of pleasing bohemianism about the whole affair which
went far towards making me take another cake. In more formal circumstances I should naturally have refrained. After tea I played the
piano and sang and everybody talked—mostly while I was singing.
It was all great fun.

TUESDAY 7TH

Such a busy day—had a play refused by William Harris. I also fell off the bus, being unused to getting off on the right hand side. I just love America.

SUNDAY 16TH

America is the place to get on. I should always like to have a little working model of Broadway at night—just to take out and look at when I feel depressed. I'm quite sure it is one of the most amazing sights in the world. I shall feel awfully offended for Piccadilly Circus when I get back.

The teasing would continue over the years. On his second visit to the United States three years later:

Ritz Carlton, New York

This is just a short line to reassure your yearning mother's heart. I am well considering I had three operations for appendicitis yesterday— was run over by a bus on Tuesday—smitten down by peritonitis on Sunday and am going into consumption tomorrow. But you mustn't *worry* because apart from these things I'm *all right*. There are certain to be Icebergs, Hurricanes, Typhoons and Torpedoes but Douglas Fairbanks I'm sure will save me if you write him a nice letter. By the way, there is a dreadfully dangerous lift in this apartment, several people are killed daily just getting in and out—and the drains are notoriously bad. Diphtheria and Typhoid are inevitable! But *Don't Worry.*

Brevort Hotel
New York
[?] September, 1921

Darling old Snig,

In case you're wondering where your wandering boy is wandering, the answer is—anywhere and everywhere!

Why did nobody tell me that the streets of New York are so hot in the summer that you could fry an egg on the pavement (sorry, sidewalk!)—always supposing you had an egg!

Everybody who is anybody—and *everybody* wants to think they're *somebody*—goes out of town and they're now beginning to trickle back in with their Long Island tans. Even so I've met some fascinating folk.

Do you remember Lynn Fontanne? She played some small parts in London, was "adopted" by Laurette Taylor—now there's a character

Noël first met Edna Ferber (1887–1968) at the
Algonquin Round Table. Observing the severe cut
of her suit, he joked, "Why, Edna, you almost look
like a man." "That's funny," she replied. "So do you,
Noël." It was the beginning of a lifelong friendship.

(and I've met her, *too*)—and came to New York. Well, she's had a
huge success in a play called *Dulcy* (she's Dulcy). I went to see her
opening night with her fiancé, an actor called Alfred Lunt and, my
dear, a star was born. Well, two stars, actually, as Alfred is also making a name for himself in these parts.

They're quite wonderful and couldn't have been kinder to me.
They haven't any money either—though they soon will have, I'm
sure—and they helped me keep body and soul together by sharing
their last crust (not quite that, really!). They're going to be huge
stars and, since we all know that yours truly is going to be one too,
we've decided that, when that great day arrives, we shall act
together in a play I shall write for us and the cosmos will have a new
galaxy.

Really, darling, the theatre here is something to wonder at. As a
successful London playwright myself—ahem! (Well, five weeks isn't
a bad start!) But I can tell you this is something in a different world.
The *speed*! Everybody seems to say their lines at such a rate you'd
think you wouldn't understand a word—but you do! And then it
suddenly struck me—that's the way people actually *talk*. Wait till I
get back to Shaftesbury Avenue!!

Well, old Snig, that's all for now. Must rush or the Astors and
Vanderbilts will think I'm not coming. Won't be long now till your

Alec Woollcott and Edna Ferber, as seen by
James Montgomery Flagg.

dear son is back to give you lots of hugs and bore everyone with his
stories and exploits, some of which actually *happened*!

Love, love, love.

•

AT FIRST GLANCE Noël's friendship with Alexander Woollcott
(1887–1943) was an unlikely one. Having returned from what he insisted
on calling "the theatre of war," Woollcott proceeded to combine the roles
of theater critic, essayist, broadcaster, sometime playwright, and occasional actor. (He was the inspiration for Sheridan Whiteside in *The Man
Who Came to Dinner,* the 1939 Kaufman-Hart play, and gloried in playing
the part on tour.)

But over and above all these roles Woollcott prided himself on being a
"personality" and the self-appointed leader of the Algonquin Round Table
for the decade that it existed. It was probably this aspect of self-promotion
that he recognized in Noël. They were both their own creations.

Woollcott began by being suspicious of this overseas interloper who
would occasionally turn up for lunch with Alfred and Lynn, but the ice
was broken the evening he asked Noël for his opinion of a play they had
both attended. Noël pronounced it "tedious," but with his distinctive
manner of speaking, the word came out "tee-jus." Woollcott was
delighted. A man who was in the habit of falling out with even his closest
friends and who never met a grudge he couldn't bear, he never quarreled
with Noël. Instead, they maintained a relationship of mutual teasing and
mock insult for the next twenty years.

Whatever activity was involved, Woollcott had to be team leader. He insisted the Algonks take up croquet, a game in which he wielded a mean mallet and reinvented the rules as he went along. Noël became a skilled player himself but he knew better than to beat Woollcott too often. After a weekend visit he wrote:

*Although at croquet I was dull, and made myself a boah*
*By choosing names in other games, less famed than Mrs. Noah*
*Although at every verbal prank I merely sniffed and snuffled,*
*Although I won at "Russian Bank" with cards you hadn't shuffled,*
*In spite of all—to coin a phrase, my literary Caesar,*
*I loved my halycon (?) nights and days with Ackie Wackie Weeza.*

Nothing was too trivial for them to debate.

May 23rd 1932

When I remember how you tossed your head and said you would not accept instruction in English pronunciation from an American, I take a special pleasure in suggesting that you look up the only pronunciation which the *Oxford Dictionary* (*not* an American product) sanctions for "inextricable."

A.W.

May 26th 1933

Dear Ackie Weeza,

I have noticed with grief just lately that you are looking increasingly under-nourished and emaciated. Now, Ackie, don't be offended at what I am going to do, and please accept the enclosed cheque in the spirit in which it is offered, which dear Ackie, is the spirit of hate, contempt, fury, jaundice, loathing, not untinged with despair.

All my love, you wicked, grasping old bitch.

Noelie Wolie Polie

August 11th 1933

You would have enjoyed an idle conversation at Neysa's [McMein] the other day. The subject of claustrophobia came up and someone said the analysts were inclined to ascribe it to delayed birth. This naturally inspired a theme song, to be called "A Womb With a View".

A. Weeza Woollcott

And so it continued for the next decade.

Neysa McMein (1890–1949) was a well-known commercial artist. Her studio
became a refuge for the "Algonks" between lunches. She and Noël became
such close friends that for years after her death he would say to Cole Lesley,
"I could have done without Neysa dying, you know."

•

ALTHOUGH HE GOT to know all the Algonks to one degree or
another, Noël had more of a rapport with some than others. There was the
beautiful artist and illustrator Neysa McMein (1890–1949). No matter
how erratic her attendance at the lunches, her studio was the next stop
after the Algonquin for anyone anxious to fill in time until the dinner
hour. While Neysa continued to paint her commissioned covers for *The
Saturday Evening Post, McCall's, Woman's Home Companion,* and just about
every other magazine, around her instant salon swirled the likes of George
Gershwin, Charlie Chaplin, Feodor Chaliapin, Mary Pickford, and Helen
Hayes.

Neysa and Noël were inseparable whenever he was in New York over
the years. And as with others in his life there was the teasing element that
Noël found essential to a close relationship. Neysa became "Beauty," and
she christened him by the same name. But when Noël seemed to step out
of line:

Your self-election to the role of Supreme Beauty I dismiss with a
coarse laugh. Super crust is the word that comes to mind. After all,
you are barely graduated from the Fumble-Paws Bird Brain ranks, so

this lack of modesty and flossy self-styling ill becomes one who has barely made the grade.

And when war came:

I resent the arrangement which makes you live 3,000 miles away, and it would have been wonderful to finish at least one of our "talks." Here was I learning about Life at a mile a minute, and we arrive at a theatre or you leave the country.

Do you suppose we will ever be together again . . . and care-free? I miss you, Beauty darling, more than I can say. Your handsome puss in an elegant frame sits in the living room. Your music is open on the piano. I have that lousy drawing of yours on my desk . . . So one way or another you are ALWAYS on my mind.

(Oh, these mad notes that foolish women write at midnight. Be sure and burn this, dear.)

Anyway, I adore you, my glorious Bird-Brain, and how about answering this just to prove to Mother that you CAN write?

She died after an abdominal operation in May 1949 but remained in what Noël called his "deepest heart." ("She always cancelled every engagement for me; this one she could not cancel.") In later years his secretary, Cole Lesley, would recall Noël often saying apropos of nothing even remotely related—"I could have done without Neysa dying, you know."

·

NOËL'S OWN SUMMATION of that first visit to New York? "It seemed, in spite of its hardness and irritating, noisy efficiency, a great and exciting place."

And then, on October 29, the message Violet had been waiting for:

DON'T FORWARD LETTERS SAILING NEXT WEEK WILL LET YOU
KNOW PARTICULARS.

NOËL

The Young Master was home and ready for *The Young Idea*.

# CHAPTER 3

# "DANCE, DANCE, DANCE,
# LITTLE LADY"

## (1922–1924)

London's leading producer of "intimate revue" in the 1910s
and 1920s—until the arrival of Charles Cochran—André
Charlot (1882–1956) gave Noël his first opportunity in
this field by staging *London Calling!* in 1923.

*In lives of leisure*
*The craze for pleasure*
*Steadily grows.*
*Cocktails and Laughter,*
*But what comes after?*
*Nobody knows.*

"POOR LITTLE RICH GIRL" (1925)

THE RETURN JOURNEY was made under rather more modest circumstances on the SS *Cedric*—even then his passage was paid for by new New York friends. There he met someone who would not normally have crossed his path.

Marie Stopes (1880–1958) was a noted feminist and leading advocate of birth control. "She had, appropriately, the eyes of a fanatic," Noël noted. They spent a great deal of a long, boring voyage together, but fortunately for him, she did not attempt readings from her master works, *Married Love* or *Wise Parenthood*—the finer points of which would in any case have been lost on him. Instead, she wanted to talk about theater and the novel, in both of which she showed a keen interest.

In the spirit that holiday friendships create, Noël rather rashly agreed to visit her on their return to England, and did so more than once. He was to realize that no good deed goes unpunished when the lady insisted on reading aloud large amounts of her own fiction and sending him off with even more of it.

111 Ebury Street
S.W.1.
[Undated]

Just a correct note to thank you very much for having me.

I read *Gold in the Wood* on the train. It has a great moment when Theckla looks at Jake with eyes full of wistful yearning and accuses him reproachfully of breaking the field mouse's home—"Poor pretty thing!"

Your writing gives me an unpleasant sensation of vilely sophisticated decadence—I don't feel quite worthy next to Robin, who, after being lassoed, gagged and bound by Jake, looks him full in the face and says, "You scamp!"

By the way, have you read Jeffery Farnol [a successful contemporary novelist of "period" fiction]? If not, do, because I'm sure he has stolen a lot from you.

Do you and your husband like *Gold in the Wood* very much?

I have a passionate desire for Theckla and Robin and Sirio and Lucy (from *Sirocco*) [a play he had written while in New York] to have a picnic together—I feel they'd get on marvelously! All among the fairies and the bracken and the mice!

Yours ever

Noël Coward

I wish you'd make Jake a sexual pervert with "saddist" tendencies.

If she detected the merest touch of irony, it certainly did nothing to deter her. After the success of *The Vortex* in 1924:

18th December 1924

Noël Coward, Esq.

Royalty Theatre

Dean Street, London W.

Oh, my dear Noël Coward!

It is now eleven hours since I parted from you, and the play exists; that is to say the play that I told you in your dressing room we must write together, you and I. You see what a vitality your play must possess, thus instantly to procreate a successor. Your play is, of course, tremendously fine and interesting but the position perfectly beastly, as you have so vividly demonstrated. The one I have just done should resolve the abominable tangle and achieve ultimately a happy ending, but by most unusual means. Anyhow I have got it. Perhaps there are fewer tantrums, but I think it contains as much dramatic interest as in your first great beginning.

Is there any reason why plays should not be serials and the vital interest created by your living characters carried on in a second complete play, independent in itself, so that those seeing it without having seen *The Vortex* would not feel too lost, but at the same time it would be of far greater interest to those who had seen *The Vortex*?

Now tell me, before I trim up the dialogue, shall we collaborate? Is it to be a play by Noël Coward and Marie Stopes, in which case the same characters Florence Lancaster, Nicky, the Husband, Helen and some of the others come in and live their lives out on Monday and Tuesday, or am I merely to do it all by myself? In that case I suppose I must not call the heroine Florence Lancaster and Nicky cannot be you, but I want him to be you, and you to have the part you have now in *The Resolution*. I think the continuity of interest in a completely fresh play about the same characters, with the further intensified drammatic [*sic*] situations which my play creates is by far the best scheme, and would give such advertising value to them both as would ensure a vital interest.

Would you let me know at once how you feel about it, because it is all red-hot in my mind, and if you are not going to be my collaborator I must finish it off myself. If you are, you and I must get at the skeleton and fill in the dialogue in harmony with *The Vortex*.

In any case I shall be producing it, I hope, early next Spring, as I am intending to take a theatre.

I hope you will understand all the millions of things I would like to see in this letter if I could only make it a million times longer.

I do hope your head is not swelled up too terrifically, but this I think is far finer than anything I expected from the mid-Atlantic.

Good wishes, congratulations and hopes for the future.

> Yours ever sincerely,
> MARIE STOPES

> Royalty Theatre
> W.1.
> December 27th 1924

Dear Dr. Stopes

Thank you so much for your letter. I am afraid I never collaborate with anyone, and, even if I did, it would not be over a sequel of *The Vortex* as, psychologically speaking, there *is* no sequel—unless of course the gardener's boy found the box of cocaine and gave it to his younger sister who took a boat to Marseilles and went into a bad house; one of those particularly bad houses for which Marseilles is justly famous.

I would rather you didn't use the names of my characters, as I feel that I have already brought *The Vortex* to an inevitable, if not altogether a successful conclusion. I do hope you have a happy New Year.

> Sincerely yours,
> NOËL COWARD

Noël did leave behind a little verse that summed up his feelings and put Marie Stopes in his personal pantheon of formidable ladies led by Mary Baker Eddy.

> *If through a mist of awful fears*
> *Your mind in anguish gropes,*
> *Dry up your panic stricken tears*
> *And fly to Marie Stopes.*

> *If you have lost life's shining goal*
> *And mixed with sex perverts and dopes,*

*For Normal soap to cleanse your soul*
*Apply to Marie Stopes.*

*And if perhaps you fail all round*
*And lie among your shattered hopes,*
*Just raise your body from the ground*
*And* crawl *to Marie Stopes.*

•

HE ARRIVED BACK in England just seven pounds richer than when he had left—still poor in everything but experience.

The family's fortunes had, if anything, deteriorated, and Noël found Violet tired and worried. He determined to do what he could to reduce the pressure on her and—with Gladys's help—searched the highways and byways of Kent to find her a country home, finally settling on a small cottage at St. Mary-in-the-Marsh, near Dymchurch. Violet would later refer to it as the first time she "left" Arthur. Meanwhile, it was Arthur who was left to run the Ebury Street boardinghouse, which he did quite happily without Violet's "supervision."

During his wanderings Noël himself fell in love with Kent and would make his own home there years later, in Goldenhurst and St. Margaret's Bay.

He also seized the opportunity to get to meet his literary idol, E. (Edith) Nesbit (1858–1924). If he had been asked to name his favorite writer, irrespective of time or genre, he would almost certainly have named her. Throughout his life he would reread the entire Nesbit canon, and one of her books, *The Enchanted Castle,* was on his bedside table the night he died.

Nesbit wrote fantasy adventure stories involving her Edwardian children protagonists, but her special appeal lay in the way she refused to talk down to her young readers. The tone of her books holds up even today, and in her time she attracted significant supporters. One of the bonds between Noël and the Queen Mother was a shared love of E. Nesbit. In 1964 Noël sent the Queen Mother a present and she replied:

Clarence House
December 2nd.

My dear Mr. Coward,

I was enchanted to find four nostalgic E. Nesbit books sitting on my table today, and I do want to send you my warmest and most grateful thanks for giving me such a delectable present.

I am longing to plunge into them again, and I am quite sure that

E. (Edith) Nesbit (1858–1924) was the most popular writer of children's stories of her time. Noël owned a complete set of her books and read them over and over. On the night he died, *The Enchanted Castle* was on his bedside table.

She saw that fully half of the chairs were occupied and by the queerest people
—THE ENCHANTED CASTLE

I shall once again be terrified of the Uglie Wugglies—oh the horror of the kid gloves clapping! Do you know, that I often take off my gloves to clap at theatres or ballet or opera, and I know that this is purely because the sound of the dull thudding of languid hands in gloves brings back vividly the dreadful Uglie-Wuglies!

The characters she refers to appear in *The Enchanted Castle.* The children put on a concert and "create" an audience out of brooms and old clothes, only to find their creations come to malevolent life. The passage is perhaps one of the most disturbing in children's fiction:

The seven members of the audience seated among the wilderness of chairs had, indeed, no insides to speak of. Their bodies were bolsters and rolled-up blankets, their spines were broom handles, and their arm and leg bones were hockey sticks and umbrellas . . . their hands were gloves stuffed out with handkerchiefs; and their faces were the paper masks painted in the afternoon by the untutored brush of Gerald, tied on to the round heads made of the ends of stuffed bolster cases. The faces were really rather dreadful . . . Their eyebrows were furious with lamp-black frowns—their eyes the size, and almost the shape, of five shilling pieces . . .

And at the end of the performance, when the humans were applauding: ". . . someone else was clapping, six or seven people, and their clapping made a dull padded sound. Nine faces instead of two were turned towards the stage, and seven out of the nine were painted, pointed paper faces. And every hand and face was alive."

When Noël met E. Nesbit, he found that she was no "sweet little old lady." Nonetheless, the literary admiration survived, and when children's novelist Noel Streatfeild was writing the 1958 Nesbit biography, *Magic and the Magician,* Noël wrote to her:

Her books have meant a very great deal to me, not only while I was a little boy of nine and onwards, but right up to the present day. I have re-read them each at least twenty times.

It was in 1922 that I first met her, she was living near Dymchurch and I went boldly and called on her. I found her absolutely charming, with greyish-white hair and a rather sharp sense of humour. Her husband, "The Skipper", and she were living in a sort of Nissen hut at Jesson St. Mary's, between Dymchurch and Littlestone.

I told her how much I admired her books and we became friends. After this first visit I saw her on and off until she died.

My favourites of her books are, in the following order, *Five Children and It, The Phoenix and the Carpet, The House of Arden, The Enchanted Castle, The Wonderful Garden,* and the Bastable books.

I can't, after all these years, remember her very clearly, but as I say, her books I never forget. She had an economy of phrase, and an unparalleled talent for evoking hot summer days in the English countryside.

He neglected to mention how he had been introduced to the writer's works. Many of her books had been serialized in *The Strand Magazine,* and Noël had been in the habit of buying back numbers for a penny each until he had acquired the whole set and could read a book straight through without having to wait for the next installment. However, when it came to *The Magic City,* a few numbers were missing. The frustrated fan was forced to steal a coral necklace from a friend of his mother's, pawn it for five shillings, and buy the complete book from the Army and Navy Stores. "In later years I told E. Nesbit of this little incident and I regret to say she was delighted."

•

A SERIES OF undated letters (but marked 1922 in the archive) give some indication of Noël's varied activities for the remainder of that year: "Jeffrey is taking me down to Cornwall this weekend . . ." ". . . This next Sunday I'm going to Oxford" [where he stayed with Lady Sybil Colefax, a noted social name collector, and met Elsa Maxwell for the first time]. "I loved [Maxwell] at once . . . all her boastfulness and noise and shrill assertiveness."

On a more domestic note, when Violet's favorite cat becomes pregnant: "I'm sorry about your pussy—cats have so little restraint."

"I've been in bed all day resting and writing—my party-going has abated a good deal and I'm settling down." What he was currently writing was a play he called *Sweet Pepper.* ("Sweet Pepper seems to be developing all right.") There is no evidence that it was ever finished, but in these years his notebooks indicate numerous plays in synopsis form that never got any further, while others would start with one title and end up as something quite different. For example, *Still Life* became *Hay Fever,* but unwilling to give up a title he liked, he used the former for one of the plays in *Tonight at 8:30,* which became *Brief Encounter* when it was turned into a film.

As the year wore on, there was *The Young Idea* to occupy him. Despite Shaw's injunctions, Noël was determined to see it staged and equally determined—despite the producer's doubts about the suitability of the casting—to star in it himself, as Sholto.

The play opened a six-week out-of-town tour in Bristol on September 25. But before they brought the show in, there was Ned Lathom.

•

NED, THIRD EARL of Lathom (1895–1930), was a peer with a passion for the theater. During the course of an all-too-short life he managed to spend the family fortune on it and died in poverty, but in 1922 he was to be Noël's Fairy Godfather.

Depressed by his own lack of success—not to mention funds—Noël plucked up the courage to ask this man he didn't know particularly well for a loan of two hundred pounds. He was refused outright. Loans, Lathom was convinced, soured friendships. Here was a *gift* of two hundred pounds. It was a gift that forged a bond.

Toward the end of the year, Lathom invited Noël to come and visit him and his sister. They were staying in Davos, where the peer was being treated for the tuberculosis that was to shadow the rest of his short life.

Noël wrote to Violet:

> Grand Hotel & Belvedere
> Davos-Platz
> Tuesday, November 29th 1922

My Lamb,

Listen—I have a slight disappointment for you. I have had a charming letter from Courtneidge [Robert, producer of *The Young Idea* and father of musical comedy star Cicely] saying he can't get any suitable dates, so we shall have to open at the Savoy straight away in February. He has arranged about keeping the cast. I shall arrive in London on the 22nd and I shall stay in London during Christmas week—then I think we'll retire in lordly state to our country seat while I write my new play, which I'm itching to do. Don't be disgruntled about not touring again—it may be for the best as I shall have time for *The Vortex*.

My holiday is being that cheap you'd never believe . . . The German mark is 30,000 to the pound. One can have lunch at the Ritz in Berlin for about two shillings . . .

On Sunday we all went up to the Schatzalp, a restaurant on top of a mountain—you go up in a mountain railway—then the unconsumptive ones and some of the consumptive too—come down in *louges* [small sleighs]. It's the most heavenly sensation in the world— two and a quarter miles zig-zagging through the trees like one long helter skelter. It's perfectly safe because when you feel you're going too fast you use your feet as brakes—and when you do fall off (which is very often) you only roll in the snow. The moment you reach the bottom you hitch on to a two-horse sleigh and gallop back through the town to the Mountain Railway again. Then once more down— one steers with a long pole! I'm sunburnt and healthy—I've never felt so well—I never wear a vest during the day—a shirt and coat are enough—it's too lovely for words.

Yesterday I went driving (with a German Baroness) right up the mountain opposite where we warmed ourselves with the most delicious hot chocolate in the world. There were deep gorges with rushing torrents at the bottom and huge icicles hanging and desolate woods of fir trees—all snow almost up to your waist if you get off the road!

I've just come in from skating at which I'm becoming quite roguish, doing figure eights *mostly* on my fanny but there—*Vive le Sport!*

Ned is being perfectly sweet. He suddenly bought me the most lovely tortoiseshell cigarette case the other day.

The leading men in the Revue will be Clifton Webb and Morris Harvey (if possible). I've done some heavenly new music. The whole thing will put me right up top and break several records.

There are some rather austere Beethoven concerts sometimes which we go and giggle at!

The hotel is full of Spaniards who teach me marvelous Spanish rhythms on the piano—and shriek and gesticulate wildly!

Goodbye now, my Sniglet. I am getting too fat—Ned and I have bread sauce with everything.

SNOOP

Grand Hotel & Belvedere
Davos-Platz
Saturday, December 2nd 1922

Darling,

I'll write more at length I've just arrived having stayed a day extra in Paris—it is perfectly heavenly—thick snow, glorious mountains and bright sunshine! And the most luxurious hotel.

Ned is *ever* so much better and perfectly sweet. I am to do all the music for the new Charlot Revue with a few extra songs interpolated, also all the words—isn't it thrilling? It will probably open in March at the Prince of Wales's with Maisie Gay and Gertrude Lawrence!

Later. I had a *huge* success in Paris.

Snoop

Lathom had funded André Charlot's most recent revue, *A–Z,* and was in a very powerful position with the impresario, who had constant trouble finding the funding for his prestigious and popular shows. On this occasion Lathom summoned Charlot from London to meet with them in Davos, and he came posthaste.

Grand Hotel
Sunday December 3rd

Darling,

I've just played all the music to Charlot and he's *delighted.* He sat without a smile and then took me aside and said they were *all* good—so that's that. I now quite definitely enter the ranks of British composers! I am very excited as the *music* is good.

I leave here on Friday.

All my love
Snoop

Grand Hotel
Tuesday December 5th

Darling Lamb,

Here is another disappointment for you. I shall have to return here for Christmas after Berlin—I had arranged to arrive in London on the 22nd, having seen Edward Molyneux in Paris—but now he is going to Cannes until the 24th, when he comes here. It is frightfully important for me to see him as he is dressing the *entire* show and Charlot wants me to produce and generally supervise . . . I do hope you won't feel miserable at Xmas without me—*please* write and say you won't be disappointed—it really is only a matter of sentiment and you really will be sensible about it. I *know* you will. We will have a Christmas day all on our own in the middle of the week—I shall bring home some rich presents from Berlin.

The Revue business is extremely unsettling—Charlot had a long talk with me today—I am to do the book, music and lyrics—if by any chance I find the whole undertaking too much for me, I am to do as much as I can and he will call someone else to fill in. He is terribly keen on my playing the lead, if Courtneidge will release me . . . Of course it will probably mean £30 a week salary to *start* with and so much more as the New Editions are produced. I must have a serious talk with Courtneidge. I don't wish to sacrifice *The Young Idea* by substituting someone inferior. The Revue will open in the second week in April. That would give me two months with *The Young Idea*. I wonder if Courtneidge will turn up trumps and let me go for such a wonderful chance. Perhaps he will suggest someone else playing *The Young Idea* altogether. If so, I'm not at all sure it wouldn't be a good plan, because it would enable me to go to America with Charlot (all expenses paid) for a fortnight in search of new ideas. He's very keen on my doing this but of course it won't be possible if I do open at the Savoy. I have a feeling that everything will come out all right in the end but I am extremely what's known as "Put About".

Charles Cochran [André Charlot's fierce rival as a producer of revues] is bringing over George M. Cohan, the famous American Actor-Author-Composer, and Charlot means to let the world see that England can produce the same combination of talents in me! When I think of the actual production with me, everything is in my favour. Anything I don't like—out! And everything I want—in! It sounds all talk but it's genuinely true—I am leaving the Business side of things to Curtis Brown [Noël's agent], because I know *nothing* about Revue terms. I shall get an advance but not until the beginning of January . . .

It really seems as tho' the chance that all the fortune tellers have foretold is coming at last. The Revue is almost certain to run a year. It's going to be colossal—I sing "The Russian Blues" with the most marvelous Molyneux Russian Ballet costume, coming on in a sort of dream Parade! Laddie Cliff is to arrange the dances—I chose him because he's so wonderful at steps—which I must learn!

The whole production will cost about seven thousand pounds to put on! And when you consider that bright particular star will be me! It's a bit breathless! Apart from being an epoch breaking achievement, it will be gorgeous to do—specially with people like Maisie and Gertie. I have written Maisie a divine burlesque musical comedy song—very vivacious with full chorus. She is to wear a fair wig and very "bitty" clothes and look quite 55. She does a parasol dance after the song with the male chorus—falling once or twice on her fanny. It's one of the *wittiest* burlesques I've ever done. She's also to sing "What love means to girls like me" and "Touring Days" with Morris Harvey (if we get him, but I think we shall). I'm writing her a cockney song and a male impersonator Burlesque—"I'm Bertie from the Bath Club but I've never learnt to swim". Gertie will sing "Prenez Garde, Lisette" (New and excellent), "Tamarisk Town", "Carrie was a Careful Girl" with full chorus in lovely Victorian dresses, all very demure, and two duets with me—"I'm so in Love With You" (Newish) and a Fortune Telling duet, "I'd Like To See" (one of the prettiest tunes I've ever done). There is also a small sketch attached to it. I am to give myself a new song to open with—with full chorus and dance—then "The Russian Blues", probably "Louise" with a wonderful mountain panorama—and "Every Peach" with two extra verses I've written—very good ones—and then I act in two or three sketches. My *clothes* (all paid for by the management) will be marvelous.

I do hope I shall be able to manage Courtneidge. Of course, I *haven't* any contract with him but still I think that makes it worse. I don't think I can possibly tackle him until after the 6th of January, because then Charlot will be able to give me a definite opening date. Another great advantage of Revue is that Charlot will release me for a month or two whenever I need a holiday! Isn't it all thrilling, darling?

Please, *please* don't be miserable about Christmas. It's damnable of it to come just now! I'm sunburnt and marvelously well—I'm afraid I'm getting fat! Constant food and *such* food!

All my love, darling
**SNOOP**

Berlin—Wilmersdorf
Guntzel Strasse 26iv
December 10th

I had an amusing journey here and laughed a good lot at the people. This is a beautifully comfortable flat with lovely food and everything I want.

Tonight I'm going to this new operette, *Madame Pompadour* to see the greatest living German Comedy Artiste, Fritzi Massary. The whole show with *her* is coming to Daly's [Theatre] later on. I have naturally booked the most expensive seats in the front row of the stalls—2/—each!

My pocket book is bulging with notes—I've *never* felt so rich—it is only the change out of 1 pound.

You say you *expect* Ned is putting up money for the Revue. Certainly he is—*it's his solely and entirely.* Charlot is on salary as Director and Producer! My music will make me a star, I hope—everyone seems to think so, even Charlot! Who is the usual taciturn manager. He's been charming to me, and asked if I'd agree to let Clifton Webb play in it *with* me! (Clifton's salary is £80) I said of course, providing that I was *indisputably* in the superior position! Aren't I a *dear*!

I'm now going for a drive before lunch—it's a beautiful city.

SNOOP

Ned (Third Earl of ) Lathom
(1895–1930). Noël's patron
for his first Charlot revue,
*London Calling!*

Tuesday and Wednesday

Darling,

I've been shopping all day, things for Ned's Davos Christmas Tree—
The shops are lovely—I'm looking out for a nice winter coat for
you . . . it's a lovely city, enormous squares and buildings and general
grandeur . . . My French has suddenly become really fluent in a
miraculous manner . . . German is a terribly funny language to listen
to—I get weak at moments and laugh in people's faces!

I leave for Davos on Monday 18th.

*Goot Nacht, mein Frau.*

Snoop Hohenzollern

Grand Hotel—Davos
Boxing Day

Darling,

We had a divine Christmas and I've had some lovely presents. Beautiful Florentine initialed handkerchiefs, etc.

Gladys Cooper is here and Maxine Elliott and Elsa Maxwell and
Molyneux. Charlot arrives on Thursday . . .

Just off *en masse* to watch ski jumping—marvelous. I'll write
tomorrow.

SNOOP

And play in *The Young Idea* he most certainly did. It opened at the Savoy
Theatre on February 1, and in general the reviews were significantly better
than they had been for *I'll Leave It to You:*

The play is going quite well—marvelous house Monday matinée and
not bad evening and tonight. I've had several more ecstatic letters,
Maxine Elliott *adored* it and has written to America post haste and
hey presto about it! . . .

We seem to be doing quite good business . . .

Nonetheless, despite his optimism and the "ecstatic letters" and the
"quite good business," the show posted the notice to close after only eight
weeks. The problem he had foreseen of not being available for his own revue
was, unfortunately, no longer a problem: "London is outraged at the play
coming off—everyone is talking about it and it's doing me a *lot* of good. I
haven't written before because I've been working hard at *The Vortex.*"

•

VIOLET RETURNED to Ebury Street that summer and firmly snatched
back the reins of office from Arthur's hands. Noël hired Lorn MacNaugh-

tan to work as his part-time secretary, sharing her services with his friend, the highly regarded young actress Meggie Albanesi. When Meggie died later that year at the tragically young age of twenty-three, Lorn began to work for him full-time, and continued to do so until her death in 1967.

The "Revue"—now titled *London Calling!* after the call sign of the exciting new medium, radio—was in active preparation. It had now been decided (though not by Noël) that entrusting the task of doing the whole show to a single pair of twenty-three-year-old hands was too much of a risk and that the writing of the book should be shared with Ronald Jeans and the music with Philip Braham. Maisie Gay had been cast, as had Gertrude Lawrence, but Clifton Webb was no longer being considered and the part to have been played by Morris Harvey would now be filled by Tubby Edlin. There remained the question of the male juvenile lead. Noël retained the power of veto and, by some strange chance, found all the names suggested unsuitable. In the end he was reluctantly persuaded to accept the role himself.

To help him with the music, he recruited a "small sharp-eyed" chain-smoking lady called Elsie April. She was to be his musical amanuensis for many years to come. When asked why, with all her skills, she had never composed anything herself, she replied, "Well, dear, I never seem to have any time."

•

*LONDON CALLING!* opened at the Duke of York's Theatre on September 4, 1923, and was hailed by most of the critics as a considerable success—except for Noël's own performance—and it certainly put Gertrude Lawrence on the West End map as an indisputable star. It ran for 316 performances.

There were, however, three particular critics whose combined thumbs were most definitely turned down—the Sitwells: Edith (1887–1964), Osbert (1892–1969), and Sacheverell (1897–1988).

One of the sketches in the show was a send-up of modern free verse, which was to remain one of Noël's pet hates. He created a fictional trio—two men and a woman—he christened The Swiss Family Whittlebot, and the Sitwells were not amused by lines such as Hernia Whittlebot's "Life is essentially a curve and Art is an oblong within that curve. My brothers and I have been brought up on Rhythm as other children are brought up on Glaxo."

A feud ensued that lasted for some forty years. Most upset was Edith, and when Noël realized that instead of seeing the joke, she was bitterly offended, he decided—but only three years later—to write her a letter of apology. She replied:

Edith Sitwell with brothers Osbert and Sacheverell.

22 Pembridge Mansions
Moscow Road
W. 2
December 6th, 1926

Dear Mr. Coward,
I accept your apology.
Yours sincerely,
Edith Sitwell

And there matters formally and uneasily rested until 1962, when Noël confided to his friend, film director George Cukor, that he had much admired Edith's (now Dame Edith) recent book on Queen Elizabeth, *The Queen and the Hive.* When he heard that Cukor was at that very moment off to see her, Noël asked him to convey his congratulations. Cukor said he would but also advised Noël to write to her himself. That evening Noël did just that.

He received first a telegram:

DELIGHTED STOP FRIENDSHIP NEVER TOO LATE INVITE YOU
BIRTHDAY CONCERT AND SUPPER FESTIVAL HALL OCTOBER 9TH
8 P.M.

EDITH SITWELL

The date was not possible for Noël but shortly afterward he received:

Dame Edith Sitwell
Flat 42
Greenhill
Hampstead
NW3
September 26th 1962

Dear Mr. Coward,

Thank you so much for your letter in answer to my telegram, and above all let me thank you for your charming previous letter, which pleased and touched me more than I can say.

I had to answer by telegram as I had acute writer's cramp (indeed I have only just emerged from bandages and a sling). How I wish that unprofessional writers would suffer sometimes from the disease!!

I am very greatly disappointed that you will not be able to come on the 9th and am very sorry for the cause [Noël had an appointment to go into hospital]. I do hope the operation won't be very painful, and that you will soon be able to escape from hospital, (Oh, those smiling Christmassy faces—Oh, those cups of tea!)

The 9th should be a day for all present to remember. Never before, I think, has anyone attended their own Memorial Service. (The Press is madly excited at my being 75, one is looking forward avidly to my funeral.)

I do hope you will find time to come and have sherry or a cocktail with me when you come to London. Do please ring me up.

I am giving Osbert your message. He is at Renishaw, [the Sitwells' Derbyshire country house] so I send you his love on his behalf. The operation was fairly successful on one side—the side of the operation. But the whole thing is dreadful and heart-breaking.

All good wishes
Yours ever
Edith Sitwell

After the celebrations (and now the "Dame" has been crossed through):

October 15th

Dear Mr. Coward

Osbert and I were so very sorry you couldn't come, so was Sachie. The concert and supper party were fun, in a way. But it was all like something macabre out of Proust. The papers excelled themselves—the *Sketch* particularly. I had never met the nice well-meaning reporter who "covered" the event, but according to him he sat beside me as my weary head sank into my pillow, and just as I was dropping asleep, I uttered these

Famous Last Words

"Be *kind* to me! Not many people are!" Very moving I think, don't you? . . . please don't forget that if you can spare the time, you are coming to see me when you are in London.

     Yours very sincerely,
     Edith Sitwell.
Osbert sends his love

Soon after, Noël paid the dame a visit.

          November 23rd
Dear Mr. Coward,
I cannot tell you what real pleasure it gave me to see you the other day. I enjoyed our talk so much. Please don't forget you have promised to come and see me again after you return on the 6th. Do ring me up any time and say you are coming.

It was so good of you to send me your *Collected Short Stories.* There are no short stories written in England in our time that I admire more. I think "Aunt Tittie", for instance, a real masterpiece. I am not a cry-baby but it brings tears to my eyes every time I read it—and I have read it over and over again. I can't think what you must have gone through, piercing into the hearts of those two forlorn human beings. The end of the story is almost unbearable. You have done more, so quietly, than most writers do by yelling at the tops of their voices.

All the stories have that extraordinary quality of reality, so that although the endings are perfect endings, one feels the people go on living after the stories, *qua* stories, are finished and one wants to know what happened to them, beyond the stories.

I am almost halfway through the book, and shall write again when I am the whole way through it.

I may say that I had a very bad nightmare, last night, about "What Mad Pursuit" [one of Noël's short stories]. I dreamt that George [Cukor] said I had to go to stay with some people in Hollywood "for a rest". But I was saved at the end, because the maid had hidden all my belongings, so I missed the boat train by two minutes!

I am having rather a harassing time with lunatics, because I was televised the other day.

One wrote to say I ought to be ashamed of myself, and that I have senile decay and softening of the brain, which—oddly enough—makes him respect me. Another has written me a very long letter about Einstein, telling me I will never get into Space or Time.

I am sending you my *Notebook* on Shakespeare. The cover is so unspeakably appalling that I nearly faint when I contemplate it. I do not know if it is meant as a portrait of me if I turn blue, or if it is supposed to represent a map.

I am not supposed to show any of my *Autobiography* to anyone at all, but I can't resist sending you my portrait of Wyndham Lewis, hoping it will make you laugh. I'm afraid it is rather a battered copy, but it is the only typescript I have got. Don't bother to return it.

Please do come and see me again very soon.

All best wishes
Yours ever
Edith Sitwell

The American masters who published my *Notebook,* not content with inflicting that scarifying cover on me, won't allow me to be an Hon. D.Litt. of Oxford. One shouldn't mind, but I do take it hard!

She sent Noël her last letter a few months later.

March 3rd 1963

Dear Mr. Coward,
I was so delighted to get your postcard.

I am obliged to send this to your address in Switzerland, because I don't have your present address. It must be heavenly being there.

Will you really give me a "Coward Original" [painting]? How much I look forward to having it. You won't forget you have promised it to me, will you?

I have been really fearfully ill—one of these mysterious viruses that baffle the doctors. Mine was turning into pneumonia, which I missed by a few hours. The whole of Harley Street practically camped out here and have now ordered me to go on a sea voyage. So I am off on Tuesday (5th) with my nurse, heading for the Pacific. (The sharks there can't be much worse than the little pets who prey on one here.) I shall be back here on the 19th of May, and shall hope so much to see you then.

If the so-much-looked-forward-to "Coward Original" should be on its way here before then, I've got a trustworthy caretaker, Miss Lewis.

A Club here have seized a poem of mine, "Still Falls the Rain" without my permission, and have recited it with their heads out of a window! Evidently they don't know it is a poem about the bombing, but think it is an advertisement for mackintoshes!

Some people might be rather cross.

Osbert has just been here and sends his love.

I look forward so much to seeing you when we both get back to England.

> Your ancient friend (ancient God knows)
> Edith

Dame Edith died in 1964, a few months after this letter was written.

# INTERMISSION

# "DEAREST DAB . . ."

## JACK WILSON (1899–1961)

> *Mad about the boy,*
> *I know it's stupid to be mad about the boy*
> *Although I'm quite aware*
> *That here and there*
> *Are traces of the cad about the boy*

"MAD ABOUT THE BOY," FROM *WORDS AND MUSIC* (1932)

## . . . AND

# "LORNIE, DEAR LORNIE . . ."

## LORN LORAINE (1894–1967)

> *Her lissome grace enchants my eyes*
> *When I am tired and worn.*
> *I cannot over-emphasize*
> *My gratitude to Lorn.*

ONE EVENING after a performance of *The Vortex* in 1925, a young man came backstage to congratulate Noël. "(He) walked nervously, and with slightly overdone truculence into my life." His entrance was to prove a distinctly mixed blessing in the years to come.

American John ("Jack") Chapman Wilson had winning ways when he chose to employ them. Cole Lesley, who was Noël's left hand from the mid-1930s—always assuming Lorn Loraine was his right—described

John ("Jack") C. Wilson (1899–1961).

Wilson in his biography as follows: "In addition to his film-star looks, Jack had an immense amount of charm, and with his sharp wit he could be so funny that one forgave, or didn't even notice, the mocking irony with which his wit was edged."

Jack was quick to pick up the contact when Noël and company arrived in New York that September to play *The Vortex,* and his persuasiveness on a personal level was such that by the time Noël was due to return to London the following March, Jack had given up his job as stockbroker to become Noël's personal manager.

On the way home Noël began to be concerned as to the effect the wise-cracking Jack would have on his cozy, close-knit little group in London.

Lorn may well have had some initial reservations herself when Noël granted Jack something she did not have, even though she had worked for him much longer: power of attorney. One can detect a certain edge in one of the verse letters she liked to leave on Noël's pillow for him to read when he returned from some social engagement:

Lorn ("Lornie") Loraine (1894–1967).

> *Just because your friend from Yale*
> *Climbs to heights you cannot scale,*
> *Don't forget your secretary*
> *Made her curtsey to Queen Mary.*

Reminding him that as a debutante she had been presented at Court—a social height that no Yalie could hope to achieve.

From December 1926 Jack could and did run Noël's business affairs, often without discussing them with Noël.

Jack's boyish charm coated most eventualities but even early in the game there were faint shadows cast. He was always inclined to be extravagant with Noël's money.

> *It's quite a big expense to us*
> *Transporting Little Dab.*
> *He never travels in a bus*
> *And seldom in a cab.*

As the youngest member of the "family" Jack was also nicknamed "Baybay," and in subsequent letters and cables the baby-talk badinage would conceal a growing concern that Noël ("Pop")—Jack's associate and lover—was not prepared to face up to for quite some time to come.

On one occasion, in 1930, Jack sailed to America while Noël stayed in England. Noël sent him a cable to the ship.

*Baybay's gone, the mousies play*
*Fifteen cheques went out today*
*Richmond Park is grey with sorrow*
*Thirty cheques go out tomorrow.*

*Darling Baybay, darling Jack*
*Just a kleptomaniac*
*Pinching gifts from Poppa's house*
*Like a predatory louse*

*Taking slyly without stint*
*Here a photo, there a print*
*Still, although you snatch and grab,*
*Poppa loves his darling Dab.*

And in that last line lies the answer to why a situation that seems clear in retrospect could not be dealt with. Noël didn't *want* to see it.

For the duration of their professional partnership this equivocal undertone continued.

·

WHEN IN 1934 Noël parted company with the C. B. Cochran management that had been so successful for him and set up his own production

Noël, Jack, and Gertie—the Three Musketeers at Goldenhurst
in the 1930s. "With his sharp wit he [Jack] could be so funny that
one forgave . . . the mocking irony with which his wit was edged."
But that was then.

company, Transatlantic Productions, with Alfred Lunt and Lynn Fontanne, Jack was made a full fourth partner. Lorn wrote:

> *Great though the love we've always loved to give*
> *To Baybay Wilson, Big Executive*
> *An added veneration we must show*
> *To Baybay Wilson, Impresario.*

Nor was it long before he began to act like one. On September 25, 1935, Noël, Lorn, and Gladys Calthrop happened to be lunching at their favorite London restaurant, The Ivy. What they saw inspired a joint creation:

> *We come to the Ivy and what do we see*
> *On this wet and horrible day?*
> *The Baybay is lunching with Vivien Leigh*
> *In order to irritate Ray.*

> *We really had not the remotest idea*
> *That Baybay was quite such a masher*
> *If this goes much further we all of us fear*
> *A cable must go to Natasha.*

(Wilson was currently paying court to Natasha Paley.)

At one point Noël even went so far as to mark Jack's "social scorecard," and one is left with a distinct feeling of the surface banter covering a genuine uneasiness.

### DON'TS FOR DAB

> *Refrain from twitting Juliet Duff*
> *On her abnormal height*
> *You've criticised her quite enough*
> *And dine with her to-night*

> *Refrain from telling Syrie Maugham*
> *She's stupid, old, and dirty*
> *It's not considered decent form;*
> *Her lunch is at 1.30.*

> *Please realise it's impolite*
> *To pan Dorothe's relations.*
> *Her party is on Tuesday night:*
> *Dancing and decorations.*

> Refrain from telling Pip Sassoon
> (It's hardly courtly, is it?)
> His skin is yellow as the moon;
> Did you enjoy your visit?
>
> Don't tell the merry Baron those
> Queer lips are too inflated.
> Quaglino's . . . then, I suppose
> Backgammon's indicated.
>
> Please do not steal a piece of jade
> From Brook House as a mascot,
> Nor murmur "Jews" as you parade
> Edwina's box at Ascot.
>
> Prends garde, cher Dab, lorsqu'à Paris
> Tu recontre la lucinge
> Ne dit pas "Princesse, je t'en prie
> Est-ce que tu est une dinge?"

When, after the war, Jack Wilson began to produce and direct on Broadway, and even to put a tentative toe in the Hollywood water, Lorn wrote:

> Long years ago when first we knew
> Our dear John Chapman W.
> His latent talents were confined
> To efforts of a simple kind.
> A homely wit, a merry sense
> Of fun at your and my expense
> A criticism here and there
> Of Peggy Wood and Mary Clare;
> A trifling bagatelle maybe
> Of error in accountancy,
> Pictures and books—a brooch or so
> Those were his limits long ago.
>
> But as the years that speed apace
> Have added girth to Baybay's face
> They've stretched the fields of enterprise
> On which he casts his penny eyes.
> Where wicked murmurs once were heard
> All Broadway trembles at his word
> The acid jokes that used to be

*Reserved for Blackheart,* [Gladys Calthrop] *you and me*
*Are now the bon mots of the day*
*In syndicated U.S.A.*
*And—Oh, it only goes to show—*
*That oaks from little acorns grow . . .*

*It used to be enough for Dab*
*To pinch, appropriate or grab*
*Such trifles as he wished to use*
*From Goldenhurst or Burton Mews.** *
*But, as a child outgrows its nurse*
*So Baybay's pocket and his purse*
*Now he finds investors just the thing*
*To suit light-fingered pilfering*
*And when he's had his fill from them . . .*
*OH, DO BE CAREFUL M.G.M.!*

*Goldenhurst was Noël's home in Kent; Burton Mews was his London office.—Ed.

•

TO BEGIN WITH, Noël had complete confidence in Jack's accounting acumen. In 1929 he is writing to Violet from New York about the Broadway success of *Bitter Sweet* but notes en passant the Wall Street crash:

> There's been a complete disaster on the New York Stock Market, everybody is losing millions . . . but it really serves them right for gambling. Thank God Jack has invested my money in gilt-edged securities and never speculated, so I'm perfectly safe, but it really is horrible, people hurling themselves off buildings like confetti.

He then returned to the *really* important news about theaterland.

Jack was simply "Jack being Jack" or he was "up to his old tricks," but this was said with indulgent affection. Even in later years, when the bloom had distinctly faded, the diary entries reveal Noël's conviction that he seems to see signs of things improving.

Then, in 1937, Jack married the beautiful and beautifully wealthy Princess Natasha (Natalia) Paley (1905–1981) at what became their home in Fairfield, Connecticut. Natasha was the daughter of Grand Duke Paul of Russia. Noël described the union as "the twenty-first fine careless rapture." It was supposed to be a simple "family" affair but turned out to be anything but. Lorn cabled Noël:

In 1937 Jack suddenly married the beautiful, and
beautifully wealthy, Princess Natasha Paley. Wherever the
marriage was made, it turned out not to be in Heaven.

*In every paper of the English Press*
*Are photographs of Dab and his Princess.*
*Although a deep dyed secret very latterly*
*All London sends its love to you and Natterly*

Jack sat out the war in America—which, as an American citizen, he
was perfectly entitled to do. Noël, on the other hand, was traveling the
world on government business overt and covert. Even if he had possessed
the business skills to run his own financial affairs, he would have been in
no position or location to do so effectively. Meanwhile, the particular
Coward store that Jack was meant to be running was receiving all too little attention—a fact that came home to Noël one day in October 1941
when he received a summons to appear in court on currency charges.

During his time in the United States in 1940 and 1941 Noël had been
funding himself on government business and, by doing so, breaking a
1939 law involving overseas currency he knew nothing about. Fortunately,
in the event he was dealt with leniently.

By now Noël was beginning to have occasional moments of doubt. Was
Jack paying enough attention to the 1941 Broadway production of *Blithe
Spirit,* a property that had overnight become one of his most valuable?
Every now and then he would question Jack's theatrical taste—but only
in the privacy of his diary. Yet in a letter to Jack he said, "I would rather
you directed it than anybody else. I have implicit faith in your taste and
discretion."

Immediately after the war, though, it became increasingly clear that Jack was paying less and less attention to Noël's work and taking on other plays. Terence Rattigan was another of Wilson's "clients," and since both Noël and Rattigan worked exclusively in London with Binkie Beaumont's H. M. Tennent Organisation, that brought Wilson into close professional contact with the most powerful figure in British theater. But Jack now saw himself as a "player" and their equal, with Broadway as his personal fiefdom.

Noël's eyes were forcibly opened to this for the first time when Binkie returned from New York in February 1946: "He told me most unhappy stories of Jack's attitude to him, to Terry and to this country . . . It all makes me feel physically sick."

A year later things deteriorated even further. When it was decided to put on an American tour of a revival of *Tonight at 8:30* (Noël's 1936 cycle of nine one-act plays), starring Gertie and with Graham Payn now playing Noël's old parts, Jack did everything possible to undermine the venture, even though he stood to make money from it. The problem for Jack was Graham. Although the relationship between Noël and Jack was by now strictly business, in simple terms Jack was jealous of the man who had taken his place in Noël's affections.

He advised Noël that Graham would never be able to get a working visa. Graham got the visa. Then Jack was heard to tell anyone who would listen that Noël was "the biggest baby-sitter in New York," with Graham being the "baby." Although he had intended to simply "get the show on the road," Noël now decided he had to stay and ensure the peace was kept.

He shared his concerns with Lorn:

[1947 Undated]

This letter will be almost exclusively about the Baybay and I would have saved it all up and said it to you but it's all rather on my mind and I wanted to get it off. Oh dear, I really am worried about him Theatrically. I have now seen several of his Westport productions and they really aren't very good. The casting of *Private Lives* apart from Tallulah is really vile. He did a new comedy the other week which he directed himself at Westport and nearly everyone in the cast was miscast and the direction was appalling. I remained silent and didn't do any finger wagging. His prestige in the Theatre here is still high but sooner or later he is bound to be rumbled and I really couldn't let him direct anything of mine unless I could come over and put the polish on (and re-cast it).

The awful thing is that the Lunts are beginning to rumble him—particularly over his miscasting, which is really his worst defect. I think the deep down truth of it all is that he hasn't really much confidence in himself and has to bolster himself up with publicity and secretaries, etc. Probably his most dangerous defect is that he isn't enthusiastic enough. When one talks to Guthrie [McClintic] or Max [Gordon] or Rodgers and Hammerstein about their forthcoming productions, they are automatically fiercely excited about them and convinced that they are going to be wonderful. I get the impression with Dab that he isn't convinced about anything and that he is perpetually terrified of committing himself and taking the slightest risk. Natasha is far from being a help as she never stops saying that everything is a bore.

I am pouring all this out to you because I am sure it is a question of character and character as you well know is unalterable. I visualize with horror a black day in the future when his star really falls. I have talked to him a bit—no finger wagging but gently. He admits blithely that his worst defect is running away from trouble. That's all very well but if you can't face trouble in the Theatre, you might just as well give up. He never dreams of opening those chocolate brown eyes before eleven o'clock in the morning and *always* sleeps in the afternoons. I *know* with every instinct in me and in spite of all protestations to the contrary that our little darling does very very little indeed! I feel in my heart that although one half of him admires and loves me as much as ever, the other half bitterly resents me.

Darling, I feel a little better having got it all off my chest. You do see my dilemma, don't you? Those years of enforced separation during the war really did a great deal of harm, as we knew they would. Wit and charm are not enough. The race is to the swift and you've got to work like mad in this world if you want to get anything and, above all, sustain anything.

With these noble and inspired sentiments, Mrs. Loraine, I will close and remain,

> Yours Affectionately
> GOD

It was then that he heard something else that disturbed him even more. The producer of the tour told him the story of an earlier thirty-week tour of *Blithe Spirit* Jack had organized.

My royalties had been eight per cent of the gross, Jack's five per cent of the gross for his kindness in letting them do it, together with five per cent of the profits. I certainly did not know about this and I don't think Lorn did either. My mind is now a seething morass of doubts.

. . . I have been observing various indications for a long while but, as usual, I discounted them, because I am always unwilling to believe other people's gossip. Then, fortunately or unfortunately, whichever way you care to look at it, I happened to overhear him on the telephone discussing me very shamefully with a comparative stranger and that gave me to think very seriously indeed. The net result was a couple of sleepless nights, a few tears, dangerously few, and a profound anger.

The next day he had it out with Jack, who immediately gave way at all points. Noël threatened to leave and sever their professional ties but was prepared to give Jack one last chance. That was the mistake that would shadow the remaining years. Jack never really believed Noël would cut the knot. He was wrong, but the final snip took too long and cost too much.

It was the nadir of their relationship. Unfortunately, it was not quite the end.

Noël began to dig deeper—with the help of Fanny Holtzmann, Gertie's lawyer and manager—and found "that my financial affairs in this country have been badly handled for twenty years and that I have been overpaying my tax for years." He hired Fanny to tidy things up.

The remaining years were a mixture of sunshine and cloud. "Jack is charming, but when he is bitchy he is horrid . . . His mind is quick but he has a destructive quality. When he is simple, he is so very sweet."

Since the early 1940s, Jack had been running the Westport Country Playhouse near his Fairfield home, one of the country's leading regional theaters, as well as producing on Broadway. Parlaying his relationship with Noël, he had managed to ingratiate himself with people such as Cole Porter, who had allowed him to direct the 1949 musical *Kiss Me, Kate*. Noël found "Jack's production excellent, fast moving and in good taste." That same year Jack acted in the same capacity on the musical version of *Gentlemen Prefer Blondes*. ("A violently successful opening.") But by now Noël detects he is suffering from "managerial grandeur."

In July 1951, Jack put on a new play of Noël's. Originally called *Home and Colonial* and intended for Gertie, it was now *Island Fling* and starring Claudette Colbert. Jack cables that they have a success, which encourages Noël to talk things over with Binkie and then to decide to fly over and see the play before it ends its limited run. This brought "another long cable from Jack literally beseeching me not to come to America. He has obviously bitched the play by bad direction and doesn't want me to see for myself . . . He is behaving like an abject fool."

In the end Noël did not make the trip after all but it was he who summarized the affair in a letter to Jack:

Dearest Dab,

You entirely misunderstood my motives in wishing to come over and see *Island Fling.* In the first place I had re-read the play carefully on my way down to stay with Binkie and realized that, although the last act got under way and had a lot of good stuff in it, the first act was heavy, over-written and dull. (I later discovered that you had changed the play into three acts which was a wise decision). When your cable arrived at Binkie's saying "Triumphant success, future plans indefinite etc., etc.," both Binkie and I decided that it was essential for me to see the play and discover where and how to re-write it before it was possibly played on the coast by Claudette or ultimately here in England by someone else.

Unfortunately, I told Natasha in Paris that I was popping over and why, and she implored me not to, saying that it would upset you, etc. This not unnaturally irritated me and, aided by a few nips of the demon Vodka I flew at her and she at me and we had a fine old scene lasting about twenty minutes, after which we giggled and Niki said it was just like old times at Fairfield! I presume that she warned you that I was on the war path. This I think, although well meant, was foolish of her because it gave you the impression that I was coming over determined not to like your production of the play. This was not true, although I must admit that from what both she and Niki told me about the cast, I was a little apprehensive. By this time I had already telephoned Lorn and my reservations on the plane were made and paid for. Then I came back and read your really quite insufferable and hysterical cables and cancelled my reservations.

I did not reply to them because your emphasis on the expense you were "ill able to afford" and your assumption that I would "automatically detest" your production, made me very angry. In the first place I would not automatically detest your production, as I am neither prejudiced, malicious nor silly, although if it was as bad as your curious behaviour has now convinced me that it was, I should have certainly detested it and said so in no uncertain terms. After all it *is* my play and I didn't ask you to do it, you asked me. The play has been read by Larry [Olivier], Vivien [Leigh], Leonora [Corbett], Gertie and Ina [Claire] and they none of them cared for it. This had already convinced me that there was something wrong with it and all I wanted to do was to see it with an audience re-action and find out if it was worth salvaging. I was also anxious to see Claudette with an eye to possible future casting. As far as the "expense" was concerned, my visit would have cost you bed and board at Fairfield for three or four days. In any event I would like to remind you that the financial burden of twenty-six years of association has been weighted far more heavily on my side than on yours.

Present circumstances are difficult but however difficult they are and continue to be, I promise you that as soon as I possibly can the existing situation will be tidied up for good and all and you need have no further financial anxieties as far as I am concerned. You say that you "get nothing" out of *Island Fling* and gave up six weeks of your summer to it. Well, dear boy, what you got out of it was a record breaking success for the Westport Theatre of which you are a director, a great deal of *réclame* and, I presume, at the end of the season, a modest addition to the kitty. The notices also, from my point of view, were far better than I expected them to be, and from your point of view, excellent. Now unhappily, owing to your lack of moral courage, I have no way of judging for myself whether your production was good, bad or indifferent, all I have to go on are reports from outsiders which, I must admit, are coming in thick and fast.

With regard to your suggestion that we sever our Theatrical association, I would like to know how really carefully you have thought about this and whether or not you truly mean it. From many angles I think it would be an excellent idea but please remember that the suggestion came from you and not from me. If in your mind I have become so unreasonable, prejudiced and fearsome in Theatrical affairs that you find any discussion of them too much of a strain, I quite agree that the sooner we pack it up the better.

At this time Jack was continually ill with a variety of reported conditions, all of which Noël suspected were another way of camouflaging his increasing alcoholism. In February 1952: "went to see Jack. He is obviously fairly ill, although I am not sure how bad really. His hair is white and he looks like an old man." He was, in fact, only fifty-three but was "becoming an egocentric bore."

By the end of the following year things had deteriorated still further. Arriving in New York, Noël went round to see Jack and Natasha and found "They were both fried and not making sense . . . I was really worried about darling Natasha, who looked puffy and jittery. Jack was as he usually is when he has had too much, petulant and silly."

In 1954:

It is a dismal sight to see him now and remember how handsome and amusing he once was. He has changed in every way so shatteringly that it is only occasionally that I can catch a glimpse of what he used to be . . . I am deeply sad about this. It is difficult to believe that the

snows of yester-year should vanish so completely. He meant so much
to me for so many years . . .

In the same year Transatlantic Productions was formally dissolved.

There was more in the same vein, all of it charting the one-way downward track that Jack was following and where he was taking Natasha. Still,
there were occasional meetings when Noël would try to convince himself
that corners had been turned.

In early 1957 Natasha took a much-needed break and visited Noël in
Jamaica on her own. When she returned to New York she wrote that when
she saw Jack she was ". . . aghast and speechless with horror." The office
must certainly be closed, and she begged Noël to have Lorn advise Jack to
that effect, since he trusted her implicitly.

Later there seemed to be a remission of sorts. Jack was his old self
again, Natasha reported. The puffy cheeks had gone; he no longer repeated
himself—he looked ten years younger. It was such a relief after the Jack
she had seen at the hospital, where he had been having hallucinations and
claimed that strange masked people were breaking into his room and pre-
venting him from sleeping. His doctor had told her that her husband was
a mental case and should be committed forthwith.

The owners of the play he was engaged to produce had fired him summarily and, while Natasha had always considered the Westport Theatre "a
stinkpot," the fact remained that if Equity were to have heard of the situation officially, Jack would undoubtedly have been barred for life. All of
this—touch wood—was fortunately now in the past.

Another painful incident played into my hands—while he was at the
hospital the people connected with *The Empress* [a play Jack was
meant to be producing] came to me to say they did not want him as
a director, as the managers [Lawrence Longner and his partners] had
gone to Roger Stevens's [another major producer] office with the
story of how drunk he was on the production of *Star Bright* and that
they did not want him near Westport.

In 1957 Noël finally cut the knot:

22nd June, 1957

Dearest Dab,
This is obviously a sad and difficult letter for me to write and I have
been hoping not to have to write it for several years.

I am truly sorry but I really cannot allow you to present me on
Broadway or my plays. I have tried for such a long, long while to stop
you drinking and to persuade you to go on a really definite cure but I

have not succeeded. When you returned from Jamaica last year I had great hopes that all was well. That was why I suggested you presenting *South Sea Bubble.* When I arrived back in New York from Bermuda and discussed the casting of the play with you I found to my dismay that you were not making sense and that you were also drinking again and pretending that you weren't.

I cannot in fairness to everyone concerned make a reappearance on Broadway after twenty years under a management that I cannot trust. This may sound very brutal to you but I am afraid I must tell you the truth as I see it and as I feel it. For you nominally to present a play is not enough and I think whoever does the work on my behalf should have the just kudos of presenting me.

This situation has been making me very unhappy for a long while. I have discussed it exhaustively with Natasha, Mrs. Bent [Jack's longtime secretary] and they have agreed with me that owing to your many years of drinking you have ruined your health to such an extent that you're no longer capable of presenting my plays, or for that matter anybody else's. Face-saving seems to me, who love the Theatre, to be a waste of time.

I had hoped that you had realized some time ago that the time had come for us to part as far as the Theatre is concerned; incidentally, you suggested this yourself when you presented *Island Fling* at Westport and refused to allow me to come over and see it. After this you presented *Quadrille* and lost the Lunts. I would also like to remind you that since the War you have had every opportunity of presenting my plays, such as *Relative Values, Peace in Our Time,* etc., but in those years you didn't seem interested.

I cannot tell you the misery it gives me to have to write to you so bluntly but, oh, my dear, there is really no alternative. I know by this I am delivering you a body-blow and I have, as I said before, been hoping against hope that I would not have to. I am desperately, desperately sorry but there really isn't anything more to be said.

> All my love,
> POPPA

In October 1961, "Natasha found Jack dead on the floor of his bedroom." In his *Diary* Noël reflected for the last time:

I cannot feel sad that he is dead. He has been less than half alive for the last ten years, a trouble and a bore to himself and to everyone else. Naturally, now that he is dead, my mind is inclined to skip the disintegration and fly back to when he was handsome, witty, charming,

Lorn Loraine (*left*), Noël's shield and defender for forty years, works with her assistant and successor, Joan Sparks (Hirst), in their Burton Mews office.

good company. What a hideous, foolish waste of life! His character was never good. Perhaps he knew that, perhaps he knew something unpleasant about himself which served as an excuse for drinking. I am almost sure he was aware of inadequacy . . . Of course I am sad. Of course I feel horrid inside. But not nearly as much as I might have. To me he died years ago.

Not that he needed to be convinced, but Jack's increasingly unpredictable behavior highlighted for Noël the pivotal role Lornie played in his life.

In *Present Laughter* he gave her a theatrical incarnation as Monica Reed, Girl Friday to actor Garry Essendine (aka Noël Coward). Early in the play there is an exchange between Daphne, a smitten fan of Garry's, and Monica:

DAPHNE: I think he's even more charming off the stage than on, don't you?

MONICA: (*with a slight smile*) I can never quite make up my mind.

DAPHNE: I expect you know him better than anybody.

MONICA: Less intimately than some, better than most.

In fact, Lorn Loraine knew the man Noël had become better than anyone.

Despite its deeply professional nature, there was a childlike quality to their relationship, which was common to all who were admitted to the inner circle of Noël's created family—Gladys Calthrop ("Blackie"), Joyce Carey ("Doycie"), and, later, Cole Lesley ("Coley" or "Toley") and Graham Payn ("Little Lad"). It was like being invited to join an exclusive club and being given your own password.

It was a concept worthy of J. M. Barrie.

For the nearly forty years they worked together, Noël and Lorn would indulge in an ongoing game of Charades in which Noël was the omniscient but kindly "Master" tolerating Lorn, the hapless servant. It was a typically English way of cloaking the deep affection that could never be adequately expressed.

Noël might write about their invariable morning ritual, when Lorn would bring him the day's post:

> *Here I sweetly lie in bed*
> *And wait for Lornie's dancing tread.*
> *Here in bed I sweetly lie*
> *Anticipating Lornie's high*
> *Well modulated senseless bray*
> *Mouthing the topics of the day.*

Or:

### REFLECTIONS BY MASTER ON AWAKENING

> *A lovely lady dressed in blue*
> *Has come to have a chat with you.*
> *The answer to my deepest prayers*
> *Is now advancing up the stairs.*
> *A little grunt, a stretch, a yawn,*
> *And then—heigh-ho! For tea with Lorn!*
> *That which supplies my carnal needs*
> *Is Lorn when hung with coloured beads.*

Rather more surprising is:

### A TRIBUTE TO LORN FROM MASTER

> *Through all these weary working days*
> *Of toil and strife and strain*

*There's one who all fatigue allays*
*And makes me gay again.*

*Her dainty, happy little face*
*Is Youth personified*
*I really could not stand the pace*
*Without her by my side*

*Her lissome grace enchants my eyes*
*When I am tired and worn*
*I cannot over-emphasize*
*My gratitude to Lorn.*

. . . until one notices that the Tribute to Lorn is *by* Lorn.

Even when there was serious work on hand the tone was still playful.
As the years went by Lorn increasingly doubled as Mother Hen as well
as Girl Friday.

*Now, Master dear, when next you do your packing*
*And you and Cole in solemn conclave sit*
*Please see that no essential thing is lacking*
*That should be in your luggage, gear or kit.*
*Please pack your peeper wash, your solo denture,*
*Your ointment, just in case of you know what,*
*And thus be sure before you start your venture*
*That all the things you're going to want you've got.*

More than most people, Noël needed the stability of his own kind of
domestic ritual, which Lorn in particular symbolized.

It was the war years that brought the degree of his dependence home to
him. During an intense theatrical tour in 1943 he was forced to recuperate
in isolation at a hotel in Tintagel, Cornwall. From there he wrote to Lorn:

*In the deep hush before the dawn*
*I hear the seagulls screaming "Lorn".*
*A baby hare cries on the leas*
*"Where is your secretary, please?"*
*A rain-drop on my window pane*
*Spells as it trickles—"L. Loraine"*
*Small shell-fish moan on rocky shores*
*"How is that pretty friend of yours?"*

*All residents at this hotel*
*Squeal at each meal—"Is Lornie well?"*
*A foreign snail squeaks from its shell*
*"Comme elle est belle! Comme elle est belle!"*
*But no wild creature has the soul*
*To long for Lorn as much as Noul.*

Then—just in case he has let his sincerity slip—the postscript . . .

Kindly return these [food ration] coupons, you fat old trout, and get me some new ones.

And so it continued until the Grim Reaper—as Noël always referred to him—decided to take Lorn in the harvest of November 21, 1967. In his *Diary* Noël recorded that he attended her memorial service. "It was well and simply done and quite intolerable. I staggered blindly away from it." A few days later he is telling himself that "there is no sense in grief, it wastes emotional energy." By this time he had little enough of his own to spare, but what he had remained hers.

# CHAPTER 4
## *THE VORTEX*

### (1924–1926)

How can we *help* ourselves? We swirl around in a vortex of beastliness.

NICKY, IN *THE VORTEX* (1924)

T HERE WAS GOOD NEWS and bad news about *London Calling!*
The bad news was that André Charlot—probably irritated by his
reduced status as a mere employee on the current project—decided to
put together a revue of his own for Broadway, made up of hits from his previous shows, and plucked Gertrude Lawrence out of Noël's show to be one
of its stars.

One piece of good news was that *André Charlot's Revue of 1924* contained
three of Noël's numbers. So now, in a roundabout way, Noël had arrived on
Broadway. Before long he had fulfilled his own obligations to the London
production and took off for New York himself, where as well as renewing
old acquaintance with the Lunts, Alexander Woollcott, and the Algonquin
crowd, he met a host of new faces, such as the "beautiful, untidy, casual"
artist Neysa McMein, Douglas Fairbanks, and Mary Pickford. He was also
a guest at Laurette Taylor's Riverside Drive house parties, where guests
were dragooned into playing her bizarre version of Charades. All in all, his
few weeks were happily oversubscribed, and he was welcomed wherever he
went. By the time he departed on the SS *Olympic,* he felt he had most definitely "arrived."

The second piece of good news was waiting back in London. Charles
Cochran—Charlot's principal rival as a producer of revues—had seen and
been impressed by *London Calling!* He invited Noël to prepare his next
revue under Cochran management, and so Noël began a personal and eventually professional relationship that would result in some of his biggest
successes.

When *On With the Dance* was successfully previewed in Manchester on
March 17, 1925, Noël cabled Cochran:

*The Vortex* (1924). Florence Lancaster (Lilian Braithwaite) enjoys one of the few happy moments with her son, Nicky (Noël), in the play that made Coward's reputation.

DEAR COCKY I DO HOPE TONIGHT WILL IN SOME SMALL
MEASURE JUSTIFY YOUR TOUCHING AND AMAZING FAITH IN ME
STOP WITH MY DEEPEST GRATITUDE I WISH YOU SUCCESS STOP
YOURS AFFECTIONATELY NOËL

Back in England Noël went to stay with Violet in Dockenfield, where he proceeded to write *Hay Fever* in just three days. If, later, anyone seeing the play should have noticed a close resemblance between Judith Bliss and her family and a certain lady on Riverside Drive, the similarity was purely intentional. The lady herself failed to see the humor in it for many years to come.

By July, Noël had several plays completed and going the rounds of London managements—*Hay Fever, Fallen Angels,* and *The Vortex*—with a marked lack of apparent interest. To keep his hand in, he wrote a fourth, *Easy Virtue,* before taking himself off for a holiday in Deauville.

Violet was not well pleased to be left alone again so soon and must have said as much:

> Royal Hotel
> Deauville
> Saturday 23rd

You poor embittered woman!

I left my address with Daddy, Curtis Brown, Charlot, Laurillard [the producer], Gladys [Calthrop] and the *Daily Graphic* and Auntie

Vida sent me my bathing dress to me—so there! I enclose a couple of smart snapshots—I'm enjoying myself—I think it's going to prove a very lucky trip—but I'll explain why later—I'm full of quite surprisingly dashing plans which look like materializing.

I expect you've had your leg amputated by this time like Sarah Bernhardt but never mind.

Good night, my poor sad old cow. Put a lamp in the window for me.

Snoop

At summer's end he was in an upbeat mood. It was, he felt, "a definite end to a chapter . . . the closing of a phase."

•

IN MANY WAYS Noël was a creative conduit, a sensor of the times he lived through. And this was never truer than in the 1920s and 1930s. Without intellectualizing it, he seemed to be able to sense the mood of the moment and to express it.

He had never forgotten the Victory Day death of actress Billie Carleton by an accidental drug overdose, and it seemed to him symbolic of the hysterical hedonism that threatened to engulf the twenties. In the 1925 song "Poor Little Rich Girl" he would speculate:

> *Cocktails and laughter*
> *But what comes after?*
> *Nobody knows.*
> *You're weaving life into a mad jazz pattern . . .*

Ironically, it was a way of life he was perfectly happy to embrace himself for much of the time, while sensing its aimless danger. *The Vortex,* in retrospect, was his personal exorcism of this postwar superficiality.

Florence Lancaster is a middle-age woman clinging tenaciously to youth by a series of affairs with men young enough to be her son. Her real son, Nicky, returns home and is appalled by what he finds. In a final confrontation he reveals that he has become a drug addict. The two of them vow to give up their self-destructive ways, but the audience is left with a strong feeling that this is not likely to happen. Both of them— and by extension their whole generation—are trapped in "a vortex of beastliness."

If *I'll Leave It to You* owed a debt to Shaw, then *The Vortex* could trace its ancestry to Shakespeare. The lord chamberlain's office had to license every play before it could be produced, and the lord chamberlain's reader reported, "If we ban this, we shall have to ban *Hamlet.*" But ban it they almost did. It was only when Noël appeared in person and argued to the lord chamberlain, Lord Cromer, that the play was, in fact, a moral tract, an *indictment* of the drug culture, that it was allowed to be staged—on November 25, 1924, at the tiny Everyman Theatre, Hampstead.

The audience reception on the first night was enthusiastic—but, then, it had been equally enthusiastic for *I'll Leave It to You* and *The Young Idea.* Even so, Noël felt an electric difference in their response. "Do you think we are all right?" asked Lilian Braithwaite, who was playing Florence. In *Present Indicative* Noël gave his retrospective verdict: "We were all right, *more* than all right. We were a smash hit."

•

PUTTING ON THE play introduced Noël to a new friend: Lilian's actress daughter, Joyce Carey (1898–1993). After the play's success, she became one of the trio of women—the other two being Gladys Calthrop and Lorn—who would form the nucleus of Noël's family. Ladylike in appearance but, like the other two, with a wicked sense of iconoclastic humor, Joyce would become a fixture in just about every Coward play or film from the 1930s onward.

When *The Vortex* transferred to the West End, a twenty-year-old actor called John Gielgud was hired as Noël's understudy. The two became good friends for the rest of their lives, though it might have given Noël pause had he known that Gielgud's program notes for the opening night of the play read, "Coward himself lacked charm and personality and played the piano too loudly, though he acted sincerely and forcefully as far as he could." A second visit, however, convinced Gielgud that Noël's perform-ance at the end of the second act was "one of the most effective things I have ever seen in the theatre."

Gielgud would also write later to Noël that "In a way I have always thought that my success in the theatre only began after *The Vortex* time."

•

A THREAD RUNNING through Noël's stage productions of the 1920s was Basil Dean (1888–1978). Dean had known Noël first as a child actor and had found him "a pimply, knobbly-kneed youngster with an assured manner." By the time of *The Vortex,* the balance of power had changed sig-nificantly, though Noël claimed he "knew Basil well and admired his work." They met up again on the SS *Majestic* to New York, after Noël had left the cast of *London Calling!,* and were to work together again almost continually for the next three or four years as writer/actor and director.

Seeing *The Vortex* convinced Dean that here was a rising star in the the-atrical firmament and quite possibly an entire galaxy. On December 16—Noël's twenty-fifth birthday—Dean was writing to him:

Basil Dean (1888–1978) gave
Noël his first serious acting
role when he directed him in
*Hannele* (1913). In the 1920s
their professional paths and
personal wills would cross
several times—with varying
results.

                                December 8th 1924

My dear Coward,
With reference to our chat on Saturday when you agreed to make a
contract with [Joseph] Bickerton and myself for the production of
the above play in America . . .

With the contracts safely signed, sealed, and delivered, the debate
turned to casting the New York production:

                                III Ebury Street
                                S.W.I.
                                February 28th

My dear Dean,
I really don't know what to suggest about the cast of *The Vortex*. I
think an English cast is extremely valuable to the play—and on the
other hand I see your point about it being expensive. If we don't have
an all English cast, I think it should be entirely American with the
exception of myself. What do you really think about this? . . .

I've got a quite splendid idea for the new play, which I shall be
starting in a week or two.

Will you cable me your opinion of *Still Life* [later *Hay Fever*], as I
have had a tentative offer for it.

The revue [*On With the Dance*] is driving me mad, but I expect it
will be a success.

Act 3 of *The Vortex* was an Oedipal confrontation that caused the lord chamberlain's reader—who had to license productions—to declare, "If we ban this, we shall have to ban *Hamlet*!"

On Monday week we all rush enthusiastically into the arms of Sir Alfred Butt [the theatrical impresario] at the Comedy, who will fondle us lovingly until our receipts drop below £2,000 a week.

Yours ever
Noël Coward

The debate continued. Dean wrote that "Madge Titheradge . . . is quite prepared to come and discuss with me the possibility of the new part . . . I have heard nothing further yet from America with regard to Laura Hope Crews . . . Can you arrange for the Globe Theatre to send me two seats for your first night next week, as I am very anxious not to miss it?"

Noël's West End calendar was filling up rapidly. *On With the Dance*—his first revue for Cochran, for which he had provided book, music, and lyrics—had enjoyed a successful tryout in Manchester. It would open at Cochran's home theater, the London Pavilion, on April 30 and run for 229 performances. There was *Fallen Angels,* with Tallulah Bankhead and Edna Best—the start of a long association for Noël with both of those very different ladies. The scandalous (for its time) story of two married women anxiously awaiting the return of a French lover they had shared years before would also succeed, and rack up 158 performances.

*On With the Dance.* Noël first saw his name in lights at the London Pavilion,
Cochran's "home" theater.

But perhaps most satisfying, to Noël at least, was Marie Tempest's
change of heart about *Hay Fever.* At the time she was, by general acclaim,
London's leading actress, and Noël had had her firmly in mind when writing the part of Judith Bliss. Miss Tempest and her director husband,
Willie Graham Browne, had found it lacking in plot and too inconsequential, and had politely turned it down. A year—and *The Vortex*—later, Tempest could now see *great* potential in it and was happy to be what she
always referred to as "Judith's *créatrice.*" The play would open its 337-
performance run at the Ambassadors on June 8, and give Noël the record
of having four shows running in the West End simultaneously.

In 1936 he would recall the experience of working with his idol in a letter to her biographer, Hector Bolitho:

Having been for so many years, in fact since she first began, a star in
every sense of the word, she wastes no time on personal inhibitions or
inferiority complexes. In fact, she takes off her coat and gets down to
the job of the moment with less shi-shi than any actress I have ever
met; she is more than amenable to direction. In fact, she begs for it.
But there is a proviso in this. The suggestions must be intelligently
and carefully phrased and she must have complete faith in the person
giving them.

So many people have written about her acting, I will content myself with mentioning only one facet and this, to me, is the strangest of all. Despite the fact that for fifty years she has performed a multitude of plays to multitudes of people, she has always contrived to remain the mistress of her tradition rather than allow any tradition to become the mistress of her.

This rather pompous epigram means that in the year 1936 she can walk on to a stage with a company of young people, experienced only in the modern, realistic school of acting, and play them off the stage with her own methods. Marie Tempest can tie up a parcel of books, speak with her back to the audience, light cigarettes, pour out drinks, do a hundred and one things with her hands and body and never lose a laugh, or mis-time a witticism. She is old-fashioned in that there is no traditional trick of the theatre that she does not know completely, and she is modern in the finest sense of the word because she has adapted and constantly readjusted her technique with the years, so that there is no staleness, no bravura posturing of another age perceptible in her performance. One never says of her, "She must have been wonderful when she was young", because that would be under-rating her. Of course she was wonderful when she was young. But to my mind, she is supremely wonderful now.

•

WITH *HAY FEVER* successfully launched, Noël took himself off to Spain for a holiday.

Calle Boticario
Genova
Palma de Mallorca
Spain
June 16th 1925

Dear Basil [no longer "Dean"]
I feel as if I had been in Spain for seventy years. There is nothing I don't know about the Spanish character—each minute inhibition has become as an open book to me. I have a very grand house here on a mountain and I walk about in sand shoes and a large straw hat fanning myself like any old world grandee.

In Barcelona on Sunday I went to my first and last bull fight. I was fortunate enough to secure a seat in the front row—and it was all too lovely. I saw fine horses gored to death and three Bulls baited and finally murdered all in the course of a half an hour, after which I left charmed and awed by the sportsmanship and refinement of the Spanish Nation.

I do hope all your funny little productions are going along all right—your office where I have enjoyed so many cups of overdrawn tea seems immeasurably remote. If you have a moment to turn from Galsworthy [*The Silver Spoon*] to Coward, you might drop me a line.

I'm awfully glad you liked *Hay Fever*. I'm very surprised it hasn't irritated the Press more—some of them seem actually to have been amused by it.

I must go and have a siesta now as it is getting too hot to do anything at all for a few hours. I am sitting on the patio of my hacienda. It is on the side of a mountain with miles of olive trees stretching down to the sea and there are coloured houses dotted about like pieces of sugar in a green cake and Palm trees and Bourganvillias vivid purple—passion flowers and lemons and then this very deep sea blue edged with Jade where it washes over the rocks.

Oh dear, I do *hate* being a successful dramatist—and why, oh why do I write unpleasant plays . . . it seems so unfair that all the good, sincere and honest failures should have to stay in London! I must think of something really lascivious to get me a longer holiday next year!

> Best love,
> NOËL

There was a small but distinctive barb in the reference to *Hay Fever*, since Dean had originally also turned it down. It was being staged now by a different management.

24th June 1925

My dear Noël,
Delighted to have a letter from you. It is very decent of you to send me news. I envy you your holiday. London has been terribly hot until yesterday, when it suddenly cooled off; as a result, theatrical business has improved at once . . .

I had a hearty laugh or two over some of the remarks in your letter. Of course, you are a demon because you promised to send me a letter that I could reprint in our News-Sheet. I am afraid the one you sent me might involve poor old Reandean [his production company] in a long and continued series of libel suits beginning with the Housekeeper who would—naturally and quite rightly—resent your animadversions upon the St. Martin's Theatre tea-making industry. Anyway, it is better to have one's tea overdrawn than under-produced, ha! ha!

You are kindly requested to write a play in the near future which would enable both partners of Reandean to have an even longer holiday than the author, than whom nobody deserves it less.

Please write me a dear, darling, seductive letter, full of polite *Daily Express*–isms and Noëlisms fit for the gentle and seductive eyes of the young ladies known to frequent the St. Martin's theatre pit.

When are you coming back? The plane trees in Piccadilly are shedding their bark in grief because of you.

Yours ever,

Basil

While continuing to work toward the American production of *The Vortex,* Dean had not been idle on other Coward fronts. He had sent the script of *Easy Virtue*—that other product of Dockenfield—to Broadway producer Charles Dillingham, who was to produce *The Vortex* in partnership with the Napoleonic and notoriously eccentric producer "Little Abe" Erlanger. Dillingham was quick to reply:

Charles Dillingham
Globe Theatre
Broadway & 46th Street, N.Y.
July 24th 1925

Dear Basil:

I have not wasted any time on *Easy Virtue,* but Miss Ina Claire has taken until now to decide that she is going in Lonsdale's play. I then tried to arrange with Miss [Lenore] Ulric but she has gone in pictures. Mme. [Alla] Nazimova read the play, thinks it is wonderful and says the first two acts are the best she has ever read. She knows Noël Coward. He sent her one of his first plays, and if he will strengthen the third act a little bit on suggestions on which they shall mutually agree, she will be glad to do it, and she is a big draw. Will you see Coward and send me a cable on the subject as she is waiting to hear from me before going elsewhere?

Yours sincerely,

C. B. DILLINGHAM

The play would be produced that December.

In August, the Coward entourage took passage on the SS *Majestic*. In addition to Noël and Basil Dean, the party included Violet, Gladys Calthrop, and Lilian Braithwaite (who was, after all, to repeat her role as Florence). Also on board, en route home from Paris, were playwright Mercedes de Acosta and her current inamorata, actress Eva Le Gallienne, who had shocked even the Parisians by appearing naked in de Acosta's play *Sandro Botticelli*. It was, said Noël, "a gay, nervous voyage and far from peaceful."

Miss de Acosta liked to boast that she could seduce anyone—man or woman—she set her mind on. And, indeed, it was rumored that she had had affairs with both Garbo and Dietrich. Although they kept in touch over the years—or, rather, de Acosta made a point of keeping in touch with *him*—Noël had distinct reservations about the lady.

She must have wondered how to take letters such as the following:

9/4/29

My dear Mercedes,

I do hope you are getting nicely secure with your [dental] plate and come to review even your own tragedies with a more detached eye . . . I'm terribly rushed at the moment, otherwise I'd write a longer letter.

All love,
NOËL

•

IF THE JOURNEY was not peaceful, there was little peace to be found on Broadway when they arrived and began to discuss the production of *The Vortex*. The plan was for it to start with a short tour and then "come in" to an Erlanger theater, but at this point the unpredictable Abe decreed that the play would most certainly *not* come to New York until Noël had rewritten the last act and eliminated "the spectacle of a son so vilely abusing the woman who gave him birth." But Noël was not to worry, Abe insisted. He (Erlanger) would come to rehearsals and tell him what to do.

The explosion that ensued removed both Erlanger and Dillingham from the production credits. The management of the show was taken over by Sam Harris and Irving Berlin.

New York was an even greater success for Noël than London had been—probably because of advance word of mouth that here was a startling new play by a startling new playwright. The company was greeted with standing ovations and rave reviews. "That night," wrote Noël of the play's opening night, "is set apart in my memory, supreme and unspoilt, gratefully and forever."

The post–New York tour, though, was not without incident, and reduced heads to an appropriate size. If Washington had been as hot as hell, Chicago was simply hell. Years later Clifton Webb, playing in the same Selwyn Theatre, saw a legend scrawled on his dressing room wall where a despairing young actor had expressed his frustrations through graffiti: NOËL COWARD DIED HERE. Since the Chicago audience had been persuaded by the badinage in the first act that they were there to watch a comedy, they laughed determinedly throughout, finding the melodramatic final act particularly hilarious.

Still, for a while it looked as though Noël were about to colonize Broad-

Noël met Gladys Calthrop (1894–1980) socially in the 1920s. She designed costumes and sets for his shows until the 1940s. Their friendship survived the professional "divorce," and she was there at Buckingham Palace in 1970 when he became "Sir Noël."

way as he had commandeered the West End. But the American production of *Hay Fever* opened in September and lasted precisely six weeks.

*Easy Virtue*—the first of his plays to have its premiere in the United States—opened on December 7 with Jane Cowl as the heroine, Larita, and with this one he did have a success. It was still running when Noël and his party boarded the SS *Olympic* the following March to return home. Basil Dean, having directed it, was now back in London, planning the English production.

The party that left was not precisely the party that had arrived the previous August. Jack Wilson was now aboard, in every sense of the word, but Gladys Calthrop had been left behind—at least for a while. The outward-bound shipboard friendship with Eva Le Galliennne had ripened, and Gladys had decided to stay on as art director of the actress's new Civic Repertory Theatre—or, as Noël dubbed it, the Civic Raspberry Company. Le Gallienne had by then broken up with Mercedes de Acosta, but whether she had begun an affair with Gladys at this time remains open to conjecture. De Acosta described Gladys as "that enchanting and beautiful person" when she first met her—a view she may have subsequently modified. A later (unsigned) cable that Gladys filed under "Eve Le Gallienne" would seem to provide a clue:

NEW YORK
JANUARY 27TH 1927
GLADYS CALTHROP 14 ST THEATRE 14 ST BETWEEN SIX AND
SEVEN

I HAVE MUCH TO SAY TO YOU THIS EVENING SO PLEASE COME
EARLY AND STAY LATE LAST NIGHT WATCHING YOU IN THE
DARKNESS YOU MADE ME THINK OF A BLACK TULIP AND GAVE
ME EXOTIC AND UNEASY DREAMS UNSIGNED

John Gielgud, who knew them all, recalled that at this period Gladys, Eva, Mercedes, and one other (possibly producer Cheryl Crawford) were known as "the Four Horsewomen of the Algonquin."

·

BACK IN LONDON, Basil was preparing for the Manchester opening of *Easy Virtue*. Jane Cowl was to reprise her role in the play before opening in London at the Duke of York's Theatre.

But that was the easy part. The hard part was the *title* of the play and an incident that would set it apart in the Coward canon.

In Dean's letter of April 22:

A curious position has arisen with regard to Manchester by John Hart, who owns the theatre, refusing to sign the contract for a play of the title *Easy Virtue*. He says he thought the title was *Easy Money*! As I am committed to Jane, the Duke of York's Theatre and all the other artists, I had to insist on the date. The only way I could insist on it temporarily was to agree that we should produce the play in Manchester under some other title. On first thoughts you may gasp at this, but I think you will quickly realise that if we handle the situation properly, we can get a lot of added advertisement for the play, and at the same time make the Watch Committee of Manchester look ridiculous because, of course, everybody knows about the play by now. I am informed the reason for the objection is because the Watch Committee would not allow a play with such a title. However, in order to be quite sure about the position, I am endeavouring to get into touch with the Watch Committee, as I want them to commit themselves definitely to the statement that they will not allow the play to be produced under that title.

I can see a good deal of mischief in your eye as I dictate this letter!

Yours ever,
D

MAY 16TH

WHAT MEANING ALTERNATIVE MANCHESTER UTTERLY
BEWILDERED STOP NOËL

MAY 18TH

MANCHESTER WATCH COMMITTEE OBJECT TO TITLE AM SOLELY
ANNOUNCING NOËL COWARD'S NEW PLAY STOP WE WILL HAVE
GRAND FUN IN PAPERS ON YOUR RETURN STOP BASIL

And indeed they did have fun. Dean was right. People who might have
been of two minds about attending now had to see what all the fuss was
about. The play was billed as *A New Play in Three Acts.* Ironically, at the
cinema next door—presumably beneath the attention of the eagle-eyed
Watch Committee—the week's attraction was a film called *Flames of Passion,* as luridly advertised as its title demanded. Not being someone to
throw such nuggets away, Noël stored this up for later use. As Celia Johnson and Trevor Howard leave the cinema in *Brief Encounter,* the poster for
the film they have just been watching reads *Flames of Passion.*

•

*EASY VIRTUE* SETTLED down into a solid run of 124 performances,
and Jane Cowl's bravura performance caught the eye of various "mature"
actresses around town.
Mrs. Patrick Campbell wrote:
August 27th 1926

I have seen *Easy Virtue* three times . . . Miss Cowl tells me she must
go back to New York Sept. 20th. Am I too old or too ugly to dare to
suggest I might take up the part? . . . If you thought there was anything in it, I would eat dry bread until the 20th so that I was at any
rate slimmer!

It was not the first time she'd petitioned Noël for work and, once again,
he did not think there was "anything in it" and said so as politely as he
knew how.
More pressing from Noël's point of view was his own commitment to
Dean as an actor in someone else's play. *The Constant Nymph* was a popular
and highly romantic novel by Margaret Kennedy. Kennedy and Dean had
collaborated on a stage version, which was to open in September. Dean—
in a maneuver typical of his authoritarian management style—offered the
leading role of Lewis Dodd to John Gielgud, then changed his mind and
decided that it would be better box office if Noël were to play the part for
the first month of the run. Noël agreed, and once again, Gielgud was
forced to play understudy, as he had in *The Vortex.*
Noël was anxious to see if he could succeed with someone else's material. The answer was—not very well and not for very long. Mrs. Patrick

Edna Best (1900–1974) starred with
Noël in *The Constant Nymph* (1926) and,
thirty years later, on live television.

Campbell exacted her own retribution by telling him very publicly on opening night that he was "the wrong type" and suggesting he should wear a beard!

On October 7 his doctor wrote: "Mr. Coward has been examined by me this morning and is suffering from severe nervous exhaustion. He has been ordered by me to remain in bed and will not be fit to act for at least a month."

John Gielgud took over once again.

It was a convenient exit strategy, and well within the proscribed month, he was to be found once again on the SS *Olympic* with Jack, en route to the United States to begin rehearsing *This Was a Man,* a new play he had written earlier in the year while in Palermo and which Dean was to direct.

To Violet:

> January 14th
> On Board S.S. *Olympic*
> Cherbourg

Darling,

I did hate leaving you so dreadfully—and I cried for a half an hour with Jack trying to comfort me. I'm so very glad that you didn't come to the front door! Oh dear—I really ought to have got over being a mother's boy by now, but I never shall!

I'm so thankful we've got the cottage because it means peace for you and something to do to take your mind off missing me. Do take care of yourself, my own darling, and drive *frightfully* slowly and don't be depressed because I'm not going to be away for long and I'll write every week reg'lar.

I'll be at the Ritz Carlton anyhow to start with. Syrie [Maugham] sends you her love—the boat isn't at all full and we're very comfortable. I'm going to rest and rest and rest and not worry about anything.

Oh darling, all my love, love, love.

Snoop

Jack also felt it politic to write:

Dear Mrs. Coward,
Just a line to say goodbye and to thank you for being so nice to me this summer. I can't realize that I've been away from home six months, for you and Noël have been so sweet and kind that I dug right in and never had a moment of the lonely, alien, homesick feeling.

As a matter of fact it's a wrench to leave England—I somehow dread New York—it seems big and noisy and strangely foreign.

Please believe that I'll do all I can to keep Noël well and happy . . . My life is open to him and Mother would be very honored and happy to have him with us all.

Again, thanks and love
JACK

# CHAPTER 5
# "WHY MUST THE SHOW GO ON?"

## (1926)

*Why must the show go on?*
*Why not announce the closing night of it?*
*The public seem to hate the sight of it,*
*Dear, and so*
*Why you should undergo*
*This terrible strain we'll never know.*

**"WHY MUST THE SHOW GO ON?" (1954)**

After the acclaim came the apprehension.

T HE INSTANT SUCCESS of *The Vortex* lured him into thinking that anything that bore the legend "by Noël Coward" was automatically a guarantee of quality and success. Plays were written too quickly and uncritically. Others were retrieved unwisely from bottom drawers. But that was all to come.

Safely arrived in New York, Noël was as good as his filial word. Every week, regular as clockwork, he shared his life with Violet:

Gladstone Hotel
114-122 East 52nd Street
New York
Wednesday

Darlingest,
I moved in here today as I was uncomfortable at the Ritz—it's far too noisy and expensive but this is very quiet and nice.

The crossing was horrible as a crossing except for two days and practically everyone was ill but Syrie [Maugham] and Jack [Wilson] and I remained superior and healthy, if a trifle apprehensive! I slept 12 hours a night firmly and now feel thoroughly rested and well.

*This Was a Man* goes into rehearsal next week with . . . a very good

Noël on the SS *Bremen* (1933)—
"I Travel Alone."

cast indeed. Gladys [Calthrop] is very gay . . . she has two first nights, one on Monday and one on Tuesday. I'm so glad I was in time for them . . .

I got your cable on arrival. I suspect *The Rat Trap* was far worse than "So-so". I'm longing to get a letter about it.

Do go to Hatchard's and get *A Deputy Was King* by G. B. Stern and put it down to my account and *read* it—it's very good and she's done me in it! Rather well at moments.

Last night I went to *Iolanthe* with Basil—it was beautifully done and the music lovely but dated. It's no use, I *hate* Gilbert and Sullivan.

All New York has rung me up and welcomed me, so I feel very cosy.

All my love, darlingest Snig

Your roving Snoop.

His next letter (October 28) was written on the stationery of "Basil Dean Inc. Presenting English Plays in America, 1674 Broadway," and scribbled at the top of the page:

Jack and I have a very grand office in this building with Noël Coward Inc. on the door in gold letters. It's very cheap, so we're going to keep it permanently—we must have somewhere to put our papers and contracts (all three!).

Darling,

I got your letter and the notices which I thought very good considering—thank God they all knew it was an early play. [In the post-*Vortex* euphoria, one of his first plays, *The Rat Trap,* had been put on at the Everyman. It did not rival *The Vortex,* running for only twelve performances.]

Everything is going very well here. I've got Francine Larrimore, A. E. Matthews and Nigel Bruce for *This Was a Man,* which is rehearsing now. It opens on the 22nd November, probably at the Klaw. Francine Larrimore is a big star and very good and Matthews is grand. Nigel arrives tomorrow—it looks like a success to me! Ruth Gordon I think is going to do *Fallen Angels* as soon as I can find someone good to play it with her.

I went to Eva's [Le Gallienne] first night on Monday and it was more frightful than anything in the world. She was terrible, the production awful and the play lousy! Two of Gladys's sets were very good. The next night they did Tchekof's *Three Sisters,* which I hear is better and Gladys has made a big success with her scenery. She's very happy and working like a beaver and it's all good experience for her.

Everyone asks after you and sends you love, particularly Fanny Ward and Mabel Webb [Mabelle Webb, Clifton's extrovert mother]. I haven't heard from [Philip] Tonge yet [Noël's boy actor competitor who was now desperately seeking to become part of the Coward entourage] but I dread the telephone.

Alfred Lunt is marvelous in an historical play at the [Theatre] Guild [*Juarez and Maximilian*] and Lynn is playing in *Mrs. Beame* [*At Mrs. Beame's*] and rehearsing Mrs. Pat's [Campbell] part in *Pygmalion*. I love being here and I'm taking everything very easily and being a good boy—Jack sends dearest love and is looking after me beautifully.

All my love, dearest darling and don't miss me *too* much.

Snoop

Noël Coward, Inc.
Wednesday, November 3rd.

Darling,

I'm inaugurating my first day in our grand new office by writing to you! It is all very dignified and I feel extremely businesslike and prosperous. The opening date of *This Was a Man* has been advanced by a week—we open cold at the Klaw Theatre on Tuesday, December 16th—my lucky date [his birthday]! It really is coming on very well—they're all going to be frightfully good. Francine Larrimore particularly. She's small and red haired and very sexy and as far as I can gather has already made plans about every man in the cast, so she ought to be well in her element!

I'm still searching wildly for someone to play *Fallen Angels* with Ruth Gordon but it's very difficult—still perseverance is my middle name! *The Constant Nymph* opens on December 9th with Glenn Anders in my part and an English girl called Beatrix Thompson as Tessa. [Basil was directing.] I think Basil should really have waited for Edna Best but he wanted to get it on quickly.

He's producing *This Was a Man* beautifully and has great ideas about *Semi-Monde* if we can raise enough money. Gladys [Calthrop] has done some grand scenery and chosen some good clothes, so *that's* all cosy!

About twenty new buildings have shot up into the air since last year and five million more motor cars, consequently one can't move anywhere.

Jane Cowl, after having talked about all the plays she was going to do and made everyone's life a burden, is going into Vaudeville with a sketch and a very much smaller salary than Nazimova, who is doing the same thing!

I went out with Laurette [Taylor, who had now forgiven Noël his trespasses] the other night and she sent you her best love—she's been kicked out of the play *she* was trying out and is raising Hell about it—altogether the flowers of the American stage are getting a bit wilted! Gertie opens next Monday in the new Gershwin show [*Oh, Kay!*]—and Jeanne Eagels opens in a new play in December [*Her Cardboard Lover*]. She was still doing *Rain* when I arrived. I haven't seen her yet.

I do wonder how the cottage [Goldenhurst] is coming along. I expect you're being a busy girl and no mistake.

How is Eric's [Noël's brother] French progressing? Tell him the moment he has completely mastered it he'd better start on Russian—difficult but commercial, so I've been told.

I'm feeling very well and I've only been out late once since I arrived.

All the love in the world, dearest darling.

    Snoop


                        November 11th

Darling

Here goes for my weekly letter.

The moment after the play opens I am going away for a fortnight to Hot Springs [he meant White Sulphur Springs] which is in the mountains and very quiet, because I want to write a little . . . I shall only send you the address in case you fall down stairs—or burn your finger or get pneumonia or have twins or something! Anyhow, I might not go at all but I don't wish you to come over peculiar and send off lots of bank notes and shirts and important letters to different addresses all over America, as it is an extremely large continent and very vague!

Nigel Bruce is driving everybody mad by being completely and abjectly stupid and trying far too hard and not listening to what he's told and it's all frightful but we feel it will be all right on the Night! Please don't be in the *least* annoyed by Swaffer's remarks. [Hannen Swaffer was an egocentric though influential London gossip journalist who had started an anti-Noël vendetta.] He doesn't worry me at all—the more frightful things he says the more sympathy I get and it doesn't matter anyhow what the papers say, good or bad, I'm far beyond being harmed in any way by the Press.

Noël found Goldenhurst in 1926. He rented it, later bought it, renovated it, and installed his parents and Auntie Vida there. It was his country retreat before and after the war, until his tax "exile" forced him to sell it in 1956.

Gertie opened in *Oh, Kay!* here on Monday and was really marvelous, she carried the whole show and made a huge success. I spend my time pursuing elusive actresses for *Fallen Angels* and am now very hot on the scent of Fay Bainter but they're all *very* tiresome ... Linda Porter [Cole's wife] arrived yesterday and I'm gracing a grand party given for her tonight ... I spent the weekend on Long Island in an enormous house party with all the Vanderbilts and Astors and Shufflebottoms—altogether Society's pet.

November 18

Darling,

I've just got a lovely long letter from you! The house does sound nice and I'm terribly glad you're pleased with it. We'll have heaps of plans when I get back.

I had a tremendous party given for me last night and it was rather fun. George Gershwin played and we all carried on like one o'clock.

Jack took me to the Yale v. Princeton Football game on Saturday. It really was a marvelous sight and terribly exciting—65,000 people all screaming their heads off. Jack lost all control and beat me on the head whenever Yale scored anything.

I shall miss you dreadfully on my First Night—it's going to be very smart and there's a huge demand for seats. I shall want my grey-haired Mother hung with Woolworth pearls to clutch! But never mind. I'll write and tell you all.

Linda [Porter] has arrived and we're all having grand fun. We went to see Lynn Fontanne play *Pygmalion* the other night—she's perfectly wonderful, much better than Mrs. Pat ever was. We spent Sunday in the country with Jeanne [Eagels] who sent you lots of love. The [Clifton] Webbs clamour for you. You needn't be afraid I shall stay away too long, because I couldn't possibly! Next year I shall probably play here and we'll have an apartment.

I met Jack's complete family and Mama is writing to you to tell you how well I look—I haven't had a day's illness since I left England except for my usual frightful heart attacks and my lumbago, varicose veins and that dreadful hacking cough that *never* stops but everyone is *very* kind and my eyesight is slowly returning!

All love, darling
Snoop

But Noël's bubble was about to burst:

November 25th
Shadowstone, Lawrenceville, New Jersey
Darling,
This is Thanksgiving Day and I'm spending it in the Wilson home en route for White Sulphur Springs.

The play, dear, has all the earmarks of being a failure! Gladys and Jack and I sat grandly in a box on the First Night and watched it falling flatter and flatter. And I must admit we got bad giggles! They were all expecting something very dirty indeed after the English Censor banning it and they were bitterly disappointed.

Francine Larrimore was very good and A. E. Matthews, too, tho' he forgot most of his lines. [Matthews later wrote to Noël and apologized—"I talked all your lines upside down."] Nigel Bruce who has never understood what it was all about from the first was all right but extremely dull and Auriol [Lee] was good but also dull—for some unknown reason they played it so slowly that there was time to go round the corner and have an ice cream soda between every line. We suffered a little during the first Act but gave up suffering after that and rather enjoyed it. I find on close reflection that I am as unmoved by failure as I am by success which is a *great* comfort. Perhaps *Fallen Angels* will go better and if it doesn't I don't really mind. I like *writing* the plays anyhow and if people don't like them that's their loss. I hope you won't be depressed about it because I'm really as bright as a button. I always get bored anyhow if everything isn't a smashing success immediately!

I've just started a play for Marie Tempest but as there are several illegitimate children in it I doubt if Lord Cromer [the lord chamberlain] will care very deeply for it. I shall finish it at White Sulphur and do it in the Spring in London.

. . . Oh dear, I've made it up with Osbert Sitwell and it's all very funny—I wrote him a note saying that as we were both in a Foreign Country we ought to put an end to the Feud, then he came round and suggested quite pleasantly that I should apologise to Edith in all the papers! I gave him an old-fashioned look and explained gently that he was very silly indeed, which he seemed to understand perfectly and we parted very amicably. It really was becoming a bore because he wasn't being asked anywhere, poor dear, owing to my popularity being the greater! So that's that.

The Queen of Roumania [Marie] with son and daughter came to the party after the First Night so we were all very grand. [Max] Reinhardt arrives in December and is very anxious to do *Semi-Monde*, which would be one in the eye for everyone and place me on such an intellectual plane that I doubt if I should ever come down! I have just eaten the most enormous Thanksgiving Dinner Turkey and plum pudding and I'm blown out like a football but look very sweet . . .

All love, my dearest darling, your unwanted unappreciated unabashed uncared for and untidy son. Snoopie.

I do hope you won't think I'm smiling through my tears!

Greenbrier
December 8th

Darling,

I'm sending this cheque early so as to get you in good time for Christmas. Will you divide it up among the family? £5 for Poppa, £5 for Baby Erik, £5 for Vivacious Vida, £2 for May, £1 for Victor and £7 for yourself? And *don't* spend it all on sweets!

We are leaving here tonight for New York. I'm feeling wonderfully well—the holiday has done me a tremendous amount of good. I've finished the comedy for Marie Tempest. It's the eighteenth century one I told you about called *The Marquise* and is very good, I think. I'll send you a script as soon as it is typed but you mustn't mention this to a soul, as they all seem so down on me in England that I may have to send it to the Censor under another name! So keep your trap shut! I shall do it about April, I should think.

*This Was a Man* is drifting along . . . Some of the Critics (the Principal ones) have said very good things about it but I fear too late to save it. I give it two or three more weeks. Jack is not coming to California with me as there is a good deal of business to be done in New York. We are going to Chicago for three days after Christmas to stay with Syrie [Maugham] and I go on from there to San Francisco to join Diana [Cooper] and Iris [Tree] and then Hollywood for a week or two . . . I get very homesick at moments and miss you terribly.

I am more or less giving up *Fallen Angels* for this season but firm plans have to be laid for next Autumn. I shall play here myself then and fling plays on like confetti!

There's no more news now, darling, so good bye—I'll write every Wednesday as usual, rain or shine—all love and several wet kisses.

Snoopie

His next letter explains the real situation:

Gladstone
December 14th

Dearest Darling,

My cable will probably have surprised you considerably. [He then strikes the line out and scribbles at the top of the letter—"I haven't sent a cable because the letter explains better" and continues] I will now proceed to explain all!

Just before I went to White Sulphur I began to feel very nervy and ill . . . So three days ago I called in a specialist who examined me thoroughly. You will be relieved to hear that organically I am completely healthy, . . . but I am in a bad way as far as nerves are concerned—he said that I have been living on nervous energy for years and now it has given out and that I must go away *at once*! . . . He said a long sea voyage was the thing and a complete break with my present interests for at least two months. I know he's right so I'm going to Sarawak . . . I sail from San Francisco on Christmas Day and go to . . . Hong Kong, where I change boats and go on to Singapore where the Rajah's [of Sarawak] yacht is sent for me. I shall stay at Sarawak for ten days . . .

I really feel the trip will do me a tremendous lot of good—I feel I must get away from all the people I know for a while, not only from the point of view of health but for my work as well. From now onwards I'm not going to work so hard anyhow . . . It will be heavenly to be stuck on a boat with *nothing* to do and I shall probably be bored stiff at first but there will be lovely places to see and I'm a *keen* traveller . . .

Nerves are extraordinary things—I sleep for eleven hours and wake up *dead* tired with my legs aching as though I'd walked ten miles! It's not serious yet as I haven't had a break down but the Doctor says I'm on the verge of one . . . I expect your vivid imagination is now at work conjuring up pictures of your beloved son gibbering like a maniac and telling everyone he's the Empress Eugénie, but as a matter of fact I'm *not* the Empress Eugénie, I'm Napoleon . . .

I'm allowed to go out at night as long as I'm *in bed* by Twelve, so you see I'm not dying.

I know I shall be dreadfully lonely and bored on that dreary boat but the Doctor says the more bored I am the better and it will be nice staying with the Sarawaks and seeing the dawn come up like Thunder out of China 'cross the bay! Wouldn't it be awful if I became a second Rudyard Kipling . . .

Oh darling, I do hope you won't cry much at the thought of two more months without me—but you do see, don't you? If I came back to England now I'd be embroiled with Marie Tempest and Basil and Films, *however* much I tried to avoid them and I should rush over to Paris and back and go to First Nights and do myself in!

I'll cable you the name of the boat and everything—and cable me on Christmas Day to San Francisco. I know I shall be terribly Mothersick. Oh Dear, Oh Dear.

All my love, my dear darling
　　　　Your Wandering boy
　　　　Robinson Crusoe

　　　　　　　　　　　　　　　　　　　Fairmont Hotel
　　　　　　　　　　　　　　　　　　　San Francisco
　　　　　　　　　　　　　　　　　　　Christmas Eve

Darling,

Here I am in California at last! I expect you have got my letter by now explaining about my trip and everything. I'm feeling very much better already but I'm more and more convinced that this is the only sensible thing to do. Jack is here with me and he goes back to New York tomorrow after I sail . . .

I get tired far too quickly and the sooner I get well away from everybody the better. I shall cable you from every port I stop at but I'm afraid it's no use writing any more after this because the letters will never reach you before I do!

My first stop is Honolulu New Year's Eve and ten days later Yokohama, after that I stop every day or two . . . The boat is quite large and I have a comfortable cabin to myself . . . I feel rather scarified going off all by myself but I know it's the only really wise plan. I've been with people much too much during these last years and a little solitude will do me good. I shall be home about the 8th of March . . . Have my little white bed at the cottage ready, as I shall probably wire you to meet me at Dover in Lulu [Violet's car] and I'll go straight to Aldington. I'm looking forward to coming home with wild excitement and my one comfort over this trip is that it's all on the way once I start! . . .

What a God-send that cottage was—it's the *greatest* comfort to me to feel you're away from Ebury Street and have a nice peaceful place to wait for your Wandering Boy!

Christmas Day

I'm finishing off this letter today. I've just got all the family cables which I loved . . . San Francisco is really divine.

We motored out to Burlinghame to lunch, everything green and fresh and roses out! The streets are steep like Edinburgh and China-town right in the middle of everything. There's a Rock just outside the town by the Golden Gate *covered* with seals! They're so sweet. I sail at four o'clock this afternoon. It's now 9:00 a.m. which means about 5 p.m. in England if you've had your Christmas dinner I expect you're all lying about stuffed. Diana and Iris send their love, they're on the same floor as we are, we had a grand party last night with Reinhardt. [They were appearing in *The Miracle,* directed by Reinhardt.] When you cable just put Well—Love because it will be expensive. I'll do the same from every port. Good bye now my darling—Give my dear love to Daddy, Vida and Erik and all. Be a good Snig and don't have too many nightmares about shipwrecks, this is not the Typhoon season!

Hugs and kisses, Snoop

At intervals for the rest of his life Noël would suffer from what were almost certainly psychosomatic conditions that, nonetheless, resulted in genuinely debilitating physical symptoms. His army experience had been one, but this time he was genuinely concerned, as indicated by the way he repeatedly justifies his decision to travel—to himself as much as Violet.

On the afternoon of that Christmas Day he waved goodbye to Jack and walked up the gangplank of the SS *President Pierce* and into another chapter of his overcrowded life.

## CHAPTER 6
# "I'M WORLD WEARY, WORLD WEARY"

### (1927)

*I'm world weary, world weary,*
*Living in a great big town,*
*I find it so dreary, so dreary.*
*Everything is grey or brown . . .*

*I can hardly wait*
*Till I see the great*
*Open spaces,*
*My loving friends will not be there,*
*I'm so sick of their*
*God-damned faces,*
*Because I'm world weary, world weary,*
*Tired of all these jumping jacks,*
*I want to get right back to nature and relax.*

**"WORLD WEARY," FROM *THIS YEAR OF GRACE* (1928)**

O N JANUARY 1, 1927, Noël cabled Violet from Honolulu:

WORLD TRIP SO FAR STAYING HERE FEW WEEKS DIVINE HERE
ADDRESS MOANA HOTEL STOP LOVE SNOOP.

But those few words did not tell the whole story.

By the time the boat docked and Noël had been escorted to the home of his local hosts, Walter and Louise Dillingham, he was running a high fever. He made his excuses and returned to the *President Pierce,* where he packed his bags and then checked into the Moana Hotel. From there he wrote to Violet:

Moana Hotel
Honolulu
January 4th 1927

Darling,

I got off the boat here on Friday feeling awful—six days of really bad sea. I wasn't sea sick at all but it made my nerves worse than ever. I had a temperature of 103! I realized that to make a long world trip one must feel *really* well and so I think I was wise to get off—I was met by friends of Florence Magee called the Dillinghams who are very rich and very nice and are virtually king and queen of Honolulu. They were very kind and sent me a charming doctor who put me to bed and has kept me there ever since until yesterday, when he took me for a drive—he says I ought to stay a month and get a real rest— you can imagine how lonely and miserable I felt being ill in a strange place but I feel grand now and I'm having tea with the Dillinghams this afternoon. I think I'm going out to their country ranch, which is divine—at the foot of the highest mountain here. It's about 30 miles by car—mostly sugar cane and banana plantations. The island is exquisite—never too hot and never anything approaching cold— flowers in masses all the year round, particularly camellias and hibiscus and roses all wild! The bathing is wonderful. There's a coral reef a mile out and the big rollers hit it and send smaller ones into the lagoons and you ride in canoes in bather dresses and are deposited high up on the beach—there are *no* sharks inside the reef! So you needn't worry. There are a few octopuses but they love them and eat them! I don't think I shall. The colouring, of course, is beyond belief, just like Robinson Crusoe—deep blue ocean—bright green lagoon—

dazzling yellow sand—enormous cocoa palms and scarlet hibiscus everywhere. I feel so rested already. I'm sure this is the right thing to do—God knows when you'll get this.

Good by, darling Snig. I'll cable every week—your photograph is a great success in a small leather frame.

SNOOP

He was putting on a brave face for her sake. Inwardly he had a suspicion that "too much had happened to me in too short a time. I had written too much, acted too much and lived far too strenuously. This was the pay-off, possibly, I thought."

He cabled faithfully.

JANUARY 9TH

HAVING LOVELY REST PALM TREES AND BLUE SEA VERY
SUNBURNT HOME END OF FEBRUARY. BE GOOD MY DARLING
LOVE TO ALL

SNOOP

After a few days the Dillinghams took him to their "ranch" at Moku-leia and left him mercifully alone to rest and recuperate. During the several weeks he stayed there he had time to take stock of who and what he was.

People, I decided, were the danger. People were greedy and preda-tory, and if you gave them the chance, they would steal unscrupu-lously the heart and soul out of you without really wanting to or even meaning to. A little extra personality; a publicized name; a little entertainment value above the average; and there they were, snatch-ing and grabbing, clamorous in their demands, draining your strength to add a little fuel to their social bonfires. Then when the time came when you were tired, no longer quite so resilient, you were pushed back into the shadows, consigned to the dust and left to moulder in the box-room like a once smart hat that is no longer fashionable.

At the end of a month of determined inactivity the siren call of civiliza-tion became insistent, and Noël embarked on the SS *Wilhelmina* to return to New York.

·

THE YEAR 1927 was not destined to be an annus mirabilis for Noël, either, even though it started our promisingly. He did indeed get back to London in time to see Marie Tempest play in *The Marquise*. As the Marquise de Kestournel, she was "everything I had envisaged; the tricorne hat, the twinkle in the eye, the swift precision of movement." For Noël, the part was a personal tribute to an actress he had adored from the first time he saw her at the age of twelve in a play called *At the Barn*.

> I was aware of her blue and mauve taffeta dress, with panniers and one of her usual crisp little hats . . . I also remember two minutes of silent acting at the end of the first act which, even at the tender age of twelve, I was bright enough to brand into my memory, where it has remained clear and unexcelled by anything I have since seen in the theatre. Marie Tempest sat alone at a tea table with a handkerchief in her right hand and a sandwich in her left, deciding in her troubled mind whether to eat or to weep. Finally, the tears won, and the sandwich went back on to the plate, and the handkerchief to her eyes . . . Into those brief two minutes was distilled the very essence of acting.

After *Hay Fever* Marie Tempest had formed her own positive opinion of her playwright:

Dame Marie Tempest (1864–1942) turned down *Hay Fever* as being too trivial, but after the success of *The Vortex,* she had a sudden change of heart (1933).

Noël is the *enfant gâté* of the theatre. At his birth two godmothers sat over his cradle, the benevolent one who gave him his superb gift, and the malignant crone who tossed in a handful of gifts, almost as good. She disappeared with a cackling laugh. Noël is aware of these gifts and he feels he must exploit them all. That is the trap which was laid by the malignant godmother.

This pompous parable is just my Victorian way of saying that I do not think he will ever quite fulfil his great promise if he does not curb his versatility. He is spending his gifts too lavishly . . . He is the most stimulating and exciting personality that has come into my life in the last ten years. I value his friendship more than I can say.

Before the play opened she wrote to Noël:

> 3 Upper George Street
> Bryanston Square
> W.1.
> February 2nd, 1927

Dearest Noël,
I do hope you are feeling well and rested again, and that you will come back to us soon again!

The play is delightful and we are producing on the 16th at the Criterion. You know what that means!—

I tried to find Gladys [Calthrop] but heard that she was in America and that left us very little time to get sketches, etc. So, we decided to get the very best possible, and Wm. Nicholson has done the scene and the men's dresses. The women's I have attended to. I may tell you that no library, picture gallery, antique furniture and silver shop have been overlooked to have everything period and correct. I do hope you will be pleased with us.

Francois Cellier is playing Estaban beautifully—Robert Harris, Jacques—Eileen Sharpe, Adrienne—Charming . . . My dearest [William Graham Browne, her husband] is going to be excellent as Raoul, and I hope for the best. Anyway, dearest, you know that we are doing our d——t!

Your writing of the play is, to me, amazing. I cannot tell you how much I love it all!

> All my love,
> MARY

*The Marquise* ran for a successful 129 performances.

•

SOMEONE ELSE who was relieved to see Noël back in London was Basil Dean, who was anxious to revive the Coward-Dean partnership. This time, however, Noël was determined not to be rushed. He would set himself and his house in order.

First came the house. When he was offered the option of buying the freehold of Goldenhurst, he took it "at a ridiculously small price" and he and Jack started the work of improving it.

With the work under way, they took off for an extended summer holiday in Europe. Noël left behind a new comedy, *Home Chat,* for Basil to mull over. On August 5 he is reassuring Noël:

I have seen the Lord Chamberlain's Office, and subject to certain alterations, I have been given to understand that both plays will be licensed. [In fact, *Home Chat* had been submitted under another name, as *To Err Is Human.*]

The alterations with regard to *Sirocco* are more than futile and need not concern you at all. The alterations with regard to the comedy are three in number and involve three good lines, one of which you can guess . . . I have said that I prefer to leave the matter over until early in October when the Lord Chamberlain will be back in town, to ask him to follow the procedure previously adopted with success, and to invite Major Gordon to witness some of our rehearsals to settle outstanding points then.

Noël wrote to Violet:

Lac d'Annecy, Savoie, France

Darling,

I haven't written before because we have been traveling all the time. We've been to Vienna [to see the German version of *The Marquise*] and Budapest, which was frightful—then a day and a night in the train to Innsbruck and up to a lake called Achen See in the middle of the Tyrol, but we hated the people so we left the next day and have now arrived here . . .

This is heavenly—a beautiful lake in the mountains just above Aix les Bains. This hotel is ten miles from a town and right on the edge of the lake with a sweet little terrace and balconies outside our rooms looking across at the most lovely mountains—it's utterly peaceful and so very lovely. I've never felt so well in my life—travelling agrees with me . . . It's quite the most beautiful place I've ever seen. We have our own little boat and bathe from it all day . . .

We've been everywhere second class and thoroughly enjoyed ourselves—not being grand is somehow a tremendous comfort for a

Noël considered Edward Molyneux
(1891–1974) a couturier in a class of his
own. (Molyneux designed Gertie's dresses
for *Private Lives*.) As a friend, Noël found
him entertaining and irritating in equal
measure.

BELOW: Molyneux's house, La Capponcina,
on Cap d'Ail, Côte d'Azur.

change. Vienna was perfectly grand—but out of season, of course.
Budapest was huge and flat and hot and stupid. The Tyrol was far, far
too crowded with pot bellied Germans in mustard coloured plush
hats and Alpenstocks tramping about everywhere.

 Goodnight, darling. I'll write again soon.

   All love
   **SNOOP**

From there they moved on to Edward Molyneux's villa, La Capponcina, on Cap d'Ail.

•

ON SEPTEMBER 6, Basil Dean wrote:

I shall (soon) be wanting to put your comedy into rehearsal with Madge [Titheradge]. I would greatly appreciate it if you would get in touch with her and chat over the cast with her. Meanwhile I am looking round for a Theatre and, if I can arrange it, I have a fancy to go to the Duke of York's where I have already done two of your plays, both of which were fairly successful, and I have a feeling that a third of your plays there may be the best success of the three.

*Home Chat* opened on October 25, but Dean was wrong. It ran for only thirty-eight performances. Noël was bitterly disappointed at its critical reception and wrote to tell Dean so in no uncertain terms:

October 1927

Dear Basil,

You still remain in my opinion the most important producer in London but I feel very definitely that light comedy is not your *métier*.

I am writing this to you because the chief value of an association like ours is the accepted fact that we can both say quite frankly what we really think.

I have now seen three satirical comedies produced by you. *This Was a Man, The Constant Wife* [Maugham] and *Home Chat* and in all three plays the primary defects have been over-meticulous business and slowness of tempo and in *Home Chat* these defects have been increased by the fact that you have been occupied in other directions and have not given the play your full attention.

To my mind the production of the play has fallen between two stools; to wit farce and serious comedy, neither of which it happens to be. Farce is indicated in bits of business such as stuffing biscuits into their mouths, the two Mothers' entrances and exits together and Paul and Mavis in their arm in arm moments and serious comedy notably in scenes at the end of the first act and last act respectively.

I don't wish you to imagine that I am blaming you entirely for my bad notices, although I think things would have been very different if the play had been played swiftly and brightly.

The reason of this letter is really a direct appeal to your intelligence with regard to *The Second Man.* I am completely convinced that this has got to be played and produced with three times the speed and finesse that has been devoted to *Home Chat.*

If in producing me you apply the same methods of measured delivery and unalterably set movements and business, I foresee grave scenes in the theatre, for I should have to stand on my own experience and knowledge and frankly refuse to accept your direction.

I am looking forward tremendously to *Sirocco* about which I have no doubts at all as far as you are concerned. You can handle serious plays with more understanding than anyone else in England.

Please accept this letter in the spirit in which it is offered as a piece of honest criticism and not as a disgruntled personal attack.

> Yours ever,
> Noël

November 1st

My dear Noël,

Of course I do not mind your critcising me. As you say, mutual frankness is the basis of our association. No doubt there is truth in what you say.

My chief concern in this matter is lest your natural chagrin at the manner in which your play has been received should not rob you of what is a sincere artist's greatest privilege; namely to profit more by his failures than by his successes. This also is written in sincere friendship.

> Yours ever
> BASIL DEAN

In his autobiography Dean recorded that the play was "a light comedy written in Noël's brightest manner, but decidedly thin, which was not surprising seeing that he had announced that he had written it in a week—an injudicious form of publicity."

In any case, by now he was mentally focused on the second play, *Sirocco.*

October 28th

Dear Noël,

You will doubtless be interested to hear that this play read very well yesterday, and I think the cast is good. I think the anticlimax of the last scene, without which the play has no point, may militate against its chances commercially, but that cannot be helped.

Noël cabled from Berlin, where he was staying:

ARRIVING EVENING TENTH WOULD LIKE IF POSSIBLE SEE PLAY
THROUGH FRIDAY AND IF CONSIDER ALTERATIONS LAST ACT
NECESSARY WILL DO THEM OVER WEEKEND STOP NOËL

Whatever changes Noël eventually made did nothing to help the play. Written in 1921, it had been consigned to the same bottom drawer as *The Rat Trap,* along with several other fledgling efforts, and should have stayed there.

On paper, *Sirocco* looked promising. The beautiful Frances Doble teamed with matinée idol and silent film star Ivor Novello. On paper was one thing. On the stage was another. The play *was* thin, and neither of the principals had the stage presence at that time to rescue it. It was hooted off the stage, and some of the galleryites spat at Noël as he left the theater. Twenty-eight performances later, the piece was history and part of the salutary lesson Noël was learning about preparing his material properly. He would later claim that he was grateful that he was forced to learn it at a critical point in his career, but at the time the taste was bitter.

The only possible reaction was to pick himself up, dust himself off, and carry on, regardless—which he proceeded to do.

•

SOME MONTHS EARLIER the Lunts had insisted he read S. N. Behrman's latest play, *The Second Man,* with which they had just had a great success in New York. In point of fact, so enthusiastic were they that they *read* it aloud to him, playing all four parts. Noël immediately agreed to act in the London production—once again a Basil Dean enterprise.

December 8th 1927

My dear Noël,

### *"THE SECOND MAN"*

I had a long talk with MacLeod today, about the general arrangements for the above play. I think they feel that it would be a good thing for the four players who are to take part in it to be featured equally {Raymond Massey, Ursula Jeans, and Zena Dare} and I must say I agree with them in this point of view. I think they will be writing to you in the course of a few days putting their views, and asking you to agree to this. Meanwhile, I am writing this private letter to suggest to you that it would be a wise gesture and would probably bear fruit. I am going to suppress my own name a good deal in this connection because just at the moment the public don't seem to be particularly fond of the Coward-Dean combination! But I regard this merely as a piece of diplomacy, and you must not take it as in any way a reflection upon your ability to carry the play over to success, and I am quite sure that you will do so. But I hope you don't mind my writing to you as a friend and making this suggestion.

>Kindest regards,
>Yours sincerely,
>BD

The play ran for 109 performances at the Playhouse Theatre—with costumes by Gladys Calthrop, who had returned earlier in the year from her Le Gallienne episode.

Before the critics could weigh in, Dean wrote:

>7 Hill Street
>Knightsbridge
>London S.W.
>Wednesday

My dear Noël,

Before I see any of the papers do let me tell you what an impression your performance made upon me. It was one of supreme distinction, and in the true line of descent from the best sources of English comedy acting, lightened by what was almost a French sense of style. Good luck to you! I hope you won't overdo things, and begin working on your nerves again. I know how fatal that is . . . am off tomorrow for a week by the sea to work, and see whether I can't pick a roasted chestnut out of the fire for myself.

>Yours ever,
>BASIL

Another letter that meant a lot to Noël was from John Gielgud.

I can't tell you how much pleasure you gave me last night, not how much I enjoyed the play but I did think your performance quite superb, and such as no-one else could possibly have equalled, in America or anywhere else. The two moments of sincerity make the most wonderful "setoff" to the rest of the characters, and that scene with the pistol in the last act is simply brilliantly done. How envious you made me of your ease and unselfconsciousness, and the way you make use of any mannerisms you have in such a way as to illuminate your character without losing it for a moment—and you manage, too, to talk at a tremendous rate without losing any words or any appearance of spontaneity, which to me would be the hardest of all.

This letter is great nonsense, but I am so glad of your tremendous success—heaven knows you deserve it. Don't bother to answer, I'll come in and see you some time if I may.

With *The Second Man* Noël certainly managed to pull his own personal chestnut out of the critical fire, and now he could move on to his revue for Cochran, *This Year of Grace.* The revue was aptly named, because 1928 was to become just that for Noël.

The Coward-Dean partnership was over. The next time their professional paths *almost* crossed would be during the war, when Dean was in charge of providing entertainment for the fighting forces.

# PART TWO

# THE YEARS OF GRACE

PART TWO

THE YEARS OF GRACE

# CHAPTER 7

# *THIS YEAR OF GRACE!*

## (1928–1929)

Were we happy in the Twenties? On the whole I think most of us were . . . I wouldn't have missed it, not—as they say—for a King's Ransom.

**LETTER TO BEVERLEY NICHOLS (1957)**

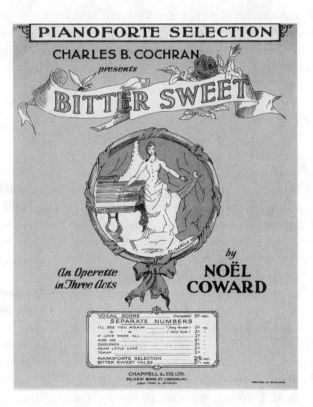

T HE YEAR 1928 proved to be the way back. Not only was Noël commended for his performance in *The Second Man* but the new Cochran revue, *This Year of Grace!*, was bubbling nicely. After a successful Manchester tryout, it opened at the London Pavilion on March 22. Starring Jessie Matthews, Sonnie Hale, and Maisie Gay, it ran for 316 performances.

The critic for *The Observer,* St John Ervine, created an alphabet of superlatives in his review: "The most amusing, the most brilliant, the cleverest . . ." and so on, until he got to "the most uberous, the most versatile, the wittiest—blow, 'x' has stopped me . . . if any person comes to me and says that there has ever, anywhere in the world, been a better revue than this, I shall probably tweak his nose."

A grateful Noël wrote to thank him: "I can't tell you how very much I appreciated your letter and I'm awfully glad to have proved to you that my real ambition is to write good stuff and not fritter away my talents on flippant nonsense . . ." And in another letter to Ervine came a rare admission:

When I read a novel like your *The Wayward Man* it makes me despair of ever writing myself because my imagination doesn't feel strong enough to reach things which have not actually happened to me— and constant repetitions of Parisian coquettes having cocktails at the Ritz bar are apt to become a bore.

Cochran wrote to Noël:

27th March 1928

My dear Noel,

Since I received your wire on the first night, for which thanks, I have told you all that I feel about your big part in the success of the revue. You have given me such brilliant material that the rest was fairly easy, but beyond that, we are all grateful for your help in production. From the moment you read me some of the book, and played the tunes, I had no doubt as to the success of the show.

I ask you to promise me one thing, and that is not to undertake a revue or any part of a revue for any other Manager. One revue a year at the London Pavilion is all you should do; also, let me remind you that you owe me a play with music and a play without music. Don't undertake to write them by Thursday next, but let me have them when the spirit moves you.

Never have I worked with an author with such pleasure as with you on *This Year of Grace!* The same goes for the lyricist and the composer.

> Yours as ever,
> CHARLES B. COCHRAN

The revue also enlisted for Noël one unlikely new fan: Virginia Woolf.

The chronology of their correspondence at the end of that year of grace is more than a little confusing, but the tone of mutual admiration is clear enough.

Noël had been introduced to Woolf in January, at a party given by society hostess Lady Sybil Colefax (1874–1950), and there appears to have been an immediate rapport. On the publication of her controversial fictional "biography" *Orlando* (1928), in which the leading character changes sex, Noël wrote her what can only be described as a fan letter—from New York, where he was then starring in the Broadway production of his show:

> I am still hot and glowing with it . . . At the risk of sounding insincere, I am completely at your feet over it. Oh, I do so congratulate you and thank you for the lovely "unbuttoned" feeling you've given me and I hope to God it will last . . . If ever I could write one page to equal in beauty your "Frozen Thames" description . . . I should feel that I really was a writer. Please when I come back to England let's meet and talk a good deal.

> November 22nd. [1928]
> 52 Tavistock Square
> W.C.1.

Dear Noel Coward,
I was enchanted to get your letter—though I had to keep it for Sybil Colefax to decipher the signature. When sure that it was yours, my heart leapt that you should have liked that innocent story and I feel—not like a dog—like a cat that is purring all over with pleasure at your praise and generosity.

> Yours,
> Virginia Woolf

> November 28th

Dear Noel Coward (but I hope you will drop Woolf—stick to Virginia)

How very charming of you to write to me! I liked your letter so much that I put off answering it. I didn't want to scribble a line. But I will now plunge, and say that it gave me immense pleasure. I can't conceive somehow why you—being such a success and all the rest of it—would like what I write. But if you do, I am, I repeat, immensely pleased.

Your secretary has sent me two books of yours, much to my delight. Now I am going into the matter of Noel Coward and his plays very seriously. I didn't like to tell you at Sybil's how some of the things in *This Year of Grace* struck me on the forehead like a bullet. And what's more, I remember them and see them enveloped in atmosphere—works of art in short . . .

I think you ought to bring off something that will put these cautious creeping novels that one has to read silently in an arm chair deep, deep in the shade.

But I must stop. I'm interrupting thousands of people who are battering at your door. But do please come to Bloomsbury when you've come back and let us discuss everything in the world shabbily over the gas-fire.

I've not a word against Argyll House [Sybil Colefax's current salon]—*but*—

> Yours ever
> VIRGINIA WOOLF

And thanks again for your letter

Their literary admiration/flirtation continued for several years. On the publication of *Flush,* in 1933, Noël wrote: "This is just to tell you how very much I enjoyed *Flush.* It is quite exquisite and the most marvelous picture of an age. I do, with all my heart, congratulate you on a very difficult job most tenderly and beautifully done."

But by now Woolf was tiring of what she saw as Noël's excessive flattery and critical of his apparent need to be a celebrity. Certainly their correspondence illustrates Noël's ambition—which was only to grow with the passing years—to be accepted by his peers as a "serious" writer. For Woolf's part, she had apparently given up on a vague ambition to draw him into the Bloomsbury net and thus—as she confides to her diary— "save him from being as clever as a bag of ferrets & trivial as a perch of canaries."

By the mid-1930s the verbal romance was over.

•

BACK TO 1928 . . .

During the year, Noël transported the rest of the Coward family— Arthur, Aunt Vida, and Erik—to join a discomfited Violet in Goldenhurst. The house at 111 Ebury Street was then sold, though Noël

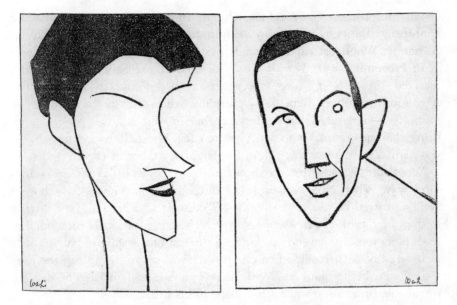

Beatrice Lillie and Noël Coward, who are the most conspicuous figures in the spotlight of "This Year of Grace," which arrives Wednesday at the Selwyn after a rapturous reception in London.

continued to rent his own suite until he bought 17 Gerald Road a couple of years later. As a mark of his increased success, he had by now descended from his cramped nest in the garrett to a lower floor and would joke, "As I moved up in the world, I moved down in the world."

The summer brought another breakthrough. Noël and Gladys Calthrop had been staying for a weekend in Surrey with a couple of friends. Just before they were leaving to return to London the lady of the house happened to put on the gramophone some new records she'd acquired of *Die Fledermaus.*

As Noël drove home the sounds of Old Vienna continued to echo in his head and he made up his mind there and then to write a romantic operetta. Parking the car under a tree on Wimbledon Common, he and Gladys worked out the complete plot and look of what became *Bitter Sweet.*

But that would have to wait its turn. His first priority was to reconquer Broadway with *This Year of Grace!*, in which he would appear himself with Beatrice Lillie. In July he and Cochran sailed for New York on the SS *Mauretania* to cast the show.

Much of the rest of the year was spent in New York. It was the most extended period he had so far spent there, and there was ample opportunity to see the many friends he had now made: the Lunts, of course; Gertie, a major Broadway fixture after *Oh, Kay!* (1926) and now appearing in the

Gershwins' *Treasure Girl;* and the Algonquin Round Tablers, who, having appropriated lunch, were now adding mandatory Sunday breakfast at Alexander Woollcott's apartment. It was a hectic place and a hectic pace.

In November *This Year of Grace!* opened at the Selwyn Theatre and received the same rapturous reception it had found in London. The Algonquin's Robert Benchley—part-time theater critic and full-time humorist—concluded that "unless someone in America is able to do something that approximates to Mr. Coward's feat we shall always feel that it was a mistake to break away from England back there in 1776."

Woollcott also admired the show but had to be his usual perverse self in some way. When Noël was singing "A Room with a View"—which even Noël admitted he did rather badly—Woollcott and Harpo Marx, sitting in their box, took out newspapers, which they ostentatiously pretended to read. Noël took his revenge by singing the rest of the song in baby talk.

Invariably with Noël, when one project was up and running, the next several were being planned. While he was playing in *This Year of Grace!* on Broadway, *Bitter Sweet* was taking shape in his mind.

The creative process was something he could never explain. The big waltz number he felt the show must have eluded him until one day, sitting in a New York taxi during rush hour, the melody of "I'll See You Again" dropped into his head ready formed. "How can a theme come to me complete like that? How can it be accounted for? Where does it come from?"

Something else came to him—the realization that the score that was emerging was far beyond the vocal range of Gertie, for whom he had set out to write it. Evelyn Laye would have been ideal but she firmly turned her back on the Coward-Cochran team when her husband, Sonnie Hale—having sung "A Room with a View" in the London production with Jessie Matthews—divorced her and ran off with Miss Matthews. Laye felt that by having written and staged the number, Noël and Cochran were to blame.

Then, by another accident, Noël literally ran into Peggy Wood in the lobby of the Algonquin. He cabled Cochran suggesting her for the part. Cochran cabled back:

> NOT SEEN PEGGY SINCE BUDDIES STOP AM TOLD SHE IS NOW
> HEAVY STOP ALSO AFRAID OF AN AMERICAN ACTRESS PLAYING
> SO ESSENTIALLY ENGLISH A PART IN LONDON.

Noël replied:

> SPENT DAY WITH WOOD STOP SHE SANG SCORE SUPERBLY STOP
> MAGNIFICENT VOICE STOP LOOKS LOVELY STOP FIGURE PERFECT
> STOP ACCENT NEGLIGIBLE STOP HAS PLAYED CANDIDA AND
> PORTIA WITH ALL ENGLISH CASTS AND ENORMOUS SUCCESS STOP

Vocal score of *Bitter Sweet* signed by the cast of the London (*left*) and Broadway (*right*) productions.

REALLY CONVINCED SHE WILL MAKE TREMENDOUS SUCCESS IN LONDON

He had his Sari.

Back in England in April of 1929 he went straight into production for a July opening. From the outset the omens were favorable. After the inevitable Manchester preview, Cochran wrote:

> 23 Montagu Street
> Portman Square W.1.
> Thursday July 18th 1927

Dear Noel,

Success, huge success is assured. Box office, American publication and all that sort of thing will be all that we hoped for.

I will actually make money at last.

But don't expect our friends of the press to do justice to your exquisite work of art. If I had the job to write a criticism I might find words to express all I feel about it. Most of them are bitten deep with prejudice and are so envious of your fine clear mind.

Ivor Novello (1893–1951) was the definitive matinee idol of his day and a friendly rival to Noël in musical theater. Noël once said of him, "The two most beautiful things in the world are Ivor's profile and my mind." (Caricature by Nerman.)

And . . . there's not one of them knows anything about music.

They all found Kern's score of *The Show Boat* commonplace and ONLY ONE NUMBER worth while.

I believe I could sit down now and give a pretty good idea of what each one will say.

Dear Noel, I am so proud . . . to have presented your very very beautiful work. I cry when I think of it.

> Yours very affectionately
> CHARLES B. COCHRAN

The quality of the show's success is perhaps best summed up in a letter from Ivor Novello, a peer without peer:

> Well, I should think it's probably Monday the what?
> Redroofs

Darling,

I've just come back from *Bitter Sweet* for the 2nd time . . . and I've got to tell you what a *lovely*, lovely thing you've done—Darling, it's sheer joy from beginning to end. The music impressed me unbelievably— it's so *gay* yet full of thought and has the most extraordinary way of reflecting the story as it goes along. The only disconcerting thing about it is that I cry the moment the first note starts and cannot stop. The whole thing is so full of regret—not only for that darling lover who died but for a vanished kindly silly darling age . . . you've created and I bless you for it and take off hat, drawers, nay *sock* suspenders to you for it.

I can play heaps of the music—my special bits are—

Bridesmaids & young men Act I

I'll See You Again (of course!)

Cleaners' chorus

Manon's Creed ("*If Love Were All*")

(Can't *bear* Little Café—very naughty in *this* show—in any other the best number!)

Bridesmaids' madrigal

Blind Man's Buff (sobbed over this)

Oh dear, I could go on for hours but I must return to my *charming* music for the Hulbert Revue [*The House That Jack Built*] over which the sick is *running* down my bib. [Jack Hulbert and his wife, Cicely Courtneidge, were a popular musical comedy team at the time and for many years to come.]

Whilst I think of it, darling, Fay [Compton] ought to play Sarah in America. She'd never quite mean what Peggy means (at least to me) but she'd sing her head off—it's her period—she's *thin* and is our best actress, let's face it—to say nothing of her *worship* of the play and her longing to play it. Do do this.

I took Bobbie [Andrews, Ivor's longtime lover] who has never loved anything so much and we have talked incessantly about it all— it's all so *clear cut* that one remembers the smallest detail. Your own mind is so unblurred and you've used it like a painter's series of brushes, all sizes, yet each stroke *definite*. This sounds nonsense but you'll know what I mean. Come back soon.

> All love
> IVOR

Max Beerbohm (1872–1956) did a series of drawings of *Bitter Sweet*'s principal characters, which he sent to Noël with his own comments:

Sentiment is out of fashion. Yet *Bitter Sweet,* which is nothing if not sentimental, has not been a dead failure. Thus we see that things that are out of fashion do not cease to exist. Sentiment goes on, unafrighted by the roarings of the young lions and lionesses of Bloomsbury. *Bitter Sweet* goes on, too; and Mr. Cochran (being a sentimentalist) has wishes that this survival should be commemorated by me in some sentimental drawings, which are here submitted to you.

That summer—with *Bitter Sweet* safely launched—Noël returned to New York to prepare the Broadway production. Not surprisingly, the

A change of Saris. Peggy Wood (*left*) hands over the *Bitter Sweet* role she played in London to Evelyn Laye (*center*), to play it on Broadway. Impresario C. B. Cochran ponders the change— but he was right both times.

show's success had produced an immediate change of heart in Evelyn Laye and she was now to be Sari after all. Before leaving England, Noël wrote to Violet:

> 111 Ebury Street
> S.W.1.
> Friday October 4th

Darlingest,

I'm scribbling this before retiring to a welcome bed, I rise at 7 o'clock to catch the boat train. Everything is going well but it's been rather wearing.

Cochran isn't coming to New York at all so I am in entire charge. Evelyn [Laye] is going to be marvellous and the whole company is good.

I leave San Francisco December 4th and will arrive in Colombo round about the first week in March [where he hoped to visit his brother, Erik].

Everything is very enjoyable. *Bitter Sweet* the greatest solid success Cochran has ever had and liable to run wonderfully. The Gramaphone [*sic*] company are sending out my records and Peggy's etc., the moment they're done.

I've been so happy to get your happy letters and excited cables—it is lovely to think you're enjoying yourself so much. I'll write regularly now but God knows when you'll get the letters. I'll cable from New York. Give my love and all to Erik.

> Always yours truly
> SNOOPIE

> Ritz-Carlton Hotel
> Madison Avenue & Forty Sixth St.
> New York
> Sunday October 13th

Darling,

This is the first moment I've had to write. The rush of arriving in this place gets worse each time I come. I've comfortably ensconced myself in a very expensive suite at the Ritz which the Management shall pay for and *like* paying for! We had a bad crossing on that filthy boat [SS *Mauretania*], very rough and several hurricanes but we weren't at all ill and enjoyed it!

All the company arrive tonight on the *Lancastria*. New York is as exciting as ever, I am going out today for lunch with the Ziegfelds in the country, we spend all the week rehearsing here and go to Boston next Sunday and open on the Tuesday.

Ina Claire and John Gilbert were on the boat and were awfully sweet and we all screamed the place down. Last night we went to see Jane Cowl in a lousy play [*Jenny*] in which she wasn't very good. Clifton and Mabel [Mabelle] send you their love. Clifton is a tremendous success in a Revue [*The Little Show*] and very pleased with himself and everyone else!

Poor Jeanne Eagels died last week just before I arrived, she dropped dead in her doctor's office, apparently heart trouble but most people seem to think the Doctor had given her an overdose of chloral or something—it's very sad and everyone is very upset about it.

> SNOOP

Give my love to young Erik and tell him I hope he's enjoyed all my long newsy letters!

Violet was now in Ceylon visiting Erik, who had taken up tea planting.

> Ritz-Carlton Hotel
> Arlington & Newbury Streets
> Boston, Massachusetts
> Wednesday October 23rd

Darling,

The show opened here last night and caused a riot, they stood up and cheered and screamed and that was that. We had an awful time.

Zigfeld [*sic*] and [Archie] Selwyn were so depressing and said everything was awful! Cockie isn't here and I'm in charge and I've had to fight every step of the way, they wanted me to alter everything and I wouldn't, now of course they're delighted and say they *knew* it was a success all along!

We've had to change our leading man (Carl) three times. Givither was no good, so we got Rosati back, when we got *him* onto the stage no-one could understand a *word or* hear a note, so I sacked him on Sunday night ["TENOR INCAPABLE OF SPEECH EVEN IN ITALIAN," Noël cabled Cochran] and we opened last night with Gerald Nodin playing it, the boy who sang "Tokay" in London and he's very good. Evelyn is marvellous and has set the Town on fire. But oh dear, it has been a business. I think it's a pretty sure success for New York, we're already sold out for twenty weeks.

We're all living here in state at the expense of the management and keep ordering very expensive food at odd hours! . . .

Give my love to Erik, and ask him kindly to make do with my letters to you because I have no time even to go to the lavatory in peace let alone write newsy letters!

All my love, darling, and take care of yourself and avoid all those nasty tropical what nots.

> Your battered but loving
> SNOOP

I think fighting agrees with me. Both Gladys and I are bursting with health and vigour.

The problem with Flo Ziegfeld that Noël refers to consisted of the impresario's trying to persuade Noël to "liven up" what he considered a rather low-key show by adding some totally superfluous Ziegfeld Girls. Noël refused point-blank and, to do him justice, Ziegfeld came to appreciate what he had. On opening night in New York he sent Noël a cable:

NOVEMBER 1ST 1929
NOEL COWARD
ZIEGFELD THEATRE

MY DEAR NOËL I WISH BITTER SWEET AS GREAT A SUCCESS AS
THE STORY YOU ARE WRITING FOR ME FOR MARILYN MILLER
STOP IN BITTER SWEET YOU HAVE DONE THE GREATEST WORK
ANY INDIVIDUAL HAS EVER DONE STOP BEST WISHES
AFFECTIONATELY STOP ZIEGFELD

On the following day:

NOVEMBER 6TH
NOEL COWARD
RITZ CARLTON HOTEL

THE THEATRE CANNOT DIE AS LONG AS IT HAS A GENIUS LIKE
YOU STOP I SINCERELY HOPE THAT YOU WILL BE ABLE TO THINK
OF A STORY SUITABLE FOR AMERICAS DANCING QUEEN MARILYN
MILLER AND THE ASTARIES [Astaires!] STOP AND YOU SHOULD
FEEL VERY HAPPY AND DELIGHTED THE PUBLIC AND CRITICS
APPRECIATED YOUR MARVELOUS EFFORT BITTER SWEET STOP
REGARDS STOP FLO

There is something of a mystery about the future show Ziegfeld repeatedly refers to and Noël's part in it. *Smiles* opened at the Ziegfeld a year later "based on a story by Noel Coward" in which three American doughboys in World War I come across a French waif and adopt her. They take her back to the United States, where she grows up to be an attractive young woman, who flirts in turn with high society, then the Salvation Army, and ends up marrying one of her benefactors.

*Smiles* starred Ziegfeld's favorite, Marilyn Miller (who had graced *Sally,* the first Broadway musical Noël had ever seen, back in 1921), Fred and Adele Astaire, Eddie Foy, Jr., and the young Bob Hope, with music by Vincent Youmans and at least one classic song, "Time on My Hands." It appeared to have all the credentials for a successful run. In fact, it lasted for just sixty-three performances.

As soon as *Bitter Sweet* opened, Noël wrote to Violet: "I've only got 283 telegrams to answer! Evelyn is weeing down her leg with excitement. She's been such a darling. I'm delighted with her success."

Laurette Taylor wrote:

The first night of *Bitter Sweet* . . . as you made your speech wreaths of laurels forming inscriptions like "Duty", "Perseverance", "Believe in your Star", etc., seemed to be hanging from either arm.

I was very proud I knew you and thankful you had that "exquisite" Evelyn Laye for "Sari". The woman you had written could not have been unless she had perfection of everything and that's a tall order.

Ritz-Carlton Hotel
Madison Avenue & Forty-sixth Street
New York
6th November

Well Darlingest,

The show opened last night and was a complete riot. It was probably
the most distinguished first night ever seen in New York, some seats
were sold for as much as $150 each! (Thirty pounds!) All the celebri-
ties were photographed coming in to the theatre and all the traffic
was specially controlled by the Police Department. Evelyn made the
most triumphant success I've ever seen when she made her entrance
in the *last* Act in the white dress they clapped and cheered for two
solid minutes and when I came on at the end they went raving mad.
How right you were about Evelyn she certainly does knock spots off
the wretched Peggy!

Tonight I took Cissie Sewell and Elsie April to see *Whoopee!* (They
deserved a treat having worked like dogs) and Eddie Cantor stepped
forward and said that he wanted to introduce the greatest Theatrical
Genius alive today and they popped a spotlight on me and I had to
stand up and bow to me great American Public! All this mind you in
the middle of somebody else's show!

I've just had a wire from Ziegfeld saying that the theatre will
never die as long as there is a Genius like me in it, which made me
laugh quietly considering how *convinced* of failure he was before we
opened in Boston. Anyhow, thank God I'm leaving on Sunday week
for Hollywood for five days, then Honolulu for four days then Japan
arriving December 20th Tokio where Jeffrey [Lord Amherst] is arriving on the same day. I got your nice long letter written just before
you arrived. I've never heard of such grandeur as *you've* been giving
out! Just the 14th Duchess of Ebony, that's what you are, my girl.
Thank you both for your cable. I wonder how Erik is getting on. I
hope I shall hear from you before I leave, if not I shall have to wait
until Tokio.

I must stop now, darling, and go to bed as I am exceedingly tired
but very relieved and happy. Give my love to Erik and a good hug to
yourself, if that's not possible get an Anaconda to do it in a *nice* way.

All love,
SNOOPIE

When the text of *Bitter Sweet* was published Noël dedicated it to Charles
Cochran: "My help in ages past, my hope for years to come." But there
were not to be too many more of them.

Santa Fe Railroad
New Mexico
20th November 10:30 p.m.

Hello Ma,

Here I am trundling across the continent. I left Chicago where Jack saw me off yesterday morning early and arrive in Hollywood tomorrow night. I've been in bed ever since I got on this train and intend to stay there, it's so lovely just relaxing after all the fuss and furor. I had a hectic time in New York everyone gave farewell parties for me and handed me expensive presents and I departed in a blaze of glory. In Chicago we saw Ethel Barrymore and Katherine [Katharine] Cornell and Mary Garden. They were all in our old friend The Lake Shore Drive and the lake was starting to freeze and it all looked exactly the same.

John Gilbert and Ina Claire are meeting me tomorrow, Charlie Chaplin is giving a large party for me, so is Ronald Coleman [*sic*] and Marion Davies. All the Movie Magnates are putting their cars at my disposal in the hopes that I'll work for them, which God forbid, but I shall use the cars and probably wee wee in them. I've caused more of a sensation in America this time than ever before, *Bittersweet* [even Noël never quite made up his mind whether this was one word or two] is the only show playing to capacity during this appalling Stock Market crash! It's really very enjoyable.

I got several letters from you including one after you had arrived, I must say it does sound lovely and I am exceedingly glad Erik isn't fat . . . When I arrive in January or February or March or whenever it is we'll discuss Erik's future which ought to be great fun taken all round. I'm bringing a movie camera with me (not a projector so we won't be able to see the films) but I shan't be happy until I have a movie of Erik on a horse. Jack says I shall *never* need a projector as none of my films ever come out—how true—but if God wills that they do, we'll show them in the barn. Good night, dears.

SNOOPIE

And so the 1920s came to a triumphant close for Noël.

When in 1957 his friend the writer Beverley Nichols was preparing a book on the twenties (*The Sweet and Twenties*) and asked Noël for his impressions of that unique decade, Noël answered him in a letter in which he also compared it to the 1950s—another decade immediately following a world war and attempting to adjust to it.

Gertrude Stein, one of the Oracles of the Twenties, once made the following pronouncement "Everything is the same and everything is

Beverley Nichols (1898–1983) and Noël. Two survivors of the
"diverting and highly exciting decade" known as the twenties.

different!" This utterance, like most of Miss Stein's, is remarkable for
a certain magnificent simplicity. However, my purpose is not to discuss Miss Stein but to consider the profundity and truth or otherwise
of her phrase as applied to the Twenties and Fifties.

I'm afraid she was right, they are awfully the same and they are
dreadfully different, so different that I might go so far as to say that
the Fifties are much much worse . . . First the similarities. The
Bright Young Things are just as determined to be bright as were
their fathers and mothers; parapets are still walked at midnight it
seems, and dinner-jacketed young men are still falling or being
pushed into swimming pools or the river to round off successful parties. The desperate endeavours of the League of Nations are perpetu-
ated by those of U.N.O. Cocktail parties, God help us, are still with
us. Most musical comedies still have to come from Broadway. The
latest dance from America—which shall be nameless because it will
have become outmoded and been replaced in the short interval before
these words get into print—is just as convulsive as the Black Bottom
and the Charleston. Skin-tight jeans are just as exaggerated as were
Oxford Bags [wide bell-bottomed trousers]. The same hectic determination to have a good time is presumably due to the fact that
younger people today are just as "Post-War" as their mothers and
fathers were and as resolved to catch up on their youth and any good
times they may have missed during the years of austerity. And I don't
blame them one bit.

I will pass lightly over the many differences for the worse—H. (or even X) Bombs, television, the general decline in standards and the crushing down of initiative, originality and ambition, the lack of incentive, etc., because your book is about the Twenties and not the Fifties and in any case one must never, never say that things were better when one was young. Of course a great many changes have been for the better; people are healthier, better paid and there is little unemployment, hardly any of those pathetic ex-servicemen's bands in the streets and no ex-officers trying to sell writing paper at one's door. Whether people are happier or not is another matter, but then happiness is well known to be elusive.

Were we happy in the Twenties? On the whole I think most of us were but we tried to hide it by appearing to be as *blasé,* world-weary and "jagged with sophistication" as we possibly could. Naturally we had a lot of fun in the process.

We all got over this period in our mental growth, or most of us did, and I can't feel we were any the worse for it. Should it be a matter for pride that we got over it without the help of psychiatry, considered so indispensable today, though not by me?

Taken all in all the Twenties was a diverting and highly exciting decade in which to live and I wouldn't have missed it, not—as they say—for a King's Ransom.

# CHAPTER 8
# "MAD DOGS AND ENGLISHMEN"
## (1930)

*In a jungle town*
*Where the sun beats down*
*To the rage of man and beast*
*The English garb*
*Of the English sahib*
*Merely gets a bit more creased.*

"MAD DOGS AND ENGLISHMEN," *WORDS AND MUSIC* (1932)

December 1929. Noël on the SS *Tenyo Maru* en route for
the Far East and a date with a dream about *Private Lives*.

AFTER A FEW DAYS in Hollywood Noël sailed for the Far East. The few days' stopover in Honolulu were fortunately less stressful than his previous visit, and then he was en route to Yokohama and Tokyo, where he was to meet Jeffrey Amherst, his traveling companion on this extended trip.

On the way, he concentrated on finding an idea for the play he had promised to write for Gertie and himself in compensation for *Bitter Sweet*, but nothing would come to him. When he arrived at Tokyo's Imperial Hotel he received word that Jeffrey had missed the connecting boat from Shanghai and would be three days late arriving.

That same night, Noël would write, "the moment I switched out the lights, Gertie appeared in a white Molyneux dress on a terrace in the South of France and refused to go again until four a.m., by which time *Private Lives,* title and all had constructed itself."

Jeffrey duly arrived, and the Eastern odyssey began in earnest.

> Tsinanfu
> China
> January 12th 1930

Darling,
I'm writing in the train on the way from Peking to Tsing Tao where we get the boat tomorrow morning for Shanghai. I had no idea you

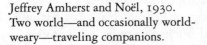

Jeffrey Amherst and Noël, 1930.
Two world—and occasionally world-
weary—traveling companions.

were sailing as early as the 1st as you said in your Japan letter you weren't leaving until February. I wired Erik from Peking to know how you were and he wired back that you were well and had sailed. I *do* hope you'll be all right and I shan't be really comfortable until I know you're safely at Goldenhurst . . . We had a nasty earthquake in Tokyo—very unpleasant . . . We really are having a lovely time. Japan was enjoyable but the Japanese are rather irritating, but still the scenery is beautiful and the Temples at Nikko and Kyoto simply glorious. We left from Shimonoseki and crossed the Japan Sea to Pusan in Korea, it was terrifically rough but we ate pickled onions and weren't sick, Jeffrey left the jar on the edge of the table and when we came in from having a breath of fresh air on deck, the entire table was carpetted with onions, very smelly but we rose above it.

From Pusan we went by train all through Korea to Mukden in Manchuria. It took two nights and a day. Korea is very lovely, snow clad mountains and bright sunshine and all the people in brilliant pinks and blues and greens, all except the married men who wear white robes and minute black top hats perched forward on their heads which look most peculiar. We arrived at Mukden at 6:00 in the morning with the temperature 35 below zero! . . . We've had a very regal time altogether because we met a Japanese Baron at the Embassy in Tokyo and he very kindly arranged for us to be met at every stop on our journey, consequently every time the train even paused, deputations of Japanese in silk hats and frock coats advanced with baskets of fruit and we all had to bow and exchange cards. Fortunately we have a lot with us because we've had to shower them like confetti, conversation was always rather difficult owing to a certain lack of Japanese idiom on our parts and no knowledge of English on theirs! But they all hiss a lot like snakes and show their teeth so everything went off very well. Mukden was too cold for comfort, and too near Siberia, so we got into a train for Peking and *what* a train! Absolutely filthy and no heating so we lay in a heap wrapped in fur coats and drank brandy for 26 hours which saved our lives. We're now heading for Shanghai after ten days of Peking which has left us quite exhausted. It's simply beautiful but we were far too popular. The first two days were too cold to bear, we nearly died until we had fur boots made which kept our feet warm in the rickshaws. The streets are fascinating and each one is called after what it sells. Jade Street, Flower Street, Crystal Street, etc.! Everything's dirt cheap owing to exchange, so we bought some things and crated them back to England to be held in Bond until we return . . .

There were two other big affairs which we graced with our presence, to say nothing of countless dinner and lunch parties. We were driven out to the Hills by Martel, the French Minister, to a lovely temple, we were carried up in swinging chairs and the view was superb, all over Peking with the coloured tiled roofs glinting in the sun. The Temple of Heaven is indescribably lovely. Pink walls and deep, deep blue roof standing in among sage-coloured winter trees; it's deserted now and was really one of the most perfect sights I've ever seen. When we left last night everyone came down to see us off and here we are bouncing across China in a slightly more comfortable train than the last one we tried . . .

Well goodbye now, my Sniglet, do take care of yourself and get well and strong by May.

Give my love and kisses to Veitch and Pop and the dear doddies. I doubt if I shall get to Ceylon until the end of February, but I've told Erik to expect me when he sees me.

         All love and hugs
         COLUMBUS

                       H.M.S. Suffolk
                       January 31st

Darling,

We're having the most lovely time sailing down to Hong Kong on a smart and shining Man of War! We met several of the officers in Shanghai and they invited us to stay over a few days and go with them instead of using the ordinary boat service, we naturally jumped at it and here we are. It was marvellous sailing down the river past all the other warships, all different nationalities, French, Italian, Japanese and American, all saluting and playing the National Anthems like mad. It's tremendously interesting to be on board a cruiser like this in full working order. We've seen everything from the Boiler Room to the Gun Turrets and the Captain very kindly allowed us to take photographs (movies) which is entirely against the rules. We spent the morning on the Bridge and I'm getting up at 4 a.m. tomorrow to watch some nice Night navigation going on.

We arrive in Hong Kong on Monday where we shall be met by fleets of Destroyers and Aeroplanes and a good deal of enjoyable fuss! We've been in Shanghai for two weeks, the first part of the time I had slight "Flu" and the last part of the time Jeffrey did, and in between while I wrote a new comedy for Gertrude Lawrence and me to do in the Autumn in London, so *no* time was wasted. It's good, I think, and anyhow gives us both marvellous acting opportunities.

Shanghai is an extraordinary place, very cold of course at this time of the year, although not as bad as Peking . . . Shanghai is such a very strange mixture and completely unlike it sounds. To start with it's on the river instead of the sea, it's tremendously modern and looks like a cross between Brussels and Huddersfield. Every nation is represented in it and the poor Chinese have to struggle with *so* many languages. We met some charming people and had a lovely time. The Chinese part of the Town was marvellous.

Last night when the Chinese New Year begins, all the shops open, fireworks going off and crowds and crowds of people all making the hell of a bloody noise if you will forgive a Biblical expression! But all highly enjoyable . . .

We say goodbye to cold weather from now on. Hong Kong, Hanoi, Saigon, Ankor, Bangkok, Singapore! We are being met at Hanoi by the Governor of Indo China and are motoring from there to Saigon, and on to Siam!

We really are having a glorious trip, everyone makes a lovely fuss of us and we get everything of the best everywhere.

We were guests of honour on the French warships yesterday and *how* we all carried on, we had to make speeches (in *exquisite* French) and Oh Dear, Oh Dear, they all sang old sea shanties and we all kissed and it was very very funny indeed!

I really must stop now as I'm being shouted for in the Ward room, it's tea time and the Navy is very particular about its tea! . . .

Ever your lovable and sweet<br>SNOOPIE

To Gladys Calthrop:

s.s. Tonkin<br>February 12th 1930

Well, old cock,

This is the first letter I've been able to write to you owing to not knowing any of your plans. Jack wired me that you were in Florida and I'm tortured with curiosity to know why and wherefore and with whom. I wonder if you ever got to Mexico? I was glad to get your cable in Honkers on Sunday saying you were fine and dandy. I'm not going into long newsy descriptions of my trip, it's all far too variegated but it really has been enthralling so far . . .

We stayed a fortnight in Shanghai and I wrote a light comedy for Gertie and me in the Autumn. It's completely trivial except for one or two slaps but it will be fun to play. I have an uneasy feeling that you won't approve of it, but I had a good think and decided that failing a really first rate emotional part for myself, I'd rather do a nice sparkling comedy with a few numbers in Act II. Both the parts are marvellous and the whole thing is very flippant and gay. And a couple of dainty sets for the old girl [Gladys] to fart about with.

It was certainly a good idea to come away like this. I feel gloriously remote and my mind is clearing up something lovely! I think there is a sporting chance of something really dandy hatching out before I'm through.

Jeff is a marvellous traveller and very funny and we pee ourselves a good deal. We met several very natty naval chaps in Shanghai and they invited us to sail with them on the H.M.S. *Suffolk* to Hong Kong. I've never in my life enjoyed anything so much. We took four days and did gunnery practice, and kept watch on the bridge all night, drinking lovely ship's cocoa and made ourselves very popular. We were shown over the ship from stem to stern as you might say, and Oh God, a really up to date warship in motion is beyond words exciting. Sitting in a gun turret alone is enough to wreck you! Talk about the poetry of Higher Mathematics, one small lever is touched and enormous guns come rushing up at you out of a pit, load themselves and fire themselves and retire down to their hole again as quick as buggery! It really was splitarsingly loverly. And all the ritual of saluting the sun, and playing "Last Post" and sailors having special roaring tunes played by the ship's band for every job they do! We gave a grand dinner to all the chaps the night before we left HK— they're all really terribly nice (no monkey business anywhere, all above board and very enjoyable). We felt thoroughly sad to say goodbye to them.

HK is I think the most beautiful place I've ever seen, specially at night with an enormous black mountain rearing itself out of the sea, covered with lights. And the most lovely harbour with thousands of ships of all sizes and sampans and junks farting 'ither and thither for all the world like tainy insects.

We're now on our way to Hanoi (capital of Indo-China). From there we are going to motor all the way through to Saigon and up to Ankor and finally Bangkok. Then down to Singapore and Java. I'm afraid India will have to be missed, there's too much to be seen up here. We're now bouncing along on a vile French ship, smaller than a channel boat, with a cargo of salt fish and Ford cars! We're the only white people on board except for one fat Frenchman and the two ship's officers, who are disagreeable sods anyway. Our cabin is filthy and filled with cockroaches and bed bugs and the food is really unbearable. Fortunately we stopped yesterday at a port called Quang Tchew Wan and buggered ashore in a sampan in a downpour of rain and bought a large supply of tinned food to last us until Saturday, when we arrive. The squalor of our cabin is lovely, what with our own lack of bathing and all the tinned food and the fish smell coming in at the window. Incidentally, it's very rough and I can't understand why we haven't been sick, but there's still time.

We met some enchanting people in Shanghai. Two twins of 22, both lovely looking with a Spanish mother. They all speak six languages each and have terrible rows in all of them! Very Sanger's Circus and highly enjoyable. Our trip alternates between complete Ambassadorial grandeur and utter squalor. We are arriving in Indo-China armed with flattering letters to the Governor, and I hope the fact that we are riddled with crabs and lice won't put him off!

We've had to talk a great deal of French here and there, which is very good for us, particularly in Shanghai where all the nicest people are French.

The other night we were nearly wrecked in HK harbour on our way to dine on the ship. Our motor sampan broke down and there we were tossing around in a howling storm, got up in our tails and diamonds, and finally reached the ship soaked. THAT was a special moment when I should have loved you to be there.

Probably Noël's most popular song. When he sang it Cole Porter swore it was the only song he'd ever heard sung in one breath.

And oh dear, all the Chinese tarts in cages! And riding along up hills in chairs! Bumping so much that your teeth rattle and your hat falls off! It's all very slapstick.

Well, old trout, I'll close now. Jeff sends love and kisses and we're wishing very, very dreadfully that you were here and oh dear, I haven't told you ANYTHING. I can't wait for our reunion in May. We've taken some really grand films and cut them and joined them ourselves. They're really pretty exciting and they will give you some idea of what we've seen.

> Goodnight, old stinks
> Love love love
> PERSEUS

Apart from *Private Lives*—which he wrote during the four days he was laid up with flu in Shanghai's Cathay Hotel—at least one other "really dandy" thing happened before Noël was through. On the long drive, he composed in his head the complex lyric for "Mad Dogs and Englishmen." When they reached the guest house that evening he sang it triumphantly to Jeffrey. "The gekko lizards and the tree frogs gave every vocal indication of enthusiasm."

To Violet:

> Phya Thai Palace
> Bangkok
> March 13th

Darlingest,

We're having almost the best time of our whole trip here. To start with it is the most beautiful city imaginable. The Temples and Pagodas and Palaces are vivid white with curly spires and minarets and sometimes towers made entirely of inlaid porcelain in the most lovely colours and designs. There is a Buddha in the Royal Pagoda made entirely of one emerald! It's about the size of a large football and it sits up very high on a gold throne! Perfectly glorious. Jeffrey happened to be at Eton with the King, so we had a private audience with him the second day we were there. He was very sweet and had read all my plays, if you please!

We conducted ourselves becomingly except that just before we went into the presence The Grand Vizier gave us glasses of soda water, we took them thinking probably it was some strange delicious Siamese nectar and had to restrain our hiccups and belches with great fortitude during the afternoon. We had to back out of the room when the Audience was over, and I saved myself in the nick of time from putting my bottom through a glass cabinet filled with china. I cast a hurried glance over my shoulder to see if I was going straight. Thank God, otherwise there would have been a slight social error!

We have been entertained lavishly by all the Siamese Grandees and we went to a special performance in the King's private Theatre, given in honour of some Danish Royalties. It was very lovely and the colours of the dresses quite indescribable. We've also been taken into all the secret shrines and temples where no Europeans are allowed, one in particular had a floor made entirely of silver!

Last night Prince Pidya gave a Siamese dinner for us. Oh Dear! We sat on the balcony under a full moon and ate and ate for hours with strange music wailing behind us. The food was very nasty and dreadfully spiced but we rose above it . . .

Your affectionate but regal<br>SNOOPIE

In Singapore, Jeffrey was struck down with his second bout of amoebic dysentery and confined to hospital. With time on his hands and *Private Lives* safely committed to paper, Noël was at something of a loose end. One evening he attended a performance of a touring English theatrical company quaintly called The Quaints. Hearing that they were about to do R. C. Sherriff's antiwar play, *Journey's End,* Noël allowed himself to be persuaded to play the hero, Stanhope. Also in the company was the young John Mills, who played Raleigh.

Even Noël admitted that he misjudged his performance and was overly emotional. On one occasion he misjudged something else, and Mills would remind him of this in a letter nearly forty years later:

9/9/67

Darling Noely,

. . . If you know anything about the theatre proper, you will be aware of two facts—that I discovered Noël Coward in Singapore, way back in 1930, and I am sure that he will agree, it is through that chance meeting—he insisted on playing Stanhope to my Raleigh—and, I thought, for a young man of his age, he gave a more than intelligent reading—in fact I saw flashes of pure magic—especially when, owing to a new piece of business which his fertile brain had invented, his tin hat fell with a nasty dull thud on my cobblers—and to be quite frank, they have never been *quite* the same since.

Playing Stanhope created a small diplomatic incident of its own. Dining with the British governor and his wife, Noël was attacked by Lady Clementi for appearing in a play that, she believed, criticized the behavior of British soldiers in time of war. This was a lady who also urged the banning of the works of W. Somerset Maugham on the grounds of immorality. When Noël and Jeffrey were safely out of her social clutches, Noël composed a verse about her:

> *Oh, Lady Clementi, you've read a lot of G. A. Henty*
> *You've not read Bertrand Russell and you've not read Dr. Freud,*
> *Which perhaps is the reason you look so unenjoyed.*
> *You're anti-sex in any form, or so I've heard it said,*
> *You're just the sort who would prefer a cup of tea instead*
> *You must have been a riot in the matrimonial bed*
> *Whoops—Lady Clementi!*

Noël couldn't resist sending the play program to Woollcott:

Alec dear,
I thought your elfin heart might be touched by this. "The Quaints" are just a band of pierrots who have developed during the last 25 years into a staunch dramatic company, unfortunately having to keep their original title owing to business reasons. I gave three performances of "Stanhope" with them and they were excellent and I was good in spots.

> All my love,
> The quaintest of the quaints.

•

KUALA LUMPUR . . . PENANG . . . where they sent a rhyming postcard to Woollcott:

> *Think kindly of your little friends*
> *And when their weary journey ends*
> *They'll come to you and clap their hands,*
> *A-brim with tales of foreign lands.*
> *So cheer high in the treble cleff*
> *For Pretty Noël and Dainty Jeff.*

Colombo (where Noël saw Erik briefly) . . . and then on to Marseilles and home. With *Journey's End* still on his mind, he dashed off his own antiwar play on the boat, *Post-Mortem*. It, too, was overemotional and has still to be professionally staged.

He did, however, show it to one or two close friends whose opinion he valued. One of them was George (later Lord) Lloyd, who wrote:

30 Portman Square, W.1.
22nd June, 1931

My dear Noël,

I have been spending three sun-baked days in the South of France
and come unwillingly back to work. I must apologise to you for my
candour over the telephone but having once seen you take a bad curtain call and witnessed your contempt for lay criticism, I felt no fear
that the blunt shafts of my brutality could do more than glance
harmlessly off your professional armour. You have said one or two
very true things. You have discerned why most men hanker after
war—for the sake of its utter freedom—you remember what
William James wrote—"The plain truth is that people want war.
They want it anyhow, for itself, and apart from each and every possible consequence. It is the final bouquet of life's fireworks." You say
some of that on page 71 and again on 76 but you say a lot of foolish
things which you don't believe and you say them in order to shock, to
*épater* and, may be, to sell. What I want to see you do is to get away
from the dull orthodoxy of today's atheism, and to free yourself from
cheap bourgeois blasphemy and to put the real case as brilliantly as
you know how to do—the Calvary that people daren't climb today
for fear of being thought stupid—the religion they daren't write lest
they be thought to rant—the love of country you daren't preach lest,

Hong Kong, 1968. Noël finally gets to fire off that "noonday gun"
he immortalized in "Mad Dogs and Englishmen." ("To reprimand
each inmate / Who's in late.")

forsooth, Bernard Shaw or Hannen Swaffer—the people you writers are so afraid of—should class you as patriotic.

Some day I believe you will dare do all these things, and then you will do them so finely that you will convert even a Celt to see the soul in a Saxon!

Yours ever
GEORGE L.

P.S. I have tried to be as unkind as I could be, but have not, I fear, been very successful. May I try again at supper?

By May he was back in England to prepare *Private Lives* for production that fall. Whatever vicissitudes he'd met and conquered on the Road to Mandalay would provide ideal toughening for his next great challenge—working with Miss Gertrude Lawrence.

# GERTRUDE LAWRENCE

### "A STAR DANCED"

A star danced . . . and under it you were born.

**THE MESSAGE DELIVERED BY A FORTUNE-TELLING MACHINE
IN BRIGHTON TO THE YOUNG GERTRUDE LAWRENCE**

T HE THREE MOST IMPORTANT women in Noël's life were undoubtedly his mother, Violet (who gave him his drive), Esmé Wynne (who inspired him to write), and Gertrude Lawrence (who was often his Muse and always his perfect complement as an actor).

Noël and Gertie first met in 1913 on the train to Liverpool. With ten other children, they had been hired by director/producer Basil Dean to appear for a three-week run of Hauptmann's *Hannele.*

She was, Noël recalled, "a vivacious child with ringlets . . . her face was far from pretty, but tremendously alive . . . She confided to me that her name was Gertrude Lawrence, but that I was to call her Gert because everyone else did . . . I loved her from then onwards."

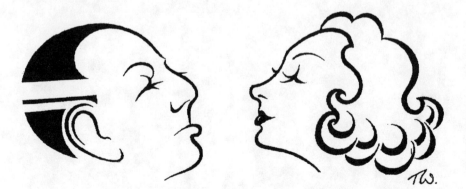

Caricatures by Tony Walton.

1924. Gertrude Lawrence and Bea Lillie starring in André Charlot's new revue.

It would be ten years before they performed together again—in his 1923 revue for producer André Charlot, *London Calling!*—and then only briefly. She introduced the song "Parisian Pierrot," which Cecil Beaton considered "the signature tune of the . . . 1920s." The show seemed set for a long run when, to Noël's horror, Charlot decided to put together a compilation of highlights from several of his previous revues and take it to Broadway as *André Charlot's Revue of 1924*. The stars were to be Jack Buchanan, Beatrice Lillie (whom Gertie had several times understudied), and Gertrude Lawrence.

Dissolve to 1929 . . . Both of them are well-established now in their own right. Leaving revue behind her, Gertie opens in a straight play, *Candle Light*. Noël sends her one of what would be a string of teasing cables:

LEGITIMATE AT LAST WON'T MOTHER BE PLEASED?

Then, that same year, on a tour of the Far East, Noël found himself waiting in the Imperial Hotel, Tokyo, for his friend and traveling companion, Jeffrey Amherst. On the night before Jeffrey was due to arrive, Noël went to bed early, but as soon as he had turned off the light, the idea for *Private Lives* came to him. By the turn of the year he was in Shanghai and,

"Sometimes I would look across the stage at Gertie and she would take my breath away." The definitive portrait of Gertie and Noël that had pride of place on his piano at Chalet Coward.

when a bout of fever confined him to bed at the Cathay Hotel, he used the time to actually *write* the play.

That turned out to be the easy part. The hard part was pinning down Gertie's butterfly mind. Noël cabled her immediately he put his pen down:

> HAVE WRITTEN DELIGHTFUL NEW COMEDY STOP GOOD PART
> FOR YOU STOP WONDERFUL ONE FOR ME STOP KEEP YOURSELF
> FREE FOR AUTUMN PRODUCTION.

He then sent her a copy and she replied:

> HAVE READ NEW PLAY STOP NOTHING WRONG THAT CAN'T BE
> FIXED STOP GERTIE

> THE ONLY THING THAT WILL NEED TO BE FIXED IS YOUR
> PERFORMANCE STOP NOËL

There then followed an avalanche of cables in which confusion soon became worse confounded. She'd committed herself to André Charlot for a new revue. Could they open in the following January instead of this September? Why didn't Noël appear in the revue with her to fill in the time? Why didn't Noël cable and ask Charlot to release her from the contract? Well, actually it wasn't so much of a *contract* as a moral obligation . . . Come to think of it, it probably *was* a contract of a sort and her lawyers were trying to get her out of it . . . She'd rather do *Private Lives* than anything . . . No, she couldn't do it at all . . .

Noël had finally had enough. When—forty pounds' worth of telegrams later—she finally remembered to give him her cable address, he wired her that he now planned to do the play with someone else anyway. He heard nothing more until he arrived back in England in May, by which time Gertie's lawyer, the redoubtable Fanny Holtzmann, had pried her free of the Charlot contract.

> La Capponcina
> Cap d'Ail
> Alpes Maritimes
> Thursday or Friday?

Darling!
Am I wrong or did I hear you mention something about a play we were going to do in London first then in America after?

Please let me know, because at present me 'ouse is full as a pig—and I would like to do something about putting up with you—sorry—I mean—well, you know—should you wish to visit me here to discuss ways and means.
> Love Gert

Dear Miss Lawrence,
With regard to your illiterate scrawl of 14th inst., Mr. Coward asks me to say that there was talk of you playing a small part in a play of his on condition that you tour and find your own clothes (same to be of reasonable quality) and understudy Jessie Matthews whom you have always imitated. [In fact, it was Matthews who had understudied and carbon-copied Gertie in the New York production of the 1924 *Charlot Revue*.] Mr. Coward will be visiting some rather important people in the South of France in mid-July and he will appear at Cap d'Ail [the location of Edward Molyneux's house, which Gertie was renting], whether you like it or not, with Mr. Wilson, on the 20th. If by chance there is no room in the rather squalid lodgings you have taken, would you be so kind as to engage several suites for Mr. W [Jack Wilson] and Mr. C [Noël] at the Hotel Mont Fleury, which will enable same Mr. W and Mr. C. to have every conceivable meal

with you and use all your toilets for their own advantage. Several complicated contracts are being sent to you by Mr. C. on the terms you agreed upon—i.e., £6.10s. a week and understudy.

With *Private Lives,* "Noël and Gertie" were to become a single entity in the public mind, creating an impression that—like the Lunts—they invariably acted together. In point of fact, they co-starred in only three original productions, of which *Private Lives* was the second and the one that defined the partnership.

Elyot Chase and Amanda Prynne are a divorced couple who meet up at the same hotel in Deauville while each is on honeymoon with a second spouse, only to discover that they are fated to be together, no matter the emotional cost to themselves or the people around them. The fictional relationship in many respects mirrored the real-life relationship between Noel and Gertie, two people deeply fond of each other but constantly bickering and testing the limits of that friendship in the certain knowledge that it is unbreakable.

Noël was both challenged and frustrated by Gertie's mercurial nature, quite opposite but somehow complementary to his own more ordered approach.

"On stage," he wrote a few years later, "she is potentially capable of anything and everything. She can be gay, sad, witty, tragic, funny and touching . . . She has, in abundance, every theatrical essential but one; critical faculty . . . But for this tantalizing lack of discrimination she could, I believe, be the greatest actress alive in the theatre today."

•

ON OCTOBER 13, 1931, *Cavalcade* opened at the Theatre Royal, Drury Lane, and Gertie was in the first-night audience.

Theatre Royal
Haymarket
S.W.1.

Noël, my darling,
Here I am down on my knees to you in humble admiration and complete adoration.

I didn't wire you last night because I felt too *near* you to mix my stupid pence worth of good wishes with those many who couldn't have been feeling as deeply as I was; but please believe me when I tell you that I spent the whole evening from eight 'til eleven with my hand tightly clasped in yours—*anything* just to feel that I might perhaps be of some subconscious support to you. As you say it's "pretty exciting to be English". But also it's pretty exciting to love you as I do!

It's horrid how I miss you but deep down it's rather grand; though not awfully satisfying!!

This you may be surprised to see is from
            "Ole Gert"

Dear old Gert,

Among all the outpourings from the great and the good and the Would-Be-Goods (as my beloved E. Nesbit might put it) nothing pleased me more than your barely decipherable scrawl!

You know me well enough to know that when I stammered about it being pretty exciting to be English, I meant every naïve word. We're a strange race and we persist in getting a lot of things wrong but we do have our hearts in the right place—and that's what matters.

When I looked down at the stage—and when I'd got over worrying about what *else* might go wrong with the mechanics—a great many things went through my mind and you were in so many of them.

I could see you on that stage at the Phoenix standing there in that damned deceptive moonlight night after night and I would make my entrance, never knowing which Gertie I would find on any particular evening. You do know, my darling, that you are a chameleon—an elegant one but still a chameleon. You never play a part the same way two nights running but it certainly keeps whoever you're playing with—in this case your author—on his tippy tip toes. And I must also admit—it's pretty exciting to be playing opposite Miss Gertrud Dagmar Lawrence-Klasen and I can't wait until the next time. And I can just hear you saying—"Well, darling, that's up to you."

I also found myself thinking back to that *first* time we played together. Do you remember Liverpool, Manchester and that tedious German play Basil was so keen on? And when we two budding thespians stuffed ourselves with peppermints and the curtain rose on the sight of two little angels being spectacularly sick! I do believe, my darling, we can do better than that and I shall endeavour to see that we do without too much further ado—and no error.

God bless you and keep you, Mother Macree!

•

REFLECTING ON HER in the mid-1930s—just before *Tonight at 8:30*—Noël mused on her complexity:

I see her now, ages away from her ringlets and black velvet military cap, sometimes a simple, wide-eyed child, sometimes a glamorous *femme du monde,* at some moments a rather boisterous "good sort", at others a weary, disillusioned woman battered by life but gallant to the last. There are many other grades also between these extremes. She appropriated beauty to herself quite early, along with all the tricks and mannerisms that go with it. In adolescence she was barely pretty. Now, without apparent effort, she gives the impression of sheer loveliness. Her grace in movement is exquisite, and her voice charming. To disentangle Gertie herself from this mutability is baffling, rather like delving for your grandmother's gold locket at the bottom of an overflowing jewel-case.

It's a little misleading to say that Noël and Gertie played together only three times. Their next joint venture, the 1936 *Tonight at 8:30,* was, in reality, nine one-act plays—ten, if one counts *Star Chamber,* which played only once at a matinée. In each they played pairs of entirely different characters, a theatrical *tour de force* that, significantly, has never since been emulated by another couple. Almost certainly a wise decision, since to do so would invite comparison with performances that have passed into legend and can now never be adequately assessed.

One of the plays was *Hands Across the Sea,* a thinly veiled parody of the superficial social life of the Mountbattens. It's impossible to know at this point in which direction Gertie erred in her portrayal of Lady Maureen "Piggie" Gilpin (Edwina Mountbatten), but it was sufficient to cause Noël in February 1936 to cable Jack—who was even then planning the subsequent American production:

Golden days at Goldenhurst. LEFT TO RIGHT: Bea Lillie, Bobbie Andrews, Gertie, and Noël.

EVERYTHING LOVELY STOP CRACKING ROW WITH GERTIE OVER
HANDS ACROSS THE SEA LASTING SEVEN MINUTES STOP HER
PERFORMANCE EXQUISITE EVER SINCE.

In March:

VERY SORRY FIND MY ENGAGEMENTS WILL NOT PERMIT ME
APPEAR UNDER YOUR BANNER IN AMERICA UNLESS I GET A
FURTHER 58 PERCENT OF THE GROSS FOR ARDUOUS TASK
RESTRAINING MISS LAWRENCE FROM BEING GROCK BEATRICE
LILLIE THEDA BARA MARY PICKFORD AND BERT LAHR ALL AT
ONCE.

The Mountbattens, incidentally, saw the play and never realized that
they were its subjects. As late as 1968 Mountbatten is writing to Noël:

> Broadlands
> Romsey
> Hampshire
> 15th October 1968

My dear Noël,
On going through my library I have just come across a copy
inscribed by you of your plays *Tonight at 8:30.*
Looking through them I suddenly remembered that you had told
Edwina and me that *Hands Across the Sea* was a skit on ourselves, and
on reading it this seems only too probable.
Can you confirm that it was written with malice aforethought, or
did it just turn into a Naval couple because you had so many Naval
friends? Did you play Commander Gilpin and did Gertie play Lady
Maureen, "Piggie"?

•

THERE IS EVIDENCE in his notebooks that Noël at least contemplated another play (*Tidewater*) for himself and Gertie both in the late
1930s and probably soon after *Tonight at 8:30,* since his tentative casting
notes include a number of the actors who had appeared with them in that.
It would also seem that he was contemplating a play-within-a-play or
"dream sequence" format, since all the principal characters double as historical characters of the Mary, Queen of Scots, period. Noël would have
played Cedric Massingham (and Bothwell), while Gertie was to have been
Loretta Gray (and Mary Stuart).

•

NOËL AND GERTIE were never to appear together again on the Broadway or West End stage. When *Tonight* was revived in 1947, Noël stood in for an indisposed Graham Payn for one matinée in San Francisco. That was their nostalgic coda. Graham's understudy "was a very very small Jewish gentleman who could neither act, dance, nor sing," so at the following day's matinée, "I popped on at an hour's notice and there was a great fuss and fume. I really did it for Gertie's sake. I couldn't let her act with that horror again."

Their careers proceeded in successful parallel.

Gertie spent most of her time in America, and on July 4, 1940, she married Richard Aldrich, a scion of one of America's many prestigious families and owner of the Cape Playhouse in Maine. The new "Mrs. A" would devote a good deal of her professional time to the playhouse in the years ahead.

On her wedding day a predictable Coward cable arrived:

> DEAR MRS A HOORAY HOORAY AT LAST YOU ARE DEFLOWERED STOP ON THIS AS ANY OTHER DAY I LOVE YOU STOP NOËL COWARD.

To which Gertie replied:

> DEAR MR. C YOU KNOW ME MY PARTS I OVERACT 'EM STOP AS FOR THE FLOWERS I'VE SEARCHED FOR HOURS STOP DOROTHY [her maid] MUST HAVE PACKED 'EM.

Soon after, producer Moss Hart was negotiating with Lawrence to play the lead in the *avant-garde* Kurt Weill–Ira Gershwin musical *Lady in the Dark.* Once again this lady dithered, and it was Noël who firmly steered her toward doing something he knew would reestablish her Broadway reputation. On the opening night he sent her another cable:

> HOPE YOU GET A WARM HAND ON YOUR OPENING.

The show was a critical and commercial success—though not with everyone. On October 25, 1941, Lynn Fontanne wrote to Noël:

> I also saw Gertie and I hate to seem such a sour puss, but because you know that I am really not, I shall confess that it was the longest and worst acted part that I have ever seen in my life. Alfred did not go with me but was waiting in the car when I came out. He asked me what it was like and all I could think of was, "But, Alfred, she *stinks.*" It's not one of my expressions, but I could think of nothing else. I was

really very amazed, as I had heard you tell about these performances which she throws from time to time and realized that I had never quite believed you. But I do, darling, oh how I do now. Apparently this is not a once in a while performance either, as I hear she is pretty much the same all the time. I wasn't very crazy about the whole show, to be exact. What is happening to me? Am I getting to be an old bitch? I do hope not. Her "Jenny" song was *wonderful* but after all, there's the whole show to be gone through!

Despite Lynn's forebodings, *Lady in the Dark* was successful enough to warrant a subsequent national tour, although wartime conditions were not likely to be what a star was accustomed to.

> American Theatre Wing
> War Service, Inc.
> September 14th 1942

Dearest old Dearest,

I am now packing away the Summer Poison Ivy Cures ready to embark upon quote an extensive tour unquote. The enclosed few modest press clippings will explain how restful the tour will seem after my holiday on Cape Cod . . .

Dearest, old Mossyface Hart seems pretty sure that our tour with the "Lady" will escape all difficulties and thus survive until June 1943—but there have been many warnings to road shows that there will be no heating and confiscations at a moment's notice of freight cars—so it seems to me that any preferences, if any, will go to the smaller companies and such big ones as ours (with *nine* baggage cars) may have to be abandoned. Anyway, whether or no, I am not signing up for *anything* to follow the "Lady" and you know of course why.

I have not been free to get back home since "Susan" [*Susan and God,* the 1937 play about which she joked, apropos Noël and Gertie, "I suppose everybody thinks *you're* playing God?"], and so the moment this is over, it's me for home. I want to know what are *your* plans. Or if you are coming here for a visit, let's do it here for a limited time and then go home together?? Oh, Angel, do let's.

I would like us to finance it ourselves 50-50 and be back again once more hand in hand at curtain calls. You know what would be really fun for a change? A really smart, chic, comedy mystery drama!!

You haven't ever written one, have you? Everybody loves a good mystery story and you could write a cert. Darling, please do it. It could start at the home of a rich woman who instructs and lends her home for a first aid class and the "victim" would be a really dead person, or something like that??

Do it, darling, let me be the victim, and let me show how much "repose" I have nowadays!!!

> All my love
> Gert

When Gertie's autobiography, *A Star Danced,* was published in 1945, Noël wrote:

> G. darling,
> I am overwhelmed. I never doubted your loyalty and your *friendship,* but to get such a proof of it, in so delightfully filial a manner, is more than my nerves can stand . . . I am afraid it is extremely difficult for me to tell you to what extent I have been touched by your views and comments on those (alas) bygone days and your efforts at making me happy have hit a bulls eye.
>
> > Lots of love
> > GUV

Gertie wrote, "I have not been home in almost seven years and am longing to get back for some war service . . ." She shared the dilemma that affected Lynn Fontanne and other British-born stars. Their lives and careers were in the United States, but a large part of their hearts were back in their homeland at war.

In the end, things were sorted out and mid-May 1944 found Gertie touring England before leading one of the first ENSA troupes to follow the Normandy landings.

A year later she has managed to write her autobiography, squeeze in a trip to Australia, and stop off in Hawaii on the way home to entertain the troops, who were lucky enough to see the Elvira in *Blithe Spirit* whom Noël had always had in mind but was never to see himself—or even *know* about until the production was history.

> August 3rd 1945

Dearest Nole,

I must explain my reasons for agreeing to do *Blythe Spirit* [*sic*] in the Hawaiian Islands. I had just come in from the most grueling trip "down under" and was tired and rather disheartened. I knew (from experience) that the men now wanted *plays.* They had had such companies as Charles Butterworth in *3's a Family*—Boris Karloff in *Arsenic* and Moss Hart in *The Man Who Came to Dinner.* They were *yelling* for *Private Lives* but the U.S.O. wouldn't pass it for troop consumption. *Skylark* was not good enough—*Susan & God* would never have passed the Chaplains on account of the title or the topic and I could hardly do a potted version of the *Lady* and *8:30* needed too many sets and versatile actors.

Yet the men wanted a play from me, and Maurice Evans had *Blythe Spirit* [*sic*] already in preparation with Milly Natwick on her way to play her original part. So John Hoysradt [Hoyt] and I decided to stay over for 4 weeks and we gave great joy to 30,000 men in that short time. I sent you the pictures, so you saw how I looked and it mattered not one bit to me whether the part had been played elsewhere by the Virgin Mary—it was a Coward play—I did a good job. I *know* I did. John was excellent, Milly, of course, was terrific and we had kept faith with the men in the services.

My plans are indefinite. I want to come home and am discussing the various ways and means with various people. It's just a case of whether to bring a new play or do the *Lady*—or come home and get a play and then take it to America afterwards. But my one aim is to re-identify myself with my own people, so if you have any ideas shoot them along to me.

Bless you, and please try to realize that I now know the labour pains of giving birth to a book and sympathize with you more than ever. One thing is certain, nobody can suggest . . . that the book was "ghosted"—it would have been a slicker job had it been; so it's my baby, and the second may bear a more marked resemblance!!

My love
GERT

Once home, she undertook a revival of *Pygmalion*.

March 28th 1946—New York

Darling,

Such a lovely surprise getting your letter—truly—my old "ticker stopped short, never to go again" when I saw that fine, reformatory handwriting!!

I am anxiously awaiting word from London about being given an assignment to write a weekly column from here; there is much of interest with G.I. Brides and the U.N.O., etc.

The play continues with standees at every performance and we shall carry on until June 15th, thus we shall (or is it "will"?) have broken all house records on tour and in N.Y. and the record for the length of the run of any production of *Pygmalion*. [They played 179 performances.]

Cedric [Hardwicke] has done a magnificent job on me, and I am convinced that you would be very proud of "Eliza Doolittle". The figures last week showed us with a total of 27,000 dollars, as against *Antigone* doing 12,000 including Cornell and Cedric!!

She continues to nag him about writing something for the two of them:

So you are writing a *book*—don't you think it would be more fun to write a jolly decent *play* for us both again? . . .

Cedric is returning to London in June to make a picture and so he would be there to direct *Pygmalion* and play "Doolittle" as well. Perhaps by that time you will have gotten an idea, and we could do the play in London first and then over here for a limited season as we did *Private Lives*. It's damn well time you came back, they need you in New York.

I had supper with Mossy last night—he is working on a new play which he will read to me when finished—but one nod from you and I would say, "I hear my master's voice".

Darling, did you hear the story of the man who took his trained bear to see the movie of *The Lost Weekend*? When asked "What's the idea?" by the theatre manager—the man explained—"Well, he *loved* the book"!!

Give my love to Mum and Lornie et al, and prepare yourself for a great big hug, soon.

GERT

Darling, do write again and tell me where you are sitting, writing, by what sea and what about.

She was constantly being given new plays for her consideration, but their past was ever present.

July 1, 1947

Dearest Noël,

Wherever I go (and we covered a lot of wherever with *Pygmalion* including Mexico City) all I hear is "Why don't you and Noël Coward get together again in a new play?" Or *Please* revive *Tonight At 8:30*!!! So many people who saw those plays want to see them again and it would seem that millions didn't see them feel furiously frustrated. Personally I do not cherish the thought of doing them again without you, any more than I would have done with *Private Lives*. BUT—it *was* revived in London most successfully without either of us, and Tallulah is going to bring it to Broadway this Autumn. So my sentiments seem rather misplaced. However, if *Private Lives* clicks over here, it will be my own fault, but it stands to reason that *someone* will get the bright idea of reviving *8:30* and we shall only have ourselves to blame.

I am reading and turning down play after play, each one has some merit or is just stupid. Also after *L.I.T.D.* [*Lady in the Dark*] and *Pygmalion* I am pretty hard to please.

Not knowing your plans or commitments, I wondered if we could have a little flutter together and revive *8:30* for a limited run here, or in London or both, as we did before? I want to come home, Noël, but if you want to do it here first and end up in London, it would be OK by me.

Please cable me "Yes" or "No", as I shall hold off everything else until I hear from you.

Much love<br>GERT

Noël was not happy at the thought of repeating himself in this way and made it clear. It was only when Fanny Holtzmann, Gertie's agent-cum-lawyer, pointed out that Gertie badly needed the money that such a tour would be likely to produce that he reluctantly agreed that six of the nine plays could be revived for an American provincial tour, with Graham Payn playing Noël's original roles.

The tour itself was modestly successful. Nonetheless, Noël's firm advice to all concerned was that under no circumstances should the production attempt a Broadway run. But, once again, the combined pleas of the ladies concerned managed to persuade him. His better judgment was sadly confirmed, and the show closed precipitately on Broadway.

The whole episode left him totally disenchanted with the Holtzmanns [Fanny and her brother]. They were "maddening throughout, screaming for hours down the telephone and never uttering a word of truth for two consecutive minutes," he wrote to Lornie. But even when it seemed to be over, it wasn't quite over.

To Lornie:

March 30th 1948

We were flung into a frenzy yesterday by a wire from Gertie saying could she come and stay for a week! Fortunately it was a funny telegram signed Hernia, so I am pretending that I don't know who it is from and am paying no attention at all. I am quite certain that the whole thing is a scheme of Fanny's. Fanny, my darling, is a lethal, boring, intriguing bitch and is determined that my life henceforward should be entirely devoted to writing plays for Gertie and directing her in everything. I have never yet written anything for Gertie that was not fraught with hideous complications. Please remind me not to write anything FOR anyone particularly ever ever again. This is all very well from Fanny's point of view on account of Gertie being her responsibility and she is anxious to pass the buck and make us all one great happy family with a firm Jewish organization in the background. I am, as you know, very fond of Gertie and she certainly behaved beautifully over all the *Eight-Thirty* business, but the thought of being alone in a house with her even for a week would drive me barmy. I take this opportunity of saying unequivocally and without any thought of compromise that I hate and loathe Fanny Holtzmann very very much indeed and, although I am perfectly willing to allow her to handle my American tax problems for the next year or so, THAT IS ALL AND THERE ISN'T ANY MORE. You can communicate this light resolve of mine to Dingo [Sir Dingwall Bateson, Noël's London lawyer] and tell him from me to be as tough as hell and leave me every loophole to escape from the clutches of that dreadful family. If it hadn't been for Little Lad [Graham Payn] and Gertie and everything I should never have got into their clutches in the first place. It doesn't really matter as long as they are kept in their place!!

The matter clearly stayed on his mind. He had now begun to refer to Fanny as "Rosie O'Grady," heroine of a Victorian music hall song, "Sweet Rosie O'Grady." The reference was certainly ironically intended, since Fanny was anything but sweet.

To Lornie (again):

May 4th

But, and here is the point, they will be very very powerful and dangerous enemies. I am now caught up with them to a certain extent and I don't really trust either of them and Rosie's gabbing and lying and intriguing bores and infuriates to such a degree that I would like to ram red hot nails up her flapping Irish nostrils and a large uncooked pineapple up her grotto. I can't bear her and she drives me dotty but, for as much as it is worth, I would rather have her for a friend than an enemy. She has immense power with all of her race and God knows they have power enough in the press and theatre to cause me a great deal of damage. I would love to shake off those clawing, pudgy fingers but I do not want personally to make a definite break unless there is a hard and fast reason for it . . . I am going to continue to be a dreamer and fluffy and silly as all hell.

Gertie needed to keep busy and she was also determined to reestablish herself at "home" in the United Kingdom. In late 1948 she opened in *September Tide,* a new play by novelist Daphne du Maurier. Noël, when he saw it that December, hated the play but felt that "Gertie really beyond all praise. I have never seen her play so beautifully or with such heart and truth. She moved me very much. I have quite decided that we must act together again in the autumn."

Finally, Noël *did* write a new play for her. It was originally called *Home and Colonial*—a soufflé of a comedy set on his mythical South Sea island British colony of Samolo. In his *Diary* (April 6, 1949) Noël described it: "Theme—Lady 'Sandra' Magnus (Diana Cooper–Edwina Mountbatten), Government House, Samolo, scandal with local Bustamente [local native politician]. There is more to it than that, but it's a heaven-sent opportunity to get in a lot of Jamaican stuff."

By early May he told Binkie Beaumont and Gertie he'd finished it, only to receive telegrams from both. They were enthusiastic about it but, owing to Gertie's tax situation, she couldn't open in it until the following April—and then she'd want to open in New York rather than London.

"This is disaster," Noël wrote. "It is typically English and topical and now is the time for it. Gertie might get away with it in America but half the point would be lost."

Later he decided to meet her halfway. They could put the play on in America—but not in New York (after the experience of *Tonight at 8:30*)—in, say, December, then bring it to London the following spring of 1950.

> 17 Fountain House
> Park Street
> W.1.
> June 27th, 1949

Dear Noël,

Rumour hath it, that should I not do your play, you are considering Ethel Merman and Nanette Fabrey [*sic*]!!! It conjured up a pretty picture, but I can only presume that these two ladies are vieing with each other for your favour in regard to your new musical.

> My dearest love,
> GERT

The idea of the play remained in her mind, but other projects took precedence. In the fall she was to make one of her rare film appearances, in Tennessee Williams's *The Glass Menagerie*.

> Cape Playhouse
> Dennis on Cape Cod
> Massachusetts
> September 14th 1949

Hullo dearest,

Well, I am now warding off the day when it will be necessary to leave for the Coast. I have written Binkie about most of the doings and goings on which led to this *impasse* but hesitated to worry you when you were still busy on *Astonished Heart* [the film of one of the plays from *Tonight at 8:30,* in which Noël was starring] or whether I would even sign the Hollywood contract. But after the phone calls, flying visits to me up here, and such enthusiasm as has been expressed, *plus* the "dough" [she received thirty thousand dollars] and the story, which Tenn. has outlined to me since seeing my test—I thought it a good chance to put my shoulder to the wheel and try for an Oscar! Warners are apparently going to make it their "prestige" picture of the year and going after the Academy Award, and even Jane Wyman has taken quite a cut in salary in order to play the lame daughter.

The plan is to make the picture in retrospect showing Amanda's memories of the sort of life she lived down south before she married a good for nothing dreamer and they are talking of making those shots in very faint colour in contrast to her present day drabness.

For the test I was rushed to New York on the Saturday night, alone in a long black and luxurious car—sent by Jack Warner—feeling rather like Mrs. Simpson! I arrived at 7 a.m. (slacks and dark glasses, of course, thought I might as well act like a screen star for a day!) I was ushered into the largest and most expensive suite . . . where I gulped down a cup of coffee, took a shower and was then whisked off to the studio on 57th St. Irving Rappa [Rapper] was there, there were flowers from Warner and [producer] Jerry Wald and Charlie Feldman in my dressing room—and even the camera man had been flown in from the Coast.

I did the "dress up" scene in costume and sashayed around the ballroom for Laura. I did the scene where she makes the dress for Laura and pads her chest out for the "gentleman caller" and I did the scene where Amanda returns after finding out that Laura has not been going to her shorthand and typing lessons. They had a girl for me to act with and, believe me, it was quite a day, ending at 7 p.m.!!!

Rappa said I did as much work without rehearsal as we would normally do in Hollywood in 2 or 3 weeks.

Strangely enough, I couldn't have felt more tired, or less interested in doing the test or in its result—but such is the way of things that everything turned out to cause a mild sensation. Sooo—the contract is signed and I am expected to be out there by about the 9th or earlier for costumes, wigs, etc., as they are sending a "double" to St. Louis on long shots for location work and we go out there later for close work.

I am now getting a little more excited than I pretend, as it was no small potatoes to beat Bette Davis and Tallulah's tests!! I think they had rather wanted Helen Hayes, too, but I don't think Helen wanted another dose of Hollywood.

After the picture is over some time in late December, Richard and I would like to go away for a few weeks *alone* . . . and from then on—well, you and Binkie can consult and we can decide. Actually, I would prefer to do *H&C* [*Home and Colonial*] around August in England, so that I could spend the summer up here . . .

But don't get windy, darling, let's see if I make a good picture or whether I retire from public life in shame!!

Ow are yer, me old cock? Give my love to *EVERYBODY*—but keep a chunk for yourself first. I have only signed with Warners for this one picture . . . but have signed with Charlie Feldman for all future stories, which does not commit me to do them unless I want to.

> All, all my love
> Shirley Picinose

.

THE FILM WAS NOT the success everyone had hoped for, and neither Warners nor any of the other studios was beating down her door for a follow-up. It was clear to both Fanny and Gertie that the future—whatever it might hold—held it on Broadway or Shaftesbury Avenue rather than Hollywood.

So, once again, *Home and Colonial* was back on the Lawrence agenda. From vacation in Florida she wrote to Jack Wilson:

> Coquina Cottage
> Naples-on-the-Gulf
> —? February, 1950

Dear Jack,
Just got the M.S., the original of which I made a special trip to Paris to see the Summer before last. I thought it most gay and very French; and next I read an adaptation which he himself [Noël] was not too crazy about, saying that it really would be quicker and more satisfactory to write a new play himself.

Gertie is referring to André Roussin's hit play *The Little Hut,* which Noël tried to adapt in 1948 as a quid pro quo for the Paris playwright adapting *Present Laughter* into French as *Joyeux Chagrins*—in which Noël appeared in Paris that year.

As you may know, we had a reading (supposedly secret and private) of *H&C* at Binkie's in London—Binkie and I really thought that the reading was to be for just us—but there was Graham, Gladys, Lorn, I believe Alan Webb and Joyce Carey.

Well, it was not a "really" private reading, was it? [The reading took place on June 13, 1949.]

The play, as far as I was concerned, was not discussed, neither were its own merits, except that Binkie said to me afterwards (as did Noël at Whitecliffs) that there was "work to be done on it."

Since then I have heard no word either from Noël or Binkie about the play, outside of rumours to the effect that Noël was planning to do Graham's musical [*Ace of Clubs*] first. Next I heard via the London mails that Kay Hammond and John Clements were to do *H&C* but not a peep out of *le maitre*!!

Gertie continued:

I have just received a letter from Binkie saying, "I don't know *what* to say about *H&C*. There are hold-ups all the way round, which of course is very exasperating.

Personally I do feel that it was up to Noël to *tell* me his plans in-as-much as it was he who gave out the statement originally that he had written the play for me.

Well, this is all for your records, and I shall read the *Island* play with much interest, especially as Nancy Mitford was Noël's neighbour at Whitecliffs!! [Mitford finally and successfully adapted *La Petite Hutte* as *The Little Hut*.]

Bless you for writing and please keep this confidentially between us. I am really rather amazed by Noël's brush-off!!

      Fondly
      Gee

She then wrote to Noël:

                 Election Day (February 23rd 1950)
Dear, dear Noley,
I had written Jack from Florida because he had sent me that Island play—and I tried to explain to him that, whilst it was a very funny play in Paris, it did not travel well. I also opened my heart to him a bit about *H&C*—only for the same reason that one could get desperate on going to Confession only to find the Cathedral closed for repairs!!

Well, he wrote me a sweet letter (after showing you mine) and it seems that you and I have been in a state with each other.

There is no need to repeat my letter to Jack—you read it—and

Binkie will tell you that I have *repeatedly* asked "What is happening to Noël's play?"

But what *is* important is that . . . you feel that I had been ill-mannered and thoughtless in not saying thank you when you wrote the play. If that is the case and I have hurt you, you *must* know it was not intentional. Surely you of all people know me to be most generous and lavish in my expressions and to have slighted you would never have occurred to me.

I came to "Whitecliffs" (alright, I brought Daphne [du Maurier]) but you had people there too and after lunch, when I thought we might *talk*—YOU went to BED—and then you slept like an old dodo until *I* came and woke you!!

You *knew* I was pleased about the play, but we never got down to any chats like chums because you were filming [*The Astonished Heart*] and I was on the wing. Lornie will tell you that I called you often and you *knew* how thrilled I was about having you on the B'cast. [She had a BBC radio show at the time and they had played the love scene from *Private Lives.*]

However—I was free to talk, not to criticize but to *talk* about the play, whereas you were working mornings and going to bed early on your picture. It all seems too bad that we should get into such a mess . . . and so I write to send my love—my deepest thanks and all the success possible when you do it with Hammond and Clements. Maybe the same initials are a good sign.

I also regret that you are offended by my references to "Graham's musical". It was not a malicious quote—it's just that habit has made all untitled plays "Somebody's musical" or "So-and-so's play".

Well, that's all that!! The election has driven everybody crazy here—it's a great night for British subjects!!!

By the way—what has 2 balls *underground,* 2 wheels *above* ground, and travels at 8 miles an hour?

You tell me.

> Fondly as ever
> GERT

On the same day she had written to Jack: "I am planning to go home this Spring in *something*—but do you really think *Island Fling* [the latest title for *Home and Colonial*] would do the trick? I don't, you know, really."

The rumor Gertie had heard had, for once, some basis in fact. Frustrated by what he saw as Gertie's dithering, Noël *had* offered the play to John Clements and his wife, Kay Hammond (the original Elvira in *Blithe Spirit*) the previous October.

It was now early 1950, though, and the timing was distinctly out of joint. There had been a British general election—the one Gertie refers to—which the ruling Labour Party had won with a vastly decreased majority, and it was obvious that their time in office was running out. A second election was inevitable in the near future and it was generally believed that Churchill's Conservative Party would be returned. Therefore, a light comedy that hinged on Labour being in power would *start* as yesterday's news.

Regretfully, Clements and Hammond decided to pass.

In June 1950 Noël had encouraged Binkie to offer *Home and Colonial* to Laurence Olivier and Vivien Leigh. Binkie reported that they disliked it intensely. It was "old-fashioned Noël Coward" and would do Olivier great harm at a sensitive point in his career. With a sigh, Noël set "poor *Home and Colonial*" aside once more and moved on.

Meanwhile, Fanny Holtzmann's mental wheels were once again spinning on behalf of her client:

CLARIDGE'S LONDON
August 5, 1950

Noël dear,

We must have crossed over the Atlantic . . . my trip was delightful; I hope yours was too. But it is getting settled or rather not getting settled on arrival which is so exhausting. This change of time ordeal is awful on the body; if one could remain in bed and adjust one's self it would be okay—oh, well, I must not complain—we saw *Ace of Clubs* the first evening and loved every moment of it. I laughed and laughed . . . it was pure fun. What a long way Graham has gone! He is magnificent. How hard he works and what a good account he gives of himself. The audience went wild over him the night we were there. *Sail Away* should be on the Hit Parade. It is a natural.

She then gets to the real subject:

Noël dear, I do wish I had come here before you left. I wanted to talk to you about Gertrude. Everyone wants her for films and she wants to come to England. I can hardly blame her for that. She is a success in her Hollywood film but her next one must be one portraying the Gertrude Lawrence Noël Coward has presented to the world in such plays as *Private Lives*. Which gave me an idea—and I shall try to stick to it and not go off in a thousand directions.

*Private Lives* is the perfect vehicle for Gertrude. Of course, you will not play in it. But would you be interested in a deal whereby you do an up-to-date version of the screenplay for Gertrude? If so, we could dictate terms for an installment payment annually, probably, as you had with *Brief Encounter,* for example. The terms are secondary; the idea is up to you.

Yes, I know Metro owns it. If you can do an adaptation in Jamaica now, I believe a great film can be made. My job would be to get the proper producer to do it and I believe we can get either MGM or Jerry Wald, perhaps, to acquire it from them. Ordinarily they refused to sell but they may this time give in. I have been talking to Ben Goetz while we dine together in his apartment, eating the food you would appreciate sent by L. B. Mayer.

Will you please let me know if you would consider doing a screenplay for Gertrude of *Private Lives* or any other of your plays? Time is short as she must report to Rodgers & H[ammerstein] in February. *Private Lives* seems so simple if you do the screenplay. Your early "NO" or possibly "YES" would be appreciated.

Noël dear, I don't want you to feel I am imposing in any way—the suggestion is humbly offered just in case you might feel in the mood to pick up the story of Elyot and Amanda any way you please and put them on celluloid—but before you do so, I shall have to get the film rights to the producer. Notice I say nothing about your directing the film in November? In England or Hollywood? All you would have to do is write the screenplay.

The chances are that if you say NO, Jerry Wald will get Nancy Mitford or someone like her, or perhaps ask Terence Rattigan to do the screenplay for money galore . . . I say "Jerry Wald", because he is searching desperately for a Noël Coward type of play for Gertrude as his first big picture under his new independent contract.

Jerry Wald, who produced *The Glass Menagerie,* had made innumerable tests of Gertie as a Glamour Girl and is delighted with the results. He feels she has that same quality on the screen as she has on the stage. I must say the flashbacks in *Glass Menagerie* prove that—she looks exquisite and will make the perfect Amanda on the screen as she did behind your footlights.

Mind if I dream? Gertie in London in a fine shooting script of *Glass Menagerie* (God forbid! Typewriter slipped)—I mean in *Private Lives,* with a screenplay by the one and only Noël Coward, scenes shot in the South of France, etc., returning to New York February. If you had a film unit, I would recommend that it be done by your own organisation as there is a gold mine in such a film—not costly to produce—with a big-time major distribution set in advance—and frozen sterling available for production. Skip all this and just know that I had the idea and put it down at once.

Take a good and happy holiday and don't work at all—unless you feel like it.

> Fondly,
> FANNY

Not surprisingly, Noël did not rise to the bait.

•

GERTIE, MEANWHILE, was moving toward the big new hit she had been looking for. She bought the rights to Margaret Landon's 1944 novel, *Anna and the King of Siam,* and persuaded Rodgers and Hammerstein to turn it into a musical for her.

Noël was initially approached to direct. No, thank you. Then would he co-star and play the king? Again, no, thank you. He was prepared to appear with Gertie only in a piece of his own, and that possibility was receding by the minute. *The King and I,* as the musical was to be called, was so budgeted that it would have to run for years rather than months to move into profit—which, of course, it did. Since Noël was never prepared to commit to long runs, this was another deciding factor. He did, however, make one valuable contribution to the show's success by suggesting the name of a young folk singer he'd heard at several parties: Yul Brynner.

When the show opened at the St. James Theatre in New York on March 29, 1951, it was clear that Rodgers and Hammerstein and Lawrence had a gold-plated hit on their hands for as long as they cared to run it.

When Gertie wrote to Noël in June she was clearly her old self again, pleased with her success and anxious to encourage her old chum in his new ventures:

> June 24th 1951

My darling Noël,

Such a beautiful photograph it is—and is framed and 'anging in me room at the Court of Siam. Blessings on your frosty pow!!!

We are all (those that are left in New York) delighted that *H&C* is being done in Dennis [the Cape Playhouse] and poor old Richard [Aldrich] is foorious that he won't be there to see it.

However, you surely chose a grand girl for the part—Claudette [Colbert] is one of my most favourite people, and I hope you will persuade her to make the high dive to Broadway. The papers here quote her as saying she does not intend to do other than play it on Farmer Brown's Circuit and then return to H'wood . . .

Colbert played at the Westport Country Playhouse under Jack Wilson's direction and then did just that. The play by now had been retitled *Island Fling*.

Did you hear the story about the woman who took her tiny child to the plumbing department to discuss fixtures and fittings for her new house?

She was talking to the manager and the child tugged at her skirt and whispered "Mummie". The woman shook her off and said, "Be quiet, mummie is busy". A while later the child pulled again at the woman and said, "Mummie, mummie". The woman said, "Stop worrying, I shan't be long now, sit down quietly and behave yourself." Later, having concluded her business, she and the manager looked for the child and found her sitting on a lavatory in the window!!

All my love, darling

"Mrs. Anna", sir

Despite the show's immediate success and the fact that it made a clean sweep of that year's Tony Awards—with Gertie winning as Best Actress—there was a fundamental problem from the very outset: Gertie's singing.

She had never had a strong voice—a fact that was generally acknowledged—and Noël would often tease her about singing off key. He once told her, "If you would sing a little *more* out of tune, darling, you would find yourself singing in thirds, which would be a *great* improvement."

He had started to write *Bitter Sweet* with her in mind back in 1929 but soon realized that what he was composing was beyond her vocal range. This time, though, the problem was exacerbated by the fact that she had to carry the leading role, and although Richard Rodgers had carefully composed songs with her limitations in mind, it soon became obvious that her singing was deteriorating to an alarming degree. Gertie herself refused to face the fact. The problem, she insisted, was purely temporary.

Dennis
Cape Cod
Mass.
January 1952

Darling Noël,

Well, whadderyerno??

After that short siege of vocal doldrums my voice suddenly returned, my spirits rose, and my hackles fairly *bristled* with vitality.

Blimey, it got hot too, just before my holiday came, but 2 weeks have gone by and I have 4 more to go before I return to the salt mines!! [Celeste Holm substituted for her during the six weeks.]

Radie H [Harris, the columnist] came back *raving* about you at the Café de Paris, and the papers here have it that you are to open at the Waldorf in the Empire Room in October. This may be just scuttlebut—nevertheless, I feel sure that it is not the best room for you. The Cotillion Room at the Sherry Netherlands has the smart Café de Paris crowd and the room is Serge Obelinski and delightfully intimate—added to which Mr. [Cecil] Beaton has a most wonderful flat up in the tower which they could give you during your engagement.

If you have not signed your contract for the Waldorf, why not have someone contact Serge for you—I know he would go *wild* to get you!

Meantime I saw Kitty Carlisle in *Lady* here last week and she was terrific, and especially exciting in the dramatic "story" part of the play. She promised to give you a big kiss for me, so give her a buzz for me, will yer, and Bonnie Prince Charming [Moss Hart] too, from his Blemish!!

Give old Lornie and Gladys my love et al. I long to get home again to see them.

♥ Anna Leonowens

A few days later she sends him a postscript with some cuttings about the show:

"When *The King and I* opened last year, most of the critical acclaim was for a relative newcomer, Yul Brynner (the King). Seeing the show again makes it evident why Gertrude Lawrence is the star. Trouper that she is, Miss Lawrence has deepened and rounded out the role of Anna (the 'I' of the show) while Brynner is now over-acting and has become so acrobatic that you expect him to do a headstand or take off on a trapeze at any moment."

I meant to put the enclosed into my last letter—it just came out before I left. So, it seems that there is not too much to worry about—I just struck a bad patch and you came and sat in it!!

Oh, dear—and it's always you I want to please above ANYONE.

♥ Dagmar

Her voice and her general health continued to deteriorate—to the point where Rodgers and Hammerstein turned to Noël for help. In his *Diary* for April 29, he writes:

Lunched with Gertie . . . Advised her to leave *The King and I* for good. I did not say they were anxious to get rid of her because of her

Noël's friend and supposedly Gertie's sometime lover, Daphne
du Maurier (1907–1989) was with Gertie in New York in those
final days and had the task of describing them to Noël later.

singing, but I think I convinced her that she ought to do a straight
play. I also said I would be prepared to rewrite *Island Fling* for her. I
am sure that, with some reconstruction, it would be a success with
her playing it.

He was overly optimistic. Gertie had no intention of leaving the cast of
*The King and I*. King George VI had just died and as she wrote to Lorn:

> February 19th 1952
> 239 East 61st Street
> New York 21, NY
>
> Everyone here very deeply distressed by the loss of our beloved King.
> Memorial services going on at all churches of all Faiths—all very
> comforting and homesick making. I long to get back. My fondest
> love to you all at No. 17 and elsewhere.

"Getting back" would be as the star of the London production of *The
King and I,* during the forthcoming coronation year of 1953, but it was not
to be. On September 6, Noël's *Diary* reads:

> A day that started gaily and ended in misery. [He had gone to the
> races at Folkestone with Cole Lesley and Gladys.] Just as I was leav-
> ing, Coley told me that it was in the Stop Press that Gertie Lawrence
> was dead. I drove home feeling dreadful . . . Poor, darling old
> Gertie—a lifelong friend. With all her overacting and silliness I have

never known her do a mean or an unkind thing. I am terribly, terribly unhappy to think that I shall never see her again.

Not for a moment had he—or, indeed, anyone else close to her—realized just how ill she was. The only exception was her friend and sometime lover Daphne du Maurier, who had traveled to New York to spend time with her while she supposedly convalesced. Later du Maurier wrote apologetically to Noël:

Menobilly—Sunday

Dear Noël,

I feel most bitterly to blame for not having got in touch with you about Gee [Gertie]. Thursday, I think it was, I sat beside the telephone wondering what to do—whether to try and find you on the telephone somewhere, but I knew your Play [*Quadrille*] was to open next week and that you might be with the company on tour, in the middle of rehearsing, etc.—and finally, I don't know what it was, a mixture of diffidence, of not wanting to seem alarmist, kept me from trying. And I was hoping every moment to have a more encouraging cable.

The thing is, I heard from Fanny Holtzmann first some ten days ago, telling me that Gee had been rushed to hospital after the Saturday matinée in great pain, tests were taken, etc., and nothing found too badly wrong but the liver, which was badly inflamed, and rest, diet, etc., would put this right. Gee had asked Fanny to write and tell me, because she did not want me to get news of it in any other way, through papers, or anything. I cabled Fanny, and Gee, and wrote to both, and then a second letter came from Fanny, after a few days, saying Gee was still in great pain, every sort of doctor had been called in, but *absolute secrecy* was to be maintained (why, for God's sake?)—no one to be told—the letter very hysterical, Noël, terribly worked up, you know how Fanny can be—and I was going about in agony of mind, not knowing what to do. But here is my fault. Fanny said "no one to be told except perhaps Noël." This is where I sat by the telephone, wondering whether to worry you, or not. Wrongly, as I see now, I decided against it. If you can forgive me, please do. Another cable, in answer to a previous one from me, came on Thursday. Doctors' reports discouraging, etc., and more specialists to be called in.

I wrote to Fanny and a tiny scrap (too late to reach her) to Gee, too. But I doubt if she was seeing any letters by then. Tommy [Daphne's husband] and I went out in the boat yesterday and then in the meantime came the last cable "Gertrude critically ill." And finally—after the News had been on the 6 o'clock—a cable that would send Gee herself rocking with that really shaking heaven-sent laugh that happened when she was really amused: "Our beloved has left us and has gone to join the immortals."

Although I have been crying all night and all day, and still can't stop, I think the wording of that cable will always make me stop short and scream with laughter. Please, dear Noël, keep this letter confidential. God knows I wish no harm to poor old Fanny, who with all her spider's web tactics I believe to have been devoted to Gee (though she probably hurried her into her grave by sitting solidly with her in the hospital, by the bedside all last Sunday according to her letter) but it was good of her to take the trouble, between her bedside vigils, to cable and to write to me, therefore the shock of Gee's death, though God damn bloody awful, hasn't taken me unawares as I feel it has you. Please forgive me, once again for keeping silent.

I had a happy letter written on the Sunday before she went back to the play grumbling at the weather but quite agog, really, to be going back to the factory, which as you know was her life, nothing else counted, except dream fantasies of being a countess from time to time, and eating sandwiches at one in the morning and having schoolgirl giggles and that wave of Cockney loyalty for waving a flag for the Queen, England and all that. She was looking forward to the coronation like a little girl of twelve ("Can we have front seats?").

I haven't felt so lost since Daddy [the actor Sir Gerald du Maurier] died. That's saying a good deal.

> With love,
> DAPHNE

> Menobilly
> September 10

Dearest Noël,

Here are the letters from Fanny, but the first I have not kept, the one that told me she was ill.

What I shall never understand is *why* they didn't spot an abcess or a tumour at once, when our lay minds jump to riddled cancer the moment anyone has a pain anywhere. But I am hoping to hear again from the wretched old bitch Fanny in a day or so, saying if an autopsy was performed, and what it was. It should have been done, if only for the sake of anyone who has a chill on the liver in future and is told to diet! However, as I told you, I'm pretty sure something was wrong and had been for some time. That real exhaustion all last year could not have been just normal fatigue. The disinclination to do anything every

Sunday but just lie on the *chaise-longue,* turban on the head, Nivea skin oil on the face, plaid rug over the knees, steam heat at full blast, enough to kill anyone, Angus the Scottie lying panting at her feet.

I remember creeping in to see if she wanted anything and kissing her silly cock-eyed nose, and she opened one eye and said—"I thought it was Angus." "It was," I said, and went. Why, oh why, should someone with the mind of somebody of ten, with whom one really had no thought in common, no topic of real conversation, no sort of outlook resembling one's own at all, who frequently lied, who never stopped doing the most infuriating things, yet have the power to so completely wrap herself around the heart that, because of her, one became bitched, buggered and bewildered? (My only outlet at the moment is foul language and useless blasphemy. Poor Tommy, no wonder he goes out sailing, rather puzzled and, I fear, a little hurt.)

You remember that dreadful straining after the high notes latterly in *The King and I* so that one's belly ached in agony for her, and which proves again there must have been something wrong? I tried to tell her not to do it, but she put on her not listening face and talked about [the war in] Korea. The night before I left, this was March— and it will be my last memory of her, she had the eternal radio switched on, it went on through the night, and suddenly your *Bitter Sweet* song came over, the "I'll See You Again" song, and she began to sing it, from her pillow, in that lilting, sexless, choir-boy voice that was her true voice, very softly, and I told her *that* was what I meant, to sing always like that, never straining, never trying to put over "big stuff"; but she said I was being sentimental, and rushed off to some new teacher who was to make her sing like [Adelina] Patti, [Nellie] Melba, [Kirsten] Flagstadt, the Works. Which probably started up the cancer of all time until it bust.

Love from
DAPHNE

Letters of condolence arrived for Noël in every post. From a mutual friend:

September 9th 1952

My dear Noël,

That was a most loving and charming article you wrote on Gertie in *The Times* and, oddly enough, if you'd died first, bits of it are exactly what she would have written about you.

Just before she left England she spent some days here when she had no need to be anything but just herself, and she talked a great deal about you.

When you write a life of her, which surely you must one day, I will tell you what she said and the part you played.

If a chameleon could be beautiful, then I would always think of it and Gertie as one, but in these days we spent here, she was telling her deep desires and wondering how she could fulfil them before it was too late. One evening she said, "You know, I'd be really happy here in England, if I could find a man who would love me, he'd have to have a nice little title (isn't the 'little' heavenly?), a place, not too big—and with it, security—I'm tired and I don't want to spend my old age working hard."

I mentioned that I thought she'd miss the being Gertrude Lawrence a bit, but "No—I'd be content with what I said—I'd stay at home and I'd want nothing else."

Bless her heart—would there be much else? And to go out of the front door, and become Lady Bountiful backed up by her too generous habits—would have satisfied her love of acting—and would have had the maximum—the best of both worlds, in fact, and why not? She felt cheated by life, and to her eternal credit, it never made her sour or spiteful.

We shall sadly miss her, shan't we?

From royal dressmaker Norman Hartnell:

> Lovel Dene
> Windsor Forest
> Berks.
> Sunday

My dear Noël,

How lovely she was—so sweet and so friendly. She was always so wonderful to me, but only now do I realize how much I have loved her and for so many years. I can scarcely write coherently—or think what to say—my throat aches and my eyes spill over with tears as I write, Noël.

Through you in *Tonight at 8:30* Gertie helped me to make my name. Do you remember a moonlight chiffon dress in "Shadow Play"? Or a black velvet in "Hearts and Flowers"? What a perfect person. Her face, her figure, her voice—and that tip-tilted nose—and her movements.

I'll tell you something:—When I was fitting those clothes for H.M. the Queen (then Princess Elizabeth) for her ill-fated trip to

Australia, we asked the Queen to walk a little. "Alas," she said, "if only I could walk across a room like Gertrude Lawrence."

That's confidential, Noël—*cela va sans dire*—but I thought you would like to know.

From your friend
NORMAN HARTNELL.

Even Fanny—like so many others—had gentle memories, if sometimes sad ones: "She had so little real happiness—all froth, living in a world of imagination, as when she bought, for example, a worn family album with photographs at Caledonia Market . . ."

•

SOME YEARS LATER, Noël and Daphne du Maurier met at a party, and naturally the conversation came round to Gertie. Daphne recalled how Gertie had so often regretted that she had never had the opportunity to sing the theme from *Bitter Sweet,* "I'll See You Again."

Noël went over to the piano, sat down, and sang the song through, but when he came to the end of it, he changed the words:

*Though the years my tears may dry,*
*And I never said goodbye,*
*I shall love you till I die . . .*

# CHAPTER 9
## *PRIVATE LIVES*
### (1930–1931)

I think very few people are completely normal, really, deep down
in their private lives . . . If all the various cosmic thingummies
fuse at the same moment, and the right spark is struck, there's no
knowing what one might do.

**AMANDA, IN *PRIVATE LIVES* (1930)**

REHEARSALS FOR *Private Lives* began in July, and a few weeks
later Noël's friend George Lloyd brought along a visitor, who confided in a letter to his sister that he found Noël "not deep but
remarkable. A hasty kind of genius."

The visitor was one Aircraftman T. E. Shaw—trying without undue success to pretend that he was not better known as T. E. Lawrence, "Lawrence of Arabia" (1888–1935). After the rehearsal the three of them lunched and there was a clear and immediate rapport between the hasty genius and the shy one.

Their go-between was well pleased with what he had achieved: ("He [Lawrence] is an odd creature but I am very fond of him and he has genius.")

The bond T. E. Lawrence and Noël had was regarding their respective writing. Lawrence was intrigued by the workings of the theater, and Noël, equally impressed by *Seven Pillars of Wisdom* (1926). Lawrence mentioned that he was working on writing about his experiences in the Royal Air Force—published posthumously as *The Mint*—and Noël asked if he could see the work in progress. This led to an exchange of letters and the occasional meeting in the months ahead.

338171 A/c Shaw
R.A.F. Mount Batten
Plymouth
15.VIII.30

Dear N.C.

Here are your R.A.F. notes. After looking at them you will agree with me that such tense and twisted prose cannot be admirable. It lacks health. Obscenity is *vieux jeu,* too: but in 1922 I was not copying the fashion!

Don't be too hard on them, though. They were meant, not for reading, but to afford me raw material for an introductory chapter to my mag.op. [*magnum opus*] on an airman's life. Unluckily I survived the Depot only to be sacked when on the point of being posted to a Squadron, the real flying unit. There followed a long spell of army life, wasting the novelty of barracks, till I broadened out into the present common-place and lasting contentment.

Obviously these notes libel our general R.A.F. life by being too violently true to an odd and insignificant part of it. So out of my head and with no formal notes I attempted a Part III to show the happiness that came after the bullying. Only happiness is such a beast to put on paper.

Meeting you was such a surprise and pleasure to me. I had often (and quite inadequately) wondered what you were like. Now I'll try to work the rehearsal you suggested into some later raid upon London. The going-round of wheels fascinates me. So I found Wednesday wholly delightful.

Yours,
T. E. Shaw

Please do not keep them longer than you can help—or I shall forget where they are, and be troubled!

> 111, Ebury Street
> S.W.1.
> Adelphi Hotel, Liverpool [where
> *Private Lives* had opened on tour]

Dear 338171,
(May I call you 338?) I am tremendously grateful to you for letting me read your R.A.F. notes. I found them even better than I expected, which is honestly saying a good deal. Now I'm faced with the problem of expressing to you my genuine and very deep admiration of your writing without treading on your over tender, hero worship, Lawrence of Arabia corns! Really, it had nothing to do with all that. I think you're a very thrilling writer indeed because you make pictures with such superb simplicity and no clichés at all, and I disagree flatly with you when you say you're photographic. Your descriptive powers far exceed flat photography. Cameras are unable to make people live in the mind as your prose succeeds in doing. China and Taffy and Skiffy and Corporal Abner are grandly written with heart and blood and bones. I found so many things I want to talk to you about which in writing would sound over effusive and pompous, so please come to London one Saturday if you possibly can.

My play was a great success in Edinburgh and we're opening here tonight in a theatre the size of Olympia, which will be very disconcerting. I am terribly glad you thought it good. I owe you a great deal for the things you said about my writing. Valuable praise is very rare and beyond words stimulating. Please come to London and see some more wheels going round, if it interests you.

I am enormously pleased that we've met.

> Yours,
> Noël Coward

> 338171 A/c Shaw
> R.A.F. Mount Batten
> Plymouth
> 6.1X.30

Dear N.C.
It is very good to laugh: and I laughed so much, and made so many people laugh over your "May I call you 338" that I became too busy and happy to acknowledge your letter.

I hope Liverpool went off well. Edinburgh—so the press said, but how they lie—went into fits over your mixed grill. I fancied you were coming thence direct to London, but clearly not. It must be very hard and uphill work winning province after province before attacking the headquarters: and London is likely to be your easiest conquest, too. The bits I saw went so swingingly.

Your praise of my R.A.F. notes pleases me, of course, more than it puzzles me. I'm damned if I can see any good in them. Some artifice— yes: some skill—yes: they even come off, here and there: but the general impression on me is dry bones. Your work is like sword-play; as quick as light. Mine a slow painful mosaic of hard words stiffly cemented together. However, it is usually opposites that fall in love. At any rate I propose to go on looking forward, keenly, to seeing more of your works and work, and perhaps of yourself, if a kind fate lets me run into you when you are not better engaged.

I'm hoping to get to London some time in October, for a week-end perhaps.

> Yours,
> T. E. Shaw

5.X.30

Dear N.C.

I was at the second night, and wondered to see how perfectly the finished product went. Just once it slipped, when she drew the curtains and the daylight took 20 seconds to come! Yet I'm not sure that the bare works you showed me that afternoon were not better. For one thing, I could not tell always when you were acting and when talking to one another. So I would suggest my coming to another rehearsal, only there seems nothing to prevent these plays of yours running for ever, and so you probably will never write any more.

Gertrude Lawrence is amazing. She acts nearly as well as yourself. I was sorry for the other two [Laurence Olivier and Adrianne Allen]. They were out of it.

The play reads astonishingly well. It gets thicker, in print, and has bones and muscles. On the stage you played with it and puffed your fancies up and about like swansdown. And one can't help laughing all the time: whereas over the book one does not do worse than chuckle or smile. For fun I took some pages and tried to strike redundant words out of your phrases. Only there were none. That's what I felt when I told you it was superb prose.

You'll be sick of letters about it, so I'll shut up. Yet I had to tell you how much delight it gave me.

> Yours,
> T. E. SHAW

111, Ebury Street
S.W.1.
10.10.30

Dear 338,

I was enormously pleased with your letter and so very much encouraged by what you say about my writing that I shall probably inflict upon you the script of a new play I've written, which will not be produced in England, only published [*Post-Mortem*]. I'd value your opinion on it very deeply, but please, if it's a bore to you to read plays, say so and I won't send it. If you have a minute in your flying visits to London, do let us meet again. There is a good deal I should like to talk to you about.

We could have supper, lunch, breakfast, dinner or tea quietly in my studio.

So please telegraph me a few days in advance when you feel like appearing.

Yours,
Noël Coward


Plymouth
10.vi.31

Dear N.C.

I have read your play (which? Why your war one, of course) twice and want to admire you. It's a fine effort, a really fine effort.

You know better than anyone what sort of a play it is; I fancied it hadn't the roots of a great success. You had something far more important to say than usual, and I fancy that in saying it you let the box-office and the stalls go hang. As argument it is first rate. As imagination magnificent: and it does you great honour as a human being. It's for that reason that I liked it so much. Mrs. Humphry [*sic*] Ward (before your time) once asked Matthew Arnold (also before your time) why he was not wholly serious. People won't like you better for being quite so serious as you are in this: but it does you honour, as I said, and gave me a thrill to read it.

Incidentally the press-man-magnate-son scene was horrifying. That would "act", surely? Only most of the rest was far above playing to any gallery.

I think it was very good of you to have done this so plainly and well. I needn't say that it's written with your usual spare exactness and skill. You deny yourself every unnecessary word.

Yours,
T. E. SHAW

No answer. It isn't a letter: I'd wanted to say how much I liked the thing, and filed to say anything worth reading: and so just report progress, gratefully.

Goldenhurst Farm
Aldington, Kent
19.6.31

Dear 338,

It's no use you writing me a letter like that and expecting no answer. It gave me tremendous pleasure and my gratitude must be expressed, particularly as I would rather you liked "Poet Noctem" [*Post-Mortem*] than most people. This may sound a trifle effusive but actually it's perfectly true.

I know all about my facility for writing adroit swift dialogue and hitting unimportant but popular nails on the head and I thought the time had come to break new ground a little. (Oh dear, self-conscious metaphors are fairly flying from my pen), but anyhow I'm *deeply* happy that you thought it good. I would very much like to see you again some time.

Yours,
N.C.

I'm doing a very fancy Production [*Cavalcade*] at Drury Lane in September, so if you want to see *real* wheels going round, let me know.

338171 A/c Shaw
R.A.F. Mount Batten
Plymouth
30.IX.31

Dear N.C.

Last week there wasn't a chance of my getting up to London for months. Today I've been warned for duty in Kent instantly, and I may be able to pass homeward via London about Monday next. It is not certain, and even if it happened, your rehearsals might have ended before then; but on the chance of it's being any use I will try and get word to you if I do arrive.

If you can gather any plain sense from that last sentence, then you are good at puzzles; but the moral is that you do nothing concerning me except sit still: If I can I will. It is very good of you to give me the chance. I have heard that it is a most unusually difficult piece of stage-tactics.

Yours,
T. E. SHAW

And there the correspondence apparently petered out. In 1935, on a deserted stretch of country road, Lawrence was killed in a motorcycle accident. However, he continued to fascinate Noël, as both a man and a dramatic phenomenon. When Terence Rattigan's play about Lawrence, *Ross*—taken from another Lawrence pseudonym—opened in 1960, Beverley Nichols recalls that after the first night:

> Noël was striding up and down a side-street in an almost too well-cut dinner jacket, bubbling with enthusiasm about the play—he is very generous about other men's work if it is good, and quite shattering if it is not. "Wasn't it wonderful", he said "to see a play in which, for once in a way, the hero was not a juvenile delinquent and the stage not cluttered up with dustbins?"

· 

TWO OTHER THINGS of significance happened that summer of 1930.

Noël completed his domestic arrangements by buying 17 Gerald Road, near fashionable Eaton Square. It was the upper part of a large house, which was immediately christened "The Studio." Soon after, he would buy a small house that backed on to it in Burton Mews, put in a connecting door, and turn that into Lorn's office. This would become his London home until 1956, and its topography is clearly echoed in Garry Essendine's flat in *Present Laughter.*

The second significant occurrence that year was more of a happy happenstance. Browsing through a tray of old books at Foyle's Charing Cross Road bookshop, Noël happened to leaf through some bound volumes of the *Illustrated London News* and his eye was caught by a photograph of British troops embarking on a troopship en route for the Boer War. Just as the sounds of *Die Fledermaus* had conjured up Old Vienna, the illustration he saw brought back childhood memories of the sights and particularly the sounds of the early part of the century.

"Extraordinary how potent cheap music can be" was a line he gave to Amanda in *Private Lives.* He might well have added "Extraordinary how emotive patriotic songs can be." He bought the set of books and went home with the martial strains of "Goodbye, Dolly Gray" and "Soldiers of the Queen" playing insistently in his head and a montage of the historic moments he and his fellow countrymen had lived through replaying in his mind.

At home later, he happened to be entertaining an old friend, writer G. B. Stern, and together they talked the idea through, each striking memories off the other. The form of the play was already taking shape. It would be a series of dramatic theatrical snapshots linked by a simple story

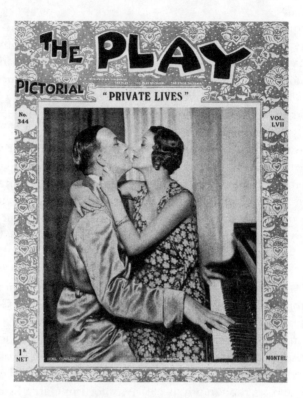

line—but what to call it? It was to be a sort of procession of history. One of the pictures showed a troop of soldiers on horseback. *CAVALCADE!*

And that was the "very fancy production at Drury Lane" Noël was in the process of devising in that last letter to Lawrence.

But first there was *Private Lives.*

•

THE SUCCESS OF *Private Lives* was immediate and absolute. The story is of a couple, Elyot (Noël) and Amanda (Gertie), who can't live with or without one another. They're divorced and remarried—Elyot to Sybil (Adrianne Allen) and Amanda to Victor (Laurence Olivier)—and now, on their second honeymoons, they find themselves at the same hotel and in adjacent suites. The hotel balcony on which Gertie appeared to Noël that night in Tokyo has now been moved to Deauville (not the Riviera), so that Elyot and Amanda can conveniently decamp for Paris once they realize the ghastly mistake they have made. Nice would have taken a day and a half!

The critics predictably found the play "thin," "brittle," "tenuous," but the public adored it and many of the people whose opinion Noël valued saw it for the breakthrough it was. It was at this point that British novelist Arnold Bennett dubbed Noël "the Congreve of our day."

G. B. Stern wrote (September 25):

Doubtless you heard my peals of silvery laughter ringing over the footlights with that individual note of pure childish delight which long ago cuddled its way down into your heart. Several times I was amused when nobody else was. Once or twice everybody else was when I wasn't . . .

It's *delightful* comedy—but I don't believe a word of it! Not that that matters. The third act pleased me, specially. I love your treatment of embarrassing situations. Yet, for the moment I'm more dazzled by your gifts as an actor than as a dramatist . . . what a perfectly finished exquisitely controlled deliciously fastidious and finally satisfying actor! Your love scene in Act 1—your silent behaviour during the breakfast scene at the end were the most excellent.

The scenes on leaving the theatre were appalling . . . the worst atrocities of the French Revolution cannot compare with them . . . a crowding fighting surging mob festering in the vortex of the maelstrom between foyer, steps and street . . . Each man for himself and women and children emphatically *not* first . . . The watching scum of the vast metropolis howled with delight at the ugly passions of the ladies and gentlemen in evening dress cavorting nakedly in the act of self-preservation . . . With my own eyes I saw H. G. Wells pick up Mrs. Arnold Bennett and hurl her thrice under the wheels of a stampeding automobile. (I can't be *quite* sure if this is accurate, so you'd better not hand it out to the Press.)

Marie Tempest wrote to say "the play was charming, so was Miss Lawrence. Dear little Adrianne was delightful and looked lovely." And there were many more letters in the same vein.

Most people took the play as an entertaining exercise in the flippant wit they had come to expect from Noël Coward, but one or two saw beyond that. One correspondent, for instance, wrote: "It struck me as the most brilliant and ingenious thing I'd seen for years—and (but I didn't really get this till later for I was too busy laughing at it)—that the study of the two chief characters went deeper than anything I'd seen of yours."

Only in recent years have some revivals of the play shown this darker side of Elyot and Amanda. Beneath the sophisticated repartee are two accidental assassins—destined to be destructive of each other and of anyone who comes emotionally close to them.

*Private Lives* was the opening production at London's new Phoenix Theatre on September 24, and its 101-performance run would have been substantially longer if Noël had not insisted that he would no longer appear for more than three months in the same show. In any case he was anxious to take the play to Broadway and consolidate the recent success of *This Year of Grace!*

•

JANUARY 1931 FOUND him back in New York and writing to Violet:

The Wyndham
42 West 58th Street
Thursday

Darling,

Well, here I am again, and I can say I'm very pleased to see the dear old place again. Oh dear, everybody is always so thrilled to see me here. I'd no idea I was so popular. I've taken a dear little apartment on the roof of a skyscraper in West 58th St. It has the most superb view and is always filled with sun. I've also got my "Town Car", which is the smartest thing you've ever seen and only about fourpence halfpenny. I've been to several plays and feel very ashamed of the English Theatre.

*Green Pastures,* the negro play, is so heartbreakingly beautiful that it wrecked me, and Lynn Fontanne's performance of Queen Elizabeth in *Elizabeth the Queen* [Maxwell Anderson] is the most superb individual performance I've ever seen in the Theatre. She looks so like all the pictures of Q.E. it takes her an hour and a half to make up every night. Alfred is lovely as Essex. I've also seen Clifton's show [*Three's a Crowd*], which is marvelous and Bart [Herbert] Marshall, who opened last night in a new play [*Tomorrow and Tomorrow*] with Gilbert Miller.

Oh dearie me, everyone is giving parties for me and I'm just the old fashioned Bell [*sic*] of New York.

Incidentally I remain

Yours sincerely
Noël Pierce Coward

The "Pierce" is silent as in Bathing [and also misspelled by Noël!].

Give a nod to Mr. Coward and Miss Veitch

The New York cast of *Private Lives* had three out of the four original principals. Adrianne Allen had a prior commitment in the United Kingdom, and Sybil was played by Jill Esmond, Laurence Olivier's then wife. The play opened at the Times Square Theatre on January 27 and ran for 256 performances. After the contractual three months, Noël and Gertie were replaced by Otto Kruger and Madge Kennedy.

Noël's Sunday letter home was religiously observed:

[Undated—? April 1931]
Friday

Hello Darling,

I've had several letters from you and enjoyed them all tip top . . .

My present plans are that when the play closes on April 25th I'm going to Bermuda with Jack for two weeks to lie in the sun and then I shall sail home about May 19th. I'm not very keen on Hollywood. I'd rather have a nice cup of cocoa, really.

The Paramount People want to equip me with a camera etc., when I go to South America in the Autumn with Jeffrey, and I think it would be fun to do a travel film on my own, I must say. And then I shall write a sort of lecture and have it recorded and synchronised with the picture afterwards.

I shall spend most of the summer bouncing backwards and forwards between Goldenhurst and London, so you'll see a lot of me. I may go to Finland in June for two weeks with Lynn and Alfred but who knows? Nothing particularly exciting is happening. I'm enjoying myself, and the play's going on exactly the same.

All love and hugs until next week.
SNOOPIE

[Undated—late April]

Darlingest,

Great excitement! Gertie was taken ill on Thursday so I have had to play five performances with the understudy who was very good but still it was agony. So we're closing for two weeks and I'm taking a holiday now instead of later. Jack and I are leaving for Havana tonight.

I'm going to play the play until May 9th instead of April the 25th to make up the 12 weeks. It's really rather a good plan because we shall be closed for Holy Week when business is always bad, and a nice fortnight in the sun will be lovely.

I'm sailing home probably in the *Europa* May 19th, so you won't have to wait very much longer before your rheumy old eyes are gladdened by the sight of your ewe lamb. Probably there will be a slight hiatus in my letters to you owing to postage difficulties but I will *write* regularly as ever. I'll also cable when I arrive. We're going around with Film Cameras so there'll be a new programme for the family when I return.

All love to all and particular hugs to yourself.
SNOOPIE

S.S. *Evangeline*
[Undated—late April/early May]

Well Darling,

Here I am writing my usual Sunday letter to you from a smallish boat in the middle of the sunny Caribbean Sea. We left Cuba this morning and we're finishing our fortnight in Nassau, where we arrive tomorrow. Havana is very, very beautiful and filled with lovely old buildings, but it's also very gay and smart and the bathing opportunities aren't so good, so we decided to return to our old favourite where we can hire a boat and go swimming around between the Islands. We are already pretty sunburnt and by the time we get back to New York I fully intend to be black.

We re-open the play tomorrow week. It feels funny having a holiday in the middle like this, and *very* enjoyable. My Spanish came in very useful in Havana, I was surprised to find out how much I knew. It really is a beautiful place. Heavenly drives in the country through Sugar Cane and Banana plantations and masses of every conceivable kind of flower.

We dined out in restaurants outside the town, with trees hung with lights and Spanish orchestras playing very softly. The Oliviers are in Nassau and are meeting us tomorrow. I am sorry to see Arnold Bennett is dead.

Well, not very long now before I shall be back at the Farm. I expect to sail home about May 19th. All love to all and particular hugs.

SNOOPIE

May 8th
Sunday

Darling,

Well, here I am back again, I found several letters from you to welcome me . . .

I had a letter from Erik asking for some money for his teeth which I am sending him. We spent the first few days of our holiday in Havana and then on to Nassau . . . Nassau was lovelier than ever. We spent all our time fishing and coasting around the islands in a motor boat. It's the best sort of holiday for me, nothing but sun and sea. The garden sounds lovely with the Daffodils coming out. I'm glad Father is fighting for dear old England. If *you* start getting Political I should think there'd be hell to pay in the dear old country!

All love Darlingest,
SNOOPIE

I'm very amused about *Bitter Sweet* re-opening again. George [Georges] Metaxa dined with me last night and told me all the news.

Metaxa had played Carl Linden in the original London production of *Bitter Sweet* and was later the subject of a Coward verse:

> *Have you heard about Georgie Metaxa?*
> *His conduct grows laxer and laxer.*
> *His poor little wife is afraid of her life*
> *For he whacks her and whacks her and whacks her.*

[Undated—May ?]
Sunday night

Hellow Darling,

How's everything? . . . Gertie is very well now and everything is going on much as usual . . . I went to the Circus for the second time tonight and went back and talked to all the animals who were very sweet and sent you their love, particularly the seals who flapped their flappers at the very mention of your name! It's a very magnificent Circus with three rings all going on at once, rather bewildering but highly enjoyable.

I'm longing to get home, if Cochran gets Drury Lane for me I shall sail about the 12th in order to start work on *Cavalcade* for September. This is secret so don't say anything except to Sasha [Violet's dachshund]. I should really rather have had the Coliseum but that's impossible. I think anyhow Drury Lane is a little more dignified and traditional.

Goodnight, my darling, until next week. Love to all
SNOOPIE

[Undated—May ?]
Thursday

Darlingest,

I've been very bad and weecked and missed writing to you on Sunday, so I shall send you a cable on or about the day you should have received the letter so that you will be comforted! Everything has descended upon me during these last three weeks and I'm rushing madly about trying to crowd everything in.

I have managed to sell the Cochran Revue [*Cochran's 1931 Revue*] songs. Three are going into the new *Little Show* ["Half-Caste Woman" and "Any Little Fish"]. Beatrice Lillie is doing two of them, and a couple more are going into the *Ziegfeld Follies,* and I have to rehearse them all, added to which Madge Kennedy and Otto Kruger are rehearsing *Private Lives* and need help. They're playing on here for a few weeks when we stop, and then go on tour for ages. I spend hours at the Dentist having all my teeth well seen to, so you see my life is full. I sail on the *Bremen* May 12th! I have fixed to open *Cavalcade* at Drury Lane on September 7th, and as it is not written yet, it looks like being a busy summer. It's all very exciting and enjoyable. I shall do most of the work at Goldenhurst, so keep the house free for me! I'm longing to get home. We're still playing to capacity and everyone thinks I'm crazy!

Love to all and violent hugs to you.

SNOOPIE

•

AFTER THE FINAL PERFORMANCE Noël sailed for home to prepare for what was to be, if anything, an even bigger triumph for him. He had consolidated his theatrical position on both sides of the Atlantic and was now—according to the *Daily Express*—the world's highest-paid writer, with an annual income of fifty thousand pounds.

But perhaps the biggest legacy he left in both places was the image of "Noël and Gertie." They would play together once more, and the legend would persist until her premature death, but this was where the magic took imperishable shape. "Sometimes in *Private Lives*," Noël wrote, "I would look across the stage at Gertie and she would simply take my breath away."

INTERMISSION

# PLAY PARADE

## "A TEMPLE OF DREAMS"

The Theatre . . . is a house of strange enchantment,
a temple of dreams.

NOËL COWARD

GEORGE BERNARD SHAW (1856–1950) was the first major
playwright to take serious notice of the young Noël, but other contemporaries soon followed suit, and it was not long before Noël
himself felt able to offer professional advice to his own contemporaries—as
he had to Esmé.

He learned one of his early lessons in 1917, from American producer
Gilbert Miller, who urged him to concentrate on plot construction before

allowing himself the license to begin writing the dialogue that always came so easily to him.

Miller said that "the construction of a play was as important as the foundations of a house, whereas dialogue, however good, could only, at best, be considered as interior decoration. No mood, however exquisite, is likely to hold the attention of an audience for two hours and a half unless it is based on a solid structure."

It was a lesson Noël was to learn the hard way in the late 1920s, when after a string of successes—*The Vortex, Easy Virtue, Hay Fever,* and *Fallen Angels*—he took out of his metaphorical suitcase a play he had tossed off on that first crowded visit to America in 1921.

He sent the play to Sir James Barrie (1860–1937), who had made encouraging noises about some of Noël's earlier work. Barrie was professionally perceptive about this one, *Sirocco:*

> Adelphi Terrace House
> Strand
> W.C.2.
> February 18th 1928

Dear Coward,

I have read *Sirocco* which you kindly sent me and in many ways I think it a brilliant piece of work. In construction and the flow of it it is probably the best of your things, as far as I know them, but I don't think it really is worthwhile doing. There is nothing special of yourself in it— in structure or in thought—to give me at least the idea that I got from *The Vortex* that a real live new dramatist was appearing. (Of course it is live to the point of violence but that is not the kind of life I mean.) Change the scene to England (leaving out Sirocco, which has nothing vital to do with the play) . . . This may be all wrong—at any rate it is the view of one who has a warm belief in you.

> Yours sincerely,
> J. M. Barrie

Don't think I am wanting you to "conceive" like your predecessors. No good in that. You belong to your time—they to theirs. Give us yourself or nothing, but your best self. (This is a little too solemn. Be gay also while you can.)

This aspect of Noël's belonging to his own time was one that was repeated by many.

•

ALTHOUGH THE THOUGHT might not have pleased Shaw, the greatest influence on the early Coward was undoubtedly W. Somerset

Noël, "Willie" Somerset Maugham (1874–1965), and Leonard Lyons at
the Villa Mauresque. From the late 1920s Noël was increasingly viewed
as "the new Somerset Maugham." Maugham cheerfully admitted that
Noël would probably "be responsible for the manner in which plays
will be written during the next thirty years."

Maugham (1874–1965). Maugham and Coward chose the basic drawing
room drama genre and then proceeded to go beyond its traditionally
accepted boundaries. For a while Coward and Maugham were professional
contemporaries, then—when Maugham literally quit the stage—they
remained wary friends, pacing around each other, as someone described it,
like a couple of panthers.

From the late 1920s comparisons between the two men were made
more and more often, and at a point Maugham himself accepted the situation with good grace. For the first published collection of three of
Noël's plays, he accepted Noël's invitation to write a preface in which he
said:

> For us English dramatists the young generation has assumed the brisk but
> determined form of Mr. Noël Coward. He knocked at the door with impa-
> tient knuckles, and then he rattled the handle, and then he burst in. After a
> moment's stupor the older playwrights welcomed him affably enough and
> retired with what dignity they could muster to the shelf which with a
> spritely gesture he indicated to them as their proper place . . . and, since
> there is no one now writing who has more obviously a gift for the theatre
> than Mr. Noël Coward, nor more influence with young writers, it is proba-
> bly his inclination and practice that will be responsible for the manner in
> which plays will be written during the next thirty years.

As the years went by Maugham became increasingly disenchanted with the medium and his own ability to contribute to it further. In 1933 he showed the script of what turned out to be his last play, *Sheppey,* to Noël, who made a number of suggestions.

Maugham replied:

> Ormonde House
> St. James's Street
> S.W.1.
> Friday

Noël my pet,

Thank you for your nice wire. I hope you will enjoy the play . . . You will notice that I took a good deal of your advice, but left some of the things you objected to. Either because I thought they sounded all right or else because the cast implored me not to make the suggested changes. This I tell you because I know it is exasperating to have one's advice asked and not taken.

> Bless you
> Willie.

After the opening night Noël wrote Maugham a polite but critical letter:

> Goldenhurst Farm
> Friday

Dearest Willie,

Well, I went to the play and I really am thankful that I read it beforehand because it seemed quite a different shape. I thought Angela Baddely [*sic*], Cicely Oates, the *manicuriste* and the little sneak-thief excellent and authentic but I thought most of the others false and theatrical. [Ralph] Richardson, I think, has a quality but it didn't seem the right one for Sheppey. I almost bowed in acknowledgment when he occasionally condescended to drop an aitch just to show he was of humblish origin. Up against the brilliantly sustained cockney of Oates and Baddely, his ringing, beautifully modulated voice was so dreadfully incongruous that it sent me off into a great Shakespearean rage!

I would like permanently to draw a veil over Laura Cowie but I fear no veil would be thick enough to cover such vintage theatricalism. Oh Willie, Willie, how very naughty of you to write a play filled with subtle implications and exquisite satire and then cheerfully allow dull witted lunatics to cast it!

I wouldn't be so violent about it except that I really do mind.

I thought the production adequate and the lighting appalling.

Do forgive me, Willie dear, for being so beastly but I do love your work so much better than anyone else's and please, please, if you *do* write another play, let me see it early and cast it for you!

All my love,
NOËL

To which Maugham replied:

Ormonde House
St. James's Street
S.W.I.
September 25th

Noël my pet,

I am sorry you were disappointed in the performance of *Sheppey*. I was a little, but I do not really care. I sat in my box at the first night feeling like a disembodied spirit. I have done with playwriting. I know now that I made a mistake in writing plays and then washing my hands of them. But it is too late to regret that I did not do something that I disliked and probably should not have done any better than the people in whose hands I left it. I cannot tell you how I loathe the theatre. It is all very well for you, you are author, actor and producer. What you give an audience is all your own; the rest of us have to content ourselves with at the best an approximation of what we see in the mind's eye. After one has got over the glamour of the stage and the excitement, I do not myself think the theatre has much to offer the writer compared with the other mediums in which he has complete independence and need consider no one.

Bless you, Willie

Maugham, nonetheless, continued to be a role model for Noël, both as a writer and as a man. In *Point Valaine* (1935) Noël creates in the character of the writer Mortimer Quinn, a hybrid version of himself and Maugham, with a romantically exaggerated philosophy of life: "I always affect to despise human nature. My role in life is so clearly marked: cynical, detached, unscrupulous, an ironic observer and recorder of other people's passions. It is a nice façade to sit behind, but a trifle bleak."

Noël and Maugham's intermittent friendship continued after the war. Maugham was every bit as playful as Noël when it came to signing his letters. It was invariably "Uncle William" or "Willie," but on one occasion he felt the need to explain: "When I was in the show business I used to call myself 'Somerset', but now that I have retired . . . I've dropped it because I can't abide swank and besides I don't need it."

In 1945 Maugham saw Noël's revue *Sigh No More* and was amused by the character called "Willy" in a song of that name who is tugged between good angels and bad:

> *Willy—Willy—Willy*
> *Don't waste your time with wrongs and rights,*
> *There can be more exciting lights,*
> *Stroll down Piccadilly,*
> *Never mind, never mind what they say,*
> *Gather rosebuds while you may,*
> *What are you afraid of,*
> *Purity can be overdone,*
> *Learn to be gay and have some fun,*
> *That's what boys are made for.*
> *There's no future in "Good", my lad*
> *So try, oh try to be bad.*

From his temporary home in Hollywood Maugham wrote: "I hope your review [revue] will be a huge success. It's no good your saying your Willie is not a portrait of me. I had long fair curls and a black belted suit. Since he is the hero, though I won't bring an action, I shall be terribly affronted. I insist on his getting the girl in the end."

At the time, Maugham, like Noël, was still in exile from his home, because of the war. The army had requisitioned Goldenhurst in Noël's case, but Maugham had an even sadder story regarding his Villa Mauresque, in Cap Ferrat:

> I shall not return to me native shores till early next year, partly because I have nowhere to go in England and partly because I can't get a visa to go to France and, even if I could, there would be no object in it, since for the moment neither labour nor materials are obtainable.
>
> The Italians occupied the villa and took my cars, the Germans occupied it next, took the yacht, emptied the wine cellar and mined the property; and then the British fleet shelled the house!

Another area in which friendly competition continued to take place between the two men was in the writing of short stories. For all his skill as a playwright and novelist, it was and is generally conceded that Maugham was the master of this particularly subtle literary form—the British

O. Henry. Noël, too, turned his hand to it. He sent Maugham his 1939 collection *To Step Aside.*

> Villa Mauresque
> Cap Ferrat
> Alpes Maritimes
> Aug. 20.

My dear Noël,

I have just finished *To Set* {*sic*} *Aside* and should like to tell you how much I enjoyed it. The Wooden Madonna is a story after my own heart, and What Mad Pursuit is perfect. It is a grand companion piece to *Hands Across the Sea.* But I'm sorry you have wasted Aunt Tittie on a short story; you had material there for a great picaresque novel . . . and it is a shame to have squandered thus such a wealth of splendid stuff. Heaven knows, I'm all for concision but there you had a subject that screamed to be treated on the grand scale.

> Willie

Whatever his flaws as a human being, both early and late, Maugham was never less than generous with his experience and advice and he continued to be Noël's first port of literary call for many years.

But perhaps his most moving communication to Noël was the letter he wrote recalling the death of his longtime companion, Gerald Haxton (1892–1944):

> Parkers Ferry
> Yemasee
> South Carolina
> February 13th 1945

My dear Noël,

I have been meaning for a long time to answer your very kind letter, but I have put it off and put it off. Since Gerald died I have been very far from well. You see, for six months I had seen him nearly every day and was anxious and worried all the time, even when I was not with him he was in my thoughts, so that after his death I broke down from the nervous strain. It is three months since he died now and I cannot get used to it. I try to forget and a dozen times a day something I come across, something I read, a stray word reminds me of him and I am overcome with my first grief.

They tell me time will help, but time flows dreadfully slowly. For thirty years he has been my pleasure and my anxiety and without him I am lost and lonely and hopeless. He was nearly twenty years younger than I and I had every right to think that he would have long survived me. He would have been terribly upset at my death, but he would have got drunk for a week or two and then reconciled himself to it, for he had a naturally happy temper but I am too old to endure so much grief. I have lived too long.

> Yours affectionately,
> WILLIE

And Maugham was to live another twenty years.

•

NOËL MET EDNA FERBER (1887–1968), a regular at the Algonquin Round Table, during his visits to New York in the early 1920s. There was the predictable initial verbal sparring, but soon they were fast friends, and she confessed that she "deeply adored" him.

The thing that drew them together initially was a shared passion for the theater. Most of the many letters they exchanged over the years were devoted to who was writing or acting in what and how well or badly they were doing it. In a typical letter to Noël, Ferber wrote:

> . . . My feeling about the theatre is so strong I am so exhilarated when I am working in it at one moment and so despondent the next that I think I act without caution, like a person in love . . . I have, I suppose, lived the life of a stage-struck Jewish nun: working very hard, occasionally running around doing good deeds. Footloose but the hands tied to the typewriter for hours daily . . .

Noël wrote back: "Dear Blighted Bernhardt . . ."

There were times when each needed to keep up the other's morale. After almost half a century of what we would now call "blockbuster" novels such as *So Big* (1924), *Show Boat* (1926), *Cimarron* (1929), *Giant* (1952), and *Ice Palace* (1958), and hit play collaborations such as *The Royal Family* (1927) and *Dinner at Eight* (1932), Ferber published her second volume of autobiography, *A Kind of Magic* (1963). In general the reviews were lukewarm, the reviewers having decided the Ferber moment was past.

Noël rallied to her support, writing:

> Darling Ferber:
> It was YOU who said that it was repetitious here and there. Well, perhaps it is, for the layman, but for a fellow writer NO. All the pains and pangs and *sturms* and *drangs,* so eloquently and vividly described, merely made me go on nodding my head like an old Buddha in a state of masochistic euphoria. That awful writer's con-

science. That ghastly and rewarding self-discipline that civilians have no idea of. Oh dear. Oh dear. I hope that every conceited amateur that lives in this great big world reads your book and has a nice quiet think and goes out to have his or her hair done.

You also said with beguiling modesty, that there were some good things in it. This, dear, was a coy understatement. There are far more than SOME good things in it. There is, for instance, the chapter on Israel: the savage accurate and loving description of New York. The bit about noise emerging incessantly from the Chatterbox and, above all, the last chapter which I suppose is the most brilliant descriptive writing you have ever done. As I said on the telephone, your use of English is, to me, endlessly satisfying. No one, in my experience, has ever equaled you in your sentimental *Un*sentimental, shrewd, affectionate, astringent, deeply understanding appraisal of your own country. (You're not the only one who likes adjectives). Nobody but you also, who I have always suspected of having a secretly baleful disposition, would have sent such a book to a poor struggling composer-lyricist on the eve of a major production [*The Girl Who Came to Supper*]. For the last three days I have been sitting in a rococo ballroom at the Bradford Hotel spearing wrong notes out of a heavy and complicated score only to return to my bedroom and be compelled to go on reading about all YOUR troubles. Not only that, I have regularly wakened at about three in the morning, eaten some chocolate (My old energy trick) and read just one more chapter. I have now, at last, finished the book. Exactly ten minutes ago and what the hell am I to do when I come home tonight? I shall buy *Life* magazine, that's what I shall do.

I must add obsequiously and slavishly that without *A Kind of Magic* this particular week might have been insupportable. So there.

I will enlarge upon all this when next I see you, which I hope will be here.

Thank you, darling Ferb, very very much indeed.

Noël Coward

Although Ferber's novels were not to Noël's personal taste, he admired them for their professionalism. When she published her novel about Alaska, *Ice Palace*, in 1958, he wrote:

Darling Ferber
I know you endured blood and sweat and tears and knocked yourself out and that we didn't see nearly as much of each other as we should have done while I was in New York. However having just finished *Ice Palace* I can only say that it was all worth it.

I was held by it from beginning to end and nobody, nobody but you could have dreamed up a Floosie called Butterfly Magrue.

The fabulous vitality of your writing is entirely undiminished and your trained observant eye misses nothing. I never thought that I should want to go to Alaska but now I do. Bridie is enchanting, both the Grandfathers utterly real and uncompromising, Christine, of course, a darling. The love story is handled with such sureness and delicacy and the devotion of those people to their own territory is moving and completely convincing.

I tremble to think what an enormous amount of research you had to do to absorb all that detail and I am lost in admiration because not once, with all the detail, does the story and the narrative quality falter. There is no dullness anywhere in the whole long book; it moves along with speed and your particular brand of urgency from the first page to the last.

I really do congratulate you, darling and thank you for such a satisfying and stimulating treat.

And years later, when he had lost track of her whereabouts: "How are you, my old duck? My voices tell me you are up to something. Your disappearances usually mean that some state of the Union is going to get it in the kisser."

•

CERTAINLY THE EXPERIENCE Noël enjoyed at the hands of his elders—and occasionally betters—encouraged him to offer comparable advice to aspiring younger writers as his own years went by. Sometimes the advice was warmly welcomed but there was a particular occasion when it most decidedly was not.

For some years after the war Noël had been concerned at the way he saw British theater going—aggravated, no doubt, by the fact that it was certainly not going his way.

The advent of John Osborne (1929–1994) and his *Look Back in Anger* (1956) seemed to crystallize a gritty, disaffected working-class attitude in contemporary playwriting that Noël found both self-satisfied and displeasing. "I wish I knew," he wrote in his *Diaries* (February 1957), "why the hero is so dreadfully cross and about what? . . . I expect my bewilderment is because I am very old indeed and cannot understand why the younger generation, instead of knocking at the door, should bash the fuck out of it." Later (May 5, 1959) he would conclude, "Destructive vituperation is too easy."

Having been exposed to a great deal more of the same, he developed the theme in a 1961 series of articles for the *Sunday Times*. This was typical:

> The theatre must be treated with respect. It is a house of strange enchantments, a temple of dreams. What it most emphatically is not and never will be is a scruffy, illiterate drill-hall serving as a temporary soap-box for propaganda.

> I am quite prepared to admit that during my fifty-odd years of theatre-going, I have on many occasions been profoundly moved by plays about the Common Man, as in my fifty-odd years of restaurant-going I have enjoyed tripe and onions, but I am not prepared to admit that an exclusive diet of either would be completely satisfying.
>
> It is dull to write incessantly about tramps and prostitutes as it is to write incessantly about dukes and duchesses and even suburban maters and paters, and it is bigoted and stupid to believe that tramps and prostitutes and under-privileged housewives frying onions and using ironing boards are automatically the salt of the earth and that nobody else is worth bothering about.

He might have remembered another quotation: "The public are asking for filth . . . the younger generation are knocking at the door of the dustbin . . . if life is worse than the stage, should the stage hold up the mirror to such distorted nature?" It was actor-manager Sir Gerald du Maurier fulminating against Noël's *own* "younger generation" in general and Noël's *The Vortex* in particular!

Not surprisingly, Noël's articles stirred up considerable controversy in the theatrical community. Naturally the "Kitchen Sink" exponents were outraged, particularly as the advice was coming from this figure from the past, as they saw him.

Critic Kenneth Tynan (1927–1980) of the *Sunday Times*'s chief competitor, *The Observer,* and personally committed as the chief protagonist of the "new" drama, snarled, "The bridge of a sinking ship, one feels, is scarcely the ideal place . . . to deliver a lecture on the technique of keeping afloat."

(Noël was to have his revenge on Tynan years later when the gamekeeper turned poacher by putting on the nude revue *Oh! Calcutta!* Leaving after the first act, Noël remarked, "I've seen quite a number of naked people and I don't think it's all that exciting.")

Tynan was not alone in consigning Noël to theatrical irrelevance at this time—as Noël realized all too well, without ever accepting the verdict. In 1964 he is writing to Adrianne Allen's husband, Bill Whitney:

> My professional demise has been predicted gleefully for years now by the same types who blame the Queen Mother for their own dreary

lives and meagre talents, and who flock to see the soggy, turgid maunderings of left-wing, often carbuncular drones about whom even Ken Tynan has begun to say "Enough" and "Whither?"

If they only had good hearts and some humour I might more easily lend an ear, but any intercourse with them leaves me bored and inordinately depressed.

·

IT WAS 1966 before fences began to be mended. First John Osborne wrote to congratulate Noël on *Suite in Three Keys,* his return to the London stage as author and actor:

May 24th 1966

Dear Noël Coward,
First things, in their way, first: it is such a pleasure for me that you are back in London. Not only with your own work but appearing in it—as you should. You should be here always. I do hope you won't stay away too long.

Now: I would like to ask a favour of you. Could you, in future, stop assessing your fellow writers to newspaper reporters? Clearly it gives them pleasure but you scarcely need their approval. I have always had the profoundest respect for you, both for what you do and as a unique and moving figure on our landscape. You are a genius. However, I think it is impertinent to pass judgement on other writers in this lordly way to gaggles of sniggering journalists. It is undignified, unkind and unnecessary. I don't need lessons in playwriting from you. The skin you inhabit is not mine. I do perfectly well and I think I manage—quite successfully—to do something no one else can. As you do. That in itself deserves the respect of reticence. In spite of your genius, your opinions on writers are mostly—not always—execrable. You admire those mincing middlebrow hounds because they offer no threats. So be it. But please say no more. I did it myself about ten years ago. About yourself, I seem to remember. I have always regretted it. You may find it hard to believe, but there is more goodwill and kindliness here for you to draw on than you might expect to find . . .

Believe me, with respect and admiration always,
Yours sincerely,
JOHN OSBORNE

Noël replied the very next day:

Noël admired Arnold Wesker's writing—if not his political
views. "Your first allegiance should be to your own rich talent
and you should go on using it . . . instead of wasting it trying
to bring culture to people who neither need it nor want it."

37 Chesham Place
S.W.1.
Wed. 25th May '66

Dear John,
I really am very grateful for your letter. It gave me a sharp and much
deserved jolt. I absolutely agree that it is unnecessary and unkind to
hand out my opinions of my colleagues to journalists. It is also
pompous. I know by the grace and firmness of your letter that you
will forgive me if I have inadvertently hurt you or even irritated you.
I think far too highly of you to wish to do either of these things. I
regret very much that since we first met years ago we have known
each other so little. This at least can be remedied if you are willing.
There is so much that I would like to talk to you about, even if our
views on plays and playwrights may differ. Please come to lunch with
me here either on Monday, Tuesday or Friday of next week or the
Monday, Tuesday or Friday of the following week. You see I am pinning you down ruthlessly for the simple reason that I would truly
like to see you. Please come. I shall not ask anyone else.
    What you said in your letter about admiration and respect is
entirely mutual . . .
          Noël

From then on the two men became friends. Osborne went on to say:
"Mr. Coward, like Miss Dietrich, is his own invention and contribution

to this century. Anyone who cannot see that should keep well away from the theatre. To be your own enduring invention seems to me to be heroic and essential. Even if you can begin to make it, it seems increasingly impossible."

•

A WRITER WHO actually did more than Osborne to define the Kitchen Sink school was Arnold Wesker. Instead of being someone from the middle class writing "down" about the "workers," Wesker was the genuine working-class article and took himself very seriously—as did some of the critics in search of new heroes.

Noël found it absurd to see Wesker compared with the likes of Tolstoy and Dickens, "when he really happens to be an over-earnest little creature obsessed by the wicked capitalists and the wrongs of the world." But clearly Noël's *Sunday Times* strictures caught Wesker's eye, and in January 1962 he rang Noël up in Switzerland and asked if he could come over. Intrigued, Noël promptly agreed.

Wesker's mission, it transpired, was to raise funds for Centre 42, a project to bring culture to the masses. Noël would have none of it, but the subsequent discussion on the nature and purpose of theater—particularly Wesker's—proved stimulating.

39 Gloucester Drive
London N.4.
January 10th 1962

Dear Noël,

I regret only one thing—that I hesitated when you asked me whether I loved my wife. To have hesitated was to betray our relationship—it was an unfair question. Otherwise my 36 hour pass was a dream, excepting the drive down to the station of Montreux—that was a nightmare. Thank you for your graciousness and hospitality.

To pursue our discussion another stage—I still don't believe you and your scepticism. God knows what happened to you in early life, but you must have landed yourself among people who (sweetly) ridiculed your earnestness, and you must have vowed pretty violently never to let yourself be vulnerable again. I do not know you well, but no real human being can be cynical without holding a profound belief in something, some values. This is all that cynicism is: damaged belief; real cynicism, that is—the rest is flippancy, passingly amusing, but nothing of account. I do not know you well, but yours must be real cynicism—it stayed with me all the way home. You are the sweetest reactionary I know.

Here is *The Kitchen.* I send it to your irreverence and as a small token of my regard and thanks.

Till I hear from you
ARNOLD

Les Avants
16.1.62

No, dear Arnold, it was not an unfair question, it might be considered impertinent perhaps, but really it was prompted by nothing more than an affectionate desire to find out as much as possible about a new friend in the very short time at our disposal. Don't reproach yourself, there was no disloyalty.

Since you left I discovered the Trilogy right under my nose in my work-room. I read it straight through with care. *Roots* is the most successful *technically* and *Jerusalem,* to me, the most moving. I find *Chicken Soup* too over-loaded with dear old Lavender-and-Old Lace-Left Wing propaganda. Sarah, of course, is fine and remains consistent throughout . . .

Now, of course, I have read *The Kitchen,* which is tremendously dramatic and bloody good theatre. I wish I had seen it. It's difficult to get its full impact from reading, which is after all just as it should be.

I have got to talk to you more . . . You *have* been victimized by those foolish men, but your talent is too rich to be lastingly affected either by over-praise or over-blame. Please, dear Arnold, don't *grumble* so much in your heart about political and Governmental injustices and stupidities. You can't change human nature. All you can do with your gifts is observe and comment with compassion and humour *and* as theatrically effectively as possible, so long as you continue to write plays.

And *please* remember that "Failure" unless written with pure genius, is rarely entertaining. I have deep sympathy for Beattie, whom I feel will eventually succeed with her own life. I have none for Dave, who is conceited, stubborn, woolly-minded and basically incompetent. I *love* Sarah who succeeds triumphantly as a human being. It seems to me that the women in the Trilogy are conceived with more depth and understanding than the men. *The Kitchen* from this point of view is a great step forward.

And now you are going to waste an enormous amount of your energy and creative talent in coping with mediocre little Bureaucrats and organizing a "Cultural Revolution"! *Do* me a favour! Leave those cheerful old girls to enjoy their Bingo. Let the great majority enjoy itself in its own way. Don't try to force them to stare at Henry Moore nudes with holes in their middles and sit on pre-fabricated mobile benches to see inevitably dodgy performances of plays in the Round. They won't go anyway. It will all turn out to be, as our mutual colleague Shakespeare said, "An expense of spirit and a waste of shame". Nor will it avail the world situation one iota for you and [playwright] Robert Bolt to spend occasional weeks in the clink in protest against humanity's yearning for self-destruction. To Hell with Centre 42! Those among the great masses who really want and need culture will manage to get it anyhow. Those who don't, won't. If this is cynicism then I am a dyed-in-the-wool old Cynic, but it just *may* be common sense. One thing is clear to me however and that is that you are a strange, vulnerable and wonderfully gifted creature. Your first allegiance is not to Humanity or Political dogmas, or world reform, but to your talent which, incidentally, you are bloody lucky to have.

When you had left the house I had pangs of guilt for having been so unresponsive to your project, but they have since died away. I am unregenerate: still hopeful and eager to contribute to the world's entertainment and transient enjoyment, but *only after* I have contributed to my own integrity. I will enlarge on this jolly little theme when we meet again and I defy you to shout me down. In the meantime I wish you success and happiness in *whatever* you do, even if it is only organizing Maypole dances in South Shields.

*Never* wear your wife's sweater again, it is *not* becoming.

Yours in Science,
NOËL

Wesker observed forty years later that Noël:

didn't always get it right. The sweater he referred to had been bought a few weeks earlier at Simpsons on Piccadilly in the department of "unisex clothes" that were just coming into fashion . . . And he didn't like *Chicken Soup with Barley* because he didn't know anything about politically quarrelling East End Jews. It read like "propaganda" to him. He might have understood more if he had seen it acted. Or just met my family!!

But Wesker did not give up so easily. On July 21 he is sending Noël a copy of his play *Chips with Everything* on Centre 42 stationery and adding a P.S.: "We are eight weeks away from our festivals, money is coming in very slowly. There is great enthusiasm, a lot of hard work from a lot of talented people, but no lucre. Are you sure you won't change your mind and help us?"

LES AVANTS
sur MONTREUX
29th July 1962

Dear Arnold,

It was sweet of you to remember to send me the play and I can't wait to read it, nor, for the matter of that, to see it again. I had a sweet telegram from your Company which pleased and touched me enormously.

I can't, or rather, *won't* help you over "Centre 42", because I really do disapprove of the whole idea. You mustn't be cross with me about this but I can't bear to think of all those talented people you mention, and you most particularly, pursuing with such ardour, a goal that I really cannot feel you will achieve successfully. As I said before, I think that your first allegiance should be to your own rich talent and that you should go on using it and enlarging it instead of wasting valuable time trying to bring art and culture to a great number of people who neither need it nor want it. After seeing *Chips* I feel more strongly about this than ever.

I *know* you have a heart that is both loving and idealistic, but you have also a great gift that should not be jettisoned for any cause however worthy. Much more has been achieved in the world by private and personal talent than by public and impersonal good works.

As well as admiration I have a great deal of affection for you and as you *know* I deplore this tiresome bee in your bonnet you can't blame me for not encouraging it to buzz!

Forgive me for my unregenerate cynicism (!) and thank you again for the play.

Love,
Noël

Friends of Centre 42
20 Fitzroy Square
London W.1.
August 4th 1962

My dear Noël,

I do not see the difference between a poster in Shaftesbury Avenue advertising a Noël Coward play to the "masses" and the poster which I now enclose (for your delight). The real difference, of course, is that the Coward play is advertised within the commercial set-up—which puts it beyond suspicion; whereas our festivals are not commercially funded—which makes us appear presumptious [*sic*]. But on the contrary it is Coward, Wesker, Osborne and the others who are presumptious—the public do not ask for their work in the beginning, whereas the trades councils have asked for us to put on a festival. *We* are being *requested.*

I don't mind your cynicism—what I do mind is that—though you cannot understand my revolution, yet you will not bless it and help it as the work of a new generation, just as your early plays were their own sort of revolution and needed to be blessed in their day.

Give us a trial, allow us to fail, permit us the chance to discover for ourselves our own mistakes—I think this is a right, surely? . . . We are not arty, we are not bumptious, we have no arrogance—we are artists taking art a step further.

Stay well for a long time
Love
ARNOLD

Les Avants
sur Montreux
September 5th 1962

My dear Arnold,
Once and for all you really must stop calling me "cynical" just because I have told you quite honestly that I do not approve of the aims and objects of "Centre 42". According to the dictionary a cynic is (1) a member of a school of Greek philosophers who taught that the essence of virtue was self-control and later came to be regarded as representing a gloomy revolt against current philosophy and social customs. (2) A captious, sneering, fault-finding person, especially one who attributes human conduct to low motives of self-interest. Frankly I do not feel that I could be described accurately as either of these. I have never for an instant thought that your enthusiasm for your project was in any way dictated by self-interest. On the contrary, as far as your brilliant talent is concerned, it seems to be dictated by a curious urge of self-destruction. In my opinion, which God knows is far from infallible, your expenditure of personal energy and time upon this immense scheme is wasting very possibly something of infinite greater value, which is your gift for writing and developing as a dramatist.

I, who have earned my living all my life by my creative talents, cannot ever agree with your rather high-flown contempt for "commercial art". In my experience, which is not inconsiderable, the ordinary run of human beings, regardless of social distinctions, infinitely prefer paying for their amusements and entertainments than having them handed out to them for nothing, or comparatively nothing. There is nothing disgraceful or contemptible in writing a successful play which a vast number of people are eager and willing to buy tickets for. You yourself should be the first to appreciate this having written a deservedly smash success. On the other hand I consider that the forming of committees to decide what sort of art and entertainment the masses should properly enjoy, is not only presumptious [*sic*] but fairly silly. I cannot for the life of me see why a hard-working provincial housewife who has spent a whole week doing her job and earning her living should not, on a Saturday and Sunday play Bingo or go to a bad movie or enjoy herself in any way she sees fit. There is after all no guarantee that your avant-garde painters and sculptors and musicians and playwrights are so tremendously necessary to culture as they naturally think they are. None of them, has as yet, stood the test of time. Personally I would rather play Bingo every night for a year than pay a return visit to *Waiting for Godot*. This of course is a personal view, but then average English men and women also have personal views and one of their most personal personal views is an inherent dislike of being bored stiff. This is not to say that I think *all* your cultural activities will inevitably bore the public, but, judging by the purple and black brochure you sent me, quite a number of them are bound to.

You mustn't be cross with me for holding these very definite views because, if you analyse them, you may find that they are based on common sense rather than cynicism. As I have told you from the first, I do not approve of your so-called cultural revolution or Centre 42 or anything to do with it. I am perfectly prepared to admit that I may be dead wrong over all this and if the future proves me to be so I shall be entirely delighted for your sake, because I am very fond of you and admire and respect your sincerity. In the meantime be a dear and stop bullying me.

Yours with wicked, cynical love,
NOËL

In June 1966 he was able to make partial amends by spending "four hours at the Old Vic in wig, eyebrows and moustache, waiting to say my five lines in Wesker's *The Kitchen*—in a memorial performance to actor/director George Devine."

•

THE OTHER CONTEMPORARY writer to whom Noël became a dedicated convert was Harold Pinter (b. 1930). To begin with he could see absolutely no merit there. This was the "surrealist school of non-playwriting." But then when he saw *The Caretaker* in May 1960, "I think I'm on to Pinter's wavelength. He is at least a genuine original." The play was "on the face of it . . . everything I hate in the theatre—squalor, repetition, lack of action, etc., but somehow it seizes hold of you."

Two years later Caretaker Films was formed—a group that included Alan Bates, Lord Birkett, Clive Donner, Pinter, Donald Pleasance, and Robert Shaw. Pinter wrote to Noël (among others):

> Fairmead Court
> Taylor Avenue
> Kew, Surrey
> 29.11.62

Dear Noël Coward,
We intend to make this film!
It would be wonderful if you could help.
Yours sincerely,
HAROLD PINTER

Noël did help, to the tune of a thousand pounds in a budget of thirty thousand. When the Hollywood backers pulled out ten days before shooting was due to begin, Birkett recalls that they had to "find 'angels', just like a West End stage show." His roll call of "angels" was an impressive one: Peter Hall (a founder of the Royal Shakespeare Company), his then wife Leslie Caron, producer Harry Salzman, Peter Sellers, Elizabeth Taylor, and Richard Burton among them. Pinter wrote again, his letters as spare as his dialogue:

> December 15th 1962

Dear Noël Coward,
I can't tell you how delighted I am at your help with *The Caretaker*!
Thank you.
We are very busy shooting. Most exciting.
Everyone sends their love and appreciation.
Why don't you come down to Hackney one day?
Warm wishes.
HAROLD PINTER

Lord Birkett, the play's producer, continues the story in a letter to the editor:

Peter Cadbury (another investor) brought Noël down to the dismal Hackney house where we were shooting. Noël stayed for two days, came to rushes in Soho with us in the evening, and finally said he had to go back home to Switzerland in the morning, but would I please send him news from time to time of how the film was going. "I'll send you lots of postcards," I said, "but what's your address in Switzerland?" Noël said, "Oh, just write 'Noël Coward, Switzerland'."

In 1965 Noël was equally impressed with Pinter's *The Homecoming* and concluded that Pinter was "a sort of cockney Ivy Compton-Burnett."

Flat 4
5 Queen's Gate Place
London S.W.7.
August 6th, 1965

Dear Noël,

. . . I can't tell you how much it means to me that you felt about the play as you did. I am so pleased.

I would love to talk to you. Perhaps one day I shall descend by parachute on to your mountain stronghold. But on the other hand, when you're next in London, please ring me, will you? And we can meet. You appear into London so swiftly and mysteriously, that there's no way of knowing that you're here.

By the way I haven't been able to write to you before this as I was in Venice all last week. I've decided now, quite conclusively, that I detest beaches, sun lotions, heat and mosquitos.

I enclose a copy of the play with all my love.

And again, many many thanks.

Yours
HAROLD

Les Avants sur Montreux
August 21st 1965

Dear Harold,

I have just read *The Homecoming* twice through. I had thought that perhaps the impeccable acting and direction might have clouded my judgement of the play itself. But I was *dead wrong*. It reads as well if not better than it plays. Your writing absolutely fascinates me. It is entirely unlike anyone else's. You cheerfully break every rule of the theatre that I was brought up to believe in, except the cardinal one of never boring for a split-second. I love your choice of words, your resolute refusal to *explain* anything and the arrogant, but triumphant demands you make on the audience's imagination. I can well see why some clots hate it, but I belong to the opposite camp—if you will forgive the expression.

Why don't you fly out here for a night or two in September? I long to talk to you. I'm going to the South of France this minute until next Wednesday . . . Please call me. I have just written *three* new plays. One long and two short, so sucks to you! I am going to grace the London stage in all three of them next March!

My love to Vivien and to you.

NOËL

In the years that followed more and more commentators came to understand the unlikely professional rapport between the two writers. The clue lay in two separate Coward lines: "Suggestion is always more interesting than statement."

And the speech in *Shadow Play* in which he has Gertrude Lawrence say, "Small talk, a lot of small talk with other thoughts going on behind."

Today a young playwright would consider it an accolade to be dubbed "Pinteresque." But Pinter could equally well be called "Cowardesque."

•

NOËL'S CONNECTIONS weren't limited to English playwrights, although he was not greatly enamored by the postwar generation of Americans, finding them too concerned with the "significance" of their work.

This disenchantment had begun with Eugene O'Neill back in the 1920s, when Noël had been coerced into sitting through—*twice!*—the whole seven acts of *Strange Interlude,* which his beloved Lynn Fontanne happened to be starring in. Noël tended to echo Alfred Lunt's verdict: "If it had had two more acts I could have sued her for desertion."

Arthur Miller (1915–2005) seemed to Noël to follow the same portentous tradition, even though he liked the man perfectly well. When told by an overexuberant playgoer that *Death of a Salesman* was not a play but an "experience," Noël murmured that he rather wished it had been a *play.*

However, in the mid-1960s Noël did establish a dialogue of sorts with the rising Edward Albee (b. 1928), whose play *Who's Afraid of Virginia Woolf?* (1962) had brought him critical acclaim.

In 1963 Noël met Albee for the first time—"Very intelligent but badly tainted with avant-garde, Beckett, etc." In 1965, on his way to Jamaica, Noël passed through New York and saw *Tiny Alice,* "altogether a maddening evening in the theatre, so nearly good and yet so bloody pretentious." He found himself "as bewildered as everyone else including the cast" and John Gielgud, "who was strained and unconvincing." Noël expressed his views to Albee, who was "very amiable about it" and later sent Noël a copy of the text.

BLUE HARBOUR
PORT MARIA
JAMAICA, WEST INDIES
18th February 1965

My dear Edward,

I have read *Tiny Alice* with the utmost concentration and considerable enjoyment. Your sense of Theatre is superb and your writing brilliant. You were right, I did get more of it from the printed page but not enough to clear up my confusion. I know now, or I think I know, what's happening but what I don't know is what *you* think is happening. Your basic premise still eludes me. I can fetch up several suitable—agreeably suitable—labels, "Destruction of Innocence", "Black Over White", "The Evil in Good", "The Good in Evil", etc., all facile and unsatisfactory. Your character drawing of Butler, the lawyer and the Cardinal clear and believable. Alice and Julien not only unbelievable but, to me, cracking bores. He seems to be a sex-obsessed prig and she an over-articulate shadow. Your other dimension is too vague for me to visualize. Perhaps my stubborn sanity clips my wings. Sex obsession and religious ecstasy, I agree, are on the same plane but it is not a plane on which I can move with much tolerance. I have enjoyed sex thoroughly, perhaps even excessively all my life but it has never, except for brief wasteful moments, twisted my reason. I suspect that my sense of humour is as stubborn as my sanity, perhaps they're the same thing. Your seduction scene neither moved, shocked or appalled me, it made me want to laugh. You must forgive me for saying these things. I have a profound respect for your rich talent and a strong affection for you, although I only know you a little. Expert use of language is to me a perpetual joy. You use it expertly all right but, I fear, too self-indulgently. Your duty to me as a playgoer and a reader is to explain whatever truths you are dealing with lucidly and accurately. I refuse to be fobbed off with a sort of metaphysical *What's My Line*!

Let me hear from you. Just an ordinary love letter will do.

NOËL

Apparently undeterred and unoffended, Albee and several colleagues proposed to stage a Coward repertory season in the fall of the following year—though for one reason or another, it never came to pass.

·

NOËL'S NATURAL EQUILIBRIUM was always to be found on the English stage, and he kept in touch with those who made an impact on it over the years.

Among those was Margaret Kennedy (1896–1967)—in whose 1926 *The Constant Nymph* he had briefly and uncomfortably starred. After the *Sunday Times* articles she wrote to him:

180 Oakwood Court
London W.14
January 15th 1961

My dear Noël,

I venture to put this point to you: The decline of the Drama is nobody's fault, and neither the dramatist nor the critic can do very much about it. This epoch is extremely unpropitious to all the arts; they are all in the doldrums, and all for the same reason.

Comedy is out. It is essentially good humoured and genial. It needs institutions, social, moral, etc., which are so well established and so much respected that everybody can afford to laugh at them. *On se moque de ce qu'on aime.* Roman Catholics are able to make irreverent jokes which shock Protestants and scandalise atheists.

Tragedy is out. It always implies some recognition of the essential nobility of Man. Man, at the moment, is not inclined to see himself as noble. He has a lot on his conscience and he may shortly be going to wipe himself out with a great big bang—or, as our poets [T. S. Eliot] prefer to believe, "not with a bang but a whimper."

What is left to the dramatist? Either farce, the resource of people who "laugh but smile no more," or some kind of tract—some petulant scrutiny of a mess.

It's not the critic's fault. Critics don't produce artists. Artists produce critics. Both flourish and decline together. Art and criticism have in the past been through these bleak, undernourished periods, though never before . . . in such an atmosphere of "smirking self congratulation".

It's this smug complacency, as though *Angst* were not a regrettable disease but a State of Grace, that can perhaps be attacked. Also the tendency to use "skill" and "entertainment" as terms of derogation. If art is going through a hard time, let's all say so, and keep on keeping on, as best we can, until the times mend.

Yours ever,
MARGARET KENNEDY

Oxford don and historian A. L. Rowse was of a similar mind:

July 18th 1962

We live in a time that is utterly antipathetic to the creative in the arts and . . . for a reason very relevant to the arts—the whole atmosphere of self-conscious, *destructive,* constant niggling critically is frightfully unpropitious psychologically to creation. If *they* were really clever they would see the point. The Elizabethan age was quite the other way: hardly any criticism, and a really clever man like Shakespeare—a damn sight cleverer, really, than any of the critical intelligences—could go forward naturally to create all the time. It did *not* mean that he was uncritical: far from it (e.g., his remarks on the technique of acting in *Hamlet*), but that he could use his critical faculty to aid his creation, refine the points, clear up the difficulties, resolve the problems.

Now, Criticism is an end in itself. And the whole circumstances of our bloody time and society immensely increase the strangle hold of the middle-men in the arts—newspapers, broadcasts, sessions of *The Critics* to criticize the Critics—and now trebled with TV!

In addition to sensitiveness and perception, our stock-in-trade, we have also today to be bloody-minded. Be Bloody-Minded! (Write a song about bloody-mindedness!)

On top of all the other boredoms, the contemporary tone is so portentous, no sense of humour, otherwise they wouldn't go on as they do. What is there worth reading that comes from them, compared with the 1920s? We had Hardy, Kipling, Shaw, Wells, Yeats still all writing, Lawrence, Virginia Woolf, Eliot, Aldous Huxley—something to excite one every publishing season. What's in a publishing season *today?*

•

WHETHER NOËL FOUND himself dealing with Angry Young Men or Anguished Older Ladies, the common denominator that had to be present was *talent.*

Enid Bagnold (1899–1991) was a writer who had started out as a novelist—*Serena Blandish* (1924) and *National Velvet* (1935)—before deciding to concentrate on writing plays. Her first major success came with the 1956 *The Chalk Garden,* in both London and New York, and she always credited Noël with helping to make it so.

Rottingdean
Sussex
June 10th 1956

My dear Noël,

I just wanted to say how you were the first to put the sword on my shoulder . . . the accolade. Up till that moment I had thought *The Chalk Garden* doomed. We had an awful out of town experience, rumours flying back to New York how bad we were . . . crows set-

Enid Bagnold (1899–1991) to Noël: "I had thought *The Chalk Garden* doomed. Then your voice. 'For those who love words, darling.' . . . it was my Mescaline, my Happiness Pill."

tling on the grave. Then girding oneself for the first night. Then coma. Apathy . . .

Then your voice. "For those who love words, darling . . ." you were saying, "for those who love words . . ." and you turned round and saw me in the gangway and kissed me. It was at the end of the first act. It was the first, first blessing I got and I shall never forget it. It carried with it all the glamour of your reputation, all the light intoxicated airy hopes I had twenty years ago . . . of pulling this off . . . it was my Mescaline, my Happiness Pill . . .

Antoine Bibesco used to say to me "Hurry, hurry! Success is only fun when you are young." In a way he was right. Here am I—the owner of a success. Haymarket full to choking and steady as a rock. Play starting two tours in America . . . and how much does it do for me? I garden, I muse sadly with disbelief. Can I ever do it again? Was it I who did it? I—fat, old and grey . . . True the money comes in, but you know what happens to the money.

I am stunned and used up . . . but perhaps not for ever.

Anyway I send this to you, my deep thanks, with love.

       Yours,

       ENID

In later letters she was not too proud to ask for advice:

29 Hyde Park Gate
S.W.7.
December 26th 1958

. . . I've been battling with another play for the past two and a half years, and it's as unclear and hazy and rambling as ever. I never seem to learn to make a clear statement. When I have a theme—it shines—and I move towards it slowly and I find I am moving into the heart of a dark, dark wood (after a year's work) and then it takes me another year to hack my way out into clarity.

In 1960 her latest play, *The Last Joke,* was dismantled by the London critics. Noël found it "elegant, unreal, impeccably acted [by Gielgud and Sir Ralph Richardson] and, on the whole, enjoyable. First act excellent, but no play really. Some lovely stylized language, lovely set, and good acting, but it really won't do." His own play in that same year, *Waiting in the Wings,* had suffered a similar critical drubbing.

Rottingdean
Sussex
October 3rd 1960

Dearest Noël,

Well, we've both been battered. But you are so full one can't get a seat. I've had a battering filled with hate. Hate because I had too much. Too many Knights, too much "lavish" . . . even married to a knight myself [Sir Roderick Jones] . . . Luckily it was so unanimous and such an onslaught that I couldn't feel a thing. As I told the *News of the World* when they rang up to know what suffering felt like—"If you take too big a dose of calomel it goes right through you . . ."

I always remember your accolade in New York—"For those who love words, darling!" Well, it's words now that they hate most of all. I forgive them hating my lack of clarity. I know that's a grave fault. But they hate and quote the words they hate and they are good ones! . . .

Love,
ENID

Noël took the trouble to write to her with his analysis of what he felt was wrong with her latest play. She replied to thank him for doing so and asked for future guidance.

Rottingdean
Sussex
Friday, Nov. 4, 1960

Dear Noël,

I read your letter which came this morning—with *great* comfort. First—in Switzerland—you are indignant with the critics, *for* me, and say you will see the play when you go to London. Next—you go and see it. Thirdly—you spot the trouble at once. I think it's coming off soon—but it's a real comfort to me that you confirm the worst trouble—the third act. It's *always* been the trouble.

In my daring moment, when I thought I held all power in my hands (i.e., at the conception—and before the play was written) it seemed to me I could pull it off. The third act had to be "out of this world" . . . i.e., halfway to heaven . . . i.e., (as it turned out)—a thing without a backbone . . . moony-mad. I thought I could re-produce, dramatically, that moment—alcohol, mescalin, vision . . . which trembles in me when I see a seagull swoop off a chimney pot and realise momentarily that there are experiences that living people never have.

But how can one do that in a play? In a poem, perhaps. But in a play—which has to go through God knows what and who knows what before it gets upright or even into rehearsal, let alone what it goes through after. I wrote 16 bloody third acts and by that time the quiver had gone out of every word and only the foolishness remained.

I am now going to bore you, perhaps. Don't bother to answer. I'm just thinking aloud. You have written so many plays and have kept them so beautifully in one mood from the beginning to the end, and obviously said what you wanted to say and not made vague hits at an ideal that hasn't come off . . . (you see I am going to ask for advice) . . . how do you manage to *keep a play growing if you have already foreseen the end?* And—if one doesn't foresee the end—then all is a gamble. I foresee something luminous but infinitely hazy, which recedes as I climb towards it. It recedes walking backwards, and often falls over its draperies into a ditch. This is what has happened this time.

Do you get all clear before you start? . . . But oh, I know it's no use asking. Every mind is an island on its own. And mine's a jungle without a clearing—where tropical plants grow—unstaked—throttling each other . . .

There! Don't bother. Nothing can be communicated. One is alone with the Thing.

Now I'm on another and I wake up in the night and say "What's the third act" and have a small nightmare and go to sleep again.

What one needs is to be the Goncourts. It seems to me it is vital to have two people working. But they must be a magic pair. One must be logical, the other not. One must have a million plots: the other only themes. And yet both must come out of the same mould—imagination.

Bless you.

Love,
ENID

Rottingdean
Sussex
November 16, 1960

Dear Noël,

I was electrified yesterday morning. And now I'll make double use of "electrified" (since I've said it) and say you turned a current on over a system. Because that's what it felt like. I've been feeling dead and doubtful and suddenly, from Switzerland, through the post, came the "charge".

So many thoughts evoked at once. To make the shape? Or to travel inside? *That* you dealt with. "Make the shape"—you say, and very firmly. What delights above all that *this* very year you say you've made a hash and had to throw away. *Comforted* isn't the word.

My God, what a job it is to write a play. First there's the theme. (Not so difficult because that's the thing that generally starts one off). Then there's the plot . . . and I see that quickly, too—but only a little way. Then there are the inhabitants. Generally I get one splendid one and forget the others have to stand up to that quality too. Then the beasts won't talk all at once. And yet when I pick up peoples' plays it all seems so straight ahead and easily-developed. I have piles here. Bjornson, Strindberg, Pirandello . . . (Six A's in search of is a pretty bitter one—about the actors, isn't it?)

I'll tell you a terrible dark secret . . . a poison I learnt from Irene S. [Selznick] I admire her so much in many ways, but the more you admire someone who isn't absolutely breathing the same air as you are the worse for you it is. She made me (in *Chalk G.* days) almost unable to write a speech that was longer than two lines. And she hashed them about so that they belonged to anyone and even cut the speeches in half and gave half away across the table. I got them nearly all back in the end, after endless arguments, some tearful and some rude and some almost shouting . . . but it's left me with a terrible doubt about "where do you put the words?" I mean a phrase seems as good here—as there. Once you begin that (coupled with cutting and pasting) and you're in the bag (of doubt).

Yes, I've been buggered about. Charles Laughton, Irene, John G. [Gielgud] . . . Glen [Byam Shaw, the director] . . . You are quite right. I really think a play had better be *wrong* than not out of one mind. And God knows how strange it is what goes home. You can say little odd things, bits of observation, trumpery nothings, and suddenly the stupidest person laughs as well as the most intelligent. The mind seems to be open at odd corners. You never know who will understand what. So it's really safest not to bother but to go on with the stuff one's got—the stuff one can make oneself. And what a box of tricks it is (the mind) and how little one knows how it works. I'm reading your book [*Pomp and Circumstance*] now (at night . . . and at four this morning) and the things that make me laugh are odd juxta-positions of thought . . . something tipped against something . . . like a spoon standing up against a jug. It's got to be done by intu-ition (yours, too, is so done) and that's the horror of play writing— that intuition is so frail, so evanescent, lets one down, and yet is the only thing that counts. Alas, my words never "tumble in". They groan out like old winches, rusty by the sea.

How can you know so much about the way mothers think? All those reflections of the heroine about her children, the rueful sighs . . . and goodness *how well done* the husband-wife relationship. I was reading at four this morning (pills no use) the bit about them both in bed, and Robin catching her ankle just before the maid swam in. The steadfast affection so beautifully under done, so that you trust them both—and trust them to say the riskiest things (that might undo it). The peculiar dry governess character of the heroine . . . (that is her own way of half hiding from me that she is beautiful and not governessy at all, and not dry). I imagine Mrs. What's her name, you only mention her name once and as it was the middle of the night I've forgotten it . . . to be a tremendous charmer. How won-derful to be able to bring that off while "full-facing" the lady. I find it's the people caught sideways who surprise one by growing unseen.

The "women relationships" together are delicious. I haven't got to Eloise's arrival yet. I'm panting for her. There's a rueful woman-pact about the lady and her chosen friends (as against the women-décor-people) which doesn't exclude the men they love. It's marvellously inside a woman's mind. The chores and the oil needed on the seat and the evoked domesticity without cataloguing it and the bits of mo-ments alone and the odd things relished. I adore your book. And, thank God it's nice and long and more nights to come. It's downstairs and I made a note or two of what I specially liked. I'll add it at the end.

Back to plays. I feel a terrible need for *two* people to write a play. It's like a session at Scotland Yard. There are always two men who talk over the crime and one sees holes in the chain of reasoning that the other doesn't.

My trouble is that I have a sort of instinct for dramatic situations but they get left about undeveloped. "More mileage needed", as Irene says. But oh, that isn't the only trouble. How much I need to do what you say and advise. How I'll try. In fact I have (since your letter) decided to abandon the second act of the mountain-of-trouble I'm building and get on and finish the third. I long to bore a clear mind like yours and see if I can get this theme into two lines for you and plot into ten lines . . . here and now. I'd like to bounce my ideas against you—like a ball on a wall. I'm doing it for *me*. You needn't even read. Throw away. But shivering against that critical face on the back of the book (it doesn't look critical there but I know it is) I might really come up with something hard . . . vomit a structure.

Now this is what one can't do in a damn play . . . follow one's twitching nose as you've followed yours, and all the minute seemingly unmentionable-worthy details and things felt to spring up and wave like delicate grasses. Everyone when they read a novel like this waves to the author as they read. Chunnering with murmurs . . . "I know! I *know*" Every page simply drips with things accurately felt and seen. They all live so brilliantly.

You must (or might be) sick of this letter—except in fairness quite a lot's about you!

Love,
ENID

The dialogue continued. In July 1966, Noël was appearing in London in *Suite in Three Keys.* Enid, who had seen it, was staying with the Lunts, who had not, and wrote from there:

TEN CHIMNEYS
GENESEE DEPOT
WISCONSIN
July 14th 1966

Darling Noël,
I've just crept through Jule's "suite" to write to you. It's Thursday, his day off, and he's left the outer door of the little room I write in—locked. It's been 90 [degrees] as you've heard, but this morning it's softly dripping, every tree-branch hanging a little lower because of the water.

I left Lynnie sewing a collar on to a white sharkskin dress (she bought for you and Jamaica but never wore) that she gave me.

If you knew (but I bet you do) how we talk of you. What a factor you are in our everyday life, which is made of plays. Old plays, plays to be, plays I haven't written, plays that you have. A continual preoccupation with that Rock. The Rock I can't climb. I can plant the Alpine flowers on it but that's all. The Rock called How you make the Story. I'm sick of the word Construction. It ceases to mean anything to me. What we want is to hold them "breathless". And the word "Construction" isn't wholly that. It's dear William Archer [a Scottish Victorian theater critic] . . . "forewarning but not foretelling" . . . and the second awful tremendous duty *la scene à faire.*

I discuss that play of yours (*Suite in Three Keys*). They haven't seen it, have they? But they will at Christmas in New York . . . I particularly say how instantly I saw what you meant about "introducing". The swift lines, like a Japanese drawing, indicating the relationships, the "tease" of a relationship all the richer for being momentarily misunderstood.

In the audience one admires backwards as well as forwards . . . You said, I think, at one moment, that audiences are stupider than writers. I don't think they are. It's extraordinary the tiny flashing motes they can perceive. Motes the Management would have thought unseeable. But if the author trusts them, they see it. (How right, in a worldly sense, that I should write a capital M and a small a.)

The fridge is humming. My teeth are comfortably beside me. Jule has lent me his bedside lamp to type by. All, all is before me. I have this gift of words *killing* me—locked in a box with no key.

Alfred said, "How you talk of death!". I said "I don't think of it and except as the Grand National jockey thinks 'Can I make it when I get into the Straight?' " It's not this death I mind. It's not having been acclaimed. You see I *believe* in myself. That is so terrible. I expect when I am writing that there should be an audience who can relish the relish I take in words! But there isn't. Or if there were, there is no management to believe in it. I wish I was 18 and on the stage (for experience) and immensely rich (another twerk, not the same one) so as to have a school of acting all my own. I wish I had been born a damned director, in swaddling clothes, with eyes like footlights and a dry voice of terrible authority. I shall say to God when I jump over the chasm, "You mucked me up!"

Noël, how kind you were. When I said it to Lynnie she said "That is the marvellous thing—among others about Noël—he *wants* to help. He *wants* one to be perfect".

I believe if I wrote a play quite suddenly that had an immense success and ran longer than yours you'd be *delighted* ("Longer than yours" is only a way of speaking).

We have been hanging naked in the pool staring into the golden eyes of toads with throbbing throats that sit along the gutter at the fringe under the grass. Alfred said, "When do you like your drink?" I said "I like to hang alcoholised in the water". And it's true. That strange element, that extraordinary shock all over the flesh and the quick recovery, and the alteration (moonwise) of weight. We had a storm in the middle of the night and the heat, and the thunder leapt into my bedroom like a devil, all among the Mazo de la Roches {a popular woman novelist of the period} and a lot fell out on the sofa.

I'll send this now or I'll be writing myself into corners and byways that will bore you, because not on the central subject. I want to say compactly—*thank you* for that wonderful evening, and to tell you again that the word "Noël" here is all their past, and our present. And the stories Alfred begins to tell (of you) and that Lynn takes from him and finishes.

We send our love
ENID

Noël managed to get through the London run of his trilogy, but impaired health and the telltale first signs of failing memory caused him to cancel his plans to take the show to Broadway that fall.

Enid voiced the general disappointment of the New York theatrical community:

Rottingdean
October 24th 1966

Dearest Noël,
Cathleen Nesbitt has just told me you are ill again and Broadway postponed. I know it will take all the courage and toughness that you have to bear this. I *ache* for you. How kind and dear you've always been to me . . . I know that you will have that marvellous golden successful time on Broadway—that it's only postponed and the deep, deep disappointment they've all felt from Alfred and Lynn down will make all the more tumultuous the welcome when you arrive there well again.

Don't drink—don't smoke—don't stay up late—don't carouse with buddies—it's worth it to be dull for a bit. By my standards you are so young.

Oh, success—success—it never grows stale—in spite of what they think.

Question: "What is better than success?"

Answer: "Having it again."

Love,

ENID

•

NOËL HIMSELF was not above *asking* for advice—if not on the writing of plays, then on the writing of novels. During the war years he wrote to his childhood friend "Peter," the novelist G. B. Stern (1890–1973):

> Caledonian Hotel, Aberdeen
> —1942
>
> Tell me, Miss Stern, do you find it difficult to write novels about a lot of people all at once—I mean, do you ever get muddled? I mean, do you sometimes find yourself having the characters say things that ought to be said by someone else? I mean, how do you manage to keep the whole God damned thing going without confusion and I really bloody well do mean that!

•

NOËL'S CLOSEST CONTEMPORARY and the dramatist with whom he is most often compared was Terence Rattigan (1911–1977).

Terence Rattigan (1911–1977) (*left*) wrote to Noël, "I sincerely believe that you and I are the last two playwrights on earth to continue to respect [the public]."

Noël admired Rattigan as the true successor in the tradition of Arthur Wing Pinero, Shaw, and Maugham as the author of the "well-made play," and in terms of commercial success Rattigan's eclipsed his own. Noël's major hits covered a wider range of genres, but none of his "serious" plays—with the possible exception of *The Vortex,* with its initial shock value—enjoyed the success of Rattigan's *The Winslow Boy* (1946), *The Browning Version* (1948), *The Deep Blue Sea* (1952), or *Ross* (1960). The two men could be most closely compared in the short play format, when Rattigan paid homage to Noël in the 1954 *Separate Tables,* where he had the same actors play different roles in two one-act plays with the same setting.

Their paths first crossed when Rattigan, as an Oxford undergraduate, was asked to review *Cavalcade* for the university tabloid, *Cherwell.* Briefed that the more serious rival magazine, *The Isis,* had given the piece a favorable notice and that *Cherwell* could not possibly follow suit, irrespective of the play's merits, Rattigan wrote, "[Coward] has the happy knack of feeling strongly what other people are feeling at the same time. If he has this ability to transform this knack into money and success, we should not begrudge them to him. But such cannot be the qualities of genius." Ironically, this was precisely the kind of comment that would in due course be applied to him.

Noël, in reality, had always been something of an icon for Rattigan. The latter's first completed play, *The Parchment,* was written in his public school days. It had two acts and a running time of approximately ten minutes. On the cover he listed his Wish List cast, which included just about every well-known actor of the day. Among them, cast as a poet in a velvet jacket, was the rising young Noël Coward.

In later years Rattigan made ample amends to Noël, who was by this time a close friend, when he wrote the preface to Mander and Mitchenson's *Theatrical Companion to Coward.* As a lyricist, Coward was, Rattigan declared, "the best of his kind since W. S. Gilbert." And "he is simply a phenomenon, and one that is unlikely to occur ever again in theatre history. Let us at least be grateful that it is our own epoch that the phenomenon has so signally adorned."

Over the years Rattigan was to be the recipient of Noël's well-intentioned but often critical "advice." When the Lunts were on tour in the United Kingdom prior to London with Rattigan's *Love in Idleness,* Noël had traveled up to Leeds to see a performance. Afterward he gave all concerned the famous Coward finger wag. Really, darlings, it would not do. On *no* account must they bring the play into town. Later Lynn sought out the wretched playwright and told him not to be depressed. Alfred would undoubtedly heed Noël's advice and want to close the play on the road, but *she* had faith in it and would talk her husband out of closing. A little while later Alfred took Rattigan aside and had the identical conversation. The Lunts were to play the piece in London and New York (retitled *O Mistress Mine*) for some four years.

Noël, as always, had the grace to admit when he was wrong, and he sent Rattigan a congratulatory first-night telegram telling him so. Rattigan replied:

> K5 Albany
> Piccadilly
> W.1.
> December 29th 1944

Dear Noël,
Many thanks for your very touching wire on the first night. I do indeed forgive you your trespasses and more than that, am most sincerely grateful to you for the probably well-deserved and certainly highly efficacious shaking up you gave us in Leeds. Also for your most generous recantation on the first night.
> Love
> Terry

Noël continued to offer his own brand of constructive criticism, which Rattigan learned to take in the spirit in which it was intended.

After *The Deep Blue Sea* (1951) Rattigan would write: "Ever since your very generous letter about *French Without Tears* fifteen years ago—you have probably forgotten writing it—I've always been deeply concerned that you should like my work . . ." And, on June 1, 1960: "There is no judgement I would rather have about a play than yours (except perhaps the public's, which, I sincerely believe, you and I are the last 2 playwrights on earth to continue to respect) and a word of praise from you is worth a paean from the press."

On July 20 he is writing to congratulate Noël on a pair of well-deserved but somewhat surprising successes:

Enormous gratters on *Private Lives* [which had just been revived at the Hampstead Theatre and would prove to be the beginning of "Dad's Renaissance"]. Wasn't it nice for you to read those notices? The sound of all those critics' Woodbine-stained teeth chewing their words must have been very agreeable to you. It was to me. [Wild Woodbines was a brand of cheap cigarettes much beloved by tabloid journalists.]
P.S. Also I hear you're going to be "National Theatred". [The revival of *Hay Fever* at Olivier's new National Theatre on the South Bank

would be the first by a living dramatist and would set the Coward snowball rolling even faster.] Any more such and I might get jealous. Enough is enough, please.

And by the time of A *Bequest to the Nation* (1970) Rattigan had learned to brush firmly aside the critical slings and arrows that "classical" playwrights—such as Noël and he had become—could predictably expect.

> 47 Rue des Vignes
> XV10
> October 6th 1970

Dear Noël,

I should have thanked you before—long before—this but . . . somehow or other, unlike you, I don't seem to get any younger, although of course I still look the merest boy—or is it that I just don't see so good these days?—anyway this sentence seems to have left out what I'm thanking you for, which is your sweet telegram for the first night of my Nelson play—years ago, it seems.

We opened in a newspaper strike, which seemed like a good idea when I read my *Daily Express,* but later, and more happily seemed a very bad idea indeed, as some very unexpected ones were very kind, and not even very patronizing.

Anyway, it presses along merrily, and I suppose, one day, we'll advertise the good notices we *did* get, and which no one in London read.

A *New Statesmannerie* will make you laugh. "Mr. Rattigan," someone wrote, with loathing, "seems to regard the Battle of Trafalgar with patriotic satisfaction, as an object (even) of pride, and not a regrettable political necessity."

I've written back—one shouldn't, but it was too good a chance to miss—that I was really *most terribly, terribly* sorry, but I *did* regard the Battle of Trafalgar with a certain pride, and if the gentleman would care to meet me one sunny afternoon in the Square of Regrettable Political Necessity, I'd try and explain why.

Was I naughty? Or just camp? Or both?

> Much, much love
> Terry

•

THEIR SHARED PROBLEMS—of professional failure and success— brought the two men close together and a genuine friendship developed.

. . . my admiration and affection for you have grown to a point where they could be covered by a much stronger word—a word, let me hastily add, that needs neither disturb John Gordon [the Calvinistic columnist for the *Sunday Express*] nor alarm yourself, but which nevertheless means simply what it says.

Love
Terry

In the 1971 Honours List, Rattigan received his knighthood. The previous year—after a wait of several decades—Noël had been given his and become the first playwright to be ennobled in the twentieth century. Rattigan writes to acknowledge Noël's cable of congratulations:

Bermuda
June 26th 1971

Darling Marquis Noël,
(If you remember, my efforts to award you a Dukedom 2 years ago were thwarted by Bermuda Cable & Wireless insisting on making it a "Dykedom"—to the consternation of all. Even they can't fuck up a "Marquisate".)

Thank you for your sweet wire which touched and delighted me. You know that you should have had yours forty years ago—at the time of *Cavalcade.* I don't think I *should* have had mine before—in fact I'm not at all sure I should have had it now—but it would have been nice, say, five years ago when "Old Blighty" [Rattigan's mother] could have swaggered about her hotel saying: "My younger son, Sir Terence . . ." etc., etc. "Your father would have had his at forty, you know, if he hadn't had that row with Curzon." (Which is true.)

The poor old love died only six weeks before, which seems a miracle of mis-timing all round.

Oh well, it's very nice anyway—and it's even nicer to have *you* congratulating me.

Much, much love,
TERRY

Over the years the friendship deepened, with both of them continuing to do what there was to be done theatrically and fully expecting by now to collect more "kicks than ha'pence" for their efforts to maintain theatrical standards. Both of them died with the outcome uncertain. Yet the rhetorical question remains—who will be revived a hundred years hence? Coward or Osborne? Rattigan or Wesker?

Despite his commercial success, Rattigan always felt a little overshadowed by Noël, for whom playwriting was only one of many achievements. But this in itself could be a double-edged sword, as Noël knew only too well.

After Rattigan's play *The Sleeping Prince* received a lukewarm reception in 1953, Noël consoled him: "Don't worry, Terence. I not only fuck up some of my plays by writing them, but I frequently fuck them up by acting in them as well."

# CHAPTER 10
# *CAVALCADE*

## (1931)

Let's drink to the hope that one day this country of ours, which
we love so much, will find Dignity and Greatness and Peace
again!

JANE MARRYOT'S TOAST, FROM *CAVALCADE* (1931)

I hope that this play has made you feel that, in spite of the trou-
blous times we are living in, it is still pretty exciting to be
English.

NOËL'S CURTAIN SPEECH ON THE FIRST NIGHT OF *CAVALCADE*

DURING HIS 1931 stay in America, Noël had had his research
material with him, and ideas for *Cavalcade* were crowding everything else out of his mind. From the ship, he sent Charles Cochran
a cable in response to the impresario's request for production details:

PART ONE ONE SMALL INTERIOR TWO DEPARTURE OF TROOPSHIP
THREE SMALL INTERIOR FOUR MAFEKING NIGHT IN LONDON
MUSIC HALL NECESSITATING PIVOT STAGE FIVE EXTERIOR
FRONT SCENE BIRDCAGE WALK SIX EDWARDIAN RECEPTION
SEVEN MILE END ROAD FULL STAGE BUT CAN BE OPENED UP
GRADUALLY AND DONE MOSTLY WITH LIGHTING PART TWO ONE
WHITE CITY FULL SET TWO SMALL INTERIOR THREE EDWARDIAN
SEASIDE RESORT FULL SET BATHING MACHINES PIERROTS ETC.
FOUR TITANIC SMALL FRONT SCENE FIVE OUTBREAK OF WAR
SMALL INTERIOR SIX VICTORIA STATION IN FOG SET AND
LIGHTING EFFECTS SEVEN AIR RAID OVER LONDON PRINCIPALLY
LIGHTING AND SOUND EIGHT INTERIOR OPENING ON TO
TRAFALGAR SQUARE ARMISTICE NIGHT FULL STAGE AND CAST
PART THREE ONE GENERAL STRIKE FULL SET TWO SMALL

"The Toast to the Future." Jane Marryot (Mary
Clare): "Let's drink to the hope that one day this
country of ours, which we love so much, will find
Dignity and Greatness and Peace again!"

INTERIOR THREE FASHIONABLE NIGHT CLUB FULL SET FOUR
SMALL INTERIOR FIVE IMPRESSIONISTIC SUMMARY OF MODERN
CIVILIZATION MOSTLY LIGHTS AND EFFECTS SIX COMPLETE
STAGE WITH PANORAMA AND UNION JACK FULL CAST
NECESSITATES ONE BEST MODERN LIGHTING EQUIPMENT
OBTAINABLE TWO COMPANY OF GUARDS THREE ORCHESTRA
FIFTY FOUR FACILITIES FOR COMPLETE BLACKOUTS FIVE FULL
WEEK OF DRESS REHEARSALS SIX THEATRE FREE FOR ALL
REHEARSALS SEVEN ABOUT A DOZEN RELIABLE ACTORS THE
REST WALKONS A FEW STRONG SINGERS EIGHT FOG EFFECT
INDIVIDUALS NECESSARY ONE FRANK COLLINS STAGE
SUPERVISION TWO DAN O'NEILL STAGE MANAGEMENT THREE
ELSIE APRIL MUSIC SUPERVISION FOUR CISSIE SEWELL CROWD
WORK FIVE GLADYS CALTHROP SUPERVISION OF COSTUMES AND
SCENERY AND YOUR OWN GENERAL SUPERVISION THIS SYNOPSIS
IS MORE OR LESS ACCURATE BUT LIABLE TO REVISION PLEASE

TAKE CARE THAT NO DETAIL OF THIS SHOULD REACH PRIVATE
OR PARTICULARLY PRESS EARS REGARDS NOEL

If Cochran flinched when he received it, there is no record of the fact, and the amazing thing is that when the show opened—a mere four months later—most of Noël's requests had been met.

All summer Noël and Gladys worked intensively at Goldenhurst—he with the book, she with the twenty-two different sets and the hundreds of costumes involved.

*Cavalcade,* as Noël envisaged it, would be a series of set pieces from British history from 1899, the year of his birth, to the present. The tableaux, so to speak, would be linked by the "Upstairs-Downstairs" stories of two families—the Marryots and their servants, the Bridges— during that period.

Current events came to Noël's accidental aid once the piece was written. There was no way during its composition for him to know that the first night, October 13, would coincide with a major economic and political crisis as the country had to come off the gold standard, an accepted symbol of national stability. An election had been called, and only a few days after the opening the Labour government was dramatically turned out of office (56–558 seats) in favor of a National coalition government led by Ramsay MacDonald. All of these issues were in the forefront of the audience's mind

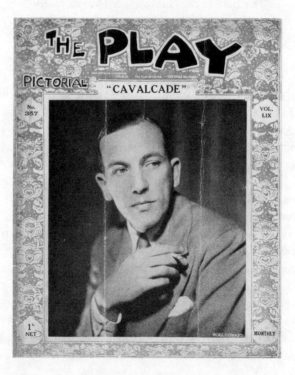

as they watched the story of their island race unfold on the massive Drury Lane stage.

Critical reaction to the play was unanimously positive, but what was even more impressive was the reaction of individual members of the audience. So many of them felt compelled to write to Noël to tell him how they felt that the Coward Archive contains a separate and substantial file entirely devoted to *Cavalcade*.

There were those who wrote of the sheer *emotion* they had experienced:

I will only tell you that you have made a very beautiful thing—and that it is a new kind of beauty. Very few people can ever do so much. [Duff Cooper]

I could not cry as I was too deeply stirred!! [Actress Yvonne Arnaud]

I don't think I have ever been so moved over any play in my life. I grisseled [grizzled] all the way through and had a lovely time. ["Boo"—Evelyn Laye]

I hope you were pleased with the reception . . . I felt that people were too wrought up to make as much noise as they would have liked to have done. An Englishman can't really applaud if he has tears in his eyes at the same time.

Before going to *Cavalcade* last night I was 34 years old—and now having lived 30 years in a flash I suppose I am 64! Which isn't very nice, is it? Or is it? . . . Please don't think me too dotty, but I had to retire to the lulu to remake my face after the Armistice scene and the old lady in charge told me pathetically that she didn't suppose she would ever have a chance of seeing the show—could you possibly do anything about it? Even if you have to take charge of the lulu yourself for the evening?!! [Lady Sheila Millbanke]

The resurrection of national pride was a recurring theme:

. . . the good it will do to the nation—"if the nation has eyes to see!" [Lord Baden Powell]

A comment that must have particularly pleased Noël came from George Bernard Shaw, who was now taking the "young author" seriously:

Noël Coward will survive in history. With *Cavalcade* alone he did more for Britain than all the generals at Waterloo.

It produces a complete jumble of emotions—There is the experience with its implications recaptured, the vague melancholy of its emotions, the regret for the things that have dropped out with it, the current sense of what has happened meanwhile, and the consciousness of the degree to which one's vision has altered, and that one is looking at it all with a cubist or at any rate an emancipated eye . . .

One wonders if the blasé little Jew who wrote *Ecclesiastes,* would alter his conclusions or find them justified—Anyway, no one can see *Cavalcade* without being started on a whole set of questions without answers—so much the most beneficial sort. [Anonymous]

I was deeply impressed, and I think you will understand why. We young persons of 20 are keen to "do our bit" to help England in its troubles, but we don't know how to set about it, and we cannot make our voices heard—we haven't the vote yet. We do appreciate, therefore, a magnificent gesture on the part of someone whose voice will be heard and listened to by thousands.

There were those who saw their own lives reflected, as in a mirror:

If anybody had told me that a play could make me live every moment of my life again, with such absolute clearness, I would have bet him any money that it was impossible. Last night proved how wrong one can be. In three hours I lived my whole life again, in every detail, ever since I can remember anything.

And there were those who were so moved—one way or another—that they simply had to get their feelings off their chests:

It does seem a pity that you should have chosen as representatives of the young people in this country such very second rate and loose-living specimens. I remember when Michael Arlen was asked why he chose to depict such a fast set (*The Green Hat*), he replied he had never been able to get the *entrée* to County rectories and could only describe the set he knew. Your play would surely have been pleasanter and truer and not lost in power if the young man killed in the war had not brought disgrace on a girl before he fell. So very many decent men were engaged in the War that it was not fair to take a libertine as a representative of a good professional class. Even the lower classes had clean minded heroes in the fighting line who in dying left no stain behind them.

Impresario C. B. Cochran.

And those who *never* wrote but just had to write:

I was down in London on Saturday on a day excursion to see the Rugby match. We were lucky enough to get seats for that night. At the time I thought eight shillings hefty for the upper circle. That is what *stalls* cost in Glasgow, where *Bitter Sweet* was an awful wash-out.

Anyway, your show was worth all the money I spent the whole day. It was absolutely great and I've been thinking about it ever since. I'm sorry I can't find words to tell you how perfect it seemed to me. Also I haven't time, as I should hate the family to come in and catch me. I was never a hero-worshiper before.

And several from fellow pros that would have particularly pleased Noël:

Who *says* the films will beat us? [Sir Cedric Hardwicke]

It moved me deeply and I'll have to confess that I felt pangs of envy, too. Because, though I know I couldn't, still how I wish I could have written such a play. I'm sending you the cleaner's bill for my best white dress, the front of which was polka-dotted with my tears. [Edna Ferber]

I cannot express in words how I felt about the play. It was wonderful to see all the actors then, and know they were all so unanimous in

their delight and tribute to you. It must be a thrilling achievement, and I'm sure you're bored with being told so, so no more.
[John Gielgud]

Ironically, one of the few dissenting—or at least questioning—voices was that of Noël's own brother, who complained to Violet: "Noël is getting a Cadillac, is he? For all his supposed patriotism, he seems to prefer most American things. I can't think why." To be fair, Erik Coward's lack of enthusiasm may have been tempered by the fact that "Big Bro" had written to him:

£500 seems rather exorbitant for a car, as it's a good deal more than I paid for my Buick, which I've had for three years—so I am sending you £300 with which I hope you'll buy a more useful car and enjoy it. P.S. I loathe writing letters.

Another critic of *Cavalcade* was Adolf Hitler. It was reported by the British ambassador in Berlin that the Führer had "laughed himself sick" at the idea of *Cavalcade.* Had he witnessed an actual performance and the committed reaction of a typical English audience, he might well have reappraised certain psychological elements of his master plan.

•

EVEN THOUGH he might have spoken of it jokingly, in many ways Noël was probably prouder of *Cavalcade* than of any other single piece of his work. Some years later, at one of those stand-up cocktail parties where one is required to balance a plate in one hand and a cup of tea precariously in another, a waiter hurried up to him with a fork. "How come *you* get a fork?" a neighboring guest asked. "Well," Noël replied, "I *did* write *Cavalcade.*"

Which is why he was so surprised and hurt a decade later when his patriotism was called into question and so much of the public adulation turned to vilification.

•

BY NOVEMBER Noël and Jack have sailed away on another of their marathon adventures—this time to South America. He arrived in Rio to find still more congratulatory mail awaiting him, including a cable from Woollcott:

NOËL COWARD HOTEL CAPOCABAN [Copacabana] RIO

ALL THE CAVALCADE NEWS DELIGHTS ME IF YOU ACCEPT A
KNIGHTHOOD NOW I SHALL BE FEARFULLY VEXED STOP
ALEXANDER WOOLLCOTT

Designer Gladys Calthrop.

Rio was hectic, and Noël had no time to write to Violet again until they reached the comparative peace of São Paulo:

Esplanada Hotel
Sao Paulo
Sunday, December 6th

Darlingest,

Well, we've got away from Rio at last. It was difficult to leave because we were having such fun. We made a striking exit—and had to jump into the train while it was going. Crowds came down to see us off and it was all very funny.

We are staying here until Wednesday when we're embarking on a lovely trip into the jungle. We travel for two days by train and then go in a special boat down the Parana River which takes a week.

We are really going with the object of filming the Igayu [Iguassu] Falls. Then we go on by train to Buenos Aires.

Oh Dear, Oh Dear, I'd almost forgotten.

A HAPPY XMAS

There.

Your sincere son
NOËL PEIRCE [correctly spelled this time]
COWARD

Plaza Hotel
Buenos Aires
Friday December 25th

Darlingest,

I haven't written for two weeks because arriving here was very hectic. We had a marvellous expedition. We were the guests of a Matè (sort of tea company) . . .

We had a special car on the train from Sao Paulo, hitched onto the end of the train, we travelled for three days in it and then arrived at the Parana River where we got on a very peculiar boat and drifted down to a place called Guayra. It was really very interesting because only *very* few white people have ever made that trip, the jungle on each side of the river is absolutely virgin forest, and quite terrifying. You can't walk more than a few yards and it's filled with snakes and orchids and parrots, etc., and it stretches on the right side for almost *two thousand* miles!

There was nowhere to spend the night except on board an ancient long-discarded pleasure steamer which had a sinister *Outward Bound* atmosphere and contained a few cockroach-infested cabins, a vast dark dining saloon and a mad steward dressed in a grayish-white bumfreezer, ominously stained blue trousers and multi-coloured carpet slippers. He had two complete rows of brilliantly gold teeth and, as it was his habit to go into gales of high-pitched laughter whenever we asked him for anything, we were almost blinded. Apart from him and us and the cockroaches, the only other living creature on board that macabre vessel was an incredibly old mongrel which had no teeth at all, gold or otherwise. Its name was Peppo. The food needless to say was disgusting . . . After our nasty meal we sat out on the deck listening to the river muttering by and chain-smoking cigarettes to discourage the insects. Later on in the evening Peppo made a determined effort to get into bed with me but I succeeded in repelling his advances and he finally retired, wheezing down the dark corridor.

We went on for days down river to the Igayu [Iguassu] Falls which are immense and twice as big as Niagara, very very beautiful. Then on for days and days, changing boats all the time, until we arrived here. The last boat was very grand and the beast of a Captain refused to allow us to come on deck or have meals in the dining room because we were not suitably dressed (Riding things). He actually sent for the Police to put us off which they refused to do. So we were sent below where we remained for two days. All the first class passengers were delighted with themselves. We remained quite happily below and gave a cocktail party to all the stewards! Then on the morning we arrived, we stepped off the boat *exquisitely* dressed, were met by a very grand car and several commissionaires etc., we cut the Captain and shook hands with all the stewards. There has been the most awful row about it, all the Directors of the line have apologised and the Papers have been full of it. I almost feel sorry for the Captain now! The first class passengers' faces were a study when we left the boat. I said very loudly in Spanish to the Head Steward that we had enjoyed the journey very much and infinitely preferred being with the real gentlemen below, than the pretentious plebians above!

  All my love and hugs, darlingest.

  SNOOP

This doesn't really feel very much like Christmas Day, although it isn't as hot here as in Rio.

Nahuel Huapi

Patagonia

January 15th 1932

Well Darling,

Here we are in the loveliest place I've yet seen. This is an *estancia* right up in the mountains on the borders of Chile. It took three days to get here from Buenos Aires. The most awful journey across the plains with dust an inch thick over everything, then five hours driving in a car, but when you get here it's certainly worth it. Nahuel Huapi is an enormous lake surrounded by snow-capped mountains and absolutely wild . . . It is quite cold even tho' it is the height of summer now, and we actually sit round a fire after dinner. In the winter (July and August) no one comes here much because it is completely snowed under! We leave on Sunday and go on into Chile, we travel by boats along the different lakes, and then ox cart and then mules until after a few days we arrive at Puerto Moutt on the Pacific coast where we get a train to Valparaiso. The only people who have done this particular journey are General Pershing, the Princes [the Prince of Wales and Prince George], and us, so we're in good company!

With Noël en route for his South American safari, agent Fanny Holtzmann managed to persuade Fox to make the movie version of *Cavalcade*, but time was of the essence. Could she have a copy of the script to send them? Strangely, Cochran didn't have one, and Lorn reported that there was only one complete script in existence and Master had taken that with him, presumably to "make revisions": "So our precious property is somewhere between here and Valparaiso. I've sent Noël a cable."

*Cavalcade*, the film (1932). The two upstairs/downstairs families.
Jane (Diana Wynyard) and Robert (Clive Brook) Marryot
(*center*), flanked by Albert (Herbert Mundin) Bridges and
Ellen (Una O'Connor). The film won the Oscar for that year.

Somehow she located him and he cabled back:

THE WOMAN IS THE WONDER WORKER OF THE AGES STOP
SCRIPT WILL WING ITS WAY TO YOU FROM CHILE STOP DO NOT
CARE WHAT HAPPENS BETWEEN SCRIPT AND SCREEN STOP YOU
MAY CHANGE IT TO BLEAK HOUSE AS LONG AS MY NAME IS
SPELLED CORRECTLY ON THE CHEQUE STOP MASTER

He found Fanny's all-American aggression a little hard to take and
would continue to do so, but on this occasion he was grateful for it and
cabled I FORGIVE YOU.

British Embassy
Santiago
Chile
January 26th

Hallo Darling,
Here we are in Chile and very lovely it is too. This town is set in a
valley high up in the Andes and down each street you see enormous
mountains stretching up to the sky. In the winter they're covered in
snow but now they're brown and purple.

We leave on Monday on a small cargo boat for Mollendo and from there we go right up to Ariguipa and La Paz and Cuzco to see all the Inca and Maya ruins then we go to Lima.

How horrid about poor little Nuts [their dog], I'm dreadfully worried about Coco, he will miss him so awfully. We must buy heaps more dogs the moment I return so that there will always be a lot left when any of them die! I know you won't approve but you're only a very stupid dolt and your opinion won't even be asked!!!

All love and hugs

SNOOPIE

Country Club
Lima
Sunday 21st February

Darling,

I arrived here and found a whole bundle of letters from you and one from Veitch. I love the snapshots of you bouncing along the promenade, very rich in your fur coats. I haven't had any letter from Erik yet but when I get to California I'll do something about the car proposition . . .

I'm so pleased about the ear trumpet [Violet was getting increasingly deaf], I shall be able to throw salted almonds into it from my end of the table. Oh Dear, Oh Dear, I'm actually quite tired of travelling for the moment, we've been going so very hard just lately. We went from La Paz to Cuzco, right across Lake Titicaca, the most lovely scenery. Cuzco is where the Incas had such a delightful time and it really *isn't* very central but undeniably beautiful. It took us two full days to get there. We went the first part of the way in the President's private car (on the train). He was going to meet his wife at Mollendo. At every stop thousands of officers and Lord Mayors and Indian Chiefs appeared and bowed and scraped and were very funny indeed.

We came back from Cuzco by auto-cavil [carvil] which is a motor car fixed to the railway line, in this we drove for sixteen hours, right over the highest point of the Andes, about 17,000 feet! It was a strange and very beautiful journey and we arrived at Araguipa [Arequipa] at 2:30 in the morning.

We stayed in Areguipa at the Quinta Bates, which is a rambling Pension kept by an old American woman who is a darling. She waited up for us and gave us tea and hot water bottles and generally treated us like children. We had a lovely week with her and completely relaxed.

Yesterday we flew here and once more we're in the tropics, thank

God, I'm so sick of high altitudes and cold. On Wednesday we sail for Panama and Jeff I think goes straight back to England while I go beetling up the coast to meet Jack who will come from New York, probably to San Diego. There's a revolution on here but we haven't seen anything of it as we're outside the Town.

Goodbye my duck I'll write again from Panama.

Your extremely affectionate
SNOOPIE

At Lima they experienced a revolution *and* an earthquake and decided Peru was perhaps a mite too "restless," and it was on to Panama, where their journey ended. Jeffrey had to return to London and Noël made plans to go to New York.

However far he traveled there was no escaping the obligations of being "Noël Coward." A pile of mail had caught up with him in Santiago, and one cable in particular cast an exciting but ominous shadow. It was from the Lunts:

OUR CONTRACT WITH THEATRE GUILD UP IN JUNE STOP WE'RE FREE STOP WHAT ABOUT IT?

He knew what that meant. From Colón, Panama, he boarded a Norwegian freighter, the SS *Toronto,* for Los Angeles, where Jack would meet him.

# CHAPTER 11
# NOËL & ALFRED & LYNN . . .
# AND THEIR DESIGN FOR LIVING

## (1921–1934)

GILDA: The human race is a let-down . . . It thinks it's progressed, but it hasn't; It thinks it's risen above the primeval slime, but it hasn't—it's still wallowing in it! . . . We've invented a few small things that make noises, but we haven't invented one big thing that creates quiet, endless peaceful quiet—something to pull over our heads like a gigantic eider-down; something to deaden the sound of our emotional yellings and screechings.

*DESIGN FOR LIVING* (1933)

DESIGN FOR LIVING

ALFRED LUNT, NOËL COWARD AND LYNN FONTANNE

ETHEL BARRYMORE
THEATRE

Lynn, Alfred, and Noël in the Lunts' home, Ten Chimneys,
Genesee Depot, Wisconsin.

·

T HE "DESIGN" STARTED back in the humid, un-air-conditioned
summer of 1921, on Noël's first impoverished visit to New York, where
he was befriended by the couple who were to become "The Lunts."

He'd met Lynn Fontanne (1887–1983) in London, where she'd grown
accustomed to the fate of playing second leads to American star Laurette
Taylor (1884–1946). In New York, where she had been taken to accompany Taylor, she was "walking out" with Alfred Lunt (1892–1977) and
living in the same West Side boarding house. Evening after evening they
would lay their plans for their stellar careers.

First, they would become stars in their own rights. Then Lynn and
Alfred would act as a team, and when they had all achieved the heady pin-
nacle of fame and acclaim, they would act together in a play that Noël
would write specially for them.

In the intervening decade, the first part of the plan had been triumphantly fulfilled. Lynn and Alfred had become the unquestioned stars
of the Theatre Guild, latterly with the power to insist that they appeared
only as a duo.

When *Private Lives* was such a hit in London, there was speculation in
the New York press that the Lunts might star in it on Broadway, but anyone who knew anything about Noël knew that the play was reserved for
Noël and Gertie—and so it proved. The Lunts, meanwhile, were being
courted by Hollywood.

The Lunts at home—caught in a typically
"unposed" moment.

In May of 1931 Lynn is writing to Noël:

The Wardell—Detroit

. . . Of course, wouldn't we have *Private Lives* dangled in front of our noses and *not* get it, but I think it is the final amalgamation into the Chinese German with a touch of Indian blood and Christian Science by persuasion play.

We are going to do a play of Bob Sherwood's next season called, but only for the moment, *Reunion in Vienna*—horrid, isn't it? I have suggested *Auf Wiedersehen* and he seems to be delighted. It is a very funny comedy—Alfred is not as hot about it as I am but I hope he is wrong—it has a marvelous part for him in it. Anyway, we are both terribly pleased to be doing a play of Bob's. We are so fond of him and he wrote it for us—not that it would make any difference if we didn't like it, of course. *Now,* I know you are laughing!

But *we* live for the end of our contract {with the Theatre Guild} when we will be free to travel and have a marvelous time and then, if we didn't retire, do the great *pot pourri* goulash chop suey curry beaten up with a grain of salt and served in London one hot night to a slightly astonished and very damp audience—what a lark it ought to be! Don't write it yet—if you do, it will be too good to keep and someone else will do it—and then you will be tired of the idea.

Noël visited Hollywood sev
times in the early 1930s. H
is seen with Douglas Fairba
and Mary Pickford (*top*) . .
(*center*) Chico Marx, Mauric
Chevalier, Herman Mankie
(writer of *Citizen Kane*), Gr
Marx (*standing*), and Harpo
(*seated*) . . . and (*bottom*) wit
Robert Montgomery (who
just played Elyot in the film
*Private Lives*).

We are terribly excited over *Cavallcade* (are there two "Ls"?) What a perfectly marvelous title, it covers the whole thing.

We go to the coast in four weeks—I think they [MGM] have decided on *The Guardsman*—we are getting quite excited about it.
Love Lynn

One *l* or two, the Lunts were not destined to see *Cavalcade*. Their *Reunion* lasted too long for their own comfort.

163 E. 36th St. NEW YORK
June 11, 1932

Baby:
We are heartsick to learn (at least *The Times* says so) that *Cavalcade* is closing. I can't believe that we're not to see it. Two seats not sold and Cochran got panicky or what? Never mind about answering if you can keep it going until we get there.

We prayed that *we'd* close by next week but no, the weather has cooled itself off and we're about selling out—so now we'll surely go on until July 2. The heat has been unbearable and it's so awfully disconcerting to kiss Lynn all over when she's so wet. I don't know what we shall do if our revue runs all summer . . .

Charlie Brackett [the producer] saw Ethel Barrymore in Providence [Rhode Island, a popular summer resort] a week or so ago and was bemoaning the fact that Alec [Woollcott] was not to be one of the caste [*sic*]. Ethel thought it rather a shame too—"Four amateurs together"—says she, etc., etc., etc., You know what she exclaimed when she heard that Helen Hayes had made a great triumph in *Coquette,* don't you?—"What, that monster!"

We (hope) to sail on the *Aquitania* August 10th.
ALFRED

By the time he reached San Francisco, where an anxious Jack was waiting for him, *Design for Living* had been written and a great weight was off Noël's mind.

He felt able to make a brief stopover in Hollywood, where he was shown the film version of *Private Lives*. Noël found it "passable." On the strength of its commercial success, Paramount bought the rights to *The Queen Was in the Parlour* (which became *Tonight Is Ours,* with Claudette Colbert and Fredric March). While he was in town Noël was able to attend one of the first production meetings at Fox for *Cavalcade.* This insider look at the studio system in action appalled him so much that he cut the visit short, although he would admit later that it was the only one of his plays up to that time that "had been filmed with taste and integrity."

Erik Coward just before his death in 1933.

Hollywood reinforced his preference for "a nice cup of cocoa." "There's America . . . and then there's Hollywood."

•

THE LUNTS DECLARED themselves delighted with *Design for Living,* and Noël sailed for home to prepare his new revue for Cochran [*Words and Music*]. He was to return at the end of the year to begin their design for rehearsing.

His summer was not to be cloudless, however. There was a cable from Erik in Colombo:

SAILING JULY THIRTEENTH ORIENT LINE OTRANTO GRANTED THREE MONTHS SICK LEAVE STOMACH ALL OUT OF ORDER DOCTORS RECOMMEND COMPLETE CHANGE NOTHING SERIOUS SO DON'T WORRY MASSES OF LOVE VERY EXCITED ERIK

When Erik arrived back in England, it was obvious that there was a great deal to worry about. Doctors confirmed that he had incurable cancer of the stomach—a fact that Violet and Noël kept from him. He joined the group at Goldenhurst until his death the following January.

•

*WORDS AND MUSIC* was successfully launched at London's Adelphi Theatre that September. In the cast, playing the juvenile, was the boy soprano Master Graham Payn. When, at his mother's instigation, Graham auditioned by singing "Nearer My God to Thee" while performing a tap dance, Noël felt he had no alternative: "We've got to have the kid in the show." During the war Noël would meet Graham again, when the young man was appearing in a series of West End revues. Their reunion would lead to a lifelong relationship.

•

BUT FOR NOW domestic matters had to take precedence over professional. Disturbed by Violet's state of mind as she nursed his brother, Noël wrote to her from Lady Mendl's house:

La Villa Trianon
Blvd. Saint Antoine
Versailles
Seine-et-Oise
September 1932
Wednesday

Darlingest,
I'm trying to take your advice about not thinking of you but it's very difficult as I find I think about you all the time.

Everything is so tragic and cruel for you and my heart aches dreadfully for you but that's no good either except that it proves even to me (who didn't need much proof) how very very much I love you.

The next letter I write to you won't be like this at all, it will be crammed with gay description. This sort of letter only makes us both cry and that's sillier than anything.

I'm saying several acid prayers to a fat contented God the Father in a dirty night gown who hates you and me and every living creature in the world.

Good night my dearest dearest darling
SNOOPIE

He had taken off for a European holiday that would end with him joining the Mediterranean fleet for a cruise on the *Queen Elizabeth,* current command of his friend Louis Mountbatten. He'd met Mountbatten and his wife, Edwina, a few years earlier, but this time together would cement their friendship and prove particularly valuable in the war that no one could envisage but that was only a few short years away.

September 1932
Orient Express
Saturday

Darlingest,
Here I am joggling along through Serbia, it's very hot and dusty but I don't mind that much and I've slept and slept standing for two nights and days. I arrive in Salonica tonight where I am to be met by several angry Greeks and tomorrow I hop onto a strange boat and go out to Lemnos where the *Queen Elizabeth* is anxiously waiting for me. I didn't realise how very much I needed to get away, apart from everything else I was physically quite exhausted.

Paris was quite peaceful, because I was staying out at Versailles and didn't see many people except the Lloyds who were staying in the house. He has given me some nice introductions for Egypt and sent off wires everywhere so I shall be made a grand fuss of!

I'll write again when I reach the ship.

> Your deeply loving
> SNOOPIE

He was a little more frank in the letter he sent to Gladys Calthrop the same day. Instead of "joggling," he was "arsing through Serbia" and, as for Paris, it had been: "quite idiotic and so was everyone in it. When we do finally retire to our mountain of contemptuous contemplation it must be a very very high one."

> H.M.S. *Queen Elizabeth*
> Wednesday October 5th 1932

Darlingest,

I've finally arrived after many very strange adventures.

The weather is absolutely lovely and I'm already very sun burnt and rested. Life on a Flagship is the acme of grandeur and very enjoyable, particularly for me as a visitor, because I sit about and watch everybody else working. All I do to contribute is to arrange the evening musical programmes with the Bandmaster and try to prevent him from playing exclusively *my* music, which he is very anxious to do! I travelled all through the earthquake zone and saw a lot of horrors, but we're well away from it here. Everyone in the ship is charming to me and I'm made a great fuss of. I have the Admiral's spare cabin and a nice servant to wait on me. There's certainly nothing to touch the Navy for charm and courtesy. At four o'clock every afternoon everybody bathes—Dickie Mountbatten has a motor boat, so I go out in that and we aquaplane round and round the Fleet. I'm going to Port Said on the 13th then we go to Cairo for a few days and back home by easy stages.

I told you my letters would be gay, didn't I?

> All my dear love.
> SNOOP

Noël's time with the Mountbattens cemented what would be an enduring friendship. They established a camaraderie that allowed mutual teasing—something Noël found essential to any close relationship.

Casa Medina<br>
Pieta<br>
Malta<br>
25th October 1932

Dear Noël,

I'm so glad you enjoyed your time with the Fleet. I need hardly tell you how much I enjoyed having you, or how good it was for me to be taken away from work for a bit . . .

You will be amused to hear that Mr. Keen [the ship's bandmaster] has now copied your style of conducting as far as it is possible for so stolid a member of the British Musical profession to and that he plays all selections at high speed. Both he and the band have been absolutely transformed by you and are 200% better than before you came.

I have never known any visitor go down with such a rush on board, particularly as our mess is rather "sticky" but your ears would have tingled to hear all the charming remarks made about you after you had gone.

> Yours,
> DICKIE

After a subsequent visit Noël would reply:

Remind me to write a very strong play about the Navy dedicated, in Russian, to the C-in-C.

Please be careful with your zippers, Dickie dear, and don't let me hear of any ugly happenings at Flotilla dances.

> Love and kisses
> Signal Bosun Coward

(I *know* Bosun ought to be spelt "Boatswain" but *I don't* care!)

In late November he sailed back to New York on the SS *Empress of Britain*. It was time to rehearse *Design*.

Violet was constantly on his mind.

2 Beekman Place<br>
New York City<br>
Saturday 10th December 1932

Darlingest,

I loved your letter—it cheered me up a lot which I know it was meant to do, but I can't bear to think of everything being so awful for you and me not there to comfort you a little bit. However, I don't

Noël, Lynn, and Alfred. A triptych each kept on their dressing room table for good luck.

intend to go on in this strain because we shall *all* cry and that's no good anyhow.

Rehearsals are going marvellously. Lynn and Alfred are simply superb and I think we're going to give the best acting in the world to the great American Public. It is bliss working with them, they're so utterly sure and concentrated on what they're doing there's no work for me at all except to try to be good in my own part!

I'm writing this in my bedroom looking right over the river, it's bitterly cold and snowing but I must say it looks very beautiful.

I've had a lot of parties given for me, there's no doubt about me being popular here—The Press fall over themselves to say nice things about me and I'm altogether New York's white headed boy. Lots of people ask after you, Judith Anderson and Pauline Lord and Mabelle Webb! I've given Philip Tonge a small part in the play and he's very good in it and I've had heartfelt letters of thanks from poor old [Mrs.] Tonge, so *that's* a good deed done! He has just one scene with me in the Second Act as the newspaper reporter. It does seem funny when I look back and remember how much in awe of him I was. Life certainly plays very strange tricks on people. Give my love to everybody and such a tremendous lot to yourself, my old darling.

SNOOP

DECEMBER 23RD.

ALL REHEARSING TERRIBLY HARD BUT ENJOYING IT VERY MUCH STOP CAVALCADE FILM OPENING HERE JANUARY FIFTEENTH THEY ARE SHOWING IT TO ME IN ADVANCE IN CLEVELAND HEAR

Gilda (Lynn), Leo (Noël), and Otto (Alfred)—a trio for life.

IT IS VERY GOOD BUT FEEL RATHER APPREHENSIVE ALL LOVE TO
ALL STOP SNOOP

He needn't have worried. The next year *Cavalcade* won three Oscars—
Best Picture, Best Director, and Best Art Direction—and took $3.5 mil-
lion at the box office. It won rave reviews but perhaps none more heartfelt
than the verdict of its apprehensive author: "It was superior in every way
than if I personally had been connected with the actual production."

Christmas Day 1932

Darlingest,
It was lovely to hear your voice this morning, it's sometimes a great
comfort to live in such a very civilised age. I think it's a grand idea
for Erik to be at Goldenhurst, I should so much rather he was there
than anywhere else. It's all very fine to tell me not to think about
you—as if I could *help* myself! But as a matter of fact I'm working so

hard that I literally haven't time to be morose or unhappy, in any case it doesn't do anybody any good.

The Play is coming along wonderfully and taken all round it is really the best acting in the world I *must* say. I've just come back from Christmas dinner with the Lunts and Constance [Collier] and the two Gladys's, Henson and Calthrop. Now I'm going to dine at Nesa [Neysa] McMein's house with Jack and a large Party. We leave for Cleveland on Friday and the whole week there is completely sold out!

All my love to all and Oh Dear, I do wish they would invent something to make Transatlantic Hugs possible?
> SNOOPIE

As well as trying to cheer his mother up as best he could from so far away, he had to write to Erik as though nothing were amiss:

> Wade Park Manor
> Cleveland
> January [?] 1933
> Friday

Well Master Erik,
I haven't written as much and as often as I should have but that's me all over—careless! The Play was a wow here and we have to have extra chairs in the aisles at every performance. We're all very good, I think, I do wish you could see it. The *Cavalcade* Picture opened in New York on Thursday night and was apparently a super riot! The notices are quite incredible, I've never read so many superlatives. They've kept it completely English and just like the play and Jack who was there said it was the most moving thing he had ever seen, when the enormous Broadway First Night Audience rose to its feet and cheered at God Save the King! They're sending me a special print of it to Pittsburgh, where I shall have a private showing on Tuesday night after the performance. I am so glad you're at Goldenhurst and away from that gloomy and depressing old B.B.C. Don't forget to play the *"Chants d'Auvergne"* on the gramophone, if you haven't already done so.

All my love to you and hand some out to everybody and get well soon.

> Your heroic National minded Patriot [presumably a little dig at Erik's reported comment]
> BRO

Hotel Schenley
Pittsburgh, PA.
January 10th 1933

Oh Darling,

A very sad letter from you today. I do wish I could do something but I know there's nothing to be done, also you might just as well write sadly because if you're cheerful I see through it and that's much worse. Christmas must have been awful and New Year's Eve! It really is amazing how much human beings have to bear sometimes.

How wonderful if he could die quietly in his sleep, I am so glad the nurses are nice and that he doesn't suspect anything.

Bear up, my darling, perhaps in the long run he will turn out to be lucky after all! Anyhow he could never go through what you're going through.

SNOOPIE

Noël's wish was granted. On January 22—two days before they opened in New York—he received a cable from his mother. Erik had indeed died peacefully in his sleep at Goldenhurst. Noël replied with a cable of his own saying that Violet and Vida must come to New York right away. He had booked them into the Beekman Towers, just around the corner from his own apartment at Beekman Place.

•

ON JANUARY 24, *Design for Living* opened at the Ethel Barrymore Theatre and was an immediate hit—so much so that Noël immediately agreed to play five months instead of his stipulated three.

For its time the play was ambiguously daring. Noël played Leo, a playwright in love with Gilda, who lives with Otto, an artist, who is also in love with Gilda. She in turn is in love with both of them. The permutations of this *ménage à trois* make up the plot. By the end of the play each of them has come to accept that they cannot live without the other two.

Because of the unusual length of the run, Noël left Beekman Place and rented a cottage at Sneden's Landing, on the Hudson River, close to Katharine Cornell and husband Guthrie McClintic. There, in whatever free time he could snatch, he began work on his first volume of autobiography, *Present Indicative*.

Meanwhile, the play continued to be the season's big hit. Noël happily reported to Gladys:

April 5, 1933

Well, Pussy:

I received yours of the whatever it was and was haighly delaighted with it. We have all got to the stage now of counting the days until May 27th. Capacity and standees at every performance and very common people, dear—not our class at all—given to spitting and coughing and belching during the quieter passages.

I have taken for two months the most enchanting little cottage at Sneedons [Sneden's], just near Kit's. It is isolated in the middle of thick woods and looking out over the river, and it takes only thirty-five minutes to get there. It really is perfectly divine, and I commute every night except Tuesdays and Fridays before matinees. I get down there, have some hot soup, and am in bed by one o'clock. I get up early every morning and work all day on my book. I am now almost half through it, well over all the deeficult war part, which I think I have managed with great tact and discretion. I do do hope you will think it good. By the time I get back to England the first draft will be practically finished, and I am going to sit at Goldenhurst and polish and revise.

I will be back about mid-July. The Lunts are coming over in September and we thought a dainty trip to Paris and Berlin might not come amiss. They are opening *Reunion in Vienna* in January, and I am beetling off with Jeff. I will give them my studio for the winter . . .

There is no particular news here. Gladys Henson continues to drink gin and gossip. Neysa and Alec are as sweet as ever. The Lunts are perfect, and everybody sends you their love. So there.

    HITLER

April 12th
### SUNDAY THE WHATEVER IT IS

Oh Dear

Here I am in my tainy cottage and it's a lovely spring day and the trees are coming out and I am suffering (as usual) from the results of a kindness! That being Bill Sykes whom I asked out, fortunately only for Sunday! His painting is really *good* I think and I journeyed down to Fourteenth Street to see it but what is this questing, galahad, chin out, striving after intellectually? It's very down getting—poor poor boy. He informed me just now that he really preferred metaphor to symbols! To which there is no adequate reply outside of "Shit!" I haven't paid much attention to him and have remained upstairs working. It's all coming along ever so. This place is really saving my reason. It's quite lovely and utterly quiet. Lynn and Alfred want you to do *Reunion in V* in January, which will be rather fun for you, hein?

We're all riding in the Circus Parade tonight on elephants—the Lunts, Neysa, . . . and me. I've had a message from Eva [Le Gallienne] rather urgent, so I'm supping with her tomorrow. Could it be money, do you think! Oh dear—very ork if it is.

I'm counting the days now until the end of the run. It's become very routine and dreary. George J. Nathan launched a heavy and not very effective attack on me in *Vanity F[air]* and has got himself into considerable *eau chaud* in consequence. I shall close now, work and drive the drooling Sykes into New York very *rapidamente* indeedy. I've come to the conclusion that the thing I hate most is a "Beauty Lover". He's quite awful about Beauty Lovers. He's sitting downstairs at the moment finding poetry in the first draft of my book! He tells me that it's full of poetry—there now! Not moonlight and veiled stars and all that nonsense but real poetic words like inkpot and sixpence! Oh Christ, and he's so very nice really, it really is dreadful. He launched off into a glowing description of you— "strong", "loyal", "beautiful", "still", etc. I contradicted the whole thing immediately and said you were weak, shifty, ugly and over fidgety. He's now very puzzled indeed.

Hasta la farting vista
SHELLEY

Tuesday

Lynn and Alfred and Neysa and I had a gorgeous ever so time at the Circus on Sunday night and rode round the ring dressed as Rajahs on very large and lovely ellies! Lynn was terrified and sat crunched up in her How de dowdah like a snail!

We dined with Madame Radua who is very old and wears white satin and rides a horse. She also shoots a whole flock of multi-coloured pigeons out of a box and they perch all over her. Her bubbies provide ample foothold for a flock of albatrosses! We asked her how she coloured the pigeons and she said—

EET ISS SOM JOB I TELL YOU
EACH FEDDER SEPARATE!

·

BY MAY, Violet was safely back in Goldenhurst:

Tuesday May 18th

Darlingest,

Well, we're closing a week earlier because we all decided we were far too tired to go on any longer. The result of this is that dense crowds are flocking to the theatre and standing five deep at every performance.

The day after you left I got a bad attack of laryngitis and couldn't speak, I really felt awful but I didn't miss one performance. I went straight into a nice quiet nursing home and went back and forth between it and the theatre, consequently with my usual remarkable recuperative powers, I was well again in a few days, but it was horrid while it lasted.

The other night I took Elsa Maxwell up to the top of the Empire State after the show and when we came down Jacobs [the driver] was white and trembling and said we had been followed by a car full of gangsters! So I called the superintendent who had a gun and also three elevator men and we went out of another entrance! The next day I got the police and they were all caught and turned out to be autograph hunters! Elsa meanwhile, without consulting me, telephoned all the newspapers! So there were headlines. I am absolutely furious with her and denied the whole thing and said that she only did it for publicity for herself. It was very annoying. I couldn't get into my dressing room for reporters and detectives with guns! And

Drawing by Lynn Fontanne.

now I'm watched wherever I go, so I'm *very safe* and *very uncomfortable!* Still I turned the tables on Elsa nicely.

They gave a farewell supper at the Algonquin on Tuesday for Alfred and Lynn and me, and sang songs about us and toasted us and generally made a hell of a fuss . . .

SNOOPIE

But before he sailed he sent a farewell cable to the Lunts:

> *Darling Alfred, dainty Lynn,*
> *Now the holidays begin.*
> *Three superb but weary hacks*
> *Comfortably may relax.*
> *No more slaps to keep the chin up,*
> *No long trains to trip our Lynn up.*
> *Let us thank benign Jehovah*
> *That the long, long trail is over!*

# CHAPTER 12

## *CONVERSATION PIECE . . .*
## AND MISSING THE POINT

### (1933–1935)

> PAUL: Tell me, do you speak French?
> EDWARD: *Oui, un peu.*
> PAUL: I never think that's enough, do you?
>
> **CONVERSATION PIECE (1934)**

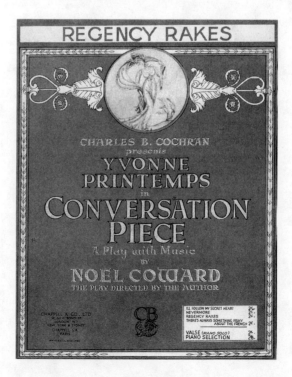

MORTIMER: I always affect to despise human nature. My role in life is so clearly marked: cynical, detached, unscrupulous, an ironic observer and recorder of other people's passions. It is a nice façade to sit behind, but a trifle bleak.

*POINT VALAINE (1935)*

NOËL MEANDERED BACK to England by way of Bermuda, where he joined HMS *Dragon* for a cruise of the Caribbean. Then on to Trinidad, with a side trip to an eccentric little island with a romantic shanty hotel called Point Balaine.

Even when he was supposed to be taking a complete break, Noël's mind was subconsciously looking for the next project, and he immediately filed away the setting for future use.

Meanwhile, on board, he came across a book called *The Regent and His Daughter,* and as had happened with *Bitter Sweet,* the sights and sounds of the Regency period began to fill his mind. On the long sea journey back to England he began work on the libretto for what became *Conversation Piece.* From the outset he knew who the star would be. On every visit to Paris— and there were many of those at this time—he would rush to see the latest operetta starring Yvonne Printemps. He would write a show for her.

Back in London he is writing to Alec Woollcott:

> 17 Gerald Road
> August 22nd

Dearest Acky-wacky-weesa,
At the moment I am working on something of which I am sure you will approve highly. It's a very small, light operette, half in French and half in English, for Yvonne Printemps and Romney Brent, which will be done here round about January or February. I am pretty excited about it. There are marvellous parts for both of them.

I am just going off to France for a couple of weeks and when I come back I shall set to work in earnest on the Printemps play and fling my house open to receive the creaking and aged bodies of Alfred and Lynn. Lorn is looking lovely; Sybil Colefax has asked quite a lot of people to lunch; Mary Sherwood [Robert's wife] is still far too small; and everything is fine and dandy.

I miss you very much, Ackie dear, and think of you in the most beautiful way imaginable . . . in fact I have been saying to myself for weeks "I really must write to the rubbishy old sod."

> Love and kisses, love and kisses, love and kisses,
> NOËL

Yvonne Printemps (1895–1977). *"Voilà, cher Noël. Une photo prisé à votre jardin."*

Back in Goldenhurst in the fall, he set to writing the score for *Conversation Piece* and making frequent trips to Paris to woo Mlle. Printemps.

The story he devised is set in Regency Brighton, where Paul, the so-called Duc de Chaucigny-Varennes has brought his ward, Melanie, from France in the hopes of rescuing both of them from imminent poverty by securing a good aristocratic marriage for her. It soon becomes clear that Melanie is in love with Paul, and all his machinations lead inevitably to a happy ending.

Cochran presented this "Romantic Comedy with Music" at His Majesty's Theatre on February 16, 1934, with Noël as Paul and Yvonne Printemps as Melanie. Mlle. Printemps's English rarely rose above the phonetic, but by the end of the run the rest of the cast were speaking adequate French.

Noël could write to Woollcott:

17 Gerald Road
April 3rd 1934

I am now giving an exquisite performance as a syphilitic French duke, fortunately only for three weeks more; Romney comes occasionally and makes hideous Siamese faces at me from the side of the stage. [Romney Brent had been the original choice as Paul but had gladly handed it over to Noël—"providing you let me still come to rehearsals and watch you find out what a bloody awful part it is".]

The play is a great success; the music and lyrics are good and the production excellent, and Gladys has done a marvellous job. The play itself I think is dull and garbled and I am faintly ashamed of it.

He also found time to write to Clifton Webb, who was appearing on Broadway in the Irving Berlin/Moss Hart revue *As Thousands Cheer* and had suggested that Noël might have indulged in a little petty larceny as far as the "Easter Parade" sequence in *Conversation Piece* was concerned.

March 27th 1934

Clifton, my little dear,

I hear weecked, disquieting rumours that you think I cribbed the tableau idea of Easter Parade for my dainty *Conversation Piece* and oh dear, oh dear, I honestly and truly never even thought of it and was absolutely delighted with the originality of my plan. Now I realise that it must have been sitting in my subconscious mind. Anyhow you will be delighted to hear it is as effective as ever and, may I say, you wicked old drab, that if I had thought of it I will tell you honestly and deeply and from my heart I *would* have stolen it without a qualm and even, if possible, have pretended that you all got the idea from me first . . . so there. In *Conversation Piece* it is actually slightly better than in *As Thousands Cheer,* because I use the silences in order to allow dialogue to be heard . . . also, instead of doing it once, I do it over and over and over again until the audiences go mad with irritation.

Any more nonsense from you and I shall not only kill myself but Rockefeller, Ghandi [Gandhi] and all the Mdvani brothers and then where will your show be? In the meanwhile perhaps you would write me a letter saying you love me very much and telling me about your life from A to Z.

Goody Goody
NOËL

In the April letter to Woollcott he also found time to bring him up to date on matters more domestic:

Dearest Ackie-Weezer,

I said to myself, I said, Ackie is getting old and weary so I will write him a letter just to cheer him up and when he is sitting over the fire in the evening, dreaming of Edna Ferber and days that are no more, he will be able to take it out (the letter, I mean) and look at it.

We are all very cosy and happy, all meaning Lynn and Alfred and Jack and me, and we intend to produce a whole lot of beautiful plays with lovely messages for the World and it's all highly delicious. Gladys has had her appendix out and Jeffrey keeps on flying possees of disgruntled old ladies backwards and forwards to and from Le Touquet.

Lorn is looking very pretty but faintly silly; she is still in love with you and constantly slavers over a rubber doll which she thinks looks like you.

Father became suddenly ill and nearly joined the feathered choir, but was reclaimed by several expensive nurses and lots of oxygen tubes. Mother is in Monte Carlo and Auntie Vida is in Madeira, having quarrelled with Mother, so everything is dandy.

Showing off his French soon began to pall, and Noël was soon happy to hand over Paul to a real Frenchman, Pierre Fresnay, later to become Yvonne's next husband. Besides, he had other things on his mind.

One of them was to leave Cochran's management to set up on his own— or, rather, with friends. Transatlantic Productions would have four principals: Noël, Alfred, Lynn, and . . . Jack Wilson.

Noël wrote to break the news to Cochran:

April 9th

My Dear Cocky,

If you were a less understanding or generous person this letter would be very difficult to write; as it is, however, I feel you will appreciate my motives completely and without prejudice.

I have decided after mature consideration to present my own and other people's plays in the future in partnership with Jack. This actually has been brewing in my mind over a period of years, and I am writing to you first in confidence because I want you to understand that there would be no question of forsaking you or breaking our tremendously happy and successful association for any other reason except that I feel this is an inevitable development of my career in the theatre.

Particularly I want you to realise how deeply grateful I am for all the generosity and courage and friendship you have shown me over everything we have done together . . . but above all, dear Cocky, I want to insist upon one important fact which, sentimental as it may seem, is on my part sincere, and that is that without your encouragement and faith in me and my work it is unlikely that I should ever have reached the position I now hold in the theatre, and that whatever may happen in the future I feel that there is a personal bond between us which has nothing to do with business or finance or production. Please understand all this and continue to give me the benefit of your invaluable friendship.

Yours affectionately,
NOËL

There was something of a hiatus before Cochran replied:

My dear Noël,
Many thanks for your letter of the 9th inst., which was found this morning under my bed, very much chewed up by my dachshund.

As you say, the development you refer to was inevitable, and I wish you and your associates the best of good fortune.

Meanwhile, believe me,

Yours as ever,
CBC

Having gone to the trouble of being emollient, Noël was somewhat put out by what he considered Cochran's dismissive reply. It was only with the perspective of time that it became clear that none of his post-Cochran musicals would enjoy the same degree of success as the shows of that illustrious decade.

·

THE SPARRING with Woollcott continued:

August [?] 1934

Dear Mr. Woollcott,
I have undergone a serious operation and have been very seriously ill and I feel that I am impelled to inform you that your book, *When Rome Something or Other* has been largely instrumental in seducing me back to life from the valley of the shadow. I was lent this volume by the Earl Amherst, an insignificant blond of my acquaintance, and was grieved to note on the fly leaf an inscription from you. This forced me to two reluctant conclusions.

(A) That you are a crawling mean old snob obviously intent upon ingratiating yourself with titled people and callously disregarding your friends of the gutter who are naturally better equipped to understand and appreciate your work, and (B)—exactly the same as (A).

Don't please imagine that I am *angry* or that I *mind* being neglected. I am only the teeniest bit *hurt*. I suggest that you remedy this unfortunate error in judgement by sending me a copy immediately, you saucy old sod.

Love and kisses, darling Acky Weesa.<br>Noelie Poelie

P.S. I noticed with delight that several of the pages were uncut.
P.P.S. I did not cut them.

At this time Woollcott had bought a shared interest in Neshobe Island, in faraway Vermont, and insisted that the Algonks—and anyone else who currently happened to be under his sway—visit, irrespective of the inconvenience to his guests. He replied to Noël from there:

Bomoseen, Vermont<br>August 11, 1934

Dear Noël,

Your little pencilled scrawl filled me with a great and unexpected longing to see you. I had heard about your illness in the most belated and roundabout fashion. Your Mr. Lunt mentioned it in a hurried letter, breaking it to me gently by saying that you had almost died and then going on laughingly to matters of more real interest to him.

I am considerably upset about this course of action pursued by the fourth and a half Earl. With the exception of Mrs. Stanley Baldwin and two or three articled clerks living near Liverpool, the entire citizenry of the British Empire has written me with great enthusiasm about *While Rome Burns,* all explaining that they had borrowed their copy from Earl Amherst. This would seem to indicate that thanks to his lordship's lavishness all sales of the book in England and the Dominions had been rendered unnecessary. I hope the little bleached son of a bitch fries in hell. As there now seems to be no hope of your buying a copy, I might as well send you one and will do so when I return to New York in October. In the interval I am happily ensconced on my island. I get news of the outside world in the form of telegrams which are telephoned from Rutland to a boatman living on the shore who takes them down in a firm Spencerian hand and gives them to his son to bring over to me in a motor boat. This makes my favorite occupation guessing what the sender really intended to say. Thus, when the Lunts recently threatened to visit me, I was thrown into an agreeable state of agitation by a distracted telegram from Alfred which said that Lynn was "too ill to take Johnny". Her condition seemed, indeed, desperate.

By the way, put an order in at Hatchard's for a copy of a new novel by Charles Brackett called *Entirely Surrounded.* The scene is our island and all the characters will be painfully recognizable. Neysa [McMein] comes off best. The portrait of Dorothy Parker (Mrs. Alan Campbell) is the most astonishingly skillful and the owner of the island is a repulsive behemoth with elfin manners whom you would be the first to recognize. He is named Thaddeus Hulbert and makes his first appearance playing backgammon with an English actor at a party. He calls a passing redhead to his side. I quote:

"The fat man clapped a plump, well-molded hand, with dice in the palm, against Henry's copper-colored hair, rubbed it back and forth. 'Now I double; do you take it?' 'Uncle Thaddeus is in wine', the fat man's opponent observed in clipped British accents. 'I take it, Duck'. Henry had seen the speaker's tired, eager, charm-furrowed face behind footlights: Nigel Farraday."

One passage I particularly like is that in which the Dorothy Parker character gropes for the *mot juste* with which to describe Harpo. She finally dismisses him as "That faun's ass."

It is a charming book; and now, my blemish, au revoir.

A. WOOLLCOTT

The rest of the year was devoted to other men's theatrical flowers. In April, in London, Noël directed S. N. Behrman's *Biography,* with Ina Claire and Laurence Olivier. Hugh "Binkie" Beaumont, assigned to co-produce it, would be almost exclusively involved with Noël's work for the next thirty years, but he considered this maiden venture a "dis-ah-ster."

Then there was the 1927 Ferber/Kaufman play *The Royal Family,* to be retitled *Theatre Royal* for its British production, out of deference to the *real* royal family.

Ferber wrote to Noël:

Pebbles
Sasco Hill, Southport, Conn.
June 28th 1934

Ever since you cabled George [Kaufman], my dear Noël, about *The Royal Family,* I've been wanting to tell you how happy I am to know that you are doing it. In all the world there's no one I'd rather see producing it.

I spoke to Jack about the Oscar Wolfe part because I was a little upset about the man chosen to play it in England. It's all none of my business, perhaps, except that I'm fond of the play, of you, and of myself. You know. Anyway, that part, though rather brief, has a curious importance . . .

Oh, forgive a doting mother's heart, sir!

I see your dear diabolical smile in all the pictures of N.C. in all the papers. It's grand to know you are to be here next winter and I hope to Gawd I'll see more of you than I saw last time. Three plays I believe it is for you this next season, and very tidy, too, and HOW does he do it is what I always say.

I'm here in Jack's house and it's practically perfect—or would be if there weren't usually ten workmen around the place hammering, pounding, digging, blasting or scraping. I have developed a green hatred against the Laboring Class as a result, and when the Revolution comes I'll be the Marie Antoinette of Connecticut.

I love you, and hope this finds you the same, and beg to remain,
                    Respectfully
                    E. FELDMAN

Since the closing of *Design for Living,* Lynn and Alfred had been playing the parts of idle country gentry. Every summer they would retire to their home in Genesee Depot, Wisconsin, and work hard at relaxing until their desire to perform propelled them like shot from a cannon back to Broadway and the inevitable tour.

Back in August, Alfred had given Noël a progress report:

                              Genesee Depot, Wisconsin
                              August 16th 1934

Dear Noeley,
Don't worry, baby, we shall be in New York November 24th, start rehearsals on the 25th and open Christmas Eve in Boston. I can't swear to be opening two weeks later at the [Ethel] Barrymore [New York], we may not be quite ready, though I hope we will.

I have never felt so well in my life and when I tell you that it is now but six a.m. and that I've been up since five o'clock, you can imagine with what happiness I welcome each day.

Lynn is getting on awfully well—though slowly. [She had recently been ill.] She should stay here a year but, of course, she won't—we can't—we're quite broke for some reason but just the same we're building like mad and enjoying every brick of it. Ever since the possibility of your coming out our one bathroom has worried us, so we decided to add a couple of new ones and work began this week. The place should be lovely and I hope to God you'll come out some day, you little bugger, and enjoy it.

The pool is a huge success and the hotter the days the nicer it is. You can't get Lynn out of it and I must say I like it myself. We have cocktails brought down, sometimes at noon, which will give you a rough idea how loose we've become.

Lynn is getting on splendidly with her French. She has a woman come out three days a week for conversation and from what snatches I catch as I pass with my hoe or my mop it all sounds very good indeed. I'm doing a bit of German (with our cook) but it's all about food and so I shall never be able to say a word outside a kitchen—which, however, is Jake with me.

My sister, Karin read *Point Valaine* and was thrilled to death—she had a miscarriage a few days later. Everyone was delighted and feel it a good omen. She says the next time she's about to have a child, won't you send her your newest play? She and Louise (my other sister) sing a lovely song, "All Abort for Alabam".

I'm having Kate Lawson work on rain effects—and Sunday is my birthday—I don't feel a day over forty. [He would, in fact, be forty-two.]

> Great love from us all,
> ALFRED

On Alfred's fiftieth birthday Noël would cable:

> *HALF A CENTURY HAS SPED*
> *OVER GRANDPA'S SILVER HEAD*
> *SILVER HAIR IS GRANDPA'S SORROW—*
> *HERE TODAY BLACK TOMORROW.*

A few days after Alfred's letter of August 16, Lynn also writes:

> August 30th 1934

Darling, darling, darling:—
This letter has been simmering inside me, what you would call deep, deep down, all summer long where all my best letters simmer and never seem to come to a boil. Is it because I watch the pot? (Five pounds over weight and can't get it down).

It seems incredible at this moment, when we are usually packed to go back to rehearsals very depressed, that we have two more months holiday. It gives me the loveliest, calmest feeling in my spine . . .

We have so much to tell you, some of it cannot be written but some can (that's good, I hear you saying, or perhaps something wittier). One is, that I have read *Pointe* [sic] *Valaine* twice and found it each time awfully exciting. I don't see how it can fail.

I have a French teacher every other day and we sit and talk, and thank God, I am at least beginning to understand what she says. I also took the French grammar to the mat, God help me, and I—*je serai* and *il sera* and *j'aurai* and *je suis monté*. Oh, just all over the place but isn't it fun? I'm afraid it is going to break my heart to stop it and learn *Pointe Valaine* . . .

Well, sweet, the time is getting short now, in a couple of months we shall see your pretty face. Until then, most beloved,

Your own,
LYNN
Lynnie Potts

As Alfred and Lynn were composing their letters Noël was holidaying in the yacht *Marra* in the Mediterranean with "Sugar," the actor Louis Hayward, who had been in the cast of *Conversation Piece*.

As Noël had left London for Cannes, where the *Marra* was due to dock, he had also left behind a production problem on *Theatre Royal*. The male lead was to be Brian Aherne, who had a contractual conflict for the pre-London tour. He first had to finish a film for MGM, and Laurence Olivier was to play the part for two weeks before Aherne arrived. However, on reflection, Noël preferred to have Olivier play for the whole run.

From the Carlton Hotel he cabled London:

> UNABLE TO RETURN BEFORE FRIDAY STOP YACHT HAS BEEN
> STORM BOUND AND HAS NOT ARRIVED YET STOP NO BOAT
> LEAVING BEFORE THURSDAY STOP HAVE PERFECT FAITH IN
> YOUR JUDGEMENT STOP SEE ONLY TWO ALTERNATIVES STOP
> EITHER SCRAP WHOLE PRODUCTION AND SUE AHERNE AND
> METRO FOR DAMAGES OR OPEN WITH OLIVIER AND FORCE
> AHERNE TO FOLLOW HIM STOP CAN THINK OF NOBODY ELSE
> FOR PART STOP IS THERE NO CHANCE OLIVIER BEING
> PERSUADED PLAY WHOLE RUN STOP WIRE ME CARLTON CANNES
> STOP IF YACHT ARRIVES TODAY WILL LEAVE IMMEDIATELY FEEL
> DREADFUL NOT BEING THERE TO HELP ALL LOVE STOP CHOOP

The *Marra* arrived and the cruise began.

•

ON AUGUST 24 Noël is writing to Violet from Ajaccio, Corsica:

This island particularly is the loveliest place. Enormous mountains and vast red cliffs going sheer down into deep blue sea. We go paddling along the coast for a few hours every day and drop anchor at night in some small harbour, well away from the shore, so as to be quiet and we sit on the deck and have cocktails and play the gramophone and sometimes go ashore to dine in some little café. We have a very good cook of our own so we don't need to budge if we don't want to. The sea is generally like glass and very clear and it's lovely to be able to pop in over the side before going to bed. Sugar has mastered his fear of the sea and is beginning to swim quite well. I take great care of myself and propel myself along with my arms so as not to return to you with giant hernias sticking out of me like melons. We're in bed by ten every night and up at seven. I think grandfather must be responsible for my sea fever! It's certainly very strong . . .

          Love and hugs.
          SNOOPIE
Sugar sends his love

The sea, unfortunately, decided not to stay "like glass," and the yacht was wrecked soon after "a terrible night in the storm with a fainting French Captain, me at the wheel, upheld by gin and my ex-appendicitis truss." Violet was never told the full story. Instead he cabled from Marseilles:

SEPTEMBER 6TH

PERFECTLY ALL RIGHT STOP LEFT YACHT FIVE DAYS BEFORE
WRECK STOP SNOOP

Years later he confided to his *Diary* that "that bestial little yacht" was "not one of the happier episodes of my life."

·

BACK IN LONDON he began rehearsals for *Theatre Royal.* The London production starred Noël's beloved Marie Tempest, equally beloved Madge Titheradge, and a fully committed Laurence Olivier. Noël tried to put Ferber's mind at rest about her "baby":

Ferber my little darling, this is just to tell you we have had our last dress rehearsal and it looks pretty good. Larry Olivier is playing Tony and is marvelous. I think you'd be delighted with the whole cast with one notable exception and that is W. Graham Browne [Miss Tempest's husband] as Oscar Wolfe who, owing to being very old indeed and unable to act at all (combining these assets with complete inaudibility) will present to a resigned public one of the most degraded characterizations of the modern Theatre—pardon the word modern.

    This unfortunately is absolutely unavoidable as Marie Tempest will not appear without him and she is beyond words superb as Fanny . . . I think you and George would be pleased with the whole performance and production. Anyhow I hope so as I've worked very hard over it and have been living all through rehearsals in a Nursing Home. I am better now, however, and shall join the play at the end of the week . . . and devote the last two weeks to polishing up. I'll be arriving in New York on the 20th so put the kettle on the hob, there's a dear and please may I tell you, dear Miss Ferber and dear Mr. Kaufman, that I think *The Royal Family* [*Theatre Royal*] is one of the most superbly written and brilliantly constructed plays that I have ever had anything to do with.

Second time proved to be lucky, and the Ferber-Kaufman piece was well received.

•

THE LUNTS were to get their wish to see Noël before New York, but not until after a November visit of his to Ottawa with Edwina Mountbatten, where the attention he received he found "all very pompous and faintly funny. The Governor General came down to Quebec to meet us with a special train and a great deal of bowing and curtesying went on . . . I have a dreary pompous day ahead of me."

Edwina was always a particular favorite of Noël's. She was a woman with an individual spirit who attracted more than her share of gossip. At different times there was speculation that she had had affairs with Paul Robeson and Indian politician Pandit Nehru.

An invitation to share her company meant a happy time and shared jokes. A proposed weekend in 1937 inspired a note for Lornie:

> *I could really not be keener*
> *On a week-end with Edwina*
> *From the moment that one rises*
> *Life's a series of surprises.*
> *On emerging from the lu-lu*
> *One's confronted by a Zulu,*
> *And one gives a sharp shrill cry on*
> *Being pounced at by a lion;*
> *So it's natural at dinner*
> *One's appreciably thinner.*
> *Still I just could not be keener*
> *On a week-end with Edwina*

From there Noël went straight to Genesee Depot "and the darling Lunts." To Violet:

The Waldorf-Astoria
New York
November 20th

Darlingest,

I had an enchanting week with Lynn and Alfred in their farm. It is so sweet, all done in bright colours—like a Swedish Farmhouse. Alfred gardens madly all day long and Lynn sews curtains, plays patience and studies her part. She almost knows it. We start rehearsing on Monday . . .

*Conversation Piece* had opened on October 23 at the 44th Street Theatre, with Yvonne Printemps and Pierre Fresnay again heading the cast. It would survive for only fifty-five performances.

On December 3 he reports that rehearsals for *Point Valaine* "are going with what is known as a swing . . . Lynn and Alfred are in a flat spin and everything looks rosy!" Though a little later he would admit: "All very difficult. Rehearsals fairly beastly. Gladys sets too heavy and highly untropical. The Lunts touchy and not happy. Finally opened in Boston on Christmas night with everything going wrong including rain effect and most of the lighting. Nobody pleased."

*Point Valaine* turned out to be an ill-considered venture. Noël had written it in a hurry, wanting to produce something "different." As Alfred would say when it was all over, with more than a touch of irony, "Well, Noely—you certainly succeeded there."

It was the story of a group of ill-assorted people who find themselves in a run-down hotel on a small island in the West Indies. The Lunts were daringly cast against type, with Lynn playing Linda, the woman with a past who owns the hotel, and Alfred as Serge, the surly Russian servant who has been her lover.

It was uncertain melodrama, a hybrid of early Tennessee Williams, who had yet to arrive on the scene, and mid–Somerset Maugham. Audiences who had come to see the Lunts be the *Lunts* did not take kindly to it.

Symptomatic of the mechanical problems that also plagued the production was the evening when Alfred was revealed standing high on a stage rock from which he was meant to jump into the sea to be devoured by sharks. Unfortunately, a stagehand had removed the mattress on which he would land. The curtain and then Alfred had to be brought down, in that order.

On January 16, 1935, the play opened at the Ethel Barrymore Theatre, scene of the Lunts' *Design for Living* triumph.

"We've had a very trying time over the play," Noël wrote to Violet in January.

The first night was awful, very dull and resentful audience. I think they all expected a gay champagne comedy and that, most emphatically, they didn't get! The press was very abusive, three good notices and the rest awful. They do hate me breaking away and trying to do something different, anyhow we are playing to marvelous business and New York is fighting wildly over the play. It has certainly been sensational all right. We ought to run comfortably until about June! So to hell with the notices as usual!

However, in his next letter he had to admit that the play was "only hic-coughing along."

Noël, who had tasted failure, could be reasonably philosophical about it, as he wrote to G. B. Stern:

> March 5th
>
> Well, dear, in spite of all our predictions, *Point Valaine* was a flop. The press and the public refused to accept our beloved Lunts spitting in each other's faces; they said a lot of very unkind things and my pants are in tatters. But, oddly enough, my darling, I have risen above it with that old world resilience which you know so well, and I am flouncing off to China on Friday to finish my book, write seventeen plays, a couple of operas and every now and then a postcard to you. I shall be back in London in June, so keep the lamp in the window.
> P.S. After all, Ibsen and Shaw got bad notices, didn't they, once? And what I always say is that we writers must be brave and true and stand by (not lie on) our convictions.

As a supportive fellow writer, "Peter" (G. B. Stern) wrote to tell him that it "*is* your best play."

The Lunts were not so forgiving. They always considered it their one and only flop, and they had long memories. Over a decade later, Alfred was to say, "All I can think and hope for is that that entire opening night audience was dead long ago."

Noël—as so often—refused to see the danger signs. From the Boston preview he had cabled Woollcott:

DECEMBER 27TH

PRESS ENTHUSIASTIC BUSINESS CAPACITY PLAY WENT WELL ALL
PERFORMANCES SWELL ALFRED SUPERB AND VERY DEPRESSED
STOP ARRIVING MONDAY MORNING PLEASE PREPARE LOVE
NEST STOP HAVE HEAVY HEAD COLD HAPPY CHRISTMAS STOP
MR. COWARD

And later:

DECEMBER 29TH

ESSIE PLEASIE KINDLY RESERVE COMFORTABLE ROOMS
AMBASSADOR WEST FOR FIFTH EARL [Amherst] AND ME STOP DO
THIS EFFICIENTLY AND WITHOUT MUDDLE STOP PUT FLOWERS
IN BOTH ROOMS CHARGED TO YOURSELF STOP AM IN NO MOOD
TO TOLERATE ANY MORE OF YOUR INCONSEQUENTIAL RADDLED
BOHEMIANISM LOVE AND WET KISSES STOP COWARD

# CHAPTER 13
## *THE SCOUNDREL . . .*
## AND STILL TRAVELING ALONE
### (1935–1936)

*The world is wide, and when my day is done*
*I shall at least have travelled free*
*Led by this wanderlust*
*That turns my eyes to far horizons . . .*
*I travel alone.*

**"I TRAVEL ALONE" (1934)**

*The Scoundrel*, Noël's first "real" film. The horse fancier is Julie Haydon.

# To VIOLET:

The Waldorf-Astoria
New York
Monday, December 3rd 1934

Darlingest,

I've got a bit of news that I know will please you. I am going at last to do a picture here at the Paramount studios. Ben Hecht and Charlie MacArthur (who did *Crime Without Passion*) are writing a special story for me and I must say it sounds pretty thrilling! . . .

The story is dramatic with a certain amount of comedy in it and I think will give me every opportunity to do my stuff. We've had a series of conferences and now they have gone off into a huddle to write it!

I'm very interested to see whether I like it or not, at any rate they do things far more quickly than the Hollywood people, so even if I hate it, it won't last long!

January [?] 1935

My picture is going to be very good, I think. The story and dialogue is marvelous but, oh dear, I'm afraid it will upset you as it is very tragic and I have to die in it! I play half of it as a dead man! I will send you a complete script soon so you can read it first and be fully prepared. I have done some good tests and they all seem to think that I'm fine, so that's that! Hope [Williams] is playing in it with me and in one restaurant scene Alfred, Lynn, Katherine [*sic*] Cornell, [Elisabeth] Bergner and Ina Claire are walking on! I'm at the studio all day. I get up at seven a.m. and don't get back until the evening when I go straight to bed. It's a hard routine but actually I rather enjoy it!

Sugar [Louis Hayward] has made the most enormous personal success (in *Point Valaine*) and is inundated with film offers. He is signing with Metro Goldwyn and getting ten thousand dollars for his first picture, fifteen thousand for the next and so on. It really is lovely for him and we are all very glad.

Noël was only receiving five thousand dollars for his own efforts, but this, he felt, was just the beginning. He wrote to Clifton Webb, "Jean Harlow had better look to her laurels."

February [?]

The film is three-quarters done and seems pretty good. Everyone concerned seems to think I am wonderful gorgeous superb and magnificent, which means that I give an excellent performance on the whole! I had a grueling time the night before last, I had to walk up and down a street (scene) for four hours in a deluge of ice cold rain with a wind machine going full blast, although I had tumblers of neat whisky after each shot it gave me a slight cold but the effect on the screen is quite extraordinary, just a sea of umbrellas and my face wandering through them. I'm drowned half way through the picture and play all the last part dead, which means no make-up, which is lovely. I have a natty little conversation with God at one point while I'm floating in a wild and ever so stormy sea! (Tank) I electrified the studio the other day by playing an emotional scene over and over again and actually crying each time without having menthol sprayed into my eyes. They are apparently unused to technical acting in the movies! . . . I'll send you some of the still photographs.

Having spent many uncomfortable hours in studio rain, Noël later turned down the lead in *The Bridge on the River Kwai*, claiming, "Everybody seemed to spend so much time under water."

The Waldorf-Astoria
New York
March 8th

Darling,

This is just a scribble before I catch my train for Hollywood.

I saw the film all through this morning and it looks fine. I'm afraid I am doomed to be a picture star but I shan't do more than one picture a year.

In fact he didn't make another until 1942.

•

THE FILM OVER, Noël took the train to the West Coast and Hollywood, where he was "the belle of the ball and feted all ends up." Word of mouth or possibly Hollywood jungle drums had been at work, and all sorts of lucrative offers were waiting for him to star, write, "write and star." He even did a screen test for Irving Thalberg at MGM. It was all very flattering but he kept his head until he was safely on the SS *Tatsuta Maru* on his way to Honolulu at the beginning of the Far East trip that would take him to China, Japan, and Singapore.

March 19th

Darlingest,

Here I am, relaxed at last. I'm afraid I didn't get time to write from Hollywood. I was only there such a short time and was on the go unceasingly . . . I can never tell you how lovely it is to be on the sea again. I've slept and slept and also written a lot of my book [*Present Indicative*] which must and *shall* be finished before I get home . . .

Well, dear, I'm afraid I shall have to fall for the movies after all. I've almost but not quite decided to do three pictures in two years for Metro Goldwyn Mayer. It only means six weeks to two months at a time and they're offering me such marvellous terms it seems a little silly to refuse. I asked for a percentage of the gross which they never give and to my amazement they said yes! So I quickly got onto a boat and disappeared. I don't intend to sign any contracts until after the Hecht/MacArthur picture has opened on Broadway April 3rd. I have a dreamy artistic feeling that I shall get a higher percentage still after that! All this is extremely secret at the moment, so don't tell a soul . . .

I was seen off by Ruth Chatterton, Ronnie Coleman [*sic*], Norma Shearer, Constance Collier, Cary Grant, etc., etc., so the commotion on the boat was terrific! They all brought hampers and flowers and God knows what so I've done very well. Constance has definitely fallen on her feet and has a fat five year contract. Isn't it lovely for her? She was practically down and out when she arrived.

The Lunts are rehearsing madly for *The Taming of the Shrew* which we [Transatlantic Productions] are doing in conjunction with the Theatre Guild, which is a good joke anyway.

> La Pietra
> Honolulu
> March 28th

Well, I've been here a week and I'm sailing tomorrow on *The Empress of Canada.* Honolulu has grown a lot since I was first here and I have had a very gay time, so much so that I shall be glad to get on the boat tomorrow. Oh dear, the parties and the picnics and the general doings!

It's very lovely sitting on the terrace in the moonlight with Hawaiian Orchestras playing and Hula dancers wiggling about. I've come home each evening hung with LEIS, which are chains of fresh flowers—carnations and jasmine and gardenias . . .

I'm getting on very well with the book . . . I made a semi-official visit to the Hospital today and went through all the wards dropping words of comfort and behaving like a good celebrity should! . . .

In June he was back in Goldenhurst and working on his "Autumn play," which turned out to be several plays. Lynn was the first to welcome him back to civilization.

> Genesee Depot
> June 18th 1935

Darling Noely:

This is to welcome the distinguished traveler from foreign parts, becomingly tanned with that peculiar keen look in his eyes that only sailors have.

We have come to roost in our little nook and cranny and I must say after a good deal of bucketing from one frightful hotel to a worse and one great auditorium to a greater, it is very pleasant.

Can't you be in New York for the opening night? You must try. It would be too lonely without you.

We are dying to have your news. Have you written another play? Have you finished your book? What you're going to do next? Do you have a regular movement every day? How is Gladys's garden coming on and did she try any new seeds, if so, did they come up?

We are still waiting for another script, preferably with a large cast of men to play alternately with the *Shrew,* as we are rather afraid there may not be a long life in Shakespeare.

I've just done such a funny thing, darling. I ran out of cold cream and Hattie had gone to bed and the light was turned out in her room so I crept into her bathroom (your bathroom) and dug the last remaining bit out of the crevices of an almost empty jar, rubbed it lightly over my face and came downstairs to continue this letter, when I was greeted with shouts of laughter. It appears I had got into the silver cream she puts on her hair and I had made my entrance with a bright silver face.

We saw *The Scoundrel* the other night and thought it most original, with some fine direction and YOU superb. The story of the picture after your death didn't come off, as far as I was concerned. I mean, I didn't *believe* it. Either I was in a very material mood or it seemed faintly absurd but, of course, we had a lovely time. The epigrams too got a little self-conscious after a while, the writing, I mean. You were always perfect and so handsome, such a beautiful face, my little Noely-Poly.

Yours ever,<br>LYNNIE GO PINNIE

·

OVER IN LONDON, Noël is preparing the nine one-act plays he and Gertie are to perform under the title *Tonight at 8:30.* As light relief, he took time off to keep up with old friends, such as Somerset Maugham:

Goldenhurst Farm<br>8/7/35

Darling Mr. Maugham,

Imagine my embarrassment on hearing obliquely from a certain lady novelist of my acquaintance [G. B. Stern] (if you'll pardon the term "lady") that you never got a copy of *Point Valaine.* Oh dear! Am I mortified, or am I mortified! Anyhow here is one and I love you very much.

Maybe your chocolate eyes will brighten when I tell you that during my recent travels in the oh so glamorous Orient I lived on an exclusive diet of Somerset Maugham, re-reading practically everything you have ever written and taking off my topi and shorts to you as being, I am afraid, a very great writer indeed.

I may appear on your doorstep suddenly during the next 3 months, so keep yourself in a state of suspended vivacity on the off chance.

All my love, Willie dear, and whack that black-browed Peter [G. B. Stern] for me with one of her own walking sticks.

Noël

17 Gerald Road
16/8/35

Darling Acky-wacky-wocky-weeza-peeza-

It was ever ever so nice to get your absolutely ripping letter all about your jolly doings and the fun you are having which, although liable to bore the fuck out of anyone less fond of you than I am, really gave me a nostalgic longing to see your pretty face again and nuzzle my head on your shoulder like I always do.

Jack and Lorn and Temple and Sybil Colefax and Mother and I are arriving at the Island next Friday week. You don't have to pay any attention to us as we are all quite content to have what you have.

Oh dear, how I wish I could! But I'm actually working like mad on a new dainty for Gertie and me for the Autumn, which I will write you more fully about later . . .

I'm going out for a provincial tour with Gertie opening on October 17th and finishing in December. Then we open in London on January 6th and will, I hope, play through till about May.

Love and big wet kisses,

Noël

•

THE SUMMER MONTHS brought bad news and good. Noël's new friend T. E. Lawrence was killed while riding his motorcycle down a deserted English country lane. The cause of the accident was never satisfactorily determined, and there was speculation about suicide.

When in 1963 Richard Aldington wrote a book viciously "deconstructing" Lawrence, Noël reflected: "I wish now I had probed a bit deeper when I knew him. Whatever they may say of him, however, he was unquestionably a great writer of the English language."

Then one Sunday at Goldenhurst Noël received a phone call from a woman claiming to be Marlene Dietrich. He hung up, assuming it was one of his friends playing a practical joke, but Dietrich rang back and told him firmly that she was calling to congratulate him on *The Scoundrel*. She later sent him a cable to "Golden Hearst Farm." (Clearly William Randolph Hearst made an indelible impression in Hollywood!) It was the beginning of a beautiful, almost forty-year friendship.

# INTERMISSION
# MARLENE DIETRICH: "OUR LEGENDARY, LOVELY MARLENE"

*We know God made trees*
*And the birds and the bees*
*And the seas for the fishes to swim in*
*We are also aware*
*That he had quite a flair*
*For creating exceptional women.*

. . . . . . . . . . . . . . . . . . . . . . .

*Though we all might enjoy*
*Seeing Helen of Troy*
*As a gay, cabaret entertainer*
*I doubt that she could*
*Be one quarter as good*
*As our legendary, lovely Marlene*

NOËL'S INTRODUCTION TO DIETRICH'S CABARET DEBUT,
AT LONDON'S CAFÉ DE PARIS (JUNE 21, 1954)

JULY 30TH 1935
MARLENE DIETRICH
PARAMOUNT STUDIOS
HOLLYWOOD
(CALIF.)

DEAR MARLENE WAS SO TOUCHED AND CHARMED TO HEAR YOUR
VOICE TONIGHT IT WAS SO SWEET OF YOU TO CALL ME SENDING
PHOTOGRAPH IMMEDIATELY MY LOVE TO YOU NOËL.

JULY 31ST
I SEE YOU EVERY NIGHT AND TALK OF YOU ALL DAY STOP
MARLENE

June 1954. "The world's most glamorous grandmother"
arrives in London for her cabaret debut at the Café de Paris.

And that was how it began—and for nearly forty years this superficially unlikely pair cared for and about each other. When Noël was in town—be it New York or Los Angeles—at the same time as Marlene she would meet his ship or plane, cook him the occasional meal like the good German hausfrau she was underneath the glamorous façade—then wave him off. He called her (fondly, it should be quickly added) his "Prussian cow" and, occasionally, "Darling Achtung."

So efficient was Marlene that he reported on one occasion that she had washed everything in sight including his hairbrush, "which was already perfectly clean."

Which is not to say that each was totally uncritical of the other. On Marlene's fiftieth birthday Noël sent her some of her favorite champagne with the accompanying verse:

> *To celebrate your birthday, most adorable Marlene,*
> *I have been to an immense amount of trouble*
> *To get you this expensive bottle of champagne*
> Please *remember that my love's in every bubble!*

She apparently drank the champagne there and then and threw the verse into the bin.

What they had in common, other than a genuine affection, was the mutual and admiring recognition that each was a magnificent self-creation. And over the years they would watch out for each other when they sensed a threat.

In the postwar years they faced similar professional problems. For both of them the ritual procession of success ground to a halt. Noël was his own factory, but the product was not in such demand. Marlene couldn't pick and choose the plum glamour roles as she once had. They had to find other creative outlets.

Noël decided to try his luck in cabaret. A successful season in 1951 at the Café de Paris led to several more and eventually to Las Vegas, where Marlene's introduction to arranger/accompanist Peter Matz was to transform the vocal quality of Noël's entire performance.

In June 1954, Noël persuaded Marlene to appear at the Café, too:

DARLING CERTAINLY THINK YOU SHOULD APPEAR CAFÉ DE PARIS
STOP ROOM AND AMBIENCE PERFECT FOR YOU STOP YOU
SHOULD GET ONE THOUSAND POUNDS A WEEK STOP MONTH OF
JULY VERY GOOD AUGUST TOO LATE IN SEASON ALL LOVE NOËL

On her opening night he introduced her with the verse quoted earlier. Later he teased her about her demanding perfectionism: "For Marlene it's

Noël took over the Actors' Orphanage from Sir Gerald du Maurier in 1934. Here he attends their annual garden party with Marlene. Never one to miss a publicity opportunity, Marlene has made sure every one of the children has a copy of her photograph.

cloth of gold on the walls and purple marmosets swinging from the chandeliers. But for me, sweet fuck all!"

Later that same year he had his own booking:

> 1/11/54
> Noël Coward
> 17 Gerald Road
> S.W.1.

Darling,

The photograph is absolutely wonderful and the dress looks like a dream and Oh, how I wish I could see you whirling on in that tiny hurricane.

I am having a lovely rich success at the *Café de Paris* and I got a beautiful laugh on the opening night by whispering "Hello" huskily through the mike and kicking an invisible cloak! I also leant against the piano with that imperious look and they cheered like anything.

> Love, Love, Love, Love
> Noël

Ironically, what brought the two of them even closer was Marlene's tangled love life. Her daughter, Maria, who was her constant companion from early childhood, records in her memoir of her mother that Marlene had affairs with, among others, Edward R. Murrow, Brian Aherne, Jean Gabin, Erich Maria Remarque, Edith Piaf, Michael Wilding, Harry Cohn, Adlai Stevenson, Frank Sinatra, and Kirk Douglas—a sexually and politically mixed bag by any estimation. But one seemed to loom larger than all the rest put together.

In 1951 she began a tempestuous affair with Yul Brynner, just beginning to establish himself in *The King and I* on Broadway. For once Marlene lost her cool.

> April 3rd, 1952

Noël, my love,

Finally I can sit down to write. After returning from the coast I rushed into recordings for my radio show to be ahead on tapings so that I can leave again at the end of the month . . . That means that I cannot take you to the boat. How sad can things get? And it's all for money, which makes it even sadder. Radio being in its last year as it seems to me, is the last easy source for quick money now and I cannot afford to say no.

My own show does not bring enough money to keep everything and everybody going.

My gilded cage life goes on quite hopelessly . . . Anybody else but

I would be on an analyst's couch by now, faded and frustrated, but every time I want to rebel I tell myself that all this is of my own choosing and that I can stop it anytime I wish. Why I don't stop it I don't know. Maybe I'm too used to get what I want. But then—why shouldn't I get what I want? If he wouldn't want me anymore it would be easy but he seems to want it very badly.

So much of that.

The Chicago Personal Appearance was fun. So much easier than films. I found out what it is I have on the stage. Balls! That's the only explanation I have for the impact of it all . . .

It is spring here so much it hurts. I want it to be last June again and drive in the open car over the Washington Bridge and have Frankfurters and drive back at sundown. But instead I look out through my golden bars and sigh like when I was sixteen. I throw all my tenderness to the children . . .

I miss you as you know always in my heart.

MARLENE

[Undated—probably early summer 1952]

Noël,

I am writing this in a hurry. I will not sign it so you don't have to be careful with this letter. Thank you for being as generous as you are . . .

Thank you also for bothering about my personal problem. I have had the *vague à larmes* all day and I felt very embarrassed to talk about my feelings because what can you say? And if you want to be helpful you might say something, I fear, you don't mean—and then I fear that and therefore I don't tell you really how much I love him. You are wiser than I, so please look well if he loves me and *how.* There are so many different kinds of love he could have, for me, I mean.

I kiss you very tenderly.

410 Park Avenue
August 11, 1952

Dearest Noël,

. . . I am stuck here just as frustrated as before. There was one ray of hope about 2 months ago, complete with moving out and taking an apartment, but it only lasted 2 weeks and things are again as they were before. It was all done very quietly on my unegotistical advice and therefore nobody noticed the two weeks interval. The reason given was again the child [Brynner's]. I do not believe that that is quite true. There are too many children not brought up in bourgoisie life who became quite extraordinary men. So I am still mystified and have no way out. I have repeatedly proposed to pull out of it all but have been implored not to. So I sat here all summer. The films offered to me were pretty bad, therefore it was easy. I'll probably do my television films soon, that will give me something to do . . .

I kiss you tenderly as always,

M

The affair limped along for several years, and Dietrich clearly felt a degree of catharsis by pouring out her feelings to someone she loved who was not a lover.

[Undated 1956]

Last week in New York, I stood at the door when he came. I was not going to do one wrong thing. He came in smiling, bottle under his coat. He came into the bedroom and told me about Paris, the fog around the Eiffel Tower, the streets, the bridges and how he thought about me. I stood there thinking this is not a dream. He is really back and he loves me. Then the hurricane broke over me for three hours and I fell asleep for the first time in two months to the day without torture and sleeping pills.

He woke at eleven, said he had an appointment at twelve. I made coffee as usual, gave him emperin as usual after a drinking night. He left as usual a little bit vague and at the door I said AS USUAL: "When will I hear from you?" and he said: "Later."

He did not call. Sinatra opened that night at the Copacabana. I went at midnight. He was there. I went home. He did not call. All day Friday I waited. As I had made plans to leave for California on Saturday. I called him at 6 p.m. I said my name and he answered. I said I was leaving Saturday and he said he was on the same plane. He said I'll see you then. My heart stopped again. There was something wrong. I thought maybe he hated himself for having come back and there would be scenes again and I said: "Won't I see you before?" And he said: "No, I have no time." I said "I want you to know there will be no complications again, no scenes, no trouble ever, no questions." He said: "Thank you, ma'am." He said: "How did you like Sinatra?" (he saw me there and smiled to me very sweetly and intimately). I said: "I thought it was terrible, Sinatra was drunk, had no voice, very unprofessional." He said, "I sat with him till 8 in the morning." Again I said: "Can't you phone me later tonight?" He said "No." I said: "What's wrong?" He said: "I want nothing anymore. I have no confidence in anyone or anything anymore. Not in you either. You asked for it."

I said: "No confidence in *me*?" He said: "Yes." I said: "Don't you love me any more?" And he said: "You said you would not ask any more questions. I have to stop, someone is coming. See you tomorrow on the plane."

Horrible night. Wanted to cancel trip, but then thought I better go because if I don't go I will reproach myself and I went.

I was taken to the plane first. He came later. Walked by me and took a seat on the other side furthest away from me in the seat section in the back of the already made-up berths. The empty plane took off. He had three drinks and went to his berth without ever looking at me, Thank God I am German. Otherwise I would have jumped out of the plane.

I went to my berth. I took a Fernando Lamas [Marlene always referred to the sleep-inducing suppositories on which she had come to rely as "Fernando Lamases," because she claimed he was the most boring actor she knew] but could not fall asleep. Dozed off and on. Then suddenly I FELT HIS HANDS ON ME AND HIS BODY FALLING HEAVILY ONTO ME. I did not know where I was only that he was there. I took his hand, heard the noise of the motors, knew he was in my berth on a plane and wanted to hide him and pull him in. He pulled himself up and half out and said something. I said: "Come here!" Still half dazed. He started to crawl back to me, then he pulled back again and said, "No, there are too many people around." I let go of his hand. I opened my shade and saw it was light. I said I dreamt this. I looked through my curtains and saw his foot in the shoes I brought from Italy on the floor of the opposite berth. He sat again on his seat of the night before.

I went over to him and said: "Good morning." He said, "Good morning. How did you sleep?" I took [Paris] Match with his story in it so I could bend down, gave it to him.

If you are still with me after reading so far, let me thank you.

Please write to me. I will be here at the Beverly Hills Hotel till February 8th. I have to work which is the worst part of it all. Work usually helps unhappy people. But my kind of work cannot be done with unhappiness. A film would be different because one is being pushed and does not have to create everything alone.

I don't know how to do it yet. I have no Lebensmut [the courage to face life]. And, without that it is difficult to exist, let alone go and dazzle people in Vegas with a performance which is a fake anyway and took always work to put it over.

Now it becomes a mountain of silly, superficial exploits, which only my sense of humor of myself could surmount.

But where do I find that?

As long as I don't know what he feels I will have no rest. If the jealousy angle is true then he must love me still. If not then why did he come back at all? Why did he call you? Why did he tell me he'd "missed me"? Why did he want me so badly?

How can one forget the one one loves when one has no pride at all and no way out like nervous breakdowns or trips around the world or jumping out of a window?

I love you and I wish I could behave in the proper fashion.

17 Gerald Road<br>29/8/52

Darling,

I've just returned from a holiday to find your sweet letter awaiting me. I am thinking of you so much. Don't get too frustrated—there is obviously nothing to be done but "wait and see"—and please, please remember that I love you dearly always.

It's the last stretch that counts.

Love and Kisses<br>NOËL

November 13, 1956

Sweetheart,

Well, the trip was hopeful in the evening. I spoke your dialogue in French (which was not as good, naturally) behind newspapers but, thank God, I had the seat beside him, but Susan Strassburg [Strasberg] sat opposite. He said "Don't let's talk about it." Twice he said that when I asked him for forgiveness. He lied, saying he had not had my letter or telegram . . . That can mean that he did not want to answer them. He said they were probably all amongst the vast mail he had picked up when he drove by the hotel for a moment coming from Boston. Then I read the book with a possible part for him and told him about it. That interested him. From then on we talked quite naturally about films. *Ten Commandments,* etc. Also drinks had by then been drunk. By the way, I forgot to say that he was drunk when I came in. Not terrible but not sober. He had six at least while we were talking. The only thing pointing to future was: "I think *The Red Badge of Courage* is the greatest film ever made. If you have time I could show it to you at Paramount."

Strassburg had by then gone to bed and we were alone talking English. I gave him the ring and the watch because I felt I should not hold on to that. He said he had not missed them. Sure not, because he wore one of the ten watches I had given him. He must be traveling with ten watches. I wrote a note—"*Je t'aime*" and put it on his briefcase which lay on his berth. His berth was *above* mine. I said

"How fitting, I should be below you this time. When we came I was *vis-à-vis* on the same level." He smiled. I was quite hopeful when I was lying in my berth. I was sorry that I had the lower one, because that probably made him feel less important in Hollywood eyes, as he reserved his so long ago. I was lying there and thought—"Be happy, he is lying up there and last night you did not know where he was." In the morning I found him sitting up two hours before landing.

I spent the time with Jean Pierre Aumont and family in the back of the plane and came there only at the end of the trip. He offered me his seat but I did not take it. Did not want to talk to Strassburg. Then we walked off the gangplank, he behind me. His man saw me and his face lit up. My friend, whom he knows, waited for me. He said—"Hallo, Max" and shook hands with him and *then* he took off like lightening [*sic*], walking so fast that his man could not keep pace and had to run. Waiting outside for the bags, he drove up with the sports Mercedes and drove off like a race-driver—and that was all.

I talked to his man last night and he said he asked if he talked to me on the plane and he said not much because of Strassburg. And that he was through with all women.

Well, I am living in this empty house. It is cold this morning and dreary. I just took a Dexomyl. I must not get depressed and miserable. I wish I could talk to you. If ever you go somewhere for any length of time where there is a phone, maybe you can call me and I call you there.

I am sending you one of the stories from a movie magazine. The dates are too funny, you might have a laugh. It seems that he was a *Doctor of Philosophy* at the Sorbonne when he was *18 years old.* And an actor with the Pitoijeffs when he was *fourteen. Before that* he had sung in Montmartre clubs and also had been with the circus. I am not interested in how old he is, but the horoscope would benefit. Or if one knew the Pitoijeffs, that would help.

But after all, only he can help and I am waiting as usual.

Michael Wilding is begging to be with me. He cannot stand the thought of my living in this empty house. He is really kind and loves me but I could not hurt him the second time, so I cannot be selfish and let him stay.

How can I learn to be self-sufficient? I think for that one has to be someone of depth, more than emotional depth, or am I not unselfish at all and have to love someone for that reason? Or is that logic that I as a woman have no right to have? He said a few days ago—"I should have married you twenty years ago" (with the accent on twenty years ago). He always claims that we *are* married. And "I love you much more now than I ever loved you". That's why I am waiting. Because it is logically impossible that he has stopped loving me the next day after he said that.

Michael said something strange to me. He had taken me to the plane when I had left for N.Y. and had seen him. He said—"I had expected him to look mysterious and slender and foreign and he looked robust and like a business man and his voice was so American." I had noticed all that too. That day at the Copacabana he looked lithe and fine, if not like an animal of the jungle but like a race-horse. He has lost that quality. Also in the expression on the *screen* he still *has* it. Did I tell you I saw *Anastasia* and that he is a *great actor* in midst of no direction and a muddled story and cast of a very low caliber??

The phone just rang but nobody was there, just that empty buzzing sound.

I love you so very much and I long for you, not only out of loneliness or to throw my burden on you. I long so for intelligence and brain food! For reading one needs a calmer mind than mine is now, always listening for a phone bell.

I got all my "wisdom" from books and great men's thoughts since my childhood, being brought up with Kant and Nietzsche and Goethe and Heine. I know all their theories and their personal experiences and all of them wanted love and nothing but. So I can only get reaffirmation of my deep conviction and little help. I need the living contact anyway.

Love love love to you, my exalted friend of the soul and the heart. And God bless you forever.

MARLENE

November 15. Still waiting

There were many such letters and Noël would typically reply:

Firefly Hill
Port Maria, Jamiaca B.W.I.

Oh, darling,

Your letter filled me with such a lot of emotions the predominant one being rage that you should allow yourself to be so humiliated and made so unhappy by a situation that really isn't worthy of you. I loathe to think of you apologizing and begging forgiveness and humbling yourself. I don't care if you did behave badly for a brief moment, considering all the devotion and loving you have given out during the last five years, you had a perfect right to. The only mistake was not to have behaved a great deal worse a long time ago. The aeroplane journey sounds a nightmare to me.

It is difficult for me to wag my finger at you from so very far away, particularly as my heart aches for you but really, darling, you must pack up this nonsensical situation once and for all. It is really beneath your dignity, not your dignity as a famous artist and a glamorous star, but your dignity as a human, only too human being. Curly is attractive, beguiling, tender and fascinating, but he is not the only man in the world who merits those delightful adjectives . . . do please try to work out for yourself a little personal philosophy and DO NOT, repeat DO NOT be so bloody vulnerable. To hell with God damned "L'Amour." It always causes far more trouble than it is worth. Don't run after it. Don't court it. Keep it waiting off stage until you're good and ready for it and even then treat it with the suspicious disdain that it deserves . . . I am sick to death of you waiting about in empty houses and apartments with your ears strained for the telephone to ring. Snap out of it, girl! A very brilliant writer once said (Could it have been me?) "Life is for the living." Well, that is all it is for, and living DOES NOT consist of staring in at other people's windows and waiting for crumbs to be thrown to you. You've carried on this hole in corner, overcharged, romantic, unrealistic nonsense long enough.

Stop it. Stop it. Stop it. Other people need you . . . Stop wasting yourself on someone who only really says tender things to you when he's drunk . . .

Unpack your sense of humor, and get on with living and ENJOY IT.

Incidentally, there is one fairly strong-minded type who will never let you down and who loves you very much indeed. Just try to guess who it is. XXXX. These are not romantic kisses. They are unromantic. Loving "Goose-Es".

Your devoted "Fernando de Lamas"

Marlene continued to unburden herself:

Dec. '56

My Love,
I waited till today to answer your letter. It deserved an answer much sooner. Besides I am not sure if I did not write something since. I have been in such an unreal world all these four weeks here that I don't really remember much. I have tried everything and I mean everything to forget the hurt, but nothing works. No avenues of escape for me. The lameness is all over me and in me and therefore I cannot shake myself into normal living. The center of my circling is no more and I zigzag through empty space like a mechanical trick design. The only desire I feel is to obliterate myself—not necessarily die—that would

give too much trouble to Maria [her daughter] and Rudy [Rudolf Sieber, her husband] but to lose the automatic signs of existing daily without creating attention, without giving away the motive. But even this desire I cannot fulfill. It would all be too complicated and dramatic and impossible. Drink makes me sick, dope I am sure would too. Well, where do we go from here? Time. Give me time. I hate to bother you with this—but if you don't hear from me that is bad, too.

MARLENE

In June of that year he had confided to his *Diary* his concern that "Marlene, with her intense preoccupation with herself and her love affairs, is also showing signs of wear and tear. How foolish to think that one can ever slam the door in the face of age. Much wiser to be polite and gracious and ask him in to lunch in advance."

It was a subject Noël could joke about but Marlene's humor tended toward the more Teutonically literal. When he once tried one of his favorite lines on her and said that all he required of his friends these days was that they survive through lunch, she gave him a puzzled look; "Why *lunch,* sweetheart?"

In 1965 he could write:

The canny old Kraut remains one of my most cherished friends . . . However, I intend to talk to her briskly about her predisposition to whining *ad nauseam* about her ageing process, as though she were the first gorgeous lady undone by Father Time. And I would dearly like to teach her something about humour, as in *sense* of humour. Unteachable, I suspect.

Preoccupied she certainly was but that didn't mean she had no time to consider her friend's needs. She was perfectly well aware that for the last decade Noël had been putting on his own brave face as, time and again, the critics wrote him off as yesterday's man. She wrote to strengthen his resolve and it must have been most welcome.

The only time Noël and Marlene ever appeared in a film together was in Mike Todd's 1956 all-star extravaganza *Around the World in 80 Days,* even though they didn't share a scene. Then, on March 23, 1958, Todd died in an air crash.

993 Park Avenue
March 24th 1958

Sweetheart,

I spent another day in a sorry-for-myself mood, (because I am sincerely sorry for Mike Todd). He would be quite astonished to hear that. I think he never dreamed that he could mean so much to me. The French have an expression which we don't have, maybe because such relationships don't exist—*Amitié amoureuse.* That's what it was exactly. I have often tried to explain the meaning. Men can have it (without any physical feelings involved) for each other and it is really friendship without carelessness in words and actions—of friends who apply lover's [*sic*] tactics—or—maybe you can say it so much better, so what am I trying to do?

Come to think of it, it is more a matter of choice—to be friends and not lovers.

Liz [Taylor, Todd's widow] went to the funeral with "a party of six". Her doctor, her dressmaker, hairdresser, etc. The intimate "family circle" the family wanted! And Mike would have been furious that I wasn't invited. So I sit here and read the papers how hysterical she was and I think of the time Jimmy Dean died and she went hysterical and behaved like a bereaved wife right in front of our Michael [Wilding]—and then when Monty Clift had the accident leaving her house, again she went hysterical and behaved the same way. Now it is real and I wonder if she can tell the difference?

Enough of that. I should concentrate to write so that you can read it. I haven't unpacked my typewriter yet and it is night and I was too lazy to unpack packages. The apartment is beautiful—at the moment I say for what—for whom? The bastard is doing a slow fade in my mind. The heart I am not so sure of.

I don't like him any more but I guess I still love him.

> But you I love
> M

Noël was not without his share of emotional problems at the time. He had brought his production of *Nude with Violin* to New York, where he played the leading role of Sebastien himself. To his chagrin, attendances began to fall away, obliging him to alternate the play with an old favorite, *Present Laughter,* before setting off on a short West Coast tour.

But that sort of thing he had learned to take in stride. What he never learned how to handle was what he called "that Old Black Magic." "This," he told his *Diary,* "is stimulating, disturbing, enjoyable, depressing, gay, tormenting, delightful, silly and sensible . . . I can already see all the old hoops being prepared for me to go through." The late-in-life and somewhat reluctant ringmaster was a young actor in the play, William Traylor.

Like Marlene, Noël now had his own "gilded cage":

Firefly Hill
Port Maria
Jamaica B.W.I
April 7th 1958

Darling,

The last matinée of *Nude* just after I had heard about Mike's death was sheer hell. Every line seemed to apply. "Until death smudged out the twinkle in his eye" . . . "He contrived to enjoy life to the full" etc., etc. I nearly went mad.

The Gilded Cage finale was played with decent reticence and was fairly upsetting, a sadness I may say not unmixed with relief. It [his young lover] called me up very tenderly in New Orleans where I broke the journey for one night, since when I haven't heard a bloody word. It has been a rather violent experience, really. I hope I have profited from it but I am definitely glad that it's over. There will probably be a *réchauffage* from time to time but it will never be quite the same.

I love you very much,
Gilded Cage II

After the booking finished, they never met again, although there was occasional correspondence.

Only one letter survives (dated January 20, 1960). In it his "friend" rambles repetitively, as he tries to decide what it is he wants to say.

He's delayed writing far too long and made several false starts and, now that he has actually put pen to paper, all that he can think of—like Proust—is remembrance of times past and other titles of the same kind, snatches of poetry, and so on.

His career, he feels, is going nowhere fast. In fact, the last year has been the worst professionally that could possibly be imagined. Nonetheless (he assures Noël), he still has "that blind faith thing."

In terms of his mental health, well, he's managed to keep things together. He's sane, and he's proud of that. But then, reading what he's written so far, it seems to him that what he's saying is about "as lucid as this ink." Put it another way, he thinks that on the whole he can now be more objective and keep his depression at bay.

Sorry if it all sounds like a "Psychology 1" course for beginners! But let's not go into all that any further, since he clearly can't convey what he wants to say. By now he's sure Noël can understand why he hasn't written before. He's just not very good at it but perhaps he'll get better as he goes on . . .

As he writes, it seems like time remembered—another title!—and it's "a rare pleasure to remember." His life would not be worthwhile if he could not occasionally "turn back the clock all the way."

Noël could report to Cole Lesley:

I arrived to find a highly sentimental and romantic letter from my friend which was very very sweet and only a very little of which I really believed. However, I telephoned him and he was rather flustered and not, I fear progressing very far with his career, and it was all most *gentile* and I felt no pangs at all which is a GOOD thing on account of me being sick of feeling pangs about anyone or anything.

To Joyce Carey:

[He] is much improved and is acting in an off Broadway artistic symbolic drama with a cast of four and an audience of thirteen. He really gave quite a good performance but the play was a trifle too poetic for me and had lines like—"The evening is putting on her diapers"!

•

THE FOLLOWING YEAR Marlene was delighted when Noël's musical (now called) *The Girl Who Came to Supper* previewed on September 28 at Boston's Colonial Theatre and gave every indication of being a smash hit for Noël.

1962. Three Christmas belles— Marti Stevens, Marlene, and Kay Thompson—decorate Chalet Coward.

933 Park Avenue
October 2nd 1963

Dearest,

In order to explain the very special joy I have I must tell you that it is much greater than the *usual* joy we always have when you write something.

Your bravado about not caring about the critics always hurt me. My own criticism [of Noël] hurt me more.

I remember talking to you once in my apartment reminding you of the great things you had done—telling you what I thought of your creations then and of old. It wasn't quite right then—you put your name to things I didn't think good enough. I searched for the reason everywhere.

Even in your personal way of living. You fought me, naturally, but I knew you felt just like I did.

"Crying all the way to the bank" attitude is fine for the lesser talents. Not right for you in my book. I worried.

Then, in Montreux—I lifted my head. But I held back—wishful thinking was not to influence me. Then, there was your voice in the street in Boston. The room, the music, the lyrics—and I knew that you were home.

I still crossed my fingers. Other elements out of your control were present. But then I put my arms around Joe [Layton]—couldn't tell him all then either—but my worries were gone. My worries for *you,* personally were gone when I put my arms around you after I heard the line: "When the kids have got you down!" Something had broken open in you—I knew that then.

Then I waited. You had beaten into me that bit about: "I *always* have bad reviews!" I never liked it. I want you to have your cake—*and* eat it.

Full houses, great reviews, money *and* glory! And inner joy about your own ability, dependability and achievement—I wanted for you. That is why I am so extra specially happy.

My love for you has nothing to do with this happiness.

Marlene

She never ceased to see herself as an unofficial *gardienne* of Noël's work.

Savoy Hotel
London
November 30th 1972

Dearest Love,

Saw [the revival production of] *Private Lives* on my first free night. God—how far away from what you wrote! It reminded me of a [TV]

New York, January 1973 . . . and Noël's last first night, as Marlene accompanies him to the revue *Oh, Coward!* Asked if he's enjoyed it, Noël replies, "One does not laugh at one's own jokes—but I went out humming the tunes."

show, *All in the Family,* the biggest hit in the U.S. Everybody was yelling and hamming it up. But the audience ate it up.

Maggie [Smith] looks worn and sad. There is something wrong—don't know what! [Her marriage to her co-star, Robert Stephens, was breaking up.] He has lightened his hair (reddish) and lost all his sex-appeal. I told him, naturally! Can't keep my mouth shut, because I know nobody tells. She plays it like a mixture of Bea Lillie, Carol Burnett, Coco Chanel (the real one) and somebody I know but cannot find the name. They are eating up the scenery. Such a Circus! But maybe you wanted that to "modernize" it. [Stephens was soon replaced by the less volatile John Standing, and Smith calmed down—relatively speaking.]

I liked you and Gertie better (MUCH). But I adored [James] Villiers [as Victor]. He is a very very good actor. I had never seen him. To hold his own in that mad surrounding is a great achievement.

> Much love as always for always,
> MARLENE

Sadly, there was not to be too much more "always."

In January of the following year Noël made his last trip to New York and paid his last visit to a theater. The show was a gala performance of the revue *Oh, Coward!,* and the lady on his arm was Marlene.

Had he enjoyed the show? he was asked: "One does not laugh at one's own jokes," he replied, then added: "I went out humming the tunes."

# CHAPTER 14
## *TONIGHT AT 8:30*

### (1935–1937)

S NOËL WROTE the individual one-act plays that would make up *Tonight at 8:30*, he sent them to his old friends the Lunts for their opinion:

Noël composing at Goldenhurst. (Note the Grinling Gibbons wood carving that he took from home to home over the years.)

Philadelphia
September 15th 1935

Darling,

I have read them all and am very excited. They are quite extraordinary. *The Astonished Heart.* What a lovely title! I recognize our psychiatrist. He was born in Genesee, do you remember? Oh, it's awfully good. It is amazing how gradually he becomes unbalanced. It gives one a strange feeling of drowning. I love the almost Proustian psychology of jealousy.

*Red Peppers* is very fine and very funny. Their utter third-rateness is so awfully pathetic. You know exactly why (aside from the pitiful business of their act) they have never been and never could be successful.

*Hands Across the Sea* is marvellous. So distressingly photographic; a whirling nightmare of chit-chat. It was quite clear to me all the way through that they were the wrong people (in case you are afraid it mightn't get over). What part shall you play in that? I suppose Peter.

*Fumed Oak* has enough material for three acts. It's wonderful. But it seems dreadfully extravagant to use all these rich plots for one-acters. Won't Gertie hate playing that unsympathetic wife? I love his remaining absolutely speechless during the first scene. It's a sure-fire trick, darling, and very exciting. I love the old mother in that.

To get to my favorite (and, of course, you already know it is the best), *Shadow Play.* Oh, darling, it is so extraordinary! I think I like it best of anything you've ever written. It is curious how that strange form of writing swings one vibrantly out into space, right out of the world somewhere in the stratosphere. It will undoubtedly be an enormous success—the whole thing.

The first play, *We Were Dancing,* aside from some very funny lines, which you can always write, I don't like at all, and I don't suppose you do either. I can tell you where I think it seems bad, and that is at the beginning when you, as an audience, should believe that these people have fallen in love,

and it only seems very silly. I don't apologize for not liking it, because I am *certain* that when you read it again you will hate it and very probably replace it, and I hope you do.

Oh, how I wish we could see some of the rehearsals. But, of course, you will do it here some time and then we shall see it. Love, love, love and good luck, my little sweet.

> Yours ever,
> LYNN

It was only when she'd seen all nine plays that she realized the sheer scope of what Noël was attempting:

We are very excited about your third bill and have no doubt whatsoever of its success. I have a hunch that changing bills like that and doing so many different things does not do the thing you had expected of it, i.e., that giving so much variety would lighten the work. I have a feeling that the job of work in the theatre of three hours hard every night is only intensified by the fact that the plays are each different and so involving further tension. And, of course, extra rehearsals, which means you are never out of the theatre. An awful lot of work to bite off in one season, Duckie! But, perhaps the entertainment part will come when you have them all and can toss them off in another season . . . such as the New York one. Or am I wrong?

1936. Noël in his dressing room before the curtain
goes up for *Tonight at 8:30*.

Gertie and Noël in *Shadow Play.*

Alec Woollcott wrote:

> Bomoseen
> Vermont
> October 8th 1935
>
> I am enchanted with all I hear about your one-act plays—snatches of information about them drift in from such witnesses as Lynn and Alfred and Ruth Gordon. Sybil [Colefax] wrote me a great deal about them and whereas I could read only a few words of her comment, they seemed to indicate that she had been favourably impressed.

October saw the beginning of a three-month tour of *Tonight at 8:30,* and it was clear—as it had been five years earlier—that the theatergoing public were anxious to resume their relationship with Noël and Gertie.

Once the tour was under way Noël sent regular progress reports back to Violet:

> October 13th
> Midland Hotel, Manchester
>
> It's a riotous success and we're playing to bigger business than has ever been known in Manchester . . . We're all dead but very happy.

We opened the second bill last night ("Hands Across the Sea", "Fumed Oak" and "Shadow Play") and it was an even greater success than the first.

> November 2nd
> Great Northern Station Hotel, Leeds

I've finished the seventh play ("Family Album")—a Victorian dainty with music and I'm now racking my brains to think of two more to make up the third bill!

Our success really is fantastic—we were sold out here completely two weeks before we arrived. It takes ages after each performance to get out of the stage door and we have to have special police to control the crowds!

From Glasgow he replied to Woollcott:

> Kings Theatre
> Glasgow
> November 4th 1935

Darling, beastly Acky-wee,

Your horrid little note arrived just as I was about to ravish my Manchester public but now that they are safely ravished I can write . . . you will be bleakly interested to hear that the short play idea is so far a triumphant success. We are now playing two bills of three plays each and by the time we get to London three bills of three plays each.

They are all brilliantly written, exquisitely directed, and I am bewitching in all of them.

Lorn sends love, Jeffrey sends love and I send a molten stream of white hot kisses.

> Yours in Christ,
> Noël

At the end of the year they took a break before the London opening and Noël, accompanied by Jeffrey Amherst set off for a holiday in Scandinavia. Christmas found them in Stockholm where they ran into Greta Garbo (1905–1990). Noël must certainly have met her in Hollywood, but their friendship blossomed in her own land and—like Dietrich's—lasted for the rest of his life.

The international press had a field day with speculation about a Garbo-Coward romance, which amused the romantically *dis*interested parties greatly. The following year, 1936, happened to be a leap year in which, by tradition, a woman is allowed to propose to the man of her choice.

Garbo sent her handwritten "proposal" to Noël:

And its Thursday—

Dear Little Coward,

Received your very loved, small and tiny letter. Dear person it almost makes me wish the newspapers in this country was right. I am so dreadfully fond of you, that I wish I could forget you. Can't think of anything more terrific than to fall in love with you. Eternaly (can't spell) occupied as you are and in need of absolutely no one and looking forward to splendid lonelyness (?) completely immune to any female charm!! Well, this might be an English lesson anyhow I take the opportunity to ask if you will be my little bride—(it's Leap Year you know). Don't accept please, I would have to come and get you right away.

How you must dislike my writing this way—but—that fluttering, tired and sad heart of mine has been in such peculiar state since a few weeks ago, but I don't suppose I know you well enough to go into that to much.

I have a very humble wish that you would write a story for me (us), if you ever have time from the theatre. I can't beg you any harder, as you will do as fits you anyhow—naturally. Besides that I would like, horribly I think, to go on dusty roads with you and tell you little fairy tales—beautiful ones about solitary figures living in white castles on top of moonlit mountains (permanent moonlight). And as finish I must tell you that what I really would like to tell you I haven't told—Darling, you are so "flippantly" serious.

•

THE FIRST PROGRAM of *Tonight at 8:30* (*Family Album, The Astonished Heart,* and *Red Peppers*) opened at London's Phoenix Theatre—scene of their 1930 *Private Lives* triumph—on January 9, 1936. Once again the success of the piece, or pieces, was limited only by Noël's willingness to play a long run.

To Woollcott:

1 Burton Mews
South Eaton Place
London S.W.1
6th February 1936

My darling Acky Poo,

You will be pleased, my little dear, that my one act play scheme is the smash hit of the town and we are playing to the most tremendous business, even in spite of the King's death. This, incidentally, has

Noël and Gertie make headlines again (1936).

been a very strange experience for the whole country. It has been very dramatic and moving and the Lying in State was quite indescribably beautiful. The whole thing has been handled with the minimum of bathos with the exception of a certain amount of nausea from the cheaper press.

I had lunch with Rebecca [West] the other day and we talked lovingly of you. Now I come to think of it I wouldn't mind a letter from you because in an odd, macabre, perverse, introverted way I am very, very, very, very, very fond of you. (Strike out as many very's as you like but leave the fond).

> Love and red hot kisses from top to *derrière.*
> Noelie-poelie

On June 20 *Tonight at 8:30* closed after 157 performances.

But before it did another long run had begun. On March 28, 1936, the twenty-seven-year-old Leonard Cole had been hired to work as some sort of general assistant and "someone to replace Charles," the cook-valet who had recently caused the Coward household considerable domestic distress before leaving abruptly. Since Noël hated the name "Leonard," the young man was summarily rechristened "Cole Lesley," and even that was quickly shortened to "Coley," which did not particularly please the *original* Coley (Porter). Coley would remain part of the Coward family until Noël's death nearly forty years later, and would subsequently run the Coward estate until his own death in 1980.

•

THE OTHER PIECE of real-life theater that year, 1936, was the royal family. On January 20, King George V had died and the throne passed to the controversial Prince of Wales, now Edward VIII, and one of Noël's least favorite people. The Princess Diana saga of the late 1990s gives some idea of the strength of feeling the British public expressed at this time.

As Prince of Wales, Edward had become involved with a twice-divorced American socialite, Wallis Simpson, and this at a time when the very word "divorce" was never mentioned in royal circles. Should Mrs. Simpson be allowed to become queen as and when Edward ascended the throne? Should he renounce the throne for "the woman he loved"?

The debate raged pro and con, with Noël most definitely con. At a dinner party with Winston Churchill, who always enjoyed being controversial, the great man grumpily observed that he couldn't see why the prince shouldn't have his "cutie." "Because England doesn't wish for a Queen Cutie!" Noël retorted.

Later in the year, Noël felt impelled to write to the one friend he thought might, through his family ties, have the influence to affect events—Mountbatten:

> Carlton Hotel
> Washington
> November 19th 1937

My Dear Dickie,

Please read this letter carefully and don't misunderstand it or think I've gone raving mad. I know perfectly well that you mind about a lot of the same things that I mind about, otherwise I wouldn't risk making such a fool of myself.

Is there anything on God's earth that can be done to put a stop to this degrading and horrible publicity about the King and Mrs. Simpson?

It is impossible to pick up any paper here without feeling sick. From coast to coast of this over large continent the King's dignity is being undermined very thoroughly and very dangerously.

English people of any position here, official or otherwise, naturally refuse to discuss it but they are all feeling it deeply. I, of course, have been badgered to death about it ever since I landed. The Press never lose an opportunity of trying to drag it into every interview I have to give.

My only reply to date has been that we love and respect the King too much to discuss his private affairs.

I am only writing to you on a sort of hunch that you might not realize the full unpleasantness of the situation here and in the hope that, it being brought to your attention, you might conceivably be able to bring a little personal influence to bear.

I should hate you to think that I am attempting to interfere with what doesn't concern me but as a matter of fact this does concern me. It most vitally concerns all of us.

Is there any way in which the King could be persuaded to make, or have made, an official statement to the American Press which would squash finally these idiotic rumours, announcements, denials, etc.?

I remember saying to the first night audience of *Cavalcade,* in an outburst of faintly theatrical patriotism, that it was pretty exciting to be English. I can only feel now, in the midst of all this scandal and vulgarity, that it's bloody uncomfortable to be English!

This letter obviously requires no answer but I should like one line from you to show that you have not misunderstood my motives in writing it.

> Yours ever
> Noël

Even as he put pen to paper, events at home were already well in train. In December, King Edward VIII abdicated, and his brother "Bertie" (Duke of York) became King George VI.

·

BEFORE HE HAD to focus on the New York production of *Tonight,* Noël took a European holiday . . . to Venice, Dubrovnik, Rhodes (where he put the final touches to *Present Indicative*), finishing up in Cairo. A significant régime change was taking place and the British high commissioner was in the process of becoming ambassador.

He wrote to Violet from the residency: "This has all been great fun—lots of red carpet and general official ding dongs. I now feel almost personally responsible for the Anglo-Egyptian Treaty!"

Back in England Anthony Eden suggested that Noël host a party for the Egyptian delegation that would be arriving on August 25 to sign the treaty.

The party was a great social success, but ever after Anthony Eden and the Mountbattens teased him that it was responsible for the erosion of

Anglo-Egyptian relations in general and for the eventual loss of the Suez Canal!

•

AT THE END of the month, Noël sailed for New York on the SS *Queen Mary* and the Broadway production of *Tonight at 8:30*.

He was to take over Alec Woollcott's riverside "digs" in the Campanile co-op building. When Woollcott had first moved in, Dorothy Parker had christened the place "Old Manse River," which she later revised to "Wit's End."

Back in April, Woollcott had confirmed the arrangements:

> April 24th 1936
>
> The routine of consent has now all been attended to. Brown started the wheels moving . . . and encountered a functionary at the real estate office who had never heard of you and turned pale when he identified you. An actor! It made him a little faint. I believe the *New Yorker* has already fashioned a paragraph on the subject. Whether the other tenants have become more tolerant of such vagrants or whether they concluded that having an actor was even preferable to having me, I don't know. I only know they have let me go without a struggle.

> 450 East 52nd Street
> Wednesday
>
> Well, we arrived in a cloud of luggage—my apartment is really heavenly. I lie in bed in the morning with the sun streaming into the room and watch the ships go by a few inches from my nose!
>
> I'm having a very busy time furnishing and buying china, glass, etc. It really is a great comfort because it's dead quiet except for the river noises which I don't mind a bit.
>
> We saw the Lunts' play [*Idiot's Delight*] on Monday night, Alfred is magnificent and Lynn very bad with a mock Russian accent.

Earlier in the year Lynn had warned Noël that their parts were not what audiences might be expecting of them—although infinitely more conventional than *Point Valaine*:

> We loved seeing darling Jack [Wilson] for a few fleeting visits. And, by the way, do tell Jack that the lighting at the dress rehearsal that he saw was perfectly terrible and had not been done at all, so don't take our appearances, mine in particular, on the strength of that, as it has all been softened down into a lovely glow, and they say we all, including Grand-pa and Grand-ma, look ravishing . . . THEY SAY!

I am supposed to be a very fakey Russian and started by patterning myself on Princess Paley, as this particular girl would do, but she turns out to be a cross between Garbo, Lady Abdey, and a good smack of Trilby . . . and this is just as good for the character in a way, as she is a girl who has her eye on every chance, even the movies, and would be quite equal to posing as Garbo just for fun.

Alfred plays a Broadway vaudevillian. It is a marvelous part and he is simply superb. Quite one of the best things he has ever done. I am very good too, but my part is not so good.

Since writing this we have also opened in New York, but you know all about that. Stood them up 81 last night, and 100 Saturday [the number of audience standees].

Old Simon Legree wants to make little Topsy work until July 4, and then take only eight weeks. Isn't he a b-i-t-c-h?

Noël's letter to Violet continues:

But last night we saw Helen Hayes as Queen Victoria [in *Victoria Regina*] and she was beyond words wonderful! She starts as a girl of eighteen and goes right through up to the Diamond Jubilee. Her make-up alone is miraculous but oh, her acting! It certainly did my heart good.

Tomorrow we go to the first night of Master Gielgud in *Hamlet*—oh Dear, oh Dear—Leslie's [Howard] doesn't open until November—however I'll let you know all.

Later (October 23) he reports: "I'm seeing Leslie's *Hamlet* tomorrow afternoon in Boston. I hear it's very good. John Gielgud's is doing quite well here but hasn't set the town on fire."

In fact, when it came to a head-to-head comparison, Gielgud won hands down. Leslie Howard's production closed early, while Gielgud broke the record for the number of Broadway performances previously held by John Barrymore (152)—a record he held until it was broken by Richard Burton in 1964.

·

TONIGHT AT 8:30 began the traditional out-of-town tour in Boston. In the audience was James Thurber reviewing it (with accompanying drawings) for a theater magazine.

It seems to me that all these plays were written wisely and well. (Mr. Coward . . . bats them off in no time at all, which appalls me.) They have at their best, a precision that moves towards the absolute. (You can go to Mr.

The astonished hands were dancing across the family fumed heart.

Maugham for a harder granite or to Mr. Huxley for a colder chisel.) . . . As far as I'm concerned Miss Lawrence could play Little Eva or even Harriet Beecher Stowe herself and he could play Grover Cleveland.

More decorous and self-contained than Boston folks, I did not rise and shout but applauded loudly . . . I liked it; hell, I was crazy about it . . . I had a swell time."

Later he wrote to friends—"We [his wife, Helen] had dinner with Coward, just the three of us, a lovely time, a swell fellow . . . he lets people talk and is very attentive. A quarter century later he would claim "Coward and I are the last of the great indestructibles."

The tour went on to Washington, D.C. As always, Noël sent Violet progress reports, interspersed with worries about what was happening in the State of Goldenhurst:

> November 1st
> The Ritz Carlton, Boston
> We had a certain amount of trouble with lights and scenery owing to the theatre staff being half-witted. *Shadow Play* is pandemonium behind the scenes. We battle our way on and off the stage in the pitch dark and try to do quick changes with all hell going on all round us.
>
> Gladys Cooper is here in *Call It a Day* and we've seen a lot of her. [Mrs.] Tonge [Philip's stage mother] is here, too. I'm afraid she's just

as unpopular as ever. Gladys and Philip Merrivale say she's an old devil in the company and never stops explaining to them that Philip (*her* Philip) would have been just as successful as I am if only he'd had my good luck.

I must say the way Father hovers between death and debauchery is nothing short of fantastic . . . I do think it's horrid for you but it really is too silly for words!

November 18th
Carlton Hotel, Washington

Washington has been buzzing round me to such an extent that I'm practically in a coma! The British Embassy gave a party for the company yesterday and we all bowed and smirked and carried on like anything. We settle into New York next week and life will become more tranquil.

Oh dear, I'm afraid we were wrong about Gielgud versus Howard. I saw Leslie in Boston as Hamlet and he was awful! He didn't do anything at all but meander through the play as tho' he were doing a word rehearsal! John, with all his staginess, was much better. Leslie's notices when he opened in New York were frightful—so that's that!

The young John Gielgud.

Noël was always to have slight reservations about what he called Gielgud's "staginess" or propensity to overact, and on at least one occasion it caused him to overreact himself:

17 Gerald Road, London SW1

September 26, 1932

My dear John,

I hear you were very hurt when I walked out of *Musical Chairs,* so I am going to be honest and tell you why.

The first reason was I thought you were overacting badly and using voice tones and elaborate emotional effects, and as I seriously think you are a grand actor it upset me very much.

The second reason was that, feeling as I did, I couldn't have come round to your dressing room and abused you roundly because there would probably have been other people present and I thought by slipping out (as I thought unnoticed) I might evade the issue.

This, I see now, was very lacking in moral courage and I am terribly sorry.

Please, dear John, forgive me for having hurt your feelings and believe me when I say I love acting and The Theatre more than anything else in the World and in this case I was genuinely upset by what I considered was a performance far below your standard.

I am going away for a holiday for a few weeks and perhaps when I come back we could have a real heart-to-heart talk about it, if you are not too angry with me.

Yours ever

Noël

Gielgud replied:

7 Upper St. Martin's Lane

W.C.2

Tuesday

Dear Noël,

Thank you very much for writing as you did. I was very upset at the time because, as you know, I have always admired you and your work so very much and also because in a way I have always thought my success in the theatre only began after *The Vortex* time. This play was my own discovery and I had much to do with the casting and getting produced so naturally I was very anxious that you of all people should like it. But you are quite right, of course. I act very badly in it sometimes, more especially I think when I know people who matter are in front. And such a small theatre as the Criterion is difficult for me who am used to the wastes of the Old Vic and His Majesty's. If I play down, they write and say I'm inaudible. And if I act too much the effect is dire. Now and again one can strike the happy mien and give a good performance. But then, it is no use trying to excuse myself. I played ever so much better today after reading your letter— and I am really glad when I get honest criticism, though sometimes it's a bit hard to decide whom to listen to and whom to ignore. One day you must produce me in a play, and I believe I might do you credit. Anyway, I think it was like you to write like that and I do appreciate it.

> Yours ever,
> John

Twenty years later Noël was to do just that.

·

ON NOVEMBER 24 *Tonight at 8:30* opened at New York's National Theatre, and Noël wrote to Violet:

> 450 East 52nd Street
> November 27th

Well, the first lot have opened and were a triumph—we begin the second bill tonight and the third on Monday. The excitement is terrific. The critics—as in London—are slightly grudging. I think they are all irritated by the tremendous fuss that goes on over everything I do. When Gertie and I came on on the first night the audience went on applauding for nearly three minutes and there we stood just mouthing at each other! We are sold out for twelve weeks and I may have to play an extra month.

I am, however, very worried about you and Father. It seems to me to be a thoroughly horrid situation . . . Oh dear, I wish I were there to be a comfort to you. I really am deeply angry over Father's behaviour—it seems to me to be common, unkind, unnecessary and supremely ridiculous.

(Mr. Coward, now approaching senility, believed himself to be in love with a lady who lived locally and had a certain "reputation.")

> December 8th

We are absolutely the smash success of the town . . . I think I'm going to do an hour on the radio once a week, it is frightfully well paying and I want to make as much as I can this season so that I can lay off for a year and have no contracts at all!

I'm happy and well and as bright as a button!

December 16th

Well darling,
Thirty-seven years ago today I popped out and oh dear, look at me now!

I must say everything is more than satisfactory here. We are apparently the biggest box office success that New York has known for years. We turn away an average of 200 people every performance.

I'm glad the Yorks are King and Queen. They will be steady and gracious and dignified which, after all, is all that is required. I am now more than a little tired of the dear Duke of Windsor and I don't care if he marries Mrs. Wallis Simpson or Nellie Wallace [a famous British music hall star]. The whole thing has been very unpleasant and quite unnecessary. I'm dreadfully sorry for poor Queen Mary.

I've known for years that he had a common mind and liked second rate people and I am sure it is a good thing for England that he abdicated.

I hope you're not still worried and irritated too much about Father and that ass of a woman . . . The whole thing is too ridiculous to do anything but laugh at!

December 30th

They did *Cavalcade* on the air the night before last and I broadcasted a speech from my dressing room in between plays! It really was fantastic. Cecil B. de Mille spoke to me from Hollywood where the thing was being done and I answered from my dressing room and then listened to the applause three thousand miles away! We certainly live in a remarkable age.

January 15th 1937

The other day I saw a private showing of Garbo in *Camille*. She has never looked so lovely or acted so well, the only disadvantage is that it makes you cry dreadfully.

January 29th

I am learning German in bits out of a book because I think it will be useful and Joyce and Alan are going to the Berlitz to learn Spanish! So the conversation in the theatre is distinctly cosmopolitan.

February 12th

I couldn't be more exhausted. I was up until six this morning running this enormous Benefit for the Flood Relief at Radio City Music Hall. The show started at 12:30 and finished at 5:00 a.m! I was Master of Ceremonies and had to introduce all the stars as well as do "Dance, Little Lady" myself with an orchestra of 70. The whole thing was incredible. There were 11 thousand people in the place itself and 100,000,000 listening in as the whole thing was broadcast all over the country. I had to make a series of tactful speeches and it was great fun although tiring.

Every star in New York appeared including Stravinsky, Helen Hayes, the Russian Ballet—Beatrice Lillie—Gladys Cooper—Luise Rainer—Gertie. Oh Dear, really. Everybody (even Sir Cedric!). (He refused to appear unless I introduced his idiotic wife too whom no one had ever heard of. So I introduced "Sir Cedric and Lady Hardwicke" and then, immediately afterwards—"Miss Beatrice Lillie and Lady Peel!" There was a nice big laugh!)

Of course I don't mind [Aunt] Ida being at Goldenhurst, she will at least keep the de Pomeroy wolf [Father's local inamorata] from the door . . . Poor Father—it is very agitating about him, isn't it? I think he really started to get a bit "ga-ga" a long time ago. I am afraid that eventually he will have to be stopped driving his car, because he is putting other people to considerable danger.

We're still jogging along. I'm now counting the days as really it has become boring. However, I'm taking a year off so my patience will be well rewarded . . . I'm going to devote most of my time to Europe and the near East.

As it turned out, the days dwindled down to a precious few.

March 11th

Well, I'm free at last—I've had a beastly eight weeks because I knew I was getting tireder and tireder. Ten days ago, on a Saturday night I started to cry during *Shadow Play*. Alan [Webb, his current lover] and Joyce [Carey] came down to Fairfield [Jack Wilson's home] with me after the show and Jack was frightfully sweet and said I was to lay off for a week, which I did, returning last Monday for the last three weeks. However, the flesh wasn't willing enough and on Tuesday night I began forgetting my lines and feeling simply awful. I barely got through the show and we realized it wasn't any good, so all the advance booking was returned the next day and we closed for good [after 118 performances]. I am actually in myself quite well but so tired I can't see straight.

I leave tomorrow for Nassau with Alan and Joyce in the sun—
then back here for a week—then Bermuda for two weeks and then
home . . .

On April 28 the SS *Normandie* duly took Noël back to England in time
for the Coronation. Here was one thing, Noël felt, that showed that England was back on the right track. But there were other, more disquieting
straws in the political wind.

# CHAPTER 15
# *OPERETTE* . . . AND STRAWS
# IN THE WIND

## (1937–1938)

*Where are the songs we sung*
*When Love in our hearts was young?*
*Where, in the limbo of the swiftly passing years,*
*Lie all our hopes and dreams and fears?*
*Where have they gone—words that rang so true*
*When Love in our hearts was new?*
*Where in the shadows that we have to pass among,*
*Lie those songs that once we sung?*

**"WHERE ARE THE SONGS WE SUNG,"** *OPERETTE* (1938)

Schloss Kammer-am-Attersee in Austria.

Eleanora von Mendelssohn (1899–1951). During a visit to her home in 1937, Noël dreamed up the idea that would become *Operette* (1938). Mendelssohn moved to New York and they remained close friends until her tragic suicide (1935).

THE NEXT TWO YEARS had something of a jigsaw quality to them and not all the pieces seemed to quite fit. And, in fact, for much of Noël's life the enormous successes were likely to be followed by a lull in which he would tackle a number of projects without being sure on which of them he should concentrate.

There were a number of positive things to be celebrated. The Coronation was certainly one. The success of his autobiography, *Present Indicative,* on both sides of the Atlantic, was another. And now he treated himself to another holiday—once again with his friends in the Royal Navy on HMS *Arethusa*. From the *Arethusa* he wrote to Lorn:

> *When I visit Venice Italy*
> *Lorn's before me pouting prettily*
> *Then again vast Yugo Slavia*
> *Reeks of Lorn's divine behavia*
> *Fishes in the Adriatic*
> *Gasp for Lorn, become ecstatic,*
> *Dive and swoop and dive again*
> *Bubbling "Viva, Lorn Loraine!"*
> *In Albania every peasant*
> *Makes a really most unpleasant*
> *Rude grimace if I refuse*

> *To tell them Lornie's latest news*
> *Serbians and Slavs and Croats*
> *Make strange noises in their throats*
> *When they sight the* Arethusa
> *Crying "Lorn! You mustn't lose her"*
> *Everywhere, now here, now there*
> *In the water, in the air,*
> *On the mountain, on the plain*
> *Comes again and yet again*
> *That persistent fierce refrain—*
> *"Viva, Viva, Lorn Loraine!"*

But this time the sailing was not entirely plain. The Mediterranean cruise stopped short at Valencia and Gibraltar. The Spanish Civil War was under way, an out-of-town tryout for what was soon to come—though few wished to see it in that light.

·

IN JULY Noël went to spend some time with Eleonora von Mendelssohn (1899–1951) at her Schloss Kammer-am-Attersee, in Austria. She would become a close friend in years to come and, when she moved to New York, one of the inner circle, until her tragic suicide.

"This place is absolutely lovely," Noël wrote to Violet. "It is an 11th century castle on a lake and dead quiet. There is nothing to do but ride and swim and read and in the evening we go and sit in the garden of the local inn and drink beer and listen to the village band, which is very brassy and plays 'The Blue Danube' while the sun sets over the lake . . . I'm staying here a week to ten days."

Here he met another of his musical theater idols from his first visit to Berlin in the early 1920s, Fritzi Massary (1882–1969), the Viennese Yvonne Printemps. Recently widowed, she was now semiretired and, being Jewish, anxious to leave Hitler's Germany. Once again the presence of a particular talent inspired Noël to create a setting for it.

He concocted a story line there and then—a "play with music," as he had done with *Conversation Piece*. ("I am writing Fritzi as herself," he wrote to Eleonora, "giving her three good songs, one in each act. The play is quite mad . . . It isn't strictly Kammer but a sort of exaggerated theatrical version of it.")

He then set it aside in favor of another treatment that featured a "play within a play," a format he had experimented with in a key sequence in *Cavalcade*. Of one thing, though, he was certain. Fritzi Massary would star. Back home in England he wrote to her offering her the lead, and sight unseen, she replied:

Fritzi Massary (1882–1969), star of *Operette*.
*"I promise I won't be kakanaiv."*

Kammer
11 August 1937

My dear Noël,
Happiness—excitement—gratitude were the feelings released in me when I read your letter. I will sing like mad—learn English till I burst and—as I told you—come when you send for me—so—October in London!

One thing I can promise you—I won't be *kaknaiv* [as naïve as shit]—I won't be *klugscheisserisch* [a smart-ass].

Have a lovely time in America with luck in everything and I hope to meet you in London as charming as only you can be!!! There is one more thing I meant to tell you—I never thought any one would ever be able to stir up so much in me again and if nothing comes of it—I am and always will be your
FRITZI

On September 12, Arthur Coward died and put several people out of their misery. Two days later, Noël—now staying with the Lunts at Genesee Depot—wrote:

Darlingest,

I am so terribly sorry not to be with you through all this. My only comfort is my complete faith in your common sense, but however sensible you are you are bound to have some horrid hours and I do wish I was near to comfort you.

I am so relieved that he died peacefully and without any struggle. I am also really relieved that he died when he did. It would have been awful both for him and for us if he had dragged on indefinitely . . .

Jack and Alan broke the news to me after the afternoon rehearsal just before the first night and it was lucky they did, as it came over the radio a half an hour later . . . The Press were after me pell mell so I hopped into a train and came straight here that night.

·

OPERETTE NEVER SEEMED to flow as his earlier shows had—neither in conception nor in execution. The story is of an Edwardian musical comedy star (Massary) who refuses to marry a British aristocrat, since he will lose his army commission if she does. Then, for some reason, there is a pastiche musical ("The Model Maid") inside the main show. While there were some charming songs, the totality was slight and more than distinctly déjà-vu—an obvious attempt to recapture Bitter Sweet. The line between the play and the play-within-a-play became so blurred that Noël recalled "peering from my box . . . and watching bewildered playgoers rustling their programmes and furtively striking matches in a frantic effort to discover where they were and what was going on."

He came to consider it "the least successful musical play I have ever done." It opened at His Majesty's Theatre on March 16 and ran for 133 performances. It is never revived.

Noël made the occasional desultory attempt to persuade himself and others that all was well. He wrote to Woollcott:

March 21st

Darling Weeza,

This is just to let you know that my Operette has opened (not the one I read to you at all) and is a smash success and anyhow very charming . . .

Everybody is very well though slightly depressed by the activities of Mr. Hitler. I am now going off to join the Navy for two months.

The summer of 1938 was spent in Europe, mostly traveling with the Mediterranean Fleet. Venice, Cyprus, Albania, Yugoslavia—wherever they went and however sybaritic the experience, there was no escaping the reality that the world he knew was seething with discontent. You could turn a myopic eye to it but not a blind one.

In early April he was in Cairo and writing to Gladys Calthrop from the British embassy:

Here I am in a gay social whirl feeling a little mizzy about *Operette* but rising above it as there is obviously nothing else to do—maybe the grosses will pick up after the political unrest has abated a bit and when Christ has once more risen like a rocket on Easter Sunday.

Life here is a fever of gay cosmopolitan junketing and at every party you hear very small dark Italians muttering "Grand Bretagne" and "Pénible" [painful, troublesome] under their breaths.

I've been taken up by the Egyptians in a big way and they show me endless mosques and monasteries and mosaics and I am very very gracious about everything and drink a great deal of fucking awful coffee.

On the fourteenth he is writing from Government House, Jerusalem:

Well Cock,
I flew here yesterday and it's a fair fucker except for the Arabs and Jews fighting and me having to *faire* the *gentil* promenade surrounded by armed guards on account of being shot in the fork. Really, the way everyone's gone on to me about the Holy Land. There isn't anything to see except places where Jesus might have done whatever it was but no one is sure because Jerusalem the G[olden] having been razed to the ground 11 times and no nonsense everything has been built over and over again on everything else and there are far too many churches. The Wailing Wall's a bit of all right tho' with a lot of Bertie Meyers really wailing like anything.

This afternoon I bathed in the Dead Sea or rather sat in it because you can't do anything else and it feels most silly.
                    Love and kisses,
                    Pontius

In Venice he ran into Ivor Novello and reported to Gladys:

He is being very sweet, I need scarcely say, and quite idiotic. He wears a pair of terra cotta rompers on the beach and has already alluded twice to the King and Queen as 'Our dear little couple'. I am waiting for the third time . . .

Valentina [the dress designer] is floating about looking the acme of something or other . . . She's wonderful with the Navy and makes lovely conversations about souls being like colours and the Piazza being a vast baroque room. There are millions of queens here all in Lanvin shorts and when Lady Pound (my late hostess in the *Aberdeen*), who is concerned at my inviting some of my "fine friends" on board, I said—"Take care of the Pansies and the Pounds will take care of themselves!" Wasn't it a lovely joke and nobody understood it but the Captain and he only dimly! *Oh la la la, comme la vie est* fucking *drôle* and no error . . .

The Italians are ever so friendly to the English and I have a shrewd suspicion that the Rome-Berlin *entente* underneath is all my eye and Betty Pollock.

> Love and tisses
> Whistler

Once more into the Breach. Oh Christ!

From Yugoslavia he reports further on Ivor's exploits with the Navy:

He wore a Panama hat and saluted with it upon arriving on board which was pretty fine. The Captain said afterwards with a gleam in his eye. "Nice fellow, thoroughly feminine without being effeminate!"

I'm so pleased you've finally finished your Book! And I take back all I said about you being an indolent bitch and now say you're as nippy and clever as paint, so there! Your telegram was flown dramatically alongside by the ship's plane and an able seaman swam with it in his mouth! Wasn't it lovely? I drink to it silently in some very nasty wine indeed made of distilled monk's blood and ammonia but it's the thought that counts.

This place [Rab] is heaven—nothing to do but bathe starko (I say!!!) and read Milton to improve my spirit and more Milton to discourage my crabs. I have been water ski-ing without conspicuous success owing to the joints of the skis going up my nose and the backs of them up my arse but I'm pressing on. I think life is absolutely ripping if only you live true—what do you think?

> SHELLEY

By way of incidental entertainment he stopped off in Rome and attended a Fascist rally, where he thought Mussolini "looked like an overripe plum squeezed into a white uniform and laughed so dreadfully and had a seat so close I had to leave for fear of being flung into jug." In retrospect, though, it would seem *comédie noire.*

Joke as he might, it was hard not to notice the widening gap between

European *angst* and the determined hedonism of the United States when he received letters like Woollcott's:

Neshobe Island
August first

Lamb of God:

I am sending this word of affection and inquiry and am moved to do so by the notion that you might be susceptible to a suggestion that you come over and sample life on the island. I will be here until October and then intermittently through October while I make brief angry visits to New York for broadcasting purposes. The island is loveliest in October, gayest in August. In the latter part of August, Neysa and the Lunts and God knows who else will be here.

I am glad Neysa is coming back. She was here in July and left a trifle the worse for wear. In one ill-starred Badminton game, I was her zealous but unwieldy partner. In one behemothian lunge at a quill, my racket struck Neysa instead—hitting her on the head and laying her out stiffer than a plank. After she had been revived and the game resumed, I flung myself into the contest with all the old ardor, leaping about like a well-nourished gazelle and coming down with all my weight, such as it is, on the little lady's foot. Later I upset her out of the canoe into the cool, sweet waters of the lake. But only once. So she left in good humor and will be back on these shores on the 21st inst.

I think there's very little chance of your responding to this suggestion, but it did seem to me there was a possibility of your being— Good God, there's a "very" in this sentence!—of your being fed up with whomever you're with at the moment of its arrival. I wish you could have come in at breakfast-time yesterday. I was having mine alone—no one else was up yet—partaking in consoling quantities of the thick, whitish honey from the Riviera which the Otis Skinners had brought over the day before from Woodstock and weeping softly because once again I had reached that final chapter of *The Brothers Karamazov,* which always lays me low. It fills me with brotherly love which wears off about noon.

Anyway, write me and tell me how you are. And how Jeff [Amherst], whom I love, is. Come to think of it, I'd rather have Jeff come over to the island than you. So please send this letter on to him without reading it. And don't think I'll listen to any of this nonsense about your both coming. I can't have this pine-scented nook crawling with Englishmen.

My obeisances to Ladi Vi.
A. WOOLLCOTT

On November 5 Noël is sending Violet "a line to say *au revoir—auf wiedersehen* and Abyssinia," as he boards the SS *Normandie* once more, heading for New York. This time it was to stage a Broadway revue, *Set to Music,* a revised version of the 1932 *Words and Music.* The star was to be his old sparring partner Beatrice Lillie, generally accepted as being one of the funniest ladies around but one who—as Noël knew to his past chagrin—was known as someone who tended not to remember the lines as written.

As she was making her own eccentric way to New York, he cabled her:

> OCTOBER 1938
> LADY PEEL
> *QUEEN MARY*
>
> PRETTY WITTY LADY PEEL
> NEVER MIND HOW SICK YOU FEEL
> NEVER MIND YOUR BROKEN HEART
> CONCENTRATE AND LEARN YOUR PART

To which she replied:

> THANKS MUSTY DUSTY NOËL C
> FOR BEASTLY WIRE TO LADY P
> TO CONCENTRATE IS HARD I FEAR
> SO NOW SHES CRYING IN HER BEER

For Gladys Calthrop, who was on the same ship as Lillie, Noël had a word of cabled advice—perhaps remembering her earlier fateful Atlantic experience with Eva Le Gallienne:

> LOCK YOUR CABIN DOOR MY DARLING
> LOCK YOUR CABIN DOOR
> OTHER THINGS THAN WAR MY DARLING
> THINGS WE ALL ABHOR MY DARLING
> THREATEN YOU ONCE MORE MY DARLING
> WHEN AWAY FROM SHORE MY DARLING
> LOCK YOUR CABIN DOOR

Other correspondence on the show had a more ominous tone. Jack cabled:

> SUGGEST YOU ENGAGE EIGHT REALLY BEAUTIFUL SHOWGIRLS
> MORE OR LESS SAME HEIGHT STOP NO PARTICULAR TALENT
> REQUIRED STOP ALSO NEED CLOSE HARMONY TRIO

But then Jack was in New York and felt none of the tensions of Munich that were hard to ignore if one was in London.

Noël replied:

> GRAVE POSSIBILITY OF WAR WITHIN NEXT FEW WEEKS OR DAYS
> STOP IF THIS HAPPENS POSTPONEMENT REVUE INEVITABLE AND
> ANNIHILATION ALL OF US PROBABLE

As it happened, it was the inevitable that was postponed, and preparations for the show continued. In his November 11 letter to Violet he reports not only theatrical progress:

> Rehearsals now getting to the hectic stage but going marvelously. Beattie is funnier than ever . . . Gladys [who was doing the sets and costumes] is practically a stretcher case, running between the revue and *Dear Octopus* [for which she was also doing sets] but I think she'll survive. I think my birthday treat is going to turn out to be a lighting rehearsal. Goody, goody, what fun!

But another piece of world theater was also being staged in parallel. On September 29 Prime Minister Neville Chamberlain had signed the Munich Agreement with Hitler and Mussolini, supposedly guaranteeing "Peace with Honour." Skeptics saw this as further evidence of appeasement toward the Nazis and Fascists, but the government was anxious to explain and justify its stance to other major powers and dispatched one of its most senior statesmen to do just that, Anthony Eden:

> We've had the most terrific excitement owing to the arrival of the Edens. The ship was late so the wretched Anthony had to be met by a special cutter and brought roaring down the river in order to be in time to make his speech. He had the most terrific reception and his speech was marvelous. I need hardly say I was sitting practically in his lap. He is tremendously popular here and I think his visit has been most useful.
>
> No more news now, darlingest. I've got to take the Edens and the Gary Coopers out to dinner.

(Ironically, Eden—who was then secretary of state for foreign affairs—resigned shortly afterward as a result of Munich.)

But politics soon took up their proper place as *Set to Music* went into rehearsal.

> I must say the show girls in this town are lovely looking and there are thousands of them, so all one has to do is just choose. We've

Bea Lillie. (Hand and cigarette by—
guess who.)

already chosen twelve of the loveliest I've ever seen and all the same
height and all different types and able to move well.

Jack is nearly going mad, what with casting the revue and *Dear
Octopus* I need hardly say he's having much more trouble with the latter because Glen Byam Shaw who's directing it hasn't got quite my
determination, and so people keep on saying they will play a part and
then they won't—and it's all *very* enjoyable!

What was less enjoyable:

There was a terrific blizzard last night and I fell on my face getting
out of a taxi into a snow drift. I'm sure the driver thought I was
drunk, which was unfair as I'd only had an onion sandwich and a
glass of milk!

December 6th

Everything is going beautifully so far and Beattie has never been so
funny in her life. I have written a new Persian song for her in which
she sings as she works at her tapestry, which she has been working on
for years, stitching her dream-lover—unfortunately at the end she
gets so carried away by her singing that she catches the wool on her

Cap d'Antibes, 1931. Bea Lillie and Noël about to go
to "a marvelous party" thrown by American socialite Elsa Maxwell—
only to find that *they* were the "entertainment."

foot without noticing and unravels the whole thing! She is very happy with her material and there haven't been any squalls yet.

> December 29
> Boston

The revue opened on Monday night and went through without a hitch. Beattie was marvelous and it really was a smash success! Of course New York may be a bit more difficult to please but I really think we're all right judging from what the audiences feel. We rehearse a little every day just to polish up bits and pieces. We are all feeling very pleased with ourselves and it certainly is a comfort after *Operette* to come into the theatre and see five rows of standees and everyone cheering and yelling!

*Set to Music* opened at New York's Music Box Theatre on January 18, 1939, and ran for a modest 129 performances. As soon as it was safely launched, Noël wrote to Violet, who was undergoing treatment in Switzerland for her chronic deafness:

> January 21st

I'm off I'm off I'm off! Isn't it lovely—particularly when I can leave a smash hit behind me!

"Off" was to spend a couple of days with Alfred and Lynn, then on to Hollywood for a week to stay with Cary Grant and then . . . "a nice comfortable suite on a nice comfortable ship and, I hope, a nice lot of sunshine!"

His original plan had been to go to Pago-Pago, but when he got to Hollywood, he changed his mind, sent Coley a cryptic cable—"BUTTERING NO PARSNIPS"—and went to his beloved Honolulu instead. (The line from Proverbs is "Fine words butter no parsnips," presumably meaning that empty words get one nowhere. Noël was saying that the offers he had received in Hollywood fell firmly into that category.)

> 1018 Ocean Front
> Santa Monica, California
> February 1st

Darlingest,

I've had a lovely week here staying with Cary Grant and Randolph Scott in a little house right on the edge of the sea. I've been whirling about from studio to studio and party to party hobnobbing with all the glamour boys and girls. I was photographed upside down and inside out with Shirley Temple whom I must say is sweet. I did an hour's broadcast on Sunday with Ronnie Coleman [*sic*], Carole Lombard, Cary and the Marx Brothers for which I was paid a thousand pounds! Of course I shan't see much of it owing to the income tax but it was a nice thought!

Norma Shearer gave a party for me last night. Everyone was there—Claudette Colbert, Tyrone Power, Gary Cooper, Marlene Dietrich, etc., etc., etc., and they're all coming in a mass to see me off at the boat tonight.

I'm going to Honolulu to stay with the Dillinghams for a few days and then find some quiet little house by the sea and just relax for a month . . .

On February 7 he found Honolulu "such a beautiful island at this time of the year when there is a certain amount of rain every day. It looks newly washed and all the flowers and trees look as tho' they had been varnished." There was "a curving sandy beach fringed with palms and soft feathery ironwood trees and a great headland of mountains in the distance. I have actually two little shacks—one to live in and one to sleep in and a little verandah on each with a rocking chair." His only company was "a fat old Japanese woman who comes in and cooks very badly."

"I'm having my one weekly outing tonight and going to a LUAU which is an Hawaiian open air dinner where they roast pigs and eat them with bread fruit and Taro, etc. Then I shall drive off to my little hideout in the moonlight!"

Then it was back to Hollywood . . . Cary Grant (again) . . . Alfred and Lynn . . . and finally home on April 1 on the *Normandie.*

•

THE EARLY SUMMER was spent writing at Goldenhurst. At the end of May he was bringing Woollcott up to date:

> 1 Burton Mews
> South Eaton Place, London S.W.1.
> 31st May 1939

Dearest pretty Aweeza,

With any luck I may come flying into your arms, burrowing my head on your shoulder, sometime during the summer. In the meantime my news is this:

A. I have written a new comedy, very gay I think, which I am going to play here in the autumn.

B. I have finished my book of short stories. There are seven of them and I can guarantee that one at least you will like.

C. We are going mad at the moment over the Actors' Orphanage because our Theatrical Garden Party is next week and I am spending every night of this week rushing madly through all the West End theatres making impassioned appeals. I am looking astonishingly pretty considering everything. You would be the first to admit this, however bitterly.

London is calming down. Nobody expects a war now for a month or two. The Prime Minister is fishing. Sybil Colefax is entertaining but not very. The bluebells are out and I sometimes throw myself down among them laughing. Peggy Wood has sailed away in a blaze of Baby talk and there is no more news whatsoever. By reading between the lines in the papers I suspect that the King and Queen are visiting Canada and America. If you should knock up against them try and behave and carry the whole thing off with what remains of your tattered dignity.

> All my love, dear Aweeza
> NOLIE POELIE

In fact, Noël wrote two plays that summer—*This Happy Breed* (a semi-sequel to *Cavalcade,* taking events up to the present) and *Such Sweet Sorrow,* which became *Present Laughter,* the new comedy he refers to. Both were intended for September production but, in the event, neither achieved it for reasons totally nontheatrical.

Noël's life was about to enter an entirely new phase, and it began that July.

# PART THREE

# NOËL'S WAR

## PERSONAL NOTE

Creative impulse, whether fine, austere,
Or light in texture, great in scope, or small,
Owes to its owner, if it's true at all,
Some moments of release. In this dark year,
When all the world is shadowed, when the time
Essential to the clear process of thought
Is so accelerated, I have sought
Relief by these excursions into rhyme.
I must explain I have no mind just now
To write light operettes, revues or plays,
Nor leisure, for these swiftly moving days
Have set my hand to quite a different plough.
I feel my spirit battered, bludgeoned, sore,
All my ideas seem pale, oppressed by doom,
Like frightened children in a burning room,
Scurrying back and forth to find the door.

**NOEL COWARD**
*Flag-wag*

LEFT: Caricature by Vicky. RIGHT: Noël's personal philosophy as he contemplated the coming war.

# CHAPTER 16
# WORLD WAR II:
# "TWENTIETH CENTURY BLUES"

(1938–1940)

*Why is it that civilized humanity*
*Must make the world so wrong?*
*In this hurly-burly of insanity*
*Our dreams cannot last long.*

"TWENTIETH CENTURY BLUES," FROM *CAVALCADE* (1931)

T HE IMPRESSION one gets of "Noël's War," as he himself recounts it in his 1954 autobiography, *Future Indefinite*, is that it began with a mysterious out-of-the-blue phone call from a Sir Campbell Stuart demanding a midnight meeting with Noël at Coward's Gerald Road house.

The naïveté of Noël's account was both false and forced—by the exigencies of the Official Secrets Act, which bound to silence for many years anyone even slightly involved in government intelligence. In fact, it was only in 1973, in the month before his death, that Noël felt able to give any real account of his wartime activities. As his interviewer remarked afterward, "It was as though he felt the need to get it on the record."

It's necessary to recall the prevailing political climate of the late 1930s. Hitler had come to power in Germany in 1933, and by 1938 it was clear he had ambitions to dominate at least Europe. In that year he annexed Austria and was laying claim to part of Czechoslovakia. In England, Neville Chamberlain was prime minister, leading a Conservative Party that was largely in favor of "appeasement." What Hitler was doing was none of Britain's business, and perhaps he was entitled to unify the German-speaking peoples. In any case, another world war was a ludicrous idea. We were only just getting over the last one.

As early as November 1932, many of Noël's friends were taking sides.

Noël went wherever he was asked to go to entertain the armed forces . . . The Antipodes or the Middle East . . . South Africa or Burma.

Some were taking a violent point of view for disarmament—if that isn't a contradiction in terms. Beverley Nichols invited Noël to a meeting at the Albert Hall. Noël sent his regrets and added:

> I'm certainly all for disarmament, providing that every other country is all for disarmament too. As now everything seems so chaotic in this delicious civilisation I should think that the really best thing to do is for all of us to slay each other as swiftly and efficiently as possible. I'd love to see you before I go.

On September 29, 1938, Chamberlain was a signatory—along with Hitler, Mussolini, and Daladier for France—to the Munich Agreement, supposedly a nonaggression pact. Chamberlain returned to London and was photographed on the steps of his aeroplane waving a piece of paper. For Noël, "the pre-war past died on the day when Mr. Neville Chamberlain returned with such gay insouciance." Noël hated very few people, but "that bloody conceited old sod" (whose neck, he claimed, was too thin for his collar) was near the top of his personal list.

Although the "appeasers" were in power, a strong countermovement was building and rallying around the controversial Winston Churchill, back in the Conservative Party but out of cabinet office. In the Civil Service— a body that maintains continuity, no matter which political party is in

Robert (later Lord) Vansittart (1881–1957). A senior diplomat at the Foreign Office, he became alarmed by the government's policy of appeasement toward Nazi Germany and recruited Noël, among others, to sound out foreign opinion on Hitler's intentions.

office—the same unofficial role was being played by Sir Robert (later Lord) Vansittart (1881–1957), permanent undersecretary at the Foreign Office from 1930 to 1937 and now a powerful Whitehall "mandarin" waiting in the wings, so to speak. Vansittart took it upon himself to build the case for rearmament, and to do that he had to piece together evidence of what Hitler was really planning and what the opinion was among Britain's European neighbors. To do that he set up a network of unofficial "agents," made up of businessmen and celebrities who had legitimate business in European cities and now a private "brief" to report back to Vansittart.

Noël was recruited as one of Vansittart's men. Precisely when is impossible to say, but early 1938 would seem likely. What Noël saw concerned him deeply, since it was in direct opposition to what many of his friends were *choosing* to see.

On September 27, 1938—two days before Munich—Blanche Lloyd, wife of Lord George Lloyd, a prominent diplomat and close friend of Noël's, was writing: "I can't help wondering a little whether that epileptic monster in Berlin is beginning to think twice—but I am dreadfully afraid that no bridge is golden enough for him to get back over—and also that he is sure that he can beat us—Well, he just *shan't*."

Noël was writing to Alec Woollcott: "We have nothing to worry about but the destruction of civilisation."

Humor is the typical British reaction to stress. Nothing, at the time, can be allowed to be serious enough to be taken seriously. It's an outward attitude that Britain's enemies consistently misinterpret as weakness. Nonetheless, concern was growing, and it was possible to find the true perspective on those strange days only a long time later.

As late as January 1970, Robert Boothby, a Tory politician and friend of Noël's for more than forty years, could write to him: "I've been going through my Munich papers. How right we both were. It is *still* frightening."

Noël to Vansittart:

5th Nov. 1938

My dear Bob,

I am terribly sorry to have missed you, however I had not very much to tell you. I had a brief but reasonably interesting time in Switzerland. I snooped around a good deal and flapped my ears and I don't think discovered much more than you know already which is A. That the Swiss, although pretty scared, behaved and are behaving pretty well and very calmly. B. That the Nazi propaganda, particularly in Zurich and Basle, is very strong but falling on the stoniest of stony ground. C. In various conversations I had and listened to it was apparent that English prestige had dropped considerably but there was no violence about this just a rather depressed acceptance of the inevitable. There was, of course, relief that war had been averted but also a certain surprised resignation that it should have been averted at such a price.

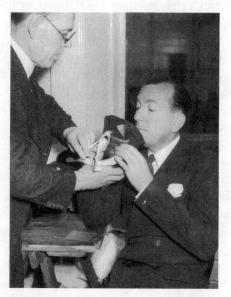

"Don't forget your gas mask!" was the cry in the early months of the war. Interestingly, Noël is being fitted for his as early as September 26, 1938—nearly a year before hostilities began.

I heard an Englishman (commercial traveller type) in the bar of the hotel in Zurich making a tremendous tirade against Duff [Cooper, First Lord of the Admiralty], Anthony [Eden] and Winston but he was very quietly and successfully squashed by a Swiss professor of sports propaganda who said, without heat, that in the opinion of the Swiss, if we'd had a few more men like that, perhaps the British Empire would not have fallen so low.

It was all a little depressing, I think and I felt that everybody was just waiting rather drearily to see what was going to happen next. I am afraid that none of this is very illuminating, however, my time was very short. I sail for America on the 5th and my address there is 450 East 52nd Street. I shall be in Washington for two weeks in January so just drop me a line when you have time and give me a few conversational leads or, if possible, defences.

My love to you both,
NOËL

On November 12, Vansittart replies:

Hotel de Paris
Monte Carlo

Your information is very much what I expected; and I think that the impressions you gleaned would be applicable to many other countries in Europe. I should expect you to have the same impression in the U.S., only more so. I shall be most interested to get your general impressions about this, for your range will be pretty wide, and it should furnish a good cross section. Try to get them on to the topic as much as possible, and let them rip. I think many will need very little encouragement! And the topic will still be a very fresh one, I should imagine, in spite of the growing calls of the parish pump.

·

IN JUNE 1939, Noël undertook a trip for Vansittart to Warsaw, Danzig, Moscow, Leningrad, Helsinki, Stockholm, Oslo, and Copenhagen "to see what was going on."

His secret mission was hardly "secret." *The Daily Sketch* reported:

Noël Coward has "Design for Politics." He left from Heston Airport to study the political situation there. He has seen a great deal of Mr. and Mrs. Anthony Eden in the last two years and in 1937 he joined the "Die-hard" Atheneum Club . . . On his departure he gave the reason for his Polish trip as he maintained his well-known "poker face" but he did not deny that his trip might have a political reason as well.

He kept Violet up to date on the lighter side of things:

In Warsaw . . . I was met by a private band of fifty men in uniform who played "God Save the King" in my honour—off key—I had to stand to attention and try not to giggle . . . The Poles are very sweet and gay and everyone drinks far too much vodka. Fortunately I have a very strong head!

[Russia] was filthy and smelly. Exactly like a whole world composed of the Whitechapel Road on August Bank Holiday. In addition to that, I was spied upon and followed everywhere because it was known that I had something to do with the British Embassy . . . The Russians, I need hardly say, opened everything and turned out all my clothes onto the platform. What they hoped to find I don't know. I had any papers of importance in my hip pocket!

[Helsinki] . . . the relief after Russia is indescribable. This town is clean and pleasant and everyone is amiable . . . I had my usual press conference when I gave out discreet information about my new plays and the magnificent strength of the English Air Force!

[Danzig is] a lovely city and seemed calm enough although there were a lot of Nazis parading about.

Dame Rebecca West (1892–1982). A distinguished writer and an old friend. Like Noël, she found after the war that she had been on the German "blacklist." "My dear," she cabled Noël, "the people we should have been seen dead with!"

I'm leaving [Oslo] this afternoon for Copenhagen which is my last port of call as far as doing my stuff goes. I'm not altogether sorry. It becomes a little wearing *constantly* having to be polite and guarded. But still I think I've done it all all right.

Wherever he went Noël found "the same fatalistic conviction that war was not only inevitable but imminent"—a perspective that could be achieved only by being outside the wishful-thinking world he had left at home.

In Danzig—a particularly sensitive location—he was spotted by the writer Lawrence Durrell being closely observed by Nazi agents. It's probable that there and then he was put on the infamous blacklist of British "agents" to be liquidated when Britain was conquered. When the list was published at the end of the war, Noël received a cable from his friend Rebecca West, who was also on the list:

MY DEAR THE PEOPLE WE SHOULD HAVE BEEN SEEN DEAD WITH.

He began to send in his reports, and on July 5 Vansittart replies to Noël in guarded terms:

In view of the uncertainty of the letter's destination it will be brief. Your letter told me much in a small compass, particularly in regard to the attitude of some people. In fact, it told me all I wanted to know. Some people are not very quick at seeing wedges, even right under their noses. I shall look forward to hearing more of your experiences directly you get back.

Vansittart fought the good fight for many years, and when he finally resigned, he unburdened himself to Noël of the feelings he had kept to himself for so long:

My dear Noël,
Oh yes, I've done right to go. The last twelve years of my thirty-nine in the public service have been a long martyrdom. For eight years my advice was rejected and for the last four it has been unsought. To have foreseen everything, and been allowed to do nothing to save, has been so huge a spiritual misery that I am glad to have been alone in it . . . Now at last I am wrenching myself—yes, it's a wrench—free from gags and trammels. I've given my life to trying to prevent two German-made wars. I've failed. I wasn't allowed to succeed. Whatever remains of my life I'm giving to the prevention of a third. But

this time on my own, by God. You may imagine how I'm looking forward to my freedom. I sometimes ask myself whether so many of my dear fellow-beings would have had to suffer and die if I had freed myself sooner. And then I dismiss the question as vanity. Well, we shall see.

Yours ever,
BOB

•

WITH THIS AS a background and a regular contact with Vansittart, the phone call from Stuart that sunny Sunday in mid-August can hardly have seemed "out of the blue."

Managing director of *The Times* and an important figure in propaganda in the First World War, Stuart was known to have moved in the corridors of power. A lunch guest at Goldenhurst that day happened to be Robert Boothby, who told Noël that Stuart probably wanted to recruit Noël for some hush-hush job when war broke out. Knowing that Boothby would be breaking his return journey to town to dine with Winston at Chartwell, Noël asked if he might accompany him. He felt badly in need of Churchill's advice on what he should do in the conflict that was about to begin.

He was still haunted by his inglorious lack of performance in the first war and was determined to make a significant contribution this time. All of which he told Churchill later that evening.

When Noël said that he wanted a job that would be associated with the navy and that would use his "intelligence," Churchill pretended to interpret the word with a capital *I*. No, no, he'd be no good at that, Churchill told Noël. Too well known. His job was to go out and sing "Mad Dogs and Englishmen" when the guns were firing. Noël reflected (but did not say) that if the guns were firing, no one would hear a word of the song.

It would not be the last time that the two men failed to see eye to eye. A day or two later Noël tried to set the record straight in a letter he drafted but may have thought better about sending:

My Dear Winston,

It was good of you to receive me yesterday so graciously and at such short notice, too. I know you had many more things on your mind than listening to *my* insignificant concerns!

Thinking about it overnight, I would like to make one thing clear to you. I fear I failed to do so properly at the time.

During the last "war to end wars" I'm conscious that I made little or no contribution—and that is something that has stayed at the back of my mind ever since. I was young and callow—but that was a reason not an excuse. This time I am determined to play as much of a part as the powers-that-be allow me.

You know of my love of the Navy—one I know you share. [Churchill was to become First Lord of the Admiralty within weeks.] I needn't elaborate on that. What I miserably failed to convey to you was that this time I want to do something that will utilize whatever *creative* intelligence I've been blessed with. You, I know, took me to mean I wanted some glamour job in Naval Intelligence. My ambitions are not so high and I simply want to clear the air on that score.

You may count on my doing whatever I am called upon to do and to do it to the best of my ability.

In sincere admiration

Noël Coward

Why didn't Noël tell Churchill that he was already involved through Vansittart? It came down to a question of political protocol. Vansittart was a professional civil servant, committed to serving the government of the day, whether he agreed with their policices or not—and in the case of their appeasement policy, he most emphatically did not. His information-gathering activities were strictly private, and discussion of them could have undermined his position at the center of power and influence. It was highly likely that the like-minded Churchill was perfectly well aware of what was going on, but he was in no position to discuss it, either. A very British situation and one perfectly understood and accepted by all concerned.

•

SURE ENOUGH, that night, back at Gerald Road, the saturnine Sir Campbell Stuart made Noël an offer he couldn't very well refuse, if he was serious about wanting to serve. He was to go to Paris immediately the war began and set up a Bureau of Propaganda, working closely with the French Commissariat d'Information. Since the French were using famous literary figures Jean Giraudoux and André Maurois to run their own operation, presumably the use of someone of Noël's stature was considered appropriate. Giraudoux himself said that he "would take it as a personal compliment" if Noël accepted the role, the role that would provide him with the opportunity "to prove my own integrity to myself."

It was a flattering offer but not what Noël had hoped for, and the very next day he consulted Vansittart again, only to be told that Vansittart agreed with the posting. (He himself was now the government's chief diplomatic adviser, a post Chamberlain intended to be purely symbolic but one that acquired teeth when Churchill became prime minister.) The die effectively had been cast before Stuart even picked up the phone.

The next two weeks were more than a little chaotic. Noël divided his time between rehearsing two new plays that were due to open in tandem that autumn at the Phoenix Theatre—*Present Laughter* and *This Happy Breed*—and being briefed by Stuart and his second-in-command, Col. Dallas Brooks. Noël was given his own deputy, David Strathallan, and on Sunday, September 3, the day war was formally declared by a lugubrious Chamberlain, the two of them traveled to Stuart's "secret" headquarters in Bletchley Park, Buckinghamshire, a country house commandeered by the SIS and a location that would come to be increasingly important as the war progressed.

Noël was formally enrolled into D section, familiarly known as the "dirty tricks department" and one that was to earn its name in more ways than one. The future spy Guy Burgess was already ensconced there, and his partner in crime, Kim Philby, would soon join him.

The fate of the plays—at least for the duration—was settled when all London theaters were officially closed. For theater folk, no statement could have been more definitive. War had become a reality.

Noël was off to fulfill a unique out-of-town booking, and Lorn and Joyce sped him on his way:

> DAYS WILL BECOME A PERPETUAL NIGHT
> NOW THAT THE MASTER HAS FLOWN OUT OF SIGHT
> FRANCE WILL HAVE DAYLIGHT AND FRANCE WILL
> HAVE DAWN
> JOYCE WILL HAVE NEITHER AND NEITHER WILL
> LORN
> BECAUSE TO THE RULES WE MUST NOT ACT
> CONTRARY
> THIS CABLE IS SIGNED LORN LORAINE AND JOYCE
> CAREY

Ironically, the very day he left the following letter was sent to him:

> MINISTRY OF INFORMATION
> SENATE HOUSE
> LONDON UNIVERSITY BUILDING
> MALET STREET, W.C.1.
> 5th September 1939

Dear Sir,
I am directed by the Minister of Information to inform you that your name has been entered on a list of authors whose services are likely to be valuable to the Ministry of Information in time of war.

The Minister will be grateful, therefore, if you will refrain from engaging yourself in any other form of national service without previously communicating with the Ministry of Information.

Please send particulars of any change of address, and all communications to me at Room 135, at the above address.

Yours faithfully,
A. D. PETERS

Peters was a highly respected literary agent. Noël instructed Lorn to reply.

Dear Mr. A. D. Peters,
Mr. Noël Coward has asked me to thank you for your letter and to tell you that he has noted the instructions contained therein. He wishes me to say, however, that he fears he will be unable to comply with these as he is going abroad today for several months. Should you wish to get in touch with him, he suggests that you should apply to the Ministry of Information or to the British Embassy in Paris.

Yours sincerely,
Lorn Loraine
Secretary

For Noël it was like acting in a surrealistic play. On September 5 he was flown across the Channel in a small plane, to find Paris in a state of suspended animation. War had not reached them, and surely never could—not with the Maginot Line. While he and Strathallan searched for office premises, their informal headquarters was the Ritz. And then—nothing. *La drôle de guerre*—the French name for the "phoney war," itself an American coinage—was well under way, and Noël found it difficult to take it seriously. He'd signed up for *this?* "I could not avoid realizing quite early on that the job I had undertaken was neither so serious or so important as I had been led to believe."

•

AT FIRST he warmed to his new task. It was like opening a new show and he sent regular (censored) reports to Violet and Gladys:

18-20 Place de la Madeleine
September 15th

Everything is going very well here and I must admit I'm enjoying it all quite a lot. To begin with the work itself is frightfully interesting and I'm beginning to understand what it's all about. I have to deal tactfully with all sorts of people and up to date I think I have got the most important ones on my side. At all events I keep getting telegrams of thanks from my Chief in England so, so far so good!

I have found the most lovely flat in the Place Vendôme just a few minutes from the office and right in the middle of everything. Also it is bang opposite the Ritz where they have the most well prepared air raid shelter, so all is well.

Don't worry about air raids. We are bound to have a few here but I don't suppose we shall have as many as London and the Germans have seventeen lines of defences to cross before they get here.

I should think in a few weeks time when things have settled down a bit I shall be able to pop home for a few days or you can come over here.

And to Gladys Calthrop on the same day:

Well, Cock,
So far, so *bien.*
It really is quite enthralling when you begin to get below the surface a bit and the jolly decent intrigues and carryings on is nobody's business . . .

Paris is beautifully "War gay". Nobody ever dresses and everybody collects at Maxim's.

September 21st

Hallo, Cock,
Hold on to everything because I think I shall be coming home for a couple of nights. Promise not to break down when you meet me at the station, you will notice many great changes in me. To begin with I have barely any nose at all owing to having picked it away and my eyes look terribly haunted and tired after all the horrors I've seen.

I have had a series of rather depressed letters from the Baybay [Jack Wilson]. Do try and cheer him up. He seems to be taking the war too big, if you know what I mean.

I am doing my own job very well apparently and everything is going down like anything and my French is getting worse and worse with every day that passes . . . I entertain nightly the highest officials to the nastiest dinners and my success passes all bounds.

Love and kisses<br>Germaine de Staël

It's a strange life and oh dear, what material for a writer!!

To Violet:

September 26th

Everything is getting more into a routine now. I get to the office every morning at 9 o'clock and then all hell breaks loose until we get our dispatches and reports done to catch the bag which leaves at 11:30. Fortunately we have now been given a boy scout who runs about Paris for us, so our legs and our time is saved.

I think after all I shall have to have a uniform of some sort and until this is approved by the authorities it's no good my coming over, as I must have it made by my own tailor and have it ready to fit when I arrive. It will, I think, be Naval!

Keep out of London the moment War really starts.

To Gladys:

October 25th

Well, Cock,

I haven't heard a peep out of you lately so I thought I'd just drop a line to remind you that I am in dire distress, having a cold and wind, to say nothing of the exhaustion following on the dashing visit of my Chief who whistled through Paris France like a dose of salts and left various articles of clothing in all directions.

The whole thing is expanding like mad, if you know what I mean, and it won't be long now before you will see my face on the French coinage.

I am, needless to say, entranced with the goings on in England. I was particularly touched by the House of Commons cheering the U-Boat Commander who sunk the *Royal Oak* and drowned eight hundred of our sailors. I think gentlemanly behaviour is really very important particularly at a moment like this when those vulgar Germans are so terribly *lacking* in decency. I'm furious with them, I really am.

I dined last Sunday evening at [interior decorator] Elsie Mendl's with the Windsors and [journalist] Godfrey Winn and it was all very glamorous. Godfrey Winn thinks our Air Force is simply marvellous and very very brave indeed and the French Army is very brave too and filled with a wonderful sort of spirit which after all is very important and a sort of touching united quality which is very important too. The Duke of Windsor thinks the German spirit is very important because they are awfully dogged and capable of really surprising endurance in the face of practically anything, which is very important.

You will gather from the above that the conversation was of a distinction *formidable*.

I had a large envelope from the Lunts in Washington with no letter inside it but all the latest notices of *The Taming of the Shrew*. I had a long letter from John Gielgud saying that he is quite all right and that Edith Evans is quite all right and that there is a possibility of Michel St. Denis [Saint-Denis] being quite all right too and so *that's* all right.

I am having daily lessons in French from a sweet old girl who has been in love with [Louis] Jouvet [the actor] for twenty years and I am making well the progress and can say a lot of very important things.

I haven't any other news whatsoever. Actually, of course, I have a lot of very secret information, because I am very mysterious and doing a very important job for my country but you couldn't expect me to tell you anything because you are so garrulous.

Keep a brave heart and look to the future for sweet bugger all.

      Love and Kisses
      Charlemagne

To Violet:

                               November 9th
I've just got back from three days up at British Army Headquarters . . . I walked about on Vimy Ridge and looked at all the remains of the last war and the whole thing seems very pointless and futile but when countries have bad diplomats and worse politicians these catastrophes are inevitable.

Before too long the whole enterprise came to have an amateur, schoolboyish air about it that rubbed off on Noël. One can picture him having read the day's mail ("Most Secret, Confidential and Dull") and increasingly frustrated that he could not get on with his real work. Other men would have filled the idle hours with crossword puzzles or the flying of paper aeroplanes. Noël's mind took to verse, and he wrote to and about anyone and everyone in a series of verse letters. (Cole Lesley would recall that in later years Noël would "re-read these letter-poems so often with reminiscent pleasure!")

There would be letters to the Coward "family" and to Lorn in particular. In October he writes to her on British embassy stationery:

        *Lornie, whose undying love*
        *Pursues me to this foreign clime,*
        *Please note from the address above*

*That master is not wasting time*
*In pinching all that he can see*
*From His Britannic Majesty.*

*Master regrets he has no news*
*To gladden Lornie's loving heart.*
*Hitler's still beastly to the Jews*
*And still the battle does not start.*

*Kindly inform my ageing Mum*
*That I am reasonably bright*
*Working for peace and joy to come*
*By giving dinners every night.*
*Give her my love and also Joyce,*
*Thus echoing your master's voice.*

*And as for you, my little dear,*
*Please rest assured of my intense*
*And most devoted and sincere*
*And most distinguished compliments,*
*And if you do not care a bit*
*You know what you can do with it!*

October 28th

*Pretty Pretty Pretty Lorn,*
*Timid as a hunted faun,*
*This engaging little rhyme*
*Merely serves to pass the time,*
*Tho' my hands with cold are numb*
*Give my love to dear old Mum,*
*Also it would make me glad*
*Now that dear Almina's mad—*
*If you shut her up alone*
*Where there was no telephone.*
*Dear Virginia Vernon's here*
*In my hair and in my ear.*
*Hoytie Wiborg too still sits*
*Drinking deeply in the Ritz,*
*And I've heard from Giraudoux*
*That he's sick to death of you.*
*Reynaud on the other hand*
*Thinks you're absolutely grand,*

*Which will prove most sinister*
*Should he be Prime Minister.*
*Gamelin and Ironside*
*Puff and blow and burst with pride*
*For I sent a carrier dove*
*Saying Lorn had sent her love.*

In this first strange year of the "phoney war," more domestic concerns would occasionally intrude, especially when they had their roots in America, which was three thousand physical miles removed, and a great deal more than that emotionally, for many Americans.

Noël had sent the Lunts a copy of *Present Laughter* hoping they might play it in the United States, but, perhaps with *Point Valaine* still fresh in memory—or perhaps it was the fact that the play would have a show-stopping part for Alfred but a relatively supporting one for Lynn:

> Technical High School Auditorium, Omaha, Nebraska
> October 22nd, 1939

Darling, darling,

Our first instinct was to ask you to make a few alterations, so that the play would be more suitable for both of us, then go ahead and do it, knowing that we would have a big hit on our hands, and that we would be doing Noly's play, all of which would make us very happy; then we thought of how long we have held out, turning down one obvious Lunt-Fontanne vehicle after another, in order not to be stuck with that kind of thing forever, and so we decided that we will not do a new play until something exciting, dramatic, and on the serious side comes along, I know the *Sea Gull* [their 1938 production] was serious and God knows too, but we only played it for five weeks in New York preparatory to leaving and doing *Amphitryon* in London.

I would not bother you with these trivialities while you are in the middle of a war, except that I do want you to thoroughly understand why we do not want to do your play and also, we feel that it is such a comedy classic and a sure fire hit, not difficult to cast, really. Meanwhile, believe it or not, we are whoopsing across the country with *The Taming of the Shrew,* and so far (we are in the first three weeks), playing to capacity business . . .

We think of you all the time, and now that the big offensive has begun, with a certain amount of anxiety, although we hope you are fairly safe. What we wouldn't give for a little heart to heart talk.

Next week we shall be in St. Louis at the same hotel, in the same rooms exactly that we saw you last and the war that we talked of then is now an accomplished fact, although, I still feel as if I am dreaming. We are keeping our thumbs crossed all the time about the repeal of the embargo. [America was neutral and officially unable to send materials to the United Kingdom.] Even if they don't repeal it, there will be factories set up in Canada and everything will be all right, although not so quick or convenient.

Since I began this letter Turkey has signed her pact with England and we are so excited and happy about it. Now Mussolini, then Russia and next America, then we will have the bugger [Hitler] cornered. I don't think he is any too sure of Russia by the quick way he hastened to ratify the pact, as soon as he heard of Turkey, and well he mightn't.

I expect you will be far too busy to wade through as far as this, but I have written while making-up every night and it has given me a nice cozy feeling of talking to you.

Au revoir, my sweet. If you want me to go on writing these rather ponderous letters and they don't bore you, let me know and I will, because there is one good thing about them, you won't have to answer them.

Love, love, love darling from us both ever your,
LYNNIE

•

IN EARLY NOVEMBER he heard that his old friend playwright, painter, novelist Clemence Dane (Winifred Ashton) had slipped and fallen in the blackout:

Saturday, November 4th

*Why did you fall, Winnie?*
*Why did you fall?*
*Were you just drunk, dear,*
*Or not drunk at all?*
*Were you preoccupied?*
*Were you in doubt?*
*Or were you merely*
*Just bashing about?*
*Were you too early,*
*Or were you too late?*
*Were you in full*
*Conversational Spate?*
*Where was dear Olwen* [Davies, her secretary],
*And what was she at?*

Letting you hiccup
And stumble like that!
What were you thinking of,
Was it a plot?
Was it a painting,
A sculpture, or what?
Was that which caused you
To fall in the street
Something unpleasant
Or charming or sweet?
What was the cause
Of this fall down the drain?
Was it some quirk
In your functional brain?
Was it your strange
Intellectual strength
Leading you sadly
To measure your length?
Once and for all, darling,
Once and for all
Why did you fall, Winnie?
Why did you fall?

(COMPOSED AND TYPED PERSONALLY BY NOËL COWARD
AMID THE HORRORS OF WAR IN PARIS 1939)


"REPLY, REPLY"

(SEE SHAKESPEARE, *MERCHANT OF VENICE*)

Noël! A string-and-scissors mind,
One with, *and* to officialdom cemented,
Ignobly, though bi-lingually, contented
With the Parisian grind,
Cannot conceive how mysticals like me
Can trip it on a lea!

It was economy
That caused the smash—
The old desire for sausages-and-mash
At Bow Street, in a bar
Where once our virgins raised a nunnery
And now policemen are.

Clemence Dane (Winifred Ashton) (1888–1965).
Dramatist, novelist, artist, sculptor, friend, and—second only to
John Gielgud—incomparable dropper of verbal bricks.

*Thither I sped to eat;*
*But, as I made my way down Floral Street,*
*(a pleasant touch*
*for one to whom the meanest flower that blows*
*Does mean so much!)*
*In the black heavens arose*
*Balloons,*
*Those oblong, argent, artificial moons,*
*And lolloped o'er the sky*
*Ever so high!*

*I thought they looked a treat,*
*So, carelessly, as Olwen trolloped by*
*I pointed out each separate silken blob.*
*I carolled: "Aren't they neat?*
*Sheer poetry of motion!*
*They rhyme, they lilt, they scan!"*

*I did not watch my feet.*

*I had no notion*
*They did not know their job.*

*I trusted them: they failed me: and I fell,*
*Hurting myself like hell!*
*Oh—what a fall was there, my countrymen!*

CLEMENCE DANE

Occasionally Noël would be able to get a seat back to England on an official plane, although he could never be sure until the last minute. Sometimes the war got in the way:

TO LORN

Monday, November 20th

*Because of vast political intrigues*
*I cannot yet my fond Mama embrace*
*Nor traverse those uncompromising leagues*
*To see your pallid and unchanging face*
*Because of vast political intrigues.*

*Because of sinister, far-reaching plots*
*And desperate excursions and alarms*
*I must forego those twin forget-me-nots*
*Men call your eyes; I must forego your charms*
*Because of sinister, far-reaching plots.*

*Because of secret work that must be done*
*I may not hear your loving, heavy tread*
*Nor see, caught by the early morning sun,*
*Your shining dentures looming o'er my bed*
*Because of secret work that must be done.*

*Because of my unconscionable task*
*I cannot yet come whirling through the air*
*Nor yet of Destiny politely ask*
*To lose myself in your three strands of hair*
*Because of my unconscionable task.*

*Next week end is pretty certain anyhow!*

On Christmas Eve his Christmas card to Lorn was another verse letter:

> *Dearest sympathetic lovely Lorn*
> *Very many years ago tomorrow*
> *Jesus Christ was definitely born*
> *Into this unpleasant vale of sorrow.*
> *Unpremeditated, this event*
> *Caused a pretty fair amount of chatter.*
> *Later years He adequately spent*
> *Wresting with mind; disowning matter*
> *Breathing new life into the newly dead,*
> *Juggling with loaves and little fishes,*
> *Walking on the water (it is said*
> *Contrary to many people's wishes!)*
> *Working several miracles a week,*
> *Making an enormous lot of speeches;*
> *Telling the conceited to be meek;*
> *Contemplating God on lonely beaches;*
> *Urging local prostitutes to pray;*
> *Blackguardly the rich and aged fossils;*
> *Emphasising every seventh day;*
> *Eating rubber rolls with His apostles*
> *All of this with amiable intent*
> *Hoping against hope the human being*
> *Might succeed in being more content*
> *Not by far, but just by further seeing.*
> *To pursue this story to its end*
> *Might show lack of taste—I'm sure you'd hate it.*
> *Must we watch the human star descend?*
> *"What the hell", we cry. "Why celebrate it?"*
> *None the less, in spite of and because*
> *I, with others, must obey convention,*
> *Making in my busy life, a pause*
> *Long enough, my darling Lorn, to mention*
> *That I hope this gay and festive time*
> *(Tho' I fear, without apparent reason)*
> *Might be gladdened by my little rhyme.*
> *Bringing comps of this delightful season.*

To Gladys he was in a less flippant mood. Once again his equivocal attitude toward organized religion comes over loud and clear:

## WITH ALL BEST WISHES FOR A MERRY CHRISTMAS. 1939

*Back to the nursery. Back to the nursery.*
*Let us enjoy this sublime anniversary*
*Full nineteen hundred and thirty-nine years*
*Let us forget the despair and the tears*
*Let us ignore all the slaughter and danger*
*(Think of the Manger! Remember the Manger!)*
*Let us envisage the star in the East*
*(Man is a murderer! Man is a beast!)*
*Let us forget that the moment is sinister*
*Let us uphold our devout Foreign Minister*
*Let us not prattle of Simon or Hoare*
*Or Mr. Chamberlain's diffident war.*
*Let us not speak of Belisha or Burgin*
*(Think of the Virgin! Remember the Virgin!)*
*Let us from ridicule turn to divinity*
*(Think of the Trinity! Think of the Trinity!)*
*Now as our day of rejoicing begins*
*(Never mind Poland—Abandon the Finns)*
*Lift up your voices "Long Live Christianity!"*
*(Cruelty, sadism, blood and insanity)*
*So that the Word across carnage is hurled*
*God's in his Heaven, all's right with the world!*

The correspondence to the "family" continued intermittently throughout the war, even when news was thin on the home ground. Winnie herself was anxious to contribute to the war effort, over and above her writing, but, like so many older women, was frustrated by finding herself confined to menial tasks. These, for her, were just as much "the perils of war" as the Blitz.

In this limbo nothing has happened and there is no interesting news to give you. So take this merely as the pleasure of hearing a voice, even if it is jammed. Jammed is the word for this war. We all move around as if in treacle. I send off a fresh batch of glowing testimonials to myself every two days to the particular department I'm supposed to be working with, but nothing happens. I also do an occasional morning of sitting at a telephone box in a cellar, but no one has ever rung me up! I can't tell you the maddening effect it has to see one's friends doing work and not being able to oneself . . .

Despairing of my Ministries, I've just taken on a temporary weekend job of cooking for policemen. If they'd rather lose the war on my sausages than win it on my German, well, that's England's loss. Olwen is coming as kitchen maid . . . By the way, I read this in the small hours in Swedenborg's *Heaven and Hell,* "The human race is the seminary of Heaven." I have done with Swedenborg!

P.S. Have just come home after frying 53 eggs and ten pounds of bacon. I smell to heaven—and feel *much* better.

Oh, how I do love shabby England . . . I didn't ever before realize quite how much; or how contented the war has made one with what one has.

IF NOËL WAS NOT entirely sure of what he was meant to be doing, some of his show business friends were even more confused. Adrianne Allen—whom he had once nicknamed "Planny Anny" (or "Anny Planny")—lived up to her nickname by writing to him suggesting he should tell Chamberlain and French prime minister Édouard Daladier that they should insist on President Roosevelt's providing a formal declaration of moral support.

Noël replied by cable:

DARLING PLANNY THOUGH INTERNATIONALLY BOSSY I AM NOT YET INTERNATIONALLY AUTHORITATIVE. FEAR GENTLEMEN YOU MENTION MIGHT CONCEIVABLY RESENT MY TELLING THEM HOW TO READ THEIR LINES.

By early 1940 he had settled into the apartment at 22 Place Vendôme and could tell Alec Woollcott something of the life he was leading, painting a rather rosier picture than he really felt for the benefit of his American friends:

January 26th 1940

I can honestly assure you I have never worked so God damned hard in my life. I am delighted to have a job that is most of the time passionately interesting, of course there are boring moments and I find it peculiar to sit this royal can down at an office desk every morning at nine o'clock! I cannot unfortunately go into details about what I am doing because of the so weecked spies who can't wait to read my letters, listen to my telephone conversations and follow me in and out of public lavatories. All I can tell you is that I am learning a whole lot of things about a whole lot of other things and I dread to think what

I shall be like at the end of it. Perhaps it will mould my character into the most fantastically beautiful shapes, making it impossible for me to play with anyone but Eva Le Gallienne and in anything but Tchekof. On the other hand, I might emerge gnarled and cruel and twisted and beat the living Jesus out of you at backgammon. In either event it is bound to be fascinating.

I hear that Ruth [Gordon] and Helen [Hayes] have been making strong representations to Jack to persuade me to give all this up and return to the theatre! If you should see them at any time you might explain sweetly and tenderly for me that the reason I cannot at the moment return to the theatre (madly important though I know it to be) is that I am an Englishman and my country is at war! If you happen to have a trumpet handy at the moment so much the better.

I am a trifle saddened by the behaviour of many of my actor countrymen of military age who scuttled off with such inelegant haste to New York or Hollywood. There really is a great deal to be done. This is a sinister and deadly war, in many ways more so than the last one. There has not been so much bloodshed as yet but, with the kind assistance of press and radio, some very dreadful things are happening to the human spirit. There is no knowing what will survive and what we shall all feel and think. I expect a lot of things will change. I certainly hope so.

The above is the address of my flat which is very natty and comfortable. I have, in addition, a smart office at 18 Place de la Madeleine and a very high Hispano which I think was made for the late Empress Frederick. It cost only a very few francs. (Have you noticed how many verys there are in this letter? Oh dear!)

I occasionally hurtle up to the front and sing firmly to the troops who are so sunk in mud that they can't escape.

All my love dearest Ackieweeza

•

LYNN WAS BUSILY keeping the home fires burning, even at a distance:

Temple Theatre, Birmingham, Ala.
January 8, 1940

Darling, darling,

We received your lovely letter intact, uncensored, it was wonderful. It made us laugh an awful lot, such a good letter and we were so glad to get it, the first since that dark curtain closed down on us.

We had a big Christmas dinner party for the company in Fort Worth, Texas, fifty of us, and very wild it was, too. We bullied the hotel into giving us quite a decent meal; daquiri cocktails, turkey,

Christmas pudding, of course, and champagne. I didn't get drunk, but I lost one of my diamond clips! Don't worry, darling, it's insured, and what with the expense of doing over the house, I had just as soon have the money and it will help pay for the party, oi, oi.

We had another party, which I enjoyed even more, on the train in the club car, quite unexpected like. It was the day of the British victory over the *Graf Spee,* it began with Frank Compton, who was a little, not very tight, suddenly beginning to sing in a very pleasing voice, "Rule Britannia", at which, everyone joined in hysterically. We went from there to all the old war songs: "Tipperary"; "Pack Up Your Troubles"; "Keep the Home Fires Burning"; "Madelon"; "It's A Long, Long Trail"; "Mademoiselle From Armentiers"; it was lovely.

The party ended up with the only German in the company (whom we strongly suspect of having pro-Nazi sympathies) standing up with Frank Compton and me, the only English, and singing with tears rolling down his cheeks, "God Save the King."

·

THE FRUSTRATIONS CONTINUED to mount for him as the phoney war dragged on. There seemed to be nothing but protocol and more protocol.

None of the things he was required to do seemed to make any practical sense to him.

·

ONE OF HIS most difficult tasks was to explain to friends and "family" *why* he was doing *what* he was doing:

January 29th, 1940

My dear Jack:

I have just had a letter from you that I feel I must answer immediately. You said in it that there was a certain movement among my friends in New York to induce you to induce me to give up the job I am doing now and return to the Theatre. I do so very much want you to explain to them that what I am doing now is, to me, even more important than a successful play however well written, well directed and well played. You will have difficulty over this. The quality that I love most in my friends of the Theatre is their hundred per cent concentration. They live far away from what is happening now and what has been happening during the last years. Do tell them also, with my love and a great deal of nostalgia, that I miss them very much and that there are many moments when I long to be with them.

Unfortunately, however, we are at war. (I hope they won't be frightened by the word "we" it is certainly not propaganda!) We are at war in defence of all that makes their performances possible.

I am sure that art and the Theatre signify a great deal in life (if they don't I have been bloody well wasting my time for thirty years) but at the moment I can't feel that they matter quite so much as they did. I admit that up to date there hasn't been overmuch bloodshed and that consequently the headlines in the press haven't been vastly entertaining, but in the meantime the war is being waged on more subtle terms. It is a very dreadful war because it is doing bad things to people's minds. It would be quite impossible for me to act in New York while my friends were fighting in Europe. I am using my intelligence and my brains for my country until the war is over. Some of my work is interesting and a lot of it is dull but at least I know I am doing the only thing possible for me. Perhaps when it is all over I might emerge from it a better writer and a better actor in which case there will be that much gained. On the other hand what has happened and is going to happen might bitch me for ever which will be that much lost! In either case I cannot help feeling that there are other things that matter more.

You can tell them for me that my life is unheroic in the extreme. I have a comfortable flat and a comfortable office (when the heat's on). Compared with what many English actors are doing, who have far more to lose than I, I am on velvet. I fully realize that several thousand miles of ocean between America and Europe make it difficult for people over there to understand what we are feeling over here. I am sure they occasionally read the press notices of this particular production, but we all know how unreliable critics can be. This play hasn't been very well directed so far and the first act, according to many, is too long and rather dull. I am afraid however that I cannot walk out on it. Please give them my love; show them this letter; thank them for thinking so well of my talent and reproach them, affectionately, for thinking so poorly of my character.

All my love
Signed Noel

•

THE WEEKS DRAGGED BY with nothing to show for their efforts that Noël could see. The Germans continued to advance—Norway, Denmark, with Holland and Belgium clearly in their sights. Chamberlain continued to see the silver lining in this blackest of storm clouds. Mr. Hitler had "missed the boat," he cheerfully claimed.

All of which made Noël fretful that he was not doing more to help his country. To him one thing was abundantly clear: the phoney war was now most definitely over. By March, Sir Campbell observed his *protégé* and had a distinct feeling of "the frenzied beating of wings." He suggested—to Noël's pleased surprise—that Noël take a six-week sabbatical, go to the United States and report back on the sentiment toward the war he found there. How strong was the isolationist movement, for instance? Which important people were saying what and to whom? Noël began to pack his bags and wrote to Violet:

March 30th

I am very gay and excited because I am going to America for a month sailing on April 20th in a nice safe American boat! I have been given six weeks leave to arrange my business affairs! (I will explain the *real* story to you verbally when I come home in about two weeks time!)

## TO NOËL GOING TO AMERICA IN WAR-TIME

### (TO ACCOMPANY A POUND OF "BEST ASSORTED SOFT-CENTRED CREAMS")

*My dearest Noël, hard it is for us*
*to lose you for six weeks to the Americas,*
*to know that you must plough the wine-dark seas*
*wearing the waistcoat of reality,*
*while we in garden-England sit at ease*
*and fuss.*

*But you know, don't you,*
*we plant our spring delight*
*of daffodils and aricas,*
*go to the latest "night"*
*or other such banality,*
*because these toys*
*help us to keep our poise?*
*Remember, won't you?*

*And, Noël, if—*
*if the fat wench in stone*
*with a smug sniff*
*waves her synthetic torch*
*of Liberty at you on your arriving*
*in New York's water-porch,*
*and chatters of a "phon-*
*y Armageddon",*

*and how the English always miss the bus,*
don't let her get away with it,
*not for one day with it!*
*Tell her we're thriving,* thriving
*upon our iron dreams:*
*Then offer her the sort of thing she's fed on*
*—soft-centred creams!*

**FROM CLEMENCE DANE, APRIL 6TH 1940**

•

WHEN THE WAR was over Noël summed up his feelings about the whole Paris episode in *Future Indefinite:*

> On looking back now on those strange, frustrating months, I find it diffi-cult to believe that I ever lived them at all. They seem in my memory to be, not exactly vague, but irrelevant, almost as though I had dreamed them.

At the time, though, the frustrations were all too real and immediate.

To Lornie:

> The bloody Americans have already started to be tiresome by refus-ing to allow me to embark at Gibraltar after all, as it infringes their neutrality laws, or some such cock. So I'm going with a diplomatic visa via Italy. Oh dear!

On April 18 he sailed from Genoa on the SS *Washington.*

# CHAPTER 17
# "THEN ALONG CAME BILL"

## (1940)

*Then along came Bill,*
*Who's not the type at all.*
*You'd meet him on the street*
*And never notice him.*

**P. G. WODEHOUSE, "BILL"**

T HE NEW WORLD, when Noël arrived, seemed more than a world away. He was plunged back into reunions with old friends he had not expected to see again until the war was over, if ever. Jack and Natasha Wilson, the Lunts, Neysa McMein, Alec Woollcott—it was as though he had never left.

Sir William ("Little Bill") Stephenson
(1896–1989). Noël's wartime spymaster.
"Little Bill saw where my celebrity value would
be useful...which was very smart of him. My
disguise would be my own reputation as
a bit of an idiot—a merry playboy."

He was soon to make a new and important one. In Paris his colleague Paul Willert, an old friend of Mrs. Roosevelt's, had given Noël a letter of introduction. Feeling that Washington was the obvious place to start his fact- or, rather, feelings-finding mission, Noël flew there and settled into the Carlton Hotel. He sent Willert's letter around by special messenger and proceeded to set up his appointments, one of which was lunch at the British embassy. There he found himself seated next to Mrs. Richard Casey, wife of the Australian minister. She reminded him that her husband had met him in Paris and had something he wished to discuss. Later Noël would recall that in that conversation "one more link was forged that was to lead me across the world."

The next day, a note arrived from Eleanor Roosevelt inviting him to dine that evening. Noël had expected a simple exchange of social pleasantries. Instead, President Roosevelt took him aside privately, mixed him a mean martini (in fact a whisky sour), and proceeded to discuss the state of the war in Europe in considerable and well-informed detail. He was clear about the fact that, while he supported the British position personally, he had to balance his own inclinations with the local political realities. In America at that point the isolationists were every bit as powerful as the appeasers had been in Britain. A focal figure was Charles Lindbergh (1902–1974), a national hero since being the first man to fly the Atlantic solo. Even then the "media halo" had its potency in the public mind.

Noël left the White House with the clear feeling that the president intended to "manage" events toward the desired outcome but that the process could not be rushed.

There was more ground to be covered and not much time to cover it. Noël returned to New York, from Los Angeles where he stayed once again with Cary Grant, who was to become another important figure in future events.

Day by day the war news got worse. The German forces continued to occupy country after country with Teutonic precision. The British Expeditionary Force was trapped at Dunkirk, and the bodies of many thousands of men were likely to litter those famous beaches. In the end some 224,000 out of 394,000 men were rescued, but that was some days off as Noël sat looking out at the Californian sun and watching people going about their daily business. He knew he had to get home.

Back in New York he found cables from Sir Campbell Stuart telling him that Chamberlain had been forced to resign. Churchill was now head of a National Government, and Noël's old friend Duff Cooper was the new minister of information and effectively their new boss. Noël immediately sent off a cable of his own to Duff, saying that he intended to return on the first available plane, something easier said than done. (There would be days to wait. The first flight he could get was not until June 8.)

Then, on June 3, he received a telegram from the president's secretary:

THE PRESIDENT WOULD LIKE TO SEE YOU TOMORROW AT
FIVE P.M. EXECUTIVE OFFICES AND MRS. ROOSEVELT HOPES YOU
WILL STAY FOR DINNER AND SPEND NIGHT AT WHITE HOUSE.
PLEASE CONFIRM.

Noël confirmed.

This time the atmosphere was both more somber and sober. Coca-Colas appeared instead of whisky sours, and the conversation focused on the war. Roosevelt was visibly moved by the epic events of Dunkirk and by Britain's unique ability to turn a devastating defeat into a moral victory. Did Noël believe his country could withstand Hitler? Noël replied that he was convinced "beyond all logic and reason" that it could and would.

Later—after making them both a martini after all—the president retired for the night and Noël accompanied Mrs. Roosevelt to an appointment she had at the annual Agricultural Students' Dance, where she spoke and Noël was persuaded to say a few words himself. Looking at those fresh young faces he realized that he was looking at the people who would, perhaps all too soon, be called upon to help correct the balance of world affairs.

On the way back to the White House, Mrs. Roosevelt instructed the driver to go via the Lincoln Memorial. The night was clear and the moon was high. President Lincoln looked out enigmatically, and Noël could only hope that the current president, like his forebear, would do everything that needed to be done to ensure that "government of the people, by the people and for the people, shall not perish from the earth."

Back at the St. Regis he wrote:

June 6th

Dear Mr. President,

You have been more than kind in giving me so much of your valuable time and I can never begin to tell you how deeply I appreciate it. Please allow me to say how much I admire your wonderful humour and sanity at a moment when the world is battering at you. It was a great privilege to be with you and there will be many times when I am back in Europe that I shall long to be in the warm friendly atmosphere of your study enjoying your very special cocktails.

I will write you immediately I arrive in England.

I do hope that the talk to the "Bright Young Things" went down all right.

With all my very best wishes to you always and again so many thanks.

Yours sincerely,<br>Noël Coward

In a draft he edited before sending the final letter he wrote:

I must admit that when I arrived in America I was decidedly unsure of what I should find and, to be sure, I have encountered a number of people who appear sceptical both of Britain's resolve and her ability to face and overcome the extreme challenges we presently face.

In my humble actor's way I have tried to convince them that, though we may inhabit a small island, we never have been or ever shall be a small people. Many years ago in a very different world in a curtain speech after one of my plays I heard myself saying that it was still pretty exciting to be English. I feel that today more than ever.

He would recall Roosevelt as being a man "who knew *everything*. He was right up to date on everything and full of candour, advice and honesty. And, of course, that immense personal charm. I'd have done anything he asked me to do."

On Sunday he took the clipper for England.

•

WHEN HE ARRIVED at Lisbon on June 9 the news he received literally stopped him in his tracks. The British ambassador, embarrassed but firm, forbade him to continue his journey to Paris and offered him a direct flight to London. Italy had entered the war, and the German tanks were rolling toward Paris. Noël tried to persuade the ambassador that it was his duty at least to go back and help evacuate the office there, but in the end he had little option but to cancel his reservation. Had he used it, he would have arrived in Paris just hours before the Germans. Since by this time he was on the Nazi blacklist, his stay there might have been terminally short.

Back in England he unashamedly pulled every string he could in an effort to land himself a real wartime job—but to no avail. He busied himself arranging for children from the Actors Orphanage to be sent to the safety of America, and for Violet and Aunt Vida to leave the bombs of London for the safe boredom of North Devon.

•

LYNN AND ALEC continued to send their "Letters from America":

Alvin Theatre, New York
June 28th

Lawrence Langer [Longner, head of the Theatre Guild] is the instigator of this wonderful idea that so nearly concerns us; the Government have accepted it and it is going through at once. I have a secret to tell you about it. They already have three of our greatest inventors and one of them is working on an invention at the moment, which he told Lawrence, if perfected, will render useless all further inventions in airoplane [*sic*] warfare. My own guess is that it possibly is something like that ray of light that stops the engines and has not yet been found efficacious, but that's just a guess. However, I have made Lawrence promise to tell me at once, although of course, it will be published right away if they get anything. [In fact, the "invention" was the splitting of the atom.]

We are very pleased over the [Wendell] Wilkie nomination and if Roosevelt doesn't run [which he did], we shall probably vote for him, unless the Democrat is better, but our vote goes to the nominee whose platform most passionately helps England.

Love from us both,<br>LYNNIE

And from Woollcott:

The Connor Hotel<br>Laramie, Wyoming<br>January 4th 1940

Dear Noël,

You must have long since discovered (and probably could yourself have foreseen) the peculiar paralysis which, since the third of September, has numbed any American with English friends to whom he might wish to write. I find, if I try writing about the war, which is now on our minds all the time, that what comes out on paper is either stale or pretentious or offensive. Or all three. When, on the other hand, I try reporting on our own doings, the most innocent and casual preoccupations suddenly sound as fatuous and shallow as a bit of iron merriment got up by Elsa Maxwell for Mrs. Hearst. Perhaps they are.

In early September I thought by this time to be up to my ass in the war and I suppose that before long it may yet take such a pattern that an unneutral American can see where his job is. In the meantime I traipse somnambulistically about the country.

•

THERE WAS TALK of a fact-finding tour to South America. On July 4 Noël's friend Lord Lloyd at the Colonial Office writes: "Please do not worry too much. All is going to be well, I am confident. Meanwhile, I have not had a line from the D.M.I. (Ministry of Information)."

On July 9 the War Office writes to Lord Lloyd at the Colonial Office to inform him that while Mr. Noël Coward is touring South America under the auspices of the British Council, he may be carrying out a few little jobs for them. Naturally, they reassure their colleagues that this must not be construed as the purpose of the trip:

MOST SECRET

In the course of his projected tour of South America on behalf of the British Council, Mr. Noël Coward will have opportunities of carrying out certain incidental work for this Directorate. This he has undertaken to do on the clearest understanding that such work will neither interfere with his programme nor be regarded as forming in any sense the purpose of his tour, which will be undertaken solely on behalf of the British Council.

In consideration, however, of the work Mr. Coward may be able to do for this Directorate, I am prepared to contribute £200 towards the expenses of the tour, and I shall be glad to hear if this suggestion meets with your approval.

Yours sincerely,
F. Beaumont Nesbit

Clearly it did not. It would, in any case, have been illegal for a government to pay someone engaged in covert activity in what were neutral countries. Wires became tangled, and on July 15 Lloyd broke the bad news:

I am very unhappy to hear that the South American trip has broken down. I stuck to my side of the bargain, but understand that the War Office would not take sufficiently the initiative to enable us to operate. Do give me a ring some time and tell me what you are intending to do.

It is perhaps not coincidental that on the fourteenth Winston Churchill's secretary had handed him a memo:

PRIME MINISTER
Mr. Noël Coward rang up. He has just come back from America. He would like to see you tonight if you can spare the time, as he has been staying with the President.

It must be assumed that the meeting took place and the likelihood is that Churchill—who had yet to make his own strong personal relationship with Roosevelt—was not best pleased to see the man he had told to go off and sing his little songs in the cannon's roar appeared to be doing the very opposite. Did this cause Churchill to intervene in Noël's future plans?

Their relationship was always an edgy one. "I had a gnawing suspicion,"

On the British battleship *Prince of Wales* in Placentia
Bay, Newfoundland, August 17, 1941. "Little Bill"
can be seen ducking as he sees the cameraman about
to snap a picture. It is the only known photograph
of him taken during World War II.

Noël wrote, "that there was something about me that he didn't like." It
may have been as simple as a clash of mighty egos with a touch of homo-
phobia thrown in on Churchill's side. There was a good deal of walking on
eggshells to be done in the years ahead.

The answer to Lord Lloyd's question was not long in coming. According
to Noël's account in *Future Indefinite,* Noël took Duff Cooper's advice,
which had remained consistent throughout: he would be of more use in
America than in England at this particular juncture, helping to assess and
perhaps shape American opinion in favor of the British side.

On July 21 he found himself making the return trip on the SS *Brittanic*
with a Ministry of Information ticket and a private letter from Cooper to
Lord Lothian, the British ambassador.

However, somewhere in that English hiatus another meeting had taken
place that Noël never referred to until the month of his death—his first
meeting with William "Little Bill" Stephenson (1896–1989).

·

STEPHENSON, THE QUIET CANADIAN, was never seen or heard
from by the general public, either during the war or after, but he was probably one of the men most influential in the winning of it.

An air ace from World War I, he had also been involved in intelligence and had become convinced that information—or even disinformation—was one of the most significant weapons in modern warfare. Between the wars, he became an inventor and a multimillionaire industrialist with wide-ranging interests. When the second war loomed, he was ideally placed, both emotionally and geographically, to be a conduit between Britain and the United States.

A physically small but compact man, Stephenson gained the sobriquet "Little Bill" to distinguish him from his friend and colleague "Big Bill" Donovan, a man he maneuvered into the role of head of the newly formed American OSS (Office of Strategic Services)—the forerunner of the modern CIA.

In *Future Indefinite,* Noël relates that his first meeting with Stephenson was in New York on that second trip in 1940, but in a 1973 interview he tells a different story. He was asked to go to St. Ermin's Hotel in Caxton Street:

Very appropriately positioned between the House of Lords and Victoria Railway Station . . . I had to meet a contact in the foyer. I waited in this squalid place and eventually a man said, "Follow me" . . . he wheeled me round and into an elevator. It was only labelled to go up three floors. To my absolute astonishment it went to the fourth floor. An immense fellow guarded the place, all scrunched up inside a porter's uniform.

He was in one of a whole series of "safe houses" that had been instantly set up near Whitehall.

Well, this was the Special Operations Executive. What we later called the Baker Street Irregulars [the gang of street urchins occasionally employed by Sherlock Holmes, since they could pass unnoticed]. Some chap was saying that President Roosevelt wanted us to do his fighting. And Little Bill was there, very calm, with those sort of hooded eyes, watching everything. And all he said was—"We could have done with Roosevelt these past few years."

Stephenson's demeanor was one that deeply impressed Noël, and he referred to it again:

When he was on the ball, his *eyes* changed. And I love watching people's personalities in action. Bill becomes someone quite different and you feel the steel. He doesn't have to raise his voice or alter his tone but he does change. He's a very deceptive man. He's so gentle but when he's cross, he's terrifying. But if Bill decided he was for you, he'd be with you right to the last shot.

Once he became prime minister, Churchill immediately appointed Stephenson head of BSC (British Security Coordination), the intelligence network in the United States. In effect, among his other duties, he would become the unofficial link between Roosevelt and Churchill, a sensitive position, since by acting for Britain in a neutral country, he was technically a spy. Churchill, a man not normally at a loss for words, sought one to describe the unique quality Stephenson would require to pull off his mission. Finally he found it: "You must be," Churchill said, "*intrepid.*" Henceforth Little Bill was A Man Called Intrepid.

On his arrival in New York, Noël went to see Stephenson again at his office in Hampshire House, Central Park South. Whatever screening had been going on at the London meeting and subsequently must have proved satisfactory, for Little Bill matter-of-factly invited Noël to become one of his "boys"—a group that included people such as Ian Fleming, Leslie Howard, David Niven, Roald Dahl, Alexander and Zoltan Korda, and Cary Grant. Stephenson inclined to the belief that celebrity was its own disguise, which meshed completely with the feelings Noël had unsuccessfully tried to convey to Churchill.

Noël was to go about being, ostensibly, nothing more or less than Noël Coward.

I was to go as an entertainer with an accompanist and sing my songs and on the side do something rather hush-hush. I was to go all the way through the continent of South America, because at that time the Nazis were running all over South America. I spoke Spanish, so that was all right.

He saw where my celebrity value would be useful and he seemed to think I ought to be as flamboyant as possible, which was very smart of him. My disguise would be my own reputation as a bit of an idiot . . . a merry playboy. It was very disarming. Very clever of him . . .

I was the perfect silly ass. Nobody . . . considered I had a sensible thought in my head and they would say all kinds of things that I'd pass along to Bill. All my reports were written for him alone—nobody else. And whether anybody ever *will* see them or be anything but bored stiff, if they do, I doubt strongly.

He later reflected on the jigsaw puzzle nature of intelligence gathering.

Some of the things seemed trivial but what anyone who has anything to do with intelligence will tell you is that you learn that the smallest detail fits into the final picture and you must be very careful, even though it sounds redundant. A whole lot of tiny things are the stuff of intelligence. In talking to people I ridiculed the whole business of intelligence, because that's the best way to get on with it—ridicule and belittle ourselves, and say what an awful lot of duffers we are, can't get the facts straight and all that sort of thing.

When he accepted the job, to begin with

I was awfully bewildered. I thought it would be more Mata Hari—and then I told myself, "Well, hardly that. I couldn't wear a jewel in my navel, which I believe she was given to doing" . . . I was never much good as a spy, really . . . So many career intelligence officers went around looking terribly mysterious—long black boots and sinister smiles. Nobody ever issued me with a false beard. In fact, the hush-hush side of it was frankly disappointing. I never had to do any disguises. Except occasionally I had to look rather idiotic—but that wasn't all that difficult. I'm a *splendid* actor!

And invisible ink? I can't read my own writing when it's supposed to be visible, so to make it invisible would be going *too* far. I learned a lot from the technical people, became expert, could have made a career of espionage—except my life's been full enough of intrigue as it is.

Those were his recollections in age and tranquillity. How much was embroidery to make a good story is open to speculation. Certainly the working relationship with Little Bill lasted for the rest of the war—no matter where Noël found himself—and the respect and friendship, for the rest of his life.

It is almost impossible to render Little Bill and the magnitude of his contribution to World War II. On the one hand, he was certainly a James Bond–like "M," a puppet master cannily twitching the strings, as his "boys" went about his business. But his real contribution was to lie in his domain of information—information on what the Germans intended to do next, so that it could be thwarted.

His was the initiative that set up the team at Bletchley to crack the German ULTRA code. That was complex enough, but it had to be done in such a way that the Nazis didn't realize it had been cracked or they would simply have changed it. In the process, Little Bill and Churchill—who had the power of final decision—were faced with horrific choices. They knew, for example, that Coventry was to be bombed on a certain night but to warn the citizens and attempt an evacuation would have been to tell the enemy *how* they knew. Coventry was bombed, with massive loss of life.

Perhaps even more devastating, since it was a personal loss, was the knowledge—gained from ULTRA—that the plane that one of Stephenson's boys, Leslie Howard, was taking from Lisbon was to be shot down and that there was nothing to be done but let it happen.

It takes a remarkable man to live with decisions like these.

•

NOËL'S POSITION in America was once again tenuous, to say the least. He had no formal credentials to show what he was doing there. To add insult to injury, he was met at the docks by a man from the British

Information Services who "implored me breathlessly to tell the Press I was arriving unofficially on my own theatrical business."

Back home, too, things were going from bad to worse. The *Daily Express* declared that, *whatever* he was doing over there, "Mr. Coward is not the man for the job. His flippant England—cocktails, countesses, caviar—is gone." In the House of Commons, Harold Nicolson, parliamentary private secretary to Duff Cooper (minister of information), did what he could to come to Noël's defense: "His qualifications are that he possesses a contact with certain sources which are very difficult to reach through ordinary sources."

The media reverberations echoed to and fro across the Atlantic. In the United States, the State Department had made official inquiries as to Noël's true status. J. Edgar Hoover's FBI opened a file on him, which has only recently been declassified. It makes fascinating, if frustrating, reading, since so much of it is heavily blacked out to protect the names of the Bureau's informants, even though all of them are certainly dead by now.

For instance, in June 1940, the American Legion in Illinois complained about pamphlets being dropped from a plane by the Communist Party, U.S.A., which read (in part):

Noël Coward is only one of a whole gang of British agents disguised as actors, novelists, writers, lecturers, etc., who are working to drag the United States into the war.

No newspaper raises the alarm about the "Fifth Column" agents.

Neither Martin Dies nor J. Edgar Hoover bursts into a sweat [they were wrong there!]. There are no midnight raids as they did against the boys of the Abraham Lincoln Brigade who faced death to fight the Fascist invasion in Spain.

On the contrary, these war-making agents are adored, entertained, banqueted and welcomed by the "best society" everywhere.

College presidents are flattered to receive them. Editors give them front page publicity. The recent Allied Ball for "relief" was organized with Noël Coward as the chief attraction for the "suckers".

The American people must awaken to this real "Fifth Column" . . .

A lengthy diatribe ends with:

KEEP AMERICA OUT OF THIS IMPERIALIST WAR!
STARVE THE WAR AND FEED AMERICA!
NO BLITZKRIEG AGAINST THE BILL OF RIGHTS!
MOTHERS SAY WE WANT OUR SONS NOT GOLD STARS
THE YANKS ARE NOT COMING!

In an August 28, 1940, "Memorandum for the Director," it is noted that in the Congressional Record for the Senate a Mr. Lundeen names several

Englishmen "supposedly engaged in disseminating propaganda designed to secure the intervention of the United States in the present war." Among those names are Lord Northcliffe, Sir Gilbert Parker, and Sir George Paish. A Mr. Holt added Sir William Wiseman "(official of Kuhn, Loeb & Co.)" and "Noël Coward (playright)" [sic].

By March 31, 1941, his every move is being monitored. In a secret "Internal Security" document, a lonely sentence isolated among the stark black censoring reveals that the "Subject" (unknown) "entertains extensively. On March 30th 1941, NOËL COWARD, British playwright, visited [name deleted] at Hotel."

On June 9, 1941, another "subject" is clearly having his or her office conversations recorded. Two of them are involved with a magazine called IN FACT, which had obviously caught the FBI's attention. They are reported to have unwrapped a package with copies of the magazine in it. And then "they mentioned the names of NOËL COWARD and [name deleted] as being agents of a foreign country."

The surveillance continued even after America had entered the war. On August 25, 1942, the Cleveland, Ohio, FBI office reported on yet another subject that in several of Noël's letters he had stated that

> he had found it necessary to travel to England and that while there he had gone to [deleted] place on the Isle of Wight and that "the usual crowd was there including NOËL COWARD and his American friend." He believes that [deleted], whom he states is [deleted], and COWARD both favor appeasement and friendship with Germany and he believes that the fact that gatherings were held at [deleted] place would be of interest to the English Government.
>
> This information is being forwarded to the Bureau for whatever action is deemed advisable.

Considering that "appeasement" had ended—with both a whimper and a bang—on September 3, 1939, and that Britain had been at war for almost three years, it is not immediately clear what possible use the special agent in charge who submitted the report can have believed his report could be. It is to be hoped that some of the bureau's other information had a little more relevance.

•

AUGUST 21, 1940, and Noël is now well into a multi-city tour of the United States on behalf of British War Relief, where "I sang my songs and spoke nicely to my hosts. I went out and opened bazaars and shut them again and carried on and behaved like a traveling celebrity."

From San Francisco he appeals to Vansittart:

### FAIRMONT HOTEL, SAN FRANCISCO

Please forgive me for not having answered your letter before. I am so sorry that the Foreign Office is agitated about my Press utterances.

I was very much distressed by the shindy in the House of Commons about me being sent over here and I am most awfully sorry if it caused you any embarrassment. I cannot help feeling a trifle embittered by the fact that although I have given up all my own affairs in order to do anything in my power to help my country I mostly seem to be getting only kicks for it.

Would it be possible to tell the State Department the truth, which is that I was sent over by the Ministry of Information to work, with your approval, at gauging various cross sections of American opinion and reporting on it? I think I should be only too delighted to register as a Government agent and I think it would do away with a lot of false rumour and wild surmise. I am most definitely not over here on personal business. If I were I should be carrying on with my own career and earning a certain amount of money.

I detect a strong note of rather dreary grievance in this letter for which I apologise, particularly as you were so sympathetic and understanding when we talked in Washington the other day. Please believe that I shall continue to do my best, as discreetly as possible, to find out anything that might be of the slightest use and contribute all I can towards winning the war. If however it were possible for me to be not quite so disowned in all directions I think it would strengthen my hand.

I have a good deal to tell you which I would prefer to do verbally when I get back.

I am very much cheered by the news from home and deeply proud and I must say I thought the Prime Minister's speech yesterday was magnificent.

When talking to the Press I am sticking to my original story that I came over on a mission to you that has now been discharged. Is this all right?

The accreditation he wanted was not forthcoming. Meanwhile, he continued with his travels for Little Bill:

In the United States I just talked about Britain under bombing . . . I had a terrible time with some of the Senators—one or two who thought we were finished. They were such silly old idiots that I didn't mind very much. In fact, I was rather sharp with them, because they really did talk such unconscionable nonsense. I put them down and pointed out that I was not doing any subversive propaganda of any sort. What I was doing was travelling around the world at the express wishes of my government to talk about the British war effort and, above all, what was happening in Britain during the air raids—to let them know how the British were taking it, etc. So I told them—"Really, calm down, keep your hair on. Nothing really dangerous is going on." They suspected me to start with, obviously, of being a spy—which, of course, technically I was, as America was a neutral country at the time.

His itinerary took in another stop in Hollywood, and while the sight of old friends was welcome, he now saw the "British community" there with new eyes. Here was their country at war, yet young men of service age continued to sit in the sun, apparently unmoved by their nation's plight. Conscious, perhaps, of the fact that there were those at home who chose to think *he* was about to become one of them, he wrote to Violet, whom (with Auntie Vida) Noël had now moved to the safety of a New York apartment: "If I ran away and refused to have anything to do with the war and lived comfortably in Hollywood, as so many of my actor friends have done, I should be ashamed to the end of my days."

There were, of course, numerous "Brits Abroad" who were anxious to do what they could to help the war effort. One of them was Lynn Fontanne. She described to Noël her collecting box:

> Alvin Theatre, New York
> June 28th, 1940
>
> I have a little tin box on my dressing table which Larry made for me out of an empty coffee can. Jim, the carpenter, made a beautiful wide slot to encourage dollars, and soldered a little Union Jack on it, and Dickie painted British Relief Fund in red and a large GIVE, in blue, and you know how I hate visitors after the play; now I am quite interested and whenever anyone wants to see me, no matter who they are, I stun them with my welcome with tin box in right hand, autograph hunters too, have to pay.
>
> Antoinette [Keith, her sister] has been trying to get to England for months, but has given up the idea in favor of taking care of a couple of evacuee children from England, and I think that will be more useful. I can't tell you how I feel when I think of those poor wretched mothers saying good-bye to their children, perhaps forever. It's the most monstrously cruel thing that ever had to happen.
>
> Vivian [Vivien Leigh] and Larry [Olivier] went up to Canada and saw the Commissioner there, I forget his name, who completely and utterly discouraged them from going over, he said that they were not needed, but now, the British Government has ordered him to come home. So it's all settled; he doesn't know when, as there are one hundred thousand young men of military age in America and they have

to wait until the facilities for getting them over are completed. Between you and me, I don't think *Hitler* would keep them waiting long, do you? Meanwhile, Larry is learning to fly every day, and has begun to like it, so that means he will be good. He says he is going to be an ace!

We are all thinking at the moment of children that are coming over. I am standing sponsor for Mrs. Michael Redgrave [actress Rachel Kempson] and her two children. I filled in the papers this afternoon. I don't know what it entails, but we are preparing for everything. I am going to take a house with a lot of rooms in case there are some left over that nobody seems to want, or perhaps we could take temporary care of some of them until they are settled. We will see, we will see what happens when they start arriving.

He brought Lorn up to date on his activities, which included his embattled attempt to bring over children from the Actors Orphanage.

September 6th, 1940

Darling Lornie:

I haven't written before because I have been on the go all the time and have now got back to my flat here slightly exhausted. First of all, I went to Hollywood where I found most of the English actors up in arms against me because they resented my having talked to the Ambassador about those who were not of military age going back. I also achieved the great distinction of being cut dead by Gladys Cooper—as you know, John Buckmaster [her son] is appearing gallantly in a night club here and I expect she felt self-conscious about it. The fussing and fuming going on over the Orphanage was something terrible. Poor old May Whitty, who was going nearly mad because all the actors kept on coming to Committee meetings and having wonderful ideas and then going away and talking to their lawyers who refused to let them do anything about anything at all. Cedric Hardwicke, oddly enough, was one of the few sensible ones . . . but as the whole thing seemed to be getting more and more chaotic every minute I put the whole thing in the hands of Fanny Holtzmann who, bore or no bore, proceeded to bash about, cut red tape and get everything straightened out in a flash. This was very noble of me really because it means that I sob and cry and shrink into corners every time I hear the telephone ring.

I don't know whether or not you know it but the Hollywood stars decided to give three weeks' performances of the entire *Tonight at Eight-Thirty* cycle in aid of the British War Relief. These were such a triumphant success that they are to do them all over again for

another three weeks. I didn't see the first bill which was young Doug
[Fairbanks] and Constance Bennett in "We Were Dancing", Basil
Rathbone and Gladys Cooper in "The Astonished Heart", and Binnie
Barnes and Reginald Gardiner in "Red Peppers". All the reports say
that Binnie was marvelous. I saw, however, the second and third
bills. Roland Young in "Fumed Oak", who played it like a dim For-
eign Office attaché and was awful, "Family Album" with Joan
Fontanne [Fontaine], Claire Trevor, Philip Merivale, etc. and Aubrey
Smith as "Burrows"—this was charmingly done and the success of
the series, "Hands Across the Sea" with Judith Anderson, Isabel
Jeans, Nigel Bruce, Ian Hunter, etc., was a lash-up on account of
Zazu Pitts never having been on the stage before and playing "Mrs.
Wadhurst". Every laugh she got went to her head and she did more
and more clowning until not one word of the play was heard. The
third bill was pretty horrible except for Bart [Herbert] Marshall,
Rosalind Russell, Una O'Connor and Edmund Gwynn [Gwenn] in
"Still Life". "Ways and Means" was played by Brian Aherne and
Greer Garson with all the lightness and speed of a performance of
*King Lear* given by a church social. But the pearl of the whole
evening was "Shadow Play" with Georges Metaxa and a rather aging,
Jewish actress called Dorothy Stone; this was terribly macabre.
Georges, who is now quite square, was completely incomprehensible
and sang very loudly indeed. Dorothy Stone danced so much that I
was afraid she would have heart failure; unfortunately she did not . . .

The shindig in the House of Commons, which was headlined in
all the papers here, caused me a great deal of inconvenience and
unpleasantness. I want you to do the following; first of all, send me a
copy of *Hansard* with a verbatim account of the debate in it, then
check up through dear Herrings on the histories of the gentlemen
saying those unpleasant things about me. There will come a day
when the pen will prove to be a great deal mightier than the sword.

The performance of the Air Force and the people of England generally, is having a tremendous effect on the people over here. I get
into awful states now and then when I read of the bombings and wish
I was there with you all very much indeed. Sometimes being so far
away is almost more than I can bear. I am astounded that Goldenhurst is still standing. Mother and Vida are apparently having a
whale of a time in Atlantic City. I only saw them the day they arrived
but they were very happy, and I expect them to come back next
week . . .

         Love, love, love—
         MASTER
         NOËL COWARD

What's going to happen to the tots? Noël leads an enthusiastic chorus of kids at the Actors' Orphanage. (Notice the girl second from left, at the back, who is clearly wondering if she should now get an agent.)

As the saying goes, "No good deed goes unpunished," and Noël's Children's Crusade was no exception. The British press remained unwilling to see even a glimmer of silver lining in the dark cloud they insisted on placing over his head. Even old friends were persuaded to have their doubts from time to time.

Beverley Nichols wrote apologetically:

> Butchers Barn
> Dane Hill
> Haywards Heath
> September 11th 1940

Dear Noël,

You will probably have seen a few words I wrote about your American visit. I wish that I hadn't written them, because they must have seemed unkind, and because I hate to think that after praising you for twenty years in all sorts of journals, I should have administered this sudden scratch. However, you must blame the quite incredible ineptitude of your press agent. You would get quite as hot as I did if I were to quote a selection of the remarks attributed to you by cable. When on top of this, it was announced that you were leaving for

Hollywood "to evacuate children", together with the other remarks about your "nerves", I am afraid that I lost my sense of humour.

Your return makes me feel a complete fool. And this letter of mine gives you a perfect opportunity of making me feel an even more complete one. However, I am quite sincere in saying that if I have done you any harm, my only wish is to undo it. I know that you are in a position where you can afford to ignore journalists. But I hope you will never feel yourself in a position where you can ignore old friends.

Yours ever,<br>Beverley

Noël writes to Gladys Calthrop:

September 12th 1940

Darling,

These last two weeks have obviously been hell and every minute fraught with anxiety and unimaginable imaginings, and it's sick my heart is with the longing to be with you. I still believe, however, that I was dead right to come back, despite the fact that my generous countrymen both in the House of Commons and in the press have done their damndest to make my job here a thousand times more difficult. When the smoke clears away and there is a respite from all this horror I shall have something to say, but now I cannot. I must say I feel deeply ashamed of the way the English press has treated me since the beginning of this war. Unfortunately, of course, a lot of the muck gets reprinted over here and in Canada. However, I am rising above it as well as I can and getting on with the job . . . I may be able to let you know more details about this later on but at present it is impossible.

I have been traveling around a great deal talking to politicians, journalists, ex-Presidents, gallant English actors and even Mormons. I am now back in my apartment here working very hard, which is all part of the plan. If you will cast your mind back to two evenings before I left London, when Winnie, Lorn and you and I ate sandwiches with J. B. Priestley, you will have an inkling of what I am up to, it is, in fact, a carefully thought out series which is what I am working on now.

I think it is time that somebody of importance in England rose up in my defense and explained the truth about my activities, since I chucked up the whole works to do a job for my country. I don't mind scurrilous attacks when I am working in the theatre and where, after all, I have my own plate to sit on, but this filth that has been heaped upon me is really beginning to get under my skin.

I am feeling awfully frustrated over this letter, for there is so much to say that is quite impossible. Please don't think from the tone of grievance that I am in a frizz for I really am digging in and holding on to hard boiled eggs like anything, but if any mealy mouthed, cowering God can think out a viler year than this one, good luck to the bugger.

Take care of yourself—

DREYFUS

And later . . .

September 27th 1940

Since my return I have discussed exhaustively how best to employ my brittle talents for the good of the cause, and at long last a jolly decent decision has been arrived at, blessed by the approval of the Ambassador and Uncle Tom Cobbley and all. It is this—I am now officially attached to the British War Relief Society, and my job is to travel around to all the key cities where I help organize and advise the various committees, in addition to making speeches, appearing at benefits, and what have you. This, as your slow moving, sluggish mind will readily perceive, provides me with an admirable excuse to wear my long black elbow gloves and that large shady hat with the red rose on it. It also gives me a dignified plate to sit on, which, I think, in time will silence the press. If there is any way that you could get hold of Walter Monckton, or Duff [Cooper], or Vansittart, or anybody of governmental importance to give an order for them to lay off me, it would be a great help, not particularly from my personal point of view, which doesn't really matter, but from the point of the job itself. It is perfectly idiotic that I, who am working for the country to the exclusion of everything else, should have my efforts undermined by a few mischievous little journalists who don't know what it is all about anyway. This, I think, actually is rather serious otherwise I wouldn't go on about it. I thought of writing, myself, to the *Times* or Winston or Duff, but I don't wish to descend into the arena with personal complaints at the moment when things of much more importance are happening. So if there is anything you can do about this privately and quietly, just have a slap at them, there's a dear, dear.

It is perfectly horrifying to read in the papers and hear over the radio about the administrative muddles taking place in London. This is, obviously, not the moment to enlarge upon it in writing, but it is really agonizing to visualize those thousands and thousands of people, not only being bombed by the Germans, but being strangled and frustrated by governmental red-tape.

The Presidential election campaign is roaring along in full swing. Mr. Wilkie started very well with a lot of personal charm and two fisted virility. Unfortunately, for his supporters, he is becoming more and more cute and pixy with every day that passes, and if he ever does get into the White House, I am afraid the only place for him will be on the chandelier.

> Send out good thoughts, my darling,
> and hold on to everything.
> NOËL

October 1st, 1940

Darling Lornie:

I haven't heard from you just lately, but you have been so frightfully good about cabling that I really mustn't grumble. It is perfectly horrifying to visualize what you must be all going through and I long so very much to be with you, because, in spite of nerve strain and lack of sleep, at least we should all be together in the big brass band. Here it feels quite obscene to be sitting in peace and security sipping a drink, and listening to the news bulletins on the radio; quite obscene and very, very horrid indeed.

I am going to Washington today to see the Ambassador about various things. I am working very hard for the British War Relief, but it looks as if I should have to do a lot of traveling in the next few months, unless, of course, something very different happens. Traveling for the British War Relief would resemble, in many ways, the traveling I did to Poland and Russia just before the war, if you know what I mean, dear. I see by the papers here that, in addition to all the horrors going on in London, there is also the usual administrative lash-up—oh dear, will we never never learn? I must say, that in spite of all personal tears and disquiet, it is a pretty exciting thing to be English, and one's national head can be carried very very high even though one's personal head may droop a bit at being so far away.

Mother and Vida are settled in a hotel just near me. They have a flat on the twenty-fifth floor with a glorious view of the river, but are extremely dissatisfied with the food. Mother says that the meat is so tough that she can't get her teeth into it. Aunty Vida's teeth, however, seem to work, on the average, pretty well. The Baybay [Jack Wilson] has procured a play by Victor Wolfson the author of *Excursion* which really is very well written, but as it deals with a frustrated New England woman who goes mad finally and kills her rival, I fear that gaiety will not be the keynote of our theatrical season. There is so very very much that I want to tell you, that it really is quite difficult.

I don't think I have any more news for you, darling. I do hope that you are not letting all this horror get you down too much. When all this is over there will be a lot to say.

With all my dearest love—
MASTER

To Gladys Calthrop:

October 11th

I'm feeling a good deal more cheerful as I at last have a job to do which will, I think, be worth doing. I've been talking a good deal lately to Dick Casey, the Australian Minister here. I think I told you about him, we originally met in Arras in November. He is a grand man, tough and with humour and very sympathetic about the dreariness of me sitting here on my fanny without anything really specific to do, apart from a few odd jobs on the side, and a fair Aunt Sally for all the mingy little journalistic twirps who like to throw mud at me across the Atlantic, and so he suggested that I beetle off to Australia for a month or two to talk about England, The British War Effort, etc: and appear at Red Cross benefits and generally make myself pleasant. Then, on my return here in January, I shall be able to explain the Australian point of view and do as much as I can to help towards an understanding between the two countries. All this seems as though it might be of use and at any rate it will be utilising my capabilities and celebrity value efficiently. I am paying my own fare but while I am there I am the guest of the Australian Government. Of course, I am very excited about it although I shall be so far way, but I feel that perhaps, in some ways, Australia will seem nearer to England than here. The British Ambassador, who has been extremely nice, was enthusiastic about the project, almost too much so I thought, in fact I detected a gleam of relief in his eye at the idea of my getting out of his hair. I suspect that the Embassy is constantly racked with anxiety lest I say something unethical and lousy. However, all is arranged, with suitable official announcements, and I fly to Los Angeles on Monday night and sail on Wednesday. I have masses of books and notes to read up on Australia and a lot of speeches to prepare and I intend to do the Australians proud.

I miss you most horribly and have dreadful nocturnal imaginings and walk up and down the room, eat a chocolate, take two aspirin and go bubbers again, tear stained but resigned. The other night I indulged in a little light cookery and have arrived reluctantly at the conclusion that it really isn't my thing on account of losing my head, getting flurried and dropping a thought too much yoke of egg between the prongs of the gas ring. By the time I had finished the kitchen was like the black hole of C[alcutta] with gas escaping in all directions and I was forced to retire to the bath room with a plate of frizzled tomatoes, two rashers of ever so black and white bacon and a slice of inadequately toasted bread with some fluff on it. I take back all I said about that hair in the pheasant. I'd understand now if I found your whole bush in it.

There is a great deal too much fart and fancy going on about the election, a convenient, if temporary refuge for escapists—after November the 4th I really don't know what they'll do.

H. G. Wells arrived the other day and proceeded to make a prize ass of himself, whereas Willie [Maugham] arrived only two days ago and did exactly the opposite, which isn't really so surprising, is it? There has been a lot to contend with here—little tiresomenesses mostly well meaning and quite maddening. It's no use going on about the bombings, so I won't but please don't go buggering about the overt too much and for Christ's sake bob down when you're spotted.

I remain, yours sincerely,
Nellie Melba

Before setting sail, Noël took a few days in Hollywood, where once again he stayed with Cary Grant. Although they had known each other for some years, they had never been particularly close friends and there was some speculation in the local community as to why—considering all the old friends he had there—Noël should visit Grant three times in just over eighteen months. Was there an affair? Unlikely, since Grant was living with Randolph Scott at the time. And if Noël was so critical of British-born men refusing to return to the old country, did his criticisms not also include Grant?

What people couldn't know was that two of Little Bill's "boys" were conferring. On his subsequent travels, Noël would frequently use the Hollywood-bound Grant as his "control." Grant himself fretted that he was not allowed to serve in the armed forces but was told that he could make a much greater contribution by staying where he was and monitoring which of his colleagues in the film colony supported which side. It's tempting to think that at this time all of Hollywood was pro-Britain, but this was not the case. Stars such as Errol Flynn were suspected of strong

Nazi sympathies. Little Bill needed to know who they were and what they were saying and doing.

Grant's role was never made public, but the fact that at the end of the war he was awarded the King's Medal for Service in the Cause of Freedom—an award given only to those who performed special intelligence services—tells its own story.

•

ON OCTOBER 16 Noël sailed from San Pedro, California, on the SS *Monterey.* Once again he was traveling alone.

# CHAPTER 18

# WORLD WAR II: "FARAWAY LAND"

## (1940–1941)

*I come from a faraway land*
*On the other side of the world,*
*A land that's primitive, crude and brave,*
*Where no one's master and no one's slave,*
*Yet one and all of us primly stand*
*When the English flag's unfurled.*
*I come from a faraway land*
*On the other side of the world.*
*The journey's long and the seas are wide*
*But it's sweet to know that there's English pride*
*On the other side of the world.*

**"FARAWAY LAND," IN** *AFTER THE BALL* **(1954)**

S.S. *Monterey*
At Sea
October 20th

DARLING LORNIE,

I'm typing this A. because you can read it more easily. B. because the censor can read it more easily and C. because the typewriter was handy although broken to bits and I fear I shall have to buy several new ones when I arrive in Honolulu tomorrow. The route of the ship has been changed at the last minute and now no one, least of all the Captain, has the faintest idea where we are going when we leave Honolulu. All that is known is that we have to go somewhere or other in the Orient and pick up a great many—too many—people and then go on to Australia if the Japanese will let us and not behave like saucy little sods and make us eat our passports and pull down

1940. Two national treasures, and
endangered species, meet . . . with the
Aussie definitely coming out on top.

our trousers and paint lotus blossoms on our bottoms, any of which
might quite conceivably happen. In the event of me being whipped
off the ship like a flash and placed in some old Yoshiwarra will you
kindly explain to the *Sunday Pictorial* that I did it for Britain and not
because I am just naturally decadent and like that sort of thing.

I only spent one night in Hollywood but I utilised it by sitting in
a projection room and seeing the film they have just made of *Bitter
Sweet.* No human tongue could ever describe what Mr. Victor Saville,
Miss Jeanette MacDonald and Mr. Nelson Eddy have done to it
between them. It is, on all counts, far and away the worst picture I
have ever seen. MacDonald and Eddy sing relentlessly from beginning to end looking like a rawhide suit case and a rocking horse
respectively. Sari never gets old or even middle aged. "Zigeuner" is a
rip snorting production number with millions of Hungarian dancers.
There is no Manon at all. Miss M elects to sing "Ladies of the Town"
and both Manon's songs, she also dances a Can-Can! There is a lot of
delightful comedy and the dialogue is much improved, at one point,
in old Vienna, she offers Carl a cocktail! Lord Shayne was wrong,

Richard (later Baron) Casey (1890–1976) and his wife. It was Casey who persuaded Noël to tour Australia and New Zealand and then the war zones.

Jeanette MacDonald and Nelson Eddy are very definitely the wrong age for Vienna. It is the vulgarest, dullest vilest muck up that I have ever seen in my life. It is in technicolour and Miss M's hair gets redder and redder until you want to scream. Oh dear, money or no money, I wish we'd hung on to that veto.

Oh Lornie, it feels very strange and not entirely nice going further and further away but, because I've got a really good job to do, I must say I feel happier than I have felt for ages. I have a lovely lot of time stretching ahead of me on board this ship in which to write and prepare speeches and broadcasts, etc. I do so very much hope I shall make a go of it. I certainly start at an advantage as I am already popular in Australia as a name, let's hope that by sheer prettiness I shall be able to round up even the most sullen dissenter. I miss you most dreadfully but I don't intend to go on about that. Take care of yourself, darling, and the children and remember that even though I am at the other side of the world, I am very very close indeed.

Love Love Love
MASTER

His route, in fact, took him from Honolulu to Yokohama, where he was told he might not disembark. This piqued his interest enough to have

himself smuggled ashore, where he found the city awash with Germans—
a fact he promptly reported back to Little Bill.

Then on to Shanghai: "Gay as bedamned . . . I'd never have believed it
had been battered to hell [by the Japanese in 1937]." "It's hardly changed
at all," he wrote to Violet. "All my old friends greeted me. The Cathay
Hotel [where he had written *Private Lives*] insisted upon my being their
guest and gave me a resplendent suite filled with flowers!"

Then Manila and, finally, Sydney. En route he had done his Australian
homework and written several of his intended broadcasts.

> Menzies Hotel
> MELBOURNE
> 3rd December 1940

Darling Lornie,

This is another communal letter to my loved ones. I have not had a
moment to write before, because to date this has been the most hectic experience of my life and makes the last rehearsals of *Cavalcade*
look like a couple of aspirin and a nice lie-down.

Now I must talk to you seriously for a moment. This is really a
much more important job than I ever anticipated. The broadcasts
that I prepared on the ship coming out, each one lasting 15 minutes,
are really good and some of the best writing I have ever done. These
are having a terrific response and are heard all over Australia twice a
week. The Government is being enormously considerate and
although the whole business is terribly strenuous, so far it has really
been a triumphant success and I am assured that I am doing a fine job
for England and for Australia.

You can imagine, with the nerve-strain of all this just beginning,
that it was a little startling to receive at the outset cables from you and
Joyce and Blackheart [Gladys Calthrop], urging me to return to England immediately. I fully realise that I am missing a great deal of history there, but on the other hand, maybe I am making a little here. As
you remember, at the beginning of this war we decided that the best
way I could do a job for the country was to make one for myself. This
is the first really valuable work I have yet done for the war.

After all this I am going to be pretty exhausted, so I am going to
get on to the Clipper to New Zealand and stop off at Canton Island,
which is a tiny place where there is nothing to do, and stay there by
myself . . . in order to sort out my impressions and prepare broadcasts
on Australia and New Zealand, which I intend to do in America.

According to this plan, I shall arrive back in America round about
the 20th February. I shall stay there for about a month, because one

of the reasons that the Australian Minister sent me here was in order to talk about the Australian war effort in America. It therefore does not look as though I could return to England before April.

Now then, I am absolutely furious about the way the cheap English press has treated me as a result of those idiotic questions in Parliament. The reason I am doing what I am doing is because I know I am really contributing to the ordinary people, not the press or the big shots. The behaviour of the latter makes me at moments feel I never want to clap eyes on England again, but this is only temporary bitterness and quite natural in the circumstances. I am longing to come back to see all of you, but it can only be for a little while because the frustration of seeing all that muddling going on scares me much more than all the bombs in Christendom.

Nobody in England has the faintest idea what the Australians are like, and when I do get back I am going to make it my business to tell them. They are simple and direct and friendly, and their feeling about England is so deep and touching that in my opinion a great deal more should be done about them, from our point of view, than has been to date. This really is being a wonderful experience.

The Australian country—what I have seen of it from aeroplanes and motor-cars—is perfectly beautiful, but, the thing that is nicest about it here is its Englishness. It is good, honest middle-class, nei-

"Accustomed as I am to public speaking . . ." Noël makes one of his very many public appearances to help the war effort.

ther common nor social. There is no snobbery around, or very little, and I should think that in future years it will turn out to be far and away the most important jewel in our Imperial crown. If, in the future, I hear anybody saying, "Darling, really the Australians are too dreary for words—those awful voices, etc., etc.," there will be bad trouble.

I will now, my little darlings, conclude this bright novel. If you would care to visit my detractors *en masse,* each holding a meat-axe, I would be delighted.

Love! Love!! Love!!!<br>MASTER

On the same day he sent a preliminary report to Duff Cooper:

My dear Duff,
This is just a brief letter to tell you how I am fareing here—actually I am fareing very well, and it seems that I am doing a good job. [He then gives a detailed summary of his activities.]

I propose to get back to the States round about the 20th February and spend a month or so there, broadcasting and generally talking about Australia and its war effort, etc. When I have done that, this particular job will be finished and some other plans will have to be made. If it really turns out to have been successful, perhaps you would help over this. As I told you in my last letter, I have been naturally upset about some of the dirty cracks in the English press about my activities, and I would like in the Spring to come back and deal with some of this. There is lots of time, unfortunately, and perhaps you could think of some way to help.

It is horrible to think what an awful time England is having. I do hope you are all well and not getting too nerve-strained and tired. Please give my love to Diana [Cooper], and please believe that I'm doing the level best I can, and intend to go on doing so until the damned war is won.

Take care of yourself,
Yours ever,<br>NOËL COWARD

HOTEL ESPLANADE<br>Perth, W.A.<br>14th December 1940

Darling Lornie,
Well, my tour is nearly over, and a fine rampage it has been. I have been charming, simple, modest, boyish (inappropriately) human,

understanding, patriotic, and absolutely unspoiled by my great success. All this vintage coquetry will not surprise you. The press have been terrifically nice to me and everything has gone down like a dinner.

I see that Lord Lothian, aided successfully by a Christian Science practitioner, has joined the feathered choir. I am now waiting anxiously to see who is going to succeed him. [Lothian, British ambassador to the United States and a devout Christian Scientist, had died of an undetermined but determinedly untreated illness, thus confirming Noël's skepticism of the teachings of Mary Baker Eddy.]

I miss you all so terribly, and here, where everything is so tremendously English, it is sometimes very upsetting. You have literally no idea what they feel about the home country here, and I am most deeply impressed with it. I intend, if I do get back to England in the Spring, to have a great deal to say about all this, and also to lay about me good and proper. I do so hope you are all holding up alright and that your cheerful cables are not only designed to keep me from worrying. I am longing to get back, and yet rather dreading to see what has happened to London. I wonder if it is as bad as I imagine it to be. Take care of yourselves, my darlings, and I will write again soon.

> Love—love—love.
> MASTER

> THE AUSTRALIA HOTEL
> Sydney, N.S.W.
> 27th December 1940

Darling Lornie.
The whole tour is over. It has been a real triumph from every angle. I have made a helluva lot of money for the war charities here and really got through to the real Australian public by my broadcasts.

. . . I am longing to come home to England, and absolutely dreading it. If I find, when I get there, the same frustrating idiocy in high circles still going on in the same old way, I shall probably do something desperate and finish up in jug.

Give all my love and let's hope that 1941 will be slightly brighter for all of us. This I doubt, but we must all be sweet and hopeful, mustn't we, and send loving thoughts through the air with such impetus that they crush the bloody skulls of the recipients.

> All love, darling, darling Lornie,
> MASTER

GRAND HOTEL
Auckland
15th January 1941

Darling Lornie,

All the cables were delayed and so I got into rather a frenzy, but by now they have all come trickling in and so all is well. I arrived here on Monday and had a tremendous welcome. This, thank God, is not going to be as strenuous as Australia. I leave here on February 1st on the Clipper and am going to stop off for a fortnight or a month on Canton Island, which is only three miles of coral reef and a hotel, in order to get all my impressions sorted and have a rest, which I shall badly need, and maybe write a little something. I had rather a nasty little collapse at the end of the Australian tour, but had a week entirely by myself in the country, and got myself right back again . . .

I really do think I have a pretty clear outline of what I intend to do this year and next year. I think our financial situation is worrying, but after the war I shall just have to paint my face and prance off again acting like buggery in all directions. At any rate, I am absorbing a hell of a lot from all these strange experiences, so something is bound to come out.

           Love, love, love,
           MASTER

With Violet he would share the concerns that were always at the back of his mind about his postwar world:

Noël with his trusty traveling companion.

It really would be rather nice to go back to London, covered with a fair amount of glory, and just tell a few home truths to those rats who have been saying beastly things about me in the press! I know you'll understand about this. Ultimately, after the war, I can't afford to have a few unanswered criticisms hanging about.

Noël wrote, "1940, in immediate retrospect, seemed to me the most difficult, complicated year I had ever lived, so many adjustments and re-adjustments and changing circumstances." But at least now it was over and he could take a short break before returning to see what London and the United States had in store for him.

•

IN LATE MARCH, after a couple of stopovers, Noël is heading back to London. A fellow passenger on the plane introduces himself and tells him that they had a mutual friend, Lord Lloyd. Noël is puzzled by the man's use of the past tense, and it is only then that he learns that his old ally, George Lloyd, died suddenly a few days earlier.

The plane's first stop is Bermuda.

# CHAPTER 19

# WORLD WAR II:
# "IN WHICH WE SERVE"

## (1941–1942)

*Be pleased to receive into thy Almighty and most
Gracious protection the persons of us thy servants,
and the Fleet in which we serve.*

FORMS OF PRAYER TO BE USED AT SEA (FIRST PRAYER)

The *Torrin* has been in one scrap after another—but even when
we have had men killed the majority survived and brought the
old ship back. Now she lies in fifteen hundred fathoms and with
her more than half our shipmates. If they had to die, what a
grand way to go, for now they lie all together with the ship we
loved, and they are in very good company. We have lost her but
they are still with her. There may be less than half the *Torrin* left
but I feel that each of us will take up the battle with even
stronger heart. Each of us knows twice as much about fighting
and each of us has twice as good a reason to fight . . .

CAPTAIN KINROSS ADDRESSING THE SURVIVORS
AT THE END OF *IN WHICH WE SERVE* (1942)

If you had never done and never do anything else, you have not
lived in vain.

ADMIRAL HOLLAND (1942)

•

THEN CAME the thunderclap. The famous telegram from London saying I wasn't to go. It was supposed to come from Winston Churchill.
I don't really believe it *did*—but anyway, it was supposed to.

Noël was recalling the incident in his 1973 interview and he was
being remarkably benevolent toward his old sparring partner, because

the "forbidance" (as Noël termed it) almost certainly *did* come from Churchill. The cable from Little Bill that was waiting for him in Bermuda reported that "A greater power than we could contradict has thwarted our intents."

The "intents" had been the significant job Stephenson was to have formally offered Noël on his return from the Antipodes, "a job which, in his opinion and in mine, would be of real value in the war effort." While Noël was in transit back home, Stephenson had received a telegram in code with no signatory:

APRIL 2ND.

FOR NOËL COWARD (A) REGRETTABLE PUBLICITY GIVEN TO YOUR
VISIT LONDON BY ENTIRE BRITISH PRESS WHICH WOULD
INCREASE ON YOUR ARRIVAL UNFORTUNATELY MAKES ENTIRE
SCHEME IMPRACTICABLE (B) COMPLETE SECRECY IS
FOUNDATION OF OUR WORK AND IT WOULD NOW BE IMPOSSIBLE
FOR ANY OF OUR PEOPLE TO CONTACT YOU IN ENGLAND
WITHOUT INCURRING PUBLICITY (C) WE ARE ALL VERY
DISAPPOINTED AS WE HAD LOOKED FORWARD TO WORKING
WITH YOU BUT THERE ARE NO FURTHER STEPS TO BE TAKEN.

To Violet Noël put on his bravest face:

> While I was in Bermuda all the nice plans I had were dashed. There
> will be more explanation of this when I get to London. I was very upset
> at the time but with my natural resilience—to say nothing of my grim
> determination—has since asserted itself and I am gay as a lark, altho'
> very very cross indeed! . . . With me everything always turns out for
> the best, because I am bloody well determined that it shall!!

At the time he most definitely *did* suspect Churchill, egged on by press
baron Max Beaverbrook (then minister of supply) whose *Daily Express*
was—and would remain—a persistent thorn in the Coward flesh.

So that appeared to be that—certainly in any formal sense. In the 1973
interview, Noël goes on to quote Little Bill's typical reaction. If one door is
closed in your face, create another: "He told me to go off and do my stuff
anyway. So I did."

He kept in direct touch with Stephenson for the rest of the war but said
nothing about it for thirty years.

·

THE RETURN TO London was far from triumphal. The job he had
anticipated with such pleasure was gone, and the British press was still at
his heels, anxious to portray his visits to Australia and New Zealand as
frivolous holidays away from real responsibilities.

Fortunately, for his morale—and even his sanity—true friends rallied to
his defense. Rebecca West wrote:

> I can't quite see what else you could do for your country, except strip
> yourself of all your clothes and sell them for War Weapons Week,
> after which your country would step in and prosecute you for inde-
> cent exposure. I can't do it. Can't adequately express my rage that
> you should have been treated in this way.

Then, within days, two other blows fell. A German bomb badly damaged the house at Gerald Road and the army commandeered Goldenhurst.
Noël was forced to evacuate himself to the Savoy Hotel until repairs could
be made. He also took advantage of an invitation from Joyce Carey to join
her for a short break in the Welsh resort of Portmeiron, where she was hoping to find the peace and quiet from London's bombs and write a play. Her
play was never written, but Noël came back from that five-day quietus
with *Blithe Spirit*.

No sooner was it written than it was put into production by Binkie
Beaumont. The play fulfilled part of the promise Noël had made to him-

self on his return—to write the play, the film, and the song that would help his fellow countrymen get through the war. *Blithe Spirit* was the play.

Charles Condomine (Cecil Parker), happily married for the second time to Ruth (Fay Compton), is visited by the ghost of his dead first wife, Elvira (Kay Hammond), conjured up by the medium Madame Arcati (Margaret Rutherford). The play fulfilled Noël's ambition in every way—though he was not to know that at the time. It opened at the St. James's Theatre on July 2 and eventually racked up 1,997 performances, creating a West End record at the time. It ran longer than the war.

Noël wrote to Jack Wilson:

> 17 Gerald Road
> S.W.1.
> July 18th 1941
>
> Dearest Dab:
>
> We have been very remiss in not writing before to tell you all about everything. The first night was terrific . . . oddly enough a really good audience. At the end our old friend in the gallery shouted "It's rubbish—take it off", which convulsed everybody and, of course, was used *ad nauseam* by my admirers in the Press, the *Daily Mirror* even going so far as to have "Noël Coward Booed" as a headline. The notices were marvellous on the whole and the business terrific even through heat waves. The performance is excellent. Fay is better than she has ever been and was lovely and easy to direct. I've cured her of all her bad mannerisms and she looks charming. Cecil is really first rate and very charming too in a pompous hen's bottom sort of way. The best performance is Kay Hammond, who is absolutely bewitching and a much finer actress than I suspected she was with a wonderful sense of timing. Edward [Molyneux] made her as simple and lovely a dress as I have ever seen and she looks a vision. She uses dead white make-up with a little green in it, green powder on face, hair and arms, scarlet lips and nails and ordinary dark eye make-up. She is covered from each side of the stage by a following green spot, almost imperceptible, wherever she goes. The great disappointment is Margaret Rutherford, whom the audience love, because the part is so good, but who is actually very, very bad indeed. She is indistinct, fussy and, beyond her personality, has no technical knowledge or resources at all. She merely fumbles and gasps and drops things and throws many of my best lines down the drain. She is despair to Fay, Cecil and Kay and mortification to me because I thought she would be marvellous. I need hardly say she got a magnificent notice. So much for that.

Well, not quite. His contemporary playwrights appreciated what he had achieved and said so. Thornton Wilder didn't see the play until a year into the run and then wrote:

The Savoy
October 10th 1942

Dear Noël,
First of all the title is genius: with *spirit* and *blithe* you already *lay the ghost* and *shroud* the death's head.

And then the whole treatment of Madame Arcati. What is genius but combining the unexpected and the self-evident—so that at the same moment you are saying both: "How surprising!" and "How true that is!"

And what a performance from Miss Rutherford—and then turning it all on Edith. By quarter to four I was saying: How the Hell can Noël get us out of this *satisfactorily*? And then you did—like that.

Elvira—perfect. That voice.

I wish you'd been Charles.

I thought Fay Compton was hitting pretty hard.

Tell the director how brilliant his work was. For instance, that moment when Elvira knows she has caused Ruth's death. Oooo!

Only thing I didn't like was the last three minutes. Hard, I call it. And a little *longeur* in the early part of Act II.

This play—and "London Pride"—and the Destroyer picture—all falling from one sleeve within two years, and such years. That's telling 'em. That's England talking.

God bless you
THORNTON

By that same July 18 post he wrote to Violet, who was still in New York:

Well Darlingest,
I've been absolutely beastly about not writing to you but so many things have been happening at once so you must forgive me. The play is a lovely smash hit and playing to marvellous business.

There are lots of projects in the air about my future activities. There was talk about me being sent back to America more or less at once but I have said that I won't go if I have to be away from England for more than a month. You mustn't be sad about this—I know I am right. The only reason I want to come to America at all at the moment is to see you. Somehow since I've been back here all my talent seems to be coming to the top again. It is undoubtedly the strongest weapon I have in my personal battle and the one thing that does not depend on Government support. My enemies have all been silenced by my return and gratifyingly furious about my success, which has really been bigger than it has ever been in this country. It is very possible that I may be able to come over for a little while at the beginning or the middle of September. If so I could help Jack with the play and do one or two things in Washington.

There is so much that I long to tell you that I cannot possibly put it in a letter but you must try to read between the lines. I am on top of the wave and really happier than I have been since the war began, apart from being so far away from you. Even so I would much rather you were in America than here. Not so much on account of the Blitzes but because of the various minor discomforts which I know you wouldn't mind a bit but that I should mind for you.

Everything, of course, has turned out quite differently from what I imagined—I certainly had no idea that I was going to come back and write a wildly successful comedy and a lot of songs and by doing so get back all the popularity that the press has been so busy trying to destroy.

There are several other schemes in the air any of which might materialise at any moment, one of them is my writing and acting and directing a film here. I am thinking about this quite seriously because I think I have quite a good idea simmering in my mind. I'll let you know further if it develops. In any case and whatever I do, I really think I shall be able to manage to come over for a short while.

When you're feeling low and depressed just remember that it really was the luckiest thing in the world that everything turned out as it did, not only for my own peace of mind but for my whole position in this country, which really was in considerable danger. Now my stock is high and I must say, as a writer, I wouldn't have missed what's going on here for anything in the world. The ordinary people are so wonderful and there is a new vitality all over the country, particularly in the badly blitzed areas, which are dreadful but somehow quite magnificent at the same time. It makes one very proud to belong.

Next came the song . . .

Standing one morning waiting for a train in a London terminus station, as Noël tells it, the platforms littered with the bomb damage of the previous night, he watched the ordinary Londoners going about their business as though nothing untoward had happened. His first reaction was to admire them for their incredible courage. Then he noticed a small wildflower stubbornly growing in a crack in the concrete. He remembered what it was called, and the parallels seemed uncanny. "Though it has a Latin name / In town and countryside / We in England call it 'London Pride.' " The song of that name was introduced into the London revue *Up and Doing* a few days later (sung by Binnie Hale), and it has become the city's unofficial anthem.

Writing war songs that would relieve the gathering gloom became a priority in Noël's mind at this time, and even more so when he received a cable from Henry Morgenthau, Jr., secretary of the treasury and Roosevelt's right hand:

US GOVT.
WASHINGTON DC
OCTOBER 14TH 1941
NOËL COWARD
SAVOY HOTEL LDN.

HAVE JUST HEARD YOUR RECORDS OF LONDON PRIDE AND CAN
ANYONE OBLIGE US WITH A BREN GUN AT THE WHITE HOUSE
WHICH WERE GIVEN TO THE PRESIDENT BY LORD LOUIS
MOUNTBATTEN STOP WOULD LIKE YOU TO BROADCAST THESE
SONGS OVER NATIONWIDE HOOKUP UNDER AUSPICES OF THE
TREASURY ON OCTOBER 21ST BETWEEN NINE AND TEN PM NEW
YORK TIME STOP DETAILS COULD BE ARRANGED BY
REPRESENTATIVE OF NBC WOULD APPRECIATE A REPLY CARE OF
TREASURY WASHINGTON.

Noël's answer was, of course, a foregone conclusion.

OCTOBER 28TH

YOUR BROADCAST LAST WEEK WAS SO WONDERFUL THAT OUR
RADIO PUBLIC WANTS MORE TEN MINUTE PROGRAMS FROM
LONDON DURING TREASURY HOUR STOP HAVE YOU OR OTHER
COMPOSERS WRITTEN ANY NEW SONGS TYPIFYING SPIRIT OF
LONDON OR ENGLAND TODAY STOP WHAT ARE MOST POPULAR
SONGS BRITISH ARMY IS SINGING STOP DEEPLY APPRECIATE
YOUR CABLING ANY SUGGESTIONS.

Songs were to become a distinct weapon in the propaganda war. In 1943 one song in particular made quite an impact. A senior American journalist sent the lyric to the president with the following note: "Thought you might be amused by Noël Coward's latest contribution to post-war planning entitled 'Don't Let's Be Beastly to the Germans.' " The lyric began:

> *Don't let's be beastly to the Germans*
> *When our Victory is ultimately won*
> *It was just those nasty Nazis who persuaded them to fight*
> *And their Beethoven and Bach are really far worse than their bite*
>
> *Let's be meek to them and turn the other cheek to them*
> *And try to bring out their latent sense of fun*
> *Let's give them full air parity*
> *And treat the rats with charity*
> *But don't let's be beastly to the Hun*

When he returned to America at the end of 1943 he had to sing the song at the president's request after dinner at the White House.

Meanwhile, back in England the song gained another influential fan. Duff Cooper, now chancellor of the Duchy of Lancaster, wrote to Noël:

Treasury Chambers
Whitehall, S.W.1.
8.7.43.

My dear Noël,

Yesterday morning I had occasion to call on the Prime Minister who was in bed when he received me and had little time to give to the business with which I was concerned. This time was curtailed by his reading to me your song about being kind to the Germans. He read parts of it twice and almost improvised a tune for it. If you have a spare copy I should love to possess it, for I despair of hearing you sing it unless we can arrange a party before you go, which should not be impossible. If I was still Minister of Information, I should insist upon it being broadcast nightly because its message is one that is much needed by all the silly, sloppy sentimental shits who form such a formidable section of fellow countrymen.

Yours ever
Duff

Churchill, too, developed a taste for the song, to go with a postprandial cigar, and at Chequers, the official country residence of British prime ministers, Noël was obliged to sing it until he was hoarse.

The only people who actively disliked the song were officials of the BBC. When it was broadcast the evening before Noël's departure for the Middle East and it was realized that the word "bloody" had been heard

Refrain 1

Don't let's be beastly to the Germans
When our victory is ultimately won
It was just those nasty Nazis who persuaded them to fight
And their Beethoven and Bach are really far worse than their bite
Let's be nice to them
And give our best advice to them
And try to remember all the good they've done
Let's sweetly sympathise again
And help the rats to rise again
But don't let's be beastly to the Hun.

Refrain 2

Don't let's be beastly to the Germans
When we've definitely got them on the run
Let us treat them very kindly as we would a valued friend
We might send them out some Bishops as a form of lease and lend
Let's be sweet to them
And day by day repeat to them
That 'sterilization' simply isn't done
Let's help the dirty swine again
To occupy the Rhine again
But don't let's be beastly to the Hun.

Refrain 3

Don't let's be beastly to the Germans
For they're civil beings when all is said and done
Tho' they gave us Science, culture, art and music to excess
They also gave us two world wars and Mr Rudolph Hess
Let's be meek to them
And turn the other cheek to them
And try to bring out their latent sense of fun
Let's give them full air parity
And treat the souls with charity
But don't let's be beastly to the Hun

Refrain 4

Don't let's be beastly to the Germans
For you can't deprive a gangster of his gun
Tho' they've been a little naughty to the Czechs and Poles and Dutch
But I don't suppose those countries really minded very much
Let's be free with them
And share the B.B.C. with them
We mustn't prevent them basking in the sun
Let's soften their defeat again
And build their bloody fleet again
But don't let's be beastly to the Hun.

Noël's draft of "Don't Let's Be Beastly to the Germans." The BBC banned
the song as being almost treasonable. Churchill resurrected it
and made Noël sing it at dinner parties until he was hoarse.

over the airwaves for the first time, the corporation issued a hasty apology and promptly banned the song for the duration. They totally failed to appreciate the irony of the sentiments being expressed—a fact that was ironic in itself.

When Noël was made aware of all this, he was coming to the end of his Middle East tour. In his *Diary* he reflected ruefully: "I am willing to admit that, as a nation, we have never been especially good at recognizing satire, but the satire of 'Don't Let's Be Beastly to the Germans' was surely not all that subtle. I must be more careful in future and double dot my I's and treble cross my t's."

But all of this was small beer compared to the international incident that arose earlier over another Coward song. The first summit meeting between Churchill and Roosevelt was to create the Atlantic Charter. At one point the two men were heard arguing loudly. The topic? Which verse preceded which other verse in Coward's "Mad Dogs and Englishmen." Each of them was adamant that he was right, and Churchill later asked Noël to adjudicate. Noël said that he hated to admit it but the *president* was right. The prime minister hunched himself deeper into his chair, glared at the messenger, and grunted, "Britain can take it!"

Noël found the same spirit wherever he went, and he tried to convey it to Jack Wilson in America:

July 18th 1941

Dear Jack,

Since I have been back I have naturally discussed my future activities with all the big shots who are still whirling about in the usual flurry of bureaucratic frustration . . . After much careful thought and discussion with Lorn and Gladys, I have come to the conclusion that the only way for me to avoid further frustration and heartbreak in the future is to utilise my own talents which puts me on a plane beyond the reach of governmental intrigue and destructiveness. I can never begin to tell you how much it means to me to be back in this country again and, apart from wanting to see Mum and you and Natasha, I honestly can't bear the thought of leaving it again—except for very brief periods—till the end of the War. The muddle and confusion and irritation is almost as bad as ever but the ordinary people are so magnificent that with all the discomforts and food rationing and cigarette shortage and blackouts I want to be with them.

The other day I went to a certain very badly blitzed coastal town [Plymouth]. The behaviour of the people in the midst of such appalling devastation was beyond praise and beyond gallantry. They were genuinely cheerful and philosophic and I never heard anyone even grumble. In the evenings between 7:30 and 9:30 there is a band on the front and the whole of the town, or what is left of it, come out and dance in the sunlight. The girls put on their bright coloured frocks and dance with the sailors and marines and soldiers. The fact that they were dancing on the exact site of a certain historic game [Sir Francis Drake's 1588 game of bowls as the Spanish Armada approached] added a little extra English nostalgia to what was one of the most touching and moving scenes I have ever seen.

Travelling in England nowadays, from the point of view of pre-War comfort, is absolute hell and yet more enjoyable than it ever was before. A few minutes after you have settled yourself in your first class carriage it fills up immediately with sailors and soldiers and wives and children. The trains are mostly all jammed, there are hardly any porters and you fight your way in and out of a restaurant car where you are lucky if you get a very nasty bit of rabbit and some floury potatoes. But what is so wonderful is that a good time is had by all and no one is even remotely disagreeable. Then of course there are the jokes . . . such an unending series of really good jokes; blitz jokes, evacuee jokes, fire-watching jokes, etc. Even Arthur Macrae's joke of going to a "friend's house for cocktails and hearing awful screams and commotion inside. Then his host opened the door look- ing very white and upset and said: 'I'm afraid the cocktail party is off, dear, my friend has just been up for his medical exam and has passed A.1.'" Arthur is in the R.A.F., Alan [Webb] is a disgruntled lance- corporal in the Sappers, Cole [Lesley] in the R.A.F. in Ireland, merry as a grig when home on leave. Our own little coterie whirls around on its own axis. Winifred gives elaborate picnic parties in the Park on summer evenings and we all sit around on the grass and have dressed crab and sausage rolls and a great deal of gin.

I am immersed in a campaign of writing topical songs. This coun- try has been sadly deficient in war songs and I think it is high time that people abroad should take a lighter view than Miss [Deanna] Durbin did when she sang "They'll Always Be an England" with tears rolling down her face as though she were bitterly depressed at the thought. I have written one of the best songs of my life called "Lon- don Pride". Binnie is doing it in the Leslie Henson revue and Gracie Fields is taking it back to Canada with her. I have also done a Home Guard song which is a satire on the Ministry of Supply. This is already a success. I broadcast both last week. I will send you the records as soon as possible. In addition to those I have done 2 more, one called "Imagine the Duchess's Feelings when Her Youngest Son went Red" and the other "There Have Been Songs in England", which is a ballad for Gracie. It seems to me that by doing this sort of thing I am help- ing what I really mind about in the best way I can. You do see, don't you, why I don't want to go away? I am no longer angry with the Hollywood actors for not coming back but profoundly sorry for them for they are missing something quite indescribable.

•

## THEN CAME THE FILM . . .

Soon after the opening of *Blithe Spirit* Noël received a three-man delegation at the Savoy. One of them was Filippo del Guidice, who ran a film production company called Two Cities; the other was producer Anthony Havelock-Allan, whom Noël had met in the early 1920s; and the third was Charles Thorpe of Columbia Pictures. Their proposition was a simple one.

They wanted Noël to make a war propaganda film. He could make anything he liked and would have complete control. His reaction was less than enthusiastic. His only real previous experience in film had been as an actor in *The Scoundrel,* in 1935, and he had rejected various overtures since. He told them he would think about it and give them an answer in a week's time.

The week turned out to be fortuitous. The following day he had arranged to dine with the Mountbattens, and over dinner Lord Louis recounted the story of the sinking off Crete, back in May, of his com-

Lord Louis (1900–1979) and Lady Edwina (1901–1960) Mountbatten. Friends of Noël's since the 1920s and now, in 1947, appointed the last viceroy and vicereine to India before its independence.

mand, the HMS *Kelly*. There and then Noël knew he had the story for his film.

In his July 18 letter to Jack Wilson, he is full of enthusiasm:

Everybody is very amiable and plans get formulated for me to do this and that but what I really want to do is to do a film for the Navy. Columbia are mad for me to do it and would give me complete control of everything, even Executives . . . I think I have got an idea . . . this, of course, may necessitate me going to sea for a bit to re-absorb a little Naval atmosphere. The Admiralty have already asked me to do this on their own. If the idea materialises I shall apply to come to America for three weeks or a month in mid-September in order to help you with *Blithe Spirit* but only if I can have my return ticket clutched in my hand and the dates all set to start the picture on my return. This I think can be managed. I hope you approve of all these strange revolutionary schemes.

Dicky's story of the Battle of Crete is one of the most heroic and agonising epics I have ever heard, although he is quite unconscious of it.

Noël pulled every diplomatic string he could. Duff Cooper was no longer minister of information but was happy to lobby his successor, Brendan Bracken:

> From the
> Chancellor of the Duchy of Lancaster
> Dorchester Hotel
> 1st July 1941

My dear Brendan,
Noël Coward came to see me this morning.

He is engaged on a film which in my opinion is of the very highest propaganda value. This film has the strongest and most enthusiastic support of the Admiralty and he is being assisted in the production of it by Lord Louis Mountbatten. He wants to go out to the United States for a very short visit in October in order to confer further with Lord Louis concerning the script of the film in order that all the technical details may be correct. He will also during this visit assist at the final stages of the production of his *Blithe Spirit*, which has been such an enormous success in London. This play, also, in my opinion, has a very high propaganda value, because, although it is in no way connected with the war, it shows the high spirits of British people after two years of fighting and their ability to produce and appreciate works of art.

Further, Noël Coward has written certain patriotic songs, which have already had great success over here and which should be sung throughout the United States, where they have been too inclined to sing nostalgic melodies regretting the loss of Paris, Venice and Vienna. His songs are about London, and his presence for a few weeks in America would contribute towards their popularity.

I therefore think that the Ministry of Information should on these three grounds do what may be possible to secure him priority for this visit, which could not last more than three weeks, as he would be obliged to return in order to get on with the production of the naval film, to which I have alluded above.

I told him I would give you my views, for what they were worth, and I hope that they may have some influence on your decision.

Yours ever,<br>DUFF

As part of his preparation, Noël called on an old naval acquaintance and was invited to travel during August with the Home Fleet at Scapa Flow and the shore installations at Plymouth.

There was another plus to his visit to Plymouth. It was Michael Redgrave (1908–1985), who would play an intermittent part in Noël's life. They had met in the mid-1930s, when Redgrave was just starting his acting career, and there seems to have been an immediate and mutual attraction. Redgrave himself—father of Vanessa, Corin, and Lynn, a latter-day acting dynasty—was bisexual, and it seems clear that at the time the war broke out he and Noël were having an affair. His wife, Rachel Kempson, told Noël years later how upset she had been when Redgrave spent his last night before reporting for service duty with Noël instead of with her.

Ordinary Seaman Michael Redgrave and his wife, Rachel Kempson.

In July of 1941 Redgrave enlisted in the navy as an Ordinary Seaman, and from time to time his and Noël's paths would cross. That summer he had asked Noël for some material to sing at a ship's concert, and Noël provided him with one of his new war-related songs, "Won't You Please Oblige Us with a Bren Gun? (Or the Home Guard Might as Well Go Home)." Redgrave had slavishly learned the song, when he received a cable from Noël about the lines in the lyric: "Colonel McNamara who / Was in Calcutta in ninety-two, / Emerged from his retirement for the war." The cable read:

PLEASE CHANGE MCNAMARA TO MONTMORENCY STOP THERE IS
A REAL AND VERY ANGRY MCNAMARA IN THE WAR OFFICE.

·

IN NOVEMBER, Redgrave is writing to Noël that a weekend they had spent in New York was "a wild and wonderful dream." Despite his determination to play an active role in the war, Redgrave found his efforts frustrated by a recurrent injury, and he had more than ample time for introspection.

25 January, 1942

I am still in the old ship, waiting for the doctor to discharge me for my crooked arm, which hasn't been right since ammunitioning ship in October. I trek off to hospital each morning. The new X-rays have been sent to some specialist for his opinion. I bide all this with fretful patience because I don't want to have to tour *Richard III* for the rest of my unnatural days. I have therefore plenty of opportunity to ruminate over my not altogether happy leave and cloudy future. I have amongst other things been bearing in mind your strictures, and especially what you said about wasting time on silly people. It is perfectly true that I do. I have tried to think why and I suppose that it is a chronic inferiority complex combining with bloody laziness. You needn't have been quite so abusive about it, because my colossal vanity is readily pierced and quite capable of being put on one side for a time. Besides, invective may sharpen your darts, but it does make you aim wildly. However, I forgive the invective, knowing that you can't help that any more than I can help being a cow on occasions. It is not for nothing that each of your plays contains a slanging match.

As an object lesson, when I was feeling at my lowest, who should be on the train but Ivor [Novello] and his entourage, and God put a lot of snow about to spin out the journey to 12 hours, and rub the lesson in. It was impossible to avoid that and almost as impossible to avoid *The Dancing Years* [the musical Ivor was touring] and supper afterwards. However, I made up for that by hearing Myra Hess play a Mozart and a Brahms Concerto (No. 2) and by taking her out to supper last night. We sat four hours over it and I didn't go dreamy once (!) Dame Myra finally became deliciously giggly but she said she doesn't mind that even with a concert today, since she has given up the vanity of playing without music.

While we are on the subject I will say that, much as I appreciate and will apply the lesson, I shall I know remain ridiculously impressionable to the end of my days. I shall be wary of politics—a lesson well learnt I think—but I shall go on falling for people until I fall into my grave . . . just as I fell in turn for . . . Edith Evans, Michel St. Denis and N.C., including a mixed bunch of blokes whom I have admired and who have influenced and shaped my life. Who knows? Perhaps it is to some extent this falling for people, a tendency which prevents me from growing up, which also makes me such an actor as I am. I can't say that it is, but it may be. And you can't say that it isn't.

As the abused but perspicacious Thornton [Wilder] says: when we are in love with someone it is not so much that we idealise their good qualities but rationalize their defects . . .

You may have better means of knowing whether officers are or are not urgently needed. But I am in a better position to know from all the candidates here and in barracks that nothing drastic is done to get the right men speedily. In my own case, as a last straw, I was asked yesterday if I would like to forego my commission temporarily and take up special sea duties speaking German!

It is a question of waste. I try to make the best of the inevitable waste of my only real talent, but I cannot abide this stupid waste of my good-will, energy and cheerfulness. I could accept the conditions of this life and the temporary loss of all that I love best until, like thousands of other men in this country, I know that good use is not being made of me and I am going to take this opportunity, if I can, to do something useful. Let no one say that they are sticking it, so why shouldn't I? The majority would be glad to do anything worthwhile, and have no chance.

You have so often said that you looked forward to us being friends always. I would like that. Please forgive my behaviour while on leave and, if possible, forget it. I was pretty unhappy and worried about a number of things. (First Vanessa was ill then Corin; Rachel far from well. And I had a bloody awful row with my mother two nights before our ding-dong and I may say that in that case it was *not* my fault at all. And you will understand that it was pretty shattering to find that with the new draft nothing I have done so far will count at all.) I had looked forward to it so much that I was almost ill with excitement, and the anti-climax was pretty devastating to the sensitive dreamer type.

I don't expect you to answer this, as you are I know very busy and I imagine, when you have time to be, very sore.

Good luck to the film. You know how much I shall be thinking of it and of you.

M.

By November of that same year, Ordinary Seaman Redgrave, M., was ordinary civilian Michael Redgrave. He and Noël remained friends and occasional colleagues for the rest of Noël's life.

•

MEANWHILE, ON-SHORE PRESS and interdepartmental arguments were raging about the making of the film. Despite Duff Cooper's intervention, Brendan Bracken tried to stop it on the grounds that it would tie up too many valuable film facilities. That, at least, was his public pose. In reality, it's more likely that he shared Fleet Street's conviction that Noël was an unsuitable person to portray a heroic naval figure. Fortunately, there were powerful voices that endorsed the project and could sway the opinions of others.

The most influential of those was Lord Louis Mountbatten—who just happened to be the king's cousin and knew everybody who mattered. In the end it was his weight that tipped the balance. And there was one other key motivation. It was *his* story. But as the weeks went by and the arguments raged, that in itself began to be a problem.

In September, Mountbatten and his wife, Edwina, are in America, and he writes to Noël with a detailed account of their official doings:

> The Plaza
> Fifth Avenue at 59th Street
> New York
> September 16th 1941

My dear Noël,
Jack Wilson has just told Edwina over the telephone that you are not coming out to the States. This is a great blow, as I do feel a meeting between us might have made a difference to your film. May I urge you to send out a copy of the scenario by air mail, preferably via the admirable Robert [Vansittart]?

If you will do this, I will look carefully through the scenario, in case there are any really important points to change . . .

The Navy Department have gone from extreme secrecy to extreme publicity of the *Illustrious* [Mountbatten's new command] and sent down a host of camera men. I do not know if any of the newsreels were sent to England; but if they were, you will be amused to see the old technique of breaking up the ship's company, and making them press more closely around me. [It was a technique Noël would use in the film.]

I insisted on all the newspaper men, camera men etc., withdrawing out of earshot when I talked to the men, but in return had to undertake to make a short statement for the newsreel.

The Americans do things in the most extraordinary way. They had no less than seven naval officers on Public Relations duty, and they solemnly suggested that the ship's company should be photographed in "V" formation, with their thumbs up.

I should have been there by now, but for this wretched Senatorial Enquiry into the alleged pro-British activities of the movie industry. [The "isolationists" were still rabid and would remain so until December 7 and Pearl Harbor made their arguments irrelevant.] I have, therefore, put off my visit until the 1st October, in the hopes that the Enquiry will be over, or the situation in this country sufficiently changed to enable me to carry out my programme.

We have both been very busy since we have been here. Edwina is in the middle of her Red Cross tour. She gives a half-hour talk without any notes, and has been a staggering success, often reducing her audience very unexpectedly to tears when describing the quiet courage of the civil population in air raids.

Do you know Miss Jessie Matthews? If so, could you prevail upon her to avoid giving the unfortunate impression which the enclosed cutting produces? It makes it hard for Edwina to convince her audience of the quiet courage of the British women when bombs are dropping round them if statements of the following type are to appear—". . . when a police car raced up Park Avenue, its siren screaming, Miss Matthews dropped the glass, spilling the liquid over the dress, leaped to her feet, her face white and her eyes wide with horror and she screamed." [He then returns to the subject that is *really* on his mind.]

There has already been talk of your film over here. Someone tells me that the *Daily Express* carried a front page story that the film was based on the *Kelly* and that my name was mentioned.

I know you will feel as horrified at this as I do, but what can we do about it? Could you issue a statement that the film is equally based on the *Cossack,* and destroyers that took part in Dunkirk (which the *Kelly* did not) and that the Captain (D) is no more me than Philip Vian, or any other captain (D)?

To sum up, whereas I am naturally proud that the story is in part based on the *Kelly,* I am sufficiently jealous of my own reputation in the Navy to wish to avoid personal publicity in this connection, and rely on you to try and undo any mischief which may have been done.

> Yours ever
> Dickie

Noël's letter must have crossed with his, but Noël was already anxious to calm Mountbatten's concerns:

September 17th 1941

My dear Dicky,

A great deal has happened since you left, so I will do this letter in sections.

1. Unfortunately the night when Gladys and I came to Chester Street [Mountbatten's London home] . . . you were feeling ill, if you remember . . . Jeanie and Kay were there. Jeanie went like an arrow from a bow, apparently, to Beaverbrook and a few days after you had left there was a charming headline in the *Daily Express* announcing that I was writing and acting a film of the story of your life. This was obviously calculated to put the Admiralty against the whole scheme. I was away at sea with Joe Vian and so knew nothing about it, but Brodger Brooking dealt with it swiftly and efficiently.

Since my arrival back in London I have discovered that a tremendous whispering campaign has been started by Brendan Bracken and Walter Monckton to the effect that it is most unsuitable for me to play a Naval Officer etc., etc. Nothing has been said to me direct but it has been repeated to me on all sides. It has been officially denied by the Admiralty that the film is based on you and also denied by me in the Press.

The scenario is progressing beautifully and I am purposely making it as little like you as possible. The moment the script is completed you shall have it. The Navy, I need hardly say, is supporting me and helping me in every way possible. I have never met so much kindness and eagerness to help. One very good thing is that owing to various preliminaries and lack of floor space at Denham I can't start shooting till mid-December, which means you will be back long before the film is done. I have changed the title from *White Ensign* to *In Which We Serve.* I really feel that it is going to be a rouser and I have told Brodger to inform the Admiralty that I shall be doing tests of myself as Captain (D) for a month before we start the actual shooting. These will be shown to anyone in the Admiralty who wishes to see them and if they then feel that I am unsuitable for the part, there

Noël and Mountbatten take a (somewhat posed) moment
to go over a point in the script for *In Which We Serve.*

will be time to get somebody else. My Captain (D) [Capt. Kinross] is
quite ordinary with an income of about £800 a year, a small country
house near Plymouth, a reasonably nice looking wife (Mrs. not Lady),
two children and a cocker spaniel. I know you will approve of all this.

Actually I am very angry about the underhand opposition going
on but fully realise that the only way to defeat it is by making the
picture not only first rate entertainment value but the finest and
most dignified tribute to the Navy possible. I have got the best camera man [Ronald Neame] and the best cutter [David Lean] in the
business and everything is under control . . .

I think that's about all the news really except that I had an
enchanting three weeks with the Navy and spent a great deal of time
in a great many ships and got a great deal of local colour and drank a
great deal of gin.

I think the newsreel of you taking over *Illustrious* is first rate.
Gladys and I spent a day in Campbell at Chatham with Captain
Pizey and are going down again to Sheerness to see them do action
stations. There was quite a flap of excitement about us coming on
board and sailors were observed peering out of scuttles and round
gun turrets. Gladys was in uniform and one rating was heard to say
to another: "Blimey, I didn't know she was going to be a bloody
Pongo." This has stuck and she is now Bloody Pongo for ever. I had a
grand time in the *Shropshire* with Jacko Barrett and the *Somali* with

Donald Bain [he of the most ripping pair of field glasses from Noël's Cornwall days]. The C. in C. was charming to me and I sang to the troops in as many ships as I could get to. The whole trip was a great success and I think you would have been pleased.

I hope all this bloody publicity won't annoy you as much as it annoys me. My voices tell me that disapproval of the project comes from very high up indeed. It is flattering to have such powerful enemies.

All my love to you both and take care of yourselves.

Even some of Noël's oldest and closest friends had their doubts about him as Captain "D." He wrote to reassure G. B. Stern when she had read the draft script:

Denham
23/4/42

Dearest Peter—or if you prefer it—Dirty Old Stinkpot,
I agree with your criticism of Captain D., but actually he is entirely true. I am hoping that my own personal qualities will eliminate some of the B'Jesus out of him. Seriously, darling, I am so very glad that you think it is so good. I must admit I mind about it being good probably more than anything I've ever done. The Navy has always been so wonderful to me that I really do want to do them proud.

The harassment continued, the most irritating coming from the Ministry of Information and in particular from the head of its Film Department, Jack Beddington, who ordained—as by Holy Writ—that "the film was exceedingly bad propaganda for the Navy, as it showed one of H.M.'s ships being sunk by enemy action." Permission was refused.

At the end of the year Mountbatten closed that particular door and firmly locked it by submitting the by then finished script to the king himself and received the following handwritten reply:

Buckingham Palace
December 23rd 1941

My dear Dickie,
I return you the script of the Film. I have read it and think it a very good and appealing way of dealing with the subject. Although the ship is lost, the spirit which animates the Royal Navy is clearly brought out in the men and the procession of ships coming along to take its place at the end demonstrates the power of the Navy.

I hope it will be a success.
Ever Yours
BERTIE

Collapse of various inflated parties.

•

THERE WERE TWO other sources of irritation that Noël could have done without as the year drew to a close. The first came on October 16 in the shape of a summons. He was accused on two counts of having broken the strict wartime currency restrictions on how much money could be taken out of the country. The irony was that on his "unofficial" trips to the United States he had paid all his own expenses—to the tune of eleven thousand pounds—and it had never been pointed out to him that, in doing so, he was breaking a law he had never heard of. And now a grateful government—or, at least, certain people within it—were determined to hound him further. A second summons related to his business affairs in the United States, a matter that he had always left entirely in Jack Wilson's hands.

Noël saw it as a clear case of wartime "celebrity baiting," an extension of the media disapproval he'd suffered since the war began. Ivor Novello received comparable treatment for using petrol in excess of the rations. As a result he even served a short prison sentence that undermined his health and almost certainly contributed to his early death.

Noël had, in fact, written to Jack about his income abroad several months earlier:

May 29th, 1941

My dear Jack,
This is a business letter and you know how idiotic I am at business letters but I really am in rather a state because it is only since I have been back that I have discovered the situation re. Englishmen who have any money in America. If the office had not been blitzed and all papers flung into confusion, this would have been attended to before.

This is the situation as far as I can see it. Any money that I have, either in cash or securities, in America must be sent immediately to Barclays Foreign Agency for sale to the British Treasury. As you know, I am in complete confusion as to what I have got and what I haven't and so you must promise to do this immediately because it has got to be done by every English person who wishes to contribute towards winning the War . . . and even if they didn't, there are terrific penalties attached, to say nothing of scandal and publicity.

I would so loathe for anyone to think for a moment that I was not doing my share in every way. After the War, if I am still sound in wind and limb, I shall just have to set to work and earn it all back again. Please at all costs get this tidied up immediately and please be sure that all future income from any source is sent straight to my account at Barclays, Covent Garden.

When the news of the summons broke, his real friends quickly rallied around. Cochran, for instance, wrote: "I beg you not to worry, I know, and all your friends know, that whatever human faults you may have, you are an extremely honest man. Your integrity can never be in doubt."

Noël replied:

28/10/41

My dear Cocky,

I can't tell you how touched I was by your very sweet letter. It was so typical of your thoughtfulness and kindness to write it. I need hardly tell you that I am completely guiltless over the whole business and intend to fight it tooth and claw—so very much helped by the complete faith of my real friends.

His counsel, Sir Dingwall Bateson, advised him to plead guilty but opposite advice came from an even stronger quarter—George Bernard Shaw:

4 Whitehall Court
London SW1
26/10/41

Dear Noël Coward,

The other day George Arliss [the film actor], being in trouble about his American securities, pleaded Guilty under the impression that he

Over the years, George Bernard Shaw (1856–1950) gave Noël two good pieces of advice: not to copy him as a playwright and not to plead guilty to a technical wartime currency offense. Noel took both to heart.

was only admitting the facts and saving the Lord Mayor useless trouble. There was nothing for it but to fine him £3,000.

He should have admitted the facts and pleaded Not Guilty, being as innocent as an unborn lamb. Of course the facts have to be established before that question arises, but when they are admitted or proved they leave the question of the innocence or guilt unsettled. There can be no guilt without intention. Arliss knew nothing about the Finance Clauses, and did not even know that he owned American securities. He was Not Guilty, and should have said so and thereby put his defence in order.

Therefore let nothing induce you to plead Guilty. If your lawyers advise you to do so, tell them that *I* advise you not to. You may know all this as well as I do; but after the Arliss case I think it safer to warn you.

GBS

Noël was quick to reply:

> 17 Gerald Road
> S.W.1.
> 28/10/41

Dear G.B.S.

I can't tell you how touched and grateful I am for your wise and kindly advice which I will most certainly follow.

I need hardly tell you I am completely innocent over the whole business and have done the best I could since the War began to work for the country. I intend to fight this tooth and claw and feel most enormously encouraged by your great kindness in writing to me.

I haven't seen you for many years and would so like to if you ever have the time.

With again, so very, very many thanks.

> Yours,
> Noël Coward

Noël did indeed take Shaw's advice. He was fined two hundred pounds and costs, a virtual victory, since the minimum fine was supposed to be five thousand.

When the whole thing was over he cabled Shaw:

> DEAR GBS THE RESULT OF MY HAVING FOLLOWED YOUR ADVICE
> IS ONLY TOO APPARENT STOP I AM ETERNALLY GRATEFUL TO
> YOU NOT ONLY FOR YOUR WISDOM BUT FOR THE DEEP KINDNESS
> THAT PROMPTED YOUR MOST OPPORTUNE AND VERY REAL HELP.

With the dust settling, Noël turned his attention to Jack Wilson, who, he felt, should have known and warned him about the situation, particularly since Noël had written to him on that very subject five months earlier. His failure to do so confirmed Noël's suspicion that Jack now had too many irons in the American fire for his (Noël's) comfort.

October 31st, 1941

I am now going to tick you off as you have never been ticked off before. I have just been through one of the most horrible and humiliating ordeals of my life with this finance case. It came at a moment when I, who always hates publicity, dreaded it most. The whole success and construction of my Naval film depends on the generous and magnificent support the Admiralty are giving me. This might at any moment have been withdrawn because they obviously cannot support a man who is dragged through the courts and who is prosecuted by the Crown for evasion of his financial responsibilities to the Government.

Yesterday in the police court it was considered by experts that on the facts I could be fined anything between £5,000 and £61,000. This, as you know, I could not possibly have paid and so should have had to go to prison. Fortunately my own personal integrity is unimpeachable, although my own personal idiocy in paying 5th rate accountants and allowing subordinates to let me down to the dust was only too apparent. I was fined £200 and £20 costs by the Magistrate thereby proving that English justice is not only based on legal facts but on moral ones as well. The Press, for once, have been kind and reported the whole case accurately with a slight bias in my favour. None of this justifies the fact that I was never told either by you or Hobbs or Dubois [Noël's accountants] or Lorn that since August 26th, 1939 it was illegal for me to spend one dollar of my American money. The fact that neither the Ministry of Information nor the British Ambassador told me either certainly mitigated in my favour but on the whole, although I left the court yesterday without a stain on my character, I feel sickeningly ashamed that such a horrible and undignified situation should ever have occurred. I had a brilliant counsel. I had my personal conviction that I was innocent. And I had a most heartening and charming letter from Bernard Shaw out of the blue the day before imploring me to plead Not Guilty. I am thankful to say I followed this advice.

Unfortunately, my troubles are not yet over, as I am being prosecuted by the Lord Mayor on the question of securities undeclared in time. In this instance I am personally equally innocent and the Government have not actually lost anything by my default and so I hope to be treated leniently but the fact remains that I have to appear in court at the Mansion House next Thursday and go through the whole business again with, presumably, a further fine. Whether the Lord Mayor views my case as generously and kindly as the Bow Street Magistrate did remains to be seen. [The local Bench of Magistrates fined him two thousand pounds.]

Now then, in future I am determined to know a great deal more about my business affairs, however much time it takes and however much it bores me. I still find it strange that after so many years of hard work I have so pitifully little money. I want a full and accurate statement of everything concerned with my finances since 1925.

I only wish to make one thing absolutely clear to you, that in future in no circumstances whatsoever must any of my financial affairs be even remotely suspect . . . I am bitterly ashamed that they ever have been, not only from the point of view of my position and reputation but from the point of view of my inside conscience. I would infinitely rather descend into my grave poverty stricken but honest (which seems extremely likely) than rich as Croesus and dishonest. This may sound noble and high-flown but it happens to be sincere. Now please think deeply and carefully over all that I have said. It is of vital importance to us all.

When he belatedly replied, Jack appeared to shrug off any suggestion that he personally was in any way to blame, which only sharpened Noël's sense of having been badly served.

A puzzling coda occurred years later. In a letter to Lornie (September 9, 1947), written from New York, Noël reports:

I had dinner with Little Bill and he very emphatically warned me not to go back to England without leaving myself a concrete reason for getting out again. Big Bill Donovan was also there and apparently has great pull with dear Dr. Dalton [at the time Chancellor of the Exchequer] and I think will do something about it for me. It really is very curious for an eminent and frightfully pretty Englishman to have to solicit help from an American in order to prevent himself being imprisoned in his own country! I shall come back in October whatever happens but really it is all a grave mess and in the worst possible taste and I am as cross as two sticks. Freedom, my arse, is what I say to myself over and over again.

Precisely who and what Stephenson feared for on Noël's behalf was never referred to again, but clearly neither he nor Donovan was the kind of man to jump at shadows. They had reason to believe that there were those in the United Kingdom with long memories and long knives probably connected to the currency restrictions that were still very much in force.

The whole episode convinced Noël of two things. The first was that, while he undoubtedly had powerful enemies in high places, he must also have equally powerful friends, unwilling to declare themselves publicly but pressing for leniency in what was obviously a "political" case. His main concern was that the publicity might have a negative effect on the film, which he had yet to start in earnest. For once his guardian angels were on duty for him. It did not.

The second was the unpleasant realization that he must keep a closer watch on Jack's financial management. It was the crystallization of a feeling that had been nagging him for some time now.

The third issue was a family matter. In August 1940, Noël had brought Violet and Auntie Vida over to New York to protect them from the bombing. It was not the easiest thing to achieve, as passages on transatlantic ships in wartime were almost impossible to obtain. He put them up initially in his own East Side apartment, then transferred them to an apartment of their own. Before long, Vida decided to return to face whatever Mr. Hitler decided to throw her way. She bought her own passage back. For her, a return was preferable to facing her sister day in, day out.

Violet Coward was not a happy woman and, as ever, her letters betrayed the fact. Left to her own devices—and despite round-the-clock attention from Noël's friends:

I joined the party at Sardi's. I was the guest of honour and they made a great fuss of me . . . Francis Lederer rushed across the room and hugged and kissed me and John [Latouche] pretended to be dreadfully jealous—all v. amusing. John kept saying he loved me for myself and not because of you!

. . . she still found much to complain about:

I have been reading your diary. It has told me so much of your life that I knew nothing of . . . but it depressed me to think of all you had done for the hopelessly muddled Government. You and I don't see eye to eye in some things. No one loves England more than I do, but if I were a man I should refuse to fight . . . I simply would not give my life up for such awful muddlers. I feel simply awful about it all. I hate this beastly war and all the emotional tomfoolery about fighting for your country, etc., etc. The Army fight because they are well paid, the Officers because it is a good profession with fairly good pay and the hope of pushing others down and getting to the top of power . . . I hate it, hate it all.

You, who have really given up so much for your country, they
shove you into Court and fine you for a mistake, when you lavished
all the money. Do you think for one moment any of those in high
places would have allowed you to get a foot in? However clever your
suggestions and superior your work, they were too afraid to let you
gain an inch . . . They don't want brains. They send fools out here
who get egg and tomatoes thrown at them. Oh, dear, what don't they
do that isn't idiotic, except from their own point of view? For God's
sake don't do any more in the way of politics, darling. Think and
look after yourself a little more . . . Oh dear, I don't know whether to
send all this or tear it up, anyhow you can do that. I feel so furious
sometimes, darling. I would love to put the lot of them up against
the wall and shoot them all. The censors will have something to read
if they open this!

I hope the film is going well, and that you may be allowed to have
the honour of impersonating a Capt. in the Navy. Please don't over-
work yourself at this film. You are not as strong as you pretend to be.

Goodnight, old dearest darling,

All love and hugs

Snig

I so long to see you again. My heart just aches for you.

Noël replied:

December 3rd, 1941

Darlingest,

I've just had a very long letter from you all about the first night and
how lovely it was and your gay carryings-on at Sardi's and the Bar-
berry Room.

Now then, Darling, I've got to speak very firmly to you. You don't
seem to realise why I have done what I have done since the War
began. The reason for me wishing to do all I can for my country has
nothing to do with governments. One of the privileges which we are
fighting for is to be able to grumble about our governments as much
as we like. Of course they have behaved very badly to me . . . they
behaved very badly to Winston Churchill for seven years . . . but that
is not the point. I am working for the country itself and the ordinary
people that belong to it. If you had been here during some of the bad
blitzes and seen what I have seen and if you had been with the Navy
as much as I have you would understand better what I mean. The reason that I didn't come back to America was that in this moment of
crisis I wanted to be here experiencing what all the people I know
and all the millions of people I *don't* know are experiencing. This is

because I happen to be English and Scots and I happen to believe and know that, if I ran away and refused to have anything to do with the War and lived comfortably in Hollywood, as so many of my actor friends have done, I should be ashamed to the end of my days. The qualities which have made me a success in life are entirely British. *Cavalcade, Bitter Sweet, Hay Fever,* everything I've ever written could never have been written by anybody but an Englishman.

Oddly enough, the people here are proud of me too. I have had thousands of letters, not only from friends but from strangers all over the country, sympathising with me over my case. The very fact that in the middle of the War there should have been headlines about it on the front page of every paper proves my fame in this country. Of course I have been very unhappy from time to time when people said beastly things about me and the Press attacked me but that is one of the penalties I must pay for having achieved the position I have. The English, in their own muddled way, considered that freedom of speech and thought and faith was something worth fighting for and dying for if necessary. I have never in my own personal struggles given way to superior force or to my enemies and I see no reason to start doing so now, either in my own cause or a National one. You must have been talking to a lot of very silly people if you imagine that the British fighting services are fighting for the pay they get. A sailor gets about fourteen shillings a week and a private in the Army seventeen and six . . . and a wife's allowance is twenty-six shillings a week. But for the gallantry and ideals of the fighting services there would *be* no England for you to come home to and no ship to bring you. I cannot feel that dying for one's country or for what one believes in is any worse than dying in bed of an illness. We all have to die sometime and if I had to die tomorrow at least I have had a magnificent run for my money. I should feel myself to be very unworthy of the traditions I come from if I allowed the malice and envy of a handful of journalists and pompous government officials to deflect me from my course for one instant. The Australian visit was one of the most thrilling, heartwarming, and exciting experiences of my life although it was hard work and whatever personal discouragements I may have had, not only since the War but during my whole life, have merely gone to enrich my talent.

Now then, the point of all this is that the only place in which you are entitled to grumble about England is *in* England itself and you must *NEVER,* while you are in America, speak against this country or even against the Government which is apparently doing its not very inspired best, because if you do you are letting me down very badly. I feel very ashamed of many of the people I know in America for their attitude over this War. It is their War as much as ours and they have allowed us to fight it for them for over two years. It was their muddles just as well as ours that brought it about and so please don't allow yourself, just because you are incensed by the way a few silly people have treated your ewe lamb, to forget that that same ewe lamb is very much loved in this country and by the great mass of the public and accepted and adopted as a distinguished friend by the whole of the Navy. This is no small achievement and if I didn't feel that in every way I was doing my best to help in what they are fighting for I would never forgive myself and would probably never write another good play in my life. You are very naughty indeed to have written those things and much naughtier to have thought them for a moment. I have inherited my fighting spirit from you, so it's all your fault anyway . . . in fact I wouldn't be surprised if you are not responsible for the whole War and it's only a matter of time before Hitler and his hordes join hands with Mrs. Tonge, Betty Hammond, Auntie Ida (at moments Auntie Vida) and other oppressed peoples to encircle you with an extremely nasty pincer movement!!

Now, having got that off my chest, the film is going along beautifully and I think it is the best thing I have written since *Cavalcade*. We don't actually start the shooting of it until 15th January but I really think it is going to be lovely. Of course, I'm thrilled about the success of *Blithe Spirit* and have read all the notices. It is still playing to wonderful business here. We are all well and everybody sends you their love. Give my dearest love to anybody who would care for it and tell them from me that England may be a very small island, vastly over-crowded, frequently badly managed but very much the best and bravest in the World.

Love and hugs to you, you wicked girl.

By the time Violet received the letter the Japanese had attacked Pearl Harbor and America was in the war.

450 East 52nd St.
January 21st 1942

I had decided not to answer your unkind letter, which made me ill. It was so unnecessary.

Lillian thought I was fretting to get home and I did not give you away. I could not have let her know that you had written me like that. The thing that hurt most was your saying that by discussing the war with my silly friends, I was letting you down badly. I have *never* discussed the war with anybody. But even if I did, I don't think what I said could hurt your prestige with the American public. I had been looking at your diary and felt miserable to think they should discuss your name in England after all you had done.

Next, you neglected me for months, because you had no time to write and then found time to type pages of a pompous lecture at me. How dared you! Hitler is not governing us yet and I have as much right to my opinions as you have even if you have spent so much time in the Navy . . . This letter will doubtless be torn to shreds like all my letters have always been by your immediate circle but I must keep up my reputation for being the "wicked old woman" you have always called me.

Please don't bother about my coming home. It is impossible anyhow and I don't much mind. I forgive you for making me so unhappy. It is passing and I shall soon get my spirits back and have no regrets. I can't always be miserable and shall probably survive all this beastly war and come back with a few more wrinkles and probably using a stick but as wicked as ever, I expect.

9 years ago today my Erik died. What a tragedy! I feel so very far away and so alone.

> Love
> SNIG

In a later letter (March 3):

Darlingest,

I had a lovely letter from you, written of course before you got my answer to your Dec. 3rd lecture letter! But I am taking it as being written after because I can't bear all this horror any longer and I have drawn down a shutter on the past. I am not going to think any more about my enemies or what anybody thinks about me. I can't be *all* bad and I have had a very rotten time but as in the nature of things I cannot have many years longer to live in this beastly world [she was seventy-eight]. I can't afford to throw away the only thing in it that is worth having and that is you and your love. So let's forget everything horrid from now on.

I have unpacked my boxes for the 3rd or 4th time and will try to be as happy as I can in luxurious New York until it is easier to get back. [She had tried several times to get a passage on a ship but had always been turned back in favor of passengers with genuine priorities.] I am trying not to bother about going home. After all, this war must end some day and if I am destined to end my career out here, well, that's that.

The river is so busy. Even destroyers and airplanes pass by, so big they block out the windows. There is a constant stream of traffic, day and night.

Write me soon, please. I shall write to you every week for the future.

Your Snig

In later letters she clearly felt it was time she paid more attention to Noël's life:

May 1st

I wrote you a grouchy letter yesterday and so I am writing again, as I fear it may have upset you . . .

I really think Vida is much happier living alone and is very fond of being boss! And she is very comfortable and contented. I like being alone, too! So the thing is for me to be contented here and patient. I really have lots to reassure me and time never hangs on my hands but your being in London is at the back of my mind all the time.

Cover of New York program for *Blithe Spirit*.

When I think of what you must have gone through when you got to Bermuda, my blood boils and my heart aches too for you, my poor old darling. I wonder and wonder how it came about, who did it and what are you doing about it. Of course it is impossible (for you) to write about it . . .

Meanwhile, Noël was pulling every string he could lay his hands on and finally managed to get her on an August plane home via Shannon. "I feel as bright as a button!" Violet wrote when she heard the news. "Or six buttons!"

•

THE WAR DID NOT entirely overshadow Noël's theatrical career. On November 4 Jack Wilson was to present the New York production of *Blithe Spirit* at the Morosco Theatre. Whom should they cast? Jack wrote:

> 10 Rockefeller Plaza
> New York
> June 9th
>
> Dearest Poppa,
> Alfred, of course, springs to mind . . . He called me up last night and they are crazy about the play, as I thought they would be, in fact even more so than I expected and Alfred was very tempted with the man's part. *She* felt, however, that the woman's part, whichever of the two she chose, was not good enough for her. I am not disappointed, as I never thought for a moment that they would do it.

Noël sent the following advice:

> As far as the New York company of *Blithe Spirit* goes I think Leonora [Corbett] will be fine. Gladys Cooper I am frightened of, because she is frightfully bad at learning words and it is a very long part needing the utmost precision. Clifton [Webb] I feel sure will be the best bet. He is a beautiful comedian and the slight hint of preciousness won't matter and I think he will give it distinction. I have a feeling Edna May Oliver will be superb as long as she does not overplay. I am sure that Edna Best would be good as Ruth but a little lacking in attack and I think on the whole, if you could bear it, Peggy [Wood] would be the best. We know what a good actress she is and she really has got drive. If I can't get over, you shall have a complete detailed script with every move marked and extra bits of business and cuts. I would

Noël and Clifton Webb (1893–1966).
A couple of song-and-dance men from
the 1920s who later turned "legit."
Webb played "Noël" in the Broadway
productions of both *Blithe Spirit* (1941)
and *Present Laughter* (1946).

rather you directed it than anybody else. I have implicit faith in your taste and discretion.

The final casting was Clifton Webb (Charles), Peggy Wood (Ruth), Leonora Corbett (Elvira), and Mildred Natwick (Madame Arcati). From the outset there were tantrums about billing and dressing rooms, which kept Jack, who was now to direct, in a perpetual spin. And since the show was a Transatlantic Production, he also had his two other partners, Alfred and Lynn, to contend with.

10.6.41

Lynn came the other afternoon for two acts and was very sweet. She was fullsome in her praise of me (which I presume, nay suspect, was politeness), was very pleased with Clifford [Clifton] indeed, and almost a little too keen about *la Bois* [Wood]. She made the suggestion that the scenes between those two should be of great tenderness and soul searching beauty and indicate a deep and resounding love. In other words, a little kiss in the first scene should be square on the lips, etc., etc. I am afraid I don't see that angle of playing it at all and must disregard her advice. She then went off the deep end about a very competent and ordinary actress playing Mrs. Bradman, called Phyllis Joyce, who she thought practically the new [Eleonora] Duse. She finds Natwick too frail, but when I tell you that her idea of perfect casting is either Ethel Barrymore or Sybil Thorndike, I think you can see what I mean when I said, as above, that Natwick from the balance angle will probably prove the best. She said it was a great role which should be played with greatness. I still maintain that, if it were, there wouldn't be any play and it would be Cornelia Otis Skinner doing *The Wives of Henry the Eighth.* The one she absolutely loathes and detests is the remaining member of the cast [Corbett]. She thought her inadequate, ugly, uninteresting, common, and can't imagine how you or I could have possibly thought her anything else under any conditions. She even went so far as to say that if we would have allowed her, she would have played the part herself, which I know darn well is not true, but when I told her so she countered by saying the only reason she had not was because you insulted her by offering her Ruth; she was very offended that you thought she was right for *that* part. All this, of course, is mere talk and doesn't mean a thing.

In time-honored theatrical tradition, of course, all differences were resolved and the play would run for 657 performances.

Some of Noël's New York friends could not resist a joke at his expense. Comedies about ghosts were not exactly new, and there had been at least two successful recent films on the subject, *Topper* (1937) and *Here Comes Mr. Jordan* (1941). In George S. Kaufman's view, Noël's play should be called *Topper Takes a Second Wife,* while Dorothy Parker's suggestion was *Here Comes Mrs. Jordan.*

·

NOËL'S CONTACT WITH Binkie Beaumont was kept very much alive. After all, even world wars end sometime, but The Theatre, laddie . . . Teasing the man who bestrode British theater was brief relief from more serious matters.

*Dearest Binkie, dearest Bink,*
*Lorn and I sincerely think*
*You have been for long enough*
*Both illiterate and rough*
*And in fact for many a year*
*Very very common, dear*
*So accept from this address*
*Hints on gentlemanliness*

*That which warns of Luftwaffe spleen*
*Is a* siren, *not sireen*
*Soldier's furlough, sweet but brief,*

*We call* leave *and never leaf*
*Use grammatical restraint*
*Is not* is correct . . . *not ain't*
*Words like* "nothing", *may we say,*
*End with G and not with K*
*Napkins,* in the smarter sets,
*Are not known as serviettes*
*Also, these are not tucked in*
*Neatly underneath the chin*
*May we add that* opposite
*Is pronounced to rhyme with* "bit".
*Should you belch at lunch or tea*
*Never* mutter "Pardon me".
*Mark these rules and, if you can,*
*Be a little gentleman.*

(WITH LOVE FROM MR. NOËL COWARD AND
MRS. LORN LORAINE) [NANCY MITFORD ANTICIPATED.]

•

NOËL WROTE TO JACK:

17 Gerald Road, S.W.1.
February 5th, 1942

Dearest Dab,

Here goes for one of our chatters. At long last we start shooting the picture today. I cannot possibly, in one letter, explain all the complications and obstructions that have been put in the way. Anyone would think I was trying to make a subversive propaganda film with the object of overthrowing the British Empire rather than a glowing tribute to the Navy. The Admiralty, of course, have been absolutely wonderful to me from the word go. I have been travelling all over the place to ships and shipyards and dockyards and Dicky has been fifty thousand rocks and so now all is well. It is scheduled for fifteen weeks and is costing one hundred and seventy thousand pounds . . . and so that is that.

Life here has been singularly bloody for the last few weeks. The Far East War news has, of course, depressed us abominably—added to which Jack Frost and Father Winter have joined their gnarled hands and frozen the sweet Jesus out of all of us. We have had weeks of snow which thaws and then freezes again and we fall down and break our legs and our faces are mauve and we cry and cry a great deal. Travelling about the country in these gala years is a fair picnic;

*In Which We Serve* (1942). A welcome break in shooting. Noël
relaxes on the Sussex Downs with co-director David Lean.

there are practically no restaurant cars and only a very scanty supply
of taxis, so if you could see your erstwhile luxurious and glamorous
Poppa footing it through the snow carrying his suitcases, you would
probably laugh hilariously. I have a meagre little "Drive yourself" car
which I hire by the week to get me to and fro between my cottage
and the studios and the days of Goldenhurst and Rolls-Royces seem
very far away indeed . . . but I am sure it is good for my soul. All I
can say is, it had *better* be!

But even with the tension of filming building up, he finds time to
update Jack on the doings of family and friends:

I dined [with friends] the other night and Cecil Beaton appeared and
we had a great rapprochement and are now staunch buddies. My
social life has been comparatively tranquil. I see, naturally, a great
deal of Dicky and Edwina [Mountbatten] . . . Sybil [Colefax] occasionally . . . and every now and then Juliet [Duff] peers down at me.
Cochran is trying frantically to raise money for another revue. Winnie [Winifred Ashton] is bounding about giving lectures and broadcasts, writing Welsh pageants, cooking meals, and knocking
ornaments over. Gladys [Calthrop] is very crisp and efficient and horribly worried inside because Hugo [her only son] is in Singapore.
Joyce [Carey] works daily at the Naval War Library and orders a lot

Four "Mädchen in Uniform": Ann Todd, Joyce Carey,
Peggy Ashcroft, and Celia Johnson.

of very refined old ladies about. Lorn is looking radiant as a Summer day and has given up wearing a hat for all time except on those occasions when she has to appear either with me, for me, or on account of me in the Police Court . . . Johnnie Mills has had a baby daughter [Juliet] to which I am Godfather. Arthur Macrae is in the R.A.F. and has got rather fat.

And now my great news. Ivor is coming back to London in *Dancing Years* and opens (and probably closes) at the Adelphi in March. As I cannot top that terrific *bon bouche,* I will now close . . . but I do want to know all that is happening to you, what your plans are, how Natasha is, how Fairfield is, how Leonora [Corbett] received my wistful little letter, how dear Clifton [Webb] is behaving, if Peggy [Wood] is as noisy as ever and how the Lunts are.

Love, love, love, love, love
POPPA

P.S. Lorn particularly requests that if you should happen to be an air-raid warden, will you please be photographed immediately and send us one, because a picture of that round beguiling face surmounted by a tin hat would cheer us up no end. We miss you terribly, terribly and quote your wickeder jokes from the past over and over again and oh dear, oh dear, when in all this Goddam chaos shall we all be together again?

Work on the film began in earnest. Noël and Gladys moved into twin cottages at Denham to be near the studio, and shortly after there was an omen of sorts. The Navy wrote to say:

January 23rd

Of course we can commission H.M.S. *Denham* for which draft there will be no lack of volunteers. We will get a representative destroyer ship's company together, with a beard or two if possible, and give all the assistance we can to the making of the film.

For the ship to have the same name as the studio in which the film was to be shot seemed an encouraging sign.

With filming now under way, Noël could report to Violet:

March 16th

Really the way they have constructed the destroyer is wonderful. It is life size and accurate in every detail, though it's made chiefly of wood and plaster. The Navy is delighted and the Commander-in-Chief at Portsmouth has lent us crowds of real sailors when I need them for the big scenes. The War Office has also let me have 300 Coldstream Guards for the Dunkirk part . . . It's tremendously hard work but I am enjoying it. We had to spend eight days in an enormous tank

In which we wait to serve. Actor Bernard Miles chats with the Duke and Duchess of Kent over a nice cup of tea.

filled with filthy fuel oil and, mercifully, warm water. You've never seen such sights as we looked. Before starting a scene we had to rub this black filth into our hair and ears and all over, then put on sopping clothes and flop in! The Kents [Duke and Duchess of Kent] came during that week and thoroughly enjoyed the spectacle. On the screen, of course, the effect is marvelous—it really looks like the open sea. Happily we are at last clean again, even our finger nails have returned to normal!

There were lighter moments in darkest Denham. Gladys was given leave from her wartime assignment in the MTC (Mechanized Transport Corps) to assist Noël by designing the film's sets and clothes. In peacetime she was notorious for her somewhat multicolored personal apparel. This she had now had to exchange for an unrelieved khaki, causing Noël to write her another of his verse letters. (For some time her nickname had been "Blackheart," commonly reduced to "Blackie.")

> *Where are the bright silk plaids of happier years*
> *And all those prawns that used to deck your ears?*
> *Where, in the mists of yesterday, oh where*
> *Is that small watch that formed a* boutonnière?
> *Where is the twist of Méchlin lace you had*
> *And called a hat before the world went mad?*
> *Where's the harpoon that fastened up your coat,*
> *Where those gay* mouchoirs d'Apache *for your throat?*
> *All, all are gone. The leopard skin, the sheath*
> *Of striped percale. But perhaps beneath*
> *Your blue and khaki, so austere and cold,*
> *My Blackheart is my Blackheart as of old,*
> *With shoulder-straps of shagreen and maybe*
> *A brassière of lapis lazuli.*

In the Coward "family" you had to get used to this kind of affectionate teasing. Sadly there was a lot less to laugh about when later in the year Gladys received news that her son, Hugo, had been killed.

·

TO VIOLET:

Denham
April 9th

Everything continues to go with a swing. Yesterday was a highly exciting day because the King and Queen and the two Princesses came and spent three hours. I received them at the main entrance with Dickie and Edwina and Gladys. We took them onto the set first—there were two hundred sailors in the dock of the ship and they all came to attention. The King took the salute and it was really very moving. It was charming of him to come in Naval uniform. I did the "Dunkirk" speech with the ship rolling and the wind blowing and a good time was had by all. After that I took them all over the ship . . . I presented most of the staff and the cast. The Royalties were really enchanting to everyone, very gay and interested and informal. After that we took them through the workshops, then to the projection room to see some of the scenes we'd already done. They seemed very impressed and couldn't have been more enthusiastic. We all had a gala tea and I sat between them both and had a long talk about a lot of things. Their effect on the studio was electric . . . Altogether it was a great success.

A progress report also went to Lynn and Alfred:

17 Gerald Road<br>S.W.1<br>30th July, 1942

Darling, darling, darling,
Jack will have told you that the film is finished except for cutting and dubbing. I really do think it's pretty good and oh how I am longing for you to see it. It's a fair old tear jerker and I hope you cry satisfactorily.

I enjoyed doing the Film in a way but it's a soul destroying business from the acting point of view. One of the good things that has emerged from it is my determination never again to sell a play of mine to the movies unless I have complete control. In order to ensure this I have formed my own permanent unit consisting of Ronald Neame, (the best camera man in the business) and David Lean, who is the only first rate cutter and director over here. They are both young and enthusiastic, expert and perfectly charming—you really will love them when you eventually meet them. David's wife [Kay Walsh], incidentally, plays the girl in my Film and is perfectly wonderful. They are making, under my supervision, a film of *This Happy Breed* while I am playing it on tour. After that I intend to do *Blithe Spirit,* probably myself, in technicolour. With this arrangement no play or story of mine can be done without my control. If, for instance, another company wishes to buy a script that we shall not have time to do ourselves, the casting and direction and choice of camera man, cutter, etc., will be controlled by my unit and so never again, I hope, shall I see bloody massacres like *Bitter Sweet, Design for Living,* etc.,

etc. It really won't entail so very much extra work for me and, although I shall not get vast Hollywood prices, I shall at least ensure that my prestige as an author will not be lowered in the eyes of millions of people by the grubby minds of a bunch of Hollywood cheap skates. I am sure you will approve of all this.

I still move dimly about in the political shadows in so far as I know pretty well what is going on. I spent an enchanting weekend with the Edens. He is in fine form although obviously working terrifically hard.

Jack will have also told that I am going off for a six months tour of the provinces. I'm madly excited about this, for to get back to the theatre again after the God damned Film industry is sheer heaven. Apart from the three plays I have to do two munitions concerts a week and various inspiring speeches, so I shall be hard at it . . . I am now going away for two weeks holiday to Wales to learn my parts and relax. What wouldn't I give for just a few days with you and Grandpa? I really do miss you so dreadfully. I suppose this bloody war will end sometime so that we can all be together again even if we're in bathchairs.

. . . Oh dear, oh dear, there's so much I want to tell you that I couldn't possibly put in a letter. I think of you such a lot and it would be lovely once more to put my little triplicate photograph frame on a stage dressing table instead of a movie one.

Love, love, love, love, love, love,<br>
NOELIE

And Gertie was anxious to tell him that the word of mouth was out in America even before the film opened in England:

American Theatre Wing<br>
War Service Inc.<br>
Gertrude Lawrence Branch<br>
Dennis, Massachusetts<br>
September 14th 1942

Dearest old Dearest,
The news of the "Coward Picture" has spread far and wide, with also many stills in *Life* mag., so naturally America is all agog and getting ready to redeem its War Bonds to buy tickets.

All my love<br>
GERT

Noël wrote a detailed account of the filming in *Future Indefinite*. All that needs to be said here is that the film was about what it is like to fight a war and what it is like to be the loved ones at home, waiting and worrying.

We see the HMS *Torrin* (aka the *Kelly*) built and fitted, taking her sea trials and then going into combat. We get to know members of her crew, and when the ship is sunk off Crete and the survivors cling to the Carley raft waiting to be picked up, we see—in a series of lengthy flashbacks—something of their private lives.

Despite his assurances to Mountbatten that this was not intended to be Mountbatten's own personal story, the fact remains that in the film, Noël as Captain D wears Mountbatten's naval cap and uses his friend's address to the men almost verbatim.

*In Which We Serve* had its premiere on September 17, 1942, and was an immediate and enormous critical success.

Edwina Mountbatten wrote:

> 15 Chester Street
> Belgrave Square
> S.W.1.

Darling Noël,

I have just had a letter from the Queen in which she says—"I hear that Noël Coward's film is superb, for he so utterly understands and loves our wonderful people." I so agree with her, but I think you know just what Dickie and I feel about the picture and how much we rejoice in your own happiness in what you have succeeded in doing for so many millions of people.

> With very much love.
> Edwina

A relieved Lord Mountbatten wrote:

> Combined Operations Headquarters
> 1A Richmond Terrace
> Whitehall S.W.1.
> 24th October, 1942

Dear Noël,

The King and Queen kept their promise and ran "In Which We Serve" at the official dinner for Mrs. Roosevelt. The party included the Prime Minister (who had seen it before and said he liked it better the second time than the first), Field Marshal Smuts [South Africa], the American Ambassador, etc. All were genuinely thrilled with it.

I liked it as much the third time as the first.

Two days later Churchill wrote to Mountbatten:

> October 26, 1942
> PRIVATE
>
> I thought Noël Coward's film *In Which We Serve* was rather more mixed than when I saw it the first time. It is conceived in the spirit of a dream passing before a man in the early stages of drowning, but in some respects the chronology is disturbed. There should be a few captions to say whether it was Crete or the North Sea where they were fighting. The two operations are so mixed up now that most people would find it difficult to follow them separately. There was at first a caption saying "Crete 1941", but this seems to have been dropped out of the later edition.
>
> As you took an interest in the film, perhaps it would be well for you to have a talk with the author on the subject.
>
> WC
> 26/X

Later Mountbatten wrote to Noël to explain and excuse Churchill's reaction. He had had to leave the room at a crucial point in the story to take a phone call about the desert war in Libya and had been understandably distracted from the film.

The king apparently "told off" the prime minister about getting muddled the second time he saw the film.

Then there was the matter of the "phantom honor." Noël appears to have been "sounded out" to see if he would accept a knighthood, should it be offered—that being the normal procedure. It was believed that His Majesty had expressed a personal interest in the matter. Although irked by the knighthood that had recently been conferred on Alexander Korda, which, Noël felt, cheapened the honor, he indicated that he would be proud to accept. But even as he did so, wheels were turning within wheels.

At the end of the year Churchill wrote to the king:

> 29 December 1942
>
> Since our conversation at luncheon today, I have examined, in consultation with the Chancellor of the Exchequer, the details of the case brought against Mr. Noël Coward. The Chancellor and Sir Richard Hopkins contend that it was one of substance and that the conferment of a Knighthood upon Mr. Coward so soon afterwards would give rise to unfavourable comment.
>
> With considerable personal reluctance I have therefore come to the conclusion that I could not advise Your Majesty to proceed with this proposal on the present occasion.
>
> > With my humble duty, I remain
> > Your Majesty's faithful subject and servant
> > WINSTON S. CHURCHILL

Meanwhile, the accolades poured in. In the Coward Archive they fill their own folder, but the following will give a sense of the emotional impact the film imparted to a whole range of people.

Douglas Fairbanks, Jr., at that time serving in the U.S. Navy himself:

> H.M.S. *Tormentor*
> September 28th
>
> Dear Noël,
>
> I tried to send a telegram last night and say all I wanted about the film but I found I had, as they say, no time in which to write a short message. I have to put it in a letter.
>
> I am back again on duty after taking the train immediately after the movie. I managed a few hours leave to come up to Town to see it. I had just come in from the sea, so I was in the right mood for the film's subject matter.
>
> It's difficult adequately to sum up my feelings about *In Which We Serve* because I am still too moved by it to offer you a detached and comprehensive report. But as I am off to "work" in a few minutes and the opportunities for writing will be scarce, I'll attempt it. I *have* to attempt it.
>
> In the first place, the film as a theatrical presentation was with-

out a flaw. I've been "born into" my job and have been working at it
for 19 years. I think I know something about it. Your picture from
beginning to end was *superb*! The writing was masterly. I will not
say that this was to be expected, as it *wasn't*. Writing for film, as
you no doubt have learned, is a very different technique from play
writing. Your construction, dialogue, dramatic inflections and
punctuation showed a thorough knowledge of what was meant
when the words "Motion Pictures" were coined. It is a *great motion
picture* from beginning to end. The direction, the editing, the acting
(*everyone*), the score made it a production of great quality. You are a
great and valuable addition to a medium which, despite its vagaries,
I dearly love and all of us, belonging primarily to films, are enriched
by having such a giant join our ranks. Especially valuable is the
contribution to the British Film Industry which your picture makes
and to the encouraging growth of Actor-Producer in movies. As a
professional I was thrilled and as a part of the audience I was moved
as I have not been moved in *any* theatre since the war began. I shall
hope to see it several times more—and enjoy a thorough emotional
massage.

I want to hear Celia Johnson's toast again—Capt. "D's" farewell
to his men—Joyce Carey before the blitz—Johnny Mills' remark
on Chamberlain's declaration of war—the look on the lad's face
[Richard Attenborough, in his film debut] as he left his post of
duty—the two lovers walking around the horse-dung in the road—
Bernard Miles all the time—the day on the downs with the dog-fight
overhead—oh, so many things . . .

As someone in the Navy, I was thrilled. Every minute of the film
was so honest that it hurt. Having served on destroyers myself I
know how honest it all was. Every sailor, regardless of nationality,
can recognise himself and his shipmates. Even though I do not
belong to the Royal Navy, I felt a chill of pride in the service itself
and linked myself in with the camaraderie of the sea. I experienced a
new, strange sort of "service" patriotism—a gladness that we are all
fighting together for the same kind of people in the same kind of
world. You have made me proud of the fleet in which I, too, in a
small way, serve.

Your profession and, most of all, your country owe you a profusion
of thanks. May I, as a friend, also offer mine?

> Yours,
> Doug

Other older friends were quick to respond. Lynn wrote:

> Martin Beck Theatre
> West 45th Street
> New York City
> December 8th, 1942

Darling, darling, darling—

We have seen the picture—that is, a few days ago—and I have been trying to arrange in my mind the best way that I can thank you and tell you about it. The effect it had on me was tremendous and I imagine it will have that same effect on everyone else. I feel not as if I had seen a picture, but as if I had gone through a great, terrifying and wonderful experience and it has left me very changed and set apart and with a deeper longing than ever to come to England, which I feel as if I must never do unless I come during the war. Both Alfred and I feel that we will never be able to look any of you in the eye unless we do that.

The script of *In Which We Serve* is itself a classic and will, I am sure, be kept in the British archives forever and ever. The acting never for once smacks of the theatre. With my acute ear, I did not once hear anybody giving a reading or a theatre-wise intonation. Another brilliantly wise thing that you did was the discretion of your own part. There were a great many other parts better than yours and yet, because of that, the simplicity and nobility of that man became more high-lighted. I forgot entirely that it was you and really can't remember what you looked like, except for one heavenly shot which I would like to have sculptured.

Joyce [Carey] was superb. Johnny Mills' performance a dream of beauty. I mention these because I know them, but it is the picture as a whole, the truth of it, the translating of that truth to the screen that only a very great artist could have done.—throwing every well-known trick overboard and using only the best tricks of all, simplicity and truth.

I thought Johnny Mills' sweetheart turned in a beautiful performance. But you don't think of it as a play of performances. You think of it as something that has happened that you know intimately about and that everyone in the cast is a friend of yours. There is no doubt that it will be a sensational success here and it will be the best ambassador that England has ever had. What are they going to do for you now? Such an achievement should have great recognition.

I wish you could be sent here on some mission so that we could see you for a minute, darling.

**XXXLYNN**

P.S. Alec had breakfast with us this morning. He is pretty well considering all he has gone through. [Woollcott was now suffering from a serious heart condition.] You know he is going to do a broadcast [on his show *The Town Crier*] about your picture?

Woollcott himself wrote:

New York City
November 12th 1942

Dear Noël,
There isn't a particle of you that I know, remember, or want. But my hat is off to you after seeing *In Which We Serve*. I've seen three or four good movies in my time. This is one of them. I saw it the other night in an airless projection room along with the oddest assembly of people. As we got into the elevator we found it was occupied by an elderly gentleman to whom I immediately knelt. Not to be outdone he knelt too. Grace [Eustis] was puzzled until I introduced him. "This," I said, "is Mr. Somerset Maugham." Howard Dietz sat in front of me. In the middle distance was Ben Hecht and I thought afterwards how paltry he must have considered the little puddle of water *he* had thrown you into [in *The Scoundrel*].

My dear Noël, this job you have done seems to me a really perfect thing. There was no moment of it from which I drew back or dissented. I went away marveling at its sure-footedness and realizing that all the ups and downs of your life (in particular the downs) had taught you to be unerring for your great occasion. All your years were a kind of preparation for this. If you had done nothing else and were never again to do anything else they would have been well spent.

Of course I have thought of all these things afterwards. At the time I just sat and cried quietly. For, after all, this picture is of courage all compact and courage is the only thing that brings the honorable moisture to these eyes.

Work as good as this, even if it were not work to such good purpose, always has commanded me. I have got in touch with the United Artists people and volunteered to go on some national broadcast program and do a spot of drum-beating for the picture just before it is released, the fee to go to the British War Relief.

Neysa McMein expressed what many of the other Algonks undoubtedly felt but, for once, didn't know how to express without having their *sang-froid* melt:

In that country that is paved with good intentions my seat is in the bag because for months I've been planning to look up some brand new adjectives and then try and tell you how I felt about *In Which We Serve.* Having been six times, each time I marvel at the beauty of your words, and the glory of your making your idea come true.

Incidentally, I behave the same way at each showing. I start out brave as all Hell, but I always end up the same way, looking a fright and too broken up to even notice the contemptuous glances given me by the tougher customers.

Basil Rathbone wrote on behalf of the "Hollywood Brits":

December 18, 1942

Dear Noël,

A Special Committee of our United Nations saw your *In Which We Serve* last night. I find myself in the hopeless position of being unable to adequately express myself about your picture which moved me more deeply than anything on celluloid has ever done before—dear Noël, it seems to me you have made a picture that must rank with the few that have the right to be handed down to posterity. As a Britisher I felt so grateful to you, but so helpless at this time. In Peace we must be true to those who lived and died so magnificently to give us another chance. I am not too well informed on all the technicalities on the making of moving pictures but I did see things I liked tremendously. Your economy of emotion, of course, and your superb dialogue—some most expert cutting, so that the story carried one along breathless. I cannot wait to see it again and I hope again and again. A magnificent human document.

It's not been easy being stuck out here at the moment of one's Country's greatest hour in her history—one's applications to return were turned down (twice) but perhaps some helpful work has been contributed in clothes and money and good will. For instance, I am going to the Los Angeles shipyards at 4 a.m. on Friday to talk to "The Graveyard Shift"!

[Ronald] Colman and [Nigel] Bruce and I went on the War Bonds Drive Tour—speaking 3 or 4 times a day all over the country and I believe one has been able, here, to favorably serve British interests. But seeing your picture makes one feel a poor thing in the face of all the real greatness and sacrifice of those at home. How are we to make Peace and the keeping of the Peace emotional? How are we to make important, for 100 years at least, what men and women and children are living and dying for today?

Dear Noël—you have such great talents do keep us *well stirred up* for as long as you live.

God bless you for *In Which We Serve* and thanks a thousand times for giving the first night receipts to British War Relief as our contribution to the United Nations Drive.

> Yours ever,
> BASIL

Fritzi Massary, Noël's *Operette* star, was also now in Hollywood:

Oh darling Noël, what a Man you are! I was sure nothing could surprise me any more—but then I went to see your picture, and there I could not close my mouth. You must know I saw you for the first time as an actor. What wonderful, wonderful work have you done. Your country can and must be proud of you.

I have many reasons to wish that the war will be over soon—one of them is that I am longing to put my arms around you again, and whisper into your ear: I admire you, and how proud am I to have you for a friend.

My life is not very colorful but I am satisfied and I know how lucky I am because I have no one in the Third Reich, no one in the war and am able to help, in a modest way, according to my possibilities. The only thing which hurts me is to be excluded from defense work for the reason of having been born in the gay city of Vienna. Give my love to your mother and to all the friends who remember me, and if it is not asking too much, have someone of your "staff" drop me a line about yourself.

> A tender embrace
> From your
> FRITZI

Binkie Beaumont also saw his old friend in a new light:

> H.M. TENNENT LTD.
> Globe Theatre
> Shaftesbury Avenue
> London W.1.
> Wednesday

My dear Noël,

I did not write to you on Monday because I went to see the film again that night and was more moved, if possible, than on Sunday. How proud you must be of such a great achievement. If your career had been in Pictures all your life, surely it would have been amazing, but having only done *The Scoundrel* as an actor, there are no words.

My first reaction was that I had seen a perfect Film, and it was only after that I realized about the direction, writing and score. The latter is so subtle—but so important . . . And then I realized how magnificent the acting was—you particularly—and the whole cast are characters and one thinks of them as "Capt. D" and "Shorty" and not actors—in fact, it is awfully hard to realize it's you, Joyce and Johnny Mills.

It's so hard to say what one likes best as the whole is perfect—a kind of magnificently gigantic News Reel—I shall never believe the week-end I spent with you at Denham watching Shots had anything to do with the Film, because I really believe that I have been to sea and lived with *The Torrin*.

How wonderfully you play the Dunkirk sequence, the whole of the farewell, the two cautions, the commissioning speech, the picnic scene and all the scenes of the Float . . . in fact, the whole thing.

Joyce has never been so good, but then nor has Celia, Johnny, Bernard Miles or any of them.

The bomb falling, the pregnant K. Walsh scenes, the cheering of the Ship, the shot of Richard Attenborough walking down the dock, the water bubbles dissolving from the Float, the empty screen after the bomb has fallen, the sound effects, Shorty breaking the news to Walter, the Chamberlain sequence, the Hardys at the Music Hall—in fact I can go on at great length and shall when I come to Bristol.

I fear this has turned out to be just another "Fan" letter and one of the thousands you will receive. "Oh, dear Mr. Coward. You are as clever as paint and far prettier than Evelyn Laye." Fancy doing three Plays and the Film Gala all in one week!

May I, at the same time, tell you how deeply I appreciate our lovely association—it makes me very proud, and at the same time stimulated to work with you—this all sounds very pompous but I hope and trust that you know what I really mean.

  Love,
  BINKIE.

Director Carol Reed (who might so easily have been the director of choice):

Never have I been more moved or excited by any Picture—No acting in Films has ever been better . . . I have just left Alex Korda who thought it perfect—we both said we hoped you were pleased enough to come back and do more of them—and then we were silent for a while—we got awfully depressed and drank to our own future.

Darling,
I couldn't speak properly when I saw you but I think you know what I felt about your great achievement.
All love, IVOR

It breathes goodness—the real deep goodness that is in England.
SYBIL THORNDIKE

When it was over, I found myself saying with wobbling lips and tearful eyes—"Isn't it wonderful?"
DAME MAY WHITTY

From his new post at the Foreign Office, Noël's old friend Anthony Eden wrote:

October 20th
Foreign Office
S.W.1.

My dear Noël,
I have just seen the film and write to thank you for it. I was moved, proud and ashamed—Proud of the Royal Navy, ashamed to be sitting at a desk myself, moved because I d——d well couldn't help being—
    You have created many and varied works of art. You have never done anything so big as this, so restrained, unselfish and inspired— No other living man could have done it.
    Thank you, Noël,
Yours ever,
ANTHONY

But there were a handful of letters that must have given Noël particular satisfaction. When del Giudice and Havelock-Allan had first approached him, the third man had been Charles Thorpe of Columbia Pictures. He soon pulled out and, since del Guidice talked a better game than he could afford to play, the film's funding soon became a critical issue and one that nearly involved calling it off in mid-production. It took a lot of persuasion on the part of a lot of influential people in the British film industry to piece together the necessary funding, and one of the key persuaders was producer Alexander Korda:

Claridges
Brook Street W.1.
20th October 1942

My dear Noël,
I have just received this cable from America sent by the Vice President and Foreign Manager of United Artists. I thought it would amuse you as, in spite of the perfectly idiotic expression, the fact still remains that they like your picture.

Yours ever,
ALEX

16TH OCTOBER 1942
ALEXANDER KORDA HOTEL CLARIDGE LONDON

WHEN YOU FORCED US TO INVEST ONE HUNDRED THOUSAND
POUNDS IN A MOTION PICTURE I THOUGHT WE HAD ALL
GONE CRAZY BUT . . . QUOTE IN WHICH WE SERVE UNQUOTE
IS POSITIVELY SENSATIONAL . . . A MRS. MINIVER ON A
BATTLESHIP CONGRATULATIONS AND THANKS
ARTHUR KELLY

Perhaps the most satisfying volte-face came from the Ministry of Information that had caused him so much trouble from the very start of the war:

MINISTRY OF INFORMATION
MALET STREET W.C.1.
9th October 1942

My dear Noël,
I hope you will consider very carefully my suggestion that you should make a film about the Army. I have never seen a really good film about the Army and I am sure you could make one which would be as rousing a success as *In Which We Serve.* I know you are very busy but perhaps you will have time to think about this suggestion early next year. I should be only too glad to write to Sir James Grigg and ask him to give you all possible facilities.

BRENDAN BRACKEN

Brendan Bracken did have his wish—but not in the way he had envisaged. In early 1943 David Niven—whom Noël had met in Hollywood back in 1938 and who was now serving in the army—is writing to him:

Eechfield
Holmwood Ridge
Langton Green
Tunbridge Wells
January 14th

Now, Chum, you have in a very real sense altered the whole course of my military career. It happened yesterday. I was sent for by the Adjutant General himself, who said—"Now, look here, Niven. I understand you know a certain amount about motion pictures and I believe you are also an adequate officer.

"Noël Coward has done a magnificent thing for the Navy with *his* film, and it is absolutely essential that there should be a film of the same importance and scope made about the Army. Now the Army is not a popular service like the Navy, nor has it had a lot of success like the Navy, nor, above all, are you Noël Coward, but at least you know the sort of people who could get this sort of film written and produced and I want you to have a go at getting this thing started"!!

I have got this far. I have signed myself up and also I have got Two Cities to say they'll make it. Carol Reed has a fair story which might do (with a lot of work).

I know you have already refused to have anything to do with an Army film. And I also know that, beside risking gilding the lily after *In Which We Serve,* you have no love of the Army as you have of the Navy. But I'm going to ask you just the same! Is there any chance of getting you interested even to the extent of keeping an eye on things behind the scenes in exchange for wads of notes from Twin Cities Film Corp?

The film was *The Way Ahead,* released in 1944. It was well received by critics and public alike, though it lacked the impact of *In Which We Serve.* There was a nice irony in that it was Reed who had first suggested to Noël that he use David Lean.

He was amused to hear from Niven that the team suffered a complete replay of the bureaucratic angst that had plagued his own film.

•

THERE WERE TO BE two bizarre postscripts to *In Which We Serve.* British prime minister Harold Wilson once famously said that "a week in politics is a long time." In international politics it can seem a little longer, but on September 23, 1943, producer Anthony Havelock-Allan is cabling Noël in Cairo from the Denham Studios, where he was now working on *This Happy Breed.* Once again the problem was the dreaded Ministry of Information:

MINISTRY OF INFORMATION WANT PERMISSION TO REMOVE
DEROGATORY REFERENCES TO THE ITALIANS IN COPIES OF IN
WHICH WE SERVE FOR EUROPEAN SHOWING THIS IN VIEW OF
SITUATION IN ITALY STOP LORN SUGGESTED THIS CABLE FOR
INSTRUCTIONS STOP WHEN APPROXIMATELY WILL YOU BE BACK
STOP

LOVE FROM US ALL.

The "situation in Italy" was that Italy had now surrendered.

And a bizarre 1944 footnote from a Paris-based friend:

At the risk of disquieting you, I must report on an item which, however much I avert my eyes, overcomes me with a slight nausea whenever I pass a certain cinema on the Champs Elysées. There would
appear to be, according to the hand-painted placard, a film entitled
*Ceux Qui Servent Sur Les Mers,* which is *"doublée en francais"* and which
features N.C. The peculiar, and to me, arresting part of this advertisement is that the portrait purporting to represent the gallant naval
officer with rakishly tilted cap, is quite clearly and without equivoca-
tion the spitting image of M. Sessue Hayakawa [a famous Japanese
film star] whom I recall from my childhood days having participated
in a great naval film called *The Battle.* I feel that this must all be very
confusing to your Parisian admirers—for whether it is N.C. trying to
look like S.H. or vice versa, I'm damned if I know—and anyway,
aren't we at war with these people?

# CHAPTER 20
# WORLD WAR II: "I TRAVEL ALONE"

## (1943–1945)

*I travel alone,*
*Sometimes I'm East,*
*Sometimes I'm West . . .*

**"I TRAVEL ALONE"**

"I travel alone," Noël liked to sing. Well, not
always entirely alone. Noël (with unidentified
friend) apparently heading South of the Border.

THE TWO COWARD PLAYS that had been in rehearsal when war was declared, *Present Laughter* and *This Happy Breed,* finally made their debut in a twenty-eight-week provincial tour under the title of *Play Parade.* Since he intended to star, Noël also threw in *Blithe Spirit* for good measure.

With him on the often wet and windy road were Joyce Carey and Judy Campbell ("a great find").

In addition to the eight performances a week, I have done concerts everywhere [he wrote to Jack], hospitals, camps, aerodromes and munition factories. I also make a security speech telling people to keep their traps shut at the end of each performance. This is at the behest of the Naval Intelligence Dept.

[Noël looked forward] to the happy, happy day when the silver lining will show through, the clouds will bugger off, the light of Victory will illuminate our ageing faces, the Slough of Despond will be left behind, peace will reign again in this tortured World . . . except for whole hearted industrial, economic and moral revolution and perpetual bickering between the victorious united nations.

The tour continued through the winter and well into the new year of 1943.

David Niven voiced one of the few issues that troubled a number of people in *This Happy Breed:*

Please give some thought to switching the P.O.W. [Prince of Wales] scene to George V, if it is anything like possible. I think people are still rather embarrassed by the Abdication but the death of the old man was the passing of something very great.

His plea fell on deaf Coward ears. The scene was his personal form of purging.

As for *Present Laughter,* Niven went on to suggest:

In the last scene when he [Garry Essendine] is cornered by the husband (Henry) and is asked point blank "Have you or have you not had an affair with Joanna?" he answers, "Yes, I have."

Now I had a distinct feeling that the audience were hoping he never would be forced to say that and hoped he would say anything but "Yes." I feel certain that, at that moment, although the husband is obviously a jerk, a great flood of sympathy goes out to him, and I

*This Happy Breed* was
one of the three plays Noël
took on tour in 1943. A
domestic moment between
Ethel (Judy Campbell)
and Frank Gibbons (Noël).

was rather sorry, because Essendine could so easily have glossed over
the question, as he had sailed through so many embarrassing
moments already and one likes him so much that one does not like to
see him stand in front of a man, whose only crimes are dullness and
the breath of a rather sordid affair in the background, and tell him he
has poked his wife.

The husband was so obviously upset when he couldn't find Joanna
on his return from Paris that the audience conclude he is very much
in love with her, and do not like to hear Essendine say those hurting
words—"Yes, I did."

Couldn't you say something really bogus instead, or couldn't there
be some diversion, so that he needn't answer at all? . . . Please don't
let him lose any sympathy even for a moment.+

The line remained in the play.
Noël wrote to Lynn:

17 Gerald Road
S.W.1.
1st February 1943

I am enjoying my tour enormously. It's so very rewarding playing in
unget-at-able places to packed jammed audiences who look upon it as
a terrific event. I am giving very good conscientious performances
and if ever I do any naughtiness, however infinitesimal, on the stage I
fly to my dressing room look balefully at our triple photographs and
say, "Lynnie, we are not amused". The troop concerts are great fun,
though rather arduous. I drove from Aberdeen to Inverness through a
blizzard in an open Army truck giving two concerts on the way and

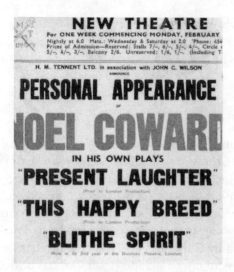

thrived on it. Practically the entire company broke down after Carlisle, so we had a week out after playing in a sea of understudies and now everybody is back again . . .

. . . Joyce is with me on tour giving excellent performances. Lorn is as pretty as a picture and typing this letter. Mother and Auntie Veitch are full of vitality and as wicked as ever. Sybil [Colefax] continues to give a series of frightening dinner parties and hasn't been known to finish a sentence since September 1939.

Oh dear, oh dear, there is so much I want to tell you and I would like to go on with this letter for hours but I must get my dear little bottom into a train and go to Northampton where I play in a theatre which is next to a boot factory, which will be a fair bugger on matinée days. I finish the tour mid April and then do a six weeks season in London with *Happy Breed* and *Present Laughter,* after which I have no definite plans.

All my love, darlings and please, please write again.
NOELIE

His letter crossed with one from Lynn that put in place the last piece in a sad puzzle. In his November letter Alec Woollcott had added a typically wry postscript:

I do not know whether you are aware that during the greater part of the time since last we met I have been on a bed of pain. For some time in the spring I was at death's door but the old fool was out. Now I am up again and, after a fashion, about. I tell you these details in case you are torn with anxiety.

Now Lynn would write:

> Martin Beck Theatre
> W. 45th St.
> New York—
> January 30th 1943

Darling,

First of all, of course, we are stunned by Alec's walking out on us like that, in spite of the warning signs. After that last operation on his gall bladder, which all the doctors said was aggravating his heart terribly and making it a good deal worse than it need be, *all* the doctors had great hope for him and, the best sign of all, he himself, was convinced he was going to live, whereas before he had made all preparations to be dead by Christmas and was convinced he would be. Then came the successful operation and he announced blithely that he was going to live. I believed it utterly and so it's a body blow. He had breakfast with us every few days. We saw him constantly. I talked to him on the telephone almost every day, so it was just as if he had walked out of our apartment five minutes ago forever and ever and ever and we shall never hear his voice or see his face again. Well, a lot of the fun in life is gone. Something you have had to face, my darling, so many times within these last years.

Woollcott had died on January 23 in the middle of one of his radio broadcasts. A world without *The Town Crier* seemed quiet indeed.

A month later the pattern of overworking followed by a temporary breakdown repeated itself for Noël. After the booking in Exeter in March he was forced to take a month to recuperate. He stayed in splendid isolation in King Arthur's Castle Hotel, Tintagel, Cornwall. He wrote to Jack:

> I left Torquay, which is filled with prosperous escapists in evening dress, and came here, which I remembered from my very far off childhood as being one of the loveliest places in the world. It really is wonderful. The hotel is old-fashioned, very comfortable and perched on the edge of a thousand foot cliff. There's nothing but sea and sky and gulls and gorse; the weather has been like summer, there are masses of wild violets and primroses and bluebells everywhere and, above all, I have had the bliss of being alone! You know how necessary this is to me every now and again. I've read a lot of books, made a lot of future plans, including a novel, a sequel to *Present Indicative* and an operette.

By the end of April he was back in action, the tour was over and he was able to fulfill his commitment to play eight weeks at the Haymarket The-

atre. Violet celebrated her eightieth birthday, and Noël wrote her a cele-
bratory verse with just a touch of irony:

## TO AN OCTOGENARIAN

### FROM HER MIDDLE-AGED SON, APRIL 20TH 1943

*Should an octogenarian wear a gay hat*
*Or some lace on her silvery hair?*
*The answer to this will be given you at*
*No. 10 Eaton Mansions, Sloane Square.*

*Should an octogenarian always be borne*
*Here and there in an invalid chair?*
*The answer to this is a volley of scorn*
*From 10 Eaton Mansions, Sloane Square.*

*Should an octogenarian wear a bright scarf*
*Or devote herself bleakly to prayer?*
*The answer to this is a hell of a laugh*
*From 10 Eaton Mansions, Sloane Square.*

·

IN A LETTER to Jack (July 19) Noël gave expression to something that
had been troubling him since the war began—the essential *differences* as
well as the similarities between Britain and America.

It is bitterly sad that you, of all people, who have been in the Country so much and love it so well should not be here, even if only for a
little, to note and absorb the extraordinary changes that have taken
place in all of us. I am worried in my mind on general terms about
the inevitable gulf that will always be between Americans and English who have stayed in America and Americans and English who
have been here. There is nothing spectacular to be observed but the
whole country has changed enormously since you knew it and I
would have so very much loved it if you could only have been with
us and become accustomed to our strangenesses. Even we don't know
how much we have altered but that we have, there can be no doubt
at all.

I am delighted to be able to tell you that Americans in England
seem to be having on the whole, a very good time. We seem to have
dropped much of our surface aloofness and are behaving with much

more genuine and generous hospitality than ever we did in the degrading days of peace. I gather this, not from the Mayfair Americans but from the ordinary ones I have met all over the country and it is a good augury for the future because, unless Americans and English really get to understand each other after this war, the whole thing will be a balls up . . .

This has turned out to be a much more serious letter than I intended it to be and please, don't misunderstand one word of it. I know America has been in the War since December 1941; I also know that you've got restrictions and rationing and transport difficulties and upsets but what you *haven't* got is the sense of immediate happenings going on all round you and that we have had incessantly. The thought processes and feelings and language of ordinary people in this Country are so tremendously different from what they were before. The bad blitzing has been over for a long time now but of course we are always having "Alerts" and sneak raiders and a few bombs dropped here and there and we all fire-watch and wake up in the middle of the night and have cups of tea and go to sleep again and the whole shape of our lives, under the surface, is completely different. We are aware in our minds all the time that invasion, either by us or by the enemy, is imminent and might occur at any moment. We are aware all the time that only twenty miles separates us from the enemy and that, however many plays we play and however many jokes we make and however many lunches we may have at the "Ivy" or "Apéritif" or Savoy or Claridges, that anything might happen at any minute and it is the fact that we are all subconsciously prepared for this that makes the difference that I am trying, so unsuccessfully, to explain.

•

AND THEN . . .

Then he accepted another booking from another source—to tour troop installations in the Middle East. In late July the HMS *Charybdis* took him to Gibraltar on the first leg of his trip.

Anxious to be on the winning side this time, Brendan Bracken wrote to General Montgomery:

> MINISTRY OF INFORMATION
> MALET STREET, W.C.1.
> 19th July, 1943

My dear General,
I am sending you this letter by hand of Noël Coward who will need no introduction to you from me. He is visiting the Mediterranean

Gibraltar 1943. On his Middle East tour, Noël visited his former Paris colleague MacFarlane— then governor—and (here) saw old theatrical friends John Perry and Anthony Quayle.

battlefields and is most anxious to see the troops under your command. He would be very glad to do all he can to entertain them during his journeys. On his return to England he has it in mind to write a film script dealing with the achievements of the Army. [At least Bracken had it in *his* mind.]

        Yours sincerely,
        BRENDAN BRACKEN

First stop was Gibraltar, where the governor was another old Paris colleague, Noël Mason-MacFarlane. MacFarlane had written to Noël back in August 1942: "I have now just received your telegram offering to arrange an all star concert party for the Rock . . . We would all be delighted to see a concert party out here of such very distinguished people and our only sorrow would be that you can't come with it. I hope so much that you will be able to fix this up . . ."

Mountbatten had given Noël a letter of introduction to General Eisenhower, Commander-in-Chief of the Allied Forces, and on August 5 Ike reported back:

Dear Dickie,
Noël Coward handed me this morning the note you sent by his hand.
I am glad you asked him to call on me. I found him most interesting

Noël somewhere in the Middle East.

and a very attractive personality. In fact, we started talking at such a great rate, I am afraid he will think I am a bit on the garrulous side. Nevertheless, I had a very enjoyable half hour, even if I am somewhat doubtful as to how he would classify it.

> Cordially,
> IKE

Gibraltar, Malta, Algiers, Iraq, Syria, Iran, Cairo—it was another jam-packed itinerary that left him tired but pleased with what he had managed to achieve.

The ubiquitous Richard Casey, now stationed in Egypt, summed up the tour when he wrote: "You did a splendid job and—to coin a phrase—you've improved the morale if not the morals of the Middle East."

•

ON HIS "bed and breakfast" wartime stopovers, Noël found himself writing many a "Bread and Butter" letter himself, frequently in verse. After a visit to Malta:

### BREAD AND BUTTER

*Dear Admiral, a Bread and Butter letter*
*To writer and receiver is a curse*
*And so this time I feel it would be better*

*To write to you in lilting, lyric verse.*
*Permit me to express appreciation*
*Of all your charming hospitality,*
*Allow me, with poetic inspiration,*
*To further your remembrance of me.*
*Remember me not as a sharp annoyance,*
*Not as an irritating, nagging pest,*
*Rather recall the swift, gay, verbal buoyance*
*Of your departed and distinguished guest.*
*Try to forget my frequent interference*
*When you saw fit to reprimand your staff,*
*Rather recall my exquisite appearance*
*Wearing a spotted Yugo-Slavian scarf.*
*Try to forgive your clumsy Flag Lieutenant,*
*Try not to spill the vials of your hate,*
*When inadvertently he hoists your pennant*
*Upside down and very much too late.*
*Try to remember when that bleating heifer,*
*Jasper, appears to have a morning chat*
*That it invariably makes him deafer*
*When unexpectedly he's shouted at!*
*When your domestic staff have disobeyed you,*
*Try, in conclusion, to remember, please,*
*God, who with such terrific wisdom made you*
*Made, with less wisdom also the Maltese.*
*And thus admitting that we're all God's creatures,*
*Gently look back in sweet humility.*
*Try to recapture my elusive features*
*And when I'm far away, remember me.*
*Yours in affectionate adieu—NC*

On those wartime travels there was another endangered species—though, fortunately, it was blissfully unaware of the fact. Many a military or other matron must have dined out on stories of how they had recently had the good fortune to meet "that charming Mr. Coward." Little did they realize how his sharp pen had pinned them down like butterflies on his private page:

## REFLECTIONS

*I often wonder why Commander F——*
*Chose such a noisy, unattractive wife.*

*It seems quite inconceivable to me*
*That such a man of such fine quality*
*Should, out of all the world, have fixed his choice*
*On anyone with such a rasping voice,*
*The thickest ankles and the smallest eyes*
*And, when undressed, wide corrugated thighs,*
*Who quite consistently wrecks every party*
*By being so abominably hearty.*
*Whose hearty, hoydenish idea of fun*
*Is so embarrassing to everyone,*
*Whose loud determination to impress*
*Meets with such very very small success,*
*Whose prowess on the tennis courts or links*
*Is so much less effective than she thinks,*
*Whose only contribution to a dance*
*Is, if her hostess gives her half a chance,*
*To keep suggesting in a piercing squeal*
*That everyone should do a Scottish Reel.*
*I cannot quite forgive Comander F——*
*For choosing such a really horrid wife.*

*Oh, why did Captain H. ——, R.N.*
*Display so little acumen*
*In picking for his better half*
*A girl with such a silly laugh*

While Noël was relaxing with the Caseys at their Mena home, outside Cairo, he was introduced to a high-ranking officer in the South African army, General Frank Theron, who repeated the invitation to visit South Africa. It was a project that had been talked about for the last two years but had been put on the back burner. With Noël's agreement, Casey cabled the South African prime minister, General Smuts, and shortly afterward came the official invitation. Noël was happy to accept it after a rest in England and the United States.

•

ON OCTOBER 10 he was back home and two months later found himself once more in New York—but a very different New York from his last visit two years earlier. The attack on Pearl Harbor, the day that, in Roosevelt's words, would "live in infamy" had changed a number of things. But not *everything:*

December 15, 1943

Darling, darling Lornie:

I won't go into any details about the trip out as that would be non-chalant talk. Sufficient to say that it was highly enjoyable. I arrived to find that Auntie had been installed in a hat-box at the St. Regis; this was changed to a suite the following day and now all is the height of luxury.

Dab [Jack Wilson] and Natasha, who you will want to know about first, of course, are sweeter than ever. The Baybay has a slightly larger face than of yore and is as wicked (if not wickeder) than ever. Everything has been more than satisfactorily discussed and it is so very lovely being with him again. Natasha is unchanged and as funny as she ever was.

On the night of my arrival I went to the first night of John Van Druten's new play [*The Voice of the Turtle*]. It was a very fashionable first night and a very pretty little play—all about a very pretty little actress who had to choose between love and a career. Judging by the way Miss Margaret Sullivan [Sullavan] overplayed it I think she was right to choose love. Everybody in New York was there and I had quite a reception. I must say that neither the play nor the audience exactly brought home the urgency of war to me, but one can't have everything.

The second night I went to *Oklahoma* with Edwina, which is quite one of the loveliest and most enchanting things I have ever seen in the theatre. Everything about it is perfect, and as for the ballets, even you would have loved them, because they were really witty . . .

I got the flu and was in bed for a couple of days, which was a great relief, as it got me out of appearing at the opening of the Civic Theatre. Gertie, apparently, ate up the scenery. I haven't seen her yet but I have talked to her on the telephone and she is quite, quite dotty.

None of these people have been in the least irritating about anything, but there are others. I went to an Orphanage Committee meeting.

Personally and privately, I was madly irritated by the whole set-up. When I get back from Washington I am going to talk to the four rebellious girls who seem to be making fair bitches of themselves. The Gould Foundation have obviously been wonderful to the children and I suspect have spoiled them forever. We are hoping that Prudence Coop will improve in character on account of the fact that she is beginning to lean emotionally in the direction of the Catholic Church. Personally, I feel that this will merely mean that she will be able to confess having stolen June Bevise's drawers, receive absolution, and make an immediate pounce for Myra McKenzie's brooch, but I may be cynical.

I will talk to May about the whole business and write you more fully later. Brian [Aherne] announced unwisely that he had always thought it was a bad plan for the children to be sent over here, because, after all, his brother's children had stayed in England through all the blitzes, to which I replied sweetly that it was very fine of him to have come over himself in order to represent the family. He then said that he had always understood that the Orphanage Fund was vastly rich in any case, to which I replied that, as far as I could remember, everything he had understood all his life has been invariably inaccurate. It was, on the whole, an exciting little meeting.

Upon breaking the seals that the censorship office had put on my *Middle East Diary* I discovered that they have cut it to shreds and made it virtually unintelligible. From the point of view of security their deletions were idiotic; it was one of the most maddening examples of bureaucratic red tape nonsense that I have ever encountered. I am writing Brendan [Bracken] about it at once.

It is quite extraordinary to see all the lights of Broadway again and to be able to eat the sort of food that one always used to be able to eat.

That's all the news for the moment, my darlings. Kindly circulate this letter among the disciples . . . Be assured, dear Mrs. Loraine, that I still think that you are the prettiest, cutest little fairy that ever stepped out of a whacking great bluebell.

Love, love, love, love, love

BELLEVUE
JAMAICA
January 9th

Darling Lornie:

Just imagine me writing you all a letter in my own pudgy hand. There is no typewriter and, at long last, I have a little time and so here goes. I had a wonderful time in New York but very exhausting and the "flu" left me with no voice at all. I dined with dear Mr. Mysterious [Little Bill] on Christmas night and he said it was idiotic of me to attempt a strenuous tour of S.A. [South Africa] without having a rest first and that one of his staff had a house in Jamaica and that he would make all arrangements which he did with paralysing efficiency.

On Sunday 2nd I gave a violent farewell cocktail party to which everybody came—it was a terrific success—all the Fighting French buried their mutual hatchets, all the Secret Cops came and brought their wives and everyone mingled like mad with everyone else. At 9:30 I was seen off by Natasha, Neysa (in whose apartment the party had been given) and Eleonora [von Mendelssohn].

I had a very rough flight and arrived in Miami the next morning. I spent two days with the Baybay who was intent on turning his vast face like a flower to the sun. On Wednesday the 5th I flew here—only four hours, popping down at Cuba for ten minutes en route. Here I was met by a Naval Commander who had had orders from the Chief that my visit was completely secret and so he whisked me out of the Airport and up to this house and here I am.

Oh dear, you'd better all prepare to weep bright green tears of envy. It is absolutely indescribably lovely. It's an old coffee plantation that used to be called "Admiral's House" because that funny little man that Winnie is so fond of lived there—the one that had that light flirtation with Emma Hamilton. His name escapes me for the moment [Horatio Nelson]. Anyhow here he lived 1500 feet up on the side of a mountain and he sat, as I am sitting now, looking over mountains, the town of Kingston in the valley and the sea. At night the lights will come up in the town and the Moon comes very soon after. The climate is perfect. I sit out at night on the terrace in my pyjamas sipping a rum punch and looking at this breath-taking view. I have a staff of ravishing coal black servants, a Chrysler car, a hammock slung between an orange tree and a palm. The garden blazes with poinsettias, hibiscus, Alamanda, Bourgainvilla, etc., etc. There are breadfruits, limes, bananas and all kinds of other tropical dainties. I eat my solitary meals on a flagged terrace. I have Jamaican curries, sweet breadfruit and yams and Yampees, which are wonderful—Coconut with everything, custard apples, cashew nuts. There is *no* telephone. There are *no* mosquitoes or snakes. The sun blazes down all day and it is just cool enough at night for one blanket! The house is fairly luxurious with masses of books and large sofas and chairs and a couple of bathrooms which don't work with great speed but after all! Macgregor, my black Major Domo, is a dream Prince and runs the whole place and calls me Dear Friend and Lord which is confusing and very, very sweet . . .

I am setting off tomorrow in the car for a two days tour of the Island. If I can find a beach with a shack on it I shall buy it. I've a feeling that this is the place I've been looking for. It's only 18 hours from New York by air and 4 from Miami. The climate varies only slightly. Everything flowers and burgeons all the year round and it's *never* cold. It reminds me of Honolulu except that it is more rich and luxuriant. I really think that as a race we must be dotty. Here is this divine place—one of the oldest British colonies and we none of us— thank God—know anything about it. That is except me and Nelson.

Now that I am out of American territory I can say what I really think. Individually, all our friends were fine but the ignorance about the War and the facts of life is abysmal. I only got really cross once, which was on New Year's Eve, when the streets were filled with drunken people celebrating, squealing and blowing squeakers. They couldn't have been more exultant if it had been Armistice Night. They're all steaming themselves up for the next election. Roosevelt is loathed among all the smarties. There's quite a lot of anti-British feeling about—mostly spread by the Hearst Press, the McCormick Press (Chicago) and the Luces, who have a lovely "down" on the British Empire, principally because Lord Linlithgow snubbed Clare in Delhi. On the other hand there are some first rate minds such as [Walter] Lippmann who see the situation a little more clearly. Our trouble is and has been all along that we are still too conciliatory. What our diplomats ought to do now is to wave the flag and keep on shouting the truth at them, which is that without the "lonely year" they would have been for ever in the *consommé*. We are continuing to be gentlemanly to the end and if I had not been hopping through on a transit visa I should have let it fly. As it was I restrained myself and bawled "Lie in the Dark" [his poem] at everyone I saw whenever I got the chance.

I think of you all so much, particularly here in this stolen Paradise where I really have time to think. It's no use sending love to you— all that is there already. If awful things happen in the next few months, and they might, cable me regularly. A Happy New Year, my darlings—the following are Tisses xxxxxxxxxx
                    MASTER


                                                    Grand Hotel
                                                    Khartoum
                                          January 29th 1944
Darling Lornie,
I've had really a fascinating journey although fairly exhausting. After Jamaica I flew to Barranquilla in Columbia [*sic*]. Here I stopped for one night and had to take on the jaw a reception and dinner given for me by the British Colony. It was quite gay and rather touching really and very "outpost of the Empire". I made a spirited speech half in English and half in Spanish on account of a bright green and pro-English Governor being present. The next day I took off and went

beetling down the Venezuelan coast to Trinidad . . . On Friday the 22nd I took off in a very large, fast plane and flew to Belem near the mouth of the Amazon . . . We stayed there long enough for breakfast and then went on to Natal where we arrived in the evening for four hours only. During this bright interim I made an appearance at an American Airmen's dance, sang and recited "Lie in the Dark" and buggered off again. We arrived at Acension Island for breakfast, a strange, volcanic rock in the middle of the South Atlantic with purple and red mountains and peculiar rocks and very bad lighting for Lynn.

At 5 o'clock that afternoon we arrived at Accra . . . It was surprisingly cool and very White Man's Burden indeed. Lots of large gentlemen in shorts carrying golf clubs just having had a "bit of a go of Malaria". From there I flew to Lagos in Nigeria which is the real school books tropics. Natives, coal black, in vivid colours, lush vegetation, palms, bananas, orchids, hibiscus, snakes, scorpions, Tze Tze flies, infantile paralysis, Blackwater Fever, Gumboils, crabs (imported naturally), moths as big as your titties, bugs, fleas and beetles. There was also Nelson Eddy but I missed him by a day. There was what is known as a "Hammatan" blowing which is a hot dusty wind from the Sahara—it must be a keen traveller for the Sahara is about two thousand miles away—anyhow it makes flying very tricky so, having dragged myself awake at five in the morning, the plane wouldn't take off. However, another much larger one thought that it would so off I went across Equatorial Africa. I spent the night at a place called Maidugeri which offers too obvious rhyming possibilities. There there were nothing but rather attractive mud houses and very, very black people indeed with very long things hanging down in front, if you know what I mean, and if you don't, Winnie is sure to. I stayed the night with the Resident and visited the English Club where there were some decent chaps and their wives who had just been exhausting themselves on the tennis courts. I must say I should have thought that the weather would have been stinking hot but not at all! In the evening we had to have a wood fire. I was most deeply offended. After a convivial evening with some of the chaps already mentioned I got up at 3 o'clock and drove off under the stars to the airport. We took off at 4 o'clock and after a couple of stops arrived in Khartoum at 3:30 . . .

We leave tomorrow for Pretoria. We arrive there on Wednesday and after a few days rehearsal with Norman [Hackforth], I shall take the plunge. I am very well indeed in spite of all my strenuous journeyings. There is no doubt about it, travelling agrees with me. I take a lot of quinine and it makes my great big violet eyes shine like bloody great beacons. I am now taking Bert to the zoo to tell the animals all about you. I will finish this when I return.

My dear, the Toucans can't bear the sight of you! Isn't it curious? I argued with them and gave them some dry toast but it was no use— "Lorn's a pig", "Lorn's a pig", they kept on saying, so I came away. There were some rather large wart hogs with tusks who were much more friendly, "Lorn's one of us" they said. It is really a very sweet zoo because most of the animals walk about with you. There was one elderly gazelle who was really a grave bore. Bert was very funny with her because she kept on nuzzling our bag of goodies and when he said "Bugger off", she butted him. Incidentally, he had a terrible voyage out, nineteen in a cabin for four. However the moment he arrived he bossed all the Arabs about, got himself driven from Suez to Cairo for four pounds, although the actual fare is five pounds ten. By the time he had been in Khartoum a week he knew everybody and was being taken off to Arab markets and shown the sights, in fact he is quite obviously a very good traveller, which is a great comfort. Will you kindly deliver the enclosed unused ticket to the redoubtable Mr. Jenkins and tell him to stuff it up his bottom and get the refund double quick chop, chop? I told the bloody fool that I wouldn't need it and that the services would fly me wherever I wanted to go but he laughed with gay communistic superiority and wouldn't believe me.

I have taken up an option on the housekeeper of his hotel especially for you. She is the most monstrous "*excusez moi*" imaginable. An evacuated Viennese Jewess of gigantic proportions who makes "Skulptur" and paints and writes modern poetry about the utterances of the soul. She is . . . quite, quite dotty.

I think this is all my news, really. The Governor and his lady are very sweet but so constricted with shyness that conversation is a trifle difficult. One of the A.D.C.'s has carbuncles. There is a sandstorm going on. I am looking fascinating. I love the widow Loraine very, very tenderly. I am also devoted to Divorcée Calthrop, Maidens [Clemence] Dane, Bowen [Olwen] and Carey.

Love, love, love, love, love, love, love, love, love, love.<br>MASTER

•

THE SOUTH AFRICAN TOUR was virtually a replica of the Antipodean—major venues alternating with troop concerts, hospital visits, broadcasts, endless meetings both formal and informal. Less of a strain this time, because Noël was now practiced in what was required. The public performances alone netted almost twenty thousand pounds for local war-related charities.

Early May found him in Bulawayo, Rhodesia. All that now stood between Noël and the trip home were a few last concerts in Nairobi and Mombasa. Then, via Cairo, to London. But just as he was packing to leave, a letter arrived from Mountbatten, now in charge of the war in Southeast Asia:

### SOUTH EAST ASIA COMMAND HEADQUARTERS
16th February 1944

My dear Noël,
I have now been round most of the Burma front where I found our troops in great heart and fighting well.

The one universal cry is for entertainment and visits from distinguished people. You can judge in what a bad way they are by the fact that the troops were even prepared to listen to me standing on a soap box and talking to them and you can imagine how much sooner they would have heard Mr. N. Coward with a mini-piano singing "Mad Dogs and Englishmen".

Joking apart, I am certain that a tour by you would be immensely appreciated out here and if you will let me know whether you can come, and if so between what dates, I will arrange to have a tour laid on for you which would include visits to British and American soldiers and airmen . . .

I can assure you that a visit to the Burma front is quite unlike any other experience. The roads which our soldiers have cut through mountainous jungle in the last three or four months are past belief and the conditions under which they work are pretty lousy.

I am telegraphing to Major General Harrison of my staff who is at present in London to contact you and see whether you would be prepared to come so that he can make the necessary arrangements with you on the spot.

Yours ever,
DICKIE

A trip of this nature would entail traveling extensively through the war zones of Assam and Burma at the height of the monsoon season. It was the last thing Noël needed, but it was a request from a source that, for obvious reasons, he found it impossible to refuse.

·

ON MAY 16 he sailed for Ceylon on HMS *Rapid* to help reassure the "Forgotten Army" (the Fourteenth Army) that they were not really forgotten. "I knew he would not have asked me to go unless he had considered it really important."

Ceylon, Calcutta ("an authentic foretaste of hell and damnation"), Delhi, Bombay—by now Noël was practiced in handling any kind of audience in any kind of context. Wherever he went there was a retinue of official "minders" to take care of the logistics—not always the easiest of tasks in wartime. Inevitably there were the occasional "lash-ups," as Noël called them.

In the eventual thank-you letter, his host recalled that "Your arrangements went well from the time you left Calcutta, except for a short period when you broke loose in your car and charged lamp posts and sea walls in Bombay."

The tone was lighthearted; the incident was not. The car Noël was traveling in was broadsided by a Navy lorry and but for a convenient palm tree would almost certainly have crashed through the seawall and into the ocean way below. It was only in the context of what he had seen elsewhere that the accident could be shrugged off.

For these few weeks he was to crisscross the subcontinent, gaining as he did so an overview of the war denied to the fighting men focused on any one area of it. One day he would be competing for his audience's attention with enemy gunfire in the next valley, another would have him going the rounds of one more hospital visit. There were endless mud-splattered rides in bumpy jeeps. All of it a far cry from the comparative luxury of his earlier tours.

Through all of it he was accompanied by the imperturbable Norman Hackforth, accompanist become friend, and The Little Treasure, the name he bestowed on the borrowed piano Norman tuned faithfully every single day.

There were moments that would stay etched in his memory long after the war was over. At Imphal, in Burma, he arrived to join Mountbatten when one of the critical battles of the war was taking place just the other side of the hills. Noël found it hard to summon up his signature sangfroid when the breeze brought the smell of piles of rotting Japanese corpses from a nearby clearing. It was at times like this that it was brought home to any touring entertainer that this was a far different booking from the kind of provincial tour he might have been used to.

By this time Noël was living on his nerves. His weight—usually about 150 pounds—had dropped to 120.

Finally he found himself back in Ceylon, where "what I had been dreading for a long time finally happened" and he did collapse. After a brief recuperation at Colombo's Galle Face Hotel, he was put on a plane for home.

Then came Mountbatten's personal message:

## SOUTH EAST ASIA COMMAND HEADQUARTERS
29th July, 1944

My dear Noël,

Although I thanked you publicly in the presence of my Staff for what you and Norman Hackforth did to entertain the Allied Forces in the South East Asia Command, I feel I must also write a private line to tell you how really deeply grateful I am.

I realise that it was at great personal inconvenience that you came on to South East Asia from South Africa and that the tour you under-took was terribly strenuous.

You have the satisfaction of knowing that you are the first British star to have come and entertained our troops at the front, and quite apart from any musical and histrionic merit that your performance may have (and I am not erudite enough to be able to judge!!!) the greatest value your visit will have is to make the men feel that they are not forgotten by the people back home . . .

Yours ever,
DICKIE

Recollections in comparative tranquillity:

## TO ADMIRAL THE LORD LOUIS MOUNTBATTEN

*It isn't for me*
*To bend the knee*
*And curtsey and cringe and pander*
*Because my JUNIOR happens to be*
*A really SUPREME Commander.*
*But nevertheless*
*I must confess*
*Dear Dickie, my stay in Kandy,*
*Apart from being a great success*
*Has made me feel fine and dandy.*
*It's been the peak*
*Of a rather bleak*
*And perilous undertaking*
*To lie in state for nearly a week*
*While history's in the making.*
*The food we had*
*(Though the films were bad)*
*Was definitely nutritious*
*And nobody but a graceless cad*

*Could say it was not delicious.*
*The roguish chaff*
*Of the Chief of Staff*
*On any official question*
*While never failing to raise a laugh*
*Was dicing with indigestion.*
*To joke with glee*
*With a C-in-C*
*When only a drab civilian*
*Could never really happen to me*
*Except in the King's Pavilion.*
*When all is done*
*And the war is won*
*How happy these days will seem—O*
*I'll shed salt tears for the games and fun*
*I shared with the dear SUPREMO*

NOËL COWARD
BREAD AND BUTTER, CEYLON, JULY 1944

And in rather more serious vein:

17 Gerald Road
S.W.1.
July 3rd 1945

My dear Dickie,

I have a sudden urge to write to you about nothing in particular and for no especial reason except that your old woman [Mountbatten's wife, Edwina] came and lunched with me the other day and we talked so much of you! She is looking lovely, as usual, and full of energy and vitality and it was a fair treat. I moaned to her rather, because I said that I would always have a slightly guilty conscience about going sick on you in Ceylon. I have a feeling I was much more tiresome than I realised at the time. Actually, of course, I was good and exhausted by South Africa even before I started. I know you understand all that, so I am not going on about it and, though I might have been rather petulant and irritating with you, I do believe, as far as the troops were concerned, that my tour was a success on the whole. I have had several pleasant repercussions from 14th Army men who have come up to me in the street and wrung me by the hand, which comforts me a great deal.

Edwina says that apart from having had a go of dysentry you are in fine form and rising above everything with your usual resilience. I have heard you twice on the radio . . . once on VE-day and once on a Naval programme a week or so later. On both occasions you said exactly the right thing in exactly the right way and were brief and to the point and extremely moving.

I hear rather discouraging reports of Basil Dean's trip to India. He certainly has a genius for antagonising not only the people who work for him but also the fighting men he should be working for. I do wish that earlier in the War we could have got ENSA on a sound working basis run by an efficient committee rather than by one man. He has much in his favour, being both energetic and determined, but he is over jealous of authority and his psychological judgement is non-existent.

Dear old *Blithe Spirit* is still playing to virtual capacity, never having missed a performance in spite of doodle-bugs and V2s since that glamorous Summer evening in 1941 when you came to the opening performance.

I hope you have by now enjoyed *This Happy Breed* and *Blithe Spirit* films; the new one, *Brief Encounter,* is practically finished and looks jolly nice.

I often think of those gay cinematic evenings in the King's Pavilion. Take care of yourself, dear Dickie, and go from strength to strength and give my love to anyone who cares for it.

       Yours ever,
       NOËL

•

WHILE NOËL WAS TOURING, the Cineguild trio—David Lean, Ronald Neame, and Anthony Havelock-Allan—had been busy filming *This Happy Breed.* Back in early 1943 Noël had told the Lunts:

> February 1st 1943
> My Film Unit [though it's doubtful if his "little dears," as he was inclined to call them, saw themselves in that light] is making *Happy Breed* in Technicolor with Robert Donat and Johnny Mills and it looks as though it might be good . . .

The announcement is a little strange, since Donat had politely but firmly turned them down a year earlier:

> 25 Davies Street
> London W.1
> April 24th 1942
>
> Dear Noël,
> I've loved reading the play. It's thick with atmosphere and your great gift for conveying essential detail in a line or two gives us a sense of depth and size far beyond the limits of the room we see. But isn't the time past for it? For me, the play fails at the big jump. Right at the end. I don't believe in the things that Frank believes in. He's human and lovable and above all he's adult and I like him enormously— until he tries to justify himself and his kind; then I'm mad with him. Rightly or wrongly, I believe it is just that very political irresponsibility that got us into another war. I don't believe he does know "what we belong to, where we come from, and where we're going". Until we do know it, with our brains and hearts and souls as well as our roots, we shall go on fighting these bloody wars. Therefore, for me, the whole play crashes at the end. (But I am only a bloody actor.) I'm immensely proud that you even thought of me.
> Yours ever,
> ROBERT

In the event, the part of Frank Gibbons was played by Robert Newton, whose drinking problem necessitated a special "fine" clause in his contract for every filming day he cost the production. By the time the film was finished Newton had left most of his salary behind.

Noël continued:

> I am exercising remote control but I want them to get used to doing films without me being actually there. As you will be interested but

not be surprised to hear that I loathe the whole Film business as much as I ever did if not more, but never again am I going to sell my plays to the movies without having the whole thing controlled by my own unit.

Even before he arrived back in England, producer Havelock-Allan is bringing him up to date on the distribution complexities that del Guidice (now Two Cities Films) has involved them in:

ANTHONY HAVELOCK-ALLAN
DENHAM 2345
BUCKS
26th April 1944

My dear Father,
I might have saved you the boredom of my letter about distribution because within ten days of my sending it, for some quid pro connection with Two Cities' future plans which has not yet emerged, Filippo had a complete change of heart and has embraced Eagle-Lion and all its works with passionate fervour. In future all Two Cities pictures will be distributed by Eagle-Lion, not only here, but in the rest of the world. It is all a little bewildering but in the best Neapolitan tradition, and only needs a little music by Rossini. However, it leaves me with an uncomfortable feeling of having treated with owlish solemnity a gay farrago which only concerned the fate of an important film and rather more than £20,000.

So far *Happiers* [*This Happy Breed*] has only been seen by a few people apart from the pre-view audience, but a tremendous enthusiasm seems to be building up for it. It went to Chequers last weekend by special request, and the comment that came back after the showing was, "A very fine film—thoroughly enjoyed it". It opens in London on Whit Sunday evening, May 28th, and the special benefit performance for the Actors' Orphanage will take place on June 1st. I imagine there is a reasonable chance of your being back in this country by then if you are not already on the Road to Mandalay.

There has been considerable labour unrest in the Studio for some time, culminating about five weeks ago in a ban from the Unions on working overtime, coupled with a policy of non-cooperation. This has slowed down progress to a snail's pace and depressed us all a very great deal. Just at the moment making pictures seems to get steadily more and more difficult, unenthusiastic and expensive, which is a great pity, since we have for the first time a golden opportunity of securing on merit our fair share of the world's screen time, which is important both economically and politically.

I have already told you in my cable about the Trade show success of *"Happiers"*, and the excellence of the Trade notices. Although nobody seems to have rumbled Bobby Newton, at least the majority have the grace to like his performance less than those of the other principals.

We sent a birthday telegram to your Mother, and David got a very sweet and very gay letter back. She wrote from North Wales about which her only complaint was that country life was turning her into a cabbage! When she returns to London she is coming down to the Studio to see *This Happy Breed*.

I don't know what the war of second front nerves is doing to the Germans, but I can tell you of one Home Guard whose equipment whenever he puts it on makes a noise like castanets.

Much love from us all,

TONY

Meanwhile, Noël's "Film Unit" had finished filming *Blithe Spirit,* and Noël turned his mind and hand to adapting *Still Life,* one of the plays in the *Tonight at 8:30* set, for the screen. It would become *Brief Encounter* and would be, along with *In Which We Serve,* one of the two films by which he is likely to be remembered.

In November he, as he put it, "dismounted graciously from my high horse" and agreed to perform for ENSA in Paris and Brussels. To see Paris again he found a slightly unsettling experience. Although the lights were bright and the boulevards bustling, he had a sense that the city somehow didn't want to meet one's eyes. In four years too many things had happened there of which it was too ashamed to speak.

He soon gave up inquiring which of his friends had been collaborators with the Germans, as everyone had contradictory, self-exculpatory versions and it merely "confirmed my belief that worse things than bombardments can happen to civilians in wartime."

He did have news of his Paris apartment before he left, though he does not record having visited it while he was there. The news came from an unlikely source. On the *Brittanic* to New York back in 1940 he had run across "a man whom I had known slightly before called Ingram Fraser." Fraser turned out to be another of Little Bill's "boys," and their paths clearly crossed more than once in future, though Noël never refers to him again. In *Future Indefinite,* Noël insists that it was Fraser who introduced him to Little Bill in New York, though later accounts—as we have seen— suggest otherwise. He refers to his "casual acquaintanceship" with Fraser, though the tone and detailed content of Fraser's letter that September rather beg that question:

21st September 1944

My Cabbage, my old—

This will be a straightforward letter, without frills. Of frills and chichi, impressions, incidents, anecdotes, there are many, too many for writing. They will have to wait until we meet. This may be quite soon, so reserve an evening.

Now, the flat. I visited it. The *concièrge* nearly fell on my neck. The place has been occupied by what must have been a particularly unpleasant pair of Gestapo hounds, never properly house-broken. The filth is indescribable, but I think it is more surface than anything else. The chief victims are the carpets, notably in the dining room, which bear an historical record of the gastronomic, alcoholic—and I much regret the coarseness—purely colic history of the inhabitants during a twelvemonth. *C'étaient des salauds, et plus que ça.* There are too some remarkable stains on the bed, notably on the brown satin headboard, which, if my deductions are correct, are a remarkable commentary on the acrobatic agility of the occupants.

The furniture seems to be more or less intact—the blue sofa and chairs in the drawing room, the desk and odd chairs do not seem to have suffered much. The dining room table and chairs are accounted for. The bedroom is a bit sparse, but recalling the soldierly simplicity—*à la* Charles X—into which you retire nocturnally, perhaps that is as it should be. The second bedroom is *sans* bed, *sans* chair, *sans* nearly everything. Likewise the kitchen, from which the *batterie de cuisine,* the *vaiselle,* and *la verrerie* have been removed by unseen hands. I might add that there is no linen, blankets, counterpanes, or more serious silver, ornaments or nicknacks. In fact the place rather looks like an *apartement meublé,* and only just *meublé* at that. No books . . .

Lest you get the wrong impression from my would-be facetiousness, the place would look 100% better after two days of a good *femme de ménage,* and the carpets taken up and cleaned. Likewise some new paint in all the rooms. The curtains are there. I also visited the servant's room, and thought I was being taken to a dungeon in the Bastille. But that is *vide, vide, vide.*

There are nasty rumours about the maid Garnier. Everyone thinks she was, is, a crook. She apparently had not only the customary *sou de franc* from the housekeeping, but about 50 centimes per franc *en plus.* Likewise, at the time of the *exode* in June 40, she cleared out with all the linen and silver and probably a lot more, anyway two trunkloads, which no one could prevent.

The general feeling is that she helped herself, but whether she did it to hide the stuff on your account or to set herself up is unknown. It might be possible to trace her in due course, but not under present conditions.

As a wind-up, I saw M. Trimbach [the landlord], and what a charmer he is. I gather that you yourself must have pressed Button A and give him something to remember you by in the way of charm and poisonality. The lease is still in his view quite valid and he is anxious that you should stay on. Whether the seven years will be considered as running from 1940 or whether you make a new lease is a matter for subsequent discussion. Likewise, how the hiatus of four rentless years is treated is something to discuss. He most certainly does not expect payment, but in the French fashion, *on s'arrangera.* Now for the immediate future, the next *trimestre* begins on 15th October, at which time Frs. 6,450 are due. On your behalf I promised that would be paid. And by the time the next quarter is due you may be here yourself and can handle the business details . . .

There has not been much time to pick up gossip about your various friends, though I am afraid that little Yvonne [Printemps] is in rather a mess. I will be getting more on that tonight, and on other mutual acquaintances, and will send you further bulletins.

Accept, my dear friend, the assurance of my sentiments the most distinguished.

> *Bien à toi*
> ORAJIO

A few weeks later Fraser is writing with more encouraging news:

> American Red Cross
> PWD/SHAEF (F.P.O.)
> B.L.A.
> November 2nd 1944

*Cher Maître,*
The flat will within the week be pristine and sweet-scented (probably *à l'eau de Javel*) and it will also have been, in military phraseology, disinfected—de-loused to you. I got hold of an admirable firm . . . which calls itself *"Tout-a-Neuf"* and that is what is being done . . .

As for the lease and the rent, Trimlach was not *en ville.* However, his office has assured me that he is counting on M. Coward to occupy the premises for many years to come. [In fact, Noël stayed on there until 1950.]

And now, you lucky beast, more good news for you—your *bonne* [Yvonne] Garnier turned up 2 weeks ago, looked up the *concierge* at

22, told him she had all your possessions *chez elle* and that you could write to her. Since then no sign. Have you got her address, which seems to be somewhere near Moulins? If so, please send, and I will cope . . .

For the time being that is about all concerning No. 22. I shall report in further detail when . . . I have seen the results of the house-cleaning.

> Farewell, sweet coz.
> Thine
> INGRAM

·

THE REST of the war was a series of snapshots for Noël.

Germany was everywhere in retreat—still dangerous to London life and limb with the V1 and V2 rockets lobbing across the Channel at a British population that had long since shown that it could take anything the enemy could throw. For most people this was almost history. The real question was what sort of society would we be living in in the postwar world?

On April 14, Franklin Roosevelt died, "a personal sadness to me," Noël wrote, "because although I did not know him really well, he had been friendly, kind and unpompous and had treated me with respect at a moment when I most needed it."

Germany would surrender unconditionally on May 7, but three days earlier Noël found himself dining with his old friend Juliet Duff at her Belgrave flat. The only other people present were Venetia Montagu—and Winston Churchill. It was an evening charged with emotion. Here was the man who had done more than any other, through his vision, courage, and determination, to give the Western world one more chance to get things right. Instinctively, the three of them rose and drank a toast to the old campaigner.

Within weeks there would be a general election. Instead of turning it into a national vote of thanks to Churchill, the British electorate turned him firmly out of office and put a Labour government into power for the next six years. There was much to celebrate, but Noël had an uneasy feeling about this supposedly brave new world.

When the Japanese finally surrendered on the fifteenth of August he wrote to Joyce Carey:

> Well, Chère,
> It looks like we've finally got what dear Neville promised us— "Peace In Our Time"—sort of. The only problem is it's nearly a decade and many thousands of lives later.

Oh dear, I really don't hate many people but the late (and decidedly not great) Mr. Chamberlain was one of them. All that ineffectual umbrella-twirling, all that unwillingness to face what was staring him in it!

What's more, I'm afraid he has bequeathed us one of those phrases that are doomed to go down in infamy (if I may misquote FDR, a *truly* great politician we have only just begun to miss).

So now it's over and I suppose I should share the general jubilation but somehow I don't. I never for a moment doubted that we should win, somehow or other, no matter how black things seemed. We British are at our best in adversity. We won the war but my concern is—how shall we win the *peace*?

As I've said so often, we betrayed so much of the past, let's try to be faithful to the future.

Your ever-loving
CASSANDRA

# PART FOUR

# *SHADOW PLAY*

"Small talk, a lot of small talk with other thoughts going on behind." *Shadow Play*, from *Tonight at 8:30*.

# CHAPTER 21

# SIGH ONCE MORE . . .
# AND A STORM IN THE PACIFIC

## (1945–1947)

PICCADILLY THEATRE
PICCADILLY CIRCUS, W.1          GERrard 4506-7
Licensed by the Lord Chamberlain to J. A. WEBB
Proprietors ...    PICCADILLY THEATRE LTD.

JOHN C. WILSON and H. M. TENNENT Ltd.

present

CYRIL                      MADGE
RITCHARD              ELLIOTT

IN

NOEL  COWARD'S

"SIGH NO MORE"

JOYCE GRENFELL    GRAHAM PAYN

MANTOVANI and HIS ORCHESTRA

EVERY EVENING at 6.45 p.m.

MATINEES : Wednesday and Saturday at 2.30 p.m.

White Cliffs, Kent, the house Noël rented immediately after the war, while Goldenhurst remained requisitioned by the army. The famous white cliffs were truly magnificent—until bits of them started landing in his garden.

I T WAS TIME to try to put life back together.

"It is so sweet to be back in London again with the people who are my own closest ones," Noël wrote. And indeed, there was a great deal to be done. He had committed to write a new revue to be called *Sigh No More,* which would star Joyce Grenfell, Cyril Ritchard, his wife, Madge Elliott, and Graham (no longer "Master") Payn, or "Little Lad," as he would become known.

He also needed a country getaway. Goldenhurst was still at the tender mercies of the army, but a friend showed him a dramatic little house, White Cliffs, at the end of the beach at St. Margaret's Bay, in Kent. Noël rented it straightaway. It was only later that he realized that bits of the famous White Cliffs were in the habit of literally dropping in like uninvited neighbors.

By October, Noël, Coley, and Graham had installed themselves there. The facilities would have to follow in their own good time.

•

AFTER HIS PROFESSIONAL BREAK with Cochran, Noël never enjoyed a really successful revue. *Set to Music* was *Words and Music* rejigged for Broadway, and Bea Lillie and *Sigh No More* suffered from ignoring the classic Cochran dictum—the result of countless productions with and

1947, and *Pacific 1860,* Noël's first postwar musical, reopened the bomb-damaged Drury Lane Theatre. Here Noël and designer Gladys Calthrop happily contemplate their star, Mary Martin, for the camera. The mutual admiration, though, was short-lived.

without Noël—that a revue couldn't easily be sustained by any one person's point of view. "The essence of revue is variety, rapidity, change of mood and contrast of line and colour . . . homogeneity can lead to monotony."

*Sigh No More* ran for 213 performances—a hit but not a palpable hit—and when Noël attended the final night, "I watched it and, apart from 'Matelot' [Graham's big number] said goodbye to it without a pang."

Much more emotional for him was the closing of *Blithe Spirit* on March 6. "It was a sad occasion, because it really could have gone on running for another year. However, four and a half years is a nice enough run." At the time those 1,997 performances set a British theatrical record.

It was time for another Coward extravaganza, and what better than a return to Drury Lane, scene of his *Cavalcade* triumph? Was it really fifteen years ago? He would reopen the bomb-damaged Theatre Royal with a major theatrical statement that would revive memories of *Bitter Sweet.*

It would be called *Scarlet Lady* and would star Irene Dunne. Miss Dunne was not available? It would be called *Samolo* and star Yvonne Printemps—but then he remembered the troubles she had with her English pronunciation. (At one point in *Conversation Piece* she had declared that "a cloud has pissed across the sun.") Very well, then, it would be called *Pacific 1860* and would star . . . Mary Martin. He wrote to her immediately.

MARCH 2ND, 1946
MARY MARTIN
PLYMOUTH THEATRE
45TH STREET
NEW YORK

DEAR MARY YOU SAID TWO YEARS AGO YOU WOULD LIKE TO
APPEAR IN LONDON STOP I AM WRITING A NEW OPERETTE FOR
NEXT AUTUMN THE SCORE IS NEARLY FINISHED AND I THINK IS
MY BEST TO DATE THE BOOK IS NOT ACTUALLY WRITTEN UNTIL
I KNOW WHETHER OR NOT YOU CAN PLAY IT STOP IT WOULD
GIVE ME SO MUCH PLEASURE TO INTRODUCE YOU TO LONDON
AUDIENCES CABLE ME IF THERE IS ANY POSSIBILITY NOËL
COWARD

Richard Halliday, Mary's husband and manager, replied the very next day. He had never known Mary "as excited and happy" and she was "completely enthusiastic" to come to London under Noël's auspices. So that was all right, he told his *Diary:* "She has youth and charm and a delightful personality. At the moment it seems all too good to be true. I do hope that later on in the year I shall not re-read this page amid gales of hollow laughter."

MARCH 5TH

MOST DELIGHTED AND EXCITED BY YOUR CABLE STOP OPENING
DATE VAGUELY SCHEDULED BEGINNING OF NOVEMBER WILL
CABLE YOU FULLER DETAILS IN A FEW DAYS STOP CAN YOU SEND
ME SOME PHOTOGRAPHS OF MARY NOT FOR PUBLICITY BUT FOR
GLADYS CALTHROP WHO IS DESIGNING THE SHOW STOP CAN
YOU ALSO TELL ME MARY'S COMFORTABLE VOCAL RANGE STOP
SO VERY MANY HOPES THAT ALL CAN BE ARRANGED
SATISFACTORILY.

Mary's vocal range was "from low G to high A, can go to C but not eight shows each week."

At this point Noël realized that he really knew very little about Miss Martin. He made it a priority to look at a couple of her film performances:

DEAR MARY HAVE JUST SEEN KISS THE BOYS AND VICTOR
HERBERT AND FOUND YOU PERFECTLY ENCHANTING IN BOTH
STOP IF ANYTHING GOES WRONG WITH OUR OPERETTE PLANS

NOW I SHALL SHOOT MYSELF STOP SHALL BE AWAY FOR A
MONTH IN FRANCE BUT ANY CABLE HERE WILL GET ME
IMMEDIATELY.

Halliday then began to ask a string of questions not only about the
piece but about the concerns that occurred to corn-fed Americans about
living conditions in austerity England. Noël began by being very understanding on both scores:

MARCH 28TH

OF COURSE ABSOLUTELY UNDERSTAND YOUR POINT OF VIEW IN
WANTING EVERYTHING CLEAR AND AGREE THIS BEST DONE
WELL AHEAD BUT QUITE CONVINCED YOU NEED HAVE NO
MISAPPREHENSION ON POINTS RAISED STOP DEVELOPMENT OF
LEADING CHARACTER AND EVOLUTION OF STORY IN FINAL
TREATMENT WILL BE SHAPED TO MARY'S PERSONALITY AND
TEMPERAMENT STOP LIVING CONDITIONS HERE GOOD ENOUGH
TO SURPRISE YOU AND ARE IMPROVING AND IF SLIGHTLY
RESTRICTED FOR GROWN UPS ARE VERY HEALTHY FOR
CHILDREN WHO ARE SPECIALLY PRIVILEGED [the Hallidays had a
year-old child, Heller] REGARDING EVERYTHING THEY NEED SUCH
AS EXTRA MILK PRIORITY IN FRUIT ALLOCATIONS AND EXTRA
CLOTHING COUPONS STOP THINK BEST PLAN FOR YOU TO LIVE
AT HYDE PARK HOTEL WHICH IS FIRST RATE AND OVERLOOKS
HYDE PARK WHICH IS LOVELY FOR CHILDREN STOP TAX
SITUATION IS WITHIN REASONABLE AND MANAGEABLE LIMITS
WILL GET ACCURATE INFORMATION ON THIS AND FORWARD IT
TO YOU STOP I AM SO VERY KEEN AND ENTHUSIASTIC OVER THIS
PROJECT SO LETS ALL DETERMINE TO BRING IT ABOUT.

At this point Neysa McMein happened to be visiting London and
offered to be an unofficial intermediary with her friends, the Hallidays:

May 25th

Your letter made an enormous hit but they were really worried about
two main points.

They were not satisfied with the story you had outlined. I
explained how you had seen the light yourself and had already made
drastic changes in the Lady's character. I also pointed out that you
could not write your book for Mary until you were sure of Mary.

Mary was entranced with her not being such a goody-goody girl. I told her what you had explained to me—i.e. getting your big tunes set. That you were in the process of writing an unsentimental and funny song for her when I left. Also pointing out that you were too good a showman to overlook any bets. She mentioned "Mad About the Boy" two or three times as a song she had always wanted to do in a night club or somewhere.

The great smash hit now is *Annie Get Your Gun* and it is perfectly wonderful. Merman puts every song over, and of course the audiences like best her funny numbers. Do, when you have the time, write a homey tough little song for Mary. (In case your memory fails you, remember that one great American characteristic is to compare everything they see with something from their home-town . . . always to its disadvantage. Also we are a race of whopping liars!)

She is worried sick about her voice not being good enough for high-toned arias (tunes). I told her your songs were beautiful and that we had listened to *her* records—so you *knew* what her voice was like.

I imagine they will want to know how big the theatre is—and of course they were anxious to have you send over the music. We argued over this for some time, my point being that it would be tragic to have the songs butchered, etc. I think she would be quite satisfied if you decided to send her two or three but you will of course decide that yourself. She is really afraid that her voice is not up to anything operatic. She wondered out loud if she should take voice lessons this summer.

She has called off her movie, and they were anxious to know what other stuff you had to do before you could get down to this show. I explained that as far as I know this was your chief concern. You might emphasise this when you write them.

Another point I thought of was her clothes. She is crazy about Mainbocher's, insisted on having him do them for her movie—and he does make her look beautiful. I imagine that sooner or later this subject will come up . . . It seems to me that Gladys could do her to a fare-you-well. But remember that Mary is a small town girl and has never been *anywhere* except Hollywood—and is scared out of her wits at the prospect of London.

What I told them on my own was that it was important that some American actress appear in London. That we had had so many delightful English stars, including the Old Vic [in the United States] and as far as I knew, not one actress or actor of any calibre is appearing on the London stage now.

Noël replied:

July 12th, 1946

Darling Beauty,

I have exchanged a lot of letters and cables with the Hallidays including a very sweet letter from Mary herself. I am quite certain they are really nice people and that we shall all like each other and I feel happy and excited about the whole thing.

After working like a dog for the last few weeks I have completed the whole operette with the exception of a small amount of music to be finished off in September; so now I am going to France for a holiday and taking the car so that I can wander about and really relax. Oh, Beauty, I do hope and believe you will like the operette now it is complete. I honestly think I've done a good job.

I am asked to send you much love by Gladys, Joyce, Graham, Lorn, Cole, Bert [Lister], Windsor Castle, the Curate of the British Museum, the cloakroom woman at the Tower of London and the Dean and several Canons of Canterbury Cathedral. There is no message from Dover Castle, so it is evidently still offended.

All my love to my dearest Beauty.

The next several weeks were taken up with Halliday haggling over details of the contract. By mid-June he is hinting that there are conflicting offers under discussion. "You know we are giving your invitation first consideration but we must begin to be definite." They remained, he said, "excited nitwits" and could not wait to arrive in September. "We are so happy we could cry and then our tears dissolve into laughter." They could not wait to "do justice to your beautiful story, your beautiful lyrics, your beautiful self."

Noël, meanwhile, took himself off to France with Graham. They drove to Biarritz to stay with Edward Molyneux, then went to Paris to reclaim the Place Vendôme apartment but, as far as the rest of the world was concerned, they were at that wonderfully convenient destination: incommunicado. The increasingly boring details were left to Lorn, who found herself dealing with two or three detailed cables and queries a day. Was the electric current alternating or direct and what was the amount? Lorn maintained her usual calm:

(HAIR DRIER OKAY BED ATTENDED TO . . . ADVISE BRING SOAP
CANDY COSMETICS UNDERWEAR AND STOCKINGS FOR YOUR
PERSONAL USE BUT NO NEED TOILET PAPER)

Then the Hallidays decided they needed to bring not only their daughter's nanny but also their secretary, and became increasingly insistent until Lorn firmly pointed out:

APPLICATION NOT GRANTED AND AM ADVISED USELESS TO PRESS
FOR IT.

By September 26 the Hallidays are safely—if somewhat sullenly—on the *Queen Mary* and Noël reenters the fray:

WE ARE DANCING WITH IMPATIENCE AND SO VERY MUCH
LONGING TO SEE YOU STOP STAY IN CABIN TILL I GET THERE SO
WE DON'T MISS EACH OTHER STOP LOVE NOËL

As he drove home after leaving them at the Savoy, Noël was, he told his *Diary,* "in a haze of happiness . . . Personally I think she has authentic magic. She is quite obviously an artist in the true sense." To begin with, he persuaded himself that she was "a dream girl . . . [with] all the mercurial charm of Gertie at her best with a sweet voice and more taste."

The troubles then began.

•

THE FIRST PROBLEM was the play itself. Noël had become besotted with his imaginary South Sea island of Samolo that he had first evoked in *We Were Dancing. Hay Fever* and *Blithe Spirit* had been written spontaneously in days, but now he spent weeks constructing a history of the island, the genealogies of the principal characters, and even the rudiments of a language. In *Conversation Piece* he had fallen into the trap of overindulging his French; this time it was Samolan. The final effect was decidedly unbalanced.

The story was conventional operetta. Mary Martin played Mme. Elena Salvador, a famous and widowed diva who visits the island after an exhausting world tour, then meets and falls in love with Kerry Stirling, younger son of a traditional Scottish Victorian family. Social pressures force them to part but, predictably, all ends happily.

Onstage, while the show was taking shape, happiness was in short supply. In truth the actual building was in no fit state to be used. There was no heating, and the winter winds found every bomb-damaged nook and cranny, while the cast was busily turning blue in their flimsy tropical costumes.

Noël wrote to Jack:

Here we are going through the familiar trouble of auditions with rows upon rows of hideous dwarfs with no voices and wild mad looking women of all ages who sing off key. As always we get a few good ones and are actually collecting a good singing company. But, of course, some, who I decide are only just good enough for chorus, are so God damned high and mighty that they want £25 a week and a single number.

The *unfamiliar* trouble we're going through is the long and bitter struggle to repair the bomb damage to the Theatre. I think it is more or less settled now but it has been a long, wearisome and idiotic fight. I have been putting additional touches to the score and I do think, honestly and truly, that it is very good.

Mary, realizing quite early on that she was badly miscast, began to show temperament. At first Noël tried to be understanding. He worried about her "general lack of understanding. However, I am sure she will get it." She did *not* get it. Instead, she fussed about her hair, refused to wear a hat or have bows on her dress. "She is at last showing signs of being tiresome . . . but I suppose she must be allowed a little latitude." And what Mary didn't choose to say to Noël, Richard Halliday was happy to say for her—loudly and repetitively. ("It was one of the most hideous, hysterical and vulgar exhibitions I have ever known in the theatre.")

Things were not helped by the financial facts of the production. Mary had insisted on 10 percent of the gross. Noël himself received no more as librettist and composer. He expressed his true feelings in private verse:

## I RESENT YOUR ATTITUDE TO MARY

*I resent your attitude to Mary.*
*It betrays a very ugly sort of mind.*
*She is innocent and pure*
*And her husband, I am sure,*
*Would consider your behaviour rather rude and* most *unkind.*
*He resents and I resent*
*And all the passers-by resent*
*Your hideous attitude to Mary*

*I resent your attitude to Mary,*
*You only send her flowers once a day*
*Tho' her voice is apt to jar,*
*She's a* very *famous star*
*And she's only taking ten per cent for acting in your play.*
*Tho' her husband's heel is rather hairy,*
*He does very nicely on her pay.*
*He resents and she resents*
*And even Sylvia C {Cecil, a cast member} resents*
*Your beastly attitude to Mary*

During rehearsal there was a sad personal note—a postscript to the war and much else. Auntie Vida Veitch, not wishing to be a bother to anyone, died peacefully in her sleep. "She looked very pathetic and little . . . [She] chose the perfect way to die. Just sleep and the light flicking out." She left an estate of £463.10s.4d.

•

*PACIFIC 1860* FINALLY opened on December 19. The critical consensus was that the postwar West End didn't need prewar Coward, especially now that Broadway had groundbreaking shows like Rodgers and Hammerstein's *Oklahoma!* Ironically it was that very show that would follow Noël into Drury Lane.

As for *Pacific 1860,* Noël "came to the sad conclusion that the fundamental trouble is that Mary, charming and sweet as she is, knows nothing about Elena, never has and never will, and although she has a delicious personality, she cannot sing. She is crammed with talent but is still too 'little' to play sophisticated parts."

He was strengthend in that belief when, on the occasion of the visit of the king and queen and Princess Margaret (January 23, 1947), Mary was heard to say to Princess Margaret of the absent Princess Elizabeth, "Give my best to your sister. Bye-bye for now." And when the following day Mary made a speech to the company, thanking them for their "good performance" for the royals, Noël briefly lost his composure with the lady— only to piece it laboriously back together the next day: "I have searched London for an olive branch but, like really agile butlers, they are very rare nowadays. To find a hatchet to bury is also difficult owing to the steel shortage. I am, therefore, sending you these flowers with my love."

But the relationship had now deteriorated too far, and Noël's attempts to patch it were counterproductive. Tired of Mary, *Pacific 1860,* "Dreary Lane," and the whole episode, he decided to set off on his first postwar visit to New York. But before he did:

Dear Noël,
I'm sorry to say I don't find it easy to be gracious about accepting the "peace-offering". Perhaps if I hadn't had less sleep in the last three weeks than I've ever had I could be more appreciative. But, I'm very weary, all over.

However, there are at least two things I'm very clear about and which I don't think you are aware of. One—you are without doubt the most charming host I've ever known and I shall always be grateful, and shall always love recalling tens—even hundreds—of wonderful moments you created and that gave me nothing but fun and pleasure.

Two—we have not had any "disagreements". I have never been

permitted to say so little or express myself so little. One just isn't allowed to disagree with a dictator—or with you or Gladys. It is fortunate and has been rewarding in the past and will be in the future, that you two found each other and understand and admire each other so perfectly. I am sure the association gives you both everything you want. But, professionally, I'm sorry to say, it has given me little that I want—and personally it has given me nothing. I found the emotional outbursts something entirely new; the unreasonable approach ugly and deplorable—they made me physically ill. I'm really writing to ask, that for all our sakes, that you accept me "for better or for worse"—but, please, both you and Gladys, stay away— "professionally" in every way—I'm incapable of going on *and* at the same time receiving *orders*. I'm tired, I'm bored. I need sleep. I'm sorry but I find I can't get sleep *and* commands from you and Gladys at the same time. And, now that it's gone so far—I can't take any more suggestions from third parties. But, of course, you also realize that "professionally," Coward and Martin just don't have anything more to offer each other. "Socially" I look forward (and will consider myself lucky) to see you again and again and again—and even more than that;—again *and* again—!!!

Have a good and successful trip—All best wishes.
MARY

January 28th 1947

My dear Mary,
I am typing this reply to your letter because I have quite a lot to say and my handwriting is difficult to read.

You said very charming things about our social and personal relationship and I do most sincerely assure you that as far as all that side of it is concerned we are absolutely quits. You and Richard couldn't possibly have been more genuinely appreciative of any small efforts I may have made to make your visit happy and you also, both of you, reciprocated everything to the full. Now, professionally speaking, I think the situation needs clarifying a little and I must say to you what is truly in my heart and mind regarding both your position and your performance in the theatre. I fully appreciate the fact that you are weary and tired and have lost sleep. So am I and so have I. It is always difficult and exhausting when something upon which one has immense faith and energy turns out to be a disappointment. I am dreadfully sad that after all our high hopes, the show has not been as successful as we thought it was going to be. However, there it is and facts must be faced.

It seems to me that you and Richard have got your theatrical values very confused. The Star System, as occasionally exemplified by (for example your *Lute Song*) [her previous show] contract should not, on the basis of logic and reason, exist in any theatre in the world.

You have personality, charm and a great deal of talent, as yet largely undeveloped. Your years in the theatre have been few; you made your first success singing, quite perfectly, "My Heart Belongs to Daddy"; your second success was *One Touch of Venus,* in which you were charming and did what was required of you gracefully and well. *Dancing In the Streets* I know little about beyond the fact that it did not come into New York. *Lute Song* I did not see but I have heard on all sides that it was beautiful to look at, dull, only moderately successful and that you were unanimously acclaimed as being charming in it. Whether or not your acting performance was accurate and according to the script I do not know, as I neither read the script nor saw you in it.

*Pacific 1860* is, according to these statistics which I think are correct, the fifth theatrical production with which you have been concerned. It is the forty-seventh theatrical production with which I have been concerned since 1920. For your performance you are paid by the management the biggest star salary payable in this Country i.e. ten per cent of the gross and have been given full transport for yourself and party. You arrived in this country full of friendliness and enthusiasm with a completely wrong conception of the part of Elena Salvador. This you have frequently admitted to me yourself. You accuse me in your letter of being a dictator. What you are really accusing me of is being a director. I have tried, with the utmost gentleness and patience, to guide and help you into understanding and playing Elena. Not only am I the director but I am also the author and creator of the character, therefore, I am afraid my conception must logically supersede yours. You worked extremely hard, not only up to production but after production, to play the part as I wished it played. You were on the verge of succeeding when, on account of some highly irrational and quite inaccurate opinions of your own about period clothes, you proceeded to throw away all that our joint efforts had so nearly achieved.

Your insistence that your position as a star entitled you to wear a dress in direct contradiction to the designer's, the director's, the author's and the management's wishes was an abuse of your position and a tacit acknowledgement that you still had no conception of the job you were being highly paid to do. It was perfectly apparent a long while ago that you had conceived a personal animosity for Gladys Calthrop but the fact remains she is an expert on period clothes and you are not. Since then you have built up in your mind an animosity towards me as a dictator. I am also an expert and know exactly how, ideally, this part should and could be played by you.

When we were rehearsing you remarked on my patience and gentleness in directing Sylvia Cecil. You may remember that both Gladys and I insisted on her wearing a wig which *she* did not wish to do. We insisted on this (A) because it was correct and in period and (B) because for her to have more or less the same coloured hair as you would have been ineffective. Do you consider this dictatorship? Or would you have preferred us to have allowed her to wear her own hair exactly as she wished?

You say you found the emotional outbursts something entirely new and the unreasonable approach ugly and deplorable. The first emotional outburst, I hasten to remind you, took place some days before production when Richard had admittedly had too much to drink and screamed a great deal of irrelevant and hysterical abuse. The second emotional outburst was when I came into your room with Lorn and asked you not to wear your Second Act dress in the First Act as it completely defeated the effect you were trying to make. You then burst into angry tears, stamped your foot, said I was out of my mind, screamed at the top of your lungs (with reference to the yellow dress), "I hate it, I hate it, I hate it" and refused point blank to wear any sort of hat in a period when only a lady of easy virtue would leave her house bare-headed. The end of this second and I hope last emotional outburst was the discarding of the yellow dress and hat in which you looked dignified and delightful and the designing and making of a new dress which, although perfectly adequate, is not a quarter as distinctive or distinguished. From that moment onwards you have proceeded to behave in a very curious way. You refused to make recordings, regardless of the fact that the making of them meant a great deal to the Company and to the show, unless I guaranteed that you had "two sides" to yourself. And that you sang, as a solo, a number which in the show is designed and executed as a duet. You also refused to appear at a photograph call until 1:30 on a Monday, thereby completely ruining the planned work of the day. It seems to me, dear Mary, that you and Richard are placing too much emphasis on the word "star" and too little on the famous theatrical word "trouper."

I am sure that by the time you have read this far you will have convinced yourself that by writing this letter to you I am behaving in an "ugly" manner with intent to hurt you. This is untrue. I am writing to you as a man of the theatre of many years standing who is full of admiration of your personality, charm and talent and who also sees, perhaps more than you realise, how many years of hard work, possible disappointments and the humble acceptance of superior knowledge lie ahead of you before you achieve the true reward that your ambition demands.

Please believe that your future career depends on your throwing away your, and above all Richard's exaggerated and grotesque conception of "Stardom" and concentrating on learning, diligently and painstakingly, to be the fine *artiste* your potential talent entitles you to be.

So much for my professional point of view.

Socially, indeed, I deeply hope that we shall meet again and again and again and I do send you my best wishes always.

He had long since become "sick to death of *Pacific 1860* and everything to do with it," and when it finally gave up the ghost after 129 performances, his sigh of relief was almost audible.

The Coward-Martin team was certainly at a parting of the ways, but it would only be temporary. They would again be "together with music"— but not just yet.

•

WHILE NOËL HAD BEEN shivering through a drafty South Pacific, he had also been trying to guide Jack through the Broadway production of *Present Laughter,* very much as he had with the earlier *Blithe Spirit.* Once again Clifton Webb was playing the leading role.

23/9/46
17 Gerald Road
S.W.1.

Darling Mr. Webb,

You poor foolish boy! Fancy attempting to play a part which being in itself small and rather thankless requires, above everything else, beauty and grace and sweetness. After all, you must remember, it was written with those qualities in mind and played with such exquisite finesse that you could have heard a bomb drop.

However, if you like, in your clumsy heavy footed way, to go stamping through the fabric of my dreams, that's entirely your affair.

I detected in your letter a certain whining note about the number of words you had to learn.

This complaint has been verified by those funny little Lunts who I hear are strutting about in some trumpery little piece [*O Mistress Mine*] and who also have trouble with their words.

Now, my Darling Little Webb, it is a question of concentration and Mary Baker Eddy . . . You must persevere, Dear Boy, and think beautiful thoughts and if you don't make an enormous success in it, I shall come and knock the B'Jesus out of you! I consign you happily to your fate! I love you very much. I also love Mabelle very much and will send her a gold tooth when I get round to it.

Now, be a good boy, Master Webb, and when in any doubts, think of Leonora Corbett.

Love and mad mad kisses

Mr. Coward

The largely socialite first night contributed to a fiasco, which the critics were quick to seize on and, although Jack soon had the numbed performers back on track and put the "bloody awful" experience behind them, the edge was taken off what might have been a considerable success.

Noël commiserated with Jack:

12th November 1946

I can't tell you how I sympathized about the obvious bloodiness of the first night. I am sure you did all you could to give them speed but I should think myself, and very much between ourselves, that the main trouble was Clifton. I am sure he plays it beautifully and I know he is a fine actor, but *Present Laughter* is not so much a play as a series of semi-autobiographical pyrotechnics, and it needs, over and

Together . . . with Chaplin. The squabbles of *Pacific 1860* behind her, Mary Martin seems to be enjoying the company of Noël and Charlie Chaplin.

above everything else, abundant physical vitality. I myself found it arduous to play and God knows I have the vitality of the devil. Clifton's method is more measured than mine and I suspect that because of this, in spite of his technical skill and wit and charm, he gives the audience time to see the wheels going round. I played it more violently than I have ever played anything, and swept everything and everybody along with me at a breakneck speed. Obviously there is nothing to be done about all this but I expect you will agree with me. I am delighted that the business is good. As you know I don't pay much attention to notices and if it's a reasonable success, so much the better.

Compared with *Blithe Spirit*'s 657 performances, it lasted just 158.

# CHAPTER 22
# THE FALLOW FORTIES

## (1947–1950)

T HE WEST END, it appeared, was not in the mood for a revue. In
fact the format that once had been glamorous, topical, and relatively
cheap to produce was in rapid decline, until it enjoyed a sort of revival
on television in the 1960s.

Nor did it find operetta any more to its taste, although it retained its

When in doubt, revive *Present Laughter.* Noël did just
that, at London's Haymarket Theatre in 1947, with
Moira Lister as the predatory Joanna Lyppiatt.

affection for the more *bravissimo* Ivor Novello version. While Noël was struggling with *Pacific 1860,* Ivor was pulling in the crowds with the even more unlikely story of a romantic highwayman in *Perchance to Dream.*

Was it possible that the common denominator in Noël's relative failures was—Noël? In the *Diaries* he asks himself the question repeatedly but always rhetorically.

No—to use another of his favorite phrases—"It was time to come out of another hole." He would star in a revival of *Present Laughter.* If Coward the dramatist wasn't a draw right now, Coward the actor certainly would be.

Then, at the back of his mind, he could feel that there was a serious play nagging to be written. It had been inspired by what he had witnessed during the war. It would be about the spirit of the British people, the way they had been let down by the promises of their leaders in those immediate prewar years and how their spirit would always ultimately triumph— even if they had actually *lost* the war. The idea was borrowed from one of Noël's favorite writers, "Saki" (H. H. Munro), who had written the post–World War I story *When William Came* based on the premise that England has been occupied by the Kaiser and his troops. Noël's version would be called—after Chamberlain's famous line—*Peace in Our Time.*

While he was in the United States in the early part of 1947 Noël duly wrote it. And while the mood was upon him, he wrote another play that September—based on his short story "What Mad Pursuit." He called it *Long Island Sound.*

*Peace in Our Time* opened in July to muted respect. It soon became clear, though, that Noël had repeated the experience of *Post-Mortem* nearly twenty years earlier. True as its observations may have been, the British public, hanging on grimly in austerity that no longer had an ennobling cause to excuse it, had no wish to be reminded of what they had just gone through, and even less to contemplate how much worse it might well have been.

When the show's probable fate became clear, Noël reflected to Lornie:

I'm fairly depressed about *Peace In Our Time* not being the smasheroo we thought it was . . . I suppose the public really don't feel like seeing anything serious at the moment and I must say I can't blame the poor sods. All the same it is disheartening . . . The Lunts read *P in our T* and were crackers about it and so were Kit [Katharine Cornell] and [her husband] Guthrie [McClintic] and so am I and so are you and if it really is a failure, I think that England is a very silly island indeed, in spite of Clive and Drake and Trafalgar and Shakespeare and Olwen [Clemence Dane's companion].

Despite an excellent cast, *Peace in Our Time* survived for only 167 performances.

By this time, however, Noël had fulfilled his commitment to *Present Laughter,* twitched his mantle blue once more, and taken Graham off on his first visit to America.

Then there was a rather self-conscious letter from Laurence Olivier. Since *Private Lives* in 1930, Olivier had been something of a *protégé* for Noël. Eight years younger, he had always been somewhat in awe of the Master, even though his own career onstage and in films was by now stellar. He was now being offered a knighthood, and his letter was like that of an ex-pupil to his old headmaster:

> I have a feeling that you would have thought more highly of me if I'd turned the bloody thing down, and I must tell you that I had always determined to do so, should the occasion arise, and Puss [Vivien Leigh] had always said "of course you'd refuse it" and I have always nodded vigorously . . . but when it came along I found that I liked the idea tremendously and so did Puss, and sighing rather regretfully to find that I just wasn't in your class, old boy, of quite justifiably sticking out for an O.M. [Order of Merit—the highest honor], decided that it felt more pompous in ME to refuse than to accept— so there you are!

What he did *not* mention was his anger that his friendly rival, Ralph Richardson, had *already* been knighted.

In later years, as the honors began to pile up for Olivier, it became a running joke between him and Noël. When Larry reported that he really couldn't understand why Oxford University would insist on making him a Doctor of Letters, he was immediately on the receiving end of a typical Coward comeback: "Doctor of four letters, I presume?"

By early August Noël was reporting from New York, where his "home-coming" was not entirely to his liking:

To Lorn [August 5]
The Baybay's wickedness over this apartment has surpassed everything. He had allowed—nay encouraged—the horrid little fuck-pig who rented it to have it all re-painted and re-furnished. He has a taste in furnishing that swings between a coloured tart and an old lady at Seaford with a parrot.

I arrived to find a very unpleasant antique ridden love-nest filled with shells and rosaries and small angry Buddhas and prettiest of all, a sodding little table made out of a zither! The dark green bedroom was like an aquarium and all the pannelling painted over in grey paint so that it looks as tho it had contracted a mild case of leprosy. With shrill trumpeting and great rage I flew to Bloomingdales and I

Laurence Olivier and Noël in earlier, happier days. They sailed together
on the *SS Normandie* in 1937.

am now having the whole place re-done with new curtains and covers
etc., etc., all of which I am cheerfully charging to the Great Wilson
Debt. Apart from this deep-dyed villainy he has been a sweet and
wriggling honey-bear and we had a lovely week-end at Fairfield with
Natasha saying *"Monstreux"* constantly and diving in and out of the
kitchen to find chicken bones for herself and her horrid dachshound.

Having got that off his chest, he turned to other news: "MCA keep on
offering me wonderful film propositions at which I laugh and snap my fingers like a gay Spanish thing. This farting typewriter still jumps like a
Springbok."

To Gladys later that month, after a visit to Katharine Cornell at
Martha's Vineyard:

It was wonderful at Kit's—really most particularly your dish—Kit
cooking steaks and lobsters over an open fire while we all sat around
sipping "Old Fashioneds". After we'd left there we drove up into the
heart of New England . . .

We had a blissful week at Martha's Vineyard and I really painted a
picture of the house without a cliff in sight but I did have a relapse
and do a tropical number with palm trees. Oh bugger this thing,
it's getting the jumps again, so this letter will look like as how I had
hiccoups!

We caught Gertie playing in Stock just outside Boston. She had elected to do the little dainty that Mary Ellis did about Mrs. FitzHerbert [wife of King George IV]. We all had supper and it was very gay and reminiscent and everyone said fuck and piss off and it was quite nostalgic. Gertie was quite good in the play although perhaps a bit piss elegant. The rest was horrid.

There was a petulant postscript to the apartment debacle:

The little sod that Dab let ruin this apartment got into a shrill rage when he found out that he was never going to be allowed to set his stinking, mincing little feet in it again, and we found that he had given orders for the telephone to be disconnected! La La but I trow there was a drumming of heels and I have had to charm a telephone gentleman into letting me have another one which these days is virtually impossible. I have also ordered a great deal of new crockery and furniture and charged it all to Dab, which may teach him to be more considerate of my possessions in future. He is now cowering in the country.

From Martha's Vineyard their itinerary took them west:

We are going to Genesee via Chicago tomorrow. Alfred and Lynn are meeting us in Chicago and we are all going with gritted teeth to see Tallulah dirty up *Private Lives*. I understand, Tallulah does everything but stuff a kipper up her twot but is playing to smash capacity! I can't feel that it is going to be an entirely pleasant evening.

1948. Tallulah Bankhead (1902–1968) revives *Private Lives*. Noël went to the Chicago tryout "with gritted teeth," but found himself pleasantly surprised. He even let the production come to Broadway.

In the event:

September 9th

We spent two hectic days with Tallulah in Chicago. I went to see her in *Private Lives* with my heart in my boots and was very pleasantly surprised. True, she did a few shrieks and growls here and there, which were not quite in the highest tradition of sophisticated comedy, but her vitality was amazing and, strange to say, she played the love scene quite beautifully. We went with Alfred and Lynn who also thought she was excellent and, as we arrived in the dressing-room afterwards, Lynn advanced, full of graciousness and said, "Tallulah, you were simply enchanting and—" whereupon Miss B cut her short and said "I don't give a fuck about you and Alfred. It's only Noël I am worrying about!" She said it in no way maliciously but merely as a statement of fact! Fortunately it was all such a gale of effusiveness and fun that nobody minded but I thought you would like to know it as an example of Dix-Huitième courtesy and tact.

After our week with the Lunts we came back and spent our two days with Tallu who, apart from getting pissed on the Sunday night and carrying on stinking, really couldn't have been sweeter. She insisted on our being her guests at the hotel, showered us with flowers and scent and wouldn't let us pay for a thing and, on top of everything insisted on giving me an enormous Augustus John painting which I collected on Sunday from her house in the country. It is a magnificent painting worth, I should think, about three thousand pounds! She explained that she wasn't mad about it herself and was going to give it to a museum but that she knew I collected pictures and would rather I had it than anyone else in the world. All this because I said she could go on playing *P.L.* for as long as she wanted and ultimately do a season in New York with it. As she is playing to smash capacity this was a reasonable gesture on my part. Altogether I was very touched by her in spite of her wildness. Incidentally she sent you all kinds of love. (Now this bloody typewriter has started jumping again and I've just had it mended— imagine!)

He had already written his thank-you letter:

[Undated—Wednesday]

Darling Tallu,

To write and thank you for the happy time you gave me is such an anti-climax. You were so gay and sweet and generous and your god damned vitality lights up all the world around you and I only hope they kept you away from the coast during the war on account of your magnetism triggering up any black out.

I'm not going to say any more about the Augustus John until I've seen it when I will write immediately but I am going to say . . . (How wonderful not to be interrupted) . . . that I am deeply touched that you should give me such a lovely and wonderful present, but not any more touched than I was by suddenly receiving two bottles of scent and, at the same time, the knowledge that, with all the weight of the years on us, you loved me very much and I loved you very much.

Thank you very much, darling, for all your sweetness and your insane generosity.

Take care of yourself and for Christ's sake, don't be a silly bitch and ruin your health by ramming "reefers" up your jacksie and generally farting about and forgetting that if your particular light flickers and even fades a little, a lot of people will be left in the dark.

My dear love to you.
NOËL

The gesture was subsequently diluted somewhat when she asked for the Augustus John painting to be returned. She had, she said, only meant it as a *loan*!

An incensed Noël wrote to Lornie: "Tallulah, apart from being a conceited slut, is a black liar. She *gave* me the bloody picture and forced it on me because she wanted to play *P.L.* in New York. There was never a question of a loan. Why in hell should I wish to be *lent* an Augustus John portrait of a pear drop? *Send it back!*"

When, a year or two later, Jack Wilson was proposing to direct the lady, Noël told Lornie: "The play he has for Tallulah is based on a Henry James novel. It is very gentle and subtle and if Miss Bankhead can discipline herself to refrain from farting to get a laugh or bouncing ping-pong balls off her tits, it might be a success."

His letter to Lorn continued:

Now I have to go and discuss drearily with Miss Lawrence the macabre possibility of her doing a revival of *To-Night at What Have You*. I shall continue—like the *Perils of Pauline*—to-morrow. In the mean time I must think of something to say to finish off this page.

Buggerbuggerbuggerbugger. That is enough. I am very pretty—I am very pretty—I am very pretty. That is better.

The production over which Noël was understandably dragging his feet was an idea of an as usually impecunious Gertie—aided and abetted by her

Tallulah and Noël in later, less happy days.

lawyer/manager Fannie Holtzmann—reviving *Tonight at 8:30*. It would be a national tour of the United States and end up on Broadway.

Following his own dictum of "never cook your cabbage twice," Noël wanted nothing to do with it. Well, the persuasive ladies suggested, what about *Graham* playing your parts?

Since their arrival, Graham had been auditioning for parts without success, and since Noël's desire for Graham's success was greater than the sum of his reservations, he finally gave in. And when it became clear that a jealous Jack, who was supposed to direct, would put every possible rock in the path of the production, Noël decided the only course open to him was to stay in the United States longer than he had originally intended to guide the project's launch.

Having kept a fatherly eye on the early part of the tour, he returned to England for Christmas, then came back to supervise the West Coast production before "bringing the show in." Despite his previous concerns, the reception the show was receiving "on the road" lulled him into thinking he might have been overly pessimistic. On the train from Hollywood to New York he wrote Coley:

Dearest Toley,
Here we are exhausted but happy on our way back to New York. "We" consist of Little Lad, Gertie, Marlene and Katie H[epburn]. It's

really quite fun and we're catching up with some sleep. Hollywood was gay but terribly wearing. I was the belle of the Thing and behaved ever so nicely and everyone outdid themselves to give parties and more parties and the whole thing was stinking with glamour. Our favourites were Irene Dunne, Clifton [Webb] and Gene Kelly but I must say everyone was really mighty sweet. Joan [Crawford] gave the largest . . . so we had a good time and watched the big shots disporting themselves. It was well done, good food and drink and the entertainment was really wonderful on account of Jack Benny, Tony Martin, Celeste Holm and Dinah Shore who all sang divinely and, as they did it as a gesture to me, I was very flattered and had to sing "Marvellous Party" out of sheer self-preservation and it topped the lot and that was jolly gratifying too.

We had a nightmare visit to Tia Juana over the Mexican border in order to get Little Lad's quota number. He drove me and Fanny and Fanny's nephew Howard; Fanny never drew breath and went on buzzing and moaning in our ears like a mad black-water beetle— four hours there and four hours back—and it was unmitigated hell except that we got the bloody number. All the agents in Hollywood have been trying to cash in on me and Del Giudice went trumpeting about and giving my script of *Long Island Sound* to all the studios and I finally got very very angry indeed and decided that in no circumstances would I have anything to do with any of it. I don't care for the movie racket much in England but in Hollywood it is much much worse.

Leonard Spigelgass who got fried that week-end at White Cliffs turned out to be a darling duck and gave a madly gay *soirée* with a whole lot of different faces. It was great fun, particularly a rather beautiful Czeck [*sic*] lady called Florence Marly who looked oddly like Peter Glenville but she spoke lovely French and Spanish and was rather sweet. Janet Gaynor and Adrian [Hollywood designer] gave a dainty dinner without really warning me that it was sixty miles away. It was nice when I got there except for Joan Fontaine's titties which kept falling about and a large rock python which was handed to me as a surprise. I didn't mind but everyone else was jolly frightened and Claudette [Colbert] had to spend the rest of the evening washing her hands in a sort of Lady Macbeth frenzy. Peggy Cummins appeared looking as though she had been carved out of opaque glass.

*Je ne crois pas vraiment* that there is any more *nouvelles* except that we are all in a slight *état* about opening next Friday. Little Lad is giving a jolly fine performance but has had to be slapped down for a slight but very perceptible tendency to overact! *Figure-toi! Le petit*

Noël watches a rehearsal of the *Tonight at 8:30* revival
at New York's National Theatre. His instincts
told him it would flop—and it did.

*violet—Quelle Bearnaise!* Give my dear dear love to all and be a sweet
Tolette and *écrire* again and again and again. La la la la.
  Le Maître.

Noël had it right the first time. The New York critics demolished
*Tonight at 8:30*. It ran for just four painful weeks. "I'll make them swallow
their damn notices yet," he wrote to Lorn. "I fear we are a flop and I have
always believed in putting geographical distance between myself and a
flop."

As he left he wrote to her about his newly confirmed personal resolution:

I have made a lot of very firm resolutions which you will thoroughly
approve of. One is that I really am *not* going to embark on any more

enterprises just because Binkie or Jack or Del [Giudice] want me to. If a lovely idea for a play comes roaring into my mind I shall do it. If fifteen gorgeous short stories attack me when I am lying in the sun I shall write them BUT I am not going to try to think of anything at all. I am also during the coming year going to see far fewer people. I have now definitely decided that I have had a basin full. They all want something from me and I really want nothing at all from them.

•

NOËL PROCEEDED TO CREATE that necessary distance by taking Graham off to Jamaica, the island in the sun that had so impressed him with its tranquillity in 1944, when "Little Bill" had packed him off there for a break before his South African tour.

> *Jamaica's an island surrounded by sea*
> *(Like Corsica, Guam and Tasmania)*
> *The tourist does not need to wear a topee*
> *Or other macabre miscellanea . . .*
> *In fact every tourist who visits these shores*
> *Can thank his benevolent Maker*
> *For taking time off from the rest of His chores*
> *To fashion the Isle of Jamaica.*

They broke their journey in New Orleans:

Our three days in New Orleans were quite fun but a trifle too hectic. Fortunately we fell in with bad company early on. A strange lady with violent black hair and a tangerine make-up and a lot of false ospreys who came from Detroit and was rather the touring rights of Tallulah only a bit more refined. She led us with unerring instinct to a nest of angry lesbians and twittering pussy willows and we drank a lot of mint juleps and looked at a great many over-wrought iron balconies. The food I must say was wonderful and what is known as the "Old Quarter" has a certain charm but it has been badly mauled by American tourists and you can see on a clear day rows and rows of Helen Hokinson [a *New Yorker* cartoonist who specialized in female foibles] ladies with rimless pince-nez and perched hats queuing up outside the Clip Joints.

We finally poured ourselves onto a dear little *bateau* called the *Alcoa Corsair*, which was the last word in modern decoration and beds came out of the wall and socked you one and then snapped back again and the Captain, who was like a Norwegian sacred cow, was clearly a stranger to the Bridge. He spent most of his sea time telling

In 1948 Noël rented Goldeneye, Ian Fleming's Jamaican retreat. Its lack of
amenities caused him to christen it "Golden Eye, Ear, Nose & Throat."

funny stories in the dining-saloon. My suspicions of his ability as a
navigator were amply justified when we arrived at Kingston and
immediately rammed the pier.

There was even something of a "clandestine" element to this particular
visit, too. Another of Little Bill's "boys" had been journalist Ian Fleming,
soon to be the creator of James Bond. Fleming shared his old boss's love of
Jamaica and had recently finished building his own house there. He called
it Goldeneye, and Noël heard it might be to let.

After a lot of good-natured haggling, he finally agreed to what he considered an exorbitant rent for something he later claimed should have been
called Golden Eye, Ear, Nose and Throat. He described it to Lorn:

The house is perched on a little thirty foot high cliff. There is an
enormous room with light walls and wide windows—no glass only
shutters—nice bedrooms with private lulus and showers. There is a
flight of cement steps leading down to an ideal little cove with white
coral sand and a reef so that we can wade out and look at all the
coloured fish through glass-bottomed buckets . . . Behind the house
are banana plantations and then green covered hills and blue mountains in the distance . . . This side of the island is quite cool all year
round and has a lovely wind that blows, not too hard, every day. I am
paying two hundred pounds a month, so you can imagine what the
rents are! That includes three servants, of course, but all the same it's
on the expensive side.

His thank-you letter to Fleming took the form of a verse:

## HOUSE GUEST

*Alas! I cannot adequately praise*
*The dignity, the virtue and the grace*
*Of this most virile and imposing place*
*Wherein I passed so many airless days.*

*Alas! I cannot accurately find*
*Words to express the hardness of the seat*
*Which, when I cheerfully sat down to eat,*
*Seared with such cunning into my behind.*

*Alas! However much I raved and roared,*
*No rhetoric, no witty diatribe*
*Could ever, even partially, describe*
*The impact of the spare-room bed—and board.*

*Alas! Were I to write 'till crack of doom*
*No typewriter, no pencil, nib nor quill*
*Could ever recapitulate the chill*
*And arid vastness of the living-room.*

*Alas! I am not someone who exclaims*
*With rapture over ancient equine prints.*
*Ah no, dear Ian, I can only wince*
*At all those horses framed in all those frames.*

*Alas! My sensitivity rebels,*
*Not at loose shutters, not at a plague of ants*
*Nor other "sub-let" bludgeonings of chance.*
*But at those hordes of ageing, fading shells.*
*Alas! If only commonsense could teach*
*The stubborn heart to heed the cunning brain,*
*You would, before you let your house again,*
*Remove the barracudas from the beach.*

*But still, my dear Commander, I admit,*
*No matter how I criticise and grouse*
*That I was strangely happy in your house—*
*In fact I'm very, very fond of it.*

Whatever reservations Noël might have had about Chez Fleming, the visit confirmed the growing attraction Jamaica held for him. Perhaps he should put down roots here, too.

"Little Lad," Noël wrote, "with a persistence born of his crude tom-tom [South African] upbringing, went beetling off on his own and found some land about seven miles from here." Before they left, Noël had bought the plot of beach land and even designed the house that was to be built there by year end. He first thought of calling it Coward's Folly, then wisely reconsidered and named it Blue Harbour.

He and Graham also found a remote hilltop site called Look-Out, so called because the pirate Sir Henry Morgan had used it for that very purpose. In his enthusiasm, Noël bought that, too, vowing to build on it in years to come when his coffers weren't quite so empty. The four-acre site cost him all of £150.

By the time they returned to New York they were full of plans, and even if the memory of *Tonight at 8:30* hadn't faded entirely, it was at least blurred around the edges.

•

BY THE END of the year Noël had stage problems of his own. He had decided he would like to play *Present Laughter* for two months in France—in French. *Joyeux Chagrins.* "I do hope it will be a success as I do not like to be associated with failures!"

It was not the best idea he ever had. The reviews were poor and the box office not much better. He wrote to Lorn: "Also feeling with insular unreason that as they (the reviews) are in French they don't matter. It seems that I am immensely aristocratic and the Left Wing hate me!"

More chagrined than *joyeux,* he boarded the *Queen Elizabeth* the following January. ("I suppose this succession of failures is good for my soul but I rather doubt it.")

•

JAMAICA HAD ENTERED his life—or perhaps he had entered Jamaica's life—at precisely the right time. It was and would remain a safe haven, a place to lay one's plans, lick one's wounds, and get things back into perspective.

When he and Graham returned there in early February 1949, the main house (Blue Harbour) was "much more ready than I had anticipated." It was also not *quite* what he had had in mind. Instead of being built in layers into the hillside, the architect had built it straight up and down like a single tower. ("My God, it's the Flatiron Building done in white sugar!") But that was soon forgotten in the pleasure Blue Harbour was to provide over the years.

He found himself with a mixed bag of occasional neighbors—Ian Fleming and his married paramour, Lady Ann Rothermere, Max Beaverbrook, and Ivor Novello among them.

When he came to see Ivor's house, it merely confirmed Noël's conviction that, whatever his other accomplishments, taste was not one of them. He reported to Lorn:

> Ivor, with typical Welsh cunning, has almost achieved the impossible, which is to find in Jamaica a house with no view at all. It is a suburban villa with several tiled bathrooms (but a scarcity of water) furnished in flowered chintz and mock mahogany. You can see the sea, which is three miles away, by standing on the dining-room table. Any mountain vista is successfully obscured by a high hedge belonging to the people next door
>
> . . . it is also deeply ensconced in the mosquito area, so that if Olive Gilbert [a close friend of Ivor's and one of his principal singers] so much as opens her twisted trap on the verandah after sundown, she will be in a malarial lather the next morning.

Noël's regular letters to Coley kept him up to date on local gossip. For instance, the long-running feud between Noël and Max Beaverbrook was at least damped down in the Jamaican air: "The Baron Beaverbrook came to lunch the other day oozing amiability and went really dotty about the *maison* and the garden and the view. There was a distinct glint of green envy in the baronial eye. He turned on masses of charm . . ."

There was also the continual *crise* of Ian and Ann. She was married to England's *other* press baron, Lord Rothermere, and, on Ann's frequent visits to the island, was living in reasonably open sin with Ian, under the eye of her husband's great rival, who had for some reason failed to focus on them or was choosing to ignore them.

In his letters to Violet, Gladys, and Lorn, Noël painted a pen portrait of the house and his life there:

> I am enchanted by the house. It is well built, solid and comfortable. The top floor is my bedroom, sitting-room, shower and verandah looking out over eighty miles of mountains and sea. Below is the main sitting-room and verandah with a comfortable bedroom alcove for Graham and a shower and lulu. Also a kitchen and servant's room. The guest-house, which is a few yards away, is one big double room, bath (shower) lulu and verandah. Up above and out of sight is the garage and the servant's quarters. There are stone steps down to the beach and little paths laid out between the almond trees and the coco palms. It really is a dream. The beach as yet is a little disappointing,

because they haven't got rid of enough rocks but that can be done in a week or so. We have a coffee-coloured chauffeur-valet, who is efficient and amiable. We have electric light and water, both of which are rare on this coast, and now we have to set to work on the garden and beach. We went into Port Maria yesterday morning and bought a lot of domestic necessities such as Polyflor wax and Brasso and hooks and scissors and cushions and paper fasteners, etc. etc!

Graham has become a gardening maniac—he pinches cuttings right and left, shoves them into the ground, croons to them and covers them and himself with manure. He is very busy bashing about and planting things upside down . . .

We have two new additions to the household; a minute white kitten called Evelyn because we are uncertain what sex it is and Evelyn will do for either!

The question was soon unequivocally settled, and a few years later: "Evelyn, who is now a grandmother, is about to have some more kittens, which really is going too far. She really is very modern in her outlook and I tremble to think what Marie Corelli would have thought of her."

Nor was that the end of the saga:

Evelyn retired into the waste paper basket yesterday morning and gave birth to three kittens! As she is a great great grandmother, I consider this no mean achievement. We have not been permitted to meet the father socially but we think he is on the common side and

Firefly, the safe haven Noël built for himself in Jamaica. He was buried there, in a spot overlooking the Spanish Main.

lives down the road with some Indians. I am thinking of re-christening the house "Cat's Cradle".

We also have a small beige puppy with a black face and white gloves. He is called Jellaby after the little boy in *Bleak House,* who keeps on getting his head caught between things.

The plumbing has proved to be a trifle eccentric and my lavatory has hiccoups and sprays my behind with cold water every now and then which is all very gay and sanitary.

When it decides to rain here there are no half measures about it. It comes down in a deluge and there is already some valuable Penicillin growing in all my shoes!

There are no dangerous insects or animals here but I have just found a beetle the size of a saucer nestling among a lot of three-halfpenny stamps. It seems fairly amiable but its expression does not inspire confidence. I have now thrown it over the verandah and I *think* it went into Graham's bedroom window.

I rather enjoy my morning shopping trips into Port Maria. Everyone is very amiable and their colours are graded from deep ebony to pale *café au lait*.

Mr. Philpot in the General Store is coal black with far more teeth than are usual and he always wrings my hand like a pump handle and we make little jokes. Then, of course, there is Madame Cecilia Chung, my Chinese groceress. She, having read in some obscure Chinese newspaper that I was renowned for being witty, goes into gales of oriental laughter when I ask quite ordinarily for Colman's mustard or Worcester sauce!

The girls in the Post Office start giggling with anticipatory delight before I get out of my car so you do see that there is never a dull moment for anybody!

Oh la la! as I always say, having acted so prettily in the French language.

I went over to tea with Jean Batten [the aviator] the other day who has a sweet but ghastly mother who was so refeened that she could hardly speak. She asked very tenderly about you and I said that you were all right except that you drank heavily and kept on falling down in Eaton Square but that everything was under control, really, on account of us living so conveniently near the police station.

I have bought the top of the mountain that I have had my eye on since last year. It is exactly five minutes from here in the car and really the view is the most fabulous in Jamaica. I am not going to spend any money on it yet beyond planting a few things but I have a feeling that in the future it might come in handy. I have several acres and the ruined remains of an old house. If in the far future I ever wanted to let this house for long or even sell it at a vast price, I could keep one of the beaches and live up top. But all that is very far in the future because I am as happy as a bee here for the present. But this coast is being bought up like mad and it is nice to think that, if it ever becomes really overcrowded, I shall have a bolt-hole. On my three acres there are oranges, limes, breadfruit, avocado pears, pimentos and all sorts of tropical deliciousnesses. The place was what is known as a "Great House" about two hundred years ago and so it is well planted. The ruins are grown over with orchids! Little wild puce coloured ones, and it really is very peaceful and sweet.

There have been great carryings on about Lady R. and Commander F. She arrived in a blaze of Jamaican publicity and announced that she was staying with me. So when a *Life* photographer arrived here we had to send Little Lad {to Goldeneye} *chaud pied* to fetch her. There then began a very natty high comedy scene in which she kept forgetting she was a house guest and asking us what we had been doing all the morning etc. We then all traipsed over to Montego Bay for a night and *Elle et Lui* discreetly (i.e. indiscreetly) had breakfast together on the balcony of his room! After this I descended upon them both and gave them a very stern lecture indeed. I must say they are very sweet but . . . I have grave fears for the *avenir.*

Jamaica was to provide a useful plot element when it came time to write his Samolan (Jamaican) novel, *Pomp and Circumstance* (1960).

Whatever its other attractions, Jamaica was not known for its haute cuisine, and Noël did not want his distinguished guests to go away hungry. He wrote again to Coley for recipe ideas:

Dearest Toley,
Thanks for yours like anything *et mille mercis pour les jolis recipes* which have caused a minor race riot *dans la cuisine.* We had some soft, damp fried bread for breakfast this morning cuddled round some old bacon rind. It was but delicious! Evan Williams, our *homme à tout faire,* is full of enthusiasm and tries like a mad thing. He is very sweet and coffee-coloured and I have to keep on buying him trousers. He will never *quite* supplant you in my affections on account of his inadequate knowledge of French (and English) and not being very good at crosswords. Little Lad alternates between savage irritation and hilarious joy at his film being postponed. Personally, of course, I am delighted because he can go on bashing about in the *jardin* and rolling in manure and generally enhancing the House Beautiful. The

What happened off the screen may well have been more
interesting than what happened on it. Here Celia Johnson
clearly has the undivided attention of the production crew,
not to mention of Graham Payn (*left*) and Joyce Carey (*right*).

H.B. as a matter of fact is coming along a treat and is a seething mass
of dark gentlemen of the sonnets hammering and fixing and smelling
jolly poignant. Mrs. Calthrop's abandoned dwelling sits on the top of
the hill with half a verandah and looks at us reproachfully every time
we pass. I seem to hear it sighing, "Please send out someone to make
me uncomfortable". [Gladys had also bought a local house in a fit of
enthusiasm but never stayed there.]

It was a year—as they were all to be from now on—of wins and losses.
In May Noël lost his beloved Neysa McMein, but in New York he made
peace with Mary Martin, who was now starring in *South Pacific*. "I hate
quarrels and feuds . . . Now all that is over and I could not be more
pleased."

Then there were what looked like being sure wins that later turned out
to be unqualified losses. One of these was the film version of *The Astonished
Heart*. Back in England in June, Noël had gone to Pinewood Studios to see
rushes featuring Celia Johnson, Margaret Leighton, and Michael Redgrave. The ladies, he felt, were exactly right, but Michael Redgrave came
across as false.

Redgrave agreed, and Noël decided to play the part that he had created
on stage in *Tonight at 8:30* himself. It occupied much of the summer but it
didn't prevent him from writing a new musical. It may be a generaliza-

Noël always referred to his painting style as "Touch-and-Gaugin." (Note the rubber gloves he had to wear after he developed an allergy to oil paint.)

tion, but it would seem that Noël's greatest and most enduring hits were written in a sudden burst of creative energy. He may have been pondering the idea for a period of time, but the actual writing seemed to flow. When a show had several false starts—for whatever reason—the final version was invariably flawed.

The new musical began life as a fable set in working-class South London—*This Happy Breed* revisited. Then he decided to make it what he called "The Romeo and Juliet musical," in which a sailor on a one-day leave finds the girl of his dreams. The title of *Hoi Polloi* is changed to *Over the Garden Wall*.

On May 19 he writes to Lornie from Jamaica:

I am working very hard on the score . . . I have constructed the book but only written a little bit of it. There's a good part for Little Lad—not the romantic lead—and I think I should like to get Pat Kirkwood . . . The music and lyrics so far are jolly good and happily free from Victorian nostalgia. [His last musical had been *Pacific 1860*.] There are no sextettes of hideous girls in white crinolines singing, "See my pretty sampler. I've stuffed it up my arse." Nor are there any opportunities for skittish jumpings up and down and clappings of hands and lines such as, "Mamma Mamma, we are going to a party, is it not agreeable—I have already pooped in my pantalettes with excitement." There will be a couple of pleasantly morose vocal numbers for Sylvia Cecil. You might make discreet enquiries about her and Kirkwood.

Before long he had changed his mind—and the approach—again:

I have just finished writing an entirely new book for the Musical and it really is jolly good and quite different from anything I have ever done before . . . It was very complicated and difficult to construct but the actual writing of it was fairly painless and I managed to do the whole thing in a week! . . . It is robust, "tough" and not a bit bittersweet but I think it is pretty exciting . . . the plot is intricate and rather complicated.

The process involved in getting a Coward show—particularly an expensive musical—onto a West End stage in these years of his professional discontent was complex and frustrating. Three managements looked at his eventual submission. Three times he was asked to rewrite, something that would have been unthinkable in the 1920s and 1930s.

Noël would always maintain that he was unaffected by his critics, who included those who influenced his work *before* it was presented. It is hard to accept that conclusion. He was constantly being told that he was old-fashioned and out of touch. Very well, then, he would show them. He would write a contemporary urban musical about Soho nightclubs and gangsters and the seedy postwar world. But it was not a world he either knew or liked, and despite some charming songs, *Ace of Clubs,* as it was finally called, was not convincing.

·

AT THE END of the year he turned fifty, and on December 16 Violet received a cable:

FIFTY YEARS AGO TODAY TEDDINGTON WAS DECKED AND
FLOWERED EVEN GOD WAS HEARD TO SAY WELL DONE VIOLET
AGNES COWARD

# A *QUADRILLE* . . . FOR TWO

### (1952–1954)

I want to do a Victorian comedy for Alfred and Lynn, if only I can get a good enough idea. We discussed it *ad nauseam . . .*

**DIARIES** (MAY 18, 1951)

Axel (Alfred) and Serena (Lynn) take their bow after a performance of *Quadrille*.

D*ESIGN FOR LIVING* had been a huge hit. *Point Valaine* had been a distinct flop. Both were twenty years ago, and Noël felt he had something to prove to his old friends as well as to postwar audiences on both sides of the Atlantic.

This time the play would open in London and then—when it had acquired the fine polish that was the Lunts' specialty—transfer to their home turf of Broadway. That was the plan.

Cecil Beaton (1904–1980) was asked to design the costumes and sets. (Noël had known Beaton since the 1920s, and for many years the relationship was a prickly one, perhaps because both men were carefully protecting their own best creations—themselves. However, the stress of the war threw them together, and a genuine mutual admiration society was born that lasted for the rest of Noël's life.)

In early 1952 Noël was able to cable the Lunts:

QUADRILLE IS FINISHED I LOVE IT VERY MUCH AND ONLY HOPE THAT YOU WILL.

Cecil wrote:

The Sherry-Netherland
Fifth Avenue at 59th Street
New York
Sunday, March 16th 1952

My Dear Noël,
I am utterly enchanted by *Quadrille.* It has the charm, the wit and frivolity of *The Importance* and is more mature and tender than anything you have ever written. I am so happy for you. It's so difficult to sustain a high average of success over the years. You have been responsible for so many of my special theatre treats: I hated having to choose my words very carefully when recently you asked me what I thought of your last couple of plays as I could not honestly feel as much enthusiasm for them as I would have liked to express. This time, however, I am completely *bouleversé.* This is your best play to date and I think you have created a masterpiece of its sort.

It has always been my ambition to do scenery and costumes for one of your plays, and I feel that I am very lucky to have been kept for this particular occasion . . . nothing on earth that I know of would prevent me from doing the job.

Saturday, 29th March
I have spent a lot of time at the costume museum getting acquainted with the period. I took Alfred and Lynn there and they were

enchanted—Lynn quite unabashed taking her clothes off there and then and getting into the bustles and *negligées*. We have even had *toiles* made by Helen Pons [the costume designer] who is a genius at getting bodices cut so that even Mrs. Braddock [a famously corpulent Labour Party MP] could have a 16 inch waist. We have patterns and measurements of all the arm seams, shoulder cuts, etc.

I have begun to have a few vague ideas about scenery but am awaiting your arrival so that I can hear your plans. It is a most enchanting epoch and one that hasn't been seen on the stage of late. Alfred spent a whole day in the Public Library in a quest for railway stations but succeeded only in catching sight of a piece of grillwork. We are all inter-comming like mad—and, as you can imagine, L and A battle in turn for the telephone mouthpiece—"What sort of ribbon could I have to tie under the chin when I first come on?" asks Lynn. "Just a minute," interrupts Alfred—"Say, what *are* we going to do about getting *shoes* of the period?" It's all a great lark—long may it remain so!

Lynn did not see the project in the light of a lark and wrote to Cecil Beaton: "It will be a lot of hard work, anxiety, worry. We will very likely fight to the death, we will hope to win through to success, but it won't be fun."

Blue Harbour—Port Maria
3rd April

Dear Cecil,

Thank you for yours like anything. Oh dear, oh dear, what a carry-on; I am so very excited over the whole business. I am delighted with your getting on with ideas about the clothes first and I have no doubts at all that they will be absolutely divine. The most important things to remember about the décor are the two quick scene-changes in Acts One and Three. I suggest you think on the lines of Serena's sitting room being fairly small and set inside the station buffet, so that in the first act we can pop it in and in the third act we can whisk it away.

I have read the *Tribune* and the *Times* notices of *The Grass Harp* [Truman Capote's play, which Beaton had designed] and you have obviously done a wonderful job. I am longing to see it and I must say I am quivering with anticipation at the thought of all the excitements ahead.

I arrive home on May 5th and heigh ho for everything.

Fondest Love
NOËL

Now Noël's correspondence with the Lunts began in earnest. Alfred writes:

> 150 East End Avenue, New York
> April 3rd, 1952
>
> Dear Noely,
> I've had several long talks with Cecil about the production, communicating to him, as tactfully as possible, your doubts, fears and desires—keeping the backgrounds simple and low in key, that the actors can be fully dimensional without distraction, the sets mobile for quick changes, the costs low—at a minimum, in fact—etc., etc., and he agrees and seems delighted over the whole thing—as a matter of fact, he and Lynn are at Mme. Pons now for a fitting of the patterns and pulling her waist in even tighter—she swears she can still breathe with ease.
>
> Her studying the part continues, as she wants every word as written and I must say it isn't easy. She has someone come in to cue her. I listen from the stairs now and then and it sounds good—though I still think Hubert overbalances the men. Axel is a darling but is weak in the second act *ensemble* scenes—and I *know* that "trip across America" speech should be lengthened. I can tell you exactly where I mean the low dull spots occur—I don't want *more* lines but truer ones here and there. Hubert is so much easier to write and in your innocent facility I think you've pulled him out of proportion—that is, if you want that lovely, tender final scene to hold up.
>
> Does this destroy the placidity of your Jamaican holiday? I truly hope not. It's a glorious play—I just want it perfect.
>
> These days are hectic, packing up the house, seeing a few plays, sitting for a portrait (damned good) and trying to keep amiable.
> Our love to you,
> GLORIA SWANSON

•

NOËL HAD COMMITMENTS in London, so the Lunts, determined to rehearse with him present, went over for the first time since the end of the war, five months before the play was due to open.

On the road, the reactions had pleased Noël. At the first reading in May: "Lovely evening. Alfred and Lynn read the first act . . . so exquisitely that the tears were in my eyes. They are *great* actors." In Manchester in July: "Opening night very exciting. Lovely audience . . . Tremendous ovation at the end—altogether satisfactory . . . Everyone very happy."

"Edinburgh . . . was enchanting . . . The audience was deeply appreciative and really warm and sweet. The ovation at the end was terrific."

The day before the London opening Cecil wrote:

8 Pelham Place
SW7

Dearest Noël,

Just a note to tell you how greatly I have enjoyed working on this enchanting play with you and to say what a happy experience for me the whole venture has been. I do trust this won't be the last of our collaborations, and that this one will be crowned with glory.

*Quadrille* opened at London's Phoenix Theatre on September 12—the same theater that had opened with Noël's *Private Lives* in 1930. The critics were kind to the Lunts, but extremely (and by now predictably) unkind to Noël.

On September 14 Cecil wrote again:

Redditch House
Broad Chalk
Salisbury

I'm afraid the critics haven't come up to my expectations—or probably they have to yours!—but *I* thought they would heap unstinted praise upon your head and tell you in no uncertain terms that the play possessed enchantment and tender qualities they hadn't expected. But the brutes have been quite clinical and ungenerous and proved themselves a grudging crabby lot. It will be fun to prove them quite superfluous, for I'm sure the play will run to delirious audiences for as long as you want.

In fact it ran for 329 performances.

•

EVEN ON THE ROAD Noël had begun to experience what other playwrights complained about with the Lunts in these years. He was forced to rewrite as they went along, when Alfred and Lynn determined that audience reaction was revealing "soft spots" in the play. The prewar Noël would have stood his ground, but by now constant criticism had begun to erode his confidence and, despite his over-protestation in his *Diaries,* he was beginning to wonder if, perhaps, his critics weren't right. Perhaps he *was* out of date.

It was ironic—and more than a little tragic—that at this point he should have been working with two old friends who had by now evolved their own method of shaping anyone's material to what they felt best suited their own stage personalities. Noël's frustration can be seen in the answer he gave to an interviewer who was asking him what it was like to direct the Lunts. "*Direct* the Lunts? When you do a play with the Lunts, nobody directs them. Oh, they have a delusion that they listen to a director, but they don't. *Quadrille,* it was said, was directed by Noël Coward. Noël Coward refused the honour." In fact, the program carried the line "Directed by the author with grateful acknowledgement to Miss Fontanne and Mr. Lunt."

Having seen the production, Edna Ferber wrote with her customary irony: "While writing this play you were, I think, somewhat touched by a remote flavour of two excellent novelists—Trollope and Ferber. Correct me if I'm wrong." Nevertheless, she had a legitimate point. There was more than a touch of "fine writing" about it.

•

WHAT STARTED WITH the London production became aggravated when the play came to New York. The Lunts returned to the United States toward the end of 1953 determined to take a long rest before embarking upon the play in late 1954.

In May, Noël is writing to Lynn and promising that "a week or so from now I will sit down on my chubby little bottom and get after tidying up *Quadrille.*"

> 17 Gerald Road, London S.W.1.
> May 24th 1954

I suggested Hugh Williams [for Hubert], because he really is a very charming actor; on the other hand John Williams [an English actor based in the United States] is also a very good actor and obviously, being in America, is more easy of access. I would be perfectly happy with him, providing you and Alfred heard him read it to you first. I have no doubts whatever about Dorothy Stickney. I saw her the other day in *Kind Sir* make the most God awful part seem quite plausible. She is a first rate actress and will be terribly valuable as Charlotte. I am certainly still holding my thumbs about coming to Genesee in September but this really rather depends on my darling Mum, who is failing, I'm afraid, and I don't intend to be far away from her as long as she is alive. [Violet died on June 30.]

A month later he wrote to them both:

> Goldenhurst
> June 26th 1954

Darling Grandma and Grandpa,
I have been sitting for a week with *Quadrille.* I read through the original published version and the prompt script with all the cuts. I have

beaten my brains out trying to find out what is wrong with it and I am afraid, looking at it with a fresh eye, that I find nothing wrong with it at all—I mean in its final version. I do think that originally the first scene was far too long and I think all the cuts are a great improvement, although I feel that if somebody really brilliant played Hubert, some of them might conceivably be put back, but as I doubt if we shall get anybody good enough, I think it would be far better to leave it as it is.

Do let us remember one thing, and that is that you both and Binkie and Jack and Cecil Beaton and I all loved this play very much when we started it, and all the weeks it was played on tour before we got to London, we still loved it very much (apart from the appalling performance of Griffith Jones [as Hubert] and the merely adequate and frequently idiotic performance of Marian Spenser). We opened in London to a dreary first-night audience and all the critics who were determined that, however good you both were, the play was *not* going to be good. From that moment onwards it was fairly inevitable that we should be assailed by doubts; however, the play ran for a year in spite of the performances above mentioned.

I have tried, hard, to think of ways of improving it and, so help me God, I can't really think of anything, beyond describing the first scene and the last scene as Prologue and Epilogue. I am unimpressed by the critics' opinion and most profoundly impressed by *our* opinion, which only suffered a slight sea-change after they, the critics, had torn the play to pieces. I genuinely think that in the original version I made a technical mistake by making the first scene so long and allowing the character of Hubert to run away with me, but this has been entirely rectified by the cuts already made; as it stands and as I last saw it at Streatham, it seems to me a very charming play indeed and I really cannot start re-writing it without spoiling its essential structure, which I still think is extremely good. If, for instance, we cut out the first scene entirely, it would leave Mr. Spevin unaccounted for and completely ruin the effect of the last scene. I believe that if Hubert and Charlotte were played even reasonably well we should have nothing to worry about.

Whoever plays Hubert must have charm and humour, and whoever plays Charlotte must be American and not an adequate English actress trying to be American. Another point I found on going over the play very carefully was that Octavia must *not* be played by a youngish character actress pretending to be old but by a really elderly woman who has experience and authority and can carry the scene without you two having to carry it for her. I would love to see Hubert played by an actor with style and charm—my suggestions

are Alan Webb, Bobby Fleming [Flemyng], possibly Basil Rathbone, who at least would know enough to get value out of the lines,
which is more than Griffith Jones ever did.

Please, please do not think that I am seeking for alibis and putting
all the blame on the actors—the casting of Griffith Jones was largely
my fault, though I had no idea he would be as bad as he ultimately
turned out to be. Marian Spenser is a competent actress but I think
her determination to be American, plus the impact of dear Griff's
laborious lack of comedy, threw the poor bitch for six.

I have racked my brains to try and think of ways of improving the
play and it is no use. My original conception remains clear in my
mind and I can't budge it. I know, with complete conviction, that if
I started re-writing and re-constructing and frigging about with it,
it would become a shambles and anyway I know that my creative talent won't work unless I really believe in what I am doing. I do, as I've
said before, love the play very much and I have a feeling that you do,
too—our mutual theatrical experience has whittled it down to its
present shape and I truly don't think we can improve upon it except
by seeing that it is well cast and well played.

This is no evasion of responsibility on my part—I am free as the
air, I have no commitments . . . and there is absolutely nothing to
prevent me from re-writing *Quadrille* from beginning to end, except
that I can see no reason whatsoever to do so. Do write to me at once,
the moment you get this letter, and let me know that you really
understand how I feel.

All dearest love, my darlings,
NOELIE

Lynn replied:

Ten Chimneys
July [?] 1954

Darling,
I am writing this in pencil because it slips along easier and no
damned pen trouble. Now, first of all, we love you and believe in
your honesty and know if you say so that it is impossible to re-write
or improve the first act—scene—or prologue. But you are wrong in
your diagnosis of our criticism of it. When you first read the play—
we both felt there was something wrong with the first scene—too
long perhaps—or was it that we were not in it—and "when *were* we
coming on?" and so on. Then we rehearsed and got immersed in the
whole thing and lost our eye—others came—Binkie and others and
said the first scene needed cutting—you cut a little before we came

to London and, after Alfred and I cut a lot, it was improved—but we felt still (*now* nothing to do with criticism because we had nothing but praise from all kinds of impressive people writers—[S. H.] Behrman—well, allright—Lord David Cecil, Bob Sherwood—Maugham—Edna Ferber—all had something different and something interesting to say)—no one said the thing that *we* felt and it is this—for what it is worth.

The first scene between those two is too fatal—we know it is going to be a failure—couldn't it be two people madly in love (he *truly*—he always is) and she certainly—a respectable girl—no fool—she knows it isn't wise to sleep with a man you want to marry—so she must be mad for him—*then* couldn't it be a gayer, more living, more over the moon with delight—so that we want them to make a success of it.

Another little technical thing. The first scene, apart from its costume, has no atmosphere of the period—the thing you are past master at—*please* do a little something about that.

I don't know why I am underlining everything—but I feel a little vehement. About Lord Herondon—Allen [Alan] Webb is a fine actor and could play him as a dapper Don Juan—if he will accept the part and if you want him, we would be willing—he is a fine actor and would realize the difficulties of the part and turn in something interesting. Bobbie Fleming [Flemyng]—no. Now Brian A'Hearne [Aherne]—you don't like him, but, he was vastly amusing in [Maugham's] *The Constant Wife* and from the meagre choice we have, he would be ours—aren't there any others? John Williams turned the part down. Perhaps darling, when you have had a little rest—first from the play—and then from the sadness of Mum's death—perhaps then you will look at it again from the point of view which I have said.

Our dearest love (the barometer says 98 in the shade today) our little suit-case in Genesee is slightly uncomfortable.

X X X LYNN

From Paris, Noël continued the debate with Lynn:

Hotel Le Président, Paris
August 4th 1954

Darling,
Now then, about your letter. It was dear and sweet and understanding of my point of view but *not* understanding of the play.

Hubert, as played by Griffith Jones and cut by you and Alfred was a dull meaningless bore. As written by me and played by a good actor with a sense of humour, he would be neither dull, meaningless nor a bore. He could *never, never* be truly in love. Serena says this herself. His only true love is himself and his enjoyment of words. If you start twitching his character about you will ruin the play.

The only outstanding difference between Brian Aherne and Griffith Jones is that Brian is less decorative and has adenoids.

He was good in *The Constant Wife* because he was playing a pompous bore without a grain of humour. Hubert is *not not not* a pompous bore, and if he is in the American production, as he was in London, the play will be seriously damaged. Do remember that in the very beginning Alfred thought Hubert such a good part that he went into his usual act and said *he* wouldn't play! I find I am firm of mind, if not more than you, because I, too, am vehement.

I love *Quadrille very, very* much. We *all* loved *Quadrille* very much . . . The first night audience in London and all the critics were determined not to like it before the curtain went up . . . I also think the whole company suffered from being directed by three very definite personalities. I still love *Quadrille* and I don't give a bugger what the critics think. They didn't like *Private Lives* either. I wrote the play lovingly for you and Alfred and, until the "clever ones" got at it, you never stopped saying how happy you were in it.

Serena is a great part for you and you played it gloriously, tenderly and beautifully, from the opening in Manchester until the last night in Streatham. Alfred was superb, in spite of occasional bouts of over-embroidery.

In his *Diary* entry covering that performance, Noël recorded that Alfred "crouched and wriggled and camped about like a massive *antiquaire* on heat. It is so depressing that so beautiful an actor can go so far wrong."

The play, in my opinion, will have a far better reception in America but, even if it doesn't, you two will triumph.

I do not agree with you when you say the first scene has no atmosphere. It is crammed with "atmosphere"! Or was, until it was cut to pieces. I have a very strong feeling that you don't want to play it at all, which would not be entirely unnatural in the circumstances.

We are old and close friends and always will be—no play good, bad or indifferent could change my love for you. I could, however, with the greatest pleasure in the world crack your silly heads together. I do *not*—underlined—think that you know as much as you think you do about playwriting and I do *not*—underlined—think that you know as much as you think you know about acting, except for your own in which you are unique! You are *very* unsure about cast.

Both John Williams and Brian Aherne are worthy, humourless and dull. But over to you, Pals. This is your decision and I will have no part of it and no blame. You will both do exactly what you want to do in the end, you always do. I would no more try and force you to engage someone I wanted for Hubert than fly. The poor bugger would be in a clinic after three weeks of rehearsal. The play is yours to do as you like with. I wrote it for you and there it *is*. I will not re-write or alter one more line. You can cut it to bits, play it backwards, engage Shirley Temple to play Octavia. I shall not be pleased but I shan't mind all that much because, unless it is played as I wrote it, I shall never come and see it. I have already explained gently in my other letter why I cannot re-write, even if I were willing to, which I most emphatically am not.

I expect this letter will make you hopping mad but that can't be helped either. I am, as you may have gathered, hopping mad myself.

Am sending over this little *billet doux* to Lorn to have typed and copied. One of the copies may very well be put in *Variety*. I reiterate that I love you dearly, dearly, dearly and however maddening you are, I always will. I also reiterate that I won't re-write *one* line, phrase or word, and please, please don't do the play at all if you don't want to and please, please do, do it if you do want to. It is as simple as that.

Some poor tortured playwright should have written this letter to you years ago.

> Love, love, love, love
> NOELLIE

He shared his frustration with Jack:

> Goldenhurst
> 13th Sept. 1954

Dearest Dab,
I think the Lunts' behaviour over this production has been dithering, indecisive and irritating to the point of lunacy. As you know, the reason I am staying outside the whole business is because I know by experience that my presence would achieve nothing except possibly a nervous breakdown for myself. They will get their own way in the long run; they always have and they always will.

I think Edna Best is a fine actress and I am devoted to her—I also think she is entirely miscast as Charlotte because, apart from her ingrained commonsense quality, she is not American and it seems idiotic to engage an Englishwoman, however good, to play an American in America . . .

As I said in my two letters to the Lunts, I have read the play in its original version and in its cut form and I cannot feel that it needs rewriting. If I did feel so, I would do it unquestioningly. On top of all this, I have just had a long conversation with poor Cecil on the telephone. He has suddenly had a request to turn the first set into an inset—also, having designed, at Lynn's request, a new dress for the second act and having received an enthusiastic letter saying she and Alfred adored it, she now changes her mind and says she has never worn blue on the stage and doesn't intend to.

All of these questions could have been hammered out and settled months ago. Although the play was written as a vehicle for the Lunts, it *is* a play for four people. I think it is pretty obvious that the Lunts will have a triumph in it and that again I shall be blamed as a bad playwright. As I am absolutely resigned to this, the only thing to do is to let them get on with it and do everything that they want to do. In any other situation I would fight all this idiocy to the last ditch, but I know perfectly well that, as things are, no good would come of it and I think it far better for the future health, wealth and happiness of John Chapman Wilson and Noël Peirce Coward for the latter to concentrate on a nice new play for himself.

I really feel a tiny bit conscience stricken at leaving you to hold those two intractable babies, but there it is, my poor dear—you must tighten your belt and get on with it and do the best you can. I thought I would like to explain this to you so that you wouldn't feel that I was casually letting you down . . . And I might also add— *"Courage, mon brave!"*

Cecil Beaton, who accompanied the U.S. production for at least part of its road tour before New York, reported:

> The Ambassador
> 341 Park Avenue
>
> Just a note hurriedly on return from Boston where I went to supervise a few details. You will be very pleased with the improvement in this production. The extra pair are so much better—Edna Best is quite wonderfully funny—very appealing and babyish—like a meringue—enormous, fluffy, creamy. Ahearne excellent in last act. The Lady Bonnington scene really comes off—an actress with authority takes charge and the girl in Joyce's part is a good fighter— much more riposte and thrust—she puts Lynn on the spot.
>
> . . . The whole thing goes extremely well. The Boston audience lapped it up—Everyone is pleased—Alfred had a lot of grumbles

against [H. M.] Tennents and listed all the items they *didn't* send. Lynn was radiant—her new clothes are a big success and she looked just as lovely as in London.

Just time for me to do a few tiddivations before N.Y. opening—but I'm sorry you weren't in Boston last night to see your play brought to life with such vitality and charm.

Jack was also at the out-of-town rehearsals and, being a longtime Lunts watcher, saw a different and more typical side of things. "Grandma" (Lynn) achieved everything she wanted without even raising her voice, whereas "Grandpa" (Alfred) chose to create scenes "reminiscent of the late Sarah Bernhardt." Not since Basil Dean had Jack seen someone make a point of bullying small part actors. Nonetheless, the results achieved were always remarkable.

The strength of Noël's comments had clearly had some effect. Alfred wrote and told him that many of the lines that had been cut in London had now been put back. When Noël replied, he expressed a different concern—that he detected a distinct chill in their friendship.

> 17 Gerald Road
> October 25th 1954

Dear Alfred,

I must say I was delighted to get your letter and I am awfully glad you put back so many of the lines and, above all, that they go so well. This must obviously be because they are spoken a great deal better than they were in London. I am really horrified over eight pieces of scenery, eleven costumes and the props being missing. I haven't the faintest idea what went wrong about this but I bloody well intend to find out. Since getting your letter I have been trying to get hold of Binkie [who was co-producing on Broadway], but have not yet succeeded. There seems to be no excuse for it or for the music not arriving. I will try and ferret out the cause of this incompetence and will let you know the result of my findings.

I hear that Brian is exceeding good and I couldn't be more pleased and of course I can't wait to see it. I thought the Boston notices were fine. The New York notices will obviously be mixed for the play but I am sure not as unanimously damning as the London ones were. I am equally certain that you and Lynn will have the triumph you so richly deserve. It is all very exciting and I am terribly thrilled.

The only thing, of course, that saddens me a little is the inside feeling I have of stiffness between you and Lynnie and me. Lynn's tart little note which started "Dear Noël" and finished "Love Lynn" was rather chilling, which I presume it was intended to be. None of this can be explained satisfactorily until we meet but it certainly must be then. It naturally makes me unhappy that my motives should be misunderstood by you two who I have loved so much for so many years.

I expect to arrive in New York in the first week of December; I shall come and see the play the night I arrive and will expect to be asked to supper after the performance. No place cards will be necessary and, if conversation should be a little stilted during the first part of the *soirée,* I hope by the end of the evening Lynnie might be induced to call me "Noelie" on leaving and even perhaps to let me kiss her hand. Failing this, I shall be forced to goose you both thoroughly as I always have and always will.

> I am,
> Yours sincerely,
> NOËL COWARD

X X X
Fuck, Fuck, Fuck.

The play opened at New York's Coronet Theatre on November 4. When he had seen the production himself, Noël wrote to Lorn:

Brian is heavy and inclined to be comical, but he has authority and looks well and compared with Griff Jones is John Barrymore on ice. Edna gives a brilliant performance, knows exactly what she's up to,

Lynn, Mountbatten, Chaplin, and Alfred at
Chalet Coward, ca. 1970.

and has her sturdy little Dutch trotters firmly embedded in the ground. I think Grandpa and Grandma are terrified of her. They did a lot of the Gestapo routine during the rehearsals—there were tremendous rows and screams, but now in the glow of success all acrimony has evaporated and the whole thing is just one big happy-ish family.

As Noël had predicted, the New York critics were kinder than their London peers, but once again, the Lunts were seen to triumph despite the play. It ran for 159 performances and could have run longer but the Lunts decided to end the run in March 1955, much to Noël's irritation. He wrote to Jack:

February 18th 1955

I am, naturally, sad about *Quadrille* but not surprised. *Quadrille* was written for four people; in London it had two, in New York it has three—the Lunts and Edna. Brian is as wrong for Hubert as Griff was, except that he has more authority and a name. For Hubert to be played as a pompous ass is entirely wrong, he should be so charming that there should be a certain amount of genuine regret that Serena is leaving him. This, neither of the Lunts have ever admitted, and of course, in the last analysis, it is my fault as a playwright. I should either have left Hubert as he is and played him myself, or reconstructed the play as a twosome. However, there has been so much spilt milk that I refuse to shed one tear over a drop of it. I think in fairness to the company, the management and me, the Lunts should at least recoup a little by playing Philadelphia, Washington, Chicago, etc., but if they feel, as you say, that "the play is not good enough", there is nothing more to be said and we must tighten our belts and rise above it.

He then went on to muse on the current state of American theater:

The American theatre, with the exception of a very few sensational hits, seems to be falling off considerably. I think that this is inevitable, because what with the Unions and Equity and one thing and another and everybody's salaries being far too high, it is impossible to have a moderate success. I always suspected that the Unions and Equity would kill the living theatre far more effectively than the talkies and television could ever do, and it looks to me as if this is coming to pass. I think the only thing to do, when eventually I appear again on Broadway, is an eight-week season with one set and a small cast, but we shall see.

# CHAPTER 23
# . . . AND THE FITFUL FIFTIES

## (1950–1954)

*A**CE OF CLUBS** opened in July 1950. It was definitely not the smash hit Noël had been looking for, and to rub it in, Frank Loesser's *Guys and Dolls* appeared on Broadway four months later to show how low life could have high impact. When Noël saw it, he was the first to admit, "It is a great evening in the theatre."

To make matters worse in what was perhaps the low point of his career, the film of *The Astonished Heart* had opened in New York to dismissive reviews, which were only echoed even more loudly later with the London opening.

Again, he put geographical distance between himself and these latest disappointments. He returned to Jamaica and buried himself in matters domestic, and in reading all twelve volumes of Proust as a soporific.

Noël, Pat Kirkwood, and Graham backstage in *Ace of Clubs*.

In an undated letter to Coley, he reports:

Dearest Tolette,

The biggest hurricane since Tallulah Bankhead has just avoided the island and is on its way to Miami. We had a dear little earthquake on Saturday morning but I was on the loo at the time and put the strange rumbling down to natural causes. Apparently in Kingston quite a lot of ladies rushed into the street holding sponges over their pussies and crying *Hilfe! Hilfe!* Apart from these minor caprices of Mother Nature's, life is very peaceful and the weather now divine. Tell Little Lad that I went to the Moneague Hotel and that we were very foolish not to go before as it is perfectly enchanting. It is run by a stout gentleman who, although far from being as normal as blueberry pie, is a really wonderful cook; his *cordon* couldn't be bluer and he has promised to take some poor wretch into his kitchen and train him or her as a cook for me next winter. Jolly good luck! His hotel is perched on the top of a highish mountain and is crammed with *goût*—you know, Bristol, Sheraton and old Spode. It is all very strange. I am going up to New York for about ten days to buy some braid and a thing for making ice cubes which is made of rubber and plugs into practically anything. I shall then return and plug it in and hope for the best.

I have now finished with Mr. Proust. He is worth reading but *Oh la la,* how jolly tiresome. I am furious about *Ace of Clubs* not being a real smash and I have come to the conclusion that if they don't care for first rate music, lyrics, dialogue and performance, they can stuff it up their collective arses and go and see *King's Rhapsody* [Ivor's last and biggest hit had opened on September 15] until *les vaches se rentrent.*

I am happy as a bee writing my stories and I have a strong suspicion that there is a novel in the offing. I need hardly tell you that this holiday has done me more good than I could have believed possible. I feel smooth as silk and look quite wonderful. Give my dearest love to all and a great deal to yourself.

•

UNFORTUNATELY, 1950 hadn't finished with Noël. In September, on a brief visit to New York, he had been asked to direct and/or star in the forthcoming Rodgers and Hammerstein musical, *The King and I,* which they had devised specifically for Gertie at her request. It would have made a lot of money for him, burnished his image, and been an undoubted hit with that combination of talents—but it would not have been *his.* He turned it down.

Instead, back in England, he had to tackle a far less appealing chore. He and Coley had to make a sad side trip to Paris to clear out the apartment in the Place Vendôme. It had been put up for sale and—mindful of the currency exchange problems of the past—Noël felt it would be unwise to try to buy it himself.

From there he traveled solo to Florence to stay with painter Derek Hill in his rather chilly little villa. It was not long before he was cabling Coley:

HAVE MOVED HOTEL EXCELSIOR COUGHING MYSELF INTO A
FIRENZE.

Fate continued to frown. Even Jamaica welcomed him back for Christmas with clouds and rain.

The year 1951 began with the mournful news that *Ace of Clubs* was closing, and a few days later Noël heard that Eleanora von Mendelssohn had committed suicide in New York. Since his 1937 visit to her Austrian *schloss* and her move to the United States, she, like Neysa, had been part of his New York "family."

He wrote to Lornie:

The horrid tragedy of poor Eleonora von Mendlsohn [Mendelssohn] upset me very much. She came to me in despair a day or two after I arrived. Her idiotic husband, who was queer as a coot and jealous of his boy friend, had thrown himself out of the window—alas only three stories—and broken himself to bits and was languishing in a public ward in a charity hospital. He and the boy friend between them had squeezed her dry and she had no money to get him moved and pay for injections to help his pain . . . Then Francesco, Eleonara's mad brother, escaped from his asylum and appeared to plague her and, of course, Toscanini kicked her around for years. Apparently this was the last straw, because that night, last Tuesday, she took several sleeping pills, then soaked a cloth in ether, placed it over her face with a pillow and a bath mat on top, and that was that! I had sessions with the doctors involved, one of whom had seen a bit of a letter she had left for her neurotic little sod of a husband. The phrase he read was—"Now perhaps you will have peace!" My only comfort is that I, at least, among her friends, really tried to help, and this she knew. She's always been fairly emotionally unbalanced—I suppose she's well out of it but Oh Dear! It was all very nasty.

There is an old superstition that bad luck comes in threes. First Eleanora, then, a day or two later, C. B. Cochran died in a domestic accident. And in early March came the news that Ivor Novello was dead. Arriving home after another triumphant performance as King Nikki in

*King's Rhapsody,* he had succumbed to a heart attack. The Grim Reaper was busy cutting a swath through Noël's friends.

As he had done so often in the past, he turned to his "family" for comfort. To Cole:

> Dearest Tolette,
> I have decided in my fluffy little mind that it would be well worth the spondulicks expended if you were to come out and be a comfort to your aged Master on account of I feel a certain lack of spiritual nourishment without you. Also the new lilos that Doycie sent me are much easier to fall off than the other ones and I long to open my lattice and watch you being constantly dashed against the reef. So just you go snaking up to the hard-faced Mrs. Loraine and keep on hissing in her ear, "Master wants Toley and money's vulgar anyhow", until by sheer persistence you wear her down.

Out of his determination to "rise above it" came at least one good thing. He set about writing a new play. Joycie happened to be staying—one of a whole string of guests who helped divert him that spring—and he was able to bounce ideas off her, very much as he had done with *Blithe Spirit* ten years earlier. Yes, it *was* about duchesses and the aristocracy, but so what? This was a world he knew and one that was changing every bit as fast as any other section of troubled postwar British society. He called the play *Relative Values.* At the back of his mind another idea was beginning to bubble—a satire on the affectations of modern art—but it would have to wait its turn. He would call it *Nude with Violin.*

And, of course, there was always his wandering child, *Home and Colonial:* written for Gertie, who had shilly-shallied; offered to John Clements and Kay Hammond, who felt its British Empire topicality had missed the moment; and about to be reincarnated that summer as *Island Fling* for Claudette Colbert at Jack's Westport Playhouse. And even then the story would not be over.

Then the *good* things began to happen.

Nineteen fifty-one was Festival of Britain Year, a halfhearted attempt on the part of the ruling Labour government to "relaunch" postwar Britain, but without the flair or the funds to do it properly. Noël, having been asked to serve on the Festival Committee, promptly resigned when he saw the state of affairs. Afterward he wrote the satirical song "Don't Make Fun of the Festival," which contained the lines: "We downtrodden British must learn to be skittish/And give an impression of devil-may-care . . ." It was the hit of that year's *The Lyric Revue,* in which Graham Payn had one of the leads.

That summer Noël made two important decisions. It was time to go

Gladys Cooper (1888–1971) and Noël were intermittent friends from their first meeting in the early 1920s. Noël always called her "The Hag"—hence her dedication, "Your loving hag."

back to Goldenhurst. He had enjoyed St. Margaret's Bay, but it lacked the peace he craved and that the prewar Goldenhurst had given him. He wrote to Jack:

July 5, 1951

I would really rather be at Goldenhurst.

I could not live in it again as it was, as it is too big to run nowadays. So this is what I plan.

I shall have my old bedroom and the library will be the main living room . . . The bar will be a dining room and will hold six comfortably and no more. The chinz, lacquer and paneled rooms will be as they were, except that I shall have a door put from the paneled room into my bathroom. I shall take away the big room entirely and also the newer part of the old house, which means the French room and bathroom, the big upstairs bathroom and Auntie Vida's bedroom. The rest of the old house will provide a nice bedroom and bathroom for Cole and an extra guest room for emergencies.

With the materials of the demolished part I am going to turn the Mauretania into a 3-roomed bungalow . . . In between my house and the old house I am going to have a walled garden and a covered way festooned with roses which will connect the two houses.

All this should cost comparatively little . . . and the demolition at Goldenhurst will mean I do not have to buy any re-building material!

He moved back on his birthday, December 16.

The second decision was to accept an invitation to appear in cabaret at the Café de Paris that autumn. His opening on October 29 was promoted as his debut, but Noël knew better. Thirty-five years earlier, when the Café was called the Elysée, he had appeared there partnered by Eileen Denis, to no noticeable effect.

This time the effect was spectacular, and the season of twenty-four performances was repeated for the next three years. The cabaret was to provide the Coward bow with a new and highly profitable string.

The fall brought another success in an area that seemed to have rejected Noël—the theater.

Earlier in the year he had written the first draft of *Relative Values,* a comedy set defiantly in yet another stately home. Even Noël was not sure if the story of a dowager countess whose son is set to marry a Hollywood glamour girl would appeal to a 1950s London audience. When the couple arrive it turns out that the countess's maid, Moxie, is the star's sister, and the star herself is anything but what she pretends to be.

As one of the characters, Crestwell, a Jeeves-like butler, observes, "Comedies of manners swiftly become obsolete when there are no longer any manners." Noël had his fingers crossed that his own prediction would be proved wrong in this case.

For once he consulted other "voices" as well as his own. He wrote to Jack:

> July 5th 1951
> Binkie's criticisms of the play were very intelligent and quite gentle. One was that the characters of Peter and Odo should either be differentiated more or made into one. Another was that the balance of the play would be improved by making it in three acts instead of two and the third criticism was that Moxie was rather indistinct as a character. Having digested all this carefully, I have lengthened and improved the first act, finishing on the "She's my sister" line. I have turned the two men into one character, which is a great improvement and have made Moxie, I think, more consistent and more true.
>
> Actually, it was not such a terrible chore and I quite enjoyed it. The present idea of casting is Gladys Cooper for Felicity, Gwen Ffrangcon-Davies for Moxie (if we can persuade her to play it), Judy Campbell for Miranda and Cecil Parker for Crestwell. None of this, of course, is definite as none of them have read it yet.

When *Relative Values* opened at the Savoy Theatre on November 28, for the first time in a long time the majority of the London critics were kind. To Jack, again:

December 3rd, 1951

Well, that's that. We had a sensational opening night; Gladys [Cooper] gave a perfectly brilliant performance and knew her words for the first time; the whole cast was good and it is a smash hit and nobody can get seats, which is all very satisfying.

On the whole he considered it had been "a good year. Let us hope that 1952 will be as amicably disposed."

Well, it was and it wasn't.

The day after Noël arrived in Jamaica he heard the news that King George VI had died, and he immediately sat down to write a letter of condolence to the queen (now Queen Elizabeth the Queen Mother). His notes show that he attempted several versions before he had it to his satisfaction.

Madam,

I heard the tragic news of the King's death the morning after my arrival in New York and I have waited to write to your Majesty until I reached the quietness of this island. I know the utter inadequacy of words of condolence but I do wish you to know how much you are in my thoughts and how very, very deeply I feel for you. The King, ever since I first had the privilege of meeting him in 1923, had always been so gracious and kind to me that I feel his loss as a personal friend. This is not as presumptuous as it sounds because all his subjects feel the same, whether they had had the honour of meeting him or not. This overwhelming sense of personal loss in the hearts of ordinary people is such an accurate and loving tribute to his quality both as a man and our King that the realization of it may, I earnestly hope, be a small comfort to you in the loneliness of your bereavement.

You said to me, such a short while ago at Dickie and Edwina's dinner party, that if ever I had anything to ask of you, I was to write to you direct, so I know that you will not misunderstand the profound affection and sympathy that prompts this letter. All I have to ask of you is to remember, amid the desolation of your personal grief, how much you are loved and honoured and the magnitude of the debt that we all of us owe to you and our beloved King for the courage and dignity and kindness that shone so steadfastly throughout the difficult years you have reigned over us.

My humble duty to you, Madam. I have the honour to be your Majesty's loyal and devoted subject.

•

BACK IN ENGLAND, Ian Fleming and Ann Rothermore took over the lease of White Cliffs and now it was Ian's turn to "criticize" the qualities of the accommodation on offer.

From Ian:

> Kemsley House
> London W.C.1
> 9th May 1952

Dear Boy,

The various repairs have been carried out. The bill comes to £100.10s.2d. I have consulted my solicitor and also the landlord and they both agree that these costs do, in fact, fall on the outgoing tenant rather than on the slim shoulders of the incoming lessor.

May I assume that a cheque will reach me in due course or would you rather work this off by writing an article for the *Sunday Chronicle* entitled "The Most Scandalous Things I Know About My Most Intimate Friends?"

> Cordially
> IAN

> May 9th

Dear Ian,

As our two solicitors seem to have completely divergent views regarding the matter about which you wrote . . . and as we offered to leave the bookshelves and you particularly asked us to remove them I am using the good old British plan of compromise and enclose a cheque for Fifty Pounds. If you do not want it I can give you a few suggestions as to what to do with it when you come to lunch on Sunday. With regards and also with smacking great kisses.

> Cordially, Noël Coward.

> 15th May

Dear Messrs. Noël Coward Incorporated.

The mixture of Scottish and Jewish blood which runs in my veins has been brought to the boil by your insolent niggardliness.

Only Ann's dainty hand has restrained me from slapping a mandamus on your meagre assets and flinging the charge of bottomry, or at least barratry, in your alleged face.

Pending the final advice of my solicitors, I shall expend your insulting *pourboire* on a hunting crop and a mills bomb and present myself at one o'clock exactly at Goldenhurst.

I shall see what Beaverbrook has to say about your behaviour at lunch today.

Tremble
IAN

By now Ian and Ann's affair was an open secret, Ann was divorced, and they were married in Jamaica that March, with Noël and Coley doubling as witnesses and the entire congregation. Noël had already warned Violet: "I shall wear long elbow gloves and give the bride away. I may even cry a little at the sheer beauty of it all."

After the event, he reported:

It was really rather sweet except that the dark gentleman who married them had the most awful breath and so the responses were rather muffled. I lost my head after it was over and began to tie the old shoe that we had brought on to *my* car but fortunately Cole stopped me in time. We threw handfuls of musty rice over them and all drove away giggling.

Noël also marked the occasion with one of his verse letters to Ian and Ann:

### DON'TS FOR MY DARLINGS

*The quivering days of waiting*
*Of wondering and suspense*
*Without regret can at least be set*
*In the Past Imperfect tense.*
*The agonies and frustrations,*
*The blowing now cold, now hot,*
*Are put to rest, and there's no more doubt*
*As to whether you will or not.*
*We all of us knew so well*
*Lo and behold, can at last be told*
*To the sound of a marriage bell.*
*All the stories that could be written,*
*The legends the world could spin*
*Of those turbulent years you've lived, my dears,*
*In excessively open sin.*
*Permit me as one who adores you,*
*An eminent* éminence grise,
*To help you in finding some method of minding*

*Your marital Qs and Ps*
*Don't, Ian, if Annie should cook you*
*A dish that you haven't enjoyed,*
*Use that as excuse for a storm of abuse*
*Of Anna or Lucien Freud.*
*Don't, Annie, when playing canasta*
*Produce a lipstick from your "sac"*
*And drop your ace with a roguish grimace*
*While giving dear Delia the pack.*
*Don't, Ian, when guests are arriving*
*By aeroplane, motor or train*
*Retire to bed with a cold in the head*
*And that ever redundant migraine.*
*Don't be too exultant, dear Annie,*
*Restrain all ebullient* bons mots,
*The one thing that vexes the old boy's old Ex's*
*Is knowing the status is quo*
*Don't either of you, I implore you,*
*Forget that one truth must be faced—*
*Although you may measure repentance at leisure—*
*You HAVEN'T been married in haste.*

Sadly the leisurely repentance remark proved prophetic and Noël watched the marriage slowly unravel until Ian's early death in 1964. He even used it as an element in his 1956 play, *Volcano*—once again set in Samolo—which, curiously, he never refers to in his *Diaries*. (It has never been produced either in the West End or on Broadway.)

•

THEN, ON SATURDAY, September 6, back in England, Noël spent the day at Folkestone races with Coley and Gladys. They bought an evening newspaper and read the news in the Stop Press. Gertie was dead. "A day that started gaily . . . ended in misery." Despite her failing health, Gertie had insisted on remaining with *The King and I*. Her sole ambition was to take it to London the following year, Coronation Year.

In the event, it was Noël who made a Coronation appearance on the West End stage and, for once, not in one of his own plays. He accepted the role of King Magnus in Shaw's *The Apple Cart* for a limited run at the Haymarket Theatre, opposite his old friend Margaret Leighton.

He learned the long part while he was in Jamaica, and wrote to Violet:

I am getting quite excited about it and I wander about spouting my long speeches to the lizards, who are mad about it . . . I expect I shall

Noël chose to play King Magnus in Shaw's *The Apple Cart* during Coronation year (1953), opposite Margaret Leighton (1922–1976). He claimed in the future he would always play kings. "It's so nice to have people getting up and down again every time you make an entrance."

throw the entire cast into a frenzy by knowing my part perfectly. As a matter of fact I have rather enjoyed learning it . . . and Magnus is a part that might have been written for me. I don't think he goes "soppy" in the last scene. He actually wins hands down.

So did Noël. The production received excellent reviews—perhaps because Noël *hadn't* written it—and the critics felt it would be bad form to dislike Shaw—at least, not when he was dealing with royalty in a Coronation year.

•

*THE APPLE CART* safely behind him, Noël took off on his ritual vacation. To Coley:

Hotel de la Poste Avallon
Well the holiday started with a bang. The bang was at six yesterday evening when the back axle broke in half in front of a War Memorial. Today we hope a Jaguar expert will arrive with a new one, in the meantime we are stranded. Napoleon, on his way from Italy in 1815, stayed one night in this hotel; we, on our way to Italy, look like stay-

ing a bloody sight longer. There is no way of leaving except by an autobus to Dijon and we have far too much luggage to get on to an autobus anyhow. Yesterday was further complicated by Little Lad having an appalling attack of wind after eating Lobster Gâteau at Barbizon made with a lot of cream and washed down with *vin rosé,* in such pain that he could not move. We hope that when he wakes the wind will have subsided, if not he will have to hobble to the local hospital and have a nice enema.

The new back axle duly arrived, was affixed and we drove off, merry as grigs, at six p.m. The car went like a bird for an hour or so and then ejected clouds of steam and stopped. We limped along to a tiny wayside garage where it was discovered that the ventilator fan had not been greased and the rubber tube which supplied the engine with water had rotted! . . . the garagist tinkered away for an hour, and off we went again to Geneva.

Hotel Palace, Montreux:
A Victorian-Edwardian hotel filled with heavy furniture and tortured woodwork. The Jaguar returned to us looking shiny and a trifle self-conscious.

Castello di Urio, Como:
Yesterday was definitely strained . . . we drove without mishap to Brigue and over the Simplon, lunched in a scruffy hotel in Domodossola, after which we drove for fifty years down the main street filled with Sunday traffic, when there was a sharp grinding noise in the gearbox and the car refused to move forwards, backwards or even sideways. In an inferno of hooting and imprecations we waited forty minutes until a garage man arrived with a truck, managed to jack up the Jaguar and tow it to the side of the road. After another forty minutes it was towed to a garage where we waited gloomily for two hours, then told the gearbox was hopelessly jammed and could not be mended under twenty-four hours! We were fairly frantic, so we hired a Lancia and its driver, loaded all the luggage on to it and drove off at breakneck speed to Como, through, I believe, lovely scenery of which I saw little as I kept my eyes tight shut. The Jaguar we hope will be returned to us tomorrow or the day after. I am seriously thinking of suing the Jaguar people for negligence, irresponsibility, arson, slander, libel and sexual perversion.

Castello di Urio,
16th August.

The Jaguar returned to us with only a slight knock in the engine. In the house, in addition to our host, there is a desiccated voluble gentleman who is the Chilean *Chargé d'Affaires,* married and has three children but travels with a boy friend who is pretty, young and fairly idiotic. He speaks French and Italian more quickly and violently than anyone I have ever met. We have, during the week, visited one Principessa and one Duchessa. The former was born Ella Walker in America and is fabulously rich. She was a friend of Mussolini and had to flee to Switzerland, where she lived for two years in an elaborate *clinique* without enough eggs. She is eighty-four, very chic, has forty-eight gardeners, twelve manservants, three cooks, one Tiepolo, one Guardi and two dim grand-nieces in white *broderie Anglaise* who seldom utter and are so *comme il faut* that it is difficult not to call them "Ma'am."

The Duchessa Sermoneta lives on the top of a mountain in a small square house which she fondly imagines is in *"le style Anglais"*. She is only about seventy, has had asthma for two years and is exceedingly grand. These rich grand, drained old ladies belong to a past that is dead-O and sigh for the times that are past-O. La Sermoneta had as guests an elderly English queen (grey moustache, *Corps Diplomatique,* beauty lover), his brother who is a Catholic priest (rather nice), and a startled young man fresh from Oxford with over-eager teeth. I don't know what he could have been doing there but I have my ideas. Mussolini, who of course they all bum-crawled to like mad, was caught and shot just near here on the border. He wasn't, however, hung upside-down until they took him to Milan.

There is to be a Ball in Biarritz on September 1st given by the Marquis de Cuevas. This is of tremendous social importance and is now in jeopardy, owing to the general strike in France. Nobody can get in touch with anybody else to find out what costume Zuki, Norman, Nada and Nell will or will not wear. It is clearly understood that Titi Something-or-other is going as a red parrot, perched on the shoulder of someone else as Man Friday. Apart from this concrete information we have little definite to go on. The excitement is reaching fever pitch and Chili Pom Pom [the Chilean *Chargé*] is beginning to show signs of strain. So, as a matter of fact, are we, and are leaving tomorrow for Lago di Garda.

·

IN JANUARY work had begun on the Jamaican house Firefly, and Noël wrote to Lornie:

The old ruin has been roofed in and a verandah made out in front where we can sit under cover and look at the fabulous view. It will be lovely to spend the day up there when there are too many people about.

Last night we took a thermos full of cocktails up . . . and sat and watched the sun set and the lights come up over the town and it really was magical. The sky changed from deep blue to yellow and pale green and then all the colour went and out came the stars and the fireflies . . . The view is really staggering, particularly when the light begins to go and the far mountains become purple against a pale lemon sky.

There is a very sweet white owl who comes and hoots at us every evening. I don't think he does it in any spirit of criticism but just to be friendly.

Jamaica being Jamaica, things do not always go according to plan:

Firefly is absolutely divine but far far from watertight. Pat Marr-Johnson's design admittedly is delightful but he is about as good a builder as Grant Tyler was an actor, and so now all the gutters have to be re-done and the outside walls rendered and possibly plastered and it's all jolly fun and I couldn't be crosser. The moral of all this being never have business dealings with friends.

Very soon, though, the place inhabited Noël every bit as much as he inhabited it. Over the years his letters to the "family" back in England recorded the many moments of relaxation.

When he, Graham, and Coley were there together, painting became a shared passion. To Lornie:

We are all painting away like crazy. Little Lad, as usual, is at work upon a very large ruined cathedral. I can't think why he has such a penchant for hysterical Gothic. Perhaps he was assaulted in childhood by a South African nun. Coley is bashing away at a lot of thin people by a river while I, swifter than the eye can follow, have finished a group of negroes and am now busy with a crowded fairground with swings and roundabouts and what should be a Ferris wheel but looks like a steel ovary. The trouble with me is that I don't know the meaning of the word *peur.*

Little Lad has done a sort of "Rose Red City", which looks a bit like Golders Green. The effect is dashing but the architecture is a bit dodgy. I keep on doing lots of people walking about and I'm sick to death of them.

Little Lad is painting a large picture of a Priest and an Acolyte in acid moonlight. He suddenly changed the Priest into a lady in a red dress, which is better really but perhaps not better enough. She is very tall and the Acolyte is crouching. It is all a great worry.

Coley is doing one of his green garden parties with a lot of thin people on a lawn. Little Lad, surprisingly, has done a cherub's head. It had a too bulging a forehead to start with and looked like it had a gumboil but that, after bitter words, has been rectified.

I am just painting hundreds and hundreds of people on beaches and esplanades. It is my new "style". My present masterpiece has to date one hundred and seventy when last counted and it isn't half done! Coley, with his passion for statistics, says that means three hundred and forty shoes.

·

IN 1954 NOËL had a date with Oscar Wilde. He accepted the challenge of turning *Lady Windermere's Fan* into a musical to be called *After the Ball.*

It was an ill-considered venture, for while he had an arm's-length admiration for Shaw, he did not have the same regard for Wilde. "What a silly, conceited, inadequate creature he was, and what a self-deceiver." Noël was convinced that, as far as the libretto was concerned, "I am forced to admit that the more Coward we can get into the script and the more Wilde we can eliminate, the happier we shall be" [from his *Diaries*].

The melodies came easily, and in his letter to Lornie from Jamaica (January 13, 1954) he could write:

It's nearly complete. I want to write one more number for the men to sing in the Darlington Rooms scene, as it seems a pity not to use all those lovely voices. I have got a rousing tune for it and am just waiting for an idea for the words to pop into my curly head . . . As far as I can see it is going to be one of the longest musical entertainments ever written, so I shall have to do snippingtons and even then I think we shall have to run special late buses to get people back from Hammersmith.

As with *Bitter Sweet,* his Muse took him over and he found that what he had composed was less a musical or even an operetta than an opera. ("I can scarcely go to the piano without a melody seeping from my fingers, usually in keys I am not used to and can't play in: it is most extraordinary and never ceases to amaze me.") There is no doubt that, subconsciously or not, he was hoping to emulate Ivor's success in this field. Even key members of the cast, such as Vanessa Lee, Peter Graves, and, most important, Mary Ellis had been Novello regulars. And that was where the problems began.

Mary Ellis had long been a major star of musical theater on both sides of the Atlantic. She had created the part of *Rose Marie* (1927) and more recently starred in Ivor's *The Dancing Years* (1939). Noël cast her automatically as Mrs. Erlynne, the glamorous mother whom Lady Windermere has never known. It was only well into rehearsals that it became all too clear that the Ellis voice was no longer up to the vocal demands of the role, and by that time it was too late to save anyone's face by delicately suggesting she abandon the part.

By this time she was living the role:

Dearest Noël,
Thank you more than I can say for the part of Mrs. Erlynne, and how you are helping her to be her best.

Oh dear, oh dear, help me to get some clothes that will make her better—not worse—no one who is ROUND should ever be asked to

When *After the Ball* opened in 1954, aesthete Stephen Tennant (1906–1987) sent Noël this illustrated letter with some costume suggestions.

wear feathers or pink *satin*!! I can look lovely in that period, I know. Pale roses, no glitter . . . plain dress in dull *moiré,* rather Yvette Guilbertish—maybe pale flamingo colours with black gloves, so I can use the same cape and fan. I am so desperate in those moulting eagle feathers and dots and sequins and frills—neither Mrs. Erlynne or me. I long to get it absolutely *right* and despise a hindrance. Also a wrap for the duet that need *not* come off—it spoils the urgency.

I will try and be all you want when you come to Manchester. This freezing hotel has set my voice back to non-resonance.

Doris Zinkeisen's costume design for Mrs. Erlynne in act 2, scene 3.

Please, *please* help me with those costumes!!! I am miserable and self-conscious in them and they do *not* do my 24 inch waist proud.

I am all homage and joy at being part of it.

Another contribution on the costumes came from aesthete Stephen Tennant:

My Dear Noël,

I've been thinking about Mrs. Erlynne's dresses in your play. Don't you think that the rather too accepted idea of the spoiled *demi-mondaine's* clothes is a little monotonous? I see no reason why Mrs. Erlynne's *toilette* should not be very subtle and melting and soft— the crude *femme-fatale* has been so over-played by Martita Hunt, P[aulette] Goddard, Isabel J[eans] and many others. Do you agree? The black lace and scarlet roses has become a tedious uniform. Mrs. Erlynne's dresses should be softer, more ravishingly melting. Mysteries, to my mind—the roses—creamy . . . pink, soft-shaded roses on a glistening brown straw hat . . . snow leopard fur. I enclose some suggestions.

With my love and longing to see you.
STEPHEN

Then came the question of the voice. From rehearsal Mary Ellis wrote:

May I compromise and HALF sing from "Lord Augustus, how do you do?" because I find my voice is in such a pickle to get to singing status just suddenly hot from the speaking. I have never done that except in this and last night the audience was ever so puzzled. In these weeks of trial and error I know I'll evolve something to please you—please let me try. I know it must be QUICK and CLEAR and GAY.

But it was too little too late. On May 24—well into the pre-London tour—Noël is telling the Lunts:

I have been having a terrible time with *After the Ball,* mainly on account of Mary Ellis's singing voice which, to coin a phrase, sounds like someone fucking the cat. I know that your sense of the urbane, sophisticated Coward wit will appreciate this simile. If you don't quite understand what it means, ask that lovable old sod you dragged to the altar. At last, by battering and bludgeoning, we have

Mrs. Erlynne (Mary Ellis) and her
daughter, Lady Windermere (Vanessa Lee).

persuaded her to sing *softly*. She plays the part beautifully, because she is a fine actress. The rest of the cast are enchanting and Graham is better than he has ever been.

Seven minutes of what Noël considered to be some of his best music had to be sacrificed on the altar of the Ellis voice, leaving the show badly balanced. Then there were those who, in retrospect, wondered whether the Wilde-Coward combination could ever have really worked. "Everything that Noël sent up, Wilde was sentimental about, and everything that Wilde sent up Noël was sentimental about . . . It was like having two funny people at a dinner party," director Robert Helpmann lamented.

To compensate for Miss Ellis's vocal shortcomings, Noël tried to fill the lacunae with more comedy for her character, but even that failed to please. "She couldn't get a laugh if she were to pull a kipper from her twat," he complained.

Since the lady apparently never actually attempted this aquatic physiological feat, the point remained unproven.

The show lasted 188 performances.

·

ON JUNE 30 Violet Coward died at the age of ninety-one with her son at her side. "It was as I always hoped it would be. I was with her close close close until her last breath . . . Fifty-four years of love and tenderness and crossness and devotion and unswerving loyalty . . . I shall never be without her in my deep mind."

# CHAPTER 24

# NESCAFÉ SOCIETY . . .
# AND THE SMALL SCREEN

## (1955–1956)

It [Las Vegas] was rather a dangerous challenge and has turned
out to be successful beyond my wildest dreams.

**LETTER TO LORNIE (JUNE 8, 1955)**

"Smile! You never know who's looking!" Noël and
Jane Powell pose by the pool at the Desert Inn,
Las Vegas. (The 1955 swimsuit fashion had
still to discover the itsy-bitsy bikini.)

Time has convinced me of one thing. Television is for appearing on, not looking at.

INTERVIEW WITH EDWARD R. MURROW (1956)

CABARET SEASONS at the Café de Paris from 1951 had proved both profitable and morale-boosting for Noël, and never more so than on a November evening in 1954 when he was visited backstage by a New York agent called Joe Glaser. Glaser suggested that Noël appear in Las Vegas and that he, Glaser, handle all the arrangements.

Of course, everything would depend on how Noël took to the place. Somehow a fee of twenty thousand pounds tax free made the place attractive sight unseen, but, nonetheless, Noël and Glaser made a sightseeing trip a few days later. By the time they left, Noël had a firm booking at Wilbur Clark's Desert Inn for the following June.

This is a fabulous madhouse. All around is desert sand with pink and purple mountains on the horizon. All the big hotels are *luxe* to the last degree. There are myriads of people tearing away at the fruit [slot] machines and gambling, gambling, gambling for twenty-four hours a day. The lighting at night is fantastic; downtown where the Golden Nugget is and the lesser dives, it is ablaze with variegated neon signs. In the classier casinos beams of light shoot down from baroque ceilings on the masses of earnest morons flinging their money down the drain. The sound is fascinating, a steady hum of conversation against a background of rhumba music and the noise of the fruit machines, the clink of silver dollars, quarters and nickels, and the subdued shouts of the croupiers. There are lots of pretty women about but I think, on the whole, sex takes a comparatively back seat. Every instinct and desire is concentrated on money. I expected that this would exasperate me but oddly enough it didn't. The whole fantasia is on such a colossal scale that it is almost stimulating. I went from hotel to hotel and looked at the supper rooms. They are all much of a muchness; expert lighting and sound, and cheerful appreciative audiences who are obviously there to have a good time. I noticed little drunkenness and much better manners than in the New York nightclubs. The gangsters who run the places are all urbane and charming. I had a feeling that if I opened a rival casino I would be battered to death with the utmost efficiency, but if I remained on my own ground as a most highly paid entertainer, I could trust them all the way. Their morals are bizarre in the extreme. They are generous, mother-worshippers, sentimental and capable of

1951 saw Noël start yet another new career, as a cabaret entertainer at London's Café de Paris. An after-show cocktail for Noël, Larry Olivier (*left*), Vivien Leigh, and Cole Lesley (*far right*). The two ladies seem to be comparing the curtain material each is using for a dress.

much kindness. They are also ruthless, cruel, violent and devoid of scruples.

Joe Glaser, whom I have taken a great shine to, never drinks, never smokes and adores his mother. My heart and reason go out to him because he at least took the trouble to fly over to London and see me at the Café and give me a concrete offer. If it all ends in smoke I don't think it will be his fault. I believe him to be honest according to his neon lights.

Now that Violet was no longer there, Goldenhurst at Christmas would have been a place of ghosts. Noël opted for Jamaica and stayed there or thereabouts for the next several months, content to let events unfold around him.

*Future Indefinite,* his second volume of autobiography, which deals with the war years, was published to good reviews. Then, in January, came an offer from CBS television. He would be paid $450,000 for three 90-minute live TV specials. If the Jamaican birds and lizards had heard him warbling "I Like America," it would not have been in the least surprising.

As the Las Vegas date grew closer Noël ran into a snag. Accompanist Norman Hackforth was refused a work permit, but once again, Marlene came to Noël's rescue and recommended a young man called Peter Matz. On May 15 Noël met the replacement in New York, and on that day Peter Matz reinvented Noël Coward, Cabaret Performer. Looking over Noël's existing arrangements, Matz was dubious. "You're not going to use *these,* are you?" Noël, who had fully intended to do just that, was quick enough to pick up the implication that the arrangements were hopelessly old-fashioned by American standards. "No, dear boy, I want you to redo them entirely."

> Sheraton Astor Hotel
> Times Square
> New York, NY
> Thursday, May 21st 1955

Darling Toley,

In that breathless hush when everything is packed upside down and Marlene is on her way to pick me up, I seize my ball plume to write to yew. All has gone well. There is a slight disappointment over Las Vegas on account of it being $30,000 a week instead of $35,000 but actually it was my mistake and not my Joe's so, I have risen above it.

The second disappointment is that Bill Paley [CBS's chief executive] is very very much frightened of *Present Laughter* and implores me to do *Blithe Spirit* to start with anyhow. Actually his arguments against *P.L.* are fairly valid, the principal one being that *Blithers* is dead safe and it would be much better to start off clean with no angry letters from repressed sex mad Mormons. He has agreed to wait until he sees the altered *P.L.* script but personally I think he's probably right and it's better to do an absolute sure fire one.

Taking a break from his Las Vegas stint, Noël (*center right*) visits Humphrey Bogart (*far left*) and chats with Van Johnson.

Marlene bright as a bee but informed me casually that *everyone's* voice conked out in Vegas on account of the dryness and the altitude! Goody Goody!

I caught a hideous cold on the plane from Miami and took some tablets called Super Anahist (which sounds like Ziegfield's [*sic*] mistress) and it cured it *at once* with no ill effects at all. A miracle! I have bought eight thousand bottles.

Columbia is recording several of my Vegas performances, so that we can take our pick.

Love love love to all

Maitre.

Later in the month he was staying with Clifton Webb and wrote to Lornie:

1005 North Rexford Drive
Beverly Hills
May 29th 1955

The new pianist, Peter Matz, is going to be all right, I think. He has worked with Kay [Thompson] for over a year, and with Mae West, is a good musician and a hard worker but of course it has meant toil and sweat, breaking him in. We work together every morning for nearly three hours and have now got to the stage where I could open on Tuesday if I had to, which is a comfort. He is a nice boy, *joli laid* with a crew haircut and good manners and when he does laugh he laughs very very quietly, if you know what I mean. I am in really splendid voice due a great deal, I think, to the man Mary [Martin] sent me to in New York [Alfred Dixon] who told me to make the O-est O in the world with my mouth and then roar like a bull-moose whenever I feel like it, which frightens everybody dreadfully. Just wait till Little Lad gets on to it, the studio will sound like a stud farm with the two of us mooing away.

After engine trouble, flying through a sandstorm and making an emergency landing at El Paso, Coley finally got here at three in the morning and has been in a whirl with Rita Hayworth and Joan Fontaine ever since. We are divinely comfortable here at Clifton's house, the staff are sweet and we have delicious television lunches, eating our salads while we press little buttons which are served on a side plate and switch from station to station. We fly to Las Vegas on Wednesday and I shan't be sorry to get there and get dug in as the weather here is exactly like any November afternoon in North Finchley. California sunshine, my foot. Claudette [Colbert] gave a dinner for me, well meant but on the dull side and the Cottens gave one the next night which was better, with an all star cast and Judy G[arland] sang and I sang and Dick Haymes sang, the latter very slowly indeed. Then yesterday was the great shindig given by the owner of the Desert Inn in my honour, which took place in his very gracious home and very lovely garden. The swimming pool was covered with thousands of roses and gardenias which went round and round till we all felt giddy, four gentlemen in blue strolled about playing violins, every star in Hollywood was there and I was photographed nearly 400 times. I took a great shine to Zsa Zsa Gabor . . . Coley spent a long time talking to a lonely lady in black, then got a shock when her skirt opened to the top of her hip and she turned out to be the cigarette girl.

I will cable you, of course, immediately after the opening on the 7th and then write again and tell you all and send the cuttings.

XXX
MASTER

Looking back on the experience, Noël wrote:

Wilbur Clark's
DESERT INN
Las Vegas, Nevada
June 8th

Darling Darling Lornie,
This will have to be a communal letter for you and Little Lad and Doycie [Joyce Carey] and Blackie [Gladys Calthrop] and all on account of there are five million telegrams, gifts, etc., to be thanked for. It was so wonderful, hearing your voice last night and it really was a fabulous occasion from every point of view. The dinner show, which we expected would be rather hard going, was, on the contrary absolutely terrific and the audience started off by applauding every single number in the Medley and from then on every number I did went better than it's ever gone. In fact there wasn't one that was even moderate. The high spot, as usual, was "Let's Do It" at the end, for which I have written an extra chorus full of local allusions all of which tore the place up. My programme was as follows:—Medley, Uncle Harry, Piccola Marina (a riot), Loch Lomond, World Weary, Nina, then off and back again with Mad Dogs, Worthington, Let's Do It and Party's Over Now.

The supper show, of course, was quite indescribable, the entire front row of tables was occupied by my chums, most of whom had been flown from Hollywood in a specially chartered plane by Frank Sinatra. There were the Nivens, Judy Garland and her husband, Joan

Noël "tears them up" at the Desert Inn.

Fontaine and hers, the Joe Cottens, the Humphrey Bogarts, Rosemary Clooney, Jane Powell, Laurence Harvey, Zsa Zsa Gabor, Peter
Glenville, etc., etc., etc. and I must honestly say I have never had
such an ovation in my life and the whole place went raving mad. Also
I have never known such warmth and generosity, Judy Garland was
in tears and told me that she and Frank Sinatra decided that I was
better than anyone they had ever seen and could give them lessons,
which couldn't have been more comforting or more sweet. If any of
you note a slight egocentric strain in this letter you will have to forgive it because it *was* rather a dangerous challenge and has turned out
to be successful beyond my wildest dreams.

Peter Matz, my pianist, is really brilliant. Not only did he play
wonderfully for me but owing to Carlton Hayes, the conductor,
being taken ill, he conducted the whole show as well, in addition to
which he has re-orchestrated every number and all those curiously
dull arrangements dreamed up by Norman and Marr Mackie have
now been thrown in the ash-can. All this he has accomplished in ten
days, so Doddie [God] was certainly on my side. Then of course all
the lighting equipment and sound equipment is perfect, I can whisper into the microphone if I want to, so I find no strain in singing.

The climate every day is between 100 and 110 but it's dry heat and
I adore it and anyway the hotel is air-conditioned. Coley and I pig
it in the most luxurious suite and I have rented a lovely automatic-

drive Ford convertible which does everything but cut my toenails, and in which we whizz up and down The Strip stopping at the men's shops to buy a few dainties for which the hotel very sweetly pays. It's deductible, dear. Tomorrow *Life* magazine is taking me an hour's ride out into the desert to photograph me in deep evening dress in colour—Mad Dogs and Englishmen, you know! There has just been a fifteen minute radio tribute to me, made by all the stars who were there last night, really very sweet and touching and I am having a copy made for my darlings to hear for themselves. Thank you one and all for all sweet cables, and dearest dearest love and kisses.

    Oh dear, Oh dear, Oh dear!

        XXXX

        MASTER

September . . . and it was time to prepare for the first of the CBS specials, a musical evening reuniting him with Mary Martin and called *Together with Music.* To prepare for it Peter Matz came down to Jamaica to work with Noël on the new numbers, with Mary and Richard Halliday to follow a few days later.

To Lornie:

                Blue Harbour

                September 12th

We had a very good journey out and got to New York a little bit late, which didn't matter as our plane for Jamaica was also a little late taking off. The boys [Charles Russell and Lance Hamilton—Noël's U.S. agents] were there all right, cheerful and efficient as ever, having got all the things we asked for, including a lovely tape recorder which has been a great help already. They seem to have done good preparatory work on the show and brought the plans for the set, which look very exciting, 68 feet in depth and with the series of curtains which will part and roll themselves up into pillars as Mary and I advance for our entrance . . .

    I immediately started work on Tuesday morning and had written two songs before the day was out! So now I have "Ninety Minutes is a Long Long Time" (which Mary and I are going to do outside our dressing room doors, wearing wrappers), then our entrance proper, "Together With Music", "Louisa Was Terribly Lonely", and also I have tidied up "What's Going to Happen to the Tots", so that it is now very topical and much funnier. Pete arrived yesterday and is enthusiastic about all four; Mary and [her husband] Dick arrive tomorrow, so our lovely peaceful week is over and I propose to stuff my ears with Q-tips from tomorrow onwards.

Back in July, Mary Martin had written to express her excitement at the prospect: "We love every word we read, every picture we see of you—and every glowing word that reaches us. So maybe we're ready to face the TV together!! . . . On September 11th I will be ready to come to you in Jamaica to work, work, work on music! Really ache to, want to."

And work they did. As with *Pacific 1860* a decade earlier, the fly in the professional ointment was Halliday. Once again he tried to impose himself and his views on the production, and one evening, in his cups, he went too far and found both Noël *and* Mary turning on him.

Unfortunately, as he had done so often with Jack—against his better judgment—Noël tried to forgive and forget. Halliday stayed involved with the production.

The broadcast aired on October 22, and a day or two later Noël wrote:

Darling Mary,
Well, I really do believe we pulled it off!

I can now admit—to you only—that, as the witching hour approached, I wondered if I had been entirely wise to call our open-ing number "Ninety Minutes is a Long, Long Time". Had we been

1956. Noël and Mary Martin join voices in the live CBS-TV production *Together with Music.* Their opening number was called "90 Minutes Is a Long, Long Time." Their audience disagreed.

doing the show in London, a veritable phalanx of my least favourite critics would have undoubtedly used the line to lead their so-called reviews!

But if what I have been hearing and reading is to be believed, we not only got away with it but we positively raised the roof.

I still feel—probably because I'm a virtual virgin in these matters—that television is a funny old medium. No real audience to play to and oi! oi!—always keep half an eye on where the camera's pointing. And yet, once we got into it, I felt the old thrill and I'm pretty sure *you* did, too.

It *was* a bit of fun, wasn't it? One of these days we really must be "Together *Again* with Music!!" Ready when you are, Miss M.

> All love,
> Noël

To French businesswoman Ginette Spanier and her husband, Paul:

> Blue Harbour
> 8th November 1955

My darling Japanese Samovars,
I came back here, flushed with triumph, as I said to Larry and Vivien, my TV success made Las Vegas look like a bad matinée at the Dundee Rep. I was really quite startled; telegrams started to arrive while the show was still on, from all over America, and from the moment it was over I was buttonholed wherever I went, the telephone never stopped ringing and I didn't have a moment to go to the loo. One night at Twenty-One I was serenaded by the entire Yale Glee Club who came up to my table and belted "Anchors Aweigh" while I was trying to have a quiet dinner with Edna Ferber.

·

THE SECOND OF the three CBS shows, then, was to be *Blithe Spirit*, due to be broadcast live in January, but before that there were other important matters to take care of.

The first was a change of residence. When Noël's financial adviser told him that he was overdrawn by nineteen thousand pounds, quite apart from paying over 19/—[19 shillings] in "supertax" for every pound he earned, Noël could see that, no matter how successful he was in the future, he was looking at an impoverished old age. He could no longer afford to be a U.K. "resident," yet to go "offshore" meant selling Goldenhurst and Gerald Road and generally liquidating any assets that tied him financially to England.

By the end of 1955 he had settled on Bermuda, a British possession but also a tax haven. Early the following year he found Spithead Lodge and made the physical and emotional move—once again stirring up the wrath of the British press in very much the same way he had in the early years of the war.

He wrote to Joyce Carey:

I could not obviously have done this while Mum was alive but even then, and all my life, I have got out of England as quickly as I could as often as I could. I think on the whole that I have not done badly by England and I also think that England has not done very well by me. The general public love me and are, I feel, proud of me but this does not apply to the press, the politicians and even the present darling Royal Family—or, if they are, they haven't made it apparent.

His move prompted letters from many of his friends. To many of them, the thought of Noël in Bermuda seemed, to say the least, a little *recherché.*

Nancy Mitford—someone Noël had come to refer to as "Pen Pal" and with whom he was now corresponding regularly—sent him an illustrated advance brochure for an institution called the College of Authors and Authors' Country Club at Goring Castle, writing:

"Here you see me burning your compromising letters to the despair of posterity." Nancy Mitford (1904–1973), Noël's "pen pal" of the 1950s.

Darling Noël,

Here you are—here's our old age provided for. You won't even have to bring your own fog with you. Those who haven't paid their income tax will be given that room marked X in the tower. I'll be in the one below . . . What I want to enquire is when you will be moving in, so as to make plans accordingly.

I'm very happy here in Torcello. It pours with freezing rain so I feel quite at home. Working all day, nothing else to do. Loved seeing you, wish it was oftener.

         Love,
         Nancy

Mitford had recently published her highly successful series of tongue-in-cheek essays on "U" and "Non-U" behavior, which purported to define socially acceptable (Upper Class) mores and manners. Noël could not resist teasing her about it in his reply:

                        July the whatever it is 1956.

Darling Pen-Buddy,

Your Authors' Club letter made me laugh like a drain, as Lady Blessington used to say. Oh Dear, what a comfort it is going to be to us all except that I warn you here and now that I shall grumble continuously about the climate. I am sending this to Rue Monsieur on account of you might have left Torcello and come winging your way back to Paris France with your manuscript under your arm and a dreadful smug gleam in your eye. I would like to be able to tell you proudly that I have written thousands of witty words since I saw you and that my novel is finished and a new play started. Unfortunately, however, it WOULD NOT BE TRUE. What is true is that I haven't written a bloody word except a short note in the third person saying that Mr. Noël Coward would be delighted to attend the Admiralty Fête and draw tickets for the Raffle. What I have been doing is what is laughingly known as "Settling In". Oh *Ma Fois and Misericorde Quelle Brouhaha!* I do not know if *Brouhaha* is really feminine or I would have brought it up before, but I shall give it the benefit of the doubt. The house is enchanting and my own little private cottage a veritable *rêve* because it goes straight down into the limpidest sea. You really will have to force your frail body (in the best sense) on to a plane and come and stay and we can sit in the lounge, which is very tastefully furnished, and have a spiffing old natter about books because as you may or may not know, I am just mad about books and you being so brainy and all, that you might give me a few ideas which, I may say, would be bitterly resented . . . I must now stop and go back to my tasks one of which is to frost a rather rubbery angel cake which I made yesterday. So ta ta for the present and drop us a p.c. when you have a sec.

> Love and kisses
> Noël

But other friends were positively dismayed at his decision to move. Laurence Olivier was one:

> Arroyo de la Miel
> Torremolinos

My dearest Noelie,
It is truly awful that I have not written to you and I am truly sorry. But I have truly felt (Jesus)—The thing is I have tried and once sat for half an hour putting nothing down for the reason that I worried that would have seemed to you smug and pompous and even hyper-critical. But it's no fucking use. If I let it go on any longer it'll be too late to write ever and turn into an idiotic puzzlement not really to be laughed off when we meet.

"That we would do we should do when we would" and I should bloody well have sat down and risked it when you made your Big Decish. I didn't because I didn't know what to say. It's always been a problem for me that I've never been able to adopt an attitude or reach a conclusion on purely logical or reasonable grounds. Doubts prompted by my feelings always get in the way. Is it too much to suppose that this hesitation is an artistic one prompted by an instinct to apprehend the real truth about a thing, and appreciate the ins and outs and pros and cons that go to make up that truth? I think you could probably guess that it is weakness both of sentiment and indolence . . . But I wouldn't like you to think that the problem is one that preoccupies me to the extent of making me brood or anything, or that I am any great hero to myself.

I couldn't write to you when I should have without sounding like a letter to *The Times*. I didn't think it suited you. I didn't feel it was up to me to be the prompter of your conscience as you've no doubt got a perfectly good one of your own; or be a depressing disturbance on a decision that you'd no doubt had a tough time making. But I couldn't go with you on it. You had prompted (?) too many other patriotic consciences—the bravery of your carriage of the flag would have made Kipling and Elgar regard you with awe. It is obvious that the country needs dough as much as it ever did anyone's blood. Your tax situation was, of course, extreme and even so your contribution couldn't make very much difference. So it was not the fact, it was the symbol that was upsetting. It could only make people who couldn't take the same course feel a little worse off, if anything. I'm not envious, darling, really I'm not. I happen to like living in England and I can suppose that perpetual Rep in Kingston would support me in the style to which I might hope to accustom myself. It just didn't feel right for you; and even with your superb technique of resolution and smart carrying out, I feel it can't be honey and almonds all the time. Darling one, make bags and bags of dough and enjoy it like hell and find the sort of peace that you have the strength of mind to achieve.

> Love always
> Your Larry Boy

The personal advice was by no means one way. When Olivier was being wooed in 1963 to take over the National Theatre as its first director, Noël wrote:

> Les Avants
>
> Darling Larry Boy,
> You have been much in my thoughts lately and I am sure everybody has been "at" you in one way or another, so I am going to pile Pelion on Ossa, Stoke on Trent and possibly Lee on Solent. *Don't* administer the National Theatre. You have clearly made it and given us some of the greatest performances of the century. Administration is more frustrating and tiring than poncing about and shouting "Ho, there!" or "I'm fair Venice's lofty cunt!" What you need is a full year off duty. Please listen carefully. Take Joanie [Plowright] and the tots—never mind about disrupting their education—fly from here to Los Angeles, from Los Angeles to Tahiti—resting for a few days to get your breath and look at the Middle Western tourists, then fly overnight to Bora-Bora and sit down for a long time. The hotel is, oddly enough, luxurious—you will have a private bungalow in the garden and live in Paradise. Once a week a ghastly cruise ship arrives. On those days you take your boat (a boat is essential) and go to one of the little islands with your lunch and wait until the coast is clear. I have done all this and it saved my life. There is nothing to do so take *War and Peace* and *Present Indicative*.
>
> If the National Theatre was not there, I could go to the movies. If *you* were not there, I could still go to the movies but I should be unable to see the screen.
>
> Noelie
> P.S. Fondest love to Joanie

P.P.S. Don't dismiss this as impossible. Nothing is impossible if you put your mind to it.
PPPPPPPPS I love you very much.

Larry Boy, needless to add, took the job.

•

NOËL HAD ALSO started work on a novel—or, rather, two novels in parallel—and in December, he wrote to Lornie:

I am getting on with my novel [*Beyond These Voices*] very well and have done forty thousand words . . . which is nearly half way. I am in full spate and writing well. I think you will like it. It is really that French Resistance melodrama I once told you about based on a rich American bitch who collaborates with the Germans, betrays a young R.A.F. pilot and then gets back into society again after the war! I am writing it as the story of the R.A.F pilot's father who is the hero of the book. I am writing it in the first person singular, not as myself but as a well-known writer who has returned to Samolo where he was born. He is sixty-one and the story is written in retrospect. He, the narrator, is Kerry Stirling, the grandson of Graham in *Pacific 1860*. [Graham's character in the play was also named Kerry Stirling.]

It is absolutely fascinating to do and all the early Samolan bits are really lovely. I am just about to embark on London in 1911, then the first war and then the Twenties, etc. I know better than anything that as long as I have time to write and invent and imagine I am happy as the day is long. I do between two and three thousand words every morning before 12 o'clock and play for the rest of the day.

At the same time he was writing *Pomp and Circumstance,* a comic novel set in Samolo and dealing with British colonial junketings. As always, he valued Lornie's opinion.

December 24th

Darling Lornie . . .
I adored your letter and I'm terribly pleased that you think so highly of *Beyond These Voices.* I shall certainly press on with it the moment I have finished *Pomp and Circumstance,* but I think it is a good idea to do the lighter one first. I agree with you about Samolan phrases. They are really only put in to create atmosphere. But when the book is finished I shall whittle them down a bit.

(*Beyond These Voices* was never finished. Noël left behind the first fifty pages or so but no notes on how the story was to develop.)

•

IN DECEMBER he made his leisurely way to Los Angeles where he had rented a furnished house at 1573 Sunset Plaza Drive, Beverly Hills.

Boulevard Nowhere
December 18th

Tolette,

Havana was un-noted by me on account of the Ambassador giving an enormous buffet dinner party for all the nobs the majority of whom were called Gonzalez-y-Lopez except for a few who were called Lopez-y-Gonzalez. They were all Sugar Barons and not one Sugar laddy for me. This is going to be a curious letter as I am doing it on the Tippa Tapper *et je ne suis pas* certain of it. The house is sweet and when the fogette lifts the view will be gorgeous. Oh dear, there is so much to tell that I don't know where to begin. Little Lad is in fine form and has landed a part in a new film with Robert Taylor. He plays a British Officer who is rather supercilious. It's apparently only a tiny bit really but there is one good scene and anyhow it is a commencement.

He is leaving Clifton's today and has taken an apartment in the same place as the boys [Charles Russell and Lance Hamilton] as we considered it unwise for him to stay here. This has caused a great fluttering in the colony and no-one knows where they're at. He has handled the Clifton situation with consummate skill and every prospect pleases, except that it was getting near the point of no return. Poor Clifton is always on the verge of Umbrage about something or other and this is not helped by Harry Pissalatums which happens very very often indeed indeedy.

The cocktail party yesterday was a riot of fun and fancy and the girls came and Erica [Marx] was mistaken for Millie Natwick by Betty Bacall who congratulated her on her wonderful performance in something or other. Tub finally said "Who *do* you think I am?" Whereupon Betty said "Mildred Natwick—Jesus Christ have I put my fucking foot in it!" And it all passed off in gales of laughter. Rock [Hudson] and Phyllis [Gates, Hudson's wife] appeared and were very sweet. Marlene gave me a wonderful set of black silk pyjamas and dressing-gown to match for traveling! The Nivens are sweet and send you particular love, so do Betty and Bogey.

I was just in time to give Charles and Ham a good finger wag on account of they were in a fair way to antagonize everyone by being too upperty and pushing. Clifton, until I insisted, refused to ask them to the party. Now, however, all is well. Oh dear, Oh dear, I have to be a psychiatrist and Nursery governess as well as the prettiest T.V. star in the world. It is all 'Ow you say—*difficile*—*mais alors il faut* press on.

Mexico was almost complete disaster on account of Peter and Vail being intolerably silly. They kept on taking wrong turnings and not knowing the way to anywhere and Vail was playing the Dauphin in *The Lark* in the Round and I had to go and sit through it wrapped in a rug with a flask of brandy and it was a bugger to end all buggers. So bad indeed that I was bereft of speech. My only comfort was when Joan [of Arc] said something about not fearing the flames, a small, miserable boy in front of me let off such a loud fart that it blew the brandy flask right out of my hand. She, Joan, was a bright amateur Jane Baxter with her arse resting on her heels and a boyish manner. I expected her to say "Mumsie, can't I play one more set with Roger?" Vail camped about and was quite inaudible and the whole thing was very very dreadful indeed . . . I managed to get one satisfactory bit of nuki and left the next morning with the greatest relief. I am sure that Mexico as a country is fascinating but Mexico City is dusty, cold, hideous and without charm of any sort.

Peter, you know, is a trifle too defeated and poor Vail is jolly asinine and not a very good driver. The only subject is THE subject and I am sick to death of THE subject.

My coloured maid is called Fredda. She has Diabetes and came from St. Ann's Bay. She is very sweet, not only because of the Diabetes.

The boys are being very good apart from their social gaffes and all is going well. I am just off to Betty's [Bacall] for the first reading.

There is really no more *nouvelles*.

Love love love and get after that turfing [at Firefly].

MASTER

P.S. My Spanish lessons stood me in good stead, because I found myself gabbing away like crazy and making witty little jokes.

The Cottens came to the party and made a very great noise.

I have a most most most wonderful car which goes fast fast fast up hill and down dale.

I am on a diet and not drinking.

My Irving ["Swifty" Lazar, his agent] sent me a Christmas Tree. I hate Christmas.

The weather is very foggy.

I do not like foggy weather.

The boiler burst the day I arrived but happily it was mended before I froze to death.

I am now very hot.

Lauren Bacall played Elvira opposite Noël in the live television production of *Blithe Spirit* in 1956. Noël reported, "She was gay and charming and a darling from first to last"— unlike some he could mention.

Claudette Colbert insisted on being filmed from only one angle, which complicated everyone's life in these early television days. In filming *Blithe Spirit,* she was so uncooperative that Noël swore he would wring her neck—if he could find it.

Did I mention that Mexico City is a cunt?

The nicest Mexican I met was Roy Boulting.

Mabelle [Webb] is very well and much brighter than her son.

Bogey, justly celebrated for his *Dix-Huitième* manners, said to Clifton at the party *apropos* their own projected Christmas Eve Rout, "Bring your fucking mother and she can wipe up her own sick!" Clifton was not pleased.

Alec Guinness was very pleased and we bowed low to each other like characters in a Restoration comedy.

It was all meant in a spirit of nice clean fun.

Betty Bacall passed out on Mabelle's bed for three hours.

All of this surprised the Rock Hudsons who are perhaps unused to high society.

Betty Bacall called Hedda Hopper a lousy bitch and kicked her up the bottie under my very eyes. Then there was an upper and downer and now they are great great friends.

*Comme la vie est étonnante, n'est-ce-pas?*

*Voila c'est tout.*

•

*BLITHE SPIRIT* was scheduled for January 17, 1956. Noël was to play Charles Condomine; Claudette Colbert, his second wife, Ruth; Lauren Bacall, his ghost wife, Elvira; and Mildred Natwick, Madame Arcati.

From the beginning there were problems.

Noël once summed up a career-long problem when he wrote: "God preserve me in future from female stars. I don't suppose He will. I really am too old and tired to go through all these tired old hoops."

He had known Colbert since the 1930s, when she appeared in the film of his play *The Queen Was in the Parlour* (*Tonight Is Ours*). In 1951 she had starred in Jack Wilson's production of *Island Fling* at the Westport Playhouse.

Noël was most decidedly *not* pleased with her in *Blithe Spirit*. The trouble began with the contract negotiations:

Blue Harbour
Port Maria, Jamaica, B.W.I
12th November 1955

Darling,

Emerge from your frizz, dry oh dry those pretty tears, all will be well eventually, so there. Agents really are tiresome sods; I had explained to my TV boys that you had said you would do it if you were free of other contracts and that your salary was 10,000. They then called up your agents, after my talking to you who demanded in high, fluting voices, 25,000. *Very confidentially,* Betty Bacall's agent also demanded 25,000 and finally, as she rightly wished to play the part, they settled for 7,000.

I hate discussing money as much as you do, particularly with friends, but as we happen to be true friends, I don't care a bugger. The actual situation is that, according to my contract with CBS, I, or rather my Company, have to pay for the cast and sets and director for each production, and believe me this is a very big item. If we are to pay Betty seven, Mildred Natwick whatever is suitable, and the other three performers and the set etc., we really can't afford to pay you more than ten without, to coin a phrase, which you will readily understand, fucking up our budget.

I *know* it's an hour and a half instead of an hour; I also know that I want you to do it terribly (I don't mean *play* it terribly) and have looked forward to us playing scenes together so very very much, so please do it, darling, and let's enjoy ourselves. And listen, listen, listen, if by any chance you *don't* want to do it for that money, I swear it won't cast the faintest, tiniest shadow on my love for you. I should only be bitterly disappointed and insult you roundly on arriving and leaving your house constantly during my stay.

I don't want to bring undue pressure to bear, but would like to point out that every dollar encircled by those pudgy French fingers will have been extracted from these gnarled Scottish fingers. I do wish, Claudette dear, that you would look at the thing in a more Christian spirit; after all, Christmas is coming very shortly and I would like you to remember (a) The Manger, (b) that God is Love there is no pain and (c) that you ate me out of house and home last Christmas and *this is all I get in return*—nothing but bitter recriminations and sordid financial squabbling.

I have painted you a picture for a Christmas present, so cast out of your mind all thought of that ermine stole, it is a very charming picture and if you don't like it I shall be on hand with some seasonable suggestions as to what you can do with it.

Love, Love, Love, Love and let me know at once which way that fluffy little Gallic mind has decided to jump.
P.S. The next ugly scene, I suppose, is going to be about billing which is, and always has been, my *bête noire.* So, I have arranged it alphabetically which will put the triumphant Betty Bacall before both of us! And if there's any argument I shall appear *under* the title myself in tiny, luminous letters and leave you two glamour pusses to straddle the farting title.

Later, recollecting the experience of the actual production in relative tranquillity, he wrote to Coley:

15th January, 1956

Darling Toley . . . . . . . .

Well it is all over and apparently a roaring triumphant success. This week has really been a nightmare right up to the moment we went on the air.

. . . Darling Claudette made a beast of herself from the word go. To begin with she wouldn't learn her lines, which as you know is not the way to please Father. She said it "wasn't her method". She then bossed everybody about, and we all had to keep on getting into Anglo-Saxon attitudes so that the correct profile of her rather large face should be presented to the camera. She had us all whirling round her like dervishes, except that for quite a while I managed to be full-face, while the camera only caught the back of her head.

There were two blazing rows at the beginning, then comparative peace, then another blazing row on Thursday when I asked her to play quicker. She was determined to play Ruth like Rebecca of Sunnybrook Farm. Then *rapprochement,* because the mutual hatred was beginning to show on the screen, and last night she winged thru still not really knowing her lines but was very good, although not quite good enough.

Betty Bacall was gay and charming and a darling from first to last and no trouble at all. She looked divine but isn't really a comedienne, although she tried like mad and really gave a first rate performance within her limits.

Millie Natwick was wonderful throughout and the others all good.

We had two previews and two kinescopes and it was only yesterday at eleven in the morning that I had to deliver a tirade and insist on close-ups and so we spent the rest of the day under the lights with Claudette screaming blue murder and carrying on like Sarah Bernhardt's Jewish aunt and me keeping cheerful and sweet with murder in my heart and only one hot dog and a dexamil in my stomach. Then came the performance and everybody came up smiling and I think, nay I am sure, that the prettiest of all contrived with harem-scarem skill to dominate the whole fucking enterprise.

On Sunday last I woke with a pain in my right leg. On Monday when we started camera rehearsals I could hardly walk, so I hobbled to a doctor and asked him to inject novocaine into the agonizing place on my right thigh. As he did so a Versailles fountain of star quality pus shot into the air, whereupon everybody said "Christ", cultures were taken, I was x-rayed and sent back to bed bright green and in screaming agony. For the next two days I stayed in bed doped to the eyes and panic-stricken while my stand-in went on with the camera blocking. On Wednesday, still in agony, I hobbled to the studio and tried to rehearse, then sent for the doctor who plunged eight times a needle the size of the Eiffel Tower into my leg. This was really terrible because he had to do it eight times and I was shrieking like mad and Charles [Russell] listening outside the door nearly fainted. However, after ten minutes the novocaine began to work and I got through the rehearsal and hobbled home to bed. The next morning Thursday Doddie [God] decided to relent and I sprang out of bed like Margot Fonteyn with no pain at all. I can only conclude that the novocaine frightened it to death. From then on we rehearsed and rehearsed with Claudette screaming about her angles and her dresses, all of which were highly unsuitable, and me screaming about my close-ups. The whole studio is a hive of incompetence and everything was bloody chaos but it is all over now and a great success and one of the nastiest weeks of my whole life has retreated into the past. That is the story of my life to date.

The Coward-Colbert relationship was later patched up, but they never worked together again.

Someone who *had* relished the experience was Lauren Bacall:

February 1956

Noël dear,

How happy you must be—safely tucked away in your own home on your private island! Away from the Rat Pack, noisy parties, blowing lines, too much booze, etc. I could hear you sigh from here as you boarded your plane. Kept up with your Eastern activities via columns. Your evenings at the theatre, Stork Club, Sardi's and various and sundry other places. There's no escaping me, you see!

Holmby Hills, Beverly Hills and all surrounding areas remain the same. We call this the never changing world. The chit-chat continues. Who's doing what to who and where and even how! Can you imagine? Our friends and enemies are unchanged. How we survive I don't know—that we do impresses me . . . Trying to adjust to the fact that . . . no one really gives a damn what you accomplish is coming slowly but steadily to me. And I'm just about convinced.

I've been thinking a good deal about our excursion into ectoplasm. As you no doubt have, I've read all our reviews—was annoyed by a few. God, I hate critics. I suppose we must be patient with them—it's their only moment in the sun—but I'm still for their complete elimination.

Anyway, darling Noël, I wanted to tell you how much I truly enjoyed our three weeks together. I learned more then than I have ever learned here. You're very special in our world—working with you was a privilege—you were marvelous to me. I thank you for having me—for everything—I am so grateful to you and I adore you!

Love,
Betty

•

BY APRIL he was back in New York and sending Cole Lesley a highly colored account of his local doings:

25 West 54th Street
Sunday April 15th 1956

Carnegie Hall was a fair bugger on account of dear [André] Kostelanetz [the conductor] with uncanny showmanship, placing me second on the bill [narrating *Carnival of the Animals*]. I spoke clearly and with great distinction and the audience was bewildered and morose and far far too large and very Sat: Nite: Pop: if you know what I mean . . .

The next day was another kettle of quite different fish, I give you my word and my Ed [Sullivan] was a dear dear and spent hours crushing the wretched Kostelanetz into the background and concentrating on this lovely little H shaped F and then we scragged Pete [Matz] off a plane to Florida and he arrived with a most curious beard and the band parts and away I went into "Mad Dogs" and the whole thing was a riot and fifty-two million Americans exactly stared and stared at me and all the New York taxi men have been most flattering ever since . . .

On Friday back I came again and moved in here. It is a curiously furnished little joint but I am quite happy. I putter about and cook myself little dainties and even wash-up afterwards. There is a gas stove which frightens me very much indeed and very very little crockery. However, there are about seventeen hundred glasses which are gradually becoming filled up with breadcrumbs and bacon fat and stock and what not . . . Unfortunately the kitchen is so very small that I couldn't even swing Croyden [his cat] in it, which I should love to do, as I miss her sorely. However, there is room for me to sit down and scrabble up my food from my cracked plate and pour the boiling water onto the Nescafé without scalding myself too much.

My coloured lady who obliges for two hours every week day is most frightfully grand and made up to kill with a lot of scarlet lipstick and rice powder. She has a wide eyed tottine which she brings on Saturdays and it sits and stares at so much unaccustomed splendour.

There is a certain amount of Chinoiserie about and several forbidding cocoa-coloured armchairs and no light at all but this has *déjà* been remedied by me popping out and buying two alabaster lamps. My bed is also cocoa-coloured and pretends to be an alluring divan and then all of a sudden it isn't and there you are in bed and reading a bad book. I persuaded dear Earl Blackwell [his landlord] to buy a brand new Steinway and he consented and so I chose it and it is very nice. His old one had bright yellow notes and a number of moths flew out every time you touched it . . .

We are cooking up a little edifying idea about doing *Relative Values* with Gladys [Cooper] and Anna Neagle as Moxie. This may assuage a little bit the blind passion that Herbert [Wilcox, Neagle's husband] has for me. She can't be all that terrible as Moxie, can she? Or can she? We are also dallying with the thought of getting N.B.C. to finance a Broadway production of a Noël Coward Revue using all the best stuff and some new numbers as well and then letting them do it afterwards as a Spectacular. This with Dora [Bryan] and Little Lad and a carefully picked cast might be a very good plan. However, all that is in the air as yet.

Miss Kay Kendall having made a cracking ass of herself and refused to play Queenie [in the TV version of *This Happy Breed*], we have now engaged Patricia Cutts who read it beautifully. We couldn't get Una O'Connor and so Norah [Howard] is playing Granny and a most glorious Sylvia appeared called Beulah Garrick and on the whole the cast looks good. We take the first plungette tomorrow. I am quite looking forward to it.

Went to hear Albanese as *Manon Lescaut* and it was a grave grave mistake on account of she didn't ought to have attempted it for several reasons. Time's Wingèd Chariot being the principal one. She sang most softly and looked like a neckless shrewmouse. Jussi Boerling did a Mary Martin and belted the living fuck out of her. He contrived this very subtly by the simple device of gripping her firmly by her shrinking shoulders, turning her bum to the audience and bellowing into her kisser. The production looked as if it had been stolen from Emil[e] Littler [British impresario, inclined to be frugal with production budgets].

A few days later was CBS's *Person to Person* with Ed Murrow, which was a fair carry-on and no error. I did it in the boys' apartment on account of my cocoa-coloured cavern looking really too beastly. The waiting about for hours was calculated to be nerve-wrecking but I refused to let it get me down and went into the kitchen and made myself a delicious Dolly's omelette and cut my finger on a tin of Dundee cake and finally appeared before the cameras calmer than any *concombre* you have ever seen. Except for a few key moments the questions and answers were genuinely impromptu and I made a few quite good jokes one of which was when Ed asked me if I did anything to relax me after a long day's work and I said "Certainly, but I have no intention of discussing it before several million people!" It was all rather a curious sensation, because there was I in the apartment and there was he in a Studio in Grand Central station and I had to snatch his questions out of the air. In any event it was apparently a great success and I crept in a personalized way into thirty-one million gracious American homes.

Meanwhile rehearsals for *This Happy Breed* continued in unnerving tranquillity. He wrote to Cole:

Patricia Cutts is a good actress and her face is very very pretty. She is however a trifle too tall and very clumsy and keeps stamping on Edna's [Best] feet and rushing blindly through doors that aren't there. Roger Moore is most pretty and acts quite nicely but veree veree softly, as though he were afraid someone might hear him. This is being remedied.

My wigs are wonderful and my clothes perfectly alright and my own performance is coming along nicely, too. We are going to do it without an audience and wander about into the garden and the kitchen and make the whole thing desperately real and true and sincere.

On May 5 he could report to Lornie:

25 West 54th Street
New York
7th May 1956

Darling Lorniegraco—
I'm sitting up in bed weighted down with laurels and on the tired side, but very, very happy. Darling, *Happy Breed* came up a treat and turned out to be an absolute triumph. It was most beautifully played and Edna was absolutely beyond words as Ethel. She played it with tenderness, humor and reality and never let go of it for a second. She was also a perfect angel all through rehearsals. She was a constant help to me rather than a hindrance. The rest of the cast were all good,

particularly Roger Moore, Patricia Cutts, Norah and the American boy who played Reg [Robert Chapman]. You will see all this for yourselves as I am bringing the kinescope with me to Paris, France. The director was one hundred per cent efficient and very nice to work with. In fact, there wasn't so much as an irritable frown from the first rehearsal to the performance.

At the end, before the credits were over, there had been over a thousand calls on the CBS switchboard. Bill Paley rang up, choked with emotion and said it was the finest thing he had ever seen in his life on TV, then Clifton and the Bogarts rang up from Hollywood, also C with E [choked with emotion]. Millions of people rang up, all with C with E. In fact, it was really the most undiluted triumph I have had, all of which goes to show that I'm very pretty indeed.

Hurray! Hurray! Hurray!

There was a sweet party afterwards at Edna's just for the company and a few common outsiders like Gladys Cooper and Rex Harrison.

I'm so thrilled about Edna being able to come back and do that so calmly and with such little fuss after six months in a mental home; she was really wonderful. This seems my big year for saving the Barmies! It's a pity Nijinski is dead—I might have written a little ballet for him.

I've really no more news except that I'm really very flushed with triumph and it's a most wonderful feeling to have vanquished my enemies by the simple reprisal of giving a good performance and I know it really was a good performance and I honestly think it has had a profound effect and that my stock in America is now higher than ever. The notices so far have been wonderful.

Love, love, love, love.

      Love
      Noël

The broadcast was watched by an audience of fifty-two million people.

# CHAPTER 25

# BUBBLES . . . AND NUDES

## (1956–1957)

HOME AND COLONIAL (unproduced) begat *Island Fling* (Westport, 1951), which begat *South Sea Bubble* (United Kingdom, 1956).

In its final incarnation, the plot hinges on Lady Alexandra Shotter, the wife of the Governor of Samolo—a cross between Lady Diana Cooper and Lady Edwina Mountbatten—*almost* becoming involved with Hali, a young firebrand native politician she is trying to wean to conservatism. He

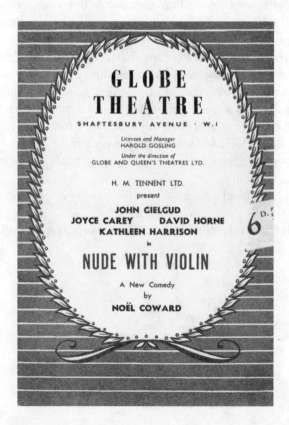

mistakes her political advances for something more amatory in nature, and when her defensive rhetoric fails, a crack over the head with a bottle has to suffice. As plots went, it was not exactly Ibsen.

Written originally for Gertie (who dithered), revised and played at Westport by Claudette Colbert, further revised and offered to Vivien Leigh (who disdainfully refused), the piece then languished until Noël heard in late 1955, to his surprise, that Vivien now saw *great* merit in it and was anxious to star in it at the earliest possible opportunity.

At this point her career was at a crossroads, her health, both physically and mentally, was suspect, and her marriage to Olivier was beginning to unravel. The play seemed something of a lifeline.

She wrote to Noël in September from her dressing room at Stratford, where she was playing Lavinia in *Titus Andronicus.* His was the best play ever written and she wanted to play *all* the female roles. Why didn't he play all the gents? But, seriously, he must co-star in it with her and direct it. They would have such fun! She had already started learning the lines, she claimed, and not one of them must be cut. She even speculated jokingly that it would make a great musical film in Todd-A-O. (Todd-A-O was the big-screen cinema format of that time developed by impresario Mike Todd.) She remained his devoted Vivien.

He wrote to Lornie:

> Blue Harbour
> September 12th 1955
>
> I had a really enthusiastic letter from Vivien about *South Sea Bubble,* saying she would like to start rehearsals second week in January if that would suit me. This is wonderful news and I am of course delighted but I really think that I cannot undertake to direct it, I would much rather Peter Brook did it and then I came back in time for the try-out, so I cabled Binkie to this effect and told Vivien that I will fly to Bermuda in December to see her and discuss all details.

Vivien wrote again a month later begging Noël to direct the play himself. She also explains her anxiety to get into immediate production—a prior film commitment in the following June or July.

Could they not do a short London season, then perhaps a TV production in New York and a film version—all of which should satisfy the financial backers? She didn't think she could manage another long run, if only because of her health. She had a history of tuberculosis and was suffering a recurrence. It would mean a stay in a clinic, having unpleasant injections, she told him, but it would be only a short stay if she behaved sensibly, which she fully intended to do, so as to be ready for the play. There was a distinct note of hysteria as she poured out her thoughts.

She knew precisely who should play the role of Hali, the male lead. Peter Finch. What did Noël think?

Noël privately thought it an extremely *bad* idea. It was an open secret that Vivien was having an affair with Finch. The part eventually went to Rank Film actor Ronald Lewis.

To Lorn:

December 24th 1955

Binkie is in New York, as you know by now, and I've had a lovely long talk to him on the telephone and apparently all is going well with the preparations. I do not think Billy Chapell [Chappell] is the ideal director of *South Sea Bubble* on account of his view of high society being confined to the area between Charing Cross Road and Dean Street. However, Larry and Vivien and Binkie think he will be right and Binkie and Vivien will supervise the social aspects of the play.

On the pre-London tour, Vivien wrote to keep him up to date with the play's progress. She felt her own performance, after a shaky start, had greatly improved and he would now not be too displeased with it. The play itself was going from strength to strength, with all the laughs coming in the right places. But oh, the theaters! The Opera House in Manchester was by no means ideal, although for some strange reason she was fond of it, which was more than could be said for Liverpool—more of a tunnel than a theater. She felt Noël would be pleased with the sets, despite the fact that they had been designed by a young man whose facial hair was entirely pink!

Noël wrote to Cole:

I haven't yet read the notices, of course, but I know in advance what to expect. They really do hate success in England, don't they? They hate and resent it with all their mean little souls. Here [in the United States] the press can frequently be cruel and vitriolic but they can also be capable of enthusiasm when they do happen to like something and at least they are interested in the Theatre.

Obviously the play is a smash hit, because it is highly entertaining and Vivien gives a lovely performance in spite of the dear first nighters and the moist cascades of faint praise. Hurray Hurray!!

The play opened at London's Lyric Theatre on April 25 and, despite the anticipated dismissive reviews, seemed to settle in for a successful commercial run.

Noël was beginning to make plans for a New York production and told Lornie:

I have decided to do a Broadway production of it under Jack's man-agement, starting rehearsals in late October. I think it is too valuable a property to be kicked round any more. I have also decided, confi-dentially but quite firmly, that Kay Kendall shall play it. I have always thought she was the only possible legitimate successor to Gertie. She has wonderful looks, immense "chic", a nice, warm basic commonness and a sense of humour and she is also wonderful to work with and will do what I tell her. To me it would be much more excit-ing to launch a new star on Broadway than have an already over-known one who would probably drive me mad. Bill Paley (privately) has agreed to put up all the money for the show on condition that he has the rights to make a TV Spectacular of it afterwards, quite agrees with all this and considers Kay is a wonderful proposition.

Jack knows nothing of all this yet but I will explain all to him when I get to New York. I have cabled the Boys to find out if Ty Power would be available to play Hali. If not I think Larry Harvey might be quite a good idea. This will put Jack back on the tracks again as a Producer and even if he breaks down again and takes to the bottle I shall be in command and will at least have the satisfaction of having given him one more chance. Somehow or other I don't think he will and if he really could be REALLY saved I should feel a great deal better. If all this turns out to be wishful thinking, I shall merely forbid him the theatre and let him get on with his drinking wherever and whenever he likes.

I have no other news except that I love Lornie very much indeed but this is such an old, old story that I am surprised Mary Martin doesn't do it on television.

Then, on July 3, Vivien wrote again to Noël in Bermuda. She had to break the news to him that she was expecting a baby and her doctor had advised her to leave the cast in three weeks' time. Noël had been in Paris a few weeks earlier, and Olivier had fully intended to travel there to see him and break the news, but script problems on his current film (*The Prince and the Showgirl*) had prevented him. She was endlessly sorry but she felt the play could continue successfully without her. Would he please write to her at once and tell her he was not *too* angry?

But Noël *was* angry—very angry indeed. Why had she and Larry waited so long to let him know?

This I consider fairly unforgivable of them, but I rose above my shock com-mendably and wrote loving congratulations . . . [He received no acknowl-edgment.] Altogether I'm sick to death of both of them at the moment. I've been bored and involved with their domestic problems for years and done all I could to help, and as they haven't even troubled to write to me, they can bloody well get on with it (*Diaries*).

He also wrote to Binkie:

Although the dubious sanctity of the Olivier's home means a great deal to me, the financial security of my own means a bloody sight more. I do not wish you to imagine that I am being in any way cynical about this inconsiderate Act of God. Oh dear me, no. Perish the thought! But I do I do I do wish that the long awaited reunion of two minds [*sic*] had been a trifle less enthusiastic and a little more thoughtful of others. I also have slight apprehensions on behalf of the imminent tot itself. It will certainly get to know a great many people in a remarkably short space of time. I also hope, for its sake, that Larry and Vivien don't go immediately into rehearsal with some particularly neurotic classic. This will be VERY BAD FOR BABY.

I cabled them and wrote to them most sympathetically but have had no reply. I presume they are too tired to write.

It wasn't long before the word got around. Joyce wrote:

Alan [Webb] and I had lunch with Proud [Vivien] and Little by Little [Olivier]. She was the same and nice but he has become a gross, prize BORE. When we were told jointly about the Baby, Alan said it was an Act of God, and Vivien said it was the best billing Larry had ever had, which I thought was very funny of her.

Noël wrote to Lornie about "the expected tot":

July 17th
Spithead Lodge
Warwick, Bermuda

Darling Lorniebubs,
I am SO SO happy for them although a teeny bit apprehensive on the tot's account. To be born into such a turbulent *ménage* might possibly be far from cosy, what with Daddy shrieking "Fuck" and bellowing *Macbeth,* and Mummy going briskly round and round different bends, and never less than twenty people to lunch, dinner and supper. I cannot either quite believe that it will remain in its present confined and uncomfortable surroundings until December the 22nd. My personal guess is that it may appear much sooner and astonish everyone . . . And I can tell you wistfully here and now if they ever

want any more material from me again at any time, they're dead out of luck.

He turned out to be morbidly prescient. Vivien left the show and had a miscarriage the next day. The show itself rapidly lost momentum. Vivien was replaced by Elizabeth Sellars.

Matters came to a head when Noël was in Dublin that September to supervise *Nude with Violin*. Vivien and Binkie flew over to see him, since Noël's offshore tax status prevented his going to London, and when it came to light that Binkie had known about the pregnancy a long time before Noël, a blazing row ensued.

Afterward Noël wrote, "I at least had the satisfaction of saying what has been fomenting in my mind for some time . . . I think and hope the air is now cleared."

Unfortunately, it was not. Olivier wrote to protest Noël's treatment of Vivien, and to give their own version of events. After calm consideration:

> Blue Harbour
> Port Maria, Jamaica, B.W.I.
> 12th January, 1957

Darling Larryboy,

If I ever had any doubts about the reality of your love for me, your letter has for ever dispelled them. Knowing you to be an indolent little cunt as far as such matters as letter-writing are concerned, the fact that you sat down and routed about in yourself to find your own truth and hand it to me has proved to me that, in spite of some painful moments here and there, we are deep friends and always will be. You couldn't have given me a more heart-filling re-assurance that you mind about me as much as I mind about you.

This is liable to be a long letter because I have a great deal to explain, so hold onto your hat, love, and press on. First of all I agree with all you say about the scene in Dublin; it was clumsy, self-indulgent and, practically all of it, quite indefensible. You are wrong in thinking it was in any way a side-wash from my "Great Decish" (I will come to all that later). The only possible excuse for it was that I had been miserably hurt by being shut away from your confidence. The idiotic spluttering fireworks were set off by Binkie saying that *he* had known your secret when he had come to Paris in June and had been expressly told by you not to say a word to anyone, even me. This, considering that I have been so intimately concerned with your and Puss's troubles for so long, made me very angry and hurt like hell. After all, you *are* both very dear to me and it *was* my play that was concerned. If only, if only you had had time to come to Paris yourself, or even let Binkie tell me, I would not only never have betrayed it to a soul, but *not* had the beastly feeling of being shut out. When, later, in Bermuda, I had the letter from you and Puss I did genuinely feel, play or no play, that this might be the solution to your troubled life together and immediately cabled and wrote to say so. To which, my darlings, I had no reply at all . . .

Please, please try to see my point in being upset over all this; it made me feel so very much further away than I actually was. Also, please wipe from your mind for ever that I am contemptuous of "the crummy little human urge" to have children. It is one of the most important urges in human life, and whatever I may have ranted and roared in my unbecoming outburst was neither valid *nor* accurate. Curiously enough I believe Puss knew this at the time. She was very upset and understanding and, *I know,* forgiving. It is more difficult for you because you weren't there and got the whole episode second-hand. I am not really trying to excuse myself over this, but it wasn't all so utterly beastly as it sounds—there were some moments of laughter and some moments of tears. I think perhaps that it was Binkie's presence that caused it to get out of hand. Not consciously, of course, he was perfectly behaved, but the awareness of an extra audience probably egged me on to be more outrageous than I either felt or wanted to be . . . the steam had been working up inside me and it had to come out. Please, darling boy, forget and forgive it. Next time, I promise, I will wag my finger at you and it won't be about anything that we any of us really mind about in the least.

Now then, about my "Great Decish". *Of course* it isn't all honey and almonds and *of course* I have had a beastly time over it. I hated the idea of selling Goldenhurst and Gerald Road and I still, sentimentally, hate the idea of having no actual home in England. I suppose I shall have to fall back on Notley [the Oliviers' country home]. It's not *too* bad in the summer!

Unfortunately, the whole business has been so distorted by the Press that it is difficult, even for those who love me, to see it clearly. To begin with, it has nothing to do with lack of patriotism; I have gone away physically from England but I have not gone away from being English and being bloody proud of it. I live in two British territories, Bermuda and Jamaica. The "Symbol" of my action has been misconstrued. I have *never* since I was young, lived in England more than I could possibly help. I love the sun and I loathe the cold, and even in the days of my early successes, I used to go off on Freighters for a month at a time. Since 1948, I have spent, on the average, less than three months a year in England. This place gives me peace and time to think and time to write.

Two years ago I was informed benignly that I was nineteen thousand pounds overdrawn and that the overdraft was guaranteed by my life insurance which is my only tax free nest egg. I then decided to return to the Café de Paris, which I didn't want to do, go to Las Vegas which was, let's face it, a considerable risk and sign a package deal TV contract which I *hated*. Happily for me these enterprises were all successful and with a little perfectly legal but adroit finagling, I managed to keep some of the dough I made. Last year my lawyer, Lornie, Cole and I went into the whole situation. Goldenhurst (five gardeners all the year round, lighting, heat, etc.) was costing a fortune. Gerald Road, very pleasant but far from inexpensive, and Jamaica with an agent and three local staff all the year round—all this of course, without investments and without capital, was sheer insanity. I was faced with the choice of giving up English residence or giving up Jamaica and I naturally chose the latter because I cannot write or get peace in England, and in Jamaica I can. The Bermuda thing is complicated and its principal advantages are too intricate to go into here, but I do so very much want you to have a clear over-all picture of my circumstances and to make you understand why I did what I did.

I have not *evaded* paying English tax by this move. My Company will pay English tax on all my English earnings except for "Bubble" and "Nude" which were contracted for with my Jamaican Company. What I have done is to avoid paying any more surtax which, if I had continued to be domiciled in England, would have completely crippled me and left me no cushion at all for my old age which is due to begin next Tuesday.

I know other people have their problems and troubles, and I think the tax laws in England as applied to artists are iniquitous, but my case is different in that I have *not* lived in England for ten years . . . As a non-resident I can not only spend three months a year there, after this financial year is over, but get on with my job of being a writer without the fear of penniless old age and sudden illness hovering over me.

Now that's enough of that "reasonable" part of the business. The abstract "Symbol" part is obviously more difficult to analyse. I can only assure you that in my deep deep heart I *know* how I feel about my country and my roots and that I never could renounce it by word or deed. The Press have as usual misrepresented the whole thing to millions of people, have given the impression that I have turned my back on my country and refused to pay my dues. In 1940 they all had another ramp at my expense and announced that I had run away from the war. This, incidentally, was one of the most hellish persecutions I have ever endured, but I did endure it and it toughened me. I know now, as I knew then, that my conscience is all right with me (except for a merry little evening in Dublin). I also know, darling, that the best way I can serve my country is *not* by sitting in it with a head cold grumbling at the climate and the telephone service, but by living further away where I can really get on with my primary job which is to become a better and better writer and a more tolerant and compassionate human being. I do *not*, I hasten to add, intend to give up being witty as all fuck and pretty as a picture.

I have turned down all TV offers from America, refused haughtily but graciously to play *My Fair Lady* for three months, refused to do a month at the Palace and refused incessant offers from Las Vegas. I *may* make a picture of *Present Laughter* later in the year but this is very vague. I list all this in reply to what you said about "Make lots of dough!" I don't particularly want to make lots of dough. All I want is enough sitting in the Bank to ensure freedom from worry during the coming years. After all I am three years off sixty!

I expect all this looks terribly garbled but I do so want you of all people to know the facts.

My house on Firefly Hill is paradise and my loved ones scrabble about down in Blue Harbour. I sometimes permit them to come up for meals and sometimes, with exquisite magnanimity, I descend to their level. They consist, at the moment, of Winifred and Gladys and Coley. Binkie, Johnny P[erry] and Terry [Rattigan] arrive tomorrow and Marilyn Monroe is just along the coast, what *more* can one ask?

I have typed all this because you wouldn't have understood one bloody word if I had written it for although my actual "writing" is improving hand over thing, my caligraphy is a sheer fucker (sorry, Mother).

Thank you again, dearest darling Larryboy. Is there any chance of you both coming here on the way to somewhere or other? I am almost certain to pop over to England some time during the summer. Give my dearest love to Puss and tell her that she's a wicked, dull, common, repulsive pig and I never want to see her again except constantly.

And that was more or less it—forgiven though never quite forgotten. Noël tied up the loose emotional ends in a letter from Blue Harbour:

February 14th 1957

Well, Darling Larry Boy,
I certainly couldn't agree with you more about what Binkie said or didn't say and who said what or didn't say what. It's all over and done

with and the only thing that's left is three people who love each other very much and always did and always will.

He then turned the subject to lighter matters. Olivier had just endured the experience of not only acting with but directing Marilyn Monroe in *The Prince and the Showgirl*—the film version of Terence Rattigan's *The Sleeping Prince*—in which he had appeared on the stage with Vivien as Mary Morgan, the role which Monroe was now attempting. At this time she was married to American playwright Arthur Miller.

In his own letter Olivier had seemed surprised that "the blond bottom looks and seems to be very good indeed," although he was less enthusiastic about Miller: "Arthur talks a great deal better than he listens, but I never found his talk very entertaining."

Noël continued the topic:

I am relieved on the whole that Mr. and Mrs. Arthur Miller disdained my invitation. I have a feeling that it just might not have been a success mad. In the first place I am not an ardent admirer of Mr. Miller's work on account of it lacking humour to an alarming degree. In the second place I once, at Clifton's in Hollywood, sat for two hours at a tiny table with Marilyn and felt, at the end of two hours, a piercing need for a whiff of oxygen. She is certainly no Madame de Staël, is she? Another reason why the lunch might have been a failure is that I was spitting mad about the tales Terry [Rattigan] told me about the silly bitch never being on time for anything and keeping you waiting for hours every day and I might, if the subject had come up, given some of my astringent views on tiresome leading ladies who are always having their hair done and pouting and making life hell for everybody. So that was something well avoided.

Now, believe it or not, I have had Johnny Ray wished on me! It will only be for a few days and I quite like him but I cannot imagine what to do with him. (The obvious answer to this might be pleasant but it really wouldn't fill in enough time!)

I shall be thinking of you bashing away at Tightarse in all those peculiar towns, but most of all I shall be thinking of flinging my arms around your darling necks somewhere, sometime and not so very far away at that.

The Oliviers were to take their Stratford production of *Titus Andronicus* on a prolonged European tour that summer. For Larry, the prospect, though emotionally draining ("darting like hysterical drunken bumblebees"), looked distinctly pleasing after "the blond bottom," and for Vivien, another stint as Lavinia meant she was working again. What matter that

Thirtysomething years on, and this time
John Gielgud plays the lead in a Noël
Coward play, the 1956 *Nude with Violin*.
Noël would play it later on Broadway.

the role carried with it one of the most depressing stage directions in
theater history: "Enter Lavinia, her hands cut off, her eyes put out and
ravished"?

•

*NUDE WITH VIOLIN* was written in early 1954 but only produced two
years later. Sir John Gielgud was to star in it as well as direct it. Having
followed Noël in *The Vortex* and *The Constant Nymph* back in the 1920s, he
was now *creating* a Coward part. As Gielgud described it to his friend Lillian Gish:

> I have Noël's new comedy *Nude With Violin* to rehearse September
> 3rd. We open in Dublin September 24th and a short tour before we
> bring it to London in October. It is a funny play—with a rather new
> kind of part for me [Sebastien]—a sort of confidential Dago valet
> who is the smooth arranger of everything—a lot of semi-farcical happenings
> going on, to do with a dead painter who has tricked the
> world into accepting as masterpieces the pictures that were painted
> by other people. It is original and neat, and seems to me the best
> thing Noël has written in years, but we shall see.

The Dublin opening was preordained by Noël's offshore tax status.
Having failed to see *South Sea Bubble* this way, he was determined to have

this production where his beady author's eye could scrutinize it. Much as he admired and liked Johnny G., he did not entirely trust his sense of contemporary comedy.

On June 11, 1956, Noël had his first meeting with Gielgud, who wrote the following day to say:

> I did so enjoy seeing you and talking over the play . . . I hope you didn't find it all too vague and problematical and I do wish you could be on hand when the time comes. You must just trust me to do my best and keep my powder dry—which, as you know, is very difficult in this revolting climate . . . Let me know if you have any more ideas and good advice from time to time.
>
> My love as ever and thank you for being so sweet.

Gielgud's traditional diffidence did nothing to calm Noël's unease. He wrote whimsically to Cole:

> And with regard to Ould Ireland, if it's me whisht heart you're thinking of, it's after being in me boot, with dread and suspicion and may the blessed Virgin have pity and keep his nibs away from the cottages [a homosexual term; Gielgud had been convicted of soliciting a few years before] and prevail upon the poor spalpeen to play divil a bit of comedy and not fuck up the whole blathering enterprise.

And more rationally, to Joyce, who was to appear in the play:

> I do hope hope hope all goes well. I have immense faith in Johnnie as a director and I know it will all be done in perfect taste. I pray he doesn't become self-conscious, but even if he does I shall have ten days to snap him out of it. He is wonderful about listening and taking direction, so all should be well . . .
>
> I am bringing a lot of "Happy" pills with me from New York which I shall munch incessantly during the performance.

16 Cowley Street
Westminster S.W.1.
18.7.56

Dear Noël,

We have begun auditions for the play and two or three people read the reporter very well. I hope we will get Peter Sallis for this part, who played for Gar Kanin, as an American, last year and was brilliant, though the play was no good. We have Patience Collier, Joyce and Kathleen Harrison, and David Horne for Jacob, but now there is the difficulty of the family.

Anne Castle [*sic*], whom you so warmly recommended, read Jane, and is, I agree, very skilled, very charming, with plenty of variety and obviously good technique. But she seems to me lacking in any sort of pertness or a lively kind of originality. Also I do feel that she is too old. True she might be Joyce's daughter, but she lacks the contrast which, it seems to me, Jane should be to her Mother. Surely she must have a twinkle in her eye, and some of the original quality of her father; which makes her Sebastien's ally?

I am having some more readings later in the week, and will try and cast Colin, Pamela and Jane together. I will also ask Joyce to come down so we can judge about the sort of ensemble we are getting.

. . . I do think that Jane and Pamela being the only non-character parts should both be very attractive, and Jane the younger of the two. Is this right? I know she cannot be a "teen-ager" because of the time factor, but do feel she should be a bit of an original, and a rebel. Anne Castle to me is a sort of leading lady, with graciousness and style.

I hate to go against your wishes in the matter because I can see what a good actress and very charming woman she is. But I do feel she would not be right in balance, and that we should try to get somebody a little more mischievous and unusual in personality. What would you think of Annie Leon?

> My love to you,
> Johnny

From Joyce, on July 21: "It's a very funny play and I am madly looking forward to it. Of course, John will drive us cuckoo . . . I imagine he is writing to you constantly?"

To Joyce, on July 30:

Oh dear, Oh dear, how you would have loved to see my reaction when Johnnie G's letter arrived explaining that Ann Castle, whom I have always wanted for Jane, was distinguished etc., etc., but not pert enough nor mischievous enough and, added in ink, poor fool, "What about Ann Leon?" I went right through the roof and had to have my laces cut. Since the acid cable I sent immediately I haven't heard from Johnnie but I have just had a lovely letter from Binkie telling me how wonderfully the reading went and enclosing a list of the cast. I noted, oddly enough, the name of Ann Castle

. . . I do so hope he isn't going to make a bollocks of it.

To Binkie on the same day:

Dearest Bink,
I am absolutely delighted that you were so pleased with the reading. The whole cast sounds fine to me. I am a teeny bit worried about David Horne being slow but he is an excellent actor and Johnny must just get after him . . .

I am more than delighted that you are pleased with Ann Castle. She was beginning to haunt me. I thought so very highly of her in Worthing, as you know, and was tremendously anxious for her to play something of mine, in fact, I made a promise to her and myself that one day this would happen. When, the other day, I got a letter from Johnnie saying that she was distinguished, charming, technically good and with a leading lady quality BUT that she wasn't pert and rebellious and mischievous enough, I gave a loud cry like a wounded lion, threw the rhubarb pie upon which I was engaged into the air and had to have feathers burned under my nose. When, later, I noted that Johnnie had written in, in ink, "What about Anne Leon?" my rage became really terrible to witness and Cole and Graham had to hide under the kitchen table. Dear John, of course, happens to be unaware that Anne Leon happens to be my greatest *bête noire* in the entire English theatre. She is cute, defiant, mischievous, rebellious, arch, debonaire and to me, entirely nauseating. She also, in my opinion, suffers from a staggering lack of talent. If by any fearful hazard she had actually been engaged, I should have been unable to look at the stage during the hideous time she was on it, all of which would have made my visit to Dublin a great waste of time. From the foregoing you may have gathered by now that I DO NOT CARE for Anne Leon.

27.7.56

Dear Noël,
Many thanks for your cable. I only found out too late that Anne Leon was a *bête noire* of yours.

Anyway, Anne Castle has now been engaged, and read the part extremely well yesterday when we had the entire company for the first time. It all seemed to balance very well, and Kathleen Harrison and Patience Collier were both extremely funny. David Horne is not over skilled and inventive, but a wonderful type for the part, and I am sure I can get a good performance out of him

We have only three weeks rehearsal and I think that will give urgency to the work, and I have told them all to learn their words before we begin. I wish you could have been here to hold the reins, but shall look forward with some trepidation, but also with great pleasure, to seeing you in Dublin.

Fond love to you, Graham and Coley.

As ever

John

P.S. I am rather in favour of the family changing after the first act and a half. Not necessarily complete changes, but say a white blouse for Jane, a tweed suit for Colin and possibly a discreet black and white number for Joyce. Binkie is inclined to think that, as a strict Catholic, Joyce particularly should stay in black throughout the play, but I think it would gay it up a bit to give them at any rate minor changes, if only to indicate the lapse of time. Once the funeral joke is over in the first act, so many black dresses on the stage might become monotonous, don't you think?

Noël duly arrived in Dublin and found, as he had anticipated, that there was much to be done. John, unsure of himself in light comedy, had given everyone too much distracting comic business so that many of the lines were lost. Noël also realized that he had his own problems as the playwright. There was cutting to be done and some rewriting, but the play *was* genuinely funny.

In his *Diaries* he wrote, "I wonder why it is that my plays are such traps for directors . . . Nobody seems capable of leaving well enough alone and allowing the words to take care of themselves."

When *Nude with Violin* opened on November 7 at London's Globe Theatre—renamed many years later The Gielgud—it received the usual scathing Coward notices but settled in for a steady run. Noël wrote to Joyce: "I am really thrilled about darling 'Nuders' being such a wonderful success, on account of I still believe, in spite of Brecht, Peggy Ashcroft, Arthur Miller, etc., that the Theatre is primarily a place of entertainment."

After the opening night was well behind him, Gielgud sent Noël a progress report:

Nov. 20th 1956

I know I have been very bad about writing but somehow it seemed absurd to put down detailed accounts of ups and downs while we were on tour. After each performance one's reactions are so instantaneous and they so often change from day to day—I didn't really want to put them on paper for you to receive a week later and perhaps fidget and fume because you were not here to correct or modify them—so I didn't write at all . . .

The Queen came with a private party. She sat in the front of the

An unspoilt Eden. During the 1930s, Anthony Eden (later the Earl of Avon) (1897–1977) was a frequent guest at Goldenhurst. Seen here with Jack and Noël. There was not too much for Eden to laugh about in years to come.

dress circle, and they tell me she seemed very amused. Fortunately, her presence did not seem to inhibit the audience at all and the play has never gone better. The company did not know until the end, which was a good thing too, as they didn't underplay—and I hope *I* didn't overplay.

Of course, I am much more fluent and certain of myself with practice and I think you would hear no more Terry tones.

Quite early in the run they had to adjust to a theatrical crisis of a more than usually serious kind. Britain attempted to take over the Suez Canal, triggering what became known as the "Suez Crisis." Gielgud reported:

We removed "Cairo" and "Port Said" last week. I felt the audience chill as we uttered them. (We have already had to change "Cyprus" in *The Chalk Garden,* first to "Suez" and then—hastily—to "Potsdam", so you see how tricky geographical references can become in a matter of hours.) "Gibraltar" and "Tangier" are not so good but the laughs still come all right.

I am very grateful for everything. Your help and advice in Dublin was quite invaluable to my performance.

As ever,
JOHN

Even at a distance Noël experienced the backwash of the Suez debacle for himself. His old friend Sir Anthony Eden, having lived in Churchill's shadow for so long, finally became prime minister in 1955. It was he who ordered the Suez invasion, only to have to backtrack in the face of Russian and American diplomatic pressure. The "defeat" broke him in spirit and health.

Then, to everyone's surprise, at the height of the global political fallout, he and his second wife, Clarissa, arrived in Jamaica to recuperate in total seclusion at Ian Fleming's Goldeneye.

Noël wrote to Lorn:

November 29th

Darling Lornie,

I haven't clapped eyes on either of the Edens yet although I had a very pleasant note from Clarissa thanking me for a small basket of goodies I left for them. She said in the note that he was feeling much better already, although he was rather fretting at being out of England!

That I expect sums the situation up fairly accurately. It really is *molto molto curioso* to think of our Prime Minister fretting away at Goldeneye while the Egyptians and the Arabs and the Israelis and the Iranians and the Syrians and the Russians are frigging away in the Middle East. I am afraid that what I once wrote in a bread and butter poem to Beatrice [Eden's late first wife] years ago is only too true. The verse finished with the gaily prophetic phrase, "The answer's a Lebanon."

I have said to myself repeatedly that all this persecution he is getting from the Press MUST prove that they are wrong and he is right, but oh dear, I am not sure at all at all and very very puzzled. The Governor, who I lunched with just after he had met them at Montego and deposited them at Goldeneye, said that Anthony looked tired but quite definitely not ill. On the other hand there are fairly well authenticated rumours that he has wakened in the night screaming several times and sent for the Guard. This of course might be accounted for by the acute discomfort of Ian's bed and the coloured prints of snakes and octopuses that festoon the peeling walls. Try as I may I CANNOT believe that he has come traipsing all the way out here in the middle of a tremendous international crisis just to REST? There must be something more than that behind it. My personal guess is that he is planning to resign and is giving himself three weeks to think it over from every angle before he takes the plunge. But of course this is only wild surmise and I may be quite quite wrong.

I am convinced that the decision to bash the Egyptians and knock Nasser for six was a good one but it should have been done much much sooner. As you said and Little Bill [Stephenson] said, a monumental example of mis-timing. The real blame, of course, lies much further back when we were idiotic enough to allow ourselves to withdraw our troops from the Canal Zone. We had a perfectly good treaty to hang on to which was valid until 1968 and with our usual misguided passion to prove to the woolly-minded Americans and the rest of the world what wonderful guys we were, we just let go our hold as we have done, with disastrous results, in so many other parts of the world.

The real doddering, fuddy-duddy Chamberlainesque villain of this gloomy little piece is, of course, John Foster Dulles. All well informed Americans, including Joe Alsop and Walter Lippman [*sic*], are perfectly aware of this. I honestly think that if we had succeeded in knocking the Egyptians out, grabbing the canal and consolidated our position everything would have been all right and the fartarsing UN could have taken over afterwards and straightened things out to its heart's content. Sadly enough, however, we had, apart from other country's interferences, our own basic English stupidity to contend with. When I read of those idiotic crowds marching about Trafalgar Square and demonstrating themselves to a standstill I felt almost as sick as I felt at the Munich time and for the same reason. I am really very surprised that Nelson didn't do a neat swallow dive from the top of his column and say "Kiss me, Hardy or not as you please but if ever I saw a lot of cunts, you're them." This might not have been as historically quotable as "England Expects" but it would certainly have been just as much to the point.

I've read the three articles you sent. But what the hell is the use of a few people writing balanced and sensible articles when the bulk of the nation is sodden with uneasy prosperity and incapable of thinking seriously about anything but Marilyn Monroe and the Football Pools. It seems to me, oh sadly, sadly, it seems to me, that we've lost our will to work, lost our sense of industry, lost our sense of pride in our heritage and above all lost our inherent conviction that we are a great race. Old Churchill, with all his personal faults, kept our real spirit alive for us for as long as he could, but look at the damned thing now.

If only if only if only our politicians could not be so unerringly relied upon to make the same mistakes over and over again.

If only we had been able to profit by the hideous experiences of the war as the defeated countries have done.

If only we were not so slavishly eager to bend the knee to our richer American allies and so girlishly prone to tremble with fear at their frown.

If only we were not so humiliatingly determined to uphold the mediocre with all our might, protect the fools and decry the intelligent, elevate the condition of the dear old honest working man to such a point that he becomes thoroughly dishonest and works as little as possible for as high wages as possible, and methodically destroy our prestige which for centuries has been the highest and most respected in the world.

Personally, I am ashamed, more generally ashamed than I have ever been since Munich and most particularly ashamed because I have been forced to leave my own country, not only because of financial reasons, but because its attitude to life and art, and specifically to me, bores me so that I find it no longer comfortable to live in.

Well, my darling, I will now close this little essay and let you know chop-chop double quick pronto if I can winkle our questionably Prime Minister out of his happy hide-away.

I have an excellent channel for gossip because his temporary secretary who has a fan of teeth, bright opaque blue eyes and is called Cora St. Aubyn, is staying with Blanche Blackwell.

Love love love love
MASTER

Eden duly resigned in January 1957. Noël wrote to Joyce:

With regard to the political situation I am feeling much much happier. Harold Macmillan is highly intelligent and I think will do a good job although he has certainly inherited a bugger's muddle. I am desperately sorry for the wretched Anthony, but I think if he had gone on any longer he'd have fallen dead, so it's just as well he did resign.

Noël had other visitors that winter: Gladys (Blackie) and Winnie (Clemence Dane). He told Lorn:

Winnie and Blackie arrived safely and only three hours late. We had reserved rooms at Sunset in case they might be exhausted but they wanted to press on and so we did. It was a lovely drive with Winnie shrieking with enthusiasm at everything she saw. When we arrived, Blackie looked like paper and was obviously worn out but not our Winnie. Oh dear no. She downed a couple of dry martinis—midnight!—and was all for swimming in the pool. This was discouraged but the next morning she was bouncing about in the pool at dawn and from then onwards. She has already painted a large picture of several oranges, very good, told us the plots of several classic novels, recited reams of poetry, dug a fork in her own neck while illustrating the way Shakespeare stabbed Marlowe, in fact she is being more wonderfully Brittania Galeish than I would have believed possible. Coley will never be quite the same again. He caught Winnie naked on a lilo with her arms outstretched, singing!

And to Joyce:

Winifred I need hardly say was quite quite tumultuous from first to last and of course said some glorious things. For instance when we were discussing harmlessly at lunch (Binkie, John, Terry, etc.) the fact of people having split personalities and secret sides to them, Winifred in her most trilling governess voice said "Of course, of course, the five John Thomases! [British slang for 'penis']" This naturally enough reduced the five John Thomases present to dreadful ill-concealed hysteria, Binkie choked, great round tears coursed down Coley's face and I talked very very loudly about something quite different.

To watch her fling herself in and out of the pool, either in what looked like a black evening dress of the 1920s or, when she thought she was unperceived, no dress at all, was indeed wonderful and curiously majestic. We haven't yet got the painting studio tidied up, but it was all well worth it. She did a lot of "Don't tell me you haven't read your Scatchwick", but I clamped down firmly on all discussions of Space Fiction on account of Space Fiction bores the fuck out of me and there's no two ways about it.

The boys all left yesterday; Binkie and John for Tobago and Terry for California via New York. Binkie was at his best and absolutely sweet, so was Terry, but really the sweetest of the lot was Johnny P[erry] who put himself out in every way he could to be of help, even to cooking a couple of meals and driving the car back and forth up and down the hill. He *is* a curious creature isn't he? I do think that on the whole he is much nicer than he used to be.

There is very little news really beyond the fact that I have decided to give myself a Sabbatical year and have refused all commitments and all offers. This gives me a wonderful feeling of freedom and I am writing verses with immense enjoyment because at the moment I do not feel like tackling a play or a book. The verses really are fairly good I think and it's certainly opening a few windows and enlarging my vocabulary. So I am feeling very happy.

Annie and Ian have arrived and are very sweet and that's all right. But what is not all right are all the other people who keep on arriv-

Binkie Beaumont (*top*), his companion John Perry (*bottom*), and Terence Rattigan (*center*). Articulate as they all were, they were rendered speechless when fellow guest Clemence Dane told the story of "the five John Thomases."

ing, all of whom have to be done something about if you will forgive the Henry Jamesian phrasing. And I wish I wish I wish that when people go on a holiday that they would *not* say "We must go to Jamaica and call on dear ole Nole."

In early 1956, during his annual pilgrimage to Jamaica, Noël wrote a play called *Volcano*. Set once again in Samolo (Jamaica), it was a thinly veiled version of real-life events. While he was carrying on his long-range affair with Ann Rothermere, Ian Fleming had not felt the need to curb his bachelor tendencies. At some point he had begun an affair with Blanche Blackwell, a local Jamaican and a friend of Noël's whose family had sold him the Firefly property.

In the play, Blanche is Adela Shelley ("a handsome woman in her mid-forties"). She is being pressed to have an affair with the local Lothario, Guy (Ian). Guy's wife, Melissa (Ann), arrives to assess her latest rival. To fill out the plot there are other guests with various romantic entanglements of their own, and the whole thing is set in the guesthouse Adela runs on the slopes of an extremely symbolic volcano that momentarily threatens to erupt and belatedly does.

Some months later, Noël sent Lorn the manuscript for her to critique, and she replied:

January 18th 1957

The first thing I want to write about is *Volcano* and how really thrilled I am that it is so frightfully good. It really is. There seems to me to be so much about it to praise and enjoy. The taut economical writing, and the wonderful atmosphere and tension of the scenes on the mountain, the sharp clarity and truth of the characters. For good actors (and of course they are going to need good actors) they are a gift from Heaven. I do think you have drawn them brilliantly and, to me, with such a sure touch that one short sentence gives so much insight into the person. For instance in Act I scene 2 when Melissa refers to her "vast daughter" you know at once that she is concrete and vinegar inside about other women, even her own adolescent daughter. And Guy's moments of genuine tenderness convince me that they really are genuine and one of the secrets of his charm. The play and the people in it have certainly worked themselves out a treat and I couldn't be more delighted.

To Joyce:

I have a strong feeling that it is good because the idea dropped complete into the mind and I wrote it with very little trouble and a great

deal of pleasure, rather like *Blithers.* It is called *Volcano.* Rather difficult to describe as it is fairly unlike anything I've done before, *Brief E*
is the nearest, I suppose, but the situations are stronger and it is less
mizzy. So now I am veree veree happee and can go off on Thursday for
the rest of my island hopping with a *coeur leger.*

Only one aspect of the play concerned Joyce, insofar as it might provide
a potentially embarrassing clue to the real-life "originals" of Noël's characters. On his first visit to Firefly Noël had been struck, in a negative way, by
Ian's "hordes of ageing, fading shells."

I am sending these two cuttings from *The Sunday Times* in case you
think it matters such wide publicity having been given to Ian's shell
collecting. I don't suppose it does but, if it is likely to, it's better to
worry about it now than later.
    I haven't heard from Binkie since I delivered the script on Monday
but there has hardly been time and anyway he will be sure to write to
you.

April 30th
To come to what is important, *Volcano,* I am extremely disappointed
that Binkie, while being impressed by a lot of it, does not care for it
a hundred per cent and has a good deal of criticism to make.
    As I understand it, there is a feeling that Adela's continued friend-
ship with Guido [Guy] plus her continued refusal to let him be her
lover makes her an unsympathetic character. There is also this prevailing idea that the only people worth considering in serious plays
are those who either live in squalor or, at the highest, do their own
housework and take the washing to the launderette. The slightly
more leisured classes are presumed to be acceptable to an audience
when in farce or light comedy but not when their deeper emotions
are involved. I think Binkie is truly unhappy about making criticisms but, of course, he is right to say what he thinks.

Noël finally wrote *two* versions of the play. In the first one—perhaps out
of deference to Blanche—he had her refuse Guy's advances. Only in the
revised version he prepared after Binkie's criticism did the dramatist take
over from the friend and make it clear that the affair *had* taken place and
was now definitely over.
    Perhaps his personal feelings for the people concerned got between him
and his characters, because the play never took off. A staged reading in
1989 and a provincial English production are the only occasions an audience has had to see the play performed.

TO NOËL'S DELIGHT, *Nude* settled in for a solid commercial London run. In May, Clifton Webb suggested that Noël should sell the film rights. Noël replied:

I would certainly like to sell *Nude with Violin* for pictures but there is still a chance that I might do it myself in NY and, until this is decided, I would like to leave it what is known as "in the air". It is not a particularly dating play, so we could either or both of us play it, even if we are kept together by Scotch tape.

(I had my hair cut yesterday because I got so sick of all that feathery stuff getting into my eyes and I now look like Yul Brynner's Aunt).

On June 24, 1957, Gielgud left the cast. Noël wrote to Joyce:

1957. Wilding took over from John Gielgud as Sebastien in *Nude,* and it was soon clear that he did not understand the role. Said Noël: "Nothing can be done until he has played it for a couple of weeks, then I shall come down with my cohorts all gleaming and beat the fuck out of him."

I expect you will have heard some repercussions about my being none too pleased when I heard that John was leaving on June 22nd. It was all news to me, and great big stars leaving great big successes is another thing I don't care for. I hope stumps will be stirred this time and someone really good be found to replace him, but there it is and I won't go on about it.

The replacement turned out to be Michael Wilding, by now a well-known film star and a past husband of the serial bride Elizabeth Taylor. Gielgud wrote his mea culpa letter:

Globe Theatre<br>Saturday, June 22nd

Dearest Noël,
I feel rather a slob to go out at this time when business is so splendid, and I am sorry to have saddled you with so much rehearsal, though I know how very much better it is for all concerned that you should have been able to take over, to say nothing of the saving of work for me! I hope Michael will have a real success.

In fact, Wilding was not a success.

Mike opened on Monday night. He was fairly all right but mumbled dreadfully and was quivering with inside nerves. He moved well and with assurance but his speech is a serious problem. Nothing can be done until he has played it for a couple of weeks, then I shall come down with my cohorts all gleaming and beat the fuck out of him.

By November it was clear that Wilding had to be replaced. Attendance had peaked immediately after he took over the part, as a direct result of his film star status, but the boost was a temporary one, and Robert Helpmann became the third and last Sebastien.
Once again Gielgud wrote to Noël:

November 11th, 1957

Dear Noël,
Today I had an excellent first rehearsal and was simply delighted not only with Bobby's [Robert Helpmann] industry and quickness but also, of course, with all the new touches and material which, with the addition of Bobby's vivacity, should revive the spirits and attack of the company, who are, not unnaturally, somewhat drooping with holding the scattered shreds of the play, as it sags under Michael's terrifying

pathological deficiencies. What you must have suffered rehearsing him I can well imagine. Even in the ten days I worked [with him] he reduced me to a helpless welter of shame and impotence, especially when he sat down on the footlights, in imitation of Danny Kaye, with a cup of tea, and gave a spirited resumé of his own inability to perform, with all the attendant reasons for it. Yet one cannot really dislike or blame him, though I came to the resentful conclusion that he is fundamentally lazy, and incapable of dealing with it in any way.

Bobby is going to be delightful—quite different to either of us—and has so much intelligence and enthusiasm that I know he will achieve a really original performance without undue labour—as he has been bright enough to lay such solid and firm foundations, and is already word perfect. His languages are poor, but I think he can pantomime them with sparkling looks and shrugs, as he already does (from you, no doubt) with the German.

The new scene with the American [journalist] is in your very best vein and you must have it put into the printed version.

   As ever,
   JOHN

Helpmann himself wrote when his first night was safely behind him:

           November 29th 1957
I can't tell you what a panic I was in, but it all went marvelously well and I don't think I let you down. Encouraged by you, of course, I was outrageous. I practically had to be carried to the wings with the weight of my jewellery. I am absolutely adoring playing it now that my nerves are subsiding a little.

He signed the letter "Margaret Erlynne," the leading character from *After the Ball,* the last show he had done with Noël.

Noël replied in kind: "What a charming woman Lady Erlynne is. Love Noël"—clearly forgetting that Mrs. Erlynne was not a lady in any sense of the word.

          ·

THE SUMMER OF 1957 found Noël staying with Edward Molyneux in Biot. From there he wrote to Joyce:

We are having a really divine hol. Edward is sweet and genial and the house is *un rêve,* exquisitely done and being most beautiful. There are several movie ladies and gentlemen about such as the Van Johnsons and Gary Coopers and last night we dined with George Schlee and Garbo on the Port at Villefranche. She was very gay and staggeringly beautiful if perhaps a tiny bit grubby and we were shown a chapel which Jean Cocteau has made, all murals, of Jesus doing the loaves and fishes lark with lots of naked young men with rather over developed cheeks and Jean Marais [Cocteau's longtime lover] expressions. Puzzling, I should think, for *les Voirs Mystiques* but *most* interesting.

Earlier in the year he had visited the Cayman Islands, where the company was rather less sophisticated.

The Caymans were rather fascinating, the people are sweet, though the natives are Baptists and madly inbred, so are inclined to gibber, but I didn't mind. There are only forty inhabitants of Cayman Brac—actually now only 37, because while I was there two deaf-mute brothers cut up their aunt into a sort of Shepherd's Pie and are now languishing in the gaol in Kingston.

•

*NUDE WITH VIOLIN'S* success decided Noël on playing in it himself for a Broadway run in the fall of that year—his first stage appearance there in twenty years. Plans were duly laid, and he wrote to Lorn to tell her that they had secured "the old Belasco," one of his favorite theaters. "I am really very pleased. It is full of great traditions, like the Haymarket, and although a bit run to seed, wonderful to play in . . . The anticipatory excitement over the production is rising steadily and all seems set fair."

It was over this production, though, that the first cracks in his long relationship with Binkie Beaumont began to appear. The London impresario suddenly demanded 2 percent of the gross from the Broadway production. Noël replied:

Dearest Bink,
This letter is difficult to write because it concerns the relationship of friendship to business and vice versa. It is particularly hard in our case to disentangle the one from the other, as we have been associates in both for so long. However, I am going to try because I have a strong feeling that, if I don't, things may go awry between us. Nobody admires your incisive business acumen more than I do, in addition to which, over our years, I have come to rely on your courage in criticism and your judgement of scripts and seldom found you wanting in either. But there is something in you, and I hope, in all of us, that is a good deal more important than sharply defined contractual obligations and it is this indefinable "something" which is caus-

ing me much concern and, to be perfectly honest, quite a lot of unhappiness. I have wanted to explain this to you before during some of our cosy, intimate dialogues, but somehow by the time I had got round to it we had both had too much gin and no good would have come of it.

In the first place let us look, as objectively as possible at my relationship with H. M. Tennent's. It seems to me in the light of remorseless sense rather than theatrical annoyance, that H.M.T. owes considerably more to me than I owe to it. As far as I can remember, and I hope I am correct in this, the firm has never lost money over any of my plays, and even if by any dastardly chance it had, it has certainly regained whatever it may have lost from such long runs as *Design For Living, Blithe Spirit, Present Laughter, Relative Values, Quadrille* and *Nude With Violin.* I think you must agree that it wouldn't have been too difficult for me to have persuaded other managements to present these plays. Therefore, the question of H.M.T. taking a big risk and providing a "shop window" for my work didn't really arise.

Which brings me with a fairly sickening thud to your demand for two per cent of the gross of the American production of *Nude With Violin.* This I salute as "shrewd business" but consider to be morally indefensible. In the first place H.M.T. have nothing whatever to do with the American production. Their contractual option to present the play in America was not taken up any more than it was with any of the other plays above mentioned. On your own wise advice I am putting it under my own management—i.e., Charles and Ham in association with Roger Stevens and the Playwrights' Company. In consideration of the fact that I have only agreed to play in it myself for twelve weeks in New York, we have been straining every nerve to keep the budget as low as possible, so that the Playwrights' Company, if the play is a success, will at least get their money back. For you to receive 2 percent of the gross will make this impossible. Also I can see no valid reason whatever why you should ask for it. Nor, in justice, can I see why you should have, or expect, any part of the American subsidiary rights. We are doing all the work on the production while you are three thousand miles away contributing nothing. The fact that you told Charles personally that those were your terms was nothing to do with the contract signed between H.M.T. and me. This, dearest Bink, comes smartly under the heading of "Pulling a fast one" and, while you are perfectly at liberty to pull fast ones with Herman Levin *et al* and even the wretched John C. Wilson, you are NOT going to be permitted to do it with me. Your sole contribution to the American production so far has been agreeing to let Joyce come over, which after all is a personal issue between you and her and me. Apart from this, far from helping the play in America, you seem to be doing a great deal to hinder it.

I would like to call to your mind a few salient features of our "business" association over the last few years.

1. I agreed to accept only five per cent author's royalty until the production had a thousand pounds in the kitty. Why? Because you asked me to and said the play couldn't go on if I didn't. Was this true? If so, why? Two more questions on this. Was this shrewd business on your part to demand it? Answer. Yes. Was it shrewd business on my part? Answer. No.

2. I came to Dublin at my own expense and redirected the play from beginning to end. This was necessary, as it had been lovingly *mis*directed and also, in the case of David Horne and Peter Sallis, seriously miscast. If I had NOT been available to do what I did, I doubt whether the play would have survived as it has.

3. Re *After the Ball.* I spent weeks in the provinces, at my own expense, re-directing and re-organizing the entire production. Had I not done so, it would, I fear, have been a dire failure instead of the moderate success it was. Question. Would it have been more businesslike of me to have clamoured for half John and Bobbie's [Helpmann] director's fees or at least have demanded expenses? Answer. According to business ethics—Yes. According to *my* ethics—No.

To return, therefore to *Nude With Violin.* Is it shrewd business for you as the London management to try and get all you can get? Answer. Certainly, if you can count on me and my management being bloody fools enough to let you get away with it. But is it, dear Bink, quite as good business as it sounds when dealing with someone like me? The answer to this is very definitely—No. I resent being made a monkey of and I also resent, very deeply, being taken for granted, which brings me to the most important point of this letter—the *clou,* as we say in France. This *clou* is our own personal relationship. To me this is far more important than any contractual obligations in the world and I suspect, in your deep heart, that it is to you, too. Ideally I know our personal feelings and our business dealings should be kept in separate compartments but it is no good ideally speaking. In our case the two are inextricably mixed. If you have any legal or contractual right to demand two per cent of the gross and a share of the subsidiary rights, you shall, of course, have them. Even so, I would doubt the wisdom of your demand in the existing circumstances. Please think carefully over all this. I am uneasy in my mind and in my heart as well.

Fondest love.

He might well have recalled Marlene's verdict on Binkie: "Noël still remains the only homosexual you can trust."

*Nude* opened on November 14.

404 East 55th Street
November 25th 1957

Darling Darling Lorniebubs,

I know you understand about me not having written before because things really have been violently hectic. However, now all is calmer. In spite of the three bad notices for the play, I have made a really triumphant personal success and we played last week to just under $32,000 which, considering the capacity of the Belasco, is just over $33,000, is jolly good. We have an $80,000 advance, so whatever happens the backers will get their money back. The public fall about in the aisles and it goes like a bomb.

Binkie came on Saturday night and seemed genuinely highly delighted, as well he might, as he's getting 1% to which he's entirely unentitled. I am fairly angry with him in my inside heart, he could have helped so much over Little Lad and hasn't lifted a finger. Also I think he behaved very badly to the Boys [Charles Russell and Lance Hamilton] over the production, trying to grab all he could and then never had the decency to send them a wire on the first night, which would have meant a great deal to them. I am being as sweet to him as always and I don't think he suspects, as yet, that there are some little rumblings of discontent going on in my inside. This will probably dawn on him later, when I write a new comedy for the London Theatre and he discovers that H.M. Tennent will not be allowed to present the play unless I get 12% as author and 2% as director and retain *all* other rights! And if he doesn't care for this, the play will be presented by Lance Hamilton and Charles Russell. The cast here really is excellent and very sweet as well, which makes a very happy and efficient ship.

Really there is nothing to grumble about except the edge being taken off the initial success by the three leading critics. Fortunately I have all the leading columnists on my side including Elsa Maxwell who, I must say, really did us proud by flying onto TV the night after we opened and quoting all the best lines and raving and roaring. I am quite definitely the Belle of the Ball and everybody is being quite exhaustingly sweet to me.

XXXXXXXXXXXXXXXXXXXXXXXXMASTER

Three days later, he wrote to Gladys:

Noël takes over the role of the suave Sebastien but with only moderate
success. It was his farewell Broadway performance. The young
American reporter, Clinton Preminger, Jr., was played by William
Traylor, with whom Noël allegedly had a late-life fling.

Oh dear, I did hope for better from Mr. Kerr of the *Tribune*—Brooks
Atkinson is well known to be gaga anyway—but it's no use, and it
has only lately dawned on me that perhaps they are all so allergic to
comedy on account of being utterly without a grain of humour themselves. Just try to think of one critic with a sense of humour or fun
and, of course, there isn't such a thing. Also, of course, in *Nude* I do
make fun of absolutely everything, including critics—no wonder
they don't care for it. The rest of the papers and especially the out of
town ones have been much less beastly, but there is no getting away
from the fact that the *Times* and *Tribune* are powerful, so we are playing to slightly under capacity. However, the audiences adore it and
raise the roof each night, so *that's* all right.

I personally am thoroughly enjoying every moment and I wish, I
wish you could see me at it in my crew-cut wig and all. The cast is
jolly sweet, so we are all happy as bees, and the only real trouble we
had was over Sally Cooper. She played it exactly like a wardress, and
exuded a curiously malevolent quality which seriously affected the
family scenes, and in the end she had to go. This, of course, was all
awful, with Gladys [Cooper] cabling from the coast, and so I let her
go without finishing her week and played with the understudy for
three performances, the latter a lady who uses her arms and hands a
great deal more than even I do, so that from the front we looked as
though we were doing a particularly arduous course in semaphore.

Apart from this, all has been plain sailing, and on the whole, great fun.

So Binkie got his 1 percent—which was probably what he realistically hoped for when asking for 2 percent—but at the cost of Noël's friendship and trust.

It turned out to be 1 percent of not very much, because the U.S. production was a distinct disappointment, despite Noël's early upbeat reports. New York audiences were apathetic about the play and found its subject matter unappealing. Week by week the auditorium took on the appearance of a man with a receding hairline, as only the seats in the middle of the rows were occupied. He found the experience distinctly humiliating and decided on a radical solution. On January 14 he wrote to Lorn from New York:

> *Nude* is only just doing all right. We are out on our own now with no more theatre parties and only a medium advance, so I intend to hurry up with *Present Laughter* and pop it on here alternately with *Nude* for the last two weeks. This, in addition to pepping up the business, will give me the chance to get *P.L.* nice and smooth for our opening in San Francisco. The news that I am doing this broke last night and this morning Jack telephoned and said "Well, I've heard of people using *New Haven* for a try-out before but New York, never." So far I am very pleased with the cast, Mona [Washbourne] is going to be excellent as Monica and Joycie better than ever as Liz. The unknown quantity so far is Eva Gabor as Joanna—she doesn't get here till Thursday, but everyone says she is a dear to work with and will certainly look lovely.

*Present Laughter* came to his rescue once again, and the succeeding tour to San Francisco and Los Angeles enabled him to end the engagement to appreciative audiences.

It turned out to be his farewell to the American stage.

# CHAPTER 26

# A DIFFERENT SKY . . .
# AND A LOOK AT *LULU*

## (1958–1959)

Noël takes possession of his new Swiss home.

*A different sky,*
*New worlds to gaze upon,*
*The strange enchantment of an unfamiliar shore,*
*One more goodbye,*
*One more illusion gone,*
*Just cut your losses*
*And begin once more.*

"SAIL AWAY," FROM *SAIL AWAY* (1961)

B ACK IN JAMAICA, Noël took the time to review his life. What did he want to do and where did he want to do it?

Bermuda, he had decided by now, was definitely not for him. Even in his first year there he had confided to Lorn, "Bermuda is all right, it's lovely in the summer, as indeed are several other places but home is where the heart is and this is where mine is—Jamaica." Two years later he wasn't even sure of that any longer. "Firefly is still lovely but the island shows more definite signs of being ruined every time I come. I *know* I have had the best of it . . . I am thinking less and less about here and more and more about Geneva. I think I need that home badly."

He had already taken a quick trip round the Caribbean but found nothing that attracted him more than Jamaica.

To Jack:

I have had a hectic ten days and have explored exhaustively Tobago and Grenada and would rather have a dear little truck run over my head than live in either of them. They are too small and everybody knows everybody else's business and, although they are very beautiful, I certainly found nothing lovelier than the view of Port Maria bay that I am looking at at this moment.

Perhaps Europe was the answer: "My brain works more clearly out of a warm climate."

He spent most of that summer on the Riviera with Edward Molyneux, at Molyneux's house in Biot, and with Maugham in Cap Ferrat, pondering his different options. To prove that his brain was indeed working clearly, he also found the time to adapt an old farce by Georges Feydeau (1862–1921), *Occupe-toi d'Amélie,* as *Look After Lulu.*

By the time he returned to Bermuda in September, his mind was made up. Europe, certainly, but France was too expensive. "You will be interested to hear," he wrote to Lorn on October 30, "that from January 1st onwards I shall be a resident of Geneva. *Won't* that be nice? And I shall be able to get as many roubles and yen and escuardos and pesetas as I need."

Chalet Coward, Les Avants, Switzerland. Noël briefly flirted with the idea
of calling it "Shilly Chalet," but the locals solved the problem for him.
"Chalet Covar" it was and is.

In January 1959, he and Coley took off on a determined Swiss house
hunt, but it was not to be in Geneva that they found Shangri-la. Symbolically their quest ended in the little village of Les Avants, high in the
mountains behind Montreux. The price was right, but there was much to
be done to turn the place into Chalet Coward. Coley took charge of that. In
late June he reported that the Petries (the previous owners) had "made a
very good, very clean getaway and I took over in brilliant sunshine."

The decision had now been made: Jamaica *and* Les Avants. Creative life
could go on.

•

AND GO ON it certainly did.

There was Lulu—intended for Shirley MacLaine, then Carol Channing,
with Vivien Leigh sulking in the wings feeling that she should have been
offered the Broadway part, which finally went to a then unknown called
Tammy Grimes, whom Noël had happened to see in cabaret.

There was also an embryonic new musical with the working title of
*Later Than Spring,* which was to be the further adventures of that born-
again hedonist widow Mrs. Wentworth Brewster (heroine of his song "The
Bar on the Piccola Marina").

There was a new play about a home for retired actresses that was nagging to be written. He called it *Waiting in the Wings.*

And ever present was "the novel," *Pomp and Circumstance,* a Samolan-set

The sitting room of Chalet Coward, as sketched by designer/choreographer/director Joe Layton.

trifle that had been evolving so long it rivaled the gestation period of a small elephant. "My novel is so light," he wrote to his U.S. publisher, Doubleday, "that you will have difficulty capturing it between hard covers."

And, as if that weren't enough, he was also writing the scenario and the music for his one and only ballet, *London Morning*—for Anton Dolin's London Festival Ballet.

Back in March (Noël told Lornie):

I had to do a two hour Television debate [*Small World*] with Ed Murrow and James Thurber in New York and Siobahn McKenna [*sic*] in Dublin! It is a fascinating programme and I had promised to do it. Thurber was dull, McKenna excellent and I was fairly chipper when I got going . . . I cannot understand this white man's magic but it certainly is remarkable that three people can chat to each other and be seen and heard doing it with a distance of thousands of miles between them. Siobahn at one point got a little hot under the collar about the British but I silenced her by saying that my father had always said that veal was unreliable and that this was how I felt about the Irish except that they had more charm. Actually, it was quite fun.

On that same visit to New York, *Look After Lulu* had opened at the Henry Miller Theatre. Noël reported to Lornie:

Cyril [Ritchard] has done an excellent production of *Lulu,* excellent visually and full of movement but, as usual, he had done his best to swamp the lines. This I have remedied to a certain extent, but on the whole, although it has a certain style, it is, I fear, basically common, although less so than I expected. Everything went smoothly and there were no dramas. Cecil [Beaton, who had designed the production] laboured beautifully and his contribution is superb.

Neither Tammy nor Roddy [MacDowall] quite came off. She made a definite success but didn't set the town on fire. He is a fine actor but lacks star quality. The success was Polly Rowles as Claire and David Hurst, a divine actor . . . George Baker who looks fine and plays it clearly and well. Binkie said he made Roddy look like an understudy. This is a slight exaggeration. He is a stronger Teddy [Edward] Woodward sort of actor and oh dear, he has HEIGHT. What a difference that makes! I am glad he got away with it because apparently Cyril was fairly odious to him at rehearsals and George hates his guts for ever and a day.

The first night performance was good and looked like a hit but the dear critics went to town. They dealt it severe blows but it is not quite done for, which in New York is surprising. I have no doubt of it whatsoever for London. I think temperamental, drunk or sober or barmy, we need Vivien or at least a big star. This experiment didn't *quite* come off. However, it is pressing on for the moment.

The show ran for only thirty-nine performances. Nonetheless, Noël made one new lifelong friend in the production, who would subsequently prove to be important in the Coward canon: Tammy Grimes.

April 16th 1962

I am sitting here looking at your photograph in Boston after one of *those* Bostonian matinées and I just thought "Dearest Noël" (to myself I said)—he got me into all this being a "star" business and then I thought *Time*—that word *time* is so precious and there's so much I have to learn and then I thought "I shall write to this beautiful, kind and oh-so-witty sir and tell him that I love him very much."

TG

•

QUITE APART from his own efforts, others were anxious to adapt his material.

Cicely Courtneidge (1893–1980) had long been a beloved actress/comedienne on the English stage. Noël had appeared with her under the direction of her father, producer Robert Courtneidge, in the 1915 *The Light Blues.* She now worked exclusively with her husband, Jack Hulbert (1892–1978), and had a suggestion to make.

Noël wrote to Lorn:

Cis Courtneidge has written a sweet letter saying that she wants to do a musical of *Hay Fever* for herself and Jack. This I really do think is a good idea and I've written and told her so. I've also told her that I cannot undertake it myself, as I am up to my eyes for months to come but have suggested Sandy Wilson. [Wilson had made his name and won Noël's approval with the 1953 *The Boy Friend.*] This is just to keep you *au courant,* as Lynn Fontanne always says. Personally I always say "Fuck", because I find it more soothing.

The project never came to anything.

And for some time Evelyn Laye had been nagging Noël into letting her do the same thing with *The Marquise.* At one point, out of sheer exhaustion, he gave in, but when the ill-conceived and doomed enterprise had dragged its way around the English provinces for a while, he called a firm halt. No, they most certainly could *not* bring it into town.

> Ritz Hotel
> Piccadilly, W.1.
> 29th July 1959

Dearest Boo,

Thank you for your very sweet letter and I am terribly glad you whisked out some of the tricks . . . Which brings me with a rush to the unpleasant part of this letter.

Honestly, darling, I do not want you to do a musical of *The Marquise,* or indeed a musical of any sort because really and truly and as a loving old friend I must tell you that your voice is not up to it. This may sound crude and cruel but I think you know me well enough to know it is not intended to be—merely to be constructive and helpful. Your looks are enchanting and you are developing into a delightful comedienne (apart from those tricks), but we must face the fact that singing voices fade with the years. I know that you did not intend to sing much in *The Marquise,* but the whole point of a musical of that sort should be that the leading lady sings the principal melodies and *The Marquise* in particular requires more operetta treatment than musical comedy treatment and even though you might get away with a couple of point numbers and play it charmingly, I still feel that "Eloise" should be sung.

I have been thinking this over very carefully and been wondering how to explain to you what I felt and I truly feel that from now onwards you should play high comedy without music. Please forgive me, dear, if this letter has hurt your feelings in any way but I am too fond of you to evade issues.

> My fondest love to you, as always,
> Noël

He now found himself facing another of his theatrical *bêtes noires*—the theatrical husband. After her divorce from Sonnie Hale, Laye had married actor Frank Lawton. Lawton had never really made the grade profession-ally but decided his mission was to be his wife's standard-bearer. He wrote an impassioned letter of complaint in which he claimed Noël had said "some cruel things which neither of us can ever forget."

Noël wrote to Lornie:

Really, I can't believe Frankie's letter. I expect she made a false scene, wept, and *made* him write it. He's an idiotic, talentless, henpecked little worm anyway. I think the only thing to do is ignore it but, if you do happen to see either of them, for God's sake make it clear that it was *not* a cruel letter but, in fact, a very gentle and kind one, which was a bloody sight more than they deserved after vulgarizing *The Marquise* as they did. Actually, if they neither of them speak to me again, I couldn't care less; they're both dull and can neither of them act. If she really thinks that letter cruel, she's a conceited cunt but alas, the world is full of conceited cunts . . .

To which Lorn replied:

Boo rang up last week. She has decided to be sensible about the whole thing . . . She said Frankie wrote his letter without her know-ing (which I doubt) and that he did it in the heat of the moment, knowing how upset she was; although she swears she didn't cry or make any sort of scene. So that's that and we are, I suppose, as we were except for having put paid to Boo's musical of *The Marquise*.

·

NOËL HAD MORE LUCK with the London version of *Lulu,* in which Vivien Leigh *did* play the lead, yet even here there were further disquieting signs of a breakdown in his relationship with Binkie.

As late as April Noël is writing to Lorn: "I haven't heard from Binkie yet whether or not or if and when he proposes to do *Lulu.*" In the same let-ter he tells her: "I have finished *Waiting in the Wings* and I think it's pretty good . . . If *Wings* is a success, we shall have something going in Lon-

1959. When the news of Larry and Vivien's
separation became public, Noël whisked Leigh off
to Chalet Coward for Christmas and—in one of
his finest performances—benignly kept the
*paparazzi* at bay.

don . . . If he [Binkie] doesn't do *Wings,* I shall give it to Toby Rowland together with *Volcano* and bugger the Pope!"

*Lulu* opened at the Royal Court on July 29, transferred to the New Theatre and managed a respectable run of 155 performances.

There was, however, one sad, discordant note—a letter from Vivien. For some years now, like the rest of her friends, Noël had been concerned about the precarious state of her health, both physical and mental. As early as 1953 David Niven had said of a recent breakdown: "I feel very strongly that she must be helped over one point . . . She has a dread of it [a mental breakdown] happening again and unless some expert can persuade her that it won't, then in my humble opinion she'll go on expecting it till it *does.*"

In that context the letter was particularly worrying.

Vivien wrote to Noël to tell him that Larry had asked her for a legal separation. She found the shock tremendous, since she had always assumed that, whatever might go wrong between them, they would stay together. She knew there was respect and love there, and surely that would sustain anything after the twenty-two years they had been together?

Yes, there had been problems, of course there had, but for her part, when she had had to choose between Larry and Peter Finch, there had been no doubt in her mind whom she would choose. She could never love anyone else as she had loved Larry.

But, she confessed, she had watched Larry change. Things seemed to improve in the months of the doomed pregnancy, and they were very happy. But then, in 1956, came *The Entertainer,* Osborne's play in which

Larry was to star, and into his life came Joan Plowright, who, Vivien felt, had now succeeded in destroying their lives.

Larry had refused Vivien's plea to try again to have a child and had gone to New York in 1957 with the play and, naturally, the lady in question. Vivien went on to tell Noël that, in fact, she and Larry now hardly lived together at all, and being alone was agony to her.

She felt she owed Noël her confidence in this matter, because of the earlier miscommunication over the baby. The only other person she had told was Sybil Thorndike, who had known Larry all his life. Sybil found it impossible to believe but sadly, Noely, it is all too true and the door is closed.

Would he please keep her secret for the time being? How would she manage? She felt her life was ended.

It was time to forgive and forget past problems. When the run ended, Noël was to take Vivien to Les Avants for Christmas and keep the "charming newspaper" men and women at a friendly but firm arm's length.

•

AT THE END of the year Coley had everything in readiness for The Master, and Noël was finally able to move into his new home in Les Avants. He couldn't wait for his friends to see it.

Christmas at Chalet Coward and (most of) the gang's
all here. Jerry Hogan, Cole Lesley, Geoffrey Johnson,
and Gladys Calthrop pose with Noël for
photographer Graham Payn.

To Clifton Webb:

This house is perfectly lovely and I can't wait for you to get your ass off those Beverly Hills and come and stay in it. It is gloriously comfortable and the view across the lake and mountains is breathtaking. It is also very convenient being only two hours from London, fifty minutes from Paris and forty minutes from Nice. We have a very *gemutlich* little social celluloid colony. Charles Chaplin, Benny and George [Benita Hume and George Sanders], the Nivens, in the next valley, Bill Holden, etc., etc. and, temporarily, the Brynners. So it is all very gay and yet quiet enough to be quiet if you want to, and I generally do. But when I don't, I just pop round the end of the lake into France and gamble at Evian, or whisk into Lausanne to hear *Turandot* or *Traviata* sung by those clever, musical Italians who will keep it up whatever you may say. Oh, do come in the Spring when the wild narcissi are all a-growing and a-blowing.

As he looked out over the mountains at a world covered in snow, it was time for reflection. In a letter to an unnamed friend he wrote:

I am now more of a perfectionist than I used to be; I take pride in being a professional. I don't write plays with the idea of giving some great thought to the world, and that isn't just coy modesty. As one gets older one doesn't feel quite so strongly any more, one discovers that everything is always going to be exactly the same with different hats on . . . If I wanted to write a play with a message, God forbid, it would undoubtedly be a comedy.

When the public is no longer interested in what I have to write, then it will be brought home to me that I am out of touch; not before. Nowadays, though, I find that I rather enjoy my downfalls; to me it's acridly funny when something flops that has taken me months to write and compose. In private I suppose I am a tremendous celebrity snob, and by celebrity I don't mean Brigitte Bardot but people of achievement like Somerset Maugham or Rebecca West. Looking back through my life I find that my personality only really changed once, and that was when I was twenty-four and I became a star and a privileged person. Yet to my inner mind I'm much the same now as I was before *The Vortex*; I'm as anxious to be good as I ever was, only now time's wingèd chariot seems to be goosing me. It doesn't bother me that I don't write in England any more. I love England but I hate the climate and I have absolutely no regrets about having left . . . looking around me I deplore the lack of style and elegance in most modern plays; I long for the glamour of great stars who used to drive up to the stage door in huge limousines. In my younger days I was tremendously keen to be a star and famous and successful; well, I have been successful for most of my life, and if at this late stage I were to have another series of resounding failures, I believe I could regard them with a certain equanimity.

# CHAPTER 27

# A VISIT TO "GREENELAND" . . . VIA *HAVANA*

## (1959–1960)

To say that Noël and Graham Greene were lifelong friends would be something of an exaggeration. In fact, they never actually met until 1949, when both were in middle age, but they had been well aware of each other for many years.

A critic, mostly of film, Greene was one of the few dissenting voices on the 1941 stage version of *Blithe Spirit,* which he found "a weary exhibition of bad taste." He continued to use Noël's work as an exemplar of what he considered outmoded and irrelevant in the theater, until finally Noël felt compelled to retaliate in verse:

"In happy memory of Hawthorne," wrote Graham Greene.

*Dear Mr. Graham Greene, I yearn*
*So much to know why you should burn*
*With such fierce indignation at*
*The very fact that I exist.*
*I've been unable to resist*
*Sitting up later than I need*
*To read in* The Spectator *what*
*Appears to be no more, no less*
*Than shocking manners. I confess*
*Bewilderment. I've seldom seen*
*Another brother-writer press*
*Such disadvantage with such mean*
*Intent to hurt. You must have been*
*For years, in secret nourishing*
*A rich, rip-snorting, flourishing*
*Black hatred for my very guts!*
*Surely all these envenomed cuts*
*At my integrity and taste*
*Must be a waste of your own time?*
*What is my crime, beyond success?*
*(But you have been successful too*
*It can't be that) I know a few*
*Politer critics than yourself*
*Who simply hate my lighter plays*
*But do they state their sharp dispraise*
*With such surprising, rising bile?*
*Oh dear me no, they merely smile.*
*A patronizing smile perhaps*
*But then these journalistic chaps*
*Unlike ourselves, dear Mr. Greene,*
*(Authors I mean) are apt to sneer*
*At what they fear to be apart*
*From that which they conceive as art.*
*You have described (also with keen,*
*Sadistic joy) my little book*
*About Australia, one look*
*At which should prove, all faults aside,*
*That I had tried, dear Mr. Greene,*
*To do a job. You then implied*
*That I had run away, afraid,*
*A renegade. I can't surmise*
*Why you should view your fellow men*
*With such unfriendly, jaundiced eyes.*

*But then, we're strangers. I can find*
*No clue, no key to your dark mind.*
*I've read your books as they appear*
*And I've enjoyed them. (Nearly all.)*
*I've racked my brains in a sincere*
*But vain endeavour to recall*
*If, anytime or anywhere,*
*In Bloomsbury or Belgrave Square,*
*In Paris or Peking or Bude,*
*I have, unwittingly, been rude,*
*Or inadvertently upset you.*
*(Did I once meet you and forget you?*
*Have I ever been your debtor?*
*Did you once write me a letter*
*That I never got—or what?)*
*If I knew, I shouldn't worry.*
*All this anguish, all this flurry,*
*This humiliating scene*
*That I'm making, Mr. Greene,*
*Is a plea for explanation*
*For a just justification*
*By what strange Gods you feel yourself empowered*
*To vent this wild expenditure of spleen*
*Upon your most sincerely*
*Noël Coward.*

When they did actually meet, Noël recorded: "Met Graham Greene at long last and belaboured him for being vile about me in the past. Actually he was rather nice."

In March 1953 he ran across Greene and his mistress, Catherine Walston, in Jamaica. "He was very agreeable and his beastliness to me in the past I have forgiven but not forgotten. He has a strange, tortured mind but, like most of God's creatures, aches to be loved."

A year later Greene is renting Blue Harbour for Mrs. Walston and himself, and making critical amends through Coley: "We went to *After the Ball* the other night and thoroughly enjoyed it. Personally I liked it better than *Bitter Sweet.*"

In January 1959 Noël was invited to play with Alec Guinness and Ralph Richardson in Carol Reed's film version of Greene's *Our Man in Havana.* Noël was to portray Hawthorne, a not very bright agent of MI-5 who decides to recruit Wormold (Guinness), a vacuum cleaner salesman, to be "our man in Havana."

In April the cast, a motley crew, arrived in a Cuba that had recently

Before he and Noël embarked on *Our Man in Havana* in
Castro's uncertain Cuba, Alec Guinness and his wife,
Merula, were Noël's house guests in Jamaica.

undergone a revolution in which Batista had been replaced by Castro.
After Noël had finished his scenes and departed, Alec Guinness kept him
informed of the film's progress, or lack of it:

> Capri—Havana
> April 26th 1959

Two or three nights ago I saw the first batch of rushes, including your
street walking and Sloppy Joe's [a scene Noël shared with Guinness].
In my opinion they were superb. Very funny, very excellent and they
look marvellous. Carol's a clever old thing—what comes on the
screen has such authority and decision and meaning. You look marvellous and the contrast between you and the Cubans creates an effect
of great brilliance without losing in any way reality.

Ernie Kovacs is very sweet and good natured but I think we are *all*
prepared to brain him. The jokes are endless and ceaseless and
exhausting to a degree. I'd far rather act with Renée Houston [a
minor English comedienne] or appear in a chorus line. Between every
take it's the gaiety or some gag he's thought up for his bloody TV
show—*and* he's a little fluffy on the lines. But good, I know. I've
become so *square* in his eyes I'm positively *cubic*.

The girl [Jo Morrow] is still full of "Hi" and "Get you" and
"Daddy-O!" and loud and bouncy but she has been told by Carol to
calm down. I believe he's told her I'm too old for all that carry on.
But I must say she performs well.

Graham Greene agreed—at least in part. In the copy of his novel that he sent to Noël, he wrote, "In happy memory of Hawthorne and in memorable horror of a certain Jo Morrow."

Burl Ives arrived last night, together with wife, guitar and personal press agent! He seems a dear—I'm sure he is—and v. good—but I *know* he's going to sing to me when we have a quiet moment in the broiling sun.

Safely back in England, Guinness became a regular correspondent. Noël had written commiserating with him on his recent foot operation:

> Kettlebrook Meadows
> Steep Marsh
> Nr. Petersfield
> August 25th 1959

. . . I was unstitched five days or so ago—I looked as if I were wearing Wardour Street perverts' boots, suitable for a cover of *London Life*—and here I am happily at home, quite comfortable in movement but walking with great dignity, like a latter day prophet. But when the green, yellow, purple and black blotches have subsided, I shall be fit to dangle a Mistinguette [Mistinguett—the French music-hall star of the 1920s] leg across the side of any blue pool with the prettiest of them.

Guinness was visited in his sick bed by Graham Greene, who had recently had a more embarrassing operation of his own.

Graham paid me a sweet visit, loaded with *paté* and cyclamen, and seemed in good form, though, I thought he sat rather gingerly on the arms of chairs.

How good that *Lulu* is such a success and that the masses are crowding in with such pleasure. And I do hope you and Coley will be crowding into that Chalet soon. How infuriating for you not to be in yet, and the *snow* presumably getting ready to come. I shall think of you snug under the eaves in the evening lamplight.

Not sure *what* is happening in my life. I was contracted (for money rather than pleasure, or rather to work off virtually the remains of my old Korda contract) to go to Hollywood in early October to make a *very* silly childish film—but after Havana I had a hankering for some funny lines for myself and to do something *without* Jo Morrow, Burl Ives and Kovacs—but I've had to do rather a lot of foot stamping (very silly people *indeed,* 20th Century Fox) and it now looks as if it's all off . . . and I shall take myself to New York to do a rather nice TV (never done one before) which they hope will help to sell Ford cars.

This is rather a ramble of a letter, isn't it? I'll bring it to a swift close. Merula [Alec Guinness's wife] sends her love. She hasn't quite got over "doing good works" a few weeks ago by taking a complete cripple lady to a *cricket match,* and the lady unbuttoned her shoes on the boundary and ate *ice cream* holding the spoon with her *toes.*

December 11th 1959

Very dear 59200,

I have just read 338's letter to you in the Collected Volume [of letters]. Of course I had read them before, but years ago, and clearly forgotten. I am glad to be reminded that someone as prosaic and critical as T. E. Lawrence appreciated your genius and fine clear prose.

I imagine you and Coley at your yodeling, shoveling the snow and emerging now and then from the gables, eaves, whatever they are, in fine feathered green hats. I shall hope to see you at it one day— perhaps next winter. Merula, Matthew [the Guinnesses' son] and a young American friend and I are off to Rome for Christmas. (I can't stand turkey, hate Merula doing all that stuffing and have always fancied myself close to the Pope at the Christmas Midnight Mass.)

We only go for five days and then almost immediately on my return Johnny Mills and I wind our kilts around each other and fling ourselves before the cameras in Highland reels [*Tunes of Glory*]. What a good thing I had those varicose veins dumped in the bin in the Clinic in August!

Nothing to report, really. I was sad to have missed you—and imagine you won't be at premiere of *Havana.* Pity but understandable. It's funny how one is *never* jealous of good actors—not in the remotest bit jealous of the huge and gay success you will make in it, but *rejoice* in it, but I shall be spitting fire if they think dear old Burl is good.

*Our Man* was released to mixed notices, with the criticism largely focused on Guinness and director Carol Reed. Guinness wrote to Noël:

January 5th 1960

How sweet of you to have written. Very touched I was—and encouraged. Most of the press were pretty beastly to me—and to the film, if it comes to that. *The Daily Mail* was sufficiently vicious for me to have written myself. I *was* dull in it—in spite of the kind things you say. I'm in a rather "I-told-you-so-mood." I *did* keep telling Carol— I ought to have characterized it all more as a shopman, perhaps with a squint, a wall eye, buck teeth and a mop of ginger hair and a Manchester accent. I don't feel bitter about it, though. I knew perfectly well what was happening while doing it—and I can't possibly blame Carol now that he is taking the rap as well as me. In fact, I don't even blame him in my heart of hearts. In spite of weaknesses, I think it is a good film—and thanks to you and Ralph [Richardson] and Ernie Kovacs an entertaining one. I might add that *so far* it is breaking all records at Leicester Square since they pulled down the old Alhambra. The critics were bound to turn on me. They do about every five years. I'm sufficiently experienced and booed at to take it in my stride. If it hadn't been for the dreary *Scapegoat* [a tedious film he made for MGM in 1959, in which he played dual roles], I might have escaped it for another year. I prefer that it should be now.

Now I have scarlet hair, a thick moustache and a Glasgow accent—not very attractive.

Love,
ALEC

February 4th 1960

I'm told we are a big success in New York with *Havana* and that notices have been appreciably better and, of course, a triumph for you. I'm rather puzzled that Ernie Kovacs hasn't been appreciated more. Since starting this letter I hear that the picture has broken *all* records in *both* cinemas in N.Y. for its first week.

I'm thoroughly enjoying my present epic [directed by Ronald Neame], though I may be slitting my throat professionally at the same time. Johnnie Mills and I have both been called, recently, Box Office poison by Mr. Davis of the Rank Org. To solve billing problems we are thinking of being billed as POISON and POISON in TUNES OF GLORY. Or perhaps, more enigmatically, POISON and IVY in etc.

Noël had written earlier:

[?] August 1959

My dear Graham,

Now that our professional paths have at long last and irrevocably crossed, I feel a tiny celebration is in order. As you know, I have recently finished playing the role of Hawthorne in *Our Man in Havana*—an experience I must admit I thoroughly enjoyed. Not only was the part beautifully written in your finest Italian hand but it gave me the opportunity to evoke all the hapless, bumbling bureaucrats I stumbled over in the war years. You must have suffered

Portrait of a man waiting
to steal a film.

the same fate yourself or even you could not conjure them up from
the vasty deep.

I very much fear that you and I got off to a sticky start all those
years ago. You clearly thought my attitude to life was a little *soufflé-*
ish and I must confess I found yours occasionally *al dente*—but
enough of this culinary argot. (You must forgive me but I have just
discovered the joys of cooking—even if my nearest and dearest don't
always share my enthusiasm for my own creations!)

Whether one agrees with some of your themes, you are without
doubt one of the finest writers in the language we both share. You are
also—rather more to my surprise and pleasure—one of the most
entertaining companions, as I discovered when you and Catherine
visited us in Jamaica . . .

So, my dear Graham, if He should give us a few more years—
always supposing there is a He and you would know more about this
than I—let us spend them separately and together, thumbing our
respective noses at those who most deserve it.

Yrs. Ever
HAWTHORNE

# CHAPTER 28
# WINGS . . . AND SAILS

## (1960–1961)

*Waiting in the Wings,*
*Older than God,*
*On we plod,*
*Waiting, waiting, waiting in the Wings.*

**"WAITING IN THE WINGS,"**
**FROM *WAITING IN THE WINGS* (1961)**

*Why do the wrong people travel, travel, travel,*
*When the right people stay back home?*
*What explains this mass mania*
*To leave Pennsylvania*
*And clack around like flocks of geese,*
*Demanding dry martinis on the Isles of Greece?*

**"WHY DO THE WRONG PEOPLE TRAVEL?"**
**FROM *SAIL AWAY* (1961)**

FOR NOËL, *Waiting in the Wings* was written from the heart. It took him back to his childhood visits with Violet to Edwardian musical comedy and those picture-postcard beauties: Lily Elsie, Violet Loraine, Gertie Millar.

But what happened when Time's wingèd chariot—no respecter of persons or legends—finally caught up with them? They would live in the memory of those who had seen and worshipped them, but they, too, would have their exits. In recent months alone he had lost an early idol, Madge Titheradge, and, well before her time, Kay Kendall. Perhaps the most shocking, because it was so unexpected, was the sudden death of Edwina Mountbatten, in February of that year. The Grim Reaper had to be kept in his place, and *Waiting in the Wings* was a statement of defiance.

Although Noël's legendary fictional ladies were literally "waiting in the wings" for their personal show to ring down the curtain in a retirement home he christened The Wings, they were determined to enjoy every moment they remained onstage.

As he often did, when he wanted a second opinion he valued, he sent the manuscript to Edna Ferber.

> August 28th 1959
> Montreux Palace
> Montreux

Noël dear, *Waiting In the Wings* is a lovely, touching, and amusing play. I don't in the least think you were being pretentious when you said you wanted to set down this play as Chekhov did his plays—without tricks and without the observance of trite usage. Here they are, these women, life has finished with them, they have nothing to expect except the final performance. But I suppose that only high tragedy and low comedy can settle for those terms.

Dear boy, after I had talked with you on the telephone I thought that my suggestions were banal. The quick reconciliation between Lotta and May coming too early . . . The son rich rather than shabby-genteel . . . Another opportunity for May or Lotta, and failure . . .

The possible appearance of a gushing gorgeous Nethersole . . . A young Doreen who is stage-struck . . . All these seemed not right. I know you rejected them at once. But I feel that this play is so good, its background and meaning and characters so dimensional and true and fresh that I want it to have one sustaining motive, a marching inevitability that isn't only death. Maybe it's Deirdre or Cora, the complainer, who might have a final go at it, and fail. It's Lotta who knows that practically every one of the girls living in The Wings has had a wonderful whirl of life, really, hundreds of times more amusing and chancey and exhilarating than all the many millions of everyday wife-and-mother women. The world owes them nothing, really, any more than it does me.

I'd like one big purple moment for them just the same. Still, I remember having seen the Russians in New York—this must have been literally decades ago—I think it was the company called the Moscow Arts Theatre in *The Lower Depths.* Certainly, I didn't know a syllable of Russian. The scene was a cellar or something. They stood or sat around and talked and talked. I don't recall that any terrific scene hit you between the eyes. But I do know that Lawrence Stallings and I came out of the theatre on that New York winter afternoon (it was a matinée) red-eyed from weeping.

So I'm prolly wrong and you're right.

I love you.

FERB

The play could so easily have been depressing—and, to be fair, there were those who found it so.

Ivy St. Helier, Noël's Manon from *Bitter Sweet,* was his first choice for Maud, but she wrote: "I beg of you not to be cross with me, but I find the subject depresses me and upsets me so much; I have an idea that you will understand how I feel and under those circumstances I would not be of any value to you as Maud . . . My love to you always."

Helen Hayes also failed to see herself in the role Noël had in mind for her: "Lotta is not for me, alas. I'd do better as one of the aged soubrettes or Diedre! Lotta, it seems to me, would be a natural for Edith Evans or Kit [Katharine Cornell] or Lynn. Dammit, it makes me furious that you never write leading roles for the likes of me!"

But for anyone who, like Noël, remembered, the play was a celebration of the spirit that made the theater the Theater.

Binkie Beaumont decided that he did not want to produce it and, as Noël discovered later, tried to dissuade leading "senior" actresses, such as Edith Evans and Gladys Cooper, from appearing in it. He told Noël that they "hated" the play, when all too often it transpired that they had not

1961. Margaret ("Peggy") Webster would direct *Waiting in the Wings,* while her companion, novelist Pamela Frankau, would acidly observe the backstage show.

even been shown the script. It was the nadir of Noël and Binkie's personal and professional relationship.

Noël decided he wanted Margaret Webster to direct. He wrote to her that he was "convinced you will do play beautifully and truly glad you want to . . . wide open for discussions and suggestions. I see it as a Chekhovian lark."

> Hotel Wellington
> 7th Ave. & 55th St.
> New York
> February 7th 1960

I am most honoured that you—&/or they—think I could direct it, and I think so too!! At least, I really ought to be able to, or I should go home and take twelve lessons and wear an "L" [learner driver's] plate. Will you be around when it is done? I do hope you would.

I ought to be more coy about this, I guess. But I would love to do it and I'll try not to burst into tears very often . . . I should think we'll have to make a Dante-esque trip from L'Inferno to Il Paradiso for the casting. (A Kafka-Coward play in this, with a cast consisting entirely of harps and dust-bins and two pianos in the pit.)

In a letter on the twenty-first Webster asks Noël to share with her his preliminary casting ideas. Already she has a few of her own:

I make only one stipulation—PLEASE NOT MARTITA [Hunt] AS ANYTHING!! She would wreck The Wings in no time flat! . . . The "straight lead" will be the trouble as always. How about Gwen [Ffrangcon-Davies]? She *is* that old, bless her, but *will* she be? One notion, which just may not have occurred to you—I'm sure all the rest have: I met Norah Blaney fairly recently . . . and she is a little duck! Don't know if she could "do" Maudie (lines, lines, lines??) but might be persuaded from retirement about 10 p.m. as Topsy. [In fact, Blaney played Maud.]

Anyway, if and when you have time, give me some of your notions and I will reciprocate with suitable thought taken. Am increasingly sure the cast and direction must be sharp—I mean for the comedy. The touching quality of the script cannot help coming through of itself, unless we are all terrible. It has everything in it but "O Come, all ye faithful" and there is an obvious cue for that!

Well into rehearsals, Webster discovers that directing a stage full of elderly ladies and gentlemen poses a set of problems over and above the usual.

> 55 Christchurch Hill
> N.W.3.
> July 25th

Dear Master,

My problem is complicated by the fact that no-one, but no-one (except Sybil [Thorndike], Lewis [Casson], Marie [Lohr] and Nora Nick [Nicholson]) ever has the smallest recollection as to where they went last time. Very occasionally they fasten triumphantly on a move, or occupation, that belongs to a quite different scene. Otherwise they float about with expressions of agonized apprehension until the moment when they know I shall say to them "NO, dear, that was where you picked up the glass and went to the piano—remember?" Maidie [Andrews] and Norah B. haven't a clue throughout; and of course Mary C [Clare] isn't really with us at all. These, however, are minor troubles, understandable because it IS a very confusing play, with so many scenes following a pattern that is the same-only-different, and further befogged by having been changed around after the first time it was set. It adds up to some rather unequal cookery. The duologue scenes are a bit over-cooked, the general scenes still haven't begun to brown. You will find, I think, an almost total lack of tempo, except in spasms. It will come with security. I hope.

Mary Clare is a serious worry [She was the original Jane Marryot in *Cavalcade*]—and I think also a serious tragedy. She is like one of those pieces of dead coal that you find in the grate the next morning. But she is also, sometimes, quite pixie! Not having uttered one of her own lines for two hours, she will suddenly come up with a splendid sentence belonging to someone else and pipe up from left field in a firm, bright voice, leaving the real speaker stupefied. Lewis has undertaken to help her; and they sit in corners going over the lines in voices of increasing volume until no-one else can hear themselves think. I am going over every one of her lines today, allocating each of the important ones to someone else! I have also arranged—and she is charmed with this—that in each scene she shall carry a brightly coloured paper-back thriller, inside which shall be—guess what! Edith Day is perfectly divine with her and steers her around all she can. Nevertheless it's a worry. BUT she brings on with her a sort of amiable ruined wreckage feeling which is a more authentic proof of The Wings than anything else that happens.

The new end works miracles. You were a wonder-boy to do it so quickly and so beautifully. It's very good for both Sybil and Marie and also for Topsy herself. I haven't staged the very end quite right and I'm not sure why. I shall find out or you will tell me. The set may help—no, it won't! Its worst disadvantage is that the hall-entrance has now retreated into a corner and I have to run a shuttle service to get people into the scene. The Topsy entrance is made extremely difficult in consequence. But there's something else I've missed somewhere. I shall need your help on the concert-party scene also! And, of course, your judgement and "eye" throughout. Sybil is quite beautiful; literally and figuratively. I think of what some critic said of [David] Garrick: "He usually perceives the finest attitudes of things." Lewis made a couple of IDIOTIC suggestions yesterday, bless him, about the last scene. I pray she will not be shaken by them. I don't think so. Marie tends to be very slow and lacking variety. I am trying to coax her into this. She's very amiable—I shall be to blame if she doesn't eventually play it very well.

We shall not have been long enough in a theatre by the time you come to have achieved much perspective; and it will be our first day with the set. So I don't know how well you will be able to *see* the play. I am inclined to think it IS—as I hoped—coming out far less "sad" than most of its readers supposed; though it will be—should be— floods of tears by N. Coward in the places designated. We must beware of tea-pot jokes, even before the audience tells us. I truly think it is very well cast; and the shortcomings will be the director's—curable by the author, because this is a willing creature. It has really been quite enjoyable so far! Graham is a great comfort, on and off the stage, and everyone is "too kind". Maybe we need some Magesterial vinegar. If so, we'll get it.

> Yours in fortitude,
> PEGGY

All in all, though, she felt encouraged. "It has ceased to be a play, it has become a group of lives."

·

WITH BINKIE OUT of the picture and other mainstream managements singularly disinterested, the project seemed to be saved by the newly formed personal and professional partnership of Michael Redgrave and American producer Fred Sadoff.

It was a less than ideal combination. Sadoff was inclined to be doctrinaire, and Redgrave, indecisive. Neither was truly experienced in this area of the theater, but since they were now "management," as the weeks went by the decibel level of their advice increased and was often contradictory and confusing to all concerned.

Things came to a head one evening over dinner at the Brompton Grill (June 15, 1960). Novelist Pamela Frankau, Margaret Webster's partner, was there to witness it and later wrote a piece of verse in the best (pastiche) tradition of Rudyard Kipling and Robert Service, those chroniclers of British Empire and derring-do:

An informal production meeting at Chalet Coward. Noël, Graham (and friend), and *Wings* producers, American Fred Sadoff and Michael Redgrave.

## THE BALLAD OF THE BROMPTON GRILL
### BY
### PAMELA KIPLING SERVICE

*Know ye the Chelsea Embankment, when the evening sunshine thins*
*On the gently slipping river? Well, that's where my story begins*
*With laughter and talk and music and a sequence of double gins.*
*(Set fair you'd say, with the Master's play and Webster's plan of the set?*
*Well, shut your damn silly trap, lad, you haven't heard anything yet).*
*Sadoff, the sloe-eyed slave-boy, nipped out of the room for a pee*
*Or that's what the Master and Webster thought, though I didn't quite agree.*
*He left his drink on the piano top; who finished it? Frankly, me.*
*And then it was time to be going. The Master put on his hat*
*An elegant little number, green as the eyes of a cat.*
*And we ran to the Rolls that was waiting, outside the Chelsea flat.*

*All of us gay and good humoured; no baby waving its rattle*
*Could match us four in cosiness as we rode out—to battle.*
*Certainly we were hungry, possibly we were high*
*But the threat of a darkening cloud came up across my psychic sky*
*"Could we do with another drink?" I asked, and the Master answered "Aye".*

*Pass me that box of Band-aids, lad, my wounds are bleeding still*
*As I fear they may be for many a day from the fight at the Brompton Grill.*
*You know the place? . . . You don't, lad? Well, if you're feeling exploratory*
*Go West from Harrods or Frasers and you'll find it facing the Oratory*
*At least you'll see where it used to be; the windows are boarded still*
*With a trace of dried blood on the lintel, lad, from the fight at the Brompton*
   *Grill.*

*"Four double dry martinis!" The Master's voice was low,*
*Clipped and keen and courteous, the voice that waiters know.*
*(And he brought them in under an hour, lad, which only goes to show)*
*I will not mention the melon. I shall not speak of the steak*
*Nor sing the praise of the sauce Bearnaise, for the storm was about to break.*
*Over the sheen of the strawberries, the shadow was coming near*
*When Sadoff, the sloe-eyed slave-boy, said "Michael will join us here."*

*Never a word spoke Webster. The Master gave no sign*
*Though I felt the point of his elbow pressing the point of mine*
*And we loosened our swords in their scabbards, lad, and dressed our battle line.*

*Then out of the night, with his pipe in his mouth and the look of a priggish*
  *preacher*
*(That he'd overdone in* A Touch of the Sun, *playing that damned school*
  *teacher)*
*Awash with whisky to strengthen his will, pink and pompous and auguring*
  *ill*
*Sir Michael entered the Brompton Grill.*

*The first of his blunt-nosed bullets smacked past me into the wall*
*But as far as I understood him, no sets were needed at all*
*And the cost of a date in Dublin, lad, was more than a village hall.*
*He huffed on his pipe and he puffed on his pipe to make his meaning plain*
*"It's all been done on a shoe-string, Son, and it's got to be done again*
*We've reaped red yield from the amateur field, we don't need tired old pros*
*To tell us of props and scenery and teach us the way it goes.*

*Two* understudies! *Good God, what next? You can't do that there 'ere!*
*Think how we opened in Stratford, Fred, with a guinea pig playing Lear."*
*Now flashes the Coward rapier.* Now *Webster goes into attack.*
*But he huffs on his pipe and he puffs on his pipe and moodily mumbles back.*
*"I didn't come here to be shouted at"—and the Master's pistols crack.*
*They aren't the sort of bullets, my lad, I'd care to riddle my skin*
*But Redgrave squats like a pink blancmange and lets them all come in,*
*While Sadoff, the sloe-eyed slave-boy, sits, as small as a safety pin.*

*Now Webster counters with* [Donald] *Wolfit. From the Master's thunderous*
  *front*
*There's less and less of the "darling boy" and more of "the silly cunt".*
*Now Webster smites on the table, the Master shoots from the hip:*
*Is Redgrave stuck on a ha'porth of tar, or does he care for the ship?*
*Well, he* doesn't *want fingers wagged at him, he offers, pouting his lip.*

*To it again go the valiant twain. The flames are shooting higher*
*I cancel my order for brandy, lad, in case they should set it on fire.*
*And one by one the guests go home, and the worn-out waiters retire.*
*(It's cut and thrust, it's "I won't"—"You must"*
*It's the ring of steel, it's a Catherine wheel*
*It's "Listen to me" and "Be damned to you"*
*It's Coward blazing and Webster too.*
*Another volley, you'd think, would do it*
*But Redgrave holds, like a pinkish suet*
*Stolidly, sludgily, sitting through it.)*

Into the flash and fury, into the smoke and flame
Into the reddened arena, the last of the waiters came
The time was long past midnight, they'd told him to bring the bill
But it's quite a risk in a row so brisk to worry about the till
And he'll tell the tale till he's old and stale of the fight that was fought to the kill
Of the bright sharp words that pierced like swords and the wounds that bled
  with a will
Of Webster's fist, and Sir Michael pissed, and the Master standing still
Elegant, cold and glorious
Superb but scarcely victorious
Flicking the blood from his finger tips in the wreck of the Brompton Grill.

And what is the end of the story? There isn't an end to tell
(Slip me a couple of codeine, lad, these bruises hurt like hell)
And I don't regret the passion and I wouldn't forego the pain
Except for one tiny point, lad,—it's all got to happen again.
So fill me another glass, lad, and help me upstairs to my bed
I shall rest, and faith I shall need it—there's Dublin and breakers ahead.

There's another fight to be fought, I fear, by the side of the Irish sea
A situation to save, boy
With Sadoff, the sloe-eyed slave-boy,
With that pink Red-dig-his-own-grave-boy
And the Master
And Webster
And me.

•

BEFORE ANY MAJOR VENTURE, Noël was in the habit of taking himself off on a holiday, and this time was no exception. This time he set off on the Road to Morocco.

To Coley:

Once in the plane found I had no less than *three* babies under 2 years old, all of whom screamed incessantly. I plugged my ears, took off my Guccis and tipped my seat back and it wouldn't come up again. *No one* could do anything about it, so I lay flat on my back, racked with cramp until we arrived at Tangier!

He arrived to find "a violent wind, grey skies and *extreme* cold" and a host whose "wild old garden [was] filled with shrieking birds, barking dogs, snarling monkeys and gasping goldfish."

One day he braved the elements and lay out on the sand when "a strange gentleman came up, sat down next to me and played delicately with my left tittie without so much as a *avec votre permission! Really!*"

Since Tangier was known to be an international focus of the gay universe, it is surprising Noël was surprised.

He moved on to Marrakech: "Marrakech is really beautiful and very much half as Golders Green. The Moroccans are *most* sweet but only wish for *one* thing, which alas I am unable to provide. However, affection is what counts."

He was invited to a "grand lunch party . . . where everyone started every sentence with *est-ce-que vous avez vu*—or *lu*—as the case may be. We had Arab food—cous-cous, etc., in fact, damp mutton but very atmospheric, dear."

The food in this hotel is lethal. I was served last night with a black rubber turd which was laughingly listed on the menu as *steak au poivre*. I sent it back with a *puce* in its *oreille* [a flea in its ear].

I have no more news . . . I am sick of my holiday, anyhow, and shall come whirling home.

·

THERE WAS ONE other important issue to trouble his mind that holiday season—a cable from Lornie telling him that her doctors had informed her she must have her left breast removed as soon as possible. While telling himself that he was confident that she would come through it, he was deeply concerned and wrote to Coley: "Be firm with Lornie. She must not be guided by second-rate doctors, she must have the best of everything."

On this occasion his confidence was justified. Lornie recovered and kept the "family" together for another seven years.

·

*WAITING IN THE WINGS* opened at the Duke of York's Theatre on September 7 and suffered what was by now the fate of anything Noël put on in the United Kingdom. The critics abused it; the public loved it. Arguably, the size of the play's natural public may have been limited, and undoubtedly the critics deterred many of them from coming, but there was general agreement in the theatrical community that the play deserved a respectable run.

Early in the new year the warning signs were too clear to ignore. Webster wrote:

January 4th 1961

Well, Master dear,

It looks perilously as if *nous avons eu le* at the Duke of York's. As you know, I've been bothered for quite a while about the patient's general health. The slow drag of bad notices does begin to tell in the end—people just haven't got it into their heads that they need bother. And it is such a HELL of a bother nowadays—pink zones and cars being towed away right and left and pouring bloody rain and all imaginable discomforts. Let's stay home and watch the Telly.

Oh—almost forgot. Would you like me to vet the prompt copy which is being done for French's edition? Or will you? You know how stage managers always put in the most idiotic things—devices to which one has been driven by some particular and desperate necessity—and leave out the really important "sign-post" directions. Under the first head, would you like some of her lines restored to Almina? She makes absolutely no sense at the moment. I don't mean Mary. She makes a lot. Has taken to saying everyone else's lines with them; or so I'm told; she has an uncanny way of *never* doing it while I'm there, even though she can't possibly know I am! The show has stayed in good shape—a bit of sledge-hammering from time to time; I told Una [Venning] she was too slow and she said "You mean it needs more bite?" and I said "Good God, no! You have the bite of a mastiff; but the gnashing of teeth makes such a noise that I can't hear the line." This went well. With Blaney.

PEGGY

*Waiting in the Wings* closed after its 188th performance.

•

BY CHRISTMAS, Noël was back in Jamaica and preparing to rise above a visit from Clifton Webb, whose mother, Mabelle, had recently died. As Noël wrote to Joyce, when the visit was safely over:

Poor Clifton, not smiling at grief—Oh dear, no—fairly bellowing at grief. Every meticulous detail of Maybelle's [*sic*] timely demise is etched firmly on our minds from the little strokey thing to the last rites including the laying out of the corpse and the last-minute putting on of the earrings which had been forgotten. You will be glad to hear that she looked very beautiful and peaceful and not contorted with cackling rage. We have now become accustomed to the whole process. First, long anecdotes about the deaths of various friends, leading inevitably to Maybelle and then floods of tears and we all gaze at each other in a wild surmise. He *is* making an effort to snap out of it but the basic truth of the matter is that he's enjoying the wallowing. He doesn't know this, of course, but it is a *leetle* bit trying. After all she *was* 91—on paper—and she *has* been on the gaga side for ages.

Then, later that same holiday:

Blanche [Blackwell] gave a birthday party for me—small and beautifully done until the last part when [she] had organized fireworks. Some careless Jamaican cunt had laid three large rockets on the terrace wall *facing* the guests and the house. These were ignited by a spark and went off. The chaos was indescribable. One rocket head missed *my* head by inches and embedded itself in the eaves. If it had hit me, I should have been blinded for life or killed! This little episode not unnaturally put a damper on the *soirée.* Everyone behaved well but there was controlled panic in the air. Poor Blanche has had nightmares ever since.

His current stay also focused for a while on some of the disillusion he was beginning to feel:

December 23rd, 1960

Very privately, darling Lornie, I have taken against Jamaica in a big way. I am grimly determined to sell Blue Harbour as soon as I possibly can and, eventually, Firefly too. The atmosphere of the whole island has changed . . . the lovely feeling of peace and isolation has almost entirely vanished. In future I shall take my sunshine holidays on board slow ships going to far off places and not be tied down to paying a lot of ungrateful sods thousands of pounds a year for nothing.

•

EARLY 1961 FOUND Noël getting down to the hard work of completing the musical that he had been toying with for some time. By now he had dispensed with Mrs. Wentworth Brewster and jettisoned the original plot of *Later Than Spring*. It was now to be called *Sail Away* and to be a vehicle for Kay Thompson.

On January 13 he wrote to Lornie from Jamaica:

I really am working like mad on *Sail Away*. I am really very excited about it. The first act is complete and I am now nearly halfway through the second. The characters have all come to life and I am really enjoying it. It was a wonderful idea having the different stories to carry through and so far I have managed to keep up the interest in all of them. I have done some lovely new songs and lyrics. Of my old stuff I am only using "Changing World", "This Is a Night for Lovers" and "Sail Away". Kay Thompson's part, Mimi Paragon, the cruise hostess, has come out marvelously. She ought to make the success of her life. I have no particular fears because, unlike *Later Than Spring,* I know where I'm going and the shape of the whole thing is clear in my mind.

The first act in nine scenes, is entirely the ship, finishing with the arrival in Europe and Gibraltar rising out of the sea. The second is a series of different places: Tangier, Naples, Athens, Venice, etc., interspersed with deck scenes in One, so that the set changes can be done easily. I intend to have it roughly finished by the beginning of February; have some auditions in New York and spend from March to June polishing the outstanding music and lyrics. The formula is wonderful because one can cut a scene entirely and substitute another without spoiling the general structure.

Back in London, *Waiting in the Wings* was faltering and would close a month later. *Pomp and Circumstance,* Noël's one and only novel to be published, had had an equally lukewarm reception in England.

I am, of course, bitterly sad about *Wings.* I suspect the long range effect of those vile notices have something to do with it. I think it is a minor miracle that we have got five months out of it. It is no use expecting that I shall ever get good notices in England, at least not until I am in my dotage, or act in a movie. But in the long run time will tell. After all *Pomp* was dismissed with faint praise, whereas in America it has had raves. As it is on the Best Seller lists in both countries I can't complain. (Oh yes, I can)

. . . Kay may appear in a week or so. Except for the sadness about *Wings* I am as happy as a bee and feel tremendously well!

And a few weeks later: "My creative genius has been churning away. I think you will be pleased with *Sail Away.* I've purposely left the script loose with unfinished gaps, because the filling up of these will depend on the personalities I encounter at auditions. I have written some really lovely new songs."

He was also having second thoughts about his second thoughts on Jamaica.

I'm hating leaving, actually, it has been lovely this time, much lovelier than I thought it was going to be at the beginning. There is no doubt about it. This place has a strange and very potent magic for me. I also seem to be able to do more work here in less time than anywhere else. It's the lovely long mornings that count. I am adoring the squeals of the Press boys but jolly cross with the idiotic public for letting me down over *Wings.* They ought to have more sense. Darling old Pompers is climbing higher and higher up all the Best Seller lists in America. It has already sold over 28,000, which is apparently fairly remarkable.

I have no more news except that my white owl said last night as it flew by—"What's happened to that silly old Twat who lives in Milner Street, SW3?"

In February he left for New York to audition. Safely back in Jamaica, he reported:

Firefly Hill<br>Sunday March 19th

Darling, Darling Lornie,

There is so much to tell you that I don't know where to begin. I have had four strenuous weeks in New York full of complications, frustrations, excitements, business discussions, auditions and what not, and here I am again at dear Firefly feeling absolutely splendid and full of piss and vinegar. In fact I have never felt so well for many years and I put it all down to two drinks a day, if that, and a carefully observed diet and a very great deal of natural vitality. This will be a long letter so put on your four-eyes, throw away your truss and get yourself into a receptive Tolstoi mood . . .

Kay Thompson, for whom I had written the part of Mimi Paragon, raved enthusiastically about the whole thing and then said she couldn't do it because she had a "thing" about appearing on Broadway. As she is on the barmy side anyhow, this did not unduly depress me and I at once contacted Elaine Stritch in Hollywood who agreed to do it sight unseen if her Television series finished in time.

I then engaged a handsome young man of six foot four with a truly glorious voice [James Hurst] who is understudying the lead in Tammy Grimes's show [*The Unsinkable Molly Brown*]. He, I am convinced, is a great find as he is comparatively unknown on Broadway. So we didn't do badly. Meanwhile I was asked if I would give an audition of the score to eight formidable ladies who organize "Theatre Parties" because, if they like it, it would ensure a big advance. I agreed, reluctantly, to do this and had the forethought to invite a Mr. Jack Small, the very tough representative of the Shuberts to be present also. Well, they all crowded into my apartment and sat about on each other's laps looking like a lot of Helen Hokinson harpies. Within about ten minutes I had got them fairly gobbling out of my hand and the principal one of them asked for thirty dates then and there which, in a big theatre will amount to a quarter of a million dollars. Better still, Mr. Small went out of his mind and has guaranteed me the Shubert Theatre, which is in a marvelous position, and a promise of the Winter Garden, if it is free by the time I want it, which it probably will be. He also, on behalf of the Shuberts, offered to put up half the backing. This, although gratifying, I viewed with slight dismay, because I do not want the Shuberts frigging about in the management on account of them being notorious for penny pinching. However, it was a step in the right direction.

I contacted Kitty Carlisle, who I knew had the right warm quality although her actual singing wasn't up to much. The next day Kitty auditioned and was completely charming and we were all delighted. The next day, however, she telephoned in tears to say that she couldn't do it after all because Moss Hart, her husband, had already had two heart attacks and they had just bought a new gracious home in Palm Springs and that her whole life would be disrupted. Against such irrefutable logic there was no argument, although I could have wished she could have told me that before wasting ten days of my time and giving the audition.

So there we were with Time's wingèd chariot bouncing along and still no leading lady. And then I heard of a woman called Jean Fenn who had sung at the Met and the City Center in opera and was a reasonably good actress as well as being a fine singer. I immediately telephoned her in California and so *she* flew to New York and gave an audition. She turned out to be tall, elegant, quite beautiful in a Nordic way and with one of the most thrilling voices I have ever heard. She led off with "Vissi D'arte" from *Tosca* and before she got to D'Arte I knew we were home. She is also longing to do a show on Broadway and seemed unassuming and sweet with no nonsense about her. So that's another find and I am absolutely delighted about her because she and James Hurst will make such lovely noises together that the more serious side of the score will be taken care of. I also interviewed a young man called Joe Layton who is the best of the up and coming choreographers and he is apparently available . . . Choreography in an American Musical is of the utmost importance and, having seen some of his work, I know he is the boy for me.

After all these goings on Roger came to me and asked me to ask Chappells to put up some money for the show. This irritated me slightly because as I am providing the music, book and lyrics and direction I don't see why I should shop around for money into the bargain. However I interviewed Max and Louis Dreyfus who said they had never backed a show before but that for me they would break their rule and put up a third. They were, in fact, absolutely staunch as they always have been with me.

Before this, however, Charles and I had had lunch with [attorney]

Don Seawell and told him the whole story, whereupon he said that he could get Mrs. Helen Bonfils . . . the third richest woman in America, to put up four hundred thousand dollars! He said "I'll have a definite answer within an hour". This, by God, he did and said that not only had she agreed immediately but had told him that he needn't have troubled to telephone her because anything by me she would back unconditionally! . . .

I don't know whether or not you met Don Seawell when he went to London. He is shrewd, wise and extremely nice. As you know, he has been the Lunts' lawyer for years and has made them a great deal of money. He also handles Mary Martin and Dick Halliday's business, which means he must know his onions and be immune to headaches . . .

Slightly exhausted by all these high powered carryings on, Coley and I stepped into a dainty Jet on Thursday for Jamaica. We graciously accepted three champagne cocktails as a present from B.O.A.C. and went off into a coma. I awoke feeling splendid. Poor Coley awoke feeling ghastly and looking bright green. He tottered off to the Gents, was sick, and returned a few minutes later minus his plate which he had dropped down the loo. Now Lornie, this is an old

Noël was deluged with messages of good wishes for *Sail Away,* but none more original than the one from Kay Thompson, who used Eloise, her fictional heroine, to proclaim proudly: "*My* mother knows Noël Coward!"

Whenever they were together—and a piano was to hand—Noël and Kay Thompson (1911–1998) would improvise duets. Here they do so at Chalet Coward. If only they had been recorded.

joke and we really cannot enlarge upon it. However, when we had landed and were going through immigration, an angelic steward, giggling hysterically, sidled up to Coley, pressed the missing teeth into his hand, and murmured "It's quite all right, sir, they have been *thoroughly* disinfected!"

I am terribly excited about *Sail Away*. I have been thinking of practically nothing else since last October and my initial enthusiasm has suffered no sea change. I have a strong feeling that it may be one of the best things I have ever done. If it turns out not to be—Fuck it.

With this tiny Patience Strong morsel of philosophy I will now close. Be assured of my sentiments the most cordial.

Your loving loving loving
MASTER

Over the years it became increasingly clear that when a show didn't come to Noël "whole," there was invariably a problem with it—usually one of construction. It happened with *Pacific 1860*. It happened with *Ace of Clubs* and *After the Ball*. And it was to happen again with *Later Than Spring/Sail Away*. He thought he had jettisoned the original plot but, in fact, he had merely transformed the Mrs. Wentworth Brewster character determined to start her life over into Verity, a woman who is running away from her marriage problems and falls into an ill-considered shipboard romance with a younger man.

To Gladys Calthrop (August 21) while the show was in rehearsal in Boston prior to opening:

> . . . it really is jolly, jolly good. Stritch is marvelous and the two young people enchanting. Fenn is beautiful, suburban, frigid and sings competently. She is also, fortunately, in a panic because she knows she's had her chance and failed and so was willing to cut her hair and wear the right clothes. Up to now she has appeared in a series of pastel iron lungs which have NOT helped. She is a dear and eager to please and last night . . . she gave the beginnings of a lovely performance, so there is still hope. What is so awful for the poor bitch is that Stritch and the show are so strong that it really only matters to *her* if she comes across or not. She is cursed with refinement and does everything "beautifully". Oh dear, I long for her to pick her nose or fart and before I'm through with her, she'll do both.

Unfortunately, he managed to do neither. The consistent audience reaction during the Boston tryout proved conclusively that the Verity/Johnny strand of the plot—originally intended as the main one—was depressing and dragging the show down. Major plot surgery was indicated.

Among the many plaudits of Noël's friends there were the occasional caveats from those, such as Edna Ferber, who knew a thing or three about putting plays together.

October 1st 1961

Dearest of Covarrs, these are next-day thoughts;

1. Your music should be heard, and it can't be heard above the noise made by the musicians playing in the orchestra. Too loud is as unhearable as too low. Not only does the orchestra drown the music, it drowns those witty, lovely and important lyrics which are, as they should be, not only lyrics but plot and character dialogue.

2. In that Arab scene, which is gloriously funny, I wish the Arab guide (Ali?) could distinctly give us those names which make up his gruesome group. They didn't come out definitely last night and they're too good to lose, certainly. Roughly, I suppose, they were something very Arabian like O'Brien, Epstein, Fromage, Schlag, Smith.

3. No woman writer ever talked like that. No woman writer ever wrote like that. If you say that you know a woman novelist who dictated her books while perched on a bit of Parthenon ruin, I'll apologize.

4. I wish we could have heard John tell off Mama Van Mier. Not a Big Scene speech. Just quietly. We knew Mimi wouldn't have him

because she already had enough unadult minds to set right, both in the children's playroom and on deck; and all over the place. Taking on John would mean taking on Mama. I wish Mimi could have introduced Mama to a hopefully helpless male fortune-hunter, younger than she and ruthless. But that's another play.

This is going to make a heavenly picture a couple of years from now.

My love to you.

Success, dear boy.

FERB

By the time *Sail Away* sailed into the Broadhurst Theatre on October 3, Elaine Stritch, the cruise hostess Mimi Paragon, was now both the romantic *and* comedic lead.

Noël had first encountered and been impressed by "Stritchie" when she was appearing in a lackluster 1958 musical called *Goldilocks.* ("Anyone who can dance with a 10 foot bear is my kind of performer.") He had no hesitation in hiring her for the show and was delighted that she became an overnight star. Nonetheless, he kept a beady Coward eye on her and an admonitory forefinger at the ready. ("My finger is an ivory spilikin.") The show is only days old before he is back in Jamaica and writing to her:

> Blue Harbour
> Port Maria
> Jamaica, B.W.I.
> October 16th 1961

Darling Stritchie,

I hope that you are well; that your cold is better; that you are singing divinely; that you are putting on weight; that you are not belting too much; that your skin is clear and free from spots and other blemishes; that you are delivering my brilliant material to the public in the manner in which it *should* be delivered; that you are not making too many God-damned suggestions; that your breath is relatively free from the sinful taint of alcohol; that you are singing the verse of "Come to me" more quickly; that you are going regularly to confession and everywhere else that is necessary to go regularly. I also hope that you are not encouraging those dear little doggies to behave in such a fashion on the stage that they bring disrepute to the fair name of Equity and add fuel to the already prevalent suspicion that our gallant little company is not, by and large, entirely normal; that you are being gracious and attentive to Pat Harty's manager; and that you are not constantly taking those silly Walter Kerrs and Agnes B.

de Mille to the Pavillon for lunch *every* day. They only exhaust you and drain your energy and however much you want to keep in with them, you must remember that your first duty is to Haila Stoddard, M.C.A. and the Catholic Church.

> I remain yours sincerely with mad hot kisses
> Annamary Dickey

The following April—rather surprisingly—finds Noël dedicating a verse to her:

> *This is the moment*
> *I wish I could fill it*
> *With someone I love*
> *But God didn't will it.*
>
> *So much fun I have had*
> *Besides which I am glad*
> *To have given or taken*
> *Something good, something bad.*
>
> *But "lights out" now and then*
> *I will wake up again*
> *And try very hard so . . . . . .*
> *Amen*

She returned the thought with an engraved cigarette box bearing the legend "The noisy one did not become a nun—Stritchie."

·

AFTER ITS BROADWAY RUN (167 performances) Noël took Stritch and the show to London's Savoy Theatre, and for a time a somewhat one-way correspondence began from wherever in the world each of them happened to be.

For Stritch it was a kind of confessional. Noël had always been critical of her drinking.

[February 28, 1963]

Now Noël, are you sitting down—ready? I don't drink at all—anything—I mean *anything,* any more and I must say it's an adventure. The results have been world shaking. I look and feel about 13 years old. I'm up at 10, do my own marketing, walk Adelaide three times a day in the park. I've been to the Laundramat [*sic*]! One of my

The context is unclear but the
attitude typical of "Stritchie."

biggest decisions in life of late is whether or not it will be V8 Juice,
plain tonic (sugar-free) or unsweetened grapefruit juice at cocktail
time.

> August 6th 1963

... Everything you said in the dressing room meant more to me
than I can ever tell you. You have a strange effect on me—every time
I see you and talk to you, I somehow immediately go on the wagon.
So what does that mean? (Unless, of course, I'm working *for* you, in
which case I double my intake.)

I've had 2 beers a day since I saw you last. Well, three today.

I was on the "Tonight" show last Thursday. There was an analyst
on the show which, of course, brought that subject up. Skitch Henderson said to me, "You're a good friend of Noël Coward's, aren't
you? And since you are, do you know if he has an analyst?"

I said, "My God no, if Noël has a problem he flies to Jamaica."
And we all decided you were a genius. I talked very little about
myself. Of course, that's because I'm not drinking.

> All my love,
> ELAINE

P.S. Tammy Grimes has been signed for *Blithe Spirit* [*High Spirits*]. So
you see, I MUST go to the Coast.

WHEN NOËL SUBSEQUENTLY took *Sail Away* to Australia (without Stritch) he was much less enamored of the proceedings:

> Goodwood Hotel
> Singapore 9
> June 6th 1963

Dear Lornie,

The whole Australian business was highly successful. *Sail Away* is a smash hit and I was the Belle of the Ball. Some of the minor performances leave a good deal to be desired. The lady who plays Dorothy Reynolds' part turned out to be a Lesbian robot who has had a skin disease for three years and was insecure in every area. I watched her with dismay at the first run through then went back to the hotel and said to Coley, "This is my biggest challenge since *Cavalcade*", so I took her aside the next morning, told her she was obviously unhappy in the part and that she must change her characterization! I got the Wardrobe to cooperate and in one afternoon I had her in slacks, drill coats, and slapping her thighs and smoking a cigar! I pretended to base the whole thing on Dorothy Sayers but was really thinking of Naomi Jacob [another lady novelist]! Anyhow she was tearfully grateful and got rounds of applause and good notices! Oh Dear!

The lady who plays Mrs. Van Mier is a cross between an ageing Jewish Princess Margaret and George Cukor. She is unable to act. Mrs. Lush is like a very squat bull dog wearing a red fright wig. She also barks. Maggie F. [Fitzgibbon] is really excellent. A good belting voice, a warm personality and the audience love her, but she isn't so good as Stritch and there's no good pretending she is. The leading man is handsome, virile, a reasonably good actor and a very nice voice. "Barnaby" is charming, *not* a dancer but clever and sings pleasantly. He used to be an usher at the Haymarket and once let me through the Pass door to see Ralph Richardson. The girl who plays Nancy is quite remarkable. She can neither sing, dance nor act, has a lisp and no top to her head! I left terse orders for her to be replaced.

On the return trip Noël took the opportunity to do a little more "travelling alone," although he doesn't appear to have been alone for long. He sent Coley regular bulletins.

From Singapore (June 11):

> I have been to one or two of *those* bars with Philip Dowson, Robin's [Maugham] friend. He is splendidly, gorgeously ghastly. Large and fat with a nervous hearty laugh and alludes to his wispy little Asiatic boy friends as "poppets"! I have taken a shine to the man who runs

this hotel. His name is Dunn [*sic*] as in Irene and his wife is bright and blonde and shrieks with maniacal laughter if I so much as ask for a salted almond, but he is a duck and we are going tomorrow to hear Master Adam Faith, who has just arrived and is giving two performances in the local stadium. I must say he seems a very sweet boy.

From the Peninsula Hotel, Hong Kong:

The sitting-room is the size of the Palais de Dance and sparsely furnished with hideously ORANGE chairs. The air-conditioning thing came away in my hand this morning and there is very very leetle *wasser* but being so *luxe* I have a tiny trickle, which I help out with a lot of Moment Suprême and Givenchy's Monsieur. The voyage on the *Chitral* was . . . fairly enhanced by the presence of R.S. who in the old days was a gynaecologist and used to fiddle about with the twats of Maud Gilroy, Ivy St. Helier and even our own dear Mrs. Loraine. He is the ship's surgeon and quite sweet and civilized if silly.

I have just been to see a "Talent" display by the tots and teenagers on board. It was fairly enjoyable on account of none of them having any talent at all. The passengers are ditchwater department . . . I will have a great deal to tell you . . . Among the things I will tell you are . . . how much I hate the American President Line . . . and the lettuce and the pressure cooked bosoms of Ancient Cornish guinea hens and the air-conditioning and how very much I hated some shirred Eggs Opéra that I had which were covered in dog shit cunningly disguised as chicken livers . . . I saw Judy's film and she sang very very slowly and very very often. [The Judy Garland film was *I Could Go On Singing.*]

> I remain your travel stained but loving
> Master

I had an enchanting encounter with the Royal Navy . . . A very tall Player's Navy Cut Able Seaman rushed at me and saluted and called me "Captain D" [from *In Which We Serve*]. He was bearded and tattooed in every direction, even his eyelids, and was carrying a small green parakeet on a bit of bamboo. He christened it "Noël" in my honour, whereupon it immediately shat in my whiskey and water. If I've told you all this before, you must rise above it.

From the SS *President Wilson,* July 1:

I have fascinated the *Maitre d'hotel* with my witty Spanish on account of he comes from Puerto Rico, so I have had specially cooked meals. I have also fascinated Captain Cox—do you mind?—who is very fond of Verdi and Puccini. I have two nice beach friends. He is handsome as the day and the American Consul in Honkers, or at least he was, now he is going to Washington to study Russian. His wife is really quite sweet but a bit wifeish . . . I have also fascinated the cruise hostess who is a very very poor man's Mimi Paragon with wild teeth. In spite of these triumphs I am leaving the ship at Honolulu with a loud fart of relief.

·

THE "TRAVEL-STAINED but loving Master" certainly put his "questing mind" to the test in some unlikely places. The previous year (1962) he felt that, having written at some length about Samolo and the South Seas in general, it might be no bad idea to see what they were really like. March found him in Tahiti and writing to Coley:

> Hotel Tahiti
> March 4th

Me *voici* sitting bollock naked in a thatched bungalow because my luggage had to stay at the *aeroport* to be decontaminated on account of Rhinoceros Beetle. This takes two hours.

Tahiti so far is divine—it is jolly *gentil* to hear *Français* spoken in *toutes directions*. I didn't much care for Suva, the social carry-on was tedious, although I avoided as much as I could by shooting off in the ketch for three days. The jet-flying is really remarkable in these parts. I've flown over two thousand miles today and feel bright as a bee. My leg is a bit better . . . I expect the no smoking [at Ed Bigg's insistence] has helped. Curiously enough I haven't minded so very dreadfully except for odd moments. I had rather a pang giving my carton of Salems to the barman at the Grand Pacific. What they say about the natives being amenable and friendly is sensationally true. I've really scarcely had a moment to myself. My bags have now arrived so I shall unpack and go for a drink on the town . . .

> Amour, Amour.
> MAITRE

> Hotel Tahiti
> March 7th

Yesterday I set forth in a tiny chug-chug boat with a Teensy Frog who's the Kon Tiki type and sailed across the Pacific in a po or something. We went to Moorea, which takes about two hours, and made a tour of the island inside the lagoon. It was breathtakingly beautiful—violent mountains standing straight up out of the sea—glorious coral and coloured fish and white sand beaches . . . the real South Sea stuff. The trouble with Tahiti is that it is devoted almost exclusively to "Con". It really is thrown at you all the time and this is 'ow you say *tres gentil* if you happen to like it . . . there is a café here on the port called Vaimar's, where one can sit watching all the cons watching all the cons watching all the cons go by. It is picturesque but fairly dull. I am now burnt black and peeling like an old snake. Perhaps when I get to Bora-Bora I will put pen to paper but I rather doubt it, this is a lackadaisical atmosphere . . . The *petites Tahitiennes* spend most of their time when not being rogered in emitting little squeaks. This is rather boring, however, I have my ear plugs.

Hotel Bora-Bora
March 15th

This is being a really wonderful holiday. I have tried to work but have not persevered because there is so much to see and do and, having come all this way, I don't want to waste any of it. I am absorbing away like an old sponge . . . The hotel, which is excellent, is run by an American married to a Tahitian singer . . . The proprietor, Alex Bougerie, has a speedboat and I have crept like a hookworm into his heart. There are very few other guests and so we spend most of every day in the boat cruising about the lagoon and fishing from the reef. I have never taken so much exercise in my life. Yesterday we paddled the *pirogue*-outrigger canoe out to the reef and back before lunch, a mile and a half each way! On the way we saw two huge stingrays having a go 'Arry Boy with a third looking on. This could only happen in a French Colonial possession. We also encountered a very nasty sea-snake which I decapitated neatly with my paddle. The reefs are glorious beyond description, if you can multiply what we see at Goldeneye about twenty times this will give you a rough ahdee. The varieties of fish are incredible and also the different sorts of coral. We went far out to the outer reef and I was snorkeling away doing nobody any harm when I saw, as in a dream, a six-foot shark coming towards me. I kept my head and slapped the water hard with my fist. It gave me a look of infinite disdain and swam under me and away. In fact the whole thing is all that one has ever dreamed about the South Sea islands. I am almost black and feeling marvelous except for my leg which, although better is not right. My bungalow is a goodish way from the main building and I have to force myself to go slow, Johnny. I smoked not at all for a month and then decided that it was too mizzy and so now I have my first cigarette with my first drink at sundown. My average is five to seven a day! I must myself say I didn't find it difficult and do feel the benefit, no more dry mouth in the night for instance. I am sure the leg is circulatory trouble and can be dealt with. I have a great deal to tell, I have taken five million photographs and am liable to be a great South Sea Bora-Bora.

     Love love love to all
MASTER

## INTERMISSION
# A CHATTER OF CHUMS

O F ALL NOËL'S many correspondents there were those who could write letters and those who were letter writers. Of these, one of the most engaging was Benita Hume (1906–1967). She had first crossed Noël's path when she played the uncredited telephone operator in the 1927 silent Hitchcock version of *Easy Virtue*. After that, she enjoyed a modestly successful film career, married Ronald Colman, and

There were those who could write letters and those who were letter writers—one of the most engaging was Benita Hume.

after his death, George Sanders. In later life she became a semi-invalid, but it did nothing to dull the sharpness of her observation on contemporary people and events.

For a while she and Sanders were also Noël's neighbors in Switzerland, and she recalls a remark of Noël's, after a visit to the Charlie Chaplins (also neighbors), that Charlie's wife, Oona O'Neill Chaplin, "sat perfectly still in a cardigan":

> *The Chaplins' house was perfectly gay*
> *And filled with all the old guard again.*
> *The actors re-acted every play,*
> *They shouted and sang of the days that were hey*
> *Wishing Irving and Tree and Péllisier*
> *Were back on the scene to be starred again.*
> *But Oona Chaplin sat perfectly still,*
> *Perfectly still, in a cardigan.*
>
> *Charlie leapt up with an* entrechat—
> *And I must say came down rather hard again,*
> *George sang "Because"—to not much applause,*
> *Then the children did cartwheels—and one lost her drawers,*
> *While Noël followed his secret heart again.*
> *But Oona Chaplin sat perfectly still.*
> *She sat perfectly still. In a cardigan.*

I'm mad about Maidstone . . . those marvelous shops. There is Mrs. Tiffin's tea shop next to Mr. Stuffin the butcher and right close by Messrs. Allchin, Smallcock and Cramphorn. "Fine coffins", they add, as if that supplied some explanation. You don't get that kind of thing just anywhere. I had to go all the way to Osaka to find a travel agency called Wei fuku tu, for instance.

We heard someone in America say that insanity is hereditary—you get it from your children!

[1965]

I am less tolerant of Christianity than you. I think it is the most appalling disease of the imagination. Rather like necrophilia.

By 1967 Hume had had ample experience of hospitals: "They tell me that for people who really want to meditate the best bet is generally regarded as taking a room in a hospital and ringing the bell."

In 1964 she and George visited Israel, where he was shooting a film:

They've settled on a language no one has spoken since Abraham and you know the number of foreigners who are about to learn it you can count on the hands of one finger. Anyhow it is really only effective in the areas of hostile prophesies and gloomy exhortations. You don't have to catch much of the Old Testament to realize it's going to be rough getting a good translation of *Blithe Spirit* in Hebrew!

Her observation of people was equally sharp:

I met Truman Capote once years ago and thought him like a tiny tendril.

Margaret Leighton . . . She's nice, isn't she? But thin, thin like shredded coconut.

Elizabeth Taylor's rather voluminous top was secured at such an astonishing height as to give the strong impression she was wearing epaulettes.

It was a game at which Noël could more than hold his own:

Our new house boy (in Jamaica) was very tall, very very silly and talked like water gurgling out of a bath.

Marina, Duchess of Kent (1906–1968), and Princess Alexandra. After the tragic death of her husband in a 1942 air crash, Noël accompanied the duchess on many social and theatrical occasions. Once, at a concert, the two stood up by mistake. The whole audience followed suit, thinking it must be the national anthem.

Coward with Clifton Webb. Two very old friends, but later encounters were not always joyful. After his mother, Mabelle, died in her nineties, Clifton was prone to lachrymose out-bursts, finally causing Noël to remark, "It must be tough to be orphaned at seventy-one."

Arlene Francis was archer than Waterloo Bridge.

To Joyce (1966), Noël wrote that film star Gloria Grahame, in *The Man Who Never Was* (1956): "looks as though someone had not stepped on but slid over her face with very greasy shoes."

We dined with Mike Todd and Liz who was hung with rubies and diamonds and looked like a pregnant Pagoda.

I have taken lately to <u>underlining</u> words here and there on account of admiring Queen Victoria <u>keenly</u>.

In fact, Noël admired many members of the royal family. The Queen Mother apart, Noël would probably have considered that two of his closest royal "chums" were the Kents, George and Marina. George, the Duke of Kent (1902–1942), died in a tragic air crash and there were strong rumors, which still persist, that he and Noël had an affair. What is certain is that Noël and Marina (1906–1968) maintained a long and loving friendship, and he was her frequent escort on social occasions. She recalled a couple:

> I can think of several occasions which *could* be amusing to read; you and I trying to undo crackly paper from sticky sweets in the front row of the stalls at an Olivier performance, and getting hopeless gig-gles in the process.
>
> That time we were at a charity film performance and the drums

started up, as they do for the National Anthem, and we both stood up and the whole theatre did likewise, and we muttered to each other, out of the corners of our mouths without moving our heads: (*You*) "Is it the Anthem?—are you quite sure?"; (*Me*) "I think it *must* be, but I thought they'd have played it at the end." (*You*—beginning to lose control) "Do we dare sit down?"; (*Me*—*panicking*) "I don't think so."

This altercation having lasted about one and a half minutes, suddenly the band burst into some popular tune and we, feeling utter fools, sat down and of course by this time were shaking with suppressed giggles.

A poisoned quill belonged to Clifton Webb (1893–1966), a friend of Noël's from 1920 revue days and a song and dance man long before he became a distinguished, if acerbic, character actor in films (*Laura, Sitting Pretty,* etc.).

He liked nothing better than to retail Hollywood gossip to his absent friend.

June 19, 1954

I understand that "Tits" Dietrich (she decided it was high time that the eye should travel north) is opening at the Café de Paris. I saw her in Las Vegas and I must say that such glorious sex and glamour has not been seen since OUR early days at the London Pavilion . . .

It has been whispered behind fans that she and Tallulah have the same bust lifter. If such is the case, the result, as you will probably note, is most gratifying. I am not sure in the case of Miss D., but I am sure in the case of Miss B the confused gentleman threw his scalpel over his shoulder and called for a derrick.

Hearing that Frank Sinatra was making the drug drama *The Man with the Golden Arm:*

November 25, 1955

It is only fair you dash off something for me—*The Man With the Plastic Prick.* It could be sensational, gorgeous and very sincere.

The three most over-rated things in the world . . . "home cooking", "home fucking" and "Texas".

Cooking at least seemed to strike a chord with Noël. By this time it was a favorite hobby.

To Clifton:

I hope that you are keeping up with your cooking. Here is a very brief recipe for a late-night snack:—

Boil and shell, very carefully, one dozen eggs, and then throw the whole fucking lot at Louella Parsons.

Love and mad, mad Mormon kisses from your drab, ex-travelling companion.

Noël to Joyce Carey:

> *There was an old Marquis of Puno*
> *Who said "There is one thing I do know*
> *A boy is all right*
> *But for perfect delight*
> *A llama is numero uno."*

·

EDNA FERBER was a regular correspondent for almost forty years. In the 1930s she shared her jaundiced view of Hollywood:

[1937]

Since *The Charge of the Light Brigade* and *Lives of a Bengal Lancer* the English colony behave like the Government with C. Aubrey Smith as Governor General and Nigel Bruce and Basil Rathbone running things. They refer to Americans as "natives."

On New York:

[1960]

The sun is brilliant, the sky a washed-out blue, the streets are being dug up in every direction in normal New York fashion, the sound of the steam shovel crashes into the brain as rows and rows of old brownstone fronts are demolished to be replaced with "luxury" apartments made of Jello and held together, evidently, with chewing gum and spit.

On pagan festivals:

[1962]

The family here tomorrow for Thanksgiving dinner—quaint tribal custom which does not prevail in your land. I have just viewed the uncooked bird—a vast plump white creature that looks appallingly like a decapitated baby.

When Noël moved into Chalet Coward, Ferber made a pilgrimage from the Palace Hotel in Montreux, where she was staying, to peer at the house in his absence:

{1961}

The house is utterly lovely, even though I saw it at half-past six on a dark and rainy evening with clouds sitting on my eye-brows, it was so livable, so beautiful, so right. The quality that impressed me most was its tranquility. One rarely sees a tranquil dwelling. I may move in, quietly, and barricade the doors and windows against your arrival. That failing, I think you should know that I've enrolled at the Girls' School at Les Avants. I'm taking the courses in Character Crushing and Advanced Curmudgeonry. I'll nip over for tea every afternoon.

She was well aware that her acerbic wit kept even her friends at a safe distance:

{1966}

All this sounds disgruntled, carping. Yet I am deeply happy to be alive. I am daily fascinated by existence, when I walk these streets, I am highly diverted, I love seeing my friends. I have a feeling of critically impending doom for our world and this depresses me, not for myself—I've had my life and loved it—but for the young ones.

{1958}

Then a little devil stirred in my memory and I thought, we-must-all-be-very-kind-to-Aunt-Jessie-for-she-hasn't-had-a-very-happy-life. But I rejected that. I have loved my life. The world owes me nothing. I've had a hell of a ride.

On death:

{1961}

Myself, I just want to be put into an old Bergdorf-Goodman paste-board box such as they use to deliver dresses, and that's that. Don't forget.

•

WHEN HE WASN'T making films David Niven (1910–1983) could turn a phrase or an anecdote with the best:

> The other night there was a sneak preview of *Salomé* [a Rita Hayworth vehicle]—all the studio executives were there and all was well when the big scene came up—the head on the tray department. Then a voice from the balcony said—"Dig those *crazy hors d'oeuvres!*" and the picture was blissfully wrecked!!

> [1960]
> I have started writing a play—the play of the century . . . at the close of the first act I have thirty-eight people, all of whom made sensational entrances, jammed like sardines in a decayed lighthouse. How do I get rid of the bastards?

> We have at Gstaad an influx of the remnants of the Kennedy family with Teddy still, last night at dinner, giving the British lots of free advice about the Irish . . . I gave a little back, suggesting that it was a pity the Irish hadn't infiltrated the English like the Scots had, thereby ensuring several Scottish Kings and Queens of England, many Prime Ministers and winding up with the best bisquit factories . . . not a big hit!

In 1972 Niven made a Japanese TV commercial for a gentleman's underarm deodorant called Who's Who?

> It took three days and was shot in Eze village [in the south of France] by a crew of 24 Japanese flown over from Tokio. There I was (only to be seen on Jap TV, thank God!) dressed as a full Colonel in the Coldstream Guards, busby, white gloves—the lot.
> A model peers out of the window as I march past—"Oh, David! I knew it was you! I'd know your smell anywhere." DN (*turning into camera and whipping out a bottle of Who's Who? from beneath his medals*) "It's Who's Who" (*Salutes—exits*)

Niven on Garbo (1972):

> G. Garbo came to see us (in Cap Ferrat) a lot. I really find professional grubbiness quite tiresome. Also, she's not very clever, is she?

Which echoed a remark Noël had made to Joyce in 1967:

> Isn't it strange grubby people being so pleased with themselves? It's a thought for the day.

1955. Old friend and another Swiss neighbor David Niven and his second wife, Hjordis, came to stay with Noël in Jamaica. Immediately upon their arrival, Niven succumbed to an attack of chicken pox and had to be quarantined. Noël wasted nothing: the incident was turned into an episode in his novel, *Pomp and Circumstance.*

The Nivens moved into a new home in the south of France, where they found the concierge "a highly unreliable lady who wears riding breeches, smokes a pipe, and I suspect keeps a pair of false teeth in her behind with which she rips off the buttons of railway seats."

In the same establishment they hired "a titty Australian blonde" who proved to be unsuitable. This was confirmed when they helped get her a job with "some German on Cap Ferrat. Apparently, she had only looked after girls before and they had two little boys. They fired her for scrubbing their sons' cocks with a nail brush."

Niven's elder son, David, Jr., was clearly a chip off the old block in Noël's view. He was also one of Noël's sixteen godchildren. Later Noël made him a present of a cocktail shaker, which bore the legend "Because, my godson dear, I rather/Think you'll turn out like your father."

•

A LATE FRIEND was playwright and librettist Hugh Wheeler (1912–1987)—perhaps best known for his collaborations with Stephen Sondheim, *A Little Night Music* (1973) and *Sweeney Todd* (1979).

He was in the habit of regaling Noël with items from the media that had struck him as amusing.

Having seen Noël on Ed Murrow's *Small World* in 1959, he wrote to congratulate him. Noël, he babbled, had been a blessed relief after the nauseous spectacle that had immediately preceded him.

Mary Martin had appeared in a show devoted to small children, whose serried ranks formed the studio audience. Mary had clearly not shed the aura of Peter Pan entirely, for her own performance—Wheeler reported—

Another of "Little Bill's Boys,"
journalist and author of the
James Bond novels, Ian Fleming,
was Noël's neighbor in Jamaica.
When Fleming finally married
Ann Rothermere, Noël was on
hand to give the groom away.

was arch and interminable. This caused the audience to peer nervously at
the studio doors, which one had a suspicion were firmly bolted and
barred—thus creating a truly "captive audience."

There was also a questionable clown who wandered among the children,
claiming that the studio lights were far too bright, weren't they, children?
But not to worry. With *their* help he knew he could blow them out. In
Wheeler's opinion, for the amount of help the children were asked to contribute to the whole enterprise, they should have had an agent! On the
clown's signal they all had to blow their little hearts out—and then Miss
Martin would be able to appear. Well, they huffed and they puffed and
they somehow contrived to blow Mary Martin on stage.

But this was only the surrealistic starter.

Mary then metamorphosed from Peter Pan into Cinderella—a role she
had played in Rodgers and Hammerstein's *Cinderella*—and proceeded to
play *all* the parts in the show by a series of frenzied costume changes. One
moment she was the fairy godmother . . . now she was Cinderella . . . now
the prince. At one point, when she was both Cinderella *and* the prince,
she contrived to waltz with herself! It was—reported Wheeler—"an Ein-
steinian complication."

But there was more to come. After the ball was over, so to speak, and
Cinderella fled, there had to be the traditional glass slipper bit. But *this*
glass slipper had not heard of tradition. The one that was produced had the
approximate dimensions of a small battleship and Mary soon made the reason clear. "The Prince has to find which foot this slipper belongs on. Now
I am going to be EVERY FOOT IN THE WORLD."

At which point Constant Viewer appears to have turned off . . .

For composer/lyricist Lionel Bart,
Noël became a second father. Bart
would be pleased to know that in
the refurbished and newly dedicated
Noël Coward Theatre, in London's
St. Martin's Lane, the second bar is
now "Lionel's Bar."

•

ANOTHER OLD FRIEND with a subversive turn of mind was Ian
Fleming (1906–1964):

[June 17, 1958]

I have a slight confession to make. While in Bombay, I met a very
beautiful girl called Indira who has intellectual pretensions as well as
a 38 inch bust. She reviews for the top Bombay weekly, which is read
by all the top gurus, and proudly showed me her book collection,
which contained one of your *opuscula*. She was so excited when I confessed to knowing you that I at once autographed the book for her,
more or less in your hand-writing and certainly on the correct note of
fatuity. I was drunk on coca-cola at the time (Bombay is dry) and it
was only afterwards that I realized I was guilty of forgery. If you wish
to get together with Stephen Spender, William Plomer and W. H.
Auden, you might scrape up enough money to bring a case and get
some damages, for I regret to say that I also autographed *their* books
together with appropriate messages to the Indian people.

A late-in-life new friend was British composer/lyricist Lionel Bart
(1930–1999). His big success was *Oliver!* (1960), and later he decided to
attempt a musical version of *The Hunchback of Notre Dame*.

I thought I'd be able to work well on my new show *Quasimodo,* but I am having a hard time at this point. All I can do is think of music, and I'm being besieged with witty suggestions for titles, etc. Somebody wants me to call it *Hunch.* Your [Elaine] Stritch lady suggests that there should be a first act finale chorus line-up of hunchbacks singing "Consider yourself one of the family."

She's a funny lady.

Joyce Carey to Noël (1963):

I dreamt that a very tall man in an ill-fitting sandy wig was brandishing a revolver at you, and you, looking smashing in a dinner jacket, stepped forward and said very grandly: "We South Americans don't know the meaning of fear!"

I know you are brave as a lion, and that you don't talk like that, but I'm worried about South America. It isn't significant? Just a figment of my congealed subconscious? R.S.V.P.

Noël to Joyce:

Three days at the Vineyard with Kit [Cornell] and Nancy [Hamilton] and Gert. It was Kit's birthday and there were great present givings and a lot of earnest ladies in trousers came in on the Sunday, seconded [*sic*] by a few dessicated [*sic*] middle-aged Queens. One of the ladies read aloud a poem to Kit which started—"Shout loud for Garbo's face, Katherine [Katharine] Cornell's voice, Bach and Coward and clear clean rage!" It went on from strength to strength, until I was under the piano (with Bach). Nan, in her cups and bright magenta, had a sharp tiff with Kit . . . It was all very enjoyable. Nan's house is really divine but I got that familiar feeling that I get sometimes at Snedens [Kit's house]. Too many breasts!

To Cole Lesley:

Croyden [the most malignant of Noël's many Jamaican cats] caught a lizard before I could stop her . . . and crunched it all up wriggling, tail and all, and sat down at my feet looking very pleased with herself and belched! It's Nature, really, whichever way you look at it, and it's the law of the jungle, too. I only wish the lizard had been Kenneth Tynan. I have been a little offish with her ever since but she hasn't noticed it.

Despite their later rapprochement, Tynan (1927–1980) remained something of an irritant to Noël. To Alfred Lunt in 1967 he wrote: "I miss you with particular anguish during our Scrabble games. Did you really play against Ken Tynan? Does he *know* any words with as few as seven letters."

To Gladys: "I am reading a lovely book called *The Gilded Cage,* all about famous international actresses, which confirms what I have long suspected and occasionally mentioned, that all famous international actresses are silly cunts. It is comforting to be supported in one's genuine beliefs."

To Ginette Spanier:

I have no other news beyond the fact that I caught a cold owing to taking a pressurized aeroplane cabin on an empty stomach. That has now gone, owing to Bismuth and Christian Science and the belief, deeply ingrained, that Life is beautiful and noble and that my heart is God's Little Acre.

To Gladys (1965):

When I was having a drink in the Excelsior Bar [Venice] a terrible American lady came up and hissed—"Are you Sir Cedric?" I replied—"Yes, and I'm dead!" and she went away. I do think life is hard.

You will be pleased to hear, though, that while I was waiting for my plane a very refined voice came over the loud speaker saying— "Would Mr. and Mrs. Berry Berry kindly report to the Information Bureau?" Life has its compensations. I longed to see Mr. and Mrs. B.B. but failed to identify them.

To Lorn, when he was staying at Chicago's Passevant Hospital in 1966 for one of his regular checkups:

I had a mad nurse who stood at the end of the bed and just stared at me with a zany look in her eye. Then she rushed at me suddenly and wrenched the intravenous feeding contraption out of my vein, hurting me considerably in the process, and so I rang for the other nurse who was an angel and she ordered the maddie out of the room and she was never seen again. I think she'd just come in off the street. Strange people come in and out without so much as a by your leave or kiss me arse or anything. A tall lady in blue satin and covered in brooches bounced in abruptly one afternoon when I was having my snooze and said, in a dreadful nasal whine, that she was counting the water pitchers. I didn't quite catch what she said and thought she was referring to those under-sea movies. Another day a hideous dwarf with a tiny cap on top of a lot of capok put her head round the door and shrieked—"How ya feeling?" I replied—"Very ill, thank you" and she said "Good!" and slammed the door.

On an earlier visit, he had had an operation to remove a gallstone and reported to film producer Sidney Box: "I presented the stone to Gladys Cooper to be worn as a brooch. She was beside herself, practically orgasmic."

·

LILLI PALMER (1914–1986) writes to Noël ("from the German-Yiddisher Cow Department") while her then husband, Rex Harrison, is playing the wicked Saladin in a film of Sir Walter Scott's *The Talisman:* "Van Johnson asked the other day what Rex was doing. 'He's jousting,' I said. Van gave a deep sigh and said in a hollow voice—'Who *isn't?*' Which gives you Hollywood in a nutshell at the present moment."

# CHAPTER 29
# GIRLS . . . AND SPIRITS

## (1962–1964)

*Dear Mr. C,*
*I wish you glee*
*With undissembled fervour,*
*As Harry Kurnitz is to me,*
*You are to* The Observer.

**LOVE FROM KEN TYNAN (1962)**

Tammy Grimes, Bea Lillie, and Edward Woodward.

I only like great and glittering success and then only for a short
time.

NOËL COWARD

I N  M I D - 1 9 6 2  Noël was approached to be involved with *two* Broadway
musicals. It was not by any means the first time he had chosen to be
double-booked, but there was one important difference—in neither case
did he have complete artistic control.

The first was to be a musical version of Terence Rattigan's Coronation
Year play, *The Sleeping Prince,* which had not been a success on Broadway
with Michael Redgrave as the Regent. Now producer Herman Levin was
seeking to repeat his 1956 triumph of *My Fair Lady,* and Noël was
asked to write the score to a book to be written by Hollywood screen-
writer Harry Kurnitz. Kurnitz was delighted at the prospect and wrote
to Noël:

> 9 Curzon Place, W.1
> Grosvenor 1051
>
> Light of the World, Lion of Shepperton, Comradely, Revolutionary
> GREETINGS.
> I am honored and pleased (in that order) that you have accepted a role
> in our panto and I swear by the Sacred Stone of Grauman's Chinese
> [Theatre] that you will in all things find me obedient, reverent,
> clean, truthful, patriotic and—pity me, I have forgotten my Boy
> Scout oath.
> I kiss the hem of thy garment.
> Your sherpa
> HARRY

As the project staggered along, Kurnitz continued to write:

> April 16th 1962
> I think you should know that I have been having a recurring dream
> in which we—you and I—are accepting The Critics' Prize For The
> Best American Musical Based On A British Play and A Warner
> Brothers' Movie and since in this dream you are always modest, unas-
> suming and give me all the credit for our huge success, I know it is a
> real dream and not some phony drunken nightmare. Herman Levin
> has told me all about your other commitments and I sympathize, of
> course, but where does that leave me? I'm not a young man any

more, Noël, and if I am to write a smash hit musical it had damn well better be SOON. That sums up my position and I close with reverent assurances of my high regard.

Ever thine,
BORIS PASTERNAK

Noël, meanwhile, was occupied with the score. He wrote to Lorn:

I am working like a slave and adoring it. I have done a number for *Sleeping Prince,* which you will adore. It's called "London's A Little Bit of All Right" and, incorporated in it are four (invented) music-hall songs. Really lovely ones. "What Ho, Mrs. Brisket", "Don't Take Our Charlie for the Army", "Saturday Night at the Rose and Crown" and "What's the Matter With a Nice Beef Stew?" They are for the Trafalgar Square scene when the young king escapes into London by himself. It needs a belter. [In the event, the part went to Tessie O'Shea.] I have virtually finished the score and I really do think that music and lyrics are among the best I've ever done.

81 Avenue Marceau
Paris 16
July 30th

Light of The World, Lion of Judah, Keeper of the 49 Umbrellas, GREETINGS:
I send thee this day, Master, one (1) complete rough (ROUGH!) draft of a musical comedy libretto as yet lamentably untitled, unfinished, unsettled and unversed. 'Tis a crude thing but replete with jokes, many of them brand new; others freshly sandblasted . . .

I have come to believe, as I believe in God, Spring, Swiss residence and Czerny *études,* that the only great first act curtain is the exit for the Coronation. I realize that this gives us a second act of the bulk of *Tristan & Isolde* but, since the whole script is now wildly over-written, I think it can be worked out. Judicious Cutting, my Hebrew editor, will help us here.

I have done some casual re-writing and, as we used to say in Culver City, polishing throughout so, if you can bear it, please hack your way through the complete text once more.

Levin was, indeed, intent on cloning his previous hit, clearly believing that the formula of an older, arrogant man humbled by a simpler young woman was surefire.

Rex Harrison didn't see it that way, however, and the search for a leading man went on.

Christopher Plummer? From a film set in Spain (where he was filming "*The Rise and Fall of the Roman Empire* or *Samuel Bronston*—I am not quite sure which") Plummer replied:

I can't possibly know how to begin to explain how awkward and frustrating my feelings have been towards the decision I made regarding your *Sleeping Prince* . . . I have always so very much wanted to work with you in the theatre (I think it's probably the dream of most actors) and I very much hope to do so some day in the future, but partly because of a half spoken promise to Jules Styne to do *Ghost Goes West,* and partly because of an actor's natural greed to jump at the chance to play two parts in the same piece instead of one, I decided against yours. I guess it was an intuitive feeling that if I missed in the diva department, I could have redeemed myself more with the added strength the two characters offered.

You know it's funny but when one admires an artist very much, as I do you, one feels very close, and usually when the parties get together at long last, the meeting is a disappointment, partly because in our silly world and our silly youth we must make ourselves feel slightly ashamed to show our real feelings of respect— particularly when the two in question are members of the same profession.

Not that this has been our case at all. In fact, on the contrary. You are perhaps the easiest and most comfortable person to meet but I would like you to know that the back slapping sort of intimacy I like to cover my shyness with, and the "I can play Noël Coward songs just as good as yooz can" kind of presumption with which I have come on so strong, has never been in any way an attempt to conceal the very strong gratitude and admiration I will always feel for you.

I wish you'd send my love to Harry Kurnitz and thank him for that night at the Savoy and yourself, too, for the dinner and the delicious score you played us. It will be wonderful. Someday think of me again for something.

Always,
CHRISTOPHER PLUMMER

*The Ghost Goes West* went west and never opened. The part of the Regent went by default to José Ferrer. Mary (the Girl) would be Florence Henderson.

Not all of Noël's friends were thrilled at the prospect. Benita Hume wrote, "*José Ferrer*? Oh my dear! I'd just as soon sit under a hair dryer as listen to him sing. George [Sanders] said to associate him with sex is disgusting, or with romance is absurd or with royalty a communistic plot."

Rehearsals for *The Girl* continued—and so did the problems. To Gladys (December 13): "Joe Layton [the director] in hospital. Me taking over. Having to write a new number on account of the lyric of 'Long Live the King, If He Can' not being VERY tactful. [Kennedy had been shot on November 22.] However, I managed it and all is well."

•

LIKE SO MANY PEOPLE, Noël remained skeptical of the supposed verdict on the Kennedy assassination as published by the Warren Commission. In 1967 he is writing to Alfred Lunt:

Nobody here took the official version seriously. Odd that the culture of pistol-packing-cowboy should also view the maverick unofficial explanation with such stuffy dubiety. I knew Jack and the whole attractive, and devoutly self-serving lot of them. I admired Jack's vigour and his capacity to throw off the cares of office in pursuit of pleasure.

To me, it is odd that your country is so dubious regarding the possibility of a clique of influential parties having the power, the motive, and the opportunity to assassinate poor Jack. That is far more credible than what is written and believed about the misfit Oswald and the gangster-vulgarian, Ruby.

Having returned to Jamaica, he wrote to Joyce:

Blue Harbour
Port Maria
Jamaica B.W.I.
December 14th [1963]

Well, Darling,
It was certainly a fabulous opening night. The audience, apart from being star-spangled, was glorious from the word "Allez". The Company responded and gave a fine performance (If they hadn't, they would have been shot by me). Tessie O'Shea stole the show and had a standing ovation of several minutes. They cheered and cheered not only at the end of the number but all through it! I really never heard anything like it. Crashing bore she may be but old pro she certainly is.

José Ferrer scuttled about on his tiny little legs and was better than he'd ever been (which was not *quite* enough) and stopped the show with "Middle-Age". Florence was perfect—absolutely fault-less. A little less knowingness and a little more inner humility and she would have made it completely. As it was she just fell short. She has been behaving rather peculiarly anyway. She suddenly refused to play the Saturday preview *matinée,* because she had a throat virus (which she didn't). She let us know an hour and a half before curtain time. This *might* have thrown the whole show and demoralized the company the day before opening. Happily, however, the understudy, Dran Seitz went on and tore the place up. Not only because she was wonderful but because she was very very good indeed and didn't fluff one line! Florence was back like a fucking greyhound for the evening performance but too late to recapture the respect she had lost from the Company. Poor Joe [Layton], still in hospital, was livid with her, so were we all. I don't *think* she'll stay off again! She was a silly girl to make such a major theatrical error. The notices were all raves except the *Times* and Walter Kerr, who at least was wonderful for Tessie, Florence and *me*! He just hated the book. I think it's a smash hit anyhow.

But a month later he is facing facts:

January 19th 1963

The show is going all right but it is not between ourselves the smash hit we hoped for. He [Ferrer] is largely to blame, I think, for being so splendidly unattractive and Florence [Henderson], between Boston and New York, *lost* the "innocent" quality.

John Gielgud was a little more generous in his verdict when he saw the show and wrote to Noël: "He [Ferrer] put over his numbers surprisingly well with, obviously, a good many hints from a master hand! How I wish you had played the part yourself. The girl is charming, but no G[ertrude] Lawrence! As John P[erry] is so fond of saying, 'We have seen some Majesty and should know.' "

*The Girl* managed to eke out 112 performances at the Broadway Theatre.

•

THERE WERE MORE dramas, alarms, and excursions on the British political scene—most notably the Profumo Affair, in which Tory Cabinet minister John Profumo, married to actress Valerie Hobson, committed the politically unpardonable sin of lying to the House of Commons about his fling with two young ladies of decidedly questionable virtue, Christine Keeler and Mandy Rice-Davies. Somewhere in the mix was a Russian spy and a society pimp, Stephen Ward, who conveniently committed suicide in his prison cell. It was a real-life plot for a B movie—and was eventually turned into one.

To Cole (June 11, 1963):

I wrote to poor Valerie just to send her my love and tell her that I was thinking of her. I said that although I didn't know all the ins and outs of the situation, etc., and then added in brackets, "Perhaps this could have been more happily put!" Now I rather wish I hadn't made that dear little joke. However, the letter has gone and she'll have to rise above it. I must say that Jack Profumo has behaved like the cuntette of all time . . . I think that people are getting sillier and sillier as the sparks fly upward and it will serve everybody bloody well right when the sparks begin to fly downward.

To Lorn, he added: "All we need now is for John Gordon [the notoriously puritanical editor of the *Sunday Express*] to be caught with a Guardsman of eighteen. I can't wait!"

Noël continued to observe the shenanigans from Jamaica, and writing to Joyce:

> August 28, 1963
>
> I expect by now the Wretched [Stephen] Ward is dead. He was sinking this morning according to *The Gleaner*. I'm not particularly sorry for him, because I think he was a smarmy horror but oh—as you say—those ghastly girls! I think I hate "Mandy Rhys Cardboard" (or "Mandy Rice Pudding") the most. What a squalid, conceited nasty little slut. *Who* I should like to know invited her to The Film Premyeer of *Cleo* [*Cleopatra*] and to the party afterwards? She was wearing a dress that she had made herself—and it *looked* like it. What is England coming to? . . . I *did* like her fainting dead away on hearing of Rachman's [her slum landord lover's] death and then opening her eyes and saying "Did he leave a Will?"

Lorn found the whole business hard to believe: "There *can't* be all this hullabaloo over two pennyworth of Rogering."

But there was, and it proved to be critical to the downfall of the Macmillan government later that year.

In his *Diary* entry for September 14, Noël would reflect: "Our history, except for stupid, squalid, social scandals, is over . . . Now my unhappiness is impersonal, then [during the war] it was personal. Then I was worried about being away when great things were happening. Now I know that it didn't matter. This is a more desolate unhappiness."

•

A LOWER-KEY but more positive note was struck that spring when the London suburban Hampstead Theatre Club decided to revive *Private Lives.* The production received surprisingly ecstatic reviews from the major critics and was soon transferred to the Duke of York's Theatre in the West End proper, where it ran for 212 performances. Unrecognized as such—except later in retrospect—its success marked the beginning of what Noël would come to call "Dad's Renaissance."

•

## BIRTHDAY ODE

### WITH LOVE FROM MASTER MARCH 6TH 1963

> *Coley now is fifty-four,*
> *Creaking on towards three score.*
> *Blow the trumpets, bang the drums.*
> *Aching joints—receding gums,*
> *Upper plate and lower plate*
> *Wretchedly inadequate.*
> *Hacking cough and thinning hair,*
> *Hernias almost everywhere.*
> *Weathered like an ancient oak,*
> *Pressing on toward a stroke.*
> *Short of breath—all passion spent*
> *Arteries hardening like cement.*
> *Shout Hosanna—shout Hooray*
> *Coley's fifty-four today.*

•

One cannot help but feel that Noël stretched himself painfully thin during 1963. Back in January he had been approached by composer Hugh Martin and lyricist Timothy Gray with a revised proposal to produce a musical version of *Blithe Spirit.* In fact, their proposal was more than just the usual outline—they had composed most of the score under the title *Faster Than Sound*—and to his great surprise, Noël found that he liked what he heard a great deal. He gave the team his blessing and even agreed to direct the piece.

Martin (b. 1915) was a highly respected composer who had worked on Broadway and later, mainly in Hollywood, with Ralph Blane (1914–1993) on such films as Judy Garland's *Meet Me in St. Louis* (1945). In fact, this was not the first time he had approached Noël with the idea.

In March 1953 Martin is writing to express the emotions he felt on seeing the Gertrude Lawrence memorial exhibition at the Museum of the City of New York:

> Next to Gertie herself it is you who dominate the small room. There is a cute letter from you advising her not to overact in *Pygmalion*. There are innumerable mentions of you by G.L. herself and her friends . . . I enjoyed seeing you listed as one of "3 Angels of Light" and one of "6 School Children" in *Hannele*.
>
> But it was the photographs of you that fascinated me. Watching you evolve from the ravishing young juvenile of "Rain Before Seven" and "Baggy Maggy"—through the matinée idol of *Private Lives* and *T.A.8:30*—into something more beautiful than either: the sardonic, sentimental, sophisticated gentleman in the photograph Miss Lawrence kept so close to her pretty head when she was making up for *The King and I*. All in all, quite a show, and it was rather wicked of you to steal it from such a very blithe spirit . . .

Then it becomes clear that there have been several earlier conversations on a possible adaptation:

> Speaking of *B.S.*, I decided not to announce it; I sensed a certain feeling from your cable that you thought I was being premature and so I was.
>
> Must confess, though, that in a dazzling flash of brilliance the other night I found the device I'd been searching for that will bridge it into a musical—will save it till I see you. (I don't relish it being vetoed by the Jamaican set before it's even worked out in my *own* mind.)

The device he was contemplating was to set the piece in Jamaica, with the hero, Charles Condomine, more closely based on Noël himself. Ruth would be played by Kay Thompson and Elvira by Judy Garland, a close friend of Martin's since *Meet Me in St. Louis,* and an even closer friend of Noël's.

To Martin's chagrin, Noël most emphatically did not approve of what he considered tampering with his work in this way.

JULY 1ST

JACK'S LETTER JUST RECEIVED TRIED PHONE YOU TERRIBLY
DISAPPOINTED BUT YOU'RE CAPTAIN PLEASE THINK OF JAMAICA
AS MERE NEW FRAME ENCLOSING UNTAMPERED WITH
MASTERPIECE JUDY GARLAND SO EXCITED AND ADORES JAMAICA
IDEA AS I DO YOU

HUGH

A few days later not even the prospect of having Judy Garland appear in the show prevented a Coward veto:

July 15th 1953

Dear Noël,

Your cable along with Jack's letter arrived this morning and was THE shock of a career checkered with them. I should probably wait a day or two and write a less emotional letter, but I feel so badly that getting this off is almost a physical necessity.

Probably one of the reasons I am not commercially in the Berlin-Porter-Rodgers category is that I never do a project unless I am terribly in love with it and this only happens to me every few years . . . I only mention this, because it's unlikely that it would happen again so soon, even though the script were written by my very favorite writer of all time, and I think you know me well enough by now to know that I mean this literally.

The musical *Blithe Spirit* would have been the most enchanting show possible—I still can't believe that you have let lawyers and agents talk you out of it. Incidentally, I am convinced that it would have made a terrible lot of money—more for you personally than revivals of the straight play would have netted you. As you undoubtedly know, there is nothing more remunerative than a really successful musical.

If a revival of the play *were* done, it seems to me that that would knock out the idea of doing a musical of it once and for all. The reason the time is so ripe for it *now* is that a good ten years have passed since the original was seen.

As far as your objection to putting it in Jamaica is concerned, I made it clear that I would abide by your decision.

Perhaps, stupidly, I have turned down several offers to write shows and films, some of which were very interesting and could have been quite important to me. Feeling secure in the blessing you gave us, I always said that I was sorry but that I had already started work on *Blithe Spirit.* Everyone in New York knows I was on the project and I have already done quite a bit of work on it. It never occurred to me to ask you for anything in writing, especially after a remark you made to Jack in connection with the Norman Wisdom show. You told him that although he had signed nothing, he was morally obligated to do the show, since he had said he would. You cited as an example the fact that you had never had a contract with Binky.

I suppose there is nothing more to be said and perhaps I shouldn't have said this much but you might as well know, as you must have suspected, how very crushed and disappointed I am.

As a consolation prize, Noël had offered Martin another property—the unproduced 1947 play *Long Island Sound.*

I read *Long Island Sound* and I think it is without a doubt one of the funniest plays you or anyone else has written. I would never have thought of it as a musical if you hadn't done so first, because to me it would seem that its great success would result from not letting its rapid fire, relentlessly witty cross talk be interrupted by songs or anything else.

Add to this the fact that, with the exception of *Pal Joey,* I can't think of a successful musical comedy which had, as your play does, only one sympathetic character. That is not to say that with the enormous advantage of a script by you as a springboard, the three of us couldn't bring it off, because I am sure we could. Not only could, but will if you say the word. I am a much better writer than I am a decider anyway. I am more than willing to leave this decision up to you and just take orders, which I shall do superbly.

Let's talk about the film M-G-M wants to make about your life. I am dying to hear if your reaction was anything other than scornful indignation. I think it would be kind of exciting myself. Heaven knows it's a fabulous story and Metro *does* make the best screen musicals in the world.

Other than getting a very spectacular garland from Garland, I haven't seen the lady for a few days so haven't been able to relay your love. But I shan't forget.

Did you know that California flowers, with the exception of one or two isolated types, have no fragrance? Don't you think this is rather symbolic?

I do hope Princess Margaret gets to marry that good looking Attaché or Equerry or whatever he is. I was secretly hoping she would marry Eddie Fisher and I think he was too!

I am enclosing a clipping from *The New Yorker* about you which you have undoubtedly already seen. I love their description of you [in *The Apple Cart*], "wearing a streamlined uniform and perfectly timing a lot of crisp Coward lines that happen to have been written by Shaw!"

And there matters rested for the best part of a decade.

By mid-year, with the title now changed to *High Spirits,* preparations were well under way. Noël took a close interest in the casting. Tammy Grimes became the first choice. To Joyce (July 19):

The cast is coming along a treat. Celeste Holm [who was eventually replaced by Louise Troy], Edward Woodward (lovely voice), Beattie

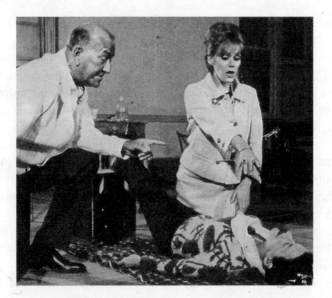

"Why, isn't that Bea Lillie pretending to be Madame Arcati?" Noël and Tammy Grimes in a rather posed pose.

[Beatrice Lillie] and Tammy Grimes. Personally, I think she'll be wonderful and provide a nice bit of competition for Lady Peel who, incidentally, is of the same opinion.

To Gladys (same date):

I had lunch with Beattie today who looked wonderful and was almost completely incoherent! I've started her learning Madame Arcati now. She ought to know the first scene by January.

To Lorn (August 2):

*Blithe Spirit* looks to me as though it might be even a bigger success than *The Girl Who Came to Supper.* Timothy Gray has done a really brilliant job on the script over which I have complete control, should it be necessary. He has very cleverly remained faithful to my original dialogue but the whole shape is quite different from *Blithe Spirit* as was and I shall add to or subtract from his additional dialogue wherever I see fit.

By the turn of the year, *The Girl Who Came to Supper* had arrived—for good or ill—and Noël was now free to "gird my fascinating loins" and concentrate on *High Spirits.*

To Joyce (January 19, 1964):

I am now plunged full fathom five into *High Spirits.* Beattie is
AGONY but, of course, has moments of brilliance. She is also trying
like mad and is very touching. Eventually she will be wonderful as
Beatrice Arcati but she has no memory at all and rehearsals are torture. However, tonight she suddenly emerged and gave a performance . . . She can't act *at all* and yet—and yet—she is a great star.
The cast is brilliant. Tammy, the closest "Elvira" to Katie Hammond
and sings like a dream. Woodward wonderful as Charles and also
sings beautifully, Louise Troy as Ruth is fine—lovely looks, good *hard*
quality, and good voice. The musical numbers excellent particularly
the "Trance" number which is pure Maskelyne and Devant [famous
stage magicians of the Victorian era]! I have little doubt that it will be
a big hit. We have two big stars who go all through the show whereas
in *Girl Who C. to S.* we only have Tessie who is on for nine minutes.

By February they are in tryout at Boston's Colonial Theatre and Noël is
bringing Joyce up to date on progress—and lack of it:

The show is going wonderfully but I am not deceived. Up to now it
is almost good. The book holds it together but the book is thrown by
Beattie who just can't do it at all . . . Not only can't she act but she
can't remember two consecutive lines. All she occasionally remembers are one or two unfunny interpolations of her own. What we all
*hoped* was that even though we had to sacrifice Madame Arcati we
should at least get Beatrice Lillie. Unhappily we only get her in spo-
radic flashes—the rest is death and age and the clanging of funeral
chimes. Last night an understudy went on for Ruth (excellent) and
had to prompt Milady several times. It's all a jolly out of Town nightmare. The critics rave, etc. We shall see.
    Tammy Grimes sings marvelously and flies more marvelously
than anyone I have ever seen. She really is brilliant. Teddy Woodward
charming as Charles, not quite a star but a beautiful actor with a
delightful singing voice. Louise Troy as Ruth is harsh and beautiful
to look at and I have a tiny suspicion that she enjoys the company of
her own sex. Both the Bradmans and Edith are fine. The sets with the
exception of two are mediocre and a bit tatty. The dresses good. The
music good. The lyrics fairly good, particularly the ones the prettiest
and best has tampered with.

From the outset Tammy Grimes was anxious to please the Master and
make up for *Lulu.*

November 21st

My dearest Noël:

Received firmly packed box of terribly English-looking frozen "stick makeup". I must say I adore the colors. I haven't the vaguest idea where to put what on my face. I realize that you are a genius and, of course, would know exactly what to do, but I am sitting here waiting, dear heart, for some kind of direction as to where the lavender goes.

Something way down deep inside does tell me where to apply the black-eye-liner, but I would appreciate it very much if, while you are sitting there, basking in the sun, and I am standing here freezing in the cold, some glimpse or direction as to how to apply these wondrous colors *dans ma visage.*

It is practically impossible to write anything anymore ever to anybody again because I am so tired, because I want to be oh so very much the most fantastic half grand, half tatty, everything that a bs (no darling, Blithe Spirit) should be.

Godspeed . . .

Lloyds of London has insured me, so when I die up there on that bloody rod you don't have to sell your Island, your grand estate or your pink and white striped jeep.

Ever thine,
TAM

The problem continued to be Bea Lillie's inability to learn her lines. In sheer frustration Noël wrote to Lorn from Boston (February 20):

> *Beatrice Lillie is a cunt*
> *No matter what you've heard*
> *Beatrice Lillie is a cunt*
> *And doesn't know a word.*
> *Beatrice Lillie is a Twat*
> *Whatever news you've had*
> *Beatrice Lillie is a Twat*
> *Who's driving Master mad.*

And to Gladys (same date):

What with trying to coax Beattie to say *one* line correctly, it has all been rather hectic . . . It is agony to watch her. Once or twice there is an echo of her old genius but they are rare. She tries so hard to be funny that I have to slip into a straitjacket whenever she comes on . . . She has had it. *Anno Domini* department. Tonight I retired to the lobby and jumped up and down . . . But she gets rave notices! Oh dear, oh dear, two major musicals in a row are a weeny bit exhausting but my strength is as the strength of ten on account of my heart being pure.

At the time he was not to know that Lillie was in the early stages of Alzheimer's, the disease that was to halt her career and devastate the last two decades of her life.

On March 24 he could write to Joyce that:

The nightmare is nearly over. It has been a curious experience. Beattie, although fairly fiendish with everyone else, has been very docile with me. She now knows it—roughly—cannot act it but—and it's a very big BUT—creates a certain beguiling magic which enchants the audience and even me! Tammy, who belongs to modern Theatre, as opposed to our Traditional kind, retired to hospital for a week with what we are told was a hairline fractured rib but which turned out to be self-induced hysteria brought on by Beattie getting the rave notices. She is now back again and merry as a grig. The sets are horrid but are being improved. Teddy Woodward is excellent and a saint. Louise Troy very good as Ruth but inclined to snarl. Gower Champion has been called in to re-do the choreography which badly needed it. He has already worked miracles and is a dear dear. I think it will probably be a hit but I'm too sick of it to care much.

Madame Arcati (Bea Lillie) en route to create
ectoplasmic havoc for the Condomines.

Before the show reached the Alvin Theatre on April 4 Champion had taken over complete artistic control. An exhausted Noël noted in his *Diaries:* "I took on far too much. I am sick of *High Spirits* and everyone connected with it. I think, galvanized by Gower, it may be a success. At any rate, I have done all I can do." And, so saying, he made a grateful exit to his beloved Jamaica.

The musical was, indeed, a success, remaining on Broadway for 375 performances.

# CHAPTER 30
# "DAD'S RENAISSANCE"

## (1964–1965)

D ESPITE NOËL'S strongly worded advice—the verbal equivalent
of "that tense and emaciated forefinger of doom," as G. B. Stern
once described it—Larry Boy *did* agree to run the new National
Theatre and clearly forgot and forgave Noël's warnings.

The biggest thing since the Beatles . . . or before them.

In fact, he went one better. In early 1964 he invited Noël to direct a revival of *Hay Fever* with an all-star cast—the first production there of the work of a living playwright. The original suggestion appears to have been made by Kenneth Tynan, whom Olivier had lured from the ranks of the caustic critics to be his right hand in charge of publicity and development. In opposite camps theatrically for most of Noël's postwar career, he and Tynan now had common cause.

In the program notes Tynan wrote for the production, he came to the revisionist conclusion that "Coward took the fat off English comic dialogue; he was the Turkish bath in which it slimmed."

Working together for the first time did a great deal to remove the tension that had historically existed between the two of them, and it was Tynan who held out the hand of reconciliation.

> The National Theatre
> 22 Duchy Street
> London S.E.1.
> 2 September 1964

I saw Marlene's triumphant opening at Edinburgh a couple of nights ago and we talked glowingly about you over supper. I then went to bed and had an extraordinary dream in which you confessed to having had an affair with Diana Cooper. "She keeps a good pillow", you said reminiscently, "but she's rather lacking in *udge*". At this I nodded sagely, though I hadn't the least idea what "*udge*" was. Perhaps one day you might care to explain.

> Ever yours,
> KEN

While flattered by Olivier's offer, Noël's initial reaction—prompted by his doctor's advice—was to stand aside from personal involvement. He wrote to Larry Boy:

> Blue Harbour Port Maria Jamaica, W.I.
> April 15th 1964

Dearest Larry Boy,
I am bitterly bitterly disappointed to have to tell you that I can't direct *Hay Fever* for you. I enclose a fairly sharp letter from my doctor which explains why. I am terribly sad about this because I was so flattered and pleased to have been asked to work for your National Theatre. *Hay Fever,* as you know, is one of my pets, but if you feel like dropping it from your programme, I shall quite understand. If, on the other hand, you want to go on with it with another director, I will do anything I can to help in discussing cast etc., etc.

Having done three large "Musicals" within a year: *Sail Away* in Australia, *The Girl Who Came to Supper* (now defunct) and lastly *High Spirits* which, from the point of view of wear and tear, was the worst of the lot, I developed what was thought to be a stomach ulcer in Philadelphia. As soon as I could and after a great deal of pain I flew to Chicago to Ed Bigg (Alfred, Lynn's and my doctor) and went into hospital for a thorough check-up. Having endured every known physical humiliation—Barium up—Barium down!—it was discovered that I was organically sound, that it wasn't—thank God—an ulcer after all, but that I was suffering from acute gastritis caused by nervous exhaustion and continuous irritation. There were many many other attendant horrors, which I won't bore you with, but the net result of the whole nightmare was that I conked out and have now been on a mild diet for eight weeks.

Obviously in this peaceful place I am getting better every day and in a few weeks time I shall be back on sizzling steaks and booze and all sorts of wickedness. However, I have learned a pretty severe lesson and have accordingly promised myself (and the doctor) not to engage in any directorial activities whatsoever for at least a year. I may write fourteen plays, seven novels, and appear in a series of ravishing movie cameos, but I would rather undertake to play *Peer Gynt on Ice* than show one actor, however talented, how to walk across the stage. (Incidentally, I find that very few actors nowadays know how to achieve this minor miracle.)

I know that you, of all people, will understand this and please believe that I wouldn't unless it were absolutely unavoidable.

It is being slowly and painfully beaten into my skull that I am no longer a precocious boy of nineteen, although when I look in the mirror at this lovely little heart-shaped face with all those pretty little jowls hanging from it, I find it hard to believe.

Please, please cable me or write to me when you get this letter saying that you understand and forgive your loving old
        Noelie.
My fond love to Joan and a very very great deal to you.

The only bright moment in the hospital was when a perfectly strange lady with orange hair bounced into my room and said "Are you Miss Davis and would you like a shampoo?" I replied coldly in the negative.

Though surprised and disappointed at Noël's decision, Olivier took the news gracefully. It was, he cabled in reply, "no good crying over milk that never got into the jug." Perhaps it was his sympathetic understanding that did the trick—or more likely the smell of the metaphorical greasepaint—

*Hay Fever* revival, National Theatre, London, 1964. "No, dear, on a *clear* day you can see Marlow—on a *very* clear day you can see Marlowe and Beaumont and Fletcher!" Noël directs Dame Edith Evans and Robert Stephens. (Photograph by Lord Snowdon and used by permission.)

but by mid-year Noël had changed his mind and agreed to direct "a cast that could have played the Albanian telephone directory"—including Dame Edith Evans, Maggie Smith, Derek Jacobi, Robert Stephens, and Lynn Redgrave.

Where the Dame was concerned, Noël found himself in territory that was depressingly familiar. In July, Olivier was writing to warn him that the lady had an unshakable "theory" about not learning her lines before she rehearsed, so he didn't honestly think there was any sense in "fussing her about it." He hastened to add that there was probably nothing to worry about since she had played the part before and must "all but know it." He felt that they could afford to let her keep the book in her hand as long as she wanted "without any undue disquiet." It was advice that was easier to give than to receive.

When the experience was safely behind him, Noël could write to Joyce:

November [?] 1964

Darling Doycie,
Well, it's all over bar the shouting and there has been a good deal of that at an encouragingly high decibel level. I do believe Dad has pulled it off this time and no error . . .

I do feel that after the trials and tribulations of Gladys [Cooper] and Bea [Lillie], who both had a wayward way with my jeweled words, I might have been spared Edith's doubtless well meant approximations.

The classic example was her insistence on saying—"On a *very* clear day you can see Marlow". Finally, when I had corrected her for the umpteenth time, pointing out that the "very" was very *very* superfluous to my intent, I heard myself saying—"No, dear, on a *clear* day you can see Marlow—on a *very* clear day you can see Marlowe and Beaumont and Fletcher." Which I was rather pleased with. You may very well hear me repeat the story and, should you be so fortunate, you are *not*—on pain of death—to stop me!

Then there was the time she took to her Christian Scientific bed with some unspecified illness and one could almost see dear Mary Baker Eddy waiting in the wings. I recalled that Lornie had once told me that on one such occasion the lady went twelve days without going to the lulu and refused to take a dose of anything, till finally in agony she *had* to get a doctor. Lornie put it exquisitely when she said—"If she ever works for us, I think a daily poop should be a clause in the contract!"

This time the doctor turned out to be my darling Maggie [Smith]. When Edith heard that "the Smith gal"—as she calls her—was word perfect and ready to go on for her, she made a recovery that should go in the record books!

The critics—now firmly convinced that they had been responsible for "rediscovering" him—were unanimous in their praise for the production, with Ronald Bryden going so far as to declare that Noël Coward was "demonstrably the greatest living English playwright."

When I tapped out this little comedy on to my typewriter in 1924 I would indeed have been astonished if anyone had told me that it was destined to re-emerge, fresh and blooming forty years later . . . One of the reasons it was hailed so warmly by the critics in 1925 was that there happened to be an ardent campaign being conducted against "Sex" plays, and *Hay Fever,* as I remarked in my first-night speech, was as clean as a whistle. True there had been no campaign against "Sex" plays lately; on the contrary rape, incontinence, perversion, sadism, psychopathology and flatulence, both verbal and physical, have for some time been sure bets in the race for critical acclaim. I was, therefore, agreeably surprised to wake up on the morning after the first night at the National Theatre and read a number of adulatory and enthusiastic notices. Such (almost) unanimous praise has not been lavished upon me for many a long year and to pretend that I am not delighted by it would be the height of affectation.

It was noted . . . that the play had no plot and that there were few if any witty lines, by which I presume is meant that the dialogue is non-epigrammatic. This I think and hope is quite true . . . To me, the essence of good comedy writing is that perfectly ordinary phrases such as "Just fancy!" should, by virtue of their context, achieve greater laughs than the most literate epigrams. Some of the biggest laughs in *Hay Fever* occur on such lines as "Go on", "No, there isn't, is there?" and "This haddock's disgusting". There are many other glittering examples of my sophistication in the same vein . . . I would add that the sort of lines above mentioned have to be impeccably delivered and that in the current performance they certainly are. In fact, I can truthfully say that never in my long years of writing and directing have I encountered a more talented, co-operative and technically efficient group of actors and my gratitude to them and my affection for them is unbounded.

But perhaps the most appreciated hosannas came from Larry Boy:

BRAVOS TO MY BELOVED ONE AND ONLY PRETTIEST AND BEST.

To which Noël replied,

WHAT A FRIGID UNGENEROUS LITTLE TELEGRAM STOP ALL I CAN SAY IS I AM NOW VERY CONCEITED INDEED AND I LOVE YOU IF POSSIBLE MORE THAN EVER STOP NOELY.

*Hay Fever* at the National. Lynn Redgrave plays Jackie Coryton in one of her first professional outings. Celia Johnson replaces Dame Edith and can presumably see Marlow clearly.

Joan Plowright (now Lady Olivier) teased the two of them that if their exchange of passionate missives had been intercepted they would both have been arrested!

•

WITH THE PLAY safely launched, Noël took another of his frequent vacations. In the summer he had been to Turkey and Italy. On returning to Rome from Istanbul, he had sent Coley one of his more memorable cables:

> I AM BACK FROM ISTANBUL WHERE I WAS KNOWN AS ENGLISH DELIGHT.

He also sampled Capri, which he enjoyed so much that he wondered what it would be like out of season. He revisited it now with Coley and Graham and soon found out. There was little delight, Italian or otherwise, to be had. "There is nowhere to go, no one to see, nowhere to eat except two crummy restaurants."

•

THE YEAR OF "Dad's Renaissance" ended on that note of anticlimax. Like so many that preceded it it had been a play with more than its share of exits.

Max Beaverbrook in June ("This long—too long—delayed occurrence requires no comment.") Much more to be mourned in August was Ian Fleming. ("It is a horrid but expected sadness.") Then in October, Cole Porter ("another figure from the merry early years"), and in December that old new "enemy friend" Edith Sitwell. ("I am sad and glad that I talked to her before I left London.")

And then, as the year turned, came the death of the ninety-year-old Winston Churchill. By hosting an all-star television tribute to the old warrior on his birthday the previous November, Noël had said his own personal farewell. In his *Diaries* he simply recorded: "Winston Churchill died this morning."

•

BACK IN JAMAICA, Noël had an unexpected visitor. The Queen Mother and Noël had been friends for many years. He had known her first as the Duchess of York, then as Queen Elizabeth, and since the accession of her daughter, Elizabeth, as Queen Elizabeth the Queen Mother. She was now to make a state visit to the island and caused a little havoc with official protocol by insisting on time being found in an already busy schedule for a visit to Noël's "mountain retreat."

The visit took place on February 24, and Noël must have put pen to paper to report to Lorn before he'd even finished waving goodbye:

The dear darling Queen Mother came up to Firefly today to lunch, in the teeth, I may say, of considerable opposition. They couldn't understand why she should want to come to such a SMALL house! The whole place was hopping with security gentlemen and vast ebony Chiefs of Police but I managed to keep them all at bay and she really had a lovely two hour feet-up. It was all a triumphant success.

There were only the Creatures (Lynnie and Alfred), Blanche [Blackwell], Coley and me and her own personal lot.

The lunch was fine—iced pea soup, Coconut Curry—or rather curry in coconuts, strawberries and Rum cream pie. The day was perfect, not a cloud.

I must say I love her more than ever. She was radiant—after a three hour drive from Spanish Town—she was sweet to everyone and insisted on having a dekko at Blue Harbour, so I drove with her through Grant's Town with all the inhabitants waving and screaming. She finally drove away—a full hour later—leaving rapture behind her.

Westminster Abbey, March 28, 1984. The service of thanksgiving for Noël's life. When Graham thanked the Queen Mother for attending, she replied simply, "I came because he was my friend."

The carry-on over the whole business has been terrific but now we can all relax and the shrubs are no longer festooned with anxious black faces.

A few days later, *The Daily Gleaner,* the local newspaper, printed a letter from one of Noël's neighbors:

Dear Sir,
We Jamaicans seldom say thanks, but this time we people of Grant's Town in St. Mary feel that we must say a big Thank You to Noël Coward for the great honour he has brought to us in having Her Majesty The Queen Mother drive through our village to lunch at his place, "Firefly". The word got around that no fuss was wanted, as it was just a private affair, so we were deprived of the opportunity of giving welcome in our way, but we were so glad of the opportunity of seeing Her Majesty on our narrow roads, so close to us. Nothing happened, and nothing could have happened as none in the area but was thrilled by the Graciousness and Beauty of Her Majesty. We felt it a great honour and were proud that Her Majesty could drive through our village and see perhaps for the first time Jamaica at first hand. There were among us some English folk on vacation from their homeland, who were as much thrilled as any of us, as they explained that there were not many people in England who had seen Her Majesty at closer range than about 50 yds. Here any of us could have touched the car as it passed.
To all of us it was a signal privilege. Indeed, we feel that we are now on the map. Thank you, Mr. Coward, and God Bless The Queen Mother.
God Save The Queen.

Joyce wrote: "I don't think I know anyone else at all who has their lav inspected for the benefit of the Queen Mum. Plumbing the heights, you might say."
Noël then received one of his most valued handwritten thank-you letters:

Clarence House
June 29th 1965

My dear Mr. Coward,
Thank you so much for the charming photographs—They bring back vividly many delightful memories of that heavenly luncheon party in Jamaica, and I am so pleased to have them.

I enjoyed it so much—Seeing your delicious house with that spectacular view, the splendid food, and those enchanting guests made it all utterly enjoyable, and a delicious moment of relaxation.

It was the nicest bit of my visit to Jamaica and I can quite see what a wonderful and inspiring place it must be to work in—I hope so much to see you when you come to England . . . Could you not come down to Sandringham for the night of Tuesday July 20th—when a famous Russian cellist (I can't spell him) is playing in one of our lovely old Churches? It would be such fun to see you, and show you dear Edwardian Sandringham.

I am, Yours very sincerely
Elizabeth R.

On March 28, 1984, the Queen Mother laid the wreath in Westminster Abbey at the service of thanksgiving for Noël's life. When Graham Payn, now the executor of the Coward estate, thanked her, she replied simply, "I came because he was my friend."

Two for the Rain. Following her visit to Jamaica, the Queen Mother ("She's a great outdoor girl") invited Noël to a picnic at Sandringham (1965). The English summer weather behaved predictably.

# CHAPTER 31
# SONGS AT TWILIGHT

## (1965–1966)

*Just a song at twilight*
*When the lights are low*
*And the flickering shadows*
*Softly come and go.*

**"LOVE'S OLD SWEET SONG"**

T HE QUEEN MOTHER'S visit clearly inspired Noël, and he immediately set to work on what would turn out to be the last of his plays
to be produced in his lifetime.

In the event, it turned out to be a trilogy. For some time he had been
mulling over the idea of writing a "farewell" play for himself and the
Lunts. Perhaps he and Alfred could play a pair of retired actors appearing

Irene Worth, Noël, and Lilli Palmer in *Come into the Garden, Maud,* a play in the
sequence *Suite in Three Keys* (1966). It would be Noël's last appearance on any stage.

Carlotta Gray (Lilli Palmer) and Hugo Latymer (Noël)
in *A Song at Twilight* (1966).

for one last performance? *Rehearsal Period? Swan Song?* But what would
there be for Lynn?

What emerged was *A Song at Twilight.* The moment he had finished the
first draft, he sent it off to Lorn posthaste:

> March 30th 1965
> Here, my darling, is my new play. I think and hope you will like it. I
> think it's quite a rouser. It is actually the first of my "Hotel Suite"
> series. I would like to play it myself with possibly Maggie Leighton
> and Irene Worth or Irene Worth and Wendy Hiller, or Maggie
> Leighton and Celia [Johnson]."

The idea for the play had been at the back of his mind for some time,
inspired by an incident recounted in *Max,* Lord David Cecil's biography of
Max Beerbohm. Beerbohm in old age was visited by a former lover, the
over-vivacious actress Constance Collier. The occasion was humorously
embarrassing in real life, but in turning it into drama, Noël admitted to
his *Diaries,* "My play is more sinister, and there is Maugham in it as well as
Max."

In Maugham's later years Noël had come to see his less likable side—
such as his failed attempt to disown his daughter, Liza, and adopt his
lover/companion Alan Searle [Gerald Haxton's successor] as his legal heir.

By the time Maugham died that same year, Noël had come to refer to him as that "scaly old crocodile."

When Emlyn Williams came to see the play, he wrote mischievously to Noël that he was *"trying* to spread the rumour that [it] was based *entirely* on J. B. Priestley, but little luck so far!"

The twist on the original anecdote that Noël provided was to make his leading character, the writer Sir Hugo Latymer, a closet homosexual. The visit of his former lover threatens to expose a secret he imagined was long since safe from discovery.

And, of course, what adds to the intrinsic interest of the play itself is that it was the one and only time that Noël dealt overtly with the subject of homosexuality. To the end of his life—even when the social climate had become more permissive—he remained firmly private in his private life, a decision that one wishes today's gay community would honor.

In April he turned to the second play, a comedy called *Come into the Garden, Maud*. Naturally he reports to Lynn and Alfred:

October 3rd, 1965

My Darlings,

This is a brief outline of my immediate plans on account of I feel you should be kept IN THE KNOW about everything that happens to your wandering boy.

I have finished my three plays, one full length one and two one hour ones, to be played on alternate nights. They all take place in one set which is a suite in the Beau Rivage Hotel, Lausanne and they only have three characters and an Italian waiter in each play.

I really do think the plays are good. Binkie is mad about them. I start rehearsing here on January 16th for two weeks. Then London for two weeks on the stage, then Dublin—February 21st for three weeks, then London March 10th with a special preview for our darling Queen Mum on the 7th.

In the meantime I have had several chins taken away in London by a brilliant plastic surgeon who, unhappily, has since died, so I cannot go back to get rid of the other six. He was a dear man and I now look an old twelve. This, of course, is a dead secret except for Ed [Bigg] whom I've already told and, of course, Louella Parsons.

The summer, to coin a phrase, has been a "fucker" and we haven't been able to see our hands before our things. (Which we were tired of doing anyway.) I have been whisking about a bit and had a peculiar week on Sam Spiegel's yacht with Burt Lancaster. I also suddenly won a thousand pounds in the Cannes Casino. Several old ladies were trampled to death I was in such a hurry to get out. I NEVER WENT BACK which proves that I have a very, very strong character as well as being beautiful as the day.

Coley sends you all sorts of love, even the love that dare not speak its name.

Love, love, love love, love
RABBIT'S BOTTOM

Although the spring and summer turned out to be a productive period, there was to be more sadness. In that same month Clemence Dane, Noël's beloved Winnie, died. A month later, Lornie was told that her cancer had returned, while in July Noël lost Irene Browne, who had played important parts in many of his shows. ("Another dear old friend gone . . . With all her grumbling and faults, she was a wonderful friend and I shall never forget her.")

It was as well he had other work to distract him. As he had written to Gladys: "I'm doing a week's work in a film with Larry [Olivier], directed by Otto Preminger [*Bunny Lake Is Missing*]. It's a terribly exciting script and a brief but effective part—an elderly drunk, queer masochist! Hurray! That's me all over, Mabel! Lovely lolly, too."

By August he had finished the third piece, *Shadows of the Evening,* and was well content with his achievement in constructing three separate plays all in the same set. (Neil Simon was not to write *Plaza Suite* until 1968.)

First there was the question of casting. Irene Worth was soon on board:

> 11 East 9th Street
> New York 10003
> May 1st 1965

Darling, clever Noël,

Fabulous—I put those plays down with such a feeling of excitement and exhilaration. I can't tell you how much I admire the 1st play—so spare, true, somehow the *first* play in spite of all the oblique plays that have been skirting the issue—so grown-up, human, vulnerable, touching, very powerful, full of pity for all men, and great dignity. You and Maggie [Margaret Leighton] will be divine in it. And I should love to play the wife.

And for the second. I think we could be very funny together. Your observation of American speech has not gone unheeded all these years—oh, Heaven preserve us—the only word you've left out is genius . . . And I already have visions of the voice and that Kitty-in-a-bad-mood snapping like a terrapin, bossing and billowing around with diamonds.

But, being an ambitious actress, Worth inevitably had a few small caveats:

I find myself greedy—in one's actor's way—asking for more and you will understand that more than anyone. Do you have plans to balance my part in the weight of the three of us? Or do you intend the season for you and Maggie, as it seems now?

It's the greatest joy to see you writing roles which ask for versatility and characterizations, such a relief from actors just playing themselves. I believe the plays will be an electric success and of course no one could be more brilliant than you and Maggie. I think she's the most dazzling actress there is today. I couldn't admire her more. Or you. I shall never forget you as King Magnus. How I wish I'd seen you with Gertie and the Lunts.

Noël, dear, I am deeply touched by your asking me to be in them. I know how high your standards are and therefore it gives me a nice feeling of self-respect for I'm always limping about thinking I'm no good. Thank you from my heart.

All admiration and love,
IRENE

Margaret Leighton, however, dithered interminably. Noël admired her talent and had enjoyed working with her in *The Astonished Heart.* She had also been a perfect foil to his King Magnus in *The Apple Cart,* as well as several audio recordings. Nonetheless, he shared the irritated affection many of her colleagues felt for her—a condition that varied by degree according to whom she happened to be married to at the time. At this point she was Mrs. Michael Wilding.

Mutual friend Terence Rattigan—even then suffering from the cancer that would finally take him off—had painted a typical picture sometime before:

> 29 Eaton Square
> London S.W.1.
> July 20th 1963

Dearest Noël.

If doctors allow I hope to get to NY for early November, so I shall have a chance to see *The Prince* [*The Girl Who Came to Supper*] before your opening—if you think I can be of any help—and, of course, at the opening itself—to which I shall ask Loopy Leighton, if she's available and not in some bin somewhere.

At the moment she is staying *chez moi* in Ischia and sounding slightly less loopy than when I saw her off at Victoria Station a week ago. (This incident, in itself, gave me a severe relapse.) She had, I think I'm not exaggerating, 36 pieces of luggage with her—she's not allowed tax-wise to come back here for a time—and we arrived five minutes before the Night Ferry was supposed to go. As I wasn't allowed past the barrier, she insisted on having a farewell drink, which *had* to be champagne, and there *is no bar* at Victoria where you can get champagne, but Victoria is a *big* station and, at one minute past take-off time, she was still looking for one, and a hundred frantic officials were looking for her—a fairly conspicuous sight, I grant, but moving at some speed through the crowd and uttering loud cries of "*Fuck* the lot of them. *Cunts.* That's what they are. All *cunts!*" I was staggering, grey-faced, I've no doubt, fifty yards behind her. Well, we didn't get our champagne, but she got her train—just—and I went to bed for five days. (That was our beloved Mag's departure from our shores.)

She's going to do Enid Bagnold's new play [*The Chinese Prime Minister*] in New York this winter, playing a lady of seventy (you can't stop her, can you—I certainly can't—from playing old ladies when she *should* be playing beautiful sex-boxes, while she still can). Anyway, it's a nice play—better than *Chalk Garden,* and Enid Bagnold is my new lover.

As for me, I'm fairly queer, I grant, but have hopes that I'm not, after all, *quite* as queer as Dr. Bodly Scott (better known as Dr. Bodkin Adams) thinks I am. Horace Evans feels fairly sure I'm not, anyway, and I have put on half a stone since May by dint of drinking some nauseating baby food, and a Swiss health drink called Rivella— or is that what you wear? . . .

Which reminds me—I can't think why—*The Daily Mail* has a competition on to find the modern equivalent of "Anyone for tennis?" I have it—but won't, I promise you, submit it. It's "Anyone for a swim at Cliveden?" [The stately home that was the setting for the Profumo scandal.]

Noël reported to Joyce on the state of play:

> Les Avants
> Sur Montreux
> SOUS LE TEMPS
> Sept. 3rd 1965

I take my electric typewriter in hand to write to my poor darling Doycie who is flogging her way through those ill-favoured provincial towns that we know so well. This will reach you in Birmingham which, you may or may not know, was the birthplace of Miss Margaret Leighton who has lately been much in my mind having made a Royal Charlie of herself. She has frigged about for four months and we've all been beating our breasts wondering whether or not Michael Wilding were or was or could or couldn't come to England. It had actually occurred to me a long time ago that I didn't want that silly mumbling ass anywhere near me, and if it is so necessary for him to be near Maggie, she had better stay out in that sub-acqueous aquarium where she can cook him unsavoury little supper dishes and drag him whimpering and belching to the nightly grind.

The "comble" 'ow you say? came when the redoubtable Hugh French (who was *excellent* as the small waiter in *Bittersweet* [*sic*]) sent Binkie a cable graciously agreeing that Michael should come to England but that Maggie couldn't commit herself as she hadn't read and approved the third play! Meanwhile, of course, we had offered the whole proposition to darling Lilli Palmer who accepted immediately, turning down two films in order to do so. I have written to the besotted Maggie explaining, fairly succinctly, the whole situation and it makes me veree veree happee to think of her and Mumbleguts crouching together over their synthetic Hollywood hearth, reading it aloud to each other. The new play [*Shadows*] really is the best of the three I think. Ask Binkie to let you read it, if he has not already done so. It's a tear jerker but not too much so, I hope. Oh dear, Oh dear, Oh dear what a silly silly girl is Miss Margaret Leighton. Actually, I am very relieved. Lilli is very intelligent, untiresome and a bloody good actress, whereas poor Maggie has, I fear, already become tainted by those awful Hollywood values and probably wouldn't be nearly so nice to work with as she used to be.

Les Avants
September 1, 1965

Dearest Maggie,

Believe me when I say that writing this letter to you is a good deal more difficult than writing any play, but it has to be done, and so here goes. Perhaps if I explain *my* point of view it may clarify things a little, for up to now it seems that you have been occupied only with your own. I am the first to understand and sympathize with your situation. I know, as an old friend, that you have been searching for personal happiness for many years and that, having at long last found it, it is natural that you should not wish it to be disturbed by even a limited season. This to me is perfectly fair and comprehensible, if perhaps a trifle exaggerated. What, however, is neither fair nor comprehensible is that you should only agree to appear in my plays if Michael is permitted to come to England with you. This surely is a personal problem between you and Michael and Hugh French? It certainly has nothing whatsoever to do with Binkie, Glen [Byam Shaw, who was the original choice to direct] or me. Personally I am very fond of Michael and would be enchanted to see him at any time, but *not* as a contractual obligation.

Over four months ago I told you of this project, which is of immense importance to me, and sent you *A Song At Twilight* and *Come Into the Garden, Maud.* You agreed to do them with me, providing certain complications were straightened out. So far so good. Now, after four months of letters, cables and telephone calls, the complications have not been straightened out. Hugh French cables to Binkie graciously permitting Michael to come to London but saying that you will not be able to commit yourself without reading and approving the *fourth* play. He adds that negotiations can now begin and says something about "adjustments" being made. I cannot quote the cable accurately as when I read the copy Binkie sent me I was so irritated that I tore it up. I have no idea what "adjustments" he had in mind and whether you or Michael or he were going to suggest them. All I do know is that I most strongly resent being treated as though I were a hack writer of movie scripts and that I consider that cable both in tone and content to be bloody impertinent. I also consider that your refusal to commit yourself to doing an unwritten one-act play by me, both pompous and silly. None of the three plays was intended to be a star vehicle for you, Irene Worth or me. They were intended to be three good plays for three first-rate actors to play to the best of their ability.

When you said in your letter that I had, in the re-written version of *A Song At Twilight* improved Hildi's part at the expense of Carlotta's (which was totally inaccurate, as I had not touched the end of the play) I knew, with a sinking heart, that our professional values were sadly at variance. If you had troubled to read the script more intelligently and more impartially, you might have noticed that my own part, out of the three, is the least sympathetic and hardest to play. In fact, dear Maggie, having with admiration and affection asked you to share this fairly exciting theatrical adventure with me, I am both offended and disappointed that your ultimate, possible acceptance should depend on such eccentric and irrelevant conditions. After discussing the situation exhaustively with Glen and Binkie, we all three decided that, all things considered, we should really be better off without you. Whereupon we decided to approach

Lilli Palmer. This may sound over-blunt, rude and unkind, but it is the truth. If you choose to place your domestic felicity above your career as an actress, you obviously have a perfect right to do so and, although as a theatre man I strongly disapprove of such a course, as a human being I cannot but sympathize with it, but you really cannot successfully serve two masters, your heart and your profession, and as, for the time being, it is the latter that I am concerned with, I have no intention of embarking on a difficult job with anyone who is liable to give it second place. Nor can I, with three parts to learn, rehearse and play, allow myself to be remotely concerned with any-one's personal emotions over and above the immediate business we are occupied with.

You have had over four months to make up your mind. It is not yet made up. Neither Binkie, Glen nor I have any more time to waste. Everything has to be finally fixed now before I go off on my travels. Both Irene Worth and Lilli Palmer accepted the offer enthu-siastically and at once without even knowing what the third play was to be about. Happily, as things have turned out, their confidence in me was not misplaced for the third (not the *fourth*) play is now fin-ished and is considered by all concerned to be the best of the three. I know this looks as though it were intended to be a nasty dig, and perhaps, in a way, it is. I shall always love you, whether you like it or not, although, at the moment my love is slightly tarnished by your lack of consideration of me as a friend and your lack of faith in me as a playwright.

We shall have to forgive and forget, shan't we?

XXXXX

Noël.

The XXXXX are kisses. If unacceptable they can be regarded as snarls.

The lady apologized profusely and returned xxxxx's. ("Yours were received most gratefully.")

•

IN EARLY OCTOBER Noël set off on his "travels," and for once he *was* traveling alone. His itinerary was to take him to Cairo, then Bombay, then on to the Seychelles for a month, where he intended to see whether this might be a suitable alternative to Jamaica. From there he would travel to Mombasa and then home, ready to start rehearsals for *Suite in Three Keys*.

As always, the journey was well documented to his loved ones, although its outcome was not the usual happy ending:

To Coley:

Taj Mahal Hotel
Bombay
October 10th 1965

I arrived here at 8:30 (Bombay time)—4.30 ours. I had full VIP treatment, on account of the Big Shot of the line being on board. He is a little like a greenish Fritzi Massary to look at, although a good deal younger. He is Unmarried and lives with a Boxer (a doggie, not a pugilist). Anyway, he drives me in style to the hotel in a Mercedes and is inviting me to meet some of his young friends! Oi! Oi! I was whisked through the Customs by a tan-coloured Angel who is coming to have a drink this evening with his "friend". I have BAD news to impart, however, for the drink will have to be Coca-Cola for this is a DRY state! I have procured a permit to buy ONE bottle of Scotch to last me the week! If only I'd been warned, I could have brought a couple. It's unobtainable today being Sunday! The Injuns are very very silly and Inja is very very dirty but, oh the bliss of being really hot.

There is an Air India Angel at Cairo called Ali Aga who pressed my hand, gave me a drink and said regretfully that he was married! Ask for him when you arrive . . . He's rather large but very sweet. The weather will be lovely for you but NOT really hot, just nice, so bring woolies. This, of course, is steaming hot and thank God I brought that quinine. I was racked with cramp immediately. It isn't the heat, you know, it's the H[umidity]! [In fact, it was the beginning of amoebic dysentery.] . . .

Mr. Bobby Kooka (The Big Fritzi Shot) is procuring a chiropodist AND a masseur who apparently goes in for weight lifting. Something tells me I've fallen on my back.

India, having achieved its independence and thrown out the hateful British, is already showing signs of utter chaos and decay. Nothing QUITE works, except the air-conditioning, which was like a pride of lions and freezes my balls off. I have silenced it. I also THINK I am going to be glad I brought the crab powder but time will tell.

It is all violently colourful but almost inconceivably filthy. Oh, those Dhoties! My suite is fairly clean but the pillows small and curious. Actually, there is an all-pervading smell everywhere which is Mother Injun . . . I shall go out to dine later on—choked to the throat with Entero-Vioform and see which way the cookies crumble.

. . . Oh dear. I DO feel a long way away, which is quite natural because I AM.

Taj Mahal Hotel
Bombay
October 15th

This certainly was a week this was. I can't wait to give you a blow by blow account. Owing to my friend, Mr. Kouka, I have been the belle of Indian *Café au Lait* Society. I also had to give a press conference, which was absolute hell and hilariously funny. They really are dreadful and as for the glamorous city, it's unbelievable. They never, having achieved independence, DREAM of cleaning the garbage out of the roads, which is lovely for the sacred cows but makes driving about a bit grungy. The heat really is intense, worse than Bangkok and the Americans as noisy as ever, only mercifully not many of them.

The snorkel mask has just arrived this afternoon, so I have sent a lot of Peter Sellers characters to get it out of Customs. I hope they succeed because I leave at eleven tomorrow morning.

There are a lot of Amateur Little Theatre movements going on. I am asked ghastly questions in high pitched voices. I met the Captain of my ship who is a dear called Bruce (Call me Spider!) The more I hear about the Seychelles the more lovely they sound.

This is a dull letter but I just wanted to let you know all was well. I THINK. Entirely owing to Entero-Vioform. I had a dreadful lunch with Mrs. David Lean, who is very morose on account of David himself being sick to death of her. She is very artistic, which perhaps explains it.

To Lorn:

Hotel des Seychelles
October 24th

The food is indescribable, God knows. I have encountered some vile cooking in my travels but nothing to touch this. I wait with bated breath for each nauseating little dish to be set before me. Curiously enough, in spite of all this, I am enjoying myself enormously . . . there are hours and hours of lovely peace which I am utilizing by reading *Martin Chuzzlewit* and learning *A Song At Twilight*. Oh darling, Mr. Dickens *is* a comfort, isn't he? Pecksniff and those ghastly daughters!

To Joyce:

Hotel des Seychelles
October 26th

Darling Doycie,

Here I am at last in The Seychelles and I must admit they are lovely islands. On the primitive side as far as creature comforts are concerned but full of lovely eccentrics and a mixed breed of natives of all shades who converse in high voices like little birds, in a Créole *patois* which I don't *believe* they understand. Unfortunately, I have struck the tail end of a cyclone so there is a fearful wind and deluges of rain. However, this will soon pass and I shall be able to fly to the lagoons. It is, of course, blissfully warm. My week in Bombay was hilarious. To add to the general fun there was a sort of black-out on account of the war with Pakistan . . . This is really the most shut-off place in the world, no newspapers, no nothing, except some occasional B.B.C. News scratching away with a lot of static.

I am going to have a dekko at some of the other islands when the weather clears. I am stuck here for a month anyhow, whether I like it or not. I have a private bungalow to *moi-même* which I share with some lizards and an occasional flying fox. The food is frankly a fucker but I have made some suggestions and things are looking up a little . . . I must now go and have a cold shower on account of there isn't a hot one.

Bessie—Bessie—Bessie

To Coley:

Hotel des Seychelles
October 26th

It is lucky I am here for five weeks because with the exception of one day, there has been a perpetual deluge and a sixty mile an hour gale. It is VERY reminiscent of Jamaica in a really bad Norther. When it clears up I am going to explore. There ARE several islands for sale. Two of them sound ideal but I'm not jumping at anything. The whole set-up is incredibly primitive and the shopping in Victoria unbelievable. If we were ever bonkers enough to embark on this wild cat enterprise, we should HAVE to get everything from the mainland, which is Mombasa, a thousand miles away—three days by ship. There is, however, one Amphibious—(aren't we all?) American plane which takes in mail once a week. The people are fascinating. The island is 99 percent Catholic and a really very funny lady Doctor has arrived, sent by the International Parent Planning Federation in London, armed with crates of contraceptives. She is a girl with a great sense of humour and looks a bit like Peggy Wood laced with Hopie [Williams]. I have taken to her. She's very funny, very bright and agreeably bawdy and, as you can imagine, her clashes with the Governor AND the clergy have been jolly enjoyable. My sharp little violet eyes see a story in this somewhere.

If we ever did come here, it would mean starting from scratch.

The water situation is all right but the natives are even more lackadaisical than the Jamaicans. Unlike Jamaica, you can get masses of fish. Like Jamaica, they are unable to cook it. Yesterday I bought an electric torch and the Indian gentleman who sold it to me looked hurt when I pointed out that it didn't work. "That," he said, "is because it has no battery." "Put one in, then," I replied. "That I cannot do, because we *have* none!" I found one incidentally at the next door shop. All this is very amusing and picturesque but I feel it MIGHT get us down after a bit.

However, I shall go and look at the island. Getting here is not so difficult if you time it right. Three hours to Cairo—four to Nairobi—one to Mombasa and three days at sea. It might—it might—it MIGHT be a good idea for *l'Avenir.*

Of course, what I am really enjoying are the people. There is a great deal of sitting round the hour before lunch and dinner and signing chits and "This round is on us," etc. . . .

Do you think you would like a shark's jaw for a Christmas present? They are comparatively inexpensive and very frightening indeed. It MIGHT just keep people out of your bedroom if you bury it at the door.

On Friday, if the weather is clearer, I am sailing to Praslin—two hours—and spending three nights in a hotel called "Pegal" on account of the proprietor and his wife being called Albert and Peggy. You do see, don't you, how the cookies crumble?

Love—love—love<br>MASTER

I love Entero-Vioform like a mother

To Coley:

November 5th

The idea of a Seychelles island is fading fairly rapidly from my mind. It is TOO inaccessible, really and very tatty indeed and if we contemplated building or doing up a house, the frustrations would drive us mad. NOTHING can be bought here, not even tin tacks. The sea between the islands is VERY rough and the boat scruffy to the point of nightmare. I spent three days in Praslin and came back in a hospital ship with little room to sit and NONE to lie down. The sea was violent. Everyone was vomiting their hearts out and a lady who was retching into an enamel basin started her labour pains as we left port. As the journey took four and a half hours, you can readily understand that the noise was considerable. I, who had lashed a deck chair, which

I had borrowed from the hotel, to the rail, tried, not very successfully, to read *Persuasion*.

A small Peter Sellers Indian Doctor officiated at the accouchement. Fortunately, we got the poor beast ashore before the poor little mite actually made his entrance, but all this in a heavy sea was a bit upsetting.

My camera packed up on me at a crucial moment and I was in despair but I kicked it and it has worked perfectly ever since. I had some Yorkshire pudding the other day. Mercy!

I have seen Praslin, La Digne and Silhouette—they are all lovely with glorious beaches but not really a patch on the Pacific. The inhabitants of all of them are as barmy as makes no matter. Life comes under the tactful heading of "Primitive." Returning to this dump was like coming back from the Taft in New Haven to the Hotel de Paris in Monte Carlo.

> Government House Seychelles
> November 8th

This is really for all loved ones, as I haven't the strength to write individual letters. I've been attacked by some sort of bug—they haven't discovered which sort yet. I was wheeled out of Government House midday Sunday and have been in this DEAR little hospital ever since.

Will now acquaint you with a decision that was in my mind long before I was stricken and that decision is that no bribe, no threat, no power human or divine will induce me anywhere near the Seychelles again. All right, all right, so the beaches are lovely, so the vegetation is luxuriant. Let them be. The standard of living is lower than a snake's arse. And the social life! Ah, Mama Mia! Everybody loathes everyone else and everyone seems to loathe the poor dear Oxfords [Lord Oxford and Asquith was the governor of the islands, known as "Ox and Ass"] who swim through their days being gracious and kindly and thinking seriously about *The Times* crossword. The other islands are very very beautiful and primitive to the point of lunacy . . . The architecture is mainly decaying wood and corrugated tin roofs. The Seychelles Club is full of atmosphere. It is also inhabited by some of the largest rats I have ever seen. Fortunately, having been laid low, I now have an excuse to get out of many of the gay entertainments arranged for me. I'm feeling weakened anyhow but perfectly all right apart from the damned squitters. I am actually surprised that I lasted for so long as I did . . .

This hospital, of course, is the last ditch. I have a terrible tin bed pan set in a worm-eaten commode. The proper loo and the showers are miles away. The noise all night and all day is deafening. There is NO privacy and in my ward at this minute a white clad nun is walking up and down apparently learning her script. Everyone has been so kind, so kind, poor things! I just thought I'd let you know these few facts of life. I have collected so many characters and ideas for short stories that I ought to be well supplied for years to come.

> Government House
> November [?]

My sojourn in the hospital was grim. It will take too long to describe it in a letter but if you take the Port Maria hospital, subtract and divide by four and then stuff it up an elephant's arse, it will give you a rough idea. It was finally discovered that I was suffering from "Round" worm which I had acquired from the water at Government House, which is apparently notorious. I've been feeling stringy all the week, added to which it has poured solidly for seven days. However, the Oxfords have been really sweet. I have stayed in my bungalow—NOT waterproof—and had special foods and now the sun has come out! ACTUALLY I FEEL FINE. Apart from the eternal "Trots" the rest did me good. It is a VERY curious place and the people!

I don't suppose that in all my travels I have endured quite so much sheer physical discomfort but somehow I haven't minded. The very idea of having a comfortable bed, hot water, clear light to read by seems like a mirage. When I get back to Les Avants, I shall wander about touching everything like [Chekhov's] Madame Ranevski [Ranevskaya].

I was wrong about the sun—it's just gone in again and rain has returned. Everything is soggy and the day before yesterday I happened to look at my "charcoal" suit and it looked as if it was covered with mother of pearl! This has now been fixed.

I have not yet been able to use my snorkel because with all the rain the sea is muddy and when the sea is muddy, the sharks come in and there are a GREAT many sharks in the Indian Ocean.

I am INFURIATED by those bloody little Beatles going to Buckingham Palace and all those "Teenagers" knocking policeman's hats off and Paul Macartney [McCartney] saying the Queen was just a "Mum". I DO know what the younger generation is coming to *non mi piace* at all, at all.

He was amused when he heard Princess Margaret quoted as saying that she presumed the Lads from Liverpool thought M.B.E. stood for "Mr. Brian Epstein," their manager.

Government House
November 21st

Oh Coley,

I will withhold from you no longer the gruesome fact that this holi-day has been a disaster. I have been horribly ill again for the last week and I have a dreadful suspicion that it MAY be Hepatitis. There is a lot of it about in these bloody islands. I am being inspected right and left and I'm beginning to feel a little better but very far from well. I sail on Thursday for Mombasa, unless I can get on to the American sea plane which goes on Wednesdays . . . I shall forego the African part of the trip and fly straight back to Geneva. Anyhow, I will wire you from Mombasa.

When I came out of hospital last week there was a steady deluge for ten days without letting up. These last few days have been lovely but too late to be of any good to me. I haven't even got enough energy to walk into the sea. Everybody is very kind and one or other of the Oxfords come and visit me every day. The food remains inde-scribable so I stick to poached eggs and corn flakes and tea.

I HATE the Seychelles and everything to do with them. Every-thing is tatty and dirty and run to seed. I share my ghastly bungalow with a rat the size of a small collie and several centipedes. I haven't quite recovered my sense of humour but there have been some black moments! I'm counting the days.

Oh, oh, oh, oh!

MASTER

It was a gaunt, emaciated Noël Coley found at Geneva airport, "more dead than alive." Nor was he over the illness, which necessitated further treatment and hospitalization in Lausanne in the first three months of 1966.

•

IRENE AND LILLI PALMER spent time with Noël in Les Avants in January discussing the plays, but the London opening had to be put off until April. When rehearsals began in March, he found himself in a posi-tion he had always despised in those who had worked for him over the years—he had trouble remembering the lines he himself had written and frequently had to be prompted by his leading ladies.

Nonetheless, when they eventually did open at the Queen's Theatre on April 14 with *A Song at Twilight,* and on the twenty-fourth with *Maud* and *Shadows of the Evening,* the reception they received was ecstatic. If this was to be Noël's last theatrical hurrah, it was a satisfyingly loud one.

John Mills wrote:

The Wick
Richmond Hill
Surrey
April 15th 1966

Your performance was quite one of the best things you have ever done (excluding perhaps Stanhope!). It was bang up to date apart from anything else, and at the next R.A.D.A. [Royal Academy of Dramatic Art] meeting I shall suggest sending the academy along *en masse* to mark, learn, and inwardly digest the way to play comedy. I don't know any actor alive today who could get laughs with, apparently, so little effort. You never compromised or went out after our sympathy for one moment.

And from Irene Worth:

April 25th 1966

Darling Noël,

There is a line in *Shadows* which has struck me so deeply and meant so much to me that I must thank you—from my heart—for such a profound and precious lesson which I shall never forget—"Life—our most important responsibility."

I do thank you with a full heart for everything, everything—I'm grateful and rejoice in your fantastic talents and sweetness and for giving me the precious experience of working with you—and to thank you for all you've done for me.

With admiration and love—
IRENE

Another anonymous correspondent wrote a perceptive critique of Noël's own performance:

He is quite wonderful and actually manages to *look* like Maugham! The gray, shrunken face, the thin, curved-down mouth, moustache and hair—and I don't think it is entirely makeup. He has submerged his own personality into the bitter, trembling, neurotic old wreck of a man and never attempts to play for sympathy. Only occasionally he uses a touch of Coward voice or mannerism to point a laugh, always brilliantly placed to relieve a moment of tension. I was most impressed by it because I have nearly always seen him play himself. Not that I'm silly enough to under-rate the technical skill in "playing himself", but it's fascinating to see him being so different; he's not only unlovable but *unlikeable,* which can't be easy for anyone with his natural charm.

His natural charm was stretched by the experience of working with Lilli Palmer, and he wrote to an unnamed friend: "The wonder is that I survived her *Song At Twilight*. What a difficult and prickly Kraut she can be. Only Claudette and Beattie were more injurious to my wayward and infinitely pathetic diverticulum."

When the tumult had ceased and the "captains and kings" had departed, Noël recognized just how much it had all taken out of him. He reluctantly decided he would not take the plays to Broadway after all.

In fact, they would not be performed there in his lifetime. It was 1974 before Jessica Tandy, Hume Cronyn, and Anne Baxter played *Noël Coward in Two Keys* (*Twilight* and *Maud*) at the Ethel Barrymore Theatre—home to *Design for Living* forty years earlier.

"One never says 'I.' " Cartoon by Gerald Hoffnung.

# CHAPTER 32
# SHADOW OF EVENING
### (1967–1973)

I would prefer Fate to allow me to go to sleep when it's my proper bedtime. I never have been one for staying up too late.

**DIARIES (1967)**

Yesterday I went to the Garrick Club where all the flags were, symbolically, at half-mast. I met a mutual acquaintance . . . In a sort of idiotic attempt not to be depressing I said—"I wonder where Noël's dining tonight and with whom—St. Joan?" To which he instantly replied—"No . . . *Ivor,* of course. He's been there quite a time, and he's sure to know all the best joints."

I know Noël would have liked that.

**BEVERLEY NICHOLS (1973)**

"*Sir* Noëlie, if you don't mind!" The newly ennobled Noël leaves the Palace with Gladys and Joyce, February 3, 1970.

AS 1967 BEGAN, Noël, with the recollection of his own failure of memory so recent, was increasingly aware that "Time's wingèd chariot is beginning to goose me."

It was another year when the Grim Reaper decided to work overtime. In June Dorothy Parker was granted the oblivion she claimed to have long sought, without any further effort on her part. "Terrible about Dorothy Parker. Of course, hers was the living death of any non-producing artist. She was a uniquely talented wit and lived so unwisely."

In the same month Spencer Tracy died. Noël immediately cabled to Katharine Hepburn, Tracy's longtime lover:

DARLING KATE

YOUR PERFORMANCE IN GUESS WHO'S COMING TO DINNER WAS
IMPECCABLE AND QUITE LOVELY STOP HOW WONDERFUL THAT
DEAR SPENCE'S LAST PERFORMANCE SHOULD BE ONE OF THE
FINEST HE HAS EVER GIVEN WHICH IS SAYING A GREAT DEAL
STOP MY FOND LOVE TO YOU.

NOËL

To which she replied: "What a wonderful, lovely looking, sensitive creature I've spent so much of my life with. I know that I am lucky—he kept me hopping and I never had time to think about myself. So—on again alone . . ."

A month later Vivien Leigh made her own exit. Noël to Larry: "She often reminded me of a Bird of Paradise. Now perhaps she can find her own."

Back in February Noël had turned his short story "Star Quality" into a three-act play. He sent it from Jamaica to Lorn:

I think it's pretty funny, whether it's too Pro-y for the great public remains to be seen. This is a DEAD, DEAD secret . . . As usual it needs a big star to play it. Obviously, I can only think of Maggie Leighton, who can't do it. I have a feeling Irene Worth might have a successful bash at it. She isn't quite a star but she's a bloody good actress . . . I wish one didn't always yearn for Gertie!

He had also written the first act of a new comedy, *Age Cannot Wither,* a sequel of a kind to *Fallen Angels* in which three sixty-ish ladies, who have been girls together since school days, meet every year to compare notes over a drink or two. It was looking distinctly promising, but the events that came so close upon one another distracted him. ("I've been too agitated by everything!") *Age Cannot Wither* was never finished, and *Star Quality* remained unproduced in his lifetime.

There was worse to come. On November 21 Lornie lost her long battle with cancer. Noël shared his grief with Joyce:

> Of course I'd known it was coming—for ages, really—but I just couldn't bear to accept it. When Gertie left us, the shock was cruel and immediate but one had to face it in public. With Mum it was one of those inevitable things one has to adjust to but with Lornie it somehow wasn't fair. It wasn't her *time*!
>
> For whatever time is left to me I shall always remember the jokes, the finger wagging, that Scots commonsense that I frequently needed but usually didn't want to hear, since she was invariably right. But most of all, I shall remember the love she brought and the dignity. She was very very special and I still can't believe when that phone rings that I shan't hear—"Now then, my darling Master, you *really* must . . ."

*Boom* (1968). Noël as the Witch of Capri, with Elizabeth Taylor as Flora Goforth, in Joseph Losey's film of the Tennessee Williams play *The Milk Train Doesn't Stop Here Anymore.*

After playing opposite Noël in *The Italian Job,*
Michael Caine claimed, "It's a bit like playing with God, actually."

WITH *SUITE* Noels's professional career reached its peak. There was nothing more he felt the need to prove, and even if there had been, his steadily deteriorating health would have prevented any serious commitment.

He appeared in Richard Rodgers's TV musical version of *Androcles and the Lion* and acted in two more films—in the 1967 *Boom,* with Elizabeth Taylor, and with Michael Caine in the 1968 *The Italian Job.* By now it would not have mattered what part he played. The legend was set and the man appreciated. He was—Noël Coward. When the film was over, Caine said he felt that playing with Noël "was a bit like playing with God." Noël did not choose to argue the point.

Then came, with delayed inevitability, *Star,* a proposed film in which "Noël Coward" was to be depicted. Gertie was to be played by Julie Andrews.

Julie . . . is about as much like Gertie as I am Edna Ferber's twin, but what can one do? I liked her athletic, careening, whilom nun in *The Sound of Music.* She is a bright, talented actress and quite attractive since she dealt with her monstrous English over-bite. It will be interesting—more interesting, I hope, than dear Gertie's actual life.

Bea Lillie said firmly that she intended to play herself in the film! The character was written out of the script.

•

LATER THAT YEAR Noël took Coley and Graham to see the South
Seas—Samolo Revisited. He could not resist writing to Gladys: "Well,
here we are in Bora-Bora. Every time I come here [he had been there in
1962], I'm dying to say that it's a bore-a bore-a but no such luck. It
remains, in fact, breathtakingly beautiful."

On the trip he wrote a verse about it to encapsulate its charm:

> *The wild lagoon in which the island lies*
> *Changes its colours with the changing skies*
> *And, lovely beyond belief,*
> *The dazzling surf upon the outer reef*
> *Murmurs its lonely, timeless lullaby*
> *Warning the heart perhaps that life is brief*
> *Measured against the sea's eternity.*

By the time the holiday was over the adventure had virtually turned
into a round-the-world trip. It would be the last.

Now came his last professional outing in *The Italian Job.* Noël played
Mr. Bridger, a criminal mastermind who organizes the "job" from the
comfort of his prison cell, which he has decorated with photographs
of the royal family. Our last glimpse is of Mr. Bridger graciously accepting
the plaudits of his fellow inmates for the successful completion of his latest coup. All in all, the role of a royalist master was a fitting symbol for the
man.

•

FOR SOME TIME NOW Noël had been battling health problems, and
he was not, he admitted, the world's best patient. Apart from the impair-
ment of his short-term memory, which he found more humiliating than
anything else, he began to suffer increasingly from arteriosclerosis, particularly in his right leg. He complained to Gladys—and anyone else who
would listen—about the regimen he had been set by his doctors.

> Can you believe it? The bloody doctors tell me I've got to pound up
> and down the road to the village every day, wet or fine, to keep the
> circulation whizzing around. That it should come to this—*walking*!
> Every morning I peer out of the window with the greatest suspicion
> to greet what I hope will *not* be a bright new day. A good downpour
> is now my idea of a good time to be had by me—"I can't possibly go
> out in *that*," I say to myself, and light up the consoling weed. Yes, I
> know it may shorten my life by a year or two but who's counting any
> more? Gather ye rosebuds—or a ciggie—while ye may is my motto

these days. And you may quote me. Of course, I suppose I *could* make very old bones indeed—look at Mum—but I'm not at all sure I want that. I've never wanted to be the last to leave any party. In fact, I was saying to Coley only the other day—"I would prefer Fate to let me go to sleep when it's my proper bedtime and not let me stay up too late." Rather poetic, I thought.

       Yours,
       LAZARUS

As it turned out, there were to be an inordinate number of late nights in the year ahead, as individuals and institutions on both sides of the Atlantic prepared to celebrate his forthcoming seventieth birthday. As the day approached, the events came so thick and fast that Noël suggested it be called Holy Week.

When it was all behind him and he was back in the safe haven of Les Avants, he could write to Joyce:

Well, dear heart,
As Cole [as in Porter] might have said—and to the best of my knowledge actually *did*—"What a swell party that was!" I could say that this beautiful heart-shaped, if slightly time-worn face, is now creased in a perpetual smile of suitably modest gratitude but that would be me being afraid to show what I *really* feel.

*Diaries:* "I sat next to the Queen Mother at lunch.
She was as dear as ever. The weather behaved with
royal consideration and it was all enchantment."
(In the background, Elizabeth Taylor and Richard Burton.)

After the Tony Awards, April 1970. Lauren Bacall, Geoffrey
Johnson, Noël, Alfred, and Cary Grant celebrate.

I have been genuinely moved by so many of the things that have
happened and been said about me—simply because nobody *needed* to
say any of them. You suddenly realize that a lot of the petty irrita-
tions of the past are just that—petty and past . . .

The moment that came closest to undoing him emotionally was the
birthday lunch given in his honor by the queen. Would he consider
accepting a knighthood, if offered? she asked. For once there was no ready
Coward riposte, and his name was duly gazetted in the 1970 New Year's
Honours List. On February 3 came the investiture and, to the accompani-
ment of a military band appropriately playing "A Life on the Ocean
Wave," Sir Noël rose on painful knee with the recognition from his country he had deserved thirty years earlier.

There was an audible sigh of relief from the ranks of the other theatrical
knights, and Sir Alec Guinness spoke for all of them when he said, "We
have been like a row of teeth with the front tooth missing. Now we can
smile again."

•

AND THAT, in effect, was the end of the Noël Coward Show. There were
no more plays, no more songs; he even stopped writing his journal. It was
as though he felt that he had delivered his curtain speech and he could now
take as many bows as the applause would allow.

The applause never stopped. He received an honorary Tony Award; he
appeared as a celebrity guest on TV talk shows. There were two anthology

Noël at Firefly, standing on the spot where
he was buried, overlooking the Spanish Main.

revues—*Cowardy Custard* in London and *Oh, Coward!* in New York—
which played to capacity for months.

It was at a gala performance of the latter that he made his last public
appearance, on January 14, 1973, with Marlene on his arm. The next day
he, Coley, and Graham left for the haven of Jamaica. There in the calm
early morning of Monday, March 26, he died peacefully.

His last words to them the previous evening had been, "Good night, my
darlings, I'll see you tomorrow."

# PERMISSIONS AND ACKNOWLEDGMENTS

I am grateful to the following individuals and organizations for permission to quote from letters to Noël. Names in parentheses indicate the executors of an estate or the copyright owners.

Edward Albee; Lauren Bacall; Enid Bagnold (Dominick Jones); Lionel Bart; Cecil Beaton (Hugo Vickers); Binkie Beaumont; (Laurence Harbottle, Harbottle & Lewis); Joyce Carey (Combined Theatrical Charities); Sir Charles B. Cochran (Laurence Harbottle, Harbottle & Lewis); Sir Winston Churchill (Anthea Morton Saner—Curtis Brown); Duff Cooper (John Julius Norwich); "Clemence Dane"/Winifred Ashton (I. R. Gibbons); Basil Dean (Martin Dean); Marlene Dietrich (Maria and Peter Riva); Robert Donat (John Donat); Dame Daphne du Maurier (Kits Browning); Mary Ellis (Josh Liveright); (Sir) Douglas Fairbanks, Jr. (Vera Fairbanks); Edna Ferber (Julie Gilbert); Ian Fleming (Kate Grimond—with permission from the Ian Fleming Will Trustees); Pamela Frankau (Timothy d'Arch Smith); Greta Garbo (Gray Horan and courtesy Harriet Brown, Inc., and the Estate of Greta Garbo); Sir John Gielgud (Ian Bradshaw on behalf of the Sir John Gielgud Charitable Trust); Graham Greene (Francis Greene); Tammy Grimes; Sir Alec Guinness (Christopher Sinclair-Stevenson); Norman Hartnell (Tim Matlin at the Norman Hartnell Estate); Sir Anthony Havelock-Allan (Lady Sara Havelock-Allan); Fanny Holtzmann (Edward Berkman and the American Jewish Archives, Cincinnati, Ohio); Marina, Duchess of Kent (HRH the Duke of Kent); Harry Kurnitz; Gertrude Lawrence (the late Pamela Clatworthy); T. E. Lawrence (Seven Pillars of Wisdom Trust); Lorn Loraine (Jane Cooper); Alfred Lunt and Lynn Fontanne (Sean Malone and the Ten Chimneys Foundation); Hugh Martin; Mary Martin (Larry Hagman); W. Somerset Maugham (Julian Hope and A. P. Watt Ltd. on behalf of The Royal Literary Fund); the late Sir John Mills; Nancy Mitford (the Duchess of Devonshire); Lord Louis Mountbatten (Lord Brabourne); Beverley Nichols (Janet Glass Agency); David Niven (David Niven Jr. and Jamie Niven); Ivor Novello (Samuel French and The Ivor Novello Trust); Lord Olivier (Laurence Harbottle, Harbottle & Lewis); John Osborne (the late Helen Osborne); Harold Pinter; Christopher Plummer; Terence Rattigan (Trustees of the Rattigan Estate); Sir Michael Redgrave (The Redgrave Family); The Royal Archives (on behalf of the late King George VI and the late Queen Elizabeth the Queen Mother); George Bernard Shaw (The Society of Authors); Dame Edith Sitwell (David Higham Associates); G. B. Stern (The Society of Authors); Elaine Stritch; James Thurber (Rosemary

Thurber); Kenneth Tynan (Matthew Tynan); Lord Robert Vansittart (Sir Colville Barclay); Margaret Webster (Diana Raymond); Sir Arnold Wesker; Thornton Wilder (Tappan Wilder); Virginia Woolf (The Society of Authors as the Literary Representative of the Estate of Virginia Woolf); Alexander Woollcott (from *The Letters of Alexander Woollcott* ca. 1944 by the Viking Press, Inc. Used by permission of Viking Penguin, a division of Penguin Group [USA] Inc.); the late Irene Worth; Esmé Wynne (Jon Wynne-Tyson).

NOTE: Every effort has been made to contact the copyright holders of letters to Noël used in this book. Should any further information come to light, we shall be glad to include it in any future editions.

So many people helped this project in so many ways that it would be impossible to name them and certainly to quantify their contribution. First and foremost, of course, the late Graham Payn, executor of the Coward Estate, for his unstinting support in this as in so many earlier Coward endeavours.

Then, in alphabetical order:

Christine Amos, Ken Bloom, Alan Brodie, Tricia Buckingham, Allison Derrett, Lisa Dowdeswell, Lisa Foster, Elizabeth Fuller, Greg Guiliana, John Hodgson, Claire Hudson, Kathryn Johnson, Geoffrey Johnson, Robert Kimball, Ed Knappman, Howard Mandelbaum, Richard Mangan, Leslie Morris, Sean Noel, Margot Peters, Silke Ronneburg, Steve Ross, Bernard Schleifer, Donald Seawell, Ken Starrett, Ray Wemmlinger, and Alice Wilson. You know who you are and what you did—

and the invaluable Rosalind Fayne, who valiantly typed and typed and typed!

# INDEX

Page numbers in *italics* refer to illustrations.

## ILLUSTRATION CREDITS

Coward Estate Archives: frontispiece, 7, 11, 14, 15, 16, 17, 21, 24, 15, 26, 31, 32, 34, 44, 47, 52, 60, 64, 65, 66, 67, 68, 80, 89, 90, 91, 95, 108, 112, 113, 118, 121, 123, 124, 128, 134, 137, 140, 147, 149, 153, 155, 156, 158, 164, 166, 167, 172, 176, 179, 180, 184, 203, 209, 223, 225, 248, 256, 278, 279, 283, 285, 292, 294, 316, 317, 329, 331, 332, 333, 334, 335, 338, 345, 351, 352, 361, 362, 366, 368, 369, 370, 372, 385, 395, 411, 419, 420, 422, 425, 435, 438, 440, 449, 458, 460, 464, 482, 484, 485, 490, 511, 514, 515, 527, 529, 532, 533, 539, 540, 544, 548, 563, 569, 575, 580, 582, 584, 586, 587, 590, 592, 594, 601, 620, 625, 630, 633, 640, 642, 644, 645, 649, 650, 656, 661, 664, 667, 677, 678, 682, 690, 691, 696, 697, 698, 702, 716, 718, 721, 723, 725, 727, 729, 745, 751, 752, 753

Barry Day Collection: 2, 5, 178, 216, 263, 264, 267, 269, 272, 275, 308, 310, 339, 428, 446, 463, 465, 503, 513, 547, 581, 610, 653, 660, 713

Geoffrey Johnson Collection: 4, 103, 284

The Players Club: 57

Algonquin Hotel: 61

Sitwell Estate: 83

Photofest: 278, 316, 536, 688, 746, 749

Ten Chimneys Foundation: 276, 277, 290, 550

Sir Arnold Wesker: 235

Carlton/Rank: 470

Rosemary Thurber: 344

Ronald Grant Archive: 111, 354

Lord Snowdon: 721

## A NOTE ON THE TYPE

This book was set in Adobe Garamond. Designed for the Adobe Corporation by Robert Slimbach, the fonts are based on types first cut by Claude Garamond (c. 1480–1561). Garamond was a pupil of Geoffroy Tory and is believed to have followed the Venetian models, although he introduced a number of important differences, and it is to him that we owe the letter we now know as "old style." He gave to his letters a certain elegance and feeling of movement that won their creator an immediate reputation and the patronage of Francis I of France.

COMPOSED BY
*North Market Street Graphics, Lancaster, Pennsylvania*

PRINTED AND BOUND BY
*Berryville Graphics, Berryville, Virginia*

DESIGNED BY
*Iris Weinstein*